FLORIDA STATE
UNIVERSITY LIBRARIES

SEP 18 1995

Tallahassee, Florida

THE FIRST
SEA LORDS

THE FIRST SEA LORDS

From Fisher to Mountbatten

Edited by
Malcolm H. Murfett

PRAEGER

Westport, Connecticut
London

DA
74
F57
1995

Library of Congress Cataloging-in-Publication Data

The first sea lords : from Fisher to Mountbatten / edited by Malcolm H. Murfett.
      p.   cm.
    Includes bibliographical references (p.) and index.
    ISBN: 0–275–94231–7 (alk. paper)
    1. Admirals—Great Britain—Biography. 2. Great Britain—History, Naval—20th century. I. Murfett, Malcolm H.
DA74.F57   1995
359′.0092—dc20   94–17009

British Library Cataloguing in Publication Data is available.

Copyright © 1995 by Malcolm H. Murfett

All rights reserved. No portion of this book may be reproduced, by any process or technique, without the express written consent of the publisher.

Library of Congress Catalog Card Number: 94–17009
ISBN: 0–275–94231–7

First published in 1995

Praeger Publishers, 88 Post Road West, Westport, CT 06881
An imprint of Greenwood Publishing Group, Inc.

Printed in the United States of America

The paper used in this book complies with the Permanent Paper Standard issued by the National Information Standards Organization (Z39.48–1984).

10 9 8 7 6 5 4 3 2 1

In memory of Barry D. Hunt, a very good friend and scholar

Contents

Preface		ix
Acknowledgments		xi
Chapter 1	The First Sea Lords (1904-1959): An Overview by *Malcolm H. Murfett*	1
Chapter 2	Admiral Sir (later Baron) John Arbuthnot Fisher (1904-1910; 1914-1915) by *Barry M. Gough*	17
Chapter 3	Admiral Sir Arthur Knyvett-Wilson, V.C. (1910-1911) by *Nicholas A. Lambert*	35
Chapter 4	Admiral Sir Francis Bridgeman-Bridgeman (1911-1912) by *Nicholas A. Lambert*	55
Chapter 5	Admiral Prince Louis of Battenberg (1912-1914) by *John B. Hattendorf*	75
Chapter 6	Admiral Sir Henry Bradwardine Jackson (1915-1916) by *Malcolm H. Murfett*	91
Chapter 7	Admiral Sir John Jellicoe (1916-1917) by *Donald M. Schurman*	101
Chapter 8	Admiral Sir Rosslyn Wemyss (1917-1919) by *James Goldrick*	113
Chapter 9	Admiral David Earl Beatty (1919-1927) by *Bryan M. Ranft*	127

Chapter 10	Admiral Sir Charles E. Madden (1927-1930) and Admiral Sir Frederick L. Field (1930-1933) by *Nicholas Tracy*	141
Chapter 11	Admiral Sir (later Baron) Ernle Chatfield (1933-1938) by *Eric J. Grove*	157
Chapter 12	Admiral Sir Roger Roland Charles Backhouse (1938-1939) by *Malcolm H. Murfett*	173
Chapter 13	Admiral Sir Dudley Pound (1939-1943) by *Robin Brodhurst*	185
Chapter 14	Admiral Viscount Cunningham of Hyndhope (1943-1946) by *Michael Simpson*	201
Chapter 15	Admiral Sir John Henry Dacres Cunningham (1946-1948) by *Malcolm H. Murfett*	217
Chapter 16	Admiral Lord Fraser of North Cape (1948-1951) by *Tom Frame*	229
Chapter 17	Admiral Sir Rhoderick McGrigor (1951-1955) by *Eric J. Grove*	249
Chapter 18	Admiral Earl Mountbatten of Burma (1955-1959) by *Geoffrey Till*	265
Select Bibliography		283
Index		297
Contributors		311

Preface

It is a rather strange fact that until now there has not been a single book devoted to the role and performance of the First Sea Lords and the degree of influence and impact each exerted on British naval policymaking in the twentieth century. While individual accounts have indeed been published on the more controversial or colorful characters appointed to this office, there has been no attempt at seeking a comprehensive coverage of all those who have occupied this position at Admiralty House. This volume of essays is intended, therefore, to rectify this omission and thereby fill an existing gap in the literature on modern British naval history. Unfortunately, even this book cannot cover all those appointed to this office in the twentieth century, and the editor recognizes that another volume will be required to do justice to those who succeeded Earl Mountbatten as First Sea Lord in the post-1959 period.

In striving to place the accomplishments of the First Sea Lords in some form of overall perspective, the contributors to this volume have sought neither to exaggerate nor to denigrate the achievements of those about whom they have written. Rather they have striven for fairness and objectivity, and hopefully, most readers will feel they have achieved this goal. In addition, the editor would like to point out that while there is obviously a need to pay attention to detail, this book is not designed to be a chronological narrative. On the contrary, it has been conceived as a more analytically based volume in which the question of "why," is addressed more often than merely "when."

A splendid compilation by Professor Robert Love Jr. on the American equivalent to this office, *The Chiefs of Naval Operations* (1980), has set the standard for this type of work. It is the editor's fervent wish that this new volume, which was written by a fine collection of established and emerging naval historians from around the world, will be seen as a comparable study, both in terms of quality and scope, to Professor Love's ground-breaking work.

Acknowledgments

I had been thinking of compiling a volume of essays on the First Sea Lords for a number of years, but because of other teaching and research commitments this project has taken a good deal of time to get off the ground. Now that it has finally made the transformation from idea into reality, I should like to acknowledge a debt of gratitude to those who have been associated with this venture in various ways over the past four years. I am particularly grateful to all my contributors for the quality of their work on this volume and the patience and understanding they have shown toward me, despite the delay in bringing this book to press.

At the outset, I talked about this project to a number of my close friends in the academic world whose advice and scholarship I both trust and admire. One of the most supportive and enthusiastic of these professionals was Barry Hunt, Dean of Arts at the Royal Military College in Canada at Kingston, Ontario. Barry was always immense fun to be with, and his sudden death in September 1992 came as a sad personal blow to me. As far as I am concerned, naval history conferences will never be the same again. Had Barry lived, he would have been a contributor to this volume of essays. Instead, this book is dedicated to him.

Another old friend, Professor Gerald Jordan of York University in Toronto, has been in touch with this project from the outset. He could always be relied upon to offer encouragement and assistance whenever I needed it. He remains someone for whom I have a very high regard. By the same token, my friend and colleague, Dr. Daniel Crosswell, has done a vast amount of work in getting the finished manuscript into camera-ready copy for the publishers. Without his considerable assistance, the publication of this book would have been delayed by several months. My gratitude to him is immense.

Apart from my splendid team of contributors and advisors, a number of other people deserve a mention for their assistance: in Singapore, Associate Professor

Edwin Lee, Dr. Brian Farrell, and Dr. Michael Smith; in London, Jonathan Franklin, Fred Lake, Tim Moreton, Professor Peter Nailor, Dr. Nicholas Rodger, Dr. Roderick Suddaby, Angus Sixsmith, Edmund Sixsmith, Captain A. B. Sainsbury, RNR, and Commander John Somerville, RN; and in the United States, Professor Jon Sumida and Dan Eades.

I should also like to extend my gratitude for the help I received from the officials and staff at the Bodleian Library in Oxford (Asquith, Attlee, and Sanders papers); the Churchill College Archive Centre in Cambridge (Alexander and Drax papers); the British Library (Cunningham of Hyndhope and Jellicoe Papers), Imperial War Museum (Millar and Whitworth Papers), Naval Library M3, Ministry of Defence Whitehall Library (Jackson papers), National Maritime Museum (Chatfield and Fraser papers) and the National Portrait Gallery in London, all of whom have consistently helped me in my research activities in recent years. Once again, further assistance and advice were also forthcoming from the officers in the search rooms at the British Public Records Office in Kew Gardens on the outskirts of London.

In addition to recording my own vote of thanks to those who assisted me in this project, I have also been asked by my contributors to record their appreciation to the following authorities for permission to quote from private correspondence. We are indebted to Her Majesty the Queen for her gracious permission to use the material in the Royal Archives at Windsor; the Masters, Fellows, and Scholars of Churchill College, Cambridge (Blake, Fisher, Edelsten, Godfrey, Dudley North, and Somerville papers); the Militärgeschichtliches Forschungsamt and the Bundesarchiv-Militärarchiv, Freiburg im Breisgau, Germany; the Bedford Estates (Arnold-White papers); the Trustees of the Broadlands Archives and the staff at the Southampton University Library (Prince Louis of Battenberg and Earl Mountbatten of Burma papers); Lord Bonham-Carter (Asquith papers); Mr. David McKenna (McKenna papers); and to the Earl of Selborne (2nd Earl of Selborne's papers).

Various excerpts from the works of the Churchill family, including extracts from the Chartwell papers, are reproduced with kind permission of Curtis Brown Group Ltd., London, on behalf of the Estate of Sir Winston S. Churchill. Copyright for this material is held by the Estate of Sir Winston S. Churchill. All Crown-copyright material used in this book is reproduced by permission of the Controller of Her Majesty's Stationery Office.

I cannot conclude this section without mentioning the important role played by my wife, Ulrike, in this particular enterprise. She has worked long hours with me on both proofreading the manuscript and compiling the index. Her involvement has improved the text immeasurably and helped to provide what I trust is a useful and reliable guide to the contents of this book. Our children: Marianne, Caroline, Nicolas, and Stephanie have never ceased to provide the light relief when the going got rough!

1

The First Sea Lords (1904–1959): An Overview

Malcolm H. Murfett

Although naval historians of the twentieth century have tended to use the official terms of First Sea Lord and Chief of Naval Staff interchangeably, it is a debatable point whether there is more than merely a semantic difference between them. Historically, the two terms were not always linked. While the title of First Sea Lord was introduced officially by the Earl of Selborne in 1904, that of Chief of Naval Staff only came into use some years later after the establishment in January 1912 of the War Staff—a slightly enlarged version of the old Naval Intelligence Division.[1] For several years thereafter, the two posts were kept separate. Although the Chief of the War Staff was theoretically subordinate to the First Sea Lord, the reality was that the former jealously guarded his independence and, in the case of Rear-Admiral Ernest Troubridge, often worked against, rather than for, the latter. As a result, a curious type of "divide and rule" policy was practiced in the Admiralty during the 1912-1915 period not only by the holders of these two offices, but also by the irrepressible Winston Churchill, the First Lord. Not surprisingly, a certain degree of acrimony and inefficiency resulted. Once Churchill fell from grace in the wake of the Dardanelles disaster, however, the independent administrative structure that he had helped to establish in the Admiralty was reformed by incorporating the Chief of Naval Staff's duties with those of the First Sea Lord. When Admiral Sir Henry Jackson (a former Chief of War Staff) was appointed to succeed Lord Fisher as First Sea Lord in late May 1915, he was also permitted to assume the role of Chief of Naval Staff. It was hardly the most propitious start to this new-found unity. In fact, it was to take several years and the administrative reforms of the Beatty years in the early 1920s to turn the Naval Staff into a modern system worthy of the name.

As the senior naval professional on the Admiralty Board, the First Sea Lord was expected to provide advice and information to his political chief, the First Lord of the Admiralty, on all naval matters. More than primus inter pares, the First Sea Lord and Chief of Naval Staff was, nonetheless, dependent on his other Sea Lords for such things as the preparation of plans, naval construction, fleet operations, personnel matters, and so forth. These duties were arduous enough without any further complications, but problems did arise with the creation in 1923 of the Chiefs of Staff Committee, a triservice subcommittee of the Committee of Imperial Defence, on which the First Sea Lord was required to sit and discuss defense issues with the Chief of the Imperial General Staff and the Chief of Air Staff. This group was charged with responsibility for tendering collective advice to the government on British defense policy. Unfortunately, in the first decade of its existence, the Chiefs of Staff (COS) Committee was to remain largely a fractious body, the competitive (rather than cooperative) instincts of which were to dominate, hindering its development. It was only with the advent of Admiral Sir Ernle Chatfield as First Sea Lord and Chief of Naval Staff in 1933 that the COS Committee really became a vital cog in the consultative machinery of the state. Chatfield not only defended the Royal Navy's interests, as any professional head would have been expected to do, but he was also gifted enough to discuss defense policy in its widest sense, and not from just the narrow point of view of the Admiralty.

Not all First Sea Lords were blessed with Chatfield's sterling abilities, however. As the years passed, the work load generated by the First Sea Lord's two, quite distinct, duties—internal Admiralty concerns and external defense responsibilities—increased substantially. Consequently, it was to become even more essential that the First Sea Lord should delegate some of his work to those around him on the Board of Admiralty and to members of his Naval Staff rather than try to do it all himself. This fact alone was to put a further premium on the selection of highly able and diligent officers as colleagues and subordinates at the Admiralty. Some of the First Sea Lords were to be more fortunate than others in having qualified and energetic staff at their disposal. Those who did not, suffered accordingly. In conclusion, it is possible to suggest, therefore, that while some individuals who were appointed First Sea Lord might have been perfectly competent in undertaking the role and duties of Chief of Naval Staff—in other words, being responsible for the work of the Admiralty—they may not have been fully equipped, either intellectually or by inclination, to become an effective First Sea Lord on the COS Committee.

While a verdict on some of the First Sea Lords has already been rendered by the academic jury, this volume of seventeen essays seeks to demonstrate the impact on naval policy made by all those who filled the office of First Sea Lord and Chief of Naval Staff from the tumultuous era of "Jacky" Fisher to Earl Mountbatten's confident stewardship of the post-Suez trauma. It was a time of momentous change for both the Admiralty and the Royal Navy, as these fine contributions reveal in detail. Sometimes the experienced, dedicated professional sailor appointed to the post of First Sea Lord proved to be a competent and resourceful administrator, a skillful and accomplished diplomat and a vigorous and obdurate defender of the Royal Navy which he loyally served. Just as frequently, however, appointees fell short of the high and demanding standards expected of the office. Clearly, it was a tall order to be judged successful in this post. For every Fisher, Beatty and Mountbatten, naval historians may point an accusing finger at Sir Arthur Knyvett-Wilson, Sir Charles Madden, or Sir Frederick Field. Success is a relative concept at the best of times. As the century drew on and a decline in British power set in, this fact was underlined with striking clarity. Once the Royal Navy's preeminent position within the defense establishment began to be eroded, the First Sea Lords were increasingly faced with the formidable challenge of trying to limit the damage that zealous ministers and bureaucrats were determined to inflict on the senior service in the name of government policy.

Barry Gough's admirable opening essay in this volume sets the office of First Sea Lord in historical perspective and goes on to demonstrate most vividly the degree to which its first incumbent, Admiral Sir "Jacky" Fisher, made the most of his appointment. As Professor Gough notes, Fisher's intelligence, vision, and supreme self-confidence were brought to bear on naval policy and ship construction in the early years of the twentieth century, and the influence he exerted on the policy making process when working with a malleable First Lord was simply prodigious. Ultimately, however, political questions and financial stringency, combined with a campaign of vitriolic denunciation fomented by Admiral Charles Beresford and his cronies within the service, managed to remove even Fisher's iron grip on the Royal Navy.

Nicholas Lambert, in a thoughtful and revealing study of Sir Arthur Knyvett-Wilson's short tenure in office, reveals that in this case, the process of finding a worthy successor to Fisher went disastrously awry. Instead of being a stolid supporter of the Fisher reforms, Wilson became a stubborn, dogmatic, and intransigent adversary of those who had assumed he would merely keep the seat warm until someone better could be appointed to his post. His unwillingness to delegate authority to his subordinates or to take even his closest advisors into his confidence won him few friends within the service. His steadfast refusal to jettison the outmoded strategical methods and old-fashioned tactical ideas with which he was personally familiar meant that some of the Fisherite reforms were stalled or even reversed. By failing to respond to the clamor for reform, Wilson became an isolated figure within the Admiralty and the service at large. Unfortunately, his personal relations with Reginald McKenna, the First Lord, plummeted to a new low, compromising any prospect of establishing a good working relationship with the Cabinet minister responsible for the Royal Navy. Moreover, his somewhat wooden and inarticulate demeanor failed to advance the cause of the Royal Navy among politicians generally. Unwilling to adapt to new thinking, Wilson found his position as Chief of Naval Staff undermined by Winston Churchill's appointment as First Lord in 1911. It did not take Churchill long to remove this handicap to change within the service.

Although Vice Admiral Prince Louis of Battenberg was Churchill's original choice as First Sea Lord in succession to Wilson, Prime Minister Herbert Asquith torpedoed his candidacy on ancestral grounds and the First Lord had to settle for appointing him to the Admiralty Board in a subordinate capacity to Admiral Sir Francis Bridgeman. Whatever the theoretical hierarchy on which Asquith insisted, however, Churchill was determined to use Battenberg as his policy advisor and wanted Bridgeman as a mere figurehead for his administration. Bridgeman soon found himself being bypassed on numerous matters. It did not help that the fledgling Naval War Staff was formed under Rear Admiral Ernest Troubridge, another personal favorite of the First Lord and an unstinting critic of Bridgeman. It is difficult not to see the First Sea Lord as an isolated and rather embattled figure at Admiralty House. Dedicated and conscientious, Bridgeman's penchant for overwork cost him his health. Ironically, his prolonged absence from the Admiralty enabled his erstwhile rival, Battenberg, to assume temporary command as acting First Sea Lord. Although Nicholas Lambert's perceptive essay on Bridgeman does expose a certain indecisiveness and lack of initiative on the First Sea Lord's behalf, it is clear that, unlike Wilson, he was not "a technological reactionary." Moreover, he had sound strategic ideas which, alas, rarely commanded undivided respect or attention from either Churchill, Battenberg, or Troubridge. It was an untenable situation in which his influence within the Admiralty and control over naval policy were marginalized while the impact and power of the First Lord and his inner circle of advisors grew proportionately. While lacking a decisive voice in the formulation of departmental policy,

Bridgeman's ineffective efforts to thwart Churchill only succeeded in irritating him and ensuring that the First Lord would seek his replacement at the earliest possible opportunity.

Churchill's choice of Battenberg as First Sea Lord to replace Bridgeman was never in doubt. Churchill and Battenberg thought alike on many issues and worked well as a team, but it was obvious who led and who followed in this relationship. As John Hattendorf indicates in his wide-ranging essay on the future Marquess of Milford Haven, Battenberg's role as First Sea Lord tends to become submerged with that of his political chief, so much so that it is difficult to discern what independent role Battenberg played as First Sea Lord. Although personally popular within the service and a loyal servant of the state, Battenberg was not responsible for any major reforms of Admiralty practice while in office. Although, as Professor Hattendorf indicates, Battenberg's nickname of "I Concur" was a trifle unfair to the First Sea Lord, the fact was that either he found little opportunity, or he chose not, to curb Churchill's powers or challenge his policy directives, save in a few isolated and relatively unimportant cases. It must be admitted, however, that Battenberg was mostly to blame for failing to lick the Admiralty into shape to face a war with the Imperial German Navy. As John Hattendorf admits, the War Staff and the War Group were ineffective in exercising operational control in the early weeks of the war, as one mishap after another befell the Royal Navy. This series of mistakes and crises was bound to create dissatisfaction with the Admiralty in many quarters. A whispering campaign was begun against Battenberg alleging that he might be suffering from a conflict of interest. These utterly unsubstantiated personal attacks found expression in both newspapers and weekly journals and were sufficient to force Battenberg's resignation. Churchill did not do much to save his loyal Chief of Naval Staff from being made the scapegoat for the Royal Navy's disastrous start to the war at sea. Instead of offering his own resignation, Churchill bade farewell to Battenberg before recalling Admiral Fisher to office as First Sea Lord.

As Professor Gough illustrates in the final part of his opening essay, the return of "Jacky" Fisher to the Admiralty as First Sea Lord in October 1914 repaid Churchill's faith in his abilities almost immediately with decisive results in the action against Admiral Graf Maximilian von Spee's squadron off the Falklands in December 1914. In the months that followed this early and spectacular success, however, Fisher's influence on Admiralty policy began to weaken as Churchill's impact on naval affairs grew steadily. As their working relationship became more onerous and compromised in the early months of 1915, Fisher, almost inexplicably, did little to challenge the First Lord's hijacking of naval policy. Times had certainly changed since those in the 1904-10 period when Fisher had dominated the proceedings at Admiralty House. When confronted with a person of Churchill's mercurial talents, however, Fisher's own gifts were neutralized to a great extent, and he became literally incapable of dictating the state of play on naval business unless Churchill wished him to do so—and he rarely chose such an option once the ill-fated Dardanelles campaign had been launched. Nonetheless, as is well known, the political fallout from this disastrous military initiative swept both these headstrong, egotistical, and remarkably able individuals from office. Their departure left a huge void at the top of the Admiralty hierarchy. Filling both positions with the appropriate personnel would not prove easy.

Unfortunately, the appointment of A. J. Balfour as First Lord and his selection of Sir Henry Jackson as First Sea Lord proved the point conclusively. Hardly inspired choices, the conservative partnership of the wily philosopher and the doughty scientist failed to provide the Admiralty and, by extension, the Royal Navy with the successful leadership that both deserved. Jackson's promotion to command the senior service, which he had served diligently for forty-seven years, may be seen as a reward for his loyalty, dependability, and administrative efficiency. He was not another Fisher, and Balfour had no intention of working with a clone of that tempestuous and opinionated character. Jackson was chosen partly, one suspects, because he was unlikely to be a thorn in the side of the Admiralty Board and his political chief. If his was expected to be merely a stop-gap appointment—he was sixty after all—he chose to ignore the possibility and worked almost incessantly, involving himself in all branches of Admiralty business, much of which could have been safely left to others to settle. Jackson's unwillingness to delegate authority to his subordinates was hardly a unique defect among the holders of his office. On the contrary, it was to be a common symptom among many First Sea Lords, who seemed determined not to share their hard-won prerogatives with any of their colleagues on the Admiralty Board. Engrossed in administrative matters, Jackson found little time or inclination to promote fresh, innovative policies. Consequently, the naval arm of the services languished under his tutelage. Opportunities for success on the high seas that did occur—the most notable being the Battle of Jutland—came and went without the stunning victory that was required to lift British morale and break the back of the Imperial German Navy. By the late autumn of 1916, this lack of a conspicuous success anywhere at sea was sufficient for dissatisfaction with the Balfour-Jackson axis to surface and gather pace in the public arena. Faced with this increasing level of dissatisfaction, Jackson wisely offered to resign to make way for the appointment of Admiral Sir John Jellicoe as his successor.

A controversial figure, pilloried by many for missing a golden opportunity to gain the elusive crushing victory over the German fleet at Jutland which the Royal Navy was built to secure, Admiral Jellicoe was nonetheless the only logical candidate to take up the mantle of First Sea Lord, which Jackson was only too pleased to lay aside in December 1916. Jellicoe's role as Chief of Naval Staff—which was much criticized for the failure to quell the submarine menace—has received a stirring defence in Donald Schurman's essay in this collection. Resisting the opportunity of jumping on the critics' bandwagon, Professor Schurman is both a persuasive and an eloquent advocate for Jellicoe, defending the First Sea Lord and pointing out that he not only introduced far-reaching reforms in how the Admiralty Board did its work, but also had done much to test the practicality of convoying before the First Lord, Eric Geddes, unceremoniously dumped him on Christmas Eve 1917 in favor of Rosslyn Wemyss. Professor Schurman has no doubts that Jellicoe's inate pessimism did not endear him to David Lloyd George, who wanted either immediate success against the U-boats or promises of success in the near future. Apart from the gloom and doom he pervaded, Jellicoe's traditional orthodoxy looked suspiciously old-fashioned, and his apparent slowness to implement new schemes aimed at controlling the submarine problem merely accentuated this impression. Moreover, his decidedly fixed views on naval strategy and general unwillingness to use the fleet in what he considered to be a reckless assault on the coast of Europe cost him the friendship of the vainglorious Douglas Haig and his friends at court, who whipped up a successful campaign to oust him.

Jellicoe departed in favor of Sir Rosslyn Wemyss, who had been brought in as Deputy First Sea Lord only three months before. In his fine essay on Wemyss, Commander James Goldrick depicts the new First Sea Lord as a court favorite who was to have a reservoir of personal support from the top that Jellicoe never enjoyed. This was perhaps just as well, since he was neither a radical reformer nor a restless innovator. Despite largely continuing the policies of his much maligned predecessor, the truth was that Wemyss was thought to represent change where Jellicoe had stood for the status quo. Unfair or not, sometimes the form of a position, and not its substance, is what counts. Wemyss was, for instance, not greatly enamored with the convoy principle, but sensibly, he did not try to interfere with the development of that system. His great strength, however, lay in his ability to cultivate and maintain good personal relations with others with whom he sought to work, such as the French, and in this respect he far eclipsed the much less convivial Jellicoe. His public relations skills deserted him, ironically, when it came to working with Admiral William Benson, the American Chief of Naval Operations. Benson thoroughly disliked, and also distrusted, Wemyss and his aristocratic attachment to the upper-class world of privilege from which he hailed. Notwithstanding the problems he had with the Americans (with the notable exception of Admiral William Sims), Wemyss's diplomatic success at the Versailles peace conference should not be underestimated. Even so, as James Goldrick points out, Wemyss's final months at the Admiralty were rather squalid ones once Geddes had left the post of First Lord. Beatty, that rampant egotist, used the opportunity to begin mounting a personal offensive against Wemyss, while Lloyd George, who had never really warmed to him, refused to recognize his talents fully or come to his aid. Unable to protect himself from these various pressures, Wemyss decided to leave office in October 1919 at the comparatively youthful age of fifty-five, feeling rather embittered at the way in which he had been sacrificed—a fate he shared with many of his predecessors, few of whom had left office willingly.

Professor Bryan Ranft, whose editorial work on *The Beatty Papers* has already been published to critical acclaim, is, perhaps understandably, more sympathetic to and supportive of David Beatty than most historians have been in the past. His clear and unequivocal message is that Beatty was an outstanding First Sea Lord who fought vigorously to defend his service from the political and economic attacks made on it. Professor Ranft indicates that by employing his wide-ranging talents and using his personal friendship with a number of highly placed politicians, Beatty did much to limit the extensive damage that the desire for disarmament and financial restraint, which is common to all post war governments, could otherwise have had on the Royal Navy. Although there was little he could do about the outcome of the Washington Conference, Beatty did his best to ward off the Geddes Axe, secure Admiralty control over the Fleet Air Arm, and establish a firm commitment to imperial defense by building the Sembawang naval base in Singapore. He was not always successful in the pursuit of these schemes, but it is difficult to conceive of any other naval figure at this time being able to do more for the service to which he was devoted than Beatty did in his eight-year period as First Sea Lord.

Nicholas Tracy, who was charged with covering the doleful period of Admiralty history between the end of the Beatty era and the beginning of the Chatfield epoch, begins his judicious essay by acknowledging that both Sir Charles Madden

(1927-30) and Sir Frederick Field (1930-33) were both regarded—at the time and subsequently—as poor First Sea Lords. Despite Professor Tracy's commendable wish to be fair to his two subjects, the fact is that comparisons are often odious, and both Madden and Field's achievements do indeed suffer if measured against those of either Beatty or Chatfield. Madden's reputation was hurt by his inability to ward off American demands for a reduction in the cruiser strength of the Royal Navy, as seen in the results of the London Naval Conference of 1930, and Field's career was irreparably damaged by his inept handling of the May Committee's report on service pay cuts and the Invergordon Mutiny, which followed in the wake of the Labour government's decision to implement these economies in the late summer of 1931. As the economic and political crises in the United Kingdom grew worse, governments changed, and First Lords came and departed, both Madden and Field appeared bereft of any political clout and were thought to be singularly ineffective in arguing the Admiralty's case before government ministers or the Establishment's bureaucrats in these most demanding of times. Field's chronic ill health and frequent absence from the scene on sick leave only made matters worse. Languishing from a lack of conviction and direction, the Admiralty wallowed in a trough of low morale and enfeeblement before being partially rescued from its enforced impotence by one of the most outstanding naval officers of his generation—Admiral Sir Ernle Chatfield.

Eric Grove's authoritative contribution on Chatfield vividly demonstrates the importance of his subject in effecting major improvements within the service and the Admiralty in his period as First Sea Lord from 1933 to 1938. These were not easy years for either of the institutions that he served so loyally, but Chatfield did a superb job in projecting a positive image for both. Displaying an adroit awareness of the importance of establishing friendly relations with those outside the service, Chatfield used his extensive contacts with influential politicians and civil servants to support his schemes and to get the Royal Navy's case a sympathetic hearing at the ministerial and Cabinet levels. Furthermore, he effectively elevated the Chiefs of Staff Committee to that of a major advisory body to the government—a status it had not hitherto been accorded. Chatfield's proudest achievement, however, must be his success in galvanizing the senior service and bringing it out of the critical slough of disillusionment and despondency to which it had plummeted under Madden and Field. In restoring the morale of the men on the lower decks, pushing through the Royal Navy's new construction and modernization programs, vastly improving the overall fighting efficiency of the fleet, and defending the service from the attacks of the Treasury mandarins, Chatfield fully deserves the glowing praise heaped on him by a naval historian of such caliber as Eric Grove.

Chatfield's retirement brought Admiral Sir Roger Backhouse to Admiralty House as First Sea Lord. Backhouse's few months in office have usually been passed over in silence by historians or dismissed peremptorily as being one of little consequence. While it is true that Backhouse's competence lay in the matériel side of the Royal Navy, he was able to focus on larger issues, such as administrative policy and strategic matters, with the zeal of a true reformer. Believing the existing administrative structure of the Admiralty to be seriously flawed, Backhouse formed the Binney Committee and instructed it to conduct an investigation into the work of the department and make recommendations for change. He was also struck by the current weakness of British military power—a dire situation exposed by the crisis over the Sudetenland—and unconvinced about the efficacy of the Main Fleet to Singapore strategy. As a result, Backhouse coaxed Admiral Sir Reginald Drax out of retirement and commissioned him to develop an independent series of war plans for use in dealing with the Royal Navy's potential enemies around the globe. In the weeks that followed, Backhouse fully supported Drax's line on the fundamental importance of the Mediterranean theater and in downgrading that of the Far Eastern. Their view was that the Italian Navy—being the weakest member of the Axis—ought to be knocked out of the war first before any full-scale attempt was made to cope with the threat posed by the Germans and the Japanese. In this and other matters Backhouse bucked the trend in naval thinking and displayed a self-confidence and a willingness to delegate rarely conceded by others. His terminal illness—a brain tumor—tragically cut short his time as Chief of Naval Staff to little more than seven months. By March 1939 he was already on sick leave.

Admiral Sir Dudley Pound inherited Backhouse's mantle as First Sea Lord in June 1939 as the Polish crisis deepened in Europe and peace became more fragile. Once European appeasement had been offically interred in September 1939, and with it Neville Chamberlain's pious hopes for the maintenance of peace, the Prime Minister took the opportunity to reshape his Cabinet team, bringing in Winston Churchill as First Lord of the Admiralty. As Robin Brodhurst points out in his sympathetic portrayal of Pound, the First Sea Lord had worked with Churchill in those ill-starred months of the Dardanelles campaign in 1915. Armed with this profound experience, Pound began to develop his own way of coping with the restless dynamo who had returned to Admiralty House to become the head of his department. On the whole, the two men worked well together; while Pound was not a slavish acolyte, as he has sometimes been depicted, he was indeed guilty of allowing Churchill, on more than one occasion, to interfere in operational matters. These interventions, it must be admitted, rarely worked. It is a moot point, however, whether Pound could have prevented Churchill from bypassing the Admiralty hierarchy and making these highly individualistic forays into the operational realm of the fleet. Robin Brodhurst intimates that Pound did very well to keep his political chief in check as much as he did. He also portrays Pound as an effective service chief who, despite working well with the other members of the COS Committee, had no intention of merely being relegated into a subordinate capacity beside the Chief of the Air Staff (CAS) and the Chief of Imperial General Staff (CIGS). Pound's stubborn and protracted struggle with Portal over air policy in 1942-43 was illustrative of his valiant fight on behalf of the Royal Navy. Realizing that success in the Battle of the Atlantic was crucial for long-term British survival in the war, Pound was prepared to go to considerable lengths to convince the allies that sufficient resources—including greater air support for his fleet—should be devoted to this vital theater of operations. His contribution to the winning of this protracted duel in the Atlantic was invaluable and should not be forgotten in any overall assessment of Pound's role as First Sea Lord. Sadly, his last few months in office were clouded by personal misfortune and chronic ill health. Few doubt that he should have retired before he did, but, as Robin Brodhurst contends, criticism that Pound was languishing years before his final demise and that the Royal Navy suffered as a result is grossly unfair and wildly inaccurate. Pound deserved much better than that.

As Michael Simpson mentions in his impressive essay, Admiral Sir Andrew Browne Cunningham made the difficult transition from being a superb naval commander afloat to a fine desk-bound Chief of Naval Staff in the Admiralty. Although known for his fiery temperament, Cunningham controlled it magnificently and deftly handled the equally tempestuous Churchill and that inveterate critic of all things British, Admiral Ernest J. King, with an astuteness and guile that almost defied belief. A protégé of Dudley Pound, Cunningham was one of the very few First Sea Lords who was prepared to delegate authority extensively to his fellow Sea Lords and their staff. Trusting in his senior commanders, he rarely interfered with their handling of operational matters and did not expect—or appreciate—such interference from others, such as Churchill or Albert Alexander. While he worked closely with the other British Chiefs of Staff and his American colleagues on the Combined Chiefs of Staff (CCOS) Committee, he was prepared to fight on behalf of the Royal Navy tirelessly and with the utmost resolution. His role as First Sea Lord encompassed both war and peace. Dr. Simpson shrewdly hints that Cunningham was definitely more effective in the former than the latter, an observation with which few would disagree. In the post war world, the Royal Navy was in for a rough time: British power, measured by virtually any yardstick, was distinctly on the wane; it had been crippled by economic inadequacy and post war reconstruction, the loss of empire, the development of atomic weapons of mass destruction, and the advent of superpower confrontation. Cunningham was not the man to preside over the destruction of his beloved fleet. He therefore chose to retire in May 1946, without rancor, leaving his chosen successor, Admiral Sir John Cunningham, with the task of defending the Royal Navy from the predatory instincts of the accountants and economists in the Treasury.

Sir John Cunningham was known in naval circles for his commanding intellect and brusque manner. Although not the dynamic fleet commander that his predecessor had been, he was thought to be more at home at the Admiralty than at sea—a singular advantage in the immediate post war world when Whitehall was destined to become the vital theater for the Royal Navy. It was Cunningham's misfortune to have joined the Admiralty Board at a time of wholesale military disarmament when politicians, civil servants, and the general public were largely united in wishing to divert public funds from the defense budget to help defray the staggering costs of implementing a National Health Service and a program of sweeping nationalization promised by the Labour government and supported overwhelmingly by the British electorate in July 1945. Cunningham's major task was as unenviable as it was herculean. It basically consisted of a prolonged course in damage limitation, one in which success could not be guaranteed and, at best, was measured in relative and transitory terms. From the outset Cunningham realized that cutbacks were unavoidable; the art for him was to try and restrict them to less crucial areas of administration and matériel. Unfortunately, regardless of the sterling qualities he brought to bear on the key issues, the task proved well beyond him. His problems had mounted once the inept Viscount Hall had been installed as First Lord. Moreover, any hopes he may have pinned on military solidarity coming to his aid were soon crippled by the promotion of Viscount Montgomery of Alamein to the position of CIGS. Thereafter, the COS Committee lacked both unity and cohesion. Above all, however, Cunningham needed a large slice of luck to ward off the blows administered by the Chancellor of the Exchequer on behalf of the Treasury and the Cabinet. Fate refused to smile on him in that way.

As Tom Frame reveals in his excellent contribution on Lord Fraser of North Cape, the new First Sea Lord was blessed with much greater luck than his predecessor. A very successful naval officer in both war and peace, Fraser was the ideal choice to succeed Sir John Cunningham as Chief of Naval Staff in September 1948. He took up his post at a time when the United Kingdom's defense policy was in a chronically anaemic state. Clement Attlee's government, nursing the sluggish British economy at home and with little wish for a military renaissance overseas, had few qualms about continuing to plunder the defense budget almost at will. Initially, there was little that Fraser and his fellow Chiefs of Staff could do, personally or collectively, to halt this slide into precipitous disarmament. Dire contingencies were planned and accounted for in the months that followed—a sign (as if such were needed) of the rapid decline in British military power around the globe. Apart from the wild rejoicing that accompanied the escape of the HMS *Amethyst* from communist detention on the Yangtze in late July 1949, there was little for Fraser and the other Sea Lords to smile about at this time—the Royal Navy had been cut to the bone and the future looked bleak indeed for the senior service. In retrospect, however, the march of international communism on the world's stage was to prove a watershed in the dismal fortunes of the British armed forces after the Second World War. Anxious that the ideological/military struggle should not be lost to any variant of Marxism-Leninism, the North Atlantic Treaty Organization (NATO) allies began reassessing their defense priorities in Asia as well as in Europe. Once the political will for the containment of the communist offensive in Korea had been articulated by Attlee's administration in the summer of 1950, the Royal Navy became an important beneficiary of the momentous change in the government's foreign and defense policy. As Dr. Frame points out unmistakably, finance—which had been previously sparce and grudging—was now provided by the Treasury for a program of accelerated naval rearmament. Fate, therefore, presented Fraser with a rare opportunity to begin the process of remodeling the naval establishment to meet its new external challenges in the 1950s. He and others would seize this chance with relish.

Admiral Sir Rhoderick McGrigor succeeded Fraser in December 1951. "Wee Mac," as he was known, proved to be one of the most underrated of all the First Sea Lords. Quiet and unassuming, he was a team player rather than a flamboyant dictator with strong, charismatic qualities. Nonetheless, he was an extremely intelligent individual who was particularly good in putting his strikingly original and perceptive ideas down on paper. An extremely able naval officer with extensive knowledge of command afloat and ashore, McGrigor worked with, rather than against, the other members of the Admiralty Board and the Chiefs of Staff Committee. While he much preferred consensus to confrontation, McGrigor was also prepared to fight long and hard for what he believed in. Imbued with strong convictions and a stubborn streak, he was a match for anyone who wished to downgrade the Royal Navy in future British defense policy. He did not win all the time, but his overall record is still remarkably impressive, as Eric Grove demonstrates in his revealing study of this largely unknown figure. McGrigor's views on the retention of the aircraft carrier and the carrier-based strike aircraft NA39 (the future Buccaneer) eventually won the day. Without his articulate and persuasive stand on behalf of the Royal Navy and the crucial role it could play in modern warfare, it is doubtful whether the Admiralty could have survived as an effective service institution. As it was, Churchill's Conservative government was far from convinced that the Royal Navy still had the potential to be of critical value to British defense policy in the 1950s. McGrigor's success in besting his critics and retaining an active and vital presence for the modern fleet in the thermonuclear age was an outstanding tribute to his outstanding intellectual drive and dogged powers of resistance. When he left office in April 1955, "Wee Mac" had established a platform on which his successor, Earl Mountbatten of Burma, could build a modern version of the Royal Navy and introduce reforms in both officer structure and training.

As Professor Geoffrey Till intimates in the final, absorbing chapter in this volume, Mountbatten moved serenely into the post of First Sea Lord—the latest in a long line of public commissions that had come his way over a fifteen-year period. As a result of his aristocratic connections, unfailingly egotistical nature, and high public profile, Mountbatten stood in complete contrast to his worthy, but largely unknown predecessor, McGrigor. When his appointment as First Sea Lord was confirmed in April 1955, he was entitled to feel that fate's wheel had eventually turned full circle. After the injustice meted out to his father, Prince Louis Battenberg, in 1914, Mountbatten became the first son of a former First Sea Lord to reach the exalted position of Chief of Naval Staff. Craving success as much for his father's memory as for his own sake, Mountbatten was prepared to use whatever power and connections he had at his disposal to win his political battles on behalf of the Royal Navy with the Conservative governments of Anthony Eden and Harold Macmillan. Professor Till evidently believes that on balance, Mountbatten did eventually achieve this objective, but only after a long, arduous, and vociferous struggle with Duncan Sandys, that most skeptical of

Defense Ministers, and the departmental advocates assembled by the Treasury and the Air Ministry. Success was certainly not guaranteed in advance, and it is to Mountbatten's considerable credit that his arguments—based on working papers fashioned for him by his excellent Naval Staff—finally prevailed over his political masters and service colleagues. He also took the opportunity to overhaul the Admiralty's administrative machinery and carried out wholesale and much-needed reforms of the Royal Navy's infrastructure. His triumphs, however, were not solely confined to the domestic stage. One of his most satisfying achievements was in fostering good relations with the leading luminaries of the U.S. Navy, Admirals Arleigh Burke and Hyman Rickover, in the aftermath of the Suez debacle. Their personal friendship became an important element in smoothing over some of the more obvious current difficulties in Anglo-American relations and setting the stage for vital naval cooperation in the future. By the time Mountbatten departed from the Admiralty, therefore, he had effectively resurrected family honor, proved the lie to the widely held belief that he was merely a lucky individual, and brought additional stature to the Royal Navy. Even to an unabashed egotist such as Mountbatten, this was a record of which to be proud.

Mountbatten's performance in office should not suggest that it was normal for a First Sea Lord and Chief of Naval Staff to be successful in this most demanding of posts. By exploring the chapters in this volume, it becomes quite apparent that, apart from the often-considerable intellectual gifts and command experience that a First Sea Lord was expected to possess, the individual also needed stamina, good health, political acumen, a willingness to delegate to able and supportive colleagues, and more than the average share of luck in order to make a positive impact on the Royal Navy and British defense policy in the twentieth century.

NOTES

The author wishes to place on record his gratitude to the National University of Singapore for its assistance in pursuit of this project.

1. Admiral Fisher, who rejoiced in arrogating power to himself at Admiralty House, is commonly associated with being the inspiration behind this change of title. It is interesting to note, however, that the duties of the First Sea Lord, in the early twentieth-century sense of that term, were remarkably similar to those performed by the First Naval Lords of the 1880s. In other words, the change of title may have done little more than create an illusion of increased power for the office holder. In a letter to the editor (30 October 1994), Dr. N. A. M. Rodger put the matter succinctly: "Surely it was purely a new name for an office whose powers and duties had not changed at all?"

2

Admiral Sir (later Baron) John Arbuthnot Fisher (1904–1910; 1914–1915)

Barry M. Gough

To "keep the Amiraltee that the English might be masters of the Narrow Sea"[1] constituted an age-old maxim of British policy, and when this objective was not maintained, England learned the cost of this failure. Even in the early twentieth century, the Empire owed its existence to the sea, and British security depended on sure lifelines of communication and supply. Thus, the ability to deploy military force to those vital locations that would ensure the maintenance of Britain's profit, as well as its power, remained the understood rule of national strategy which was always oceanic and global in perspective.

A ready understanding of these features of British preeminence at sea was held by John Arbuthnot Fisher, who was made Knight Commander of the Order of the Bath (KCB) in 1894 and made a peer of the realm under the title of first Baron Fisher of Kilverstone in 1909. His life spanned three reigns, and he knew personally three successive monarchs, Victoria, Edward VII, and George V. His connections with the crown were significant to what might be called his rise and fall from favor. His advancement owed much to Victoria's ability to "spot talent," his powerful position at the height of his administrative career owed much to Edward's warm support for him as a ruler of the Navy, and his final years in office were typified by distant relations between Fisher and George. Indeed, had the latter monarch had his way against the powerful demands of Winston Churchill and the tacit support of the Prime Minister, Herbert Asquith, Fisher would not have been First Sea Lord for the second time, during the Great War. These details may be mentioned here because Fisher's life was worked out on a very broad canvas of historical change, in which political power was eminently fluid (even fragile) and responsive to domestic demands for social welfare legislation, in which political parties and governments debated widely on the subjects of "guns and butter," and in which technological innovation was daily changing, not only the type of firepower and its deployment, but also the very means of countering such in the hands of enemies, real or possible.

That Fisher's life also spanned the period between relative peace and total war should be remembered. Born into the age of Pax Britannica, and serving in the Royal Navy when it showed the flag in distant waters, he was responsible for a revolution in strategic deployment (or redeployment, as in the days of his celebrated hero, Horatio Lord Nelson) of great ships in home waters. In his own way he played out a policy for the contraction of England's naval forces to the Narrow Seas, and with others who flourished in the Edwardian age, he was engrossed in, but not perplexed by, the defense problems of Great Britain and the empire. That his professional life ended so ignominiously and his final departure from the Admiralty was so unsatisfactory are telling commentaries about his personality; equally important, they are an indication of how the Navy had fallen from grace as the premier component of Britain's armed services. If the legacies of the Battle of Jutland bedeviled the Royal Navy during the years of peace that followed the Armistice, the notorious departure of Fisher from the Admiralty after the Dardanelles disaster, the failure of the government and its necessary reconstitution under David Lloyd George, and the growing reality that the Royal Navy could not become an effective *offensive* instrument in directing the course of the war in Europe all served to indicate that the traditional and time-honored relations of crowns and cabinets with sea lords would be the stuff of close scrutiny, and even suspicion.

Fisher, as was the case with many naval officers, expressed an abiding interest in the history of the service. He regarded it as an obligation to maintain the Navy's traditions, to glorify the memory of Nelson and other great fighting admirals, and to "engage the enemy more closely."[2] His various sayings on these matters are well known, some of them were based on texts in the Bible while others were the result of his own imagination. His enthusiasm knew no bounds and was only matched by his energy; he never did things in halves. His correspondence, which he wrote in violet ink, was punctuated by graphic images, prognostications, and images of an age gone by. In Classical Greece his heroic image would have found full scope, and small wonder that the more confined field of play afforded by fin de siècle Britain did not afford him enough room to work out his schemes and designs, which in the end were tragic to his nation and to himself.

As to his knowledge of the history of naval administration, which is of particular interest here, it can be clearly stated that he was an iconoclast: indeed, he was party, with various politicians and statesmen (Lord Esher and the Earl of Selborne in particular), to the shaping of a revolution, or evolution, in naval administration. Had he had his way, in later years he would have become Lord High Admiral, a title that appears in records dating from the reign of Edward III, and Fisher himself refered to the necessity of an "Admiralissimo." On other occasions he mentioned becoming Comptroller, or Controller, of the Navy, the former designation having been taken up by the distinguished Charles Middleton, first Lord Barham, who assumed supreme control over naval administration during the French and American wars and concentrated forces in the Western Squadron. That Fisher was to resume the strategy of Barham and to turn away from the deployment of fleets and units on distant stations is a tribute to his recognition of how some of his predecessors had dealt with meeting the needs of the day and preparing for great struggles. That he was to embrace technological invention and promote the readying of the fleet for a different type of war than had ever been seen at sea may tell volumes about the times and circumstances in which he lived; however, it is also clear that he was a revolutionary—even a visionary—about the role technology plays in the pursuit and maintenance of power. These matters, and others that are the subject of ongoing inquiry, will disclose and portray the complexities of the problems that Fisher and others in the Royal Navy were facing. Furthermore, they will contribute to an explanation of the changing interplay of Cabinet members, particularly Prime Ministers and First Lords of the Admiralty, with flag officers and others who were seeking to ensure the primacy of the fleet and its readiness for war.

History may not be kind to Fisher in the end, and from the easy perspectives of a century's hindsight, it will be tempting to savage his achievements.[3] Even so, at the height of his influence he was regarded as the savior of the fleet, and such accolades were heaped on him by the press. We expect far too much to assume that all his life and all his activities would have been correct in pursuing that perfection of objectives: a Navy that could have determined the future course of international history; this was a reality (if it ever actually existed) that ended at Trafalgar. Of one matter, however, we can be assured: like Nelson, he was convinced that the British could never be too strong at sea. Nonetheless, it is in Fisher's means and methods of maintaining that strength that have captivated historians, and in such brief compass as is allowed here, only highlights of a larger, grander, heroic, and more tragic story can be told.[4]

The constitutional aspects of Fisher's career, especially as First Sea Lord, here command our attention. For that reason, some long views of history may be pertinent. From the earliest times of the Royal Navy, men-of-war and their control rested in the Sovereign. During the late thirteenth and early fourteenth centuries, military command of naval forces was conferred in certain individuals known as Admiral (formerly Captain-General). In due course, the Lord High Admiral administered the fleet and came to be directly responsible to the Monarch. In modern times, until 1 April 1964, when the Ministry of Defence undertook unified control of sea, land, and air forces, certain officers known as the Lords Commissioners of the Admiralty (and their committee, the Board of Admiralty) held responsibility, by commission, for military and administrative aspects of the Royal Navy.

The Admiralty thus held its power by regal and political appointment, and its membership fluctuated according to the national needs of the day. Even so, the Admiralty always married civil power with professional competence, and if internal contests for authority emerged (as they often did), this reflected rather naturally the ever-persisting struggle over requirements and resources. Almost invariably, the First Lord of the Admiralty, a politician and statesman, directed the overall affairs of the Admiralty as well as advocating naval matters in the Privy Council, or Cabinet, and in Parliament. More often than not, he was assisted by an additional Civil Officer of the Admiralty, likewise a Member of Parliament, and invariably from the House of Commons (where the First Lord of the Admiralty was not always to be found, being, as he often was, a member of the House of Lords). Boards of Admiralty were reconstituted as administrations changed. Far less frequently, they were "reformed," or modified, according to the will of the Cabinet; during the nineteenth century, Sir James Graham's changes of 1832 and those implemented by George Goschen in 1872 signified adjustments in Whitehall to fluctuating political needs which, more often than not, reflected financial exigencies and changing strategic realities.[5]

The reforms effected by Goschen established the pattern for the Board of Admiralty for the next ninety-two years. The supremacy of the First Lord of the Admiralty was recognized, the principle of other members of the Board being individually responsible to the First Lord was also acknowledged, and the collective right of the full Board to give advice to the First Lord was agreed upon.[6] The service members of the Board were Naval Lords, or Sea Lords, and in consequence of the reforms put into existence under the Earl of Selborne, the principal of these naval lords became First Sea Lord. That he was the first among equals is questionable on constitutional grounds; in actuality, however, the domineering instincts of Fisher and his behind-the-scenes activities, which were for him a way of life, established him as primus inter pares.

The position of First Sea Lord, and that of his predecessors for the previous two centuries, included serving as principal naval advisor to the First Lord. He was in charge of "operations." As time advanced, however, his duties seemed ever-growing, embracing a number of other assignments including Chief of the Naval Staff. A deputy chief was introduced during the Great War, and then, towards its close, a Deputy First Sea Lord. The First Sea Lord could recommend the key appointments and, thus, influence the patronage capabilities of the Admiralty. In the First Lord of the Admiralty, by contrast, was vested the political power, and he shouldered the responsibilities in and out of Parliament for the Navy's fighting effectiveness and its deployment. The distinctions between the political and the professional were appreciated, if a little reluctantly, by Fisher. But the same could be said of his political counterpart. Winston Churchill attempted to dominate his First Sea Lord, and may have succeeded, and in a moment of perplexity Fisher admitted that he could not out argue the persistent First Lord. (No one could.) Thus are to be explained many of the complexities of Fisher's tenures as First Sea Lord.[7]

Ninety-nine years to the day, on the eve of the Battle of Trafalgar, Sir John Fisher arrived at the Admiralty as First Sea Lord. He was ready to take up the challenges of preparing the Navy for what he foresaw would be its supreme test. He wanted that professional assignment more than any other, and although his correspondence suggests that there were occasions when he did not seek the position, we now know that such statements of non-interest were merely ruses to cultivate the attention of would-be supporters. John Fisher had entered the Navy in 1854, aged thirteen, having endured a hard life for the previous seven years.[8] Within twenty years he had emerged as a dynamic and progressive officer interested in matériel and the technical inventions of his age (and their potential deployment in war): steam, armor, electricity, machinery and torpedoes. He commanded HMS *Excellent*, the Navy's gunnery school, served as Director of Naval Ordnance and Torpedoes, and came to the Admiralty as Third Sea Lord and Controller from 1892 to 1897. In 1902-3, he became Second Sea Lord in charge of fleet personnel. During this rise to authority, he fought in the China Seas and in the Alexandra forts bombardment and served as Captain of the *Inflexible*, the greatest battleship of the early 1880s. He commanded the North America and West Indies Stations, and later, the Mediterranean Station. He was a British delegate to the Hague Conference on Disarmament 1899 and served as Commander-in-Chief at Portsmouth immediately before he took up duties as First Sea Lord.

Even before he came to Whitehall as First Sea Lord, his influence was already widely accepted and many of his reforms were already in place. "I trust that Admiral Fisher does not worry you by too many schemes," confided Prince Louis of Battenberg, then Director of Naval Intelligence, to the First Lord of the Admiralty. "I never knew a man with quite so many irons in the fire at one time."[9] In particular his new scheme of entry for the training of officers, whereby all executive officers, engineers, and marines were to be entered at the young age of twelve and to be trained ashore for four years in colleges before going to sea, was radical and wide-sweeping. Although this measure had broad political support, it met with some resistance from officers of the old school, but they were unable to deflect the scheme, which was promulgated in 1902.[10] That all officers were now to have four years of engineering training ashore was novel for the Royal Navy, but it was a sign of the times. Equally important aspects of Fisher's guiding hand in state naval policy were his personal involvement with the opening of the Royal Naval College at Osborne, his experience in administering and supervising the building of new battleships as authorized by the Naval Defence Act of 1889, and his prominent role, in 1903, as a member of a committee instructed to recommend reforms in the organization of the War Office. From the latter derived a system of an Army Council, which was to be modeled on the Board of Admiralty. The following year, the Committee of Imperial Defence (CID), the precursor of the War Cabinets and the present Ministry of Defence, was given a permanent secretariat and mandated to coordinate inter service war planning. As of yet, however, no grand British strategy had developed; in fact, rivalry between the services characterized the disjointed nature of war planning.[11]

Meanwhile, Fisher gingerly worked the back rooms, especially through the all-knowing, all-seeing "fixer," Lord Esher, and through his friends or associates in government or the armed services, such as H. O. Arnold-Forster, the Secretary of State for War, and Colonel Maurice Hankey, R.M., Secretary of the CID. All these tactics were preliminary to his own direct method of achieving his reforms and were part of the informal, and sometimes alienating, Admiralty backroom diplomacy that was Fisher's hallmark.

Once in office as First Sea Lord, Fisher continued his changes uninterruptedly, and the prestige of the office lent more credence to his several interrelated moves toward a new fleet and revamped naval organization. Whereas before he had had to maintain a somewhat lower profile, in his new, more august, position, he was able to carry First Lords of the Admiralty along with him. Earl Cawdor, who became First Lord when Selborne went to South Africa as Governor-General, enthusiastically embraced Fisher's schemes, and in the Cawdor Memorandum of November 1905, a general statement of Admiralty naval policy was promulgated. Under this scheme economies were made in the naval estimates, and at the same time the "all-big-gun" fast battleship, *Dreadnought*, revolutionized the fleet's composition. This vessel was launched in February 1906 and completed in December of that year; this rapid achievement was a triumph for organization and a tribute to Fisher's grinding determination to hasten the work of contractors and government dockyards in the readying of a radical new fleet.[12]

Meanwhile, Fisher had put in place his new scheme for the "distribution and mobilization" of the fleet, which called for an end to the old "foreign" stations, the institution of cruiser squadrons, and the concentration of force in home waters. Fisher held that overseas commitments drained the strength of the Navy and tended, as in the case of Canada, to engender dependence by the Dominion on imperial support; instead, nations such as Canada should cultivate friendship with their neighbors in this case, the United States. Fisher knew that recently resolved differences with the United States lessened the possibility of war in that quarter. The Caribbean had become little more than an American lake. Japan's ascendancy in the Western Pacific, France's growing attachment to British policy, and Russia's willing accord with France all indicated that Britain's Navy could shed itself of traditional duties. The new rival, Fisher foresaw (and he was not alone in this), was Imperial Germany. Britain's "splendid isolation" ended with several diplomatic arrangements.

Equally important to Fisher's way of thinking were the new tools of maritime war: wireless telegraphy, torpedoes, torpedo boat destroyers, mines, submarines, new guns, steel hulls, and steam turbines, all of which made sea power potentially effective, provided ships and especially bases were available. Financial realities lay at the root of the reorganization, too.[13] The "new conditions" of which Fisher spoke in his memorandum to Cabinet of October 1904 necessitated a concentration of naval strength and the closing of the Pacific, South East Coast of America, and North American stations.[14] Only the Channel, Atlantic, Mediterranean, and Eastern commands remained, while a new cruiser squadron based on Gibraltar was to defend British interests in the Western Atlantic as required. Great dockyards of yesteryear—Halifax, Port Royal, Esquimalt among others—were scaled down, while others were closed altogether. Gunboats and old-fashioned cruisers went to the scrapyard or were sold. Fisher's scheme was instituted against high-level advice in the Admiralty, such as that of Sir Cyprian Bridge, former Director of Naval Intelligence, but it had broad political appeal, and it was carried.[15] The cost to the Royal Navy in terms of its failure to build a good degree of unanimity on the wisdom of the policy cannot be accurately calculated. Certainly, however, this policy contributed mightily to the anti-Fisher campaign, which was itself fed by Fisher's devious nature in cultivating friends in and out of the Navy for his own plans and in discounting and discrediting the arguments of his opponents, chief among whom was the quixotic Admiral Charles Beresford. Yet another result of the fleet reorganization was the fear of abandonment by Canada, Australia, and some of the other dominions, and this in its own way contributed to the birth of new naval services, which were established in Canada and Australia.[16]

For much of the balance of his first term as First Sea Lord, Fisher was preoccupied with ship construction and the construction of the Rosyth dockyard. Though he was obliged to consent to a reduction in the target of four capital ships being built each year, as the Cawdor memorandum had proclaimed, he found in the First Lord of the Admiralty, Lord Tweedmouth, a loyal and a keen defender of naval estimates. Soon, however, politics overwhelmed him. Parliamentary assaults on the Navy, along with the campaign brought forward by Beresford, gnawed at the First Sea Lord. His extensive correspondence on these matters reveals that he must have been distracted by the political questions.[17] How great an effect this had on his professional capabilities, we can only surmise. As a biographer who knew him well commented:

It was an anxious time and feeling himself with his back to the wall, he began to show towards his opponents, particularly those who belonged to his own profession, a vindictiveness which tended to foster personal rancor and division among the personnel of the great sea service, hitherto singularly free from these evils.[18]

A Cabinet inquiry took up Beresford's charges of intimidation and favoritism existing at the Admiralty and, in conclusion, it tended toward defending Fisher and the policies of Reginald McKenna, the First Lord of the Admiralty, who had taken up the duties from Lord Tweedmouth in April 1908.[19] Nonetheless, Fisher was compromised by the report, and it was a painful blow to him. He felt betrayed by what had happened, and he despised many political heads of the day for not backing him against the unconstitutional activities of Beresford, which he regarded as treasonous. Meanwhile, in January 1909, Beresford had been terminated as Commander-in-Chief of the Channel Fleet, while by the summer of that same year, Fisher's authority had begun to flag. An arrangement was effected so that Fisher would resign and be created a peer on the occasion of the King's Birthday, 9 November. His resignation was effective on 25 January 1910, his sixth-ninth birthday.

Fisher was succeeded by his old associate, Sir Arthur Wilson. The tributes on his retirement were glowing, and they spoke of his energy, persuasiveness, courage, and reformist capabilities. Even so, many a person breathed a sigh of relief that trouble had exited from the Admiralty. In his first term as First Sea Lord, Fisher had accomplished miraculous changes, leading to advances that are well known. That he left behind difficult legacies can be equally understood. The Admiralty understandably became more cautious, and the First Lord and the Board issued a minute, dated 4 March, that gave the corporate position: "The measures which are associated with his name and have been adopted by successive governments will prove of far reaching and lasting benefit to the naval service and the country."[20]

Fisher returned as First Sea Lord in October 1914, mainly at the insistence of Winston Churchill, then First Lord of the Admiralty. Prince Louis of Battenberg, the First Sea Lord, had been driven to the painful conclusion that his birth and parentage impaired his usefulness on the Board of Admiralty, and consequently, he resigned.[21] Winston turned immediately to Fisher, for the two of them had liked each other from the first day of meeting and had mutually promoted each others' enthusiasms and causes. Equally restless, energetic, egotistic, and heroic in nature, they made quite a pair, and if the study of the war on the British side is a study in combinations of personalities, as has been claimed, then the Churchill-Fisher duo is one of the most splendid examples. That the two men were to exit together, over the Dardanelles difficulties is symptomatic of their partnership (which, however, became strained in its latter days).

Fisher returned to the Admiralty on 29 October 1914. He arrived in time to deploy two battlecruisers, perhaps his favorite ship design innovation, to the Falkland Islands to intercept and destroy Admiral von Spee's squadron on 8 December. This was a celebrated victory. These vessels were detached from the Grand Fleet (another of his creations), and their deployment was in keeping with his understood strategy of mobile force to be speedily sent to the place of need. At this time, Fisher also made early plans for constructing a vast armada of smaller vessels, some 600 of every type, for he believed that a long war would be fought against Germany and the Central Powers. The wisdom of his plans is demonstrated, for these ships "proved a godsend when the Germans, in 1917, launched their unrestricted submarine attack on commerce."[22] He took a keen interest in the development of small, non-rigid airships to be used as scouts to detect enemy submarines. Above all, in late 1914, he pressed forward his plans (which were never realized) to deploy military forces on the coast of Northern Europe, especially Germany, in order to provide a diversion from the Western Front as it was developing at that time. His policies revolved around the theme of projecting small armies by sea, and he saw the British Army as a projectile to be hurled by the Navy. Fisher's pre-war "Baltic Scheme," though later revived, never attracted the support of his political and military superior. He intended to use Russian troops on the Pomeranian coast, some ninety miles from Berlin, and he proposed to mine the North Sea on a vast scale, thus hemming in the Imperial German High Seas Fleet. His policies never were developed along the lines of "Copenhagening" the German Fleet, though the enemy considered that a prospect. However, he always contended that the Baltic was a place Britannia ought to rule, and to the end of his years he held the view that British naval preeminence had been sorely wasted. In actuality, such a scheme would have been disastrous, for inshore operations on a grand scale would have been impossible given the possibilities of German mines, torpedoes, and submarines. Fisher's Baltic strategy had been formulated for the age of sail. Still he adhered, mistakenly, to his adage, "Hit how you like, when you like, where you like." "I backed him all I could," recollected Churchill. "He was far more often right than wrong, and his drive and life-force made the Admiralty quiver like one of his great ships at its highest speed."[23]

Fisher worked amicably with Churchill at the outset of the partnership, but the First Sea Lord grew increasingly impatient with Churchill's political meddling in service matters. Churchill's "fatal error," Sir John Jellicoe recollected, "was [an] inability to realize his own limitations as a civilian with, it is true, some early experience of military service but quite ignorant of naval affairs."[24] His sea knowledge showed a superficiality that was quite astonishing, commented Sir George Clarke, who also remarked that the strategic mistakes were rooted in the political foundations of the state.[25] Against the impulsive and adventurous activities Churchill was wont to foist upon the Senior Service, Fisher was unprepared and incapable of responding. It was not that he was growing old and had gone past his prime, for Maurice Hankey of the CID, who worked with him closely, stated that he was at the zenith of his powers: "He was probably the most remarkable man of his day. He possessed an extraordinary driving power, and swept away all obstacles."[26]

Increasingly Fisher turned to the Grand Fleet, as the main British naval deterrent, and to his chosen Admiral, Sir John Jellicoe, who commanded it. Based at Scapa Flow in the Orkney Islands, Jellicoe did not enjoy the best of health, and Fisher was concerned that this might have undercut morale. Fisher worried about the defences of Scapa and the best base of operations for the battlecruiser squadrons. He was always confident (more so than Jellicoe) that the strength of the Grand Fleet was equal to any task that lay ahead of it. He was always concerned, however, about the composition of the smaller vessels of the Navy.[27]

Fisher followed the Dogger Bank action of January 1915 with keen interest, and he concluded that the disposition of the dreadnoughts and battlecruisers was too far away from the likely scene of any grand encounter.[28] He was also critical of Beatty and his subordinates for not finishing off wounded German vessels. He tended to dismiss the problems attendant on enemy mine laying, and at the same time, advanced the latest state of his Baltic scheme before members of the Cabinet. Upon hearing the updated scheme, Lloyd George replied diplomatically that the matter would have to be brought before Cabinet: "We poor ignorant civilians must necessarily defer in these matters on the guidance of experts like yourself."[29] The politician was flattering the professional in this case, however, and Fisher was led to the belief that his scheme had not died in the water.

It was at this particular juncture that the Dardanelles scheme was drawn up, mainly, it seems, because of the government's response to urgent demands of the Czar of Russia, Nicholas II, that pressure be exerted on the Eastern Front so that Russian armies would not collapse. Fisher advised right from the beginning that any strengthening of the Mediterranean naval force would mean a corresponding weakening of the Grand Fleet, and he persisted in that view. Churchill, along with Lord Kitchener and Maurice Hankey, pushed for a Turkish plan. Fisher always maintained that the Director of Military Operations and Intelligence at the War Office, Major-General Charles Callwell, was correct in his views that any attack upon the Gallipoli Peninsula was likely to prove an extremely difficult operation.[30] Fisher had harbored eastern ambitions, however, and at one time worked in concert with Kitchener for developing a scheme for a waterway from Alexandretta to the Persian Gulf.[31] Nonetheless, during hostilities Fisher was not as inclined to imperial gains and legacies, and he worried about naval units in such an encounter. Eventually the matter came to Cabinet. Fisher concurred with the decision, and Churchill testified to the Dardanelles Inquiry that the Admiralty, with Fisher's agreement, had decided to undertake the task that the War Council had powerfully pressed on them. "I strongly urged him to undertake the operation, and he definitely consented to do so," testified Churchill, to which he added, "I state this positively."[32] The reasons against the operation were many, but what counted greatly in Fisher's mind was that the Army would be involved in what amounted to a combined operation. This turned him away, and he advised Churchill that the scheme should be aborted.[33] He proposed the Baltic and Zeebrugge as better alternatives. Fisher could not stand up to Churchill, Asquith, Arthur Balfour, and their supporters, however, despite support from other naval officers, and he bowed to the political will. He threatened resignation, and he urged the Prime Minister to remember that naval concentration and preponderance in the North Sea was the first requirement.[34] Unity in war was necessary, and he could no longer claim that unity existed between himself and the First Lord. But another matter had arisen: the nation and its politicians had become preoccupied with the British Expeditionary Force and its problems, and the Navy was being increasingly seen as an unused offensive force.[35] Fisher thought that the Cabinet was weak at the center and needed "one man." In any event, on 28 January 1915, the War Council agreed to abandon a naval attack on Zeebrugge and decided on the Dardanelles operation. This meeting's result greatly modified that of the previous meeting's discussion, at which Churchill had announced that the ultimate object of the Navy was to obtain access to the Baltic.[36]

The Dardanelles operations and disaster cannot be recounted and analyzed here, complex as they are. Suffice it to say that insufficient intelligence was acquired concerning Turkish forts and guns, shallow waters prohibited certain naval actions, and enemy mines proved an ample deterrent. Accordingly, the British imperial initiative faltered—and with it fell the government that had concocted the scheme. Following the decision to undertake the expedition, Fisher had grown silent, and he brooded over the difficulties. Again he pondered resignation.[37] Churchill, incessantly continued to press upon the First Sea Lord new demands.[38] Fisher was unable to acquiesce and simply stated to the Prime Minister his inability to continue as First Sea Lord.[39] "I find it increasingly difficult to adjust myself to the increasingly daily requirements of the Dardanelles to meet your views," he wrote to Churchill on 15 May. "As you truly said yesterday, I am in the position of continually vetoing your proposals. This is not fair to you, besides being extremely distasteful to me."[40]

The Board of Admiralty immediately took up the matter and considered Fisher's position. They concluded that there were two reasons for the resignation: disagreement as to conduct of naval operations in the Dardanelles and dissatisfaction with the procedure adopted for "the executive control of the Fleet."

They reported their opinion, to the First Lord among others, that the present method of controlling operations had been taken out of the hands of the First Sea Lord and was thus "open to very grave objection." In other words, the First Sea Lord's professional rights, and even his customary constitutional position, had been violated. The Admiralty Board recognized that it was faced with a national crisis of the greatest magnitude; not only would Fisher's resignation lead to disastrous consequences that must be averted, but in addition, Churchill, as well as Fisher, had to be prevailed on to moderate and reconsider their actions in the light of the national interest and instead to follow the advice given to them by the Admiralty Board.[41] This was an urgent and belated plea for unity at the Admiralty, for Churchill to correct his ways, and for Fisher to reconsider his decision to resign.

On 18 May 1915, British newspapers announced Fisher's resignation, but even at the last hour Fisher was drawing up a six-point demand stating that he would continue in power but only on condition that Churchill would go and that he would remain in the position equivalent to Lord High Admiral, or, as he put it privately, "Admiralissimo."[42] To Asquith he wrote, tellingly: "The 60 per cent of my time and energy which I have exhausted on nine First Lords *in the past* I wish *in the future* to devote to the successful prosecution of the War. That is my *sole* reason for the six conditions."[43]

Doubtless, Fisher found the political aspects of his job debilitating, yet at the same time he found them exhilarating. He liked being at the center. Even in the last act of the drama he is seen as attempting to manipulate himself into a higher office, past Churchill, and if the Board of Admiralty's correspondence with the First Lord (quoted here) is to be taken at face value, we can assume that Fisher had the Board's full support. Working in the shadows were those who had other opinions and advice to tender the politicians.[44] Churchill went, too, in the government reorganization, though he retained a minor office.

"You appear to have brought the fabric of government down with you," Lord Esher confided to his old friend Fisher, "necessitating a reconstruction which will make it more suitable to carry on the business of war." In that sense, observed Esher with a true political eye, Fisher had performed the greatest service to the nation.[45] Sir Roger Keyes commented on Fisher's ouster:

The Navy lost in the course of a few days the services of an Admiral who was one of its outstanding figures of the last hundred years—and the greatest producer of material in its history—and of an Administrator to whom it owed, in a great measure, its readiness for war in August, 1914.[46]

For some time Fisher dreamed of a return to the Admiralty. He served as Chairman of the Board of Invention and Research, all the while criticizing the ineffectiveness and inaction of those at the Admiralty. Not everyone shared Esher's enthusiasm for Fisher's achievements or agreed with Keyes's professional assessment of Fisher's readying of the fleet for war and administration of the Navy. It is undoubtedly true, however, that Fisher brought down the Asquith government, played an active part in the Dardanelles inquiry, and for awhile, bestrode the naval world of his era like a colossus. When the Imperial German Fleet surrendered to the Royal Navy, however, he was not there, and had not even been invited to be there, either because he had been forgotten or, more likely, kept conveniently out of the way.

NOTES

The author acknowledges with thanks the assistance of Wilfrid Laurier University and a Senior Research Fellowship that allowed research to be undertaken in London and Cambridge. See also note 4 below.

1. From Adam Moleyns's poem *The Libelle of Englyshe Polycye* [1436 ed.], ed. by Sir George Warner (Oxford: Clarendon Press, 1926).
2. This quotation is a reference to the last signal which Nelson flew in HMS *Victory* at the Battle of Trafalgar on 21 October 1805.
3. "The failures of Fisher's radical policies on capital ship design, the related poor performance of the British battle cruisers at Jutland, and defective Admiralty leadership during the war, were in large part the result not simply of prewar policy disagreements with the Admiralty, nor of random glitches in the functioning of the bureaucracy, nor again of personal idiosyncrasy with retard to the delegation of work, but of financial limitations, structural defects in the administrative system, and what might be called the Admiralty's culture of counterproductive practices that were the outgrowth of chronic prewar administrative undermanning." In Jon Sumida, "British Naval Administration and Policy in the Age of Fisher," *Journal of Military History*, 54 (January 1990): 1-26. These broad-sweeping conclusions invite further investigation and will point the way to new studies, which will be valuable in themselves. They may or may not advance the general view, put forward long ago by Arthur J. Marder, that the Royal Navy dragged itself into the modern world and was hardly fit for the challenges it faced. See Marder, *The Anatomy of British Sea Power* (New York: Knopf, 1940), and, by the same author, *From the Dreadnought to Scapa Flow: The Royal Navy in the Fisher Era, 1904-1919.* Vol. 1, *The Road to War, 1904-1914* (London: Oxford University Press, 1961).
4. The principal materials on which this study is based are the Fisher Papers in the Churchill College Archives, Cambridge. I wish to thank Correlli Barnett and his staff for their assistance, and I wish to thank the Master and Fellows of Churchill College for electing me Archive Fellow Commoner, thus enabling me to explore the Fisher, Esher, Churchill, and other papers over a number of years. A more complete examination of the life of Sir John Fisher is proposed in biographical form. Fisher's correspondence is

abstracted in Arthur J. Marder, *Fear God and Dread Nought* (London: Jonathan Cape, 1952-59). Biographies of Fisher include Richard Hough, *First Sea Lord* (London: George Allen and Unwin, 1969) and R. Mackay, *Fisher of Kilverstone* (Oxford, U.K.: Clarendon Press, 1973); the latter is based on the Fisher Papers. The laudatory *Life of Lord Fisher of Kilverstone, Admiral of the Fleet* by Admiral Sir R. H. Bacon (2 vols.; London: Hodder and Stoughton, 1929) must be treated with care; nonetheless, it contains many gems. Profiles for a new biography of Fisher to explore the complex political matrix of his era are suggested by Dudley Barker, *Prominent Edwardians* (London: George Allen and Unwin, 1969), 13-99, and especially Richard Ollard, *Fisher & Cunningham: A Study in the Personalities of the Churchill Era* (London: Constable, 1991).

5. [Francis H. Miller] *The Origin and Constitution of the Admiralty and Navy Boards* (London: HMSO, 1884); a copy of this rare work will be found in ADM 1/6740, Public Record Office (PRO), Kew Gardens, London. On the history of the Admiralty, see Sir Oswyn A. R. Murray's ten-part series, "The Admiralty," published in the *Mariner's Mirror*, 23-25 (1937-39). Two relatively recent works may be consulted: Leslie Gardiner, *The British Admiralty* (Edinburgh: Blackwood and Sons, 1968) and N. A. M. Rodger, *The Admiralty*, Offices of State Series (Lavenham, U.K.: Terence Dalton, 1979). For a critique of naval administration in the nineteenth century and on the eve of the Selborne/Fisher reforms, see W. Laird Clowes, *The Royal Navy* (London: Sampson, Low and Co., 1897-1913), 6: 188ff., 7: 1ff., esp. 10. See also (the possibly Beresford-inspired) Sir John Henry Briggs, *Naval Administrations 1827 to 1892: The Experience of 65 Years* (London: Sampson Low, Marston, 1897).

6. Murray, "The Admiralty," *Mariner's Mirror*, 23 (1937):24, 24 (1938):476.

7. Fisher was not the only First Sea Lord to feel the grinding push of Churchill. See Stephen W. Roskill, *Churchill and the Admirals* (London: Collins, 1977) and Richard Ollard, "Churchill and the Navy," in Robert Blake and William Roger Louis, eds., *Churchill: A Major New Assessment of His Life in Peace and War* (New York: W. W. Norton, 1993), 375-95.

8. Lord Fisher, *Memories* (London: Hodder and Stoughton, 1919), 138.

9. He continued, "You will probably consider me his accomplice. I can at least take credit for having effectually 'knocked the bottom' (I use his own words) out of several of the most startling." Quoted in Admiral Mark Kerr, *Prince Louis of Battenberg* (London: Longmans Green, 1934), 151; see also Brian Connell, *Manifest Destiny: A Study in Five Profiles of the Rise and Influence of the Mountbatten Family* (London: Cassell, 1953), 39.

10. Biography of "John Arbuthnot Fisher", in George Smith, ed., *Dictionary of National Biography, 1912-1921* (London: Oxford University Press, 1927), 183.

11. For an introduction to this subject, consult Norman H. Gibbs, "The Origins of Imperial Defence," in John B. Hattendorf and Robert S. Jordan, eds., *Maritime Strategy and the Balance of Power; Britain and America in the Twentieth Century* (New York: St. Martin's Press, 1989), 23-36.

12. An introduction to the complexities of designing and building dreadnoughts and super dreadnoughts is provided in E. L. Attwood, *The Modern Warship* (Cambridge, U.K.: Cambridge University Press, 1914).

13. "Financial Effects of Fleet Re-Organization," confidential, Selborne Papers, 1904-1905; see also "Naval Necessities" and related papers, in Lt.Cdr. P. K. Kemp, ed., *The Papers of Admiral Sir John Fisher*, vol.1 (London: Navy Records Society, 1960).

14. The policy was made public in the celebrated memorandum of the Earl of Selborne, the First Lord of the Admiralty, dated 6 December 1905: "Distribution and Mobilization of the Fleet." It is printed in *Parliamentary Papers*, 68 (Cmd. 2335) (1905).

15. Bridge's assault was published in the *Cornhill Magazine*, May 1905; Fisher's "Remarks on Admiral Sir Cyprian Bridge's Criticisms on Recent Naval Reforms [May 1905]," are in Crease (Fisher) Papers, Box 1, no. 13, 4, Ministry of Defence, Whitehall Library, London. For another assault on Fisher, possibly by another "anti-Fisherite," Reginald Custance, see *Blackwood's Magazine*, May 1905.

16. Barry Gough, "The End of Pax Britannica and the Origins of the Royal Canadian Navy: Shifting Strategic Demands of an Empire at Sea," in W. A. B. Douglas, ed., *The RCN in Transition, 1910-1985* (Vancouver, B.C., Canada: University of British Columbia Press, 1988), 90-103. See also Roger Sarty, "Canadian Maritime Defence, 1892-1914," *Canadian Historical Review*, 71, no. 4 (1990): 462-90, and Donald C. Gordon, "The Admiralty and Dominion Navies, 1902-1914," *Journal of Modern History*, 33 (1961): 407-22.

17. These are to be seen in the Fisher correspondence, Churchill College, Cambridge.

18. "John Arbuthnot Fisher", in Smith, ed., *Dictionary of National Biography*, 185.

19. "Report of the Sub-Committee of the Committee of Imperial Defence Appointed to Inquire into Certain Questions of Naval Policy Raised by Lord Charles Beresford," *Parliamentary Papers*, (Cmd. 256), (1909). Fisher's abhorrence of the report and his attempts to respond privately can be traced in his own papers, and particularly in his letters to Lord Esher, 3 September 1909 and 27 October 1909, Esher Papers (ESHR) 10/43, Churchill College.

20. Admiralty Memorandum of 4 March 1910, quoted in Taprell Dorling, *Men o' War* (London: Phillip Allan, 1929), 240.

21. Winston Churchill, *The World Crisis*, vol. 1: *1911-1914* (London: Thornton Butterworth, 1923), 400-1.

22. [Arthur J. Marder] "John Arbuthnot Fisher," in Peter Kemp, ed., *The Oxford Companion to Ships and the Sea* (London: Oxford University Press, 1976), 309.

23. Churchill, *World Crisis*, 1:433.

24. Jellicoe's autobiographical notes, British Library Add. Mss. 49038, 239-50; see also A. Temple Patterson, ed., *The Jellicoe Papers*, vol. 1 (London: Navy Records Society, 1966), quotation on 26-27.

25. Lord Sydenham et al., *The World Crisis by Winston Churchill: A Criticism*, 2nd ed. (London: Hutchinson, 1927), 7, 10-11.

26. Lord Hankey, *The Supreme Command 1914-1918*, vol. 1 (London: George Allen and Unwin, 1961), 145.

27. Fisher to Churchill, 20 January 1915, Fisher Papers (FISR) 1/18, Churchill College.

28. Fisher to Beatty, 25 January 1915, FISR 1/18, Churchill College.

29. Lloyd George to Fisher, 30 January 1915, FISR 1/18, Churchill College.

30. See Churchill Papers, 13/27, Churchill College; see also Martin Gilbert, ed., *Winston S. Churchill, Companion vol. 3* (London, Heinemann, 1972), 81-82.

31. Briton C. Busch, *Britain, India, and the Arabs, 1914-1921* (Berkeley: University of California Press, 1971), 115-16.

32. Dardanelles Inquiry, "Statement by Mr. Churchill upon the Dardanelles Operation to the End of the First Phase." Secret copy in FISR 1/23, Churchill College.

33. Ibid., 90.

34. Fisher to Asquith, 28 January 1915, FISR 1/18, Churchill College.

35. For a later view on this, see Hankey to Fisher, 21 January 1915 [1916], FISR 1/18, Churchill College.

36. War Council Minutes, 1915, 238, copy, ESHR 17/5, Churchill College.

37. Hankey, *Supreme Command,* 1:267.

38. Fisher to [?], 14 May 1915, FISR 1/19, Churchill College.

39. Ibid.

40. Fisher to Churchill, 15 May 1915, copy, FISR 1/19, Churchill College.

41. Board of Admiralty Memo to Churchill as First Lord and to First Sea Lord, 16 May 1915, FISR 1/19, Churchill College.

42. See Fisher to Asquith, 19 May 1915, FISR 1/19, Churchill College.

43. Ibid.

44. See, for instance, the role of one of them as described in Admiral Sir William James, *The Eyes of the Navy: A Biographical Study of Admiral Sir Reginald Hall* (London: Methuen, 1955), 82ff.

45. Esher to Fisher, 19 May 1915, FISR 1/19, Churchill College.

46. Keyes, *Naval Memoirs* 1:455-56, quoted in Arthur J. Marder, *From the Dreadnought to Scapa Flow*, vol. 2, *The War Years: To the Eve of Jutland, 1914-1916* (London: Oxford University Press, 1965), 293.

3

Admiral Sir Arthur Knyvett-Wilson, V.C. (1910–1911)

Nicholas A. Lambert

Sir Arthur Knyvett-Wilson was made First Sea Lord by an Admiralty letter of patent dated 25 January 1910. He remained the senior professional member on the Board of Admiralty until 12 December 1911. Without doubt, the selection of Arthur Wilson to succeed John Fisher was an unexpected choice. When Reginald McKenna, the First Lord of the Admiralty, offered him the post, Wilson had been retired from the Navy for almost three years. In March 1907, he had been compelled to give up the post of Commander-in-Chief after reaching his sixty-fifth birthday: the age limit for his rank.[1] On relinquishing command Wilson had been promoted Admiral of the Fleet, apparently in order to enable the Admiralty to offer him the Presidency of the Naval War College.[2] For some reason Wilson had not accepted the post. Nevertheless, this final step in rank had allowed him to remain on the active list for an additional five years.

The appointment of a retired officer as First Sea Lord was, even by the standards of the day, most unusual. Normally, one of the twelve full Admirals on the active list would have been expected to fill the post. McKenna's decision to choose Wilson stemmed largely from his agreement with Fisher that whoever succeeded him as First Sea Lord must not reverse the reforms he had introduced over the previous five years. Fisher's policies had seriously divided the senior leadership of the Royal Navy, although his opponents, collectively known as the "Syndicate of Discontent," were not offering the government a coherent alternative program. The difficulty in selecting Fisher's replacement from the list of Admirals was that at least five of them were leading members of the Syndicate. These included Charles Beresford, Reginald Custance, Lewis Beaumont, Arthur Moore, and Ashton Curzon-Howe.[3]

In contrast with some of the other non-Syndicate candidates, such as William May, Charles Drury, Wilmot Fawkes, and Francis Bridgeman, Arthur Wilson had seniority and experience and commanded respect. He also had been one of the few officers who had managed to avoid entanglement in the Fisher-Beresford dispute.[4] This allowed McKenna to put Wilson's name forward as a compromise candidate who would heal the rift between the various factions within the service.[5] Wilson had made his professional reputation as a torpedo officer. While still only a Lieutenant, he had served on the committee that, in 1870, had recommended the adoption of the Whitehead Torpedo for naval service.[6] In 1884 he had been awarded the Victoria Cross for gallantry while leading a naval brigade in the Sudan. His administrative experience was extensive. Between 1887 and 1901 he had served successively as Assistant Director of Naval Ordnance and Torpedoes (1887-89), Captain of the Torpedo School (1889-92), and Third Naval Lord and Controller (1897-1901). From 1901 until his retirement he had commanded the Channel Squadron with great distinction, becoming Commander-in-Chief of the Home Fleet and the senior Admiral afloat in 1903.[7] In 1909, Wilson had been appointed advisor to the CID.

Wilson's most important qualification was that he claimed to support Fisher's policies and reforms. Indeed, as recently as June 1909, he had endorsed the Admiralty's strategic policy to the committee appointed to investigate criticisms of Fisher's war planning leveled by Admiral Charles Beresford.[8] That Wilson also appears to have agreed with Fisher's radical ideas on capital ship design was a bonus.[9] Before taking office, Wilson promised to maintain the broad lines of Admiralty policy.[10] It had been only with the greatest difficulty, however, that McKenna, with aid from Fisher and the King, managed to persuade Wilson "how necessary it [was] in the interests of the service that [he] should become First Sea Lord in succession to Sir John Fisher."[11]

From the beginning, Wilson's appointment as First Sea Lord was only intended as an interim measure until a more suitable candidate emerged. Although McKenna and Fisher were truly anxious for Wilson to accept the post, they never intended for him to remain longer than two years.[12] In March 1912, he would again be forced to retire, on reaching the age of seventy. Meanwhile, the plan was for McKenna to manipulate the flag-list: advancing promising Vice Admirals who supported Fisher's policies, while at the same time keeping as many opponents as possible unemployed. With a liberal use of the regulation that empowered the First Lord to place on the retired list any Admiral who had not been employed for more than two years, effective opposition to Admiralty policy from within the service would thus be eradicated.[13] It is significant that just before Fisher left office, all major appointments had been filled "as far in advance as possible."[14] The success of the strategem, however, rested on the office of the First Sea Lord remaining closed to the Syndicate for two years.

Wilson was not to have taken over from Fisher until April 1910.[15] However, the decision at the end of November 1909 by the Liberal Prime Minister, Herbert Asquith, to dissolve Parliament in the new year convinced Fisher that he must retire before the General Election.[16] Fisher wanted his heir safely established at the Admiralty "on 25th January so as to avoid any difficulties in the event of a change of government and consequent change in the First Lord of the Admiralty."[17] Fisher's decision to leave early was another deliberate ploy to block the Syndicate of Discontent. If the Conservative party gained power, Admiral Arthur Moore was expected to become First Sea Lord. Fisher was equally worried that should the Liberals retain power, Asquith might take the opportunity of replacing McKenna with a minister who was more sympathetic to the appeals from the radicals in the government for reductions in naval expenditure, and who might also succumb to pressure to appoint members of the Syndicate of Discontent to the Board of Admiralty.[18] Fisher was confident, however, that no new government would risk the controversy of sacking Wilson after only a few days service as First Sea Lord. In a letter to the King's private secretary, Fisher gloated: "I don't think any intrigues can now displace Wilson after his being thus appointed before the General Election—It has been a knock-down blow to the Beresford Party and totally unexpected by them and the approval seems universal."[19] In his eagerness to thwart the Syndicate, Fisher evidently did not heed the undercurrent of friction between McKenna and Wilson. It appears that McKenna was apprehensive that, assuming he would be asked to remain First Lord after the election, he might find it difficult to work comfortably alongside Wilson for two entire years. He was clearly unhappy at being rushed into selecting his new senior advisor. McKenna recognized, moreover, that by taking the unusual step of recalling a retired officer, to an extent he was mortgaging his own reputation to Wilson's success. It would be probably too embarrassing for McKenna to dismiss Wilson. On the eve of Fisher's retirement, the First Lord privately confessed that he was seriously worried the appointment might have been a mistake.[20]

In agreeing to select Fisher's nominee, McKenna deliberately ignored several of Wilson's shortcomings. Foremost was his abrasive personality, which the First Lord rightly suspected would generate disharmony among the members of the

Board.[21] It was also well known that Wilson was not very articulate. In an era of financial limitation and strong competition for limited government resources from the Army and social reformers, it was essential for the First Sea Lord to possess considerable skills in debate in order to argue effectively the Admiralty's case to politicians.[22] The minutes of the CID show that, usually, Wilson remained silent. Later, Fisher nearly admitted his oversight: "Wilson though splendid and unsurpassed, was not a Machiavelli, and these lawyers in the Cabinet just walked round him. [W]hen a cunning rogue talks at you, you must talk back! Dear old Wilson only smiled!"[23] At the two meetings at which Wilson did speak at any length he made a very poor impression, making mistakes that reflected on both his own competence and that of the Admiralty.[24] McKenna was painfully aware of the damage Wilson was causing to the Admiralty's standing. Throughout 1911, he desperately tried to persuade Fisher to return to England and take over from Wilson the brief of advocating the Navy's case before the CID.[25] McKenna and Fisher also chose to disregard objections raised by Francis Bridgeman, who had served under Wilson in the Channel Fleet. The Second Sea Lord warned: "I know from experience with him that there is no joy to be found in serving either with him or under him! Deadly dull and uncompromising as you know! He will never consult anyone and is impatient in argument, even to being impossible!"[26] Significantly, McKenna only consulted his immediate advisors about Wilson. According to Fisher, only "three or four persons" knew of the appointment before it was published on 2 December 1910. The secrecy was deliberate. The fear was that if this news leaked out before it was confirmed, criticism might thwart the appointment: "Wilson would be got at and persuaded he was keeping the bread out of someone else's mouth etc. This was done before when we wanted Wilson as Head of the Naval War College."[27] Seemingly, none of the four knew or remembered that nine years earlier Wilson had been "removed" by Lord Selborne from the post of Controller, "where he was an utter failure and a mischievous failure too."[28] Wilson had been accused of interfering with the work of his subordinates and failing to support official policy and had been guilty of repeatedly making decisions without consulting the rest of the Board.[29] Under his leadership the Controllers department had become acutely overcentralized, thereby contributing to the delays in the shipbuilding program.[30] To get rid of Wilson, Selborne had offered him the first vacant appointment at sea. Publicly, however, no hint was ever given that Wilson had, in fact, been expelled from Whitehall.[31]

As a fleet commander, however, Wilson proved an unexpected success. By the time Lord Selborne was replaced at First Lord in 1905, Wilson had managed, not only to resurrect his career, but further, to have earned himself a reputation as one of the best Admirals in the Royal Navy. Furthermore, by the time McKenna became First Lord, none of the senior Admiralty officers who had worked alongside Wilson were still in service. Lord Walter Kerr (Senior Naval Lord), William White (Director of Naval Construction), and John Dunston (Engineer-in-Chief) had all been retired for many years. Lord Selborne had been Governor of South Africa since 1905.

On returning to the Admiralty in 1910, Wilson quickly demonstrated that he had not changed his ways. The evidence is overwhelming that as First Sea Lord, Wilson was widely regarded as obstinate, high-handed, and resistant to change. Throughout his tenure, relations between the First Sea Lord and the other members of the Board always remained strictly formal. Most people who came into contact with him agreed that he possessed "that total disregard for the opinions of other people which is the mark of a true autocrat."[32] In his diary, Captain Ernest Troubridge, the Naval Secretary, recorded that Wilson started to display his autocratic tendencies almost as soon as he arrived at Whitehall.[33] Francis Bridgeman, the Second Sea Lord, was affronted at being told publicly by Wilson that he was "only his second."[34] He was further alienated at being treated "as if he were a second lieutenant on board a ship."[35] The source of antagonism between the two men appears to have been a disagreement over the Second Sea Lord's handling of personnel matters. Wilson was determined to have things done his way. Bridgeman was sufficiently upset to threaten resignation no less than three times in one week. On the last occasion he must have appeared determined, because Troubridge was ordered to arrange for his replacement by Vice Admiral Sir George Callaghan.[36]

As he had anticipated, McKenna, too, became increasingly irritated by his new First Sea Lord.[37] He found Wilson to be particularly obstinate over appointments, wanting only officers at the Admiralty whom he personally knew.[38] After just twelve months, the First Lord longed for Wilson's retirement and frequently discussed potential replacements with Baron Fisher.[39] Other members of the Board, including the Controller, Rear Admiral John Jellicoe, also moaned that Wilson "will never consult with the other Sea Lords."[40] Meanwhile, officers in the fleet joked that so long as Wilson remained, the other Sea Lords could "be relied upon to occupy the same humble position as the junior flag-officers in the old Channel Fleet under him."[41]

Wilson's tendency to centralize extended outside the Admiralty building. In March 1910, he controlled the maneuvers of the second battle squadron off Portugal from Whitehall by wireless. According to Bridgeman, the First Sea Lord was intimately involved in the maneuvers:

> Wilson took the opportunity of moving this division throughout the whole of its course. He started them off by Wireless Telegraphy at a fixed hour. He fixed the course of every ship, as well as the rate of speed. [H]e had a bed put in his room at the Admiralty and kept the whole wireless electric staff in the office up all night while he chattered away to the Captains of every ship. His head seems full of every detail. [H]e knows the currents and lights and the shore and the prevailing winds over the whole distance.[42]

Such extraordinary interference with the operational control of warships cannot have been appreciated by the flag-officers afloat. Wilson's popularity was further damaged by the Admiralty's poor administrative record during his period of tenure.[43] The issue of orders that were often peremptory and frequently contained mistakes created resentment and confusion on the part of senior officers.[44] Loud and justifiable complaints from the lower deck over pay and conditions were ignored. The record on matériel policy was equally poor. The refusal to correct known mistakes in capital ship design (positioning the fire-control platforms behind the fore-funnel) was both stupid and expensive to rectify.[45] Other poor decisions had longer term implications for the efficiency of the Navy, some of which were to have a disastrous impact after the outbreak of war in 1914.

The best-documented example, for which Wilson himself appears to have been mainly responsible, was the decision to reverse the policy of fitting all modern capital ships with a mechanized fire-control system designed by the civilian inventor Arthur Pollen.[46] In that system's place, Wilson authorized the purchase of far less sophisticated equipment that had been invented by a naval officer, Commander Frederick Dreyer, a favorite who had served as his gunnery staff officer in the Channel Fleet.

The Wilson Board was also responsible for choosing not to address known problems with 12" armour-piercing (APC) shells that were uncovered at the end of 1909, during the Edinburgh firing experiments.[47] The trials had revealed that when fired at ranges beyond 9,000 yards, all existing 12" caliber APC shells had a tendency "to break-up on striking four inch K.C. armour" instead of penetrating it and then exploding.[48] Wilson's response was to evade the problem (and the cost of ordering new outfits of shells for sixteen dreadnoughts) by proposing changes in battle tactics: he suggested that capital ships use high-explosive shells at longer ranges in order to cripple the enemy's fire-control equipment, before closing to ranges at which the defective APC shells could penetrate armor.[49] Doubtless, he was encouraged to take this course by the knowledge that the cost of buying new outfits of shells would have been almost £400,000, more than the total sum spent on submarine construction in 1910.[50] New evidence, however, suggests that the results of the Edinburgh trials were not completely ignored. In 1909, the Navy had already decided to abandon the 12" gun in favor of a 13.5" caliber gun for all its new capital ships. In 1910, the breech of the 13.5" gun was modified to allow the firing of a new, heavier, specially strengthened, 1,400 pound shell.[51] This shell was successfully tested in April 1912.[52]

To dismiss Wilson as a reactionary would be too harsh. There is no indication that he ever blocked innovation without some justification for his decisions, although his reluctance to confide in his subordinates did tend to convey this impression. This assessment is also indicated by his record as a pioneering underwater-weapon's specialist. Possibly, however, Wilson's extensive experience with early torpedoes and mines may have taught him to be overly pessimistic about the difficulties associated with the adoption of new weapon systems. For instance, his opposition to the Pollen fire-control system (which he did not fully understand) appears to have been based on his general distrust of complex mechanical systems, which he feared were unduly susceptible to breakdown. Generally speaking, this concern was not unreasonable, if in this particular instance not justified, and it was shared by other officers, including the Director of Naval Ordnance, Captain Reginald Bacon, a progressive officer who had supervised the introduction of the submarine into the Navy.[53]

Wilson also liked to take his time when considering problems. While he was First Sea Lord a noticeable lack of urgency characterized decision making at the Admiralty. Two weeks after taking office, Wilson agreed to a plea from the Commander-in-Chief to have the experimental Scott Director transferred from his flagship, HMS *Dreadnought*, to another ship, thereby delaying the final trials for three months.[54] Flag officers who had served with Wilson, such as Vice Admiral Sir George Neville, knew that generally he would refuse changes of policy "on principle," but that given time, he could change his mind, provided "he really [went] into the matter."[55] The effects of Wilson's painstaking administrative habits were compounded by his unwillingness to delegate decisions. Although he was prepared to accept the advice of favored specialist officers such as Dreyer (gunnery), Captain (S) Roger Keyes (submarine policy), and Jellicoe (ship design), generally he only listened when their views conformed with the direction of his own. Unfortunately, his lack of up-to-date technical knowledge and unwillingness to consult widely made Wilson vulnerable to pernicious advice—such as in the case of Dreyer's malicious evaluation of the Pollen fire-control system.[56]

Most of Wilson's ideas on the character of modern naval warfare appear to have been the product of his experiences as a fleet commander. Even one of his oldest admirers, Jellicoe, admitted that "Sir Arthur Wilson was never a strategist. A brilliant handler of fleets but nothing more."[57] Unfortunately, during his short retirement many of his tactical ideas had already become outdated. While he had been Commander-in-Chief, the Royal Navy had not yet formed its first squadron of dreadnoughts. Consequently, he never had the opportunity to practice the new battle tactics for which the all-big gun ships had been designed; these were based on the controlled and deliberate fire of heavy guns at long range. In 1908, Wilson had been asked to umpire the trials of the Pollen system aboard HMS *Ariadne*. The simple tactical scenarios he devised (which did not adequately test the Pollen equipment) were indicative of his dated views of battle tactics. His hostility toward Pollen revealed his disinclination to admit that his understanding of a problem could be imperfect. Wilson's idea of extreme range for naval artillery was 8,000 yards, at a time when the battle range for HMS *Dreadnought* was generally accepted to be about 10,000 yards. He also remained convinced that to hit at this range, the firing ship would have to steer a course parallel to that of the target. The Pollen system, however, was designed to cope with ranges beyond 12,000 yards even while the firing ship was changing course.[58]

More serious, however, was the fact that Wilson had retired one year before the first large-scale exercises had been held between capital ships and submarines. Wilson's personal experience of submarines was limited to umpiring the very first maneuvres between the Channel Squadron and the Navy's handful of prototype submarine boats, held off Portsmouth in 1904.[59] At the time the exercises had been condemned as totally unrealistic, but this had not altered Wilson's own deductions about the capabilities of submarines.[60] Needless to say, by 1910 the performance of submarines had improved dramatically.

Wilson's perceptions of the conditions of modern naval warfare may not have been at the forefront of naval thinking when he became First Sea Lord, but he was still able to rely on considerable support within the service for his strategic and tactical ideas—whether or not he cared for it. Quite simply, there was no consensus within the Navy on how the fleet should be deployed in war against Germany, the nature and purpose of the blockade to be employed, or even the correct battle tactics. (Accordingly, Wilson's failure to consult and his habit of listening only to like-minded officers takes on far greater significance.) As late as

1910, many fleet officers still failed to appreciate the extent to which the advent of the submarine had changed the conditions of war at sea. Many had not yet been won over to the dreadnought concept. There were still squadron commanders serving in the Home Fleet, such as Rear Admiral Doveton Sturdee, who questioned the claimed superiority of the all-big-gun ship, arguing that "if the range can be kept in to such a distance that the 6" gun can penetrate the opponents armour, one of the chief advantages of the heavy gun is gone; this is the case at 6000 yards." Sturdee proved that the idea of actions being fought at such short ranges was plausible:

[T]aking the whole year round there are, in the North Sea, on average, twenty-five days out of thirty on which you cannot see 10,000 yards, and [given] that about 6000 yards is the distance at which fire will be opened, . . . one of the greatest advantages of the Dreadnought will disappear at once.[61]

Admiral Sir William May, the Commander-in-Chief, confessed that he, too, anticipated that battle ranges in the North Sea would be as low as 6,000 yards.[62] Even some of Fisher's keenest supporters, such as Reginald Bacon, also accepted the idea that battle ranges would be short. This conviction had implications that extended beyond battleship tactics and gunnery policy. In 1910, a survey of flag-officers found that the majority believed that as a consequence, torpedo craft must play a major role in future battle fleet engagements.[63] In turn, this had an impact on fleet tactics and ship design. When, in 1910, May demanded the reintroduction of the intermediate 6" gun battery on all new battleships, he had behind him tremendous support in the fleet.[64] Secondary armament, however, was *fundamentally* antagonistic to the all-big-gun "dreadnought principle" envisioned by Fisher and Jellicoe.[65] It is significant that only after Jellicoe left the Controller's office in 1911 were battleships given a 6" gun battery. Nevertheless, when one realizes the extent to which opinions in the Navy conflict over many questions, some of Wilson's policies become more understandable. For instance, mechanized fire control was not essential for short-range actions. Indeed, most officers agreed that it would slow rates of fire and thus prove a major disadvantage.[66] In addition, armor-piercing shells were perfectly efficient at ranges under 9,000 yards and the proposal that battleships should fire high explosive shells while closing the range was practicable.

If Wilson's ideas for surface ship warfare were reasonable (given his experience), his views on submarines certainly were not. In early 1911, Fisher expressed his concern to Jellicoe that seemingly, Wilson did not "realise the immense alteration in both tactics and strategy which the development of the submarine now causes."[67] Wilson's ideas as to the capabilities and, particularly, the weaknesses of submarines were very confused. At the same time that he accepted that British submarines could be an effective force for harbor defense, he argued that it was imperative for the Royal Navy to maintain a close blockade of German ports, primarily in order to prevent German submarines escaping to the open sea, where they could attack the battle fleet. "I see no way of stopping this," Wilson told a meeting of the CID in 1913, "except catching them in shoal water at the mouths of their own rivers."[68] "I think that the advent of the submarine is the reason which makes the close blockade absolutely necessary."[69]

Wilson's misconceptions appear to have emanated from his own interpretations of the exercises he had umpired, in 1904, between submarines and his Channel Squadron.[70] He had noted that submarines found it difficult to maneuver in shallow waters. He had also noticed that the submarines had rarely attempted to attack difficult targets, such as small destroyers or picket boats.[71] (In fact, the submarines had been maneuvering to attack the battleships.) Subsequently, Wilson had managed to convince himself that the inability to attack small targets, coupled with the threat of being rammed by a destroyer, would deter submarines from putting to sea, a fallacy that he continued to believe until as late as 1915.[72] Wilson simply would not listen to warnings from the successive Inspecting Captains of Submarines, Sydney Hall and Roger Keyes, that his views were mistaken, that submarines could easily "dive under light craft," and that consequently, "there should be no difficulty in getting a number of submariners to sea past an inshore blockading squadron of light craft."[73] Roger Keyes predicted that if a blockade squadron were to be deployed close inshore "off the coast of an enemy possessing submarines, it would court certain disaster."[74]

As for his efforts to create detailed war plans against Germany, Wilson's idea of the contemporary operational environment facing the Royal Navy was exposed as being dangerously outdated. Before giving an outline of Wilson's plans, certain circumstances must be understood. First, when Wilson took office, the Admiralty had not yet agreed on a definite plan for war against Germany, beyond the broad objective of using naval force to impose a distant commercial blockade. The traditional method of formulating war plans was for the Admiralty to issue guidelines, or "War Orders," to the Admiral responsible for operational control of the fleet, who would, in turn, draw up the detailed plan.[75] When Fisher had been First Sea Lord and Charles Beresford, the Commander-in-Chief, this system had broken down, however, because the two men had held fundamentally different ideas about strategy.[76] No plan, as a consequence, had been agreed to.[77]

Second, the interpretation of all documents relating to war planning from the period 1910-12, is greatly complicated by the fact that the Admiralty plans had to conform to "the provisions of the Declaration of London which relate to the declaration and enforcement of a blockade of an enemy's port."[78] For instance, the draft plans under consideration in August 1911 included the names and addresses of all the Burgermeisters on the German Coast who were to have been notified by a naval officer that a blockade had been declared.[79] The failure of Parliament to ratify the treaty in 1911 resulted in major changes being made to the war plans.[80] Sadly, it is not possible to identify them all because the relevant papers are missing from the Admiralty records. When Wilson left office at the end of 1911, the Admiralty still had not yet sent the Commander-in-Chief copies of its new plan for war against Germany.[81]

Despite the absence of key documents, the available records show that, to a lesser or greater degree, the successive Commanders-in-Chief, William May, Francis Bridgeman and George Callaghan, all had disagreements with Wilson over his War Orders. More significantly, they also suggest that, contrary to popular belief, Wilson's ideas on naval strategy differed radically from those of his predecessor. Fisher always accepted that some minor changes to his plan for war would be inevitable.[82] It is certain that when he handed over the reins to Wilson, however, Fisher had no plan to deploy an inshore squadron off the German ports "to prevent the enemy breaking out without being reported and brought to action."[83] Nor can he have thought that Wilson would ever adopt such a plan. As recently as 1909, Wilson had told the Beresford enquiry that while he had been Commander-in-Chief he had considered a close blockade to have been impracticable.[84] Under Fisher, the Admiralty had developed the plan to impose a distant commercial blockade, and distant naval blockade was also envisaged. All modern armored warships were to have been kept out of the southern half of the North Sea. Fisher had wanted to use only flotilla craft to operate between the German coast and the east coast of England. Moreover, his plans had involved the use of British submarines off the German ports.[85]

Under Wilson, the Royal Navy's strategic policy against Germany regressed toward a more "traditional" strategy. Wilson's plan called for the "blockade of the whole German North Sea coast," enforced by an inshore squadron of light craft supported by cruisers. He also envisaged the bombardment of German ports and the capture of islands along the enemy littoral. The Wilson strategy rested upon his absolute confidence in the ability of the stronger British battle fleet to engage and defeat the High Sea Fleet in battle whenever it emerged to break up the blockade. Of course, the practicality of this strategy relied on the battle fleet being kept on station dangerously close to the enemy coast.[86] Critics warned that torpedo boats, submarines, and contact mines made a close blockade totally unrealistic. At the time, however, many senior officers other than the First Sea Lord did not accept this assertion. In principle, Admiral May supported Wilson's strategy of a close naval blockade of German ports, as did his junior Admirals Berkeley Milne and Doveton Sturdee.[87] May objected only to certain details of Wilson's plan. For instance, May far better recognized the capabilities of existing submarines. He repeatedly begged Wilson to release a couple of flotillas from harbor defense duties to support the inshore blockade squadron that was scheduled to operate in the Heligoland Bight, but not until March 1911 did the First Sea Lord finally consider deploying British submarines for oversea operations.[88] By this time, May had been replaced as Commander-in-Chief by Admiral Sir Francis Bridgeman.

Wilson was to have far more serious disagreements with Bridgeman and his second in command, Vice Admiral Sir George Callaghan. The surviving correspondence indicates that both these Admirals openly questioned the practicality of a close blockade. In August 1911, Callaghan predicted that the Royal Navy had insufficient destroyers to maintain permanently an inshore squadron in the Heligoland Bight.[89] The solution to this problem, responded Wilson, was to capture the island of Heligoland for use as a base by the inshore squadron—a plan that alarmed the senior officers of the Home Fleet.[90] In September, Bridgeman, who was almost certainly encouraged by Callaghan, refused to endorse the draft orders for the Commodore (T) commanding the inshore squadron because of doubts "as to the exact nature of the watch required and the policy to be perused with regard to Heligoland."[91] Bridgeman had been given ample justification for his decision by the abysmal performance of the First Destroyer Flotilla, under the command of Commodore (T) Lewis Bayly, in an exercise to test the practicality of close blockade against a port defended by submarines.[92] Wilson's reaction to the dissent of the fleet commander is unknown. Possibly, he did not have time to reply before he was replaced as First Sea Lord several weeks later.

Interestingly, Callaghan did not learn all the details of the war plans until after he took command of the Home Fleet in November 1911. When he read Wilson's secret orders to the Commander-in-Chief, entitled "Notes on Operations in the North Sea," he confessed to being astonished. In this paper Wilson outlined his strategic ideas, including the plan for the capture of Heligoland. More controversially, Wilson also proposed deploying the fleet to bombard systematically German coastal fortifications. Callaghan's reaction was immediately to inform the Admiralty of his grave objections to the War Orders, particularly "the employment of a portion of the main fleet in operations against land defences."[93] He also requested a complete review of "the whole question of the Heligoland Bight blockade" in view of the Navy's shortage of destroyers.[94] Bridgeman, who was now First Sea Lord, entirely agreed.

In the autumn of 1911, others started to question Wilson's competence following his dismal performance during the Agadir crisis, involving Britain, France, and Germany, earlier in the summer. His failure to press the Cabinet to sanction the issue of a "warning telegram" at the height of the crisis was the principal cause of the fleet's unpreparedness. Francis Bridgeman, the Commander-in-Chief, who feared surprise attack by German submarines and torpedo boats was furious at the result: "[Our] Cabinet will permit no precautions being taken to prevent a surprise. I was forbidden to take the fleet to sea or take the necessary precautions while lying in harbour—exception being taken even to getting the nets out at night."[95] Both Bridgeman and Rear Admiral Sir Charles Ottley, the Secretary of CID, had pressed for the warning telegram to be sent, but the government demurred out of fear of precipitating conflict. Wilson did not insist, nor did he consult any of his colleagues. Rear Admiral Charles Madden, the Fourth Sea Lord, complained to the First Lord that none of the other Sea Lords "know what the Government thinks of the situation, or whether they consider special precautions against 'bolts from the blue' are necessary."[96] The Naval War Council was not summoned. Rear Admiral Alexander Bethell, the Director of Naval Intelligence (DNI), was on vacation. The reason for Wilson's failure to insist on sending the warning telegram probably will never be known. It may be significant, however, that both Bridgeman and Jellicoe maintained that Wilson always became "pliant" when placed under pressure by politicians.[97] Jellicoe, more cynically, claimed that "the least appeal to his sense of duty [would] cause him to agree to anything. He never asserted himself as First Sea Lord."[98] (Whether McKenna would have agreed with this statement appears somewhat questionable.)

Wilson's performance during the Agadir crisis also attracted criticism from members of the Cabinet. After the emergency meeting of the CID on 23 August 1911, summoned ostensibly to decide "the action to be taken in the event of intervention in a European war," there was a consensus among those present that the First Sea Lord's performance had been exceptionally poor. His plan for war against Germany, involving the capture of Heligoland and amphibious assaults on the German coast, had been savagely criticized by the military experts and also by the Home Secretary, Winston Churchill, although it had not been actually condemned.[99] Fortunately, from a naval perspective, the Army's plan to send its entire striking force of six divisions to the Continent was not adopted either; on reflection, "even Churchill no longer believed in it."[100]

The politicians actually displayed far more interest at the want of cooperation between the two services than in thinking about the practicability of the alternative war plans. Immediately after the meeting, the Admiralty was instructed to assist the War Office to complete the details of its plan to send an expeditionary force to the Continent. This order should not, however, be regarded as an endorsement of the continental strategy by the Prime Minister. Furthermore, at this stage there was no pressure from Asquith for administrative reform at the Admiralty, although it seems that McKenna himself suggested to Wilson the idea of creating a Naval Staff.[101]

The collapse of confidence in the Admiralty and the decision by the Prime Minister to impose administrative reform occurred a month later, at the end of September, after the War Office had complained to Asquith that they could "get no reply from the Admiralty to their request to be furnished with revised tables in regard to their sea transport of the expeditionary force."[102] Apparently Admiral Groome and Captain Christian were away on vacation from the Admiralty Transport Department. McKenna's candid admission that he "knew nothing whatever about the matter"[103] cost him his ministerial portfolio.[104] In October he was replaced as First Lord by Winston Churchill, who was sent to the Admiralty with the express purpose of setting up a Naval Staff.[105]

Wilson's emphatic rejection of Churchill's proposal to form a Naval War Staff led directly to his dismissal only three months before he was due to retire.[106] Ironically, however, Wilson's main objections to the scheme that had been put to him were later proved to have been well founded. The idea that Winston Churchill created a proper Naval Staff is a myth. Effectively, all he did was to rename the old Naval Intelligence Department, add three extra clerks, and place a different officer in charge with the title Chief of the War Staff. Wilson was opposed strongly to the confusion of authority for strategic policy between the Board of Admiralty (First Sea Lord) and the War Staff (Chief of Naval Staff).[107] Indeed, after Churchill was replaced in 1915, these two offices were merged. No attempt was made before the war to rectify the principal "structural defects" inside the Admiralty.[108]

Wilson left office in 1911 with his professional reputation severely damaged among naval and political leaders. It was, therefore, all the more surprising that Churchill recalled him to the Admiralty in August 1914 as a strategic advisor: there is no surprise that this was not well received by the Navy. A number of officers seriously doubted his sanity after he again put forward his plan to capture Heligoland at a conference of flag-officers held in September 1914.[109] Churchill's proposal to recall Wilson as First Sea Lord after Fisher's resignation in May 1915 provoked horror. Jellicoe, the Commander-in-Chief, claimed:

[T]he flag officers afloat are even more distrustful of Sir Arthur Wilson than of Winston Churchill and we should have no confidence whatever in an administration headed by him. I greatly fear that he will eventually be First Sea Lord and I as well as all the rest would view that as a national disaster.[110]

Admiral Sir Stanley Colville, himself no "Fisherite," saw the price of replacing Fisher with Wilson as too high: "If old 'Tugs' [Wilson] was to succeed him [Fisher]—well we better make peace at once!"[111]

Arthur Wilson's term as First Sea Lord proved to be regrettable both for his own reputation and for the Royal Navy. Those qualities that had made him the most respected fleet commander of his day sadly did not translate into making him a good First Sea Lord. Wilson's horizon did not extend beyond his experience as a tactician. His greatest shortcoming was that in an age of rapid technological progress, he was unprepared to accept the limitations of his own experiences and unwilling to listen to informed opinion. As an administrator, it was said that "he would have ruined the Roman Empire."[112]

Whether any of the other candidates who rivaled him for the post in 1910 would have proved better administrators, is, of course, an open question. It is difficult to imagine any of them being much better strategists. All possessed the same limited outlook on naval warfare, all being shackled by the same experiences, which is why they had all been passed over in favor of Wilson. As the caretaker for Fisher's naval policy, Wilson succeeded in maintaining only the facade of continuity. In fact, he made significant changes in policy. It is ironic that for all Fisher's efforts, Wilson's strategic outlook proved little different to that held by the many Admirals who had been disbarred from selection for their association with Beresford and the Syndicate of Discontent.

NOTES

Excerpts in this chapter are reproduced with permission of Curtis Brown Group Ltd., London, on behalf of the Estate of Sir Winston S. Churchill. Copyright the Estate of Sir Winston S. Churchill.

1. Admiral Sir Edward Bradford, *Admiral of the Fleet Sir Arthur Knyvett-Wilson* (London: John Murray, 1923), 221.
2. Fisher to Ponsonby, 3 Nov. 1909, in Marder, *Fear God and Dread Nought*, 2:276.
3. *Navy List 1910* (January edition correct to November 1909).
4. Rhodri Williams, *Defending the Empire* (New Haven, Conn.: Yale University Press, 1991), 127-37.
5. Quoting Beresford to Balfour, 12 Dec. 1909, in Arthur Marder, *From the Dreadnought to Scapa Flow*, 212.
6. Bradford, *Admiral of the Fleet*, 30-31.
7. Ibid.
8. CAB 16/9A, 305-16.
9. Conversation with Jon Sumida. Also see Fisher to Esher, 13 Sept. 1909, in Marder, *Fear God*, 264.
10. Fisher to White, 13 Nov. 1909, in Marder,. *Fear God*, 277.
11. McKenna to Wilson, 19 Nov. 1909; Wilson to McKenna, 20 Nov. 1909, McKenna Papers (MCKN) 3/9, f. 43a.
12. Fisher to Mrs McKenna, [?] Dec. 1910, in Marder, *Fear God*, 2:344; Fisher to McKenna, 23 Feb. 1911, in Marder, *Fear God*, 2:356.
13. Fisher to McKenna, 25 Aug. 1910, in ibid., 2:337. References to the importance of appointments are also found in Troubridge Mss., Diary entries 7 Jan. 1910 to 24 Jan. 1910; Fisher to McKenna, 1 Feb. 1910, in Marder, *Fear God*, 2:302; Fisher to Mrs McKenna, 14 Dec. 1911, in ibid., 421; Fisher to Balfour, 23 Oct. 1910, in ibid., 3:32.
14. Troubridge Mss. Diary entry 7 Jan. 1910. See also entry for 1 Feb. 1910. Letter from Noel to McKenna, 12 Feb. 1909, in Ruddock Mackay, *Fisher of Kilverstone* (Oxford: Clarendon Press, 1973), 412.
15. McKenna to Knollys, 20 Oct. 1909, Royal Archive (RA) W59/89.
16. Fisher to McKenna, 17 Dec. 1909, in Marder, *Fear God*, 2:284.
17. Fisher to King Edward VII, 27 Nov. 1909, RA W59/93.
18. Fisher to Esher, 27 Oct. 1909, in Marder, *Fear God*, 2:274.
19. Fisher to Knollys, 1 Dec. 1909, RA W59/93a.
20. Esher to M. V. Brett, 4 Jan. 1910, in M. V. Brett, ed., *The Journals and Letters of Reginald Viscount Esher* (London: Nicholson and Watson, 1934), 2:433.
21. Ibid.
22. Asquith Mss. 6, f. 14, Bodleian Library, Oxford. Cabinet Minutes, 1 Mar. 1911.
23. Fisher to Mrs Cecil Fisher, 2 Dec. 1911, in Marder, *Fear God*, 2:417.
24. 110th Cabinet Meeting (Cab. mtg.), 24 Mar. 1911, CAB 2/1, 4. Also Ottley memorandum, 114th Cab. mtg., 23 Aug. 1911, CAB 4/3/2/126B.
25. Fisher to Esher, 10 Oct. 1911, in Marder, *Fear God*, 2:390.
26. Bridgeman to Fisher, 21 Nov. 1909, in ibid., 2:282.
27. Fisher to Ponsonby, 3 Nov. 1909, in ibid., 2:276.

28. Selborne to Balfour, 20 May 1915, Additional Manuscripts (Add Mss.) 49707, f. 251, British Library, London.

29. "Memorandum" by Selborne, 1901, Selborne Mss. 158, f. 146/158. See also Bradford, *Admiral of the Fleet*, 153-55.

30. Bradford, *Admiral of the Fleet*, 153-55.

31. Ibid., 154.

32. Pollen to Slade, 6 Jan. 1911, Slade Mss., National Maritime Museum, London.

33. Diary entry 7 Jan. 1910, Troubridge Mss., Imperial War Museum, London.

34. Ibid.

35. Lord Esher, conversation with McKenna, 4 Jan. 1910, in Marder, *From the Dreadnought to Scapa Flow*, 1:213.

36. Fisher to McKenna, 17 Jan. 1910, FISR 1/9 FP439.

37. Fisher to Ottley, 25 Feb. 1910, FISR 1/9 FP474.

38. McKenna to Knollys, 29 Jan. 1910, MCKN 3/6. Fisher to McKenna, 12 Jan. 1911, FISR 1/10.

39. Fisher to McKenna, 20 Aug. 1911, MCKN 6/3. See also McKenna to Wilson, 6 July 1911, MCKN, 3/22, f. 54. Fisher to McKenna, 23 Feb. 1911, in Marder, *Fear God*, 2:356; Fisher to Jellicoe, 9 May 1911, in Marder, *Fear God*, 2:369; Fisher to McKenna, 12 July 1911, in Marder, *Fear God*, 2:377; Fisher to Reginald Henderson, 29 Sept. 1911, in Marder, *Fear God*, 2:386. Fisher to White, 1 Oct. 1911, in Marder, *Fear God*, 2:387.

40. Jellicoe to Hamilton, 19 May 1915, Hamilton Mss. 125, National Maritime Museum, London.

41. Battenberg to Hamilton, 5 Dec. 1910, Hamilton Mss. 118A.

42. Sanders to Balfour, 7 Mar. 1910, Add. Mss. 49766. See also "Naval War Council Minutes", 22 Feb. 1910 mtg., ADM 116/3090.

43. Scott to White, 29 Nov. 1911 and others, Arnold-White Mss. WHI 172, National Maritime Museum, London.

44. Battenberg to Hamilton, 5 Dec. 1910, Hamilton Mss. 118a.

45. Scott to White, 5 May 1912, Arnold-White Mss. WHI 63. For evidence that the defects were anticipated, see Battenberg to Hamilton, 5 Dec. 1910, Hamilton Mss. 118a. See also Jellicoe to Churchill, 27 Feb. 1912, CHART 13/8, f. 87.

46. Jon Sumida, *In Defence of Naval Supremacy* (London: Unwin Hyman, 1989), 196-202. Pollen to McKenna, 12 Apr. 1910, MCKN 3/15.

47. "Edinburgh Experiments", 7 Feb. 1910, ADM 1/8145.

48. Ships Covers No. 268 (Iron Duke class battleships), f. 35, "Trials with A.P. shells against armour", 24 Oct. 1910, G18281/10.

49. Sumida, *In Defence*, 206-7. For use of High Explosive (HE) shells by 12" battleships, see John Campbell, *The Fighting at Jutland* (London: Conway, 1983), 349.

50. Cost of equipment for 12" guns: AP shell, £46, total number of shells, 9,000; expenditure on submarines in 1910, £321,000, Vickers Papers 665, f. 212.

51. Ships Covers No. 338 (King George V class), f. 86. "As to the Adoption of 1400lb Projectiles for 13.5" BL guns, Mk.V, for the Equipment of New Ships", Rear Admiral Archibald Moore (D.N.O.), 10 Jan. 1911.

52. Churchill to Fisher, 12 Apr. 1912, CHART 8/177, f. 24.

53. Sumida, *In Defence*, 123-26.

54. "Director Firing Gear", request for transfer of experimental gear from Captain of HMS *Dreadnought* (Herbert Richmond) to May, 9 Dec. 1909. Note refusal by Bridgeman in 1909, ADM 1/8145.

55. Neville to Keyes, 28 Jan. 1911, KP4/13.
56. Sumida, *In Defence*, 130, 217-21.
57. Jellicoe to Hamilton, 19 May 1914, Hamilton Mss. 125.
58. Sumida, *In Defence*, 126-30.
59. "Report of Manoeuvres between Home Fleet and submarines", by Admiral Wilson, 22 Mar. 1903, ADM 1/7795.
60. Report by Captain Bacon, 24 Mar. 1903, ADM 1/7795.
61. Sturdee to Sanders, n.d. [1909-10], Sanders Mss. 758, f. 97.
62. "Employment of Destroyers in Fleet Action", May to Admiralty, 17 May 1910; also remarks by DNI (Bethell), 15 June 1910, ADM 1/8120.
63. Ibid. See also "Design of British Destroyers", December 1915, 6, Richmond Mss., RIC 2/5, National Maritime Museum, London.
64. Ibid.
65. Fisher to McKenna, 22 Nov. 1911, MCKN 6/3.
66. May to Admiralty, 16 Apr. 1910, May Mss. 9.
67. Fisher to Jellicoe, 10 Jan. 1911, Add Mss. 49006, f. 6.
68. Churchill quoting Wilson's report, P.2741, 3 Dec. 1913, CAB 16/28A, 324.
69. Testimony of Wilson, 3 Dec. 1913, P.2661, CAB 16/28A, 311.
70. ADM 1/7795.
71. Ibid. Also Minute by Wilson, 16 Apr. 1910, G0230/10. Ships Covers No. 338, f. 38.
72. Wilson to Bradford, 14 Feb. 1915, in Bradford, *Admiral of the Fleet*, 193, 242.
73. Keyes to V.A. Commanding 3rd & 4th Divisions (Battenberg), 3 July 1911, KP4/13.
74. Keyes to R.A. Commanding Blue Fleet (Lewis Bayly), 1 July 1911, KP4/13.
75. McKenna to Beresford, Q.733, CAB 16/9A, 68.
76. Questions put to Beresford and his replies, Q.788; 793; 794; 838; 636, CAB 16/9A, 68.
77. Meeting of War Council, 13 Oct. 1909, ADM 116/3090.
78. Memorandum "Blockade of North Sea Coast of Germany", sent to Foreign Office on 2 Feb. 1911, M0146/11. Also memo by A/DNI (King-Hall), "Arrangements in case of Blockade of German Ports and Coasts", 6 Dec. 1910, ADM 1/8132.
79. Letter M01137/11, Admiralty to Bridgeman and Callaghan, 31 Aug. 1911, ADM 1/8132.
80. Docket, "Addenda to Preliminary War Orders", Minute by Flint (Head of M branch); and also Minute by Duff (DNM), 11 Dec. 1911, ADM 1/8132.
81. Correspondence between Bridgeman and Callaghan with the Admiralty from 31 August 1911 clearly shows that the War Plan was still only in the draft stage.
82. Fisher to Grey, 23 Jan. 1908, in Marder, *Fear God*, 2:155; Fisher to Tweedmouth, 23 Jan. 1908, in Marder, *Fear God*, 2:157.
83. May to Bayly, January 1911, enclosing "Preliminary War Orders for Commodore T". Approved by Admiralty, 1 Mar. 1911, ADM 116/3096.
84. Especially questions 2529, 2539, 2540, 2554, 2598, 2601, and 2602 in CAB 16/9A, 305-16.
85. Nicholas A. Lambert "The Influence of the Submarine upon Naval Strategy: 1898-1914" (Unpublished D.Phil. dissertation, Oxford University, 1992).
86. 114th mtg. of Committee of Imperial Defence (CID), 23 Aug. 1911, CAB 2/1.
87. Sturdee to Sanders, n.d. [1909-10], Sanders Mss. 758, f. 97.

88. Memorandum by Wilson: "Revision of War Orders for Submarines", 23 Mar. 1911. For evidence that Wilson was probably persuaded by Fisher, see Fisher to Jellicoe, 10 Jan. 1911, Add. Mss. 49006, ADM 116/3096.

89. "Blockade of North Sea Coast of German Empire", Vice Admiral Callaghan to Admiralty, 31 Aug. 1911, ADM 1/8132.

90. Paragraph 3, ibid.

91. "War Plans -- Pages 1 to 24: Remarks by C.in.C. H.F., 9:1:12.", Section VII: "Watch on German Rivers", ADM 116/3096.

92. Keyes to R.A. commanding Blue Fleet (Lewis Bayly), 1 July 1911, KP4/13.

93. "War Plans—Pages 1-24. Remarks by C.in.C. H.F., 9:1:12". Section X, ADM 116/3096.

94. Ibid.

95. Bridgeman to Battenberg, 30 Sept. 1911, Battenberg Mss. T9/44.

96. Madden to McKenna, 28 July 1911, MCKN 4/4.

97. Sanders to Balfour, 14 Feb. 1911, Add Mss. 49767, f. 99.

98. Jellicoe to Hamilton, 19 May 1915, Hamilton Mss. 125.

99. Hankey to Fisher, 24 Aug. 1911. See also FISR 1/10, FP530A.

100. "Notes on Conversation 20:10:11", between McKenna and Asquith, 3, MCKN 4/2.

101. Wilson to Churchill, n/d., in Bradford, *Admiral of the Fleet,* 229.

102. Asquith to McKenna, 18 Sept. 1911, MCKN 4/1. McKenna to Asquith, 19 Sept. 1911, Asquith Mss. 13, f. 43.

103. McKenna to Asquith, 19 Sept. 1911, Asquith Mss. 13, f. 43. *See* also Haldane to Asquith, 25 Sept. 1911, ibid., f. 48.

104. Diary entry 4 Oct. 1911, ESHR 12/1.

105. Hankey to Esher, 5 Oct. 1911 and 24 Oct. 1911, Esher to Asquith, 6 Oct. 1910, Hankey Mss. 4/3.

106. Churchill to Asquith, 16 Nov. 1911, Asquith Mss. 11, f. 58. Churchill to Asquith, 5 Nov. 1911, CHART 13/1, f. 8.

107. Bradford, *Admiral of the Fleet,* 229-35.

108. Jon Sumida, "British Naval Administration and Policy in the Age of Fisher", *Journal of Military History,* 54 (January 1990):1-26.

109. Colville to Hamilton, 10 Nov. 1914, Hamilton Mss. 117. Bradford, *Admiral of the Fleet,* 241-44. See also Admiral John Jellicoe, *The Grand Fleet* (London: Cassell, 1919).

110. Jellicoe to Hamilton, 19 May 1915, 22 May 1915, Hamilton Mss. 125. See also Jellicoe to McKenna, 23 May 1915, MCKN 3/22, f. 85.

111. Colville to Hamilton, 14 May 1915, Hamilton Mss. 125.

112. Fisher to Churchill, 27 Jan. 1913, CHART 13/21, f. 4.

4

Admiral Sir Francis Bridgeman-Bridgeman (1911–1912)

Nicholas A. Lambert

Admiral Sir Francis Bridgeman was asked by Winston Churchill to join the Board of Admiralty as First Sea Lord on 16 November 1911.[1] Three weeks later he formally replaced Sir Arthur Wilson as the senior professional member of the Admiralty Board, occupying that position until his dismissal on 28 November 1912. Like his predecessor, Francis Bridgeman was not an obvious choice for the post of First Sea Lord. He had held the rank of Admiral for less than six months. More important, only seven months earlier, Bridgeman had been appointed Commander-in-Chief of the combined Home Fleets, a seagoing command to which he had always aspired and which he had expected to hold for at least two years.

Originally, Churchill had wanted Vice Admiral Prince Louis of Battenberg to become his new senior advisor. The First Lord had convinced himself that he and Battenberg had been "in cordial agreement" with each other "on nearly every important question of naval policy."[2] Churchill's nominee, however, had been rejected by the Prime Minister. Asquith had been warned by a Cabinet colleague that appointing an officer of German ancestry as head of the Royal Navy would be politically unpopular.[3] Moreover, even if the Prime Minister had not vetoed Battenberg's selection, it is unlikely that the rest of the Navy would have accepted him as First Sea Lord.[4] Holding the rank of Vice Admiral, he was junior to several officers commanding squadrons at sea.[5] In addition, he had never held office as a Lord Commissioner of the Admiralty; his experience outside the fleet was limited to two years as Director of Naval Intelligence. Since 1905, Battenberg had been given continuous employment afloat.

Despite being prevented from officially appointing Battenberg First Sea Lord, Churchill was evidently determined to employ Prince Louis as his "principal councillor" in the Admiralty.[6] Before resuming his search to find a replacement for Sir Arthur Wilson, the First Lord offered Battenberg his pick of the other seats on the Board of Admiralty.[7] Subsequently, he was appointed Second Sea Lord in December 1911. Even then, Churchill had still had not given up the hope that sometime in the future he might be able to offer his preferred advisor the senior post.[8] In the meantime, it only remained to find an officer senior to Battenberg to fill the office of First Sea Lord.[9]

Like Reginald McKenna, his predecessor, Churchill found no obviously suitable First Sea Lord among the admirals then on the active list. Indeed, Churchill considered the field of selection to be so poor that he contemplated emulating McKenna by recalling another retired Admiral of the Fleet: Lord Fisher. Political expediency, however, constrained the First Lord to limiting Fisher's role to that of unofficial advisor.[10] Resigned to choosing a second-rate First Sea Lord, Churchill focused on looking for an officer who would not resent his intention of relying on Battenberg for advice on major policy matters; however, he also wanted an admiral who would command the respect of the fleet and whose public reputation would help restore some of the confidence in the Admiralty that had been lost by Sir Arthur Wilson.[11] This ruled out Admirals Hedworth Lambton, John Durnford, and Edmond Poe. On Fisher's advice, Churchill also dropped the idea of selecting Admiral William May, after being warned not only that would he be an unpopular choice with the Navy, but also because May and Battenberg strongly disliked each other.[12] Eventually, by the process of elimination, Churchill settled on Francis Bridgeman: "Bridgeman begged and begged to be excused, but Winston was insistent and so Bridgeman yielded, sorely against his own wishes."[13]

There can be little doubt that in Churchill's mind the main reason for picking Bridgeman was indeed to instill confidence in his Board.[14] Fisher, who endorsed the selection, guaranteed that "Bridgeman would cast a 'halo' of integrity and firmness round the Board."[15] Fisher also assured the First Lord that Bridgeman knew his own limitations, that he was willing to delegate, and that in the past he had not resented greater responsibilities being given to junior admirals whom he acknowledged to be more talented than himself.[16] Fisher had good reasons for believing this to be true. Less than a year earlier, Bridgeman, who was then Commander-in-Chief, had promised that in event of war he would rely on Fisher's protégé, Vice Admiral John Jellicoe, for guidance on battle tactics.[17]

Unfortunately, no one told Bridgeman before he became First Sea Lord that he was only expected to act as the figurehead of the administration. Worse, it also emerged that Bridgeman did not, in fact, regard Battenberg as a better man. Indeed, he was positively indignant at suggestions in the press that Battenberg was expected to be the real man in charge at the Admiralty.[18] Bridgeman, however, chose to regard the stories as uninformed speculation, apparently not yet suspecting that this was actually Churchill's intention. Shortly after taking office, Bridgeman wrote Fisher to assure him that he had no intention of remaining passive and that he had already developed a good working relationship with the First Lord.[19]

Sadly, Churchill was to allow Bridgeman very few opportunities to demonstrate his talents. In matters pertaining to strategic policy, which was theoretically the principal business of the First Sea Lord, Bridgeman had to compete with the embryonic Naval War Staff. The First Sea Lord was not given much say in the reconstitution of the Naval Intelligence Division into the War Staff. That task was officially entrusted to Battenberg,[20] assisted by Vice Admiral Sir Henry Jackson, President of the War College at Portsmouth, and Rear Admiral Sir Charles Ottley and Captain Maurice Hankey, RMA, the Secretaries to the Committee of Imperial Defence.[21] Bridgeman was not allowed even to help choose the first Chief of the Naval Staff. When he arrived at Whitehall, he learned that the appointment had already been given to the Naval Secretary, Rear Admiral Ernest Troubridge, an officer who seems to have had little respect for Bridgeman.[22] Troubridge had been deliberately selected by Churchill, not only for his "great abilities" and "rare war experience," but more ominously, because the First Lord wanted the position filled with an officer who "is 'my man' and knows my whole mind and wishes."[23]

Officially, the Chief of the Naval Staff was a subordinate of the First Sea Lord, but Troubridge quickly developed a tendency to report directly to Churchill. Moreover, there can be little doubt that the First Lord encouraged him to do this. Originally, Churchill had wanted the chain of command from the Naval Staff to lead directly to his office. This proposal had been firmly opposed by the Sea Lords as constituting a potential threat to their authority. Consequently, Troubridge's defiance verged on insubordination; it was certainly resented by the First Sea Lord. Knowing that Churchill had been sent to the Admiralty with the express purpose of setting up a Naval Staff, however, and having promised to lend his support to the project, Bridgeman could not easily have raised strong protests so soon after its formation. Besides, after his predecessor had voiced objections to the organization of the Naval Staff, he had been summarily dismissed.

Possibly the reason for Churchill's apparent reluctance to trust the First Sea Lord's judgment was due to a warning from Fisher that, although Bridgeman "would *command immense confidence* . . . he has no genius whatever for administration."[24] Judging from Bridgeman's performance as Second Sea Lord between 1909 and 1911, this evaluation appears to have been fairly accurate.[25] While in charge of personnel matters, he had become absorbed by the problems of his department, tending to forget the wider perspective of naval policy-making.[26] During discussions on forthcoming naval estimates, Bridgeman had tended to disregard the political and financial aspects of policy-making. He had repeatedly pressed McKenna to ask the Cabinet for larger increases in naval expenditure than the First Lord knew he could secure.[27] Bridgeman's myopia was compounded by his tendency to threaten resignation whenever his recommendations were overruled. Because he was always easy to mollify, these outbursts made him appear volatile and temperamental. This was an irritating habit that he also exhibited as First Sea Lord. To an ambitious First Lord it could also appear menacing. It was probably a threat to resign that convinced Churchill he must "strike first" by sacking Bridgeman in November 1912.[28]

Bridgeman's efforts to exert his right to have the dominant voice in the formulation of policy was seriously hampered by recurrent bouts of poor health that he suffered throughout 1912. Like many contemporary senior officers working at the Admiralty, the breakdown of Bridgeman's health was probably due to the strain of overwork.[29] His determination to plough methodically through all his paperwork meant that he frequently worked long hours for seven days a week, without taking any vacations.[30] Bridgeman was away sick for periods during the months of April, September, and November. Over the course of the year he managed to miss three Admiralty Board meetings. More important, he was also absent from three out of six meetings of the CID.[31] Even so, for some reason he was careful to be "away from the office for never more than the inside of a fortnight at a time and very few weekends."[32] In his absence Battenberg was openly allowed to perform the duties of First Sea Lord.

In strong contrast to his predecessor, Bridgeman displayed an unusual willingness to listen and take advice from almost any quarter. He consulted widely on nearly every question involving a change in policy—possibly to an extreme. At times Bridgeman appeared to interpret the role of the First Sea Lord as the judge of various options put before him. He was noticeably reluctant himself to initiate change.³³ In 1911, as Commander-in-Chief, Bridgeman had complained to the Admiralty of major shortcomings in gunnery policy, particularly with existing methods of training fire-control teams. The result had been the appointment of a committee to investigate the problems.³⁴ When the final report was submitted to Bridgeman (by then First Sea Lord), however, he exhibited an unwillingness to address the problems squarely or to recommend specific changes in policy or personnel.³⁵ Instead, he appeared content that since the problems had been identified, matters could safely be left with the Controller and the Director of Naval Ordnance.

A number of letters in Churchill's private papers indicate that at other times the First Lord experienced difficulties in getting Bridgeman to express definite opinions on a subject, or when he did, to give the reasons for his views.³⁶ On one occasion, after Bridgeman failed to pass comment on the War Staff's assessment of the lessons learned from the 1912 maneuvers, Churchill returned the papers, a list of questions, and a peremptory note instructing the First Sea Lord: "[Y]ou are the principal naval authority in the state; and I must refer to you for guidance on this subject. What is your advice? I have noted down a few of the principal points which seem to me to require personal treatment at your hands."³⁷ Bridgeman appeared much more confident when dealing with matériel policy, where he could apply his extensive experience as a fleet commander. During his tenure as First Sea Lord, significant changes were made in the Admiralty's capital ship construction policy. Since 1905, the Royal Navy had been building two different types of large armoured warships, represented by the battleship HMS *Dreadnought* and the so-called battlecruiser, HMS *Invincible*.³⁸ In 1912, the Admiralty decided to revert to building a single type. The concept of the fast battleship was a deliberate attempt to eliminate the battlecruiser from the organization of the Royal Navy and simultaneously to induce the German Navy also to give up the construction of these vessels.³⁹ The battlecruiser had evolved from the need to build a new type of warship to outperform the French armored cruisers being built at the turn of the century for commerce raiding.⁴⁰ Now that the German battle fleet had become the focus of the Royal Navy's attention, many officers believed that no more battlecruisers should be built. Furthermore, it was important for trade protection reasons to avoid encouraging the Germans to build more of these vessels. German battlecruisers, when deployed against British commerce, could overwhelm any trade protection vessel they encountered except another battlecruiser. They were perceived as being a far greater threat to Britain's maritime supremacy than German battleships.

According to Churchill, Bridgeman strongly supported the idea of building "a division of ships fast enough to seize the advantageous position and yet strong enough in gun-power and armour as any battleship afloat."[41] In his memoirs he explained that Bridgeman's support for the program stemmed from his lack of confidence in even the latest British battlecruisers. This sounds plausible. Bridgeman, although a disciple of Fisher, had never liked the battlecruiser concept. In 1908 he had been given the responsibility for the initial tactical trials with the Invincible-class and had concluded that they could not be employed in a line of battle; battlecruisers, he had reported, "must never be considered as dreadnoughts. . . . [T]hey cannot work with battleships. . . . [T]hey must be deployed as cruisers."[42] The following year, Bridgeman, who was then Second Sea Lord, had been primarily responsible for preventing Fisher from laying down all eight armored vessels of the 1909 program as Lion-class battlecruisers.[43]

Another important procurement question to confront Bridgeman was whether the battleships of the 1912 program should be armed with new model 15" guns.[44] Not being a gunnery expert, the First Sea Lord acceded to the advice of his Controller, Rear Admiral Charles Briggs, who was urging Churchill not to order a full equipment of guns before the test of an experimental gun toward the end of the year.[45] Accordingly, the First and Third Sea Lords advised that the big-gun fast battleship project should be deferred for a year and the 1912 appropriation for battleships spent on repeats of the 1911 design. Churchill, however, rejected this counsel as timid. Spurred on by Fisher, the First Lord directed the fast battleships to be ordered immediately and that all five be armed with 15" guns. He arrogantly told his indecisive First Sea Lord, "[R]isks have to be run in peace as in war, and courage in design now may win a battle later on."[46] Actually this decision was not as much of a gamble as Churchill implied in his war memoirs, *The World Crisis*.[47] The guns were to be designed and built by the Elswick Ordnance Company, a subsidiary of Armstrong-Whitworth & Co. Ltd., the most experienced firm in the world at manufacturing naval ordnance.[48] Indeed, Elswick had been building 14" caliber guns for the United States and also Japan since 1908, and did not anticipate any difficulties in building the larger caliber gun.[49]

Bridgeman cannot, however, be accused of being a technological reactionary. Generally, he was very willing actively to encourage the development of new equipment. As Second Sea Lord he had moved the Navy one step closer to providing direct assistance to private firms engaged in weapon system development by authorizing the secondment of two gunnery officers to Arthur

Pollen's firm, which was developing an advanced fire-control table for the Navy. Bridgeman, though, had not been prepared to establish the precedent of making the Royal Navy assume actual responsibility for any of the cost of research and development. The officers' salaries had been paid by the Argo Company.[50] Thus, Admiral Sir Percy Scott's unqualified accusation that in 1912 the First Sea Lord had worked against the adoption of his director firing gear conveys a totally misleading impression of Bridgeman's attitude toward innovation.[51] Bridgeman always maintained that before a new invention could be adopted, its superiority over existing equipment must be clearly demonstrated in competitive trials. Considering the growing sophistication of naval equipment, and the consequent difficulty in achieving instant perfection, as in the case of the Scott Director, this policy was perhaps a little short-sighted. Nonetheless, it was normal procedure. When eventually, at the end of 1912, the value of the Scott Director fitted in the battleship HMS *Thunderer* had been proved conclusively, Bridgeman wrote to Battenberg to express his delight at the result.[52]

Bridgeman's contribution to Admiralty policy-making was not entirely negative. Most valuable was his willingness to consider questions of policy afresh, unhindered by the traditional ways of doing things. Bridgeman had a much clearer understanding than his predecessor of the modern conditions of naval warfare, and consequently, when viewing a problem his perspective was generally sound. For instance, unlike most of his contemporaries, Bridgeman anticipated the vulnerability of battleships to torpedo attack, particularly torpedoes fired from submarines. Commenting on the design of the 1912 battleships, he suggested that the recent trend of reacting to every extension in the range of the torpedo by further adding to the secondary armament of battleships appeared questionable:

An enormous amount of money is devoted to providing men and material as a defence against torpedo craft, but it is an open question whether we are likely to get an adequate return for it and it may be that our efforts are futile and that we are dealing with the problem in an altogether out-of-date manner which has not been sufficiently criticised.[53]

Instead, Bridgeman proposed that "the money and weight might be better expended on the hull underwater and in adding to the number of our own small craft," which were better able to ward off from the battle fleet any hostile torpedo craft.[54] Bridgeman believed it to be inevitable that a percentage of long-range torpedoes fired at a battle squadron would find their mark. He submitted that the most appropriate response would be to minimize the potential damage that a torpedo hit could inflict.

During his administration, Bridgeman received no support from within the Admiralty for his proposal to review the standard of secondary armament given to battleships.[55] It was probably to his credit, however, that just before the Admiralty was due to finalise the design of the Queen Elizabeth-class battleships, an additional set of plans were drawn up, incorporating far more extensive measures for underwater protection. The new design, which was the one adopted by the Board in June, provided the battleships with a hull strengthened by armored longitudinal bulkheads and a comprehensive internal subdivision. The added protection against torpedoes was provided at the expense of reducing the thickness of the main armor belts by one inch.[56] This change set a precedent in British capital ship design. It should also be noted that John Fisher was at the same time expressing very similar ideas on warship construction.[57]

If the evidence shows that Bridgeman failed to display much initiative while performing his administrative duties, he did exhibit far greater aptitude for the formulation of strategic policy. It is also in this area of business that Bridgeman's working relationship with his colleagues is best illustrated, particularly the difficulty he experienced in exerting his right to have the dominant voice in policy making. Not only did Bridgeman have to contend with Troubridge and the Naval War Staff, but as expected, Battenberg was also quietly challenging the First Sea Lord's authority, an endeavor in which he was aided and abetted by Churchill. At the First Lord's instigation, Battenberg was authorized to attend meetings of the CID, thereby giving him direct access to all secret documents on national strategic policy.[58]

It is difficult, however, to estimate how much Churchill actually did rely on Battenberg or any other naval officer. Few men proved able to cope with Churchill's forceful personality or recognize his deviousness in getting his own way. Although he always consulted widely, at the same time he was extremely selective in the advice he took. Bridgeman claimed that Churchill swiftly discounted Battenberg's advice after he discovered him to be "utterly deficient in technical knowledge."[59] Privately, Bridgeman was also contemptuous of his Second Sea Lord's abilities, claiming that he could "never tackle papers—he could write voluminously and in well chosen language on any subject, but they rarely stood close examination [and] . . . his knowledge was superficial."[60] These remarks cannot have been motivated entirely by resentment. It will be remembered that even before he took office, Bridgeman had not appeared to hold Battenberg's talents in high esteem.

In January 1912, Admiral George Callaghan, the Commander-in-Chief of the Home Fleets, submitted to the Admiralty that the official plan for war against Germany, as outlined in Arthur Wilson's secret memorandum to the fleet commander, was quite unworkable.[61] Both Bridgeman and Churchill entirely agreed that the strategy of close blockade should be abandoned in favor of some sort of observation blockade. Bridgeman's contribution to the new plan was restricted to providing the War Staff with only "a general direction as to the rough distribution of the various units" of the fleet.[62] The task of composing the war orders and fixing the exact station of each squadron was entrusted to Troubridge and his staff. The Chief of Naval Staff was still supposed to consult regularly with the First Sea Lord, but Bridgeman became increasingly aware that the Chief of the War Staff was attacking his authority by sending correspondence relating to the draft war plans directly to Churchill.[63] In March, Bridgeman protested that this should stop.[64]

The First Sea Lord also had to cope with growing interference from the First Lord in strategic matters of a technical nature that were not strictly his responsibility.[65] As Churchill grew more confident in his abilities, Bridgeman retained steadily less influence at the Admiralty, being seemingly unable to restrain the enthusiasm of the First Lord. At the end of March, just before the new War Orders were to have been issued to the fleet,[66] the First Lord suddenly directed the War Staff to re-write them.[67] In response, an indignant Troubridge appealed to Bridgeman not to allow this "dangerous innovation" to go unchecked.

It is indeed a grave danger that the experience of many years at sea, of many manoeuvres designed to illustrate naval war . . . should be set aside for what can be described as experimental distribution and experimental happenings that suggest themselves to a vivid brain which pictures a scene that bears no relation to actualities.[68]

Churchill's action takes on greater significance if, as Troubridge claimed, the war plans had already been endorsed by both the First and Second Sea Lords.[69] It is strange that Bridgeman did not raise serious objection to a civilian overruling staff officers on a strategic matter; possibly, he shared Churchill's misgivings. The War Staff plan had called for the establishment of "an immense cordon of cruisers and destroyers, supported by the battle fleet from the coast of Norway to a point on the east coast of England."[70] The observation line ran approximately along the fifth line of longitude east of Greenwich.[71] There is no question that this plan was little more realistic than the old one, as it required an enormous number of small craft to be kept on station scattered across the North Sea. Unfortunately it is impossible to establish to what extent the plan had been initially supported by

Bridgeman. Contrary to the assertion of one eminent naval historian, this war plan was never adopted.[72]

The First Lord justified his unprecedented behavior by claiming that "outside the Admiralty it [the plan] was generally condemned by naval opinion."[73] By "naval opinion" Churchill appears to have meant Admiral Callaghan. Recently, the two men had been discussing the draft plans, and it is reasonable to assume that the First Lord had been persuaded by the Commander-in-Chief that the idea of an observation line drawn on a map of the North Sea in Whitehall would not work in practice.[74] Churchill had tremendous confidence in Callaghan, so too did Bridgeman.[75] As Commander-in-Chief, Bridgeman had always paid close attention to Callaghan's opinion. In his memoirs, however, Churchill gave himself far too much credit for having persuaded the Navy to adopt a more realistic distant blockade strategy.[76] The available evidence tends to suggest that it was, in fact, Callaghan who led the Navy toward formally adopting the distant blockade.[77]

In April, the Commander-in-Chief was officially informed that the original war plan drawn up by Wilson, which prescribed "the blockade by the British fleet of the whole German coast on the North Sea is to be considered cancelled."[78] Thereafter, he was left with considerable latitude in the disposition of his cruiser squadrons and destroyers.[79] It was not until November 1912 that the Admiralty finally issued Callaghan with acceptable war plans (probably inspired by him), which had been written by the War Staff.[80] During 1912, Callaghan appears to have had a far more important influence in naval war planning than either Bridgeman, Troubridge, or Churchill, by repeatedly rejecting as unsuitable the plans sent to him.[81] This officer deserves to be remembered for much more than simply being the admiral who was replaced by Jellicoe on the eve of war.

The biggest strategic problem to face the Admiralty during 1912 was how to respond to the new German Naval Law, the *Novelle*, which provided the German Navy with a large increase in the number of full-time personnel and enabled the High Seas Fleet to maintain in full commission a third battle squadron. After only a short deliberation, the Admiralty resolved to recall the battle squadron stationed in the Mediterranean, primarily to release the crews to man dreadnoughts then under construction.[82] The plan, which was laid before Parliament in March, called for a simple reshuffling of battle squadrons from Malta to Gibraltar and from Gibraltar to Portland.[83] There was nothing desperate about the Admiralty's response to events in the North Sea. The redistribution of the fleet conformed to the direction of the Admiralty's strategic thinking.[84] Even before learning the contents of the *Novelle*, Churchill had been seriously considering advice from Lord Fisher to withdraw the battleships anyway.[85] Fisher had been urging him to "let the French take care of the Mediterranean and a hot time they will have of it with submarines poking about in that lake! We are well out of it!"[86] There are reasons to believe that Bridgeman also supported this advice; these will be explained below.

Diplomatic, political, and military interests, however, conspired to oppose the Navy's proposal to evacuate the Mediterranean.[87] Such a fundamental shift in policy, opponents argued, would have a dramatic impact on foreign policy and thus could not be decided by the Admiralty unilaterally. In April, the Prime Minister was persuaded to allow the Navy's plan to be examined by the CID.[88] At the end of May, Asquith conducted a preliminary investigation at Malta where he took the opportunity of consulting the Viceroy of Egypt, Field Marshal Lord Kitchener, who was an acknowledged expert on the Eastern Mediterranean. Also present were Churchill, Battenberg, and the Naval Secretary, Rear Admiral David Beatty, as well as representatives from the military and diplomatic services.

At the meeting Kitchener presented a formidable case against the Admiralty's plan to evacuate the fleet from Malta, based on the need to uphold British prestige in the region. This, he insisted, should be the paramount aim of British policy; it depended on the continuing presence of a battle squadron inside the Mediterranean. Kitchener's views were strongly endorsed by the Foreign Office, which advised that, in addition, a strong Royal Navy presence in the Mediterranean was the best deterrent to keep Italy, and possibly also Spain, from gravitating toward the Triple Alliance.[89] Under enormous pressure, Churchill offered a compromise: the Navy was prepared to station two battlecruisers in the Mediterranean, albeit based on Gibraltar, and a reinforced cruiser squadron at Malta. The Admiralty's opponents did not appear satisfied: they wanted the addition of at least a third battlecruiser.[90] Nothing, however, was decided at the meeting.

There is no question that Bridgeman was not consulted over the Malta compromise. A memorandum by the First Sea Lord, dated 9 June, makes it quite clear that he was unhappy at the transfer of two battlecruisers from the North Sea. He found himself forced to admit, however, that "the question of prestige (about which Lord Kitchener makes a strong point) has a great deal in it."[91] With reluctance, therefore, he accepted that the Malta compromise "would for the next two years perhaps be the best that could be done." He added, "But it should be on the understanding that their places must be filled in the Home Fleets by two others of new construction."[92] Reporting the First Sea Lord's opinions to the Cabinet, however, Churchill deliberately misrepresented Bridgeman's views, exaggerating his enthusiasm for the agreement and omitting his insistence on the building of two additional battlecruisers.[93] The First Lord intimated that additional construction would be needed only if the Cabinet insisted on sending a third capital ship to the Mediterranean.[94] Bridgeman maintained that Churchill was "always very secretive as to what passes in the Cabinet."[95]

Despite Churchill's pleading and threats, the Malta compromise was rejected at a meeting of the CID, on 4 July 1912, as providing insufficient protection to British interests in the Mediterranean. The Admiralty was instructed to maintain at Malta "a battle fleet equal to a one-power Mediterranean standard excluding France."[96] Churchill did, however, manage to extract an agreement that the Navy would not be compelled to dispatch battleships until new dreadnoughts (then under construction) had been completed, in or around 1915.[97] In return, he promised the Cabinet that in the interim, he would move a complete squadron of four battlecruisers to the Mediterranean.[98] Again, the First Sea Lord was apparently not consulted. Churchill's revised formula was agreed at the next meeting of the CID on 11 July. During all the discussions, the First Lord had been careful to present the opinion of the Admiralty as being unanimous. Throughout, the First Sea Lord had remained very quiet.

At the first meeting of the CID, in July, Lord Fisher had provided the politicians with an alternative solution. Fisher's strategic vision was radically different to that of Churchill and most senior naval officers.[99] He suggested that only flotilla craft should be retained in the Mediterranean. The former First Sea Lord claimed that he "had absolute confidence in the power of the submarine and did not believe that any heavy ship was safe from them in narrow waters. Therefore if we had an adequate flotilla of submarines and destroyers at Malta, Gibraltar and Alexandria, no battleship could move in the Mediterranean."[100] Churchill emphatically rejected this theory. The First Lord stated categorically to the assembly that "the Board of Admiralty did not entirely accept Fisher's views on submarines. They did not think they could deny the open waters of the Mediterranean to battleships."[101] This was not entirely true. Evidence suggests that in a free vote, Bridgeman would have given his support to Fisher.[102] There is no question that Bridgeman did not approve of the Mediterranean compromise. Afterwards, he confided in a friend that "Winston" had been entirely responsible for "the mess" over the Mediterranean arrangements—suggesting that the proposed formulas had been concocted solely by the impulsive First Lord.[103]

Before Churchill left for Malta in May, Bridgeman had implored him to "please think and talk about submarines and destroyers together with their bases in the Mediterranean. I am convinced of their necessity and let them be doled out with no meagre hand!"[104] The following month, after the First Lord came back with the Malta compromise, Bridgeman concluded his appraisal of the agreement by reemphasising the argument that "in addition to these two battle-cruisers, it is undoubtedly important that the destroyer and submarine force should be increased."[105] Rough figures at the end of the document indicate that Bridgeman envisaged more than doubling the number of flotilla craft stationed at Malta and sending new flotillas to Alexandria. Bridgeman's confidence in the capabilities of flotilla craft is also suggested by his views on the danger to capital ships posed by torpedoes. Ultimately, in October, Bridgeman made a very clear statement of his confidence in the power of the submarine. In conversation with Jack Sanders, the private secretary to the former Conservative leader Arthur Balfour, the First Sea Lord let slip that he was trying to have the Navy's War Plans amended to provide for submarines to establish a close blockade of German ports in the North Sea.[106]

The First Lord's action indicates clearly that he constantly paid more attention to his own strategic ideas or possibly those of his other naval advisors than he did to the views put forward by Bridgeman. Troubridge and Battenberg were certainly opposed to the concept of "flotilla defence." In February, the Chief of Naval Staff had considered, but instantly rejected, the idea of relying just on flotilla craft in the Mediterranean, convinced that "generally speaking flotillas of torpedo craft left in the eastern basin of the Mediterranean on the withdrawal of our battle-fleet would soon fall an easy prey to a Mediterranean enemy [with battleships]."[107] Battenberg, too, was violently opposed to any notion of a battle fleet being intimidated from operating in waters patrolled by hostile flotilla craft. After the CID meeting on 4 July, he addressed to Churchill a forceful memorandum, condemning these "quite novel principles of the art of war at sea."[108] A scheme involving the supplementing of an inferior Mediterranean battle squadron with large numbers of submarines was examined by the War Staff. The Director of the Operations Division declared he was not entirely averse to the idea, but insisted that "the substitution of battleships for submarines should be kept within strict limits until the development of the submarine had proceeded much further."[109] Interest petered out after Bridgeman was dismissed as First Sea Lord. Incidentally, submarines were given only a minor role in the 1912 War Plans.

Another major shift in British naval policy during 1912 was the decision by the Admiralty not to reestablish a fleet in the Pacific. In 1909, Fisher had drawn up a plan to send an armored squadron to the China station, thereby allowing the British Empire to reduce its dependance on the Japanese alliance. Simultaneously, the defenses at Hong Kong dockyard were upgraded. Fisher made a tremendous effort to encourage material participation as well as financial assistance from the Dominions.[110] This was rewarded by the contribution of a fleet unit each from New Zealand and Australia. At the 1909 Colonial Conference, the Admiralty agreed to match these ships with two Royal Navy battlecruisers. The squadron was to be complete by the end of 1912. Fisher also hoped that later he might persuade India, South Africa, and Canada to contribute additional battlecruisers to the new Pacific fleet. All these ships were to be regarded as "additional" to the warships kept in European waters.

One of Churchill's first acts on becoming First Lord was to ask his Cabinet colleague Lewis Harcourt, the Colonial Secretary, for assistance in extricating the Admiralty from the 1909 naval colonial agreement and for help to pressure the New Zealand government into allowing its battlecruiser to be kept in the North Sea.[111] In their place, Churchill proposed to send old armored cruisers. Bridgeman placed no obstacles in front of Churchill, honestly believing that such powerful warships as battlecruisers were not really needed in the Pacific at that time. The First Sea Lord probably did not realize that Churchill's motives were purely financial. It is significant that the First Lord first proposed the change in policy before the Admiralty learned of the planned expansion of the German Fleet. Moreover, evidence shows that since 1910, Winston Churchill, who was then Home Secretary and a leading member of the "economist" wing of the Cabinet, had been trying to prevent the dispatch of the colonial dreadnoughts to the other end of the world. Churchill had also wanted the Admiralty to include these "additional" warships in calculations of the Royal Navy's strength deployed against Germany. If the Cabinet had agreed to count these vessels as part of the naval standard in European waters, this would have allowed the government to cut substantially future capital ship construction.[112] Although Reginald McKenna had wavered under this Churchillian barrage, he had been bolstered by the refusal of his First Sea Lord to even consider the idea. Wilson had been determined not to break the colonial agreement for fear of losing the potential additional ships.[113]

Churchill's plan in 1912, to present the Liberal government with a reduction in the naval construction budget over the next few years, was dashed after the

Cabinet unexpectedly refused to endorse the planned evacuation of the Mediterranean. Nevertheless, his earlier decision not to reestablish the Pacific Fleet fortuitously enabled him to meet this unwanted responsibility at no extra cost to the taxpayer.[114] He explained his plan to the Cabinet: "The late Board of Admiralty had proposed to send *Indomitable* to China, and to let *New Zealand* go there too. We have stopped *Indomitable* and we have been allowed to keep *New Zealand.* We are therefore two to the good on these."[115] The Admiralty overall, and Bridgeman in particular, did not seem the least bit interested in the impact that this blatant breach of faith with the Dominions might have on Imperial relations. This has not yet been fully explored. Certainly, the Australian government was furious at the Admiralty for reneging on its agreement.[116] The arguments, however, were cut short in 1914 with the advent of war.

In the autumn Bridgeman became more bellicose in his attempts to contain Churchill's interference. He had "serious disagreements with the First Lord on more than one occasion"—grave enough to induce him to threaten resignation.[117] In October, he led a rebellion of the Sea Lords against Churchill's handling of negotiations with the Canadian government for the offer of money to build three dreadnoughts.[118] In the same month he managed to extract from Churchill a grudging apology to the Sea Lords for his peremptory language in official minutes.[119] The following month, the two had another row over the distribution of appointments for flag-officers, after Churchill forced Bridgeman to break a promise to Rear Admiral Rosslyn Wemyss by giving Troubridge the command of the First Cruiser Squadron. There was another dispute over whether to retain Admiral Sir Arthur Murray Farquhar on the active list by making him Commander-in-Chief of Reserves and Coast Guard.

On 14 November Churchill secretly offered Battenberg the office of the First Sea Lord, quietly working to be rid of Bridgeman at the first opportunity.[120] On 28 November, while the First Sea Lord was taking a vacation,[121] Churchill surprised Bridgeman by suggesting he should resign on the grounds of ill-health.[122] After a short struggle Bridgeman capitulated after Churchill threatened to publish private letters to Battenberg and Beatty in which Bridgeman had admitted that his health had at times been poor. Afterwards, he insisted he had not "voluntarily resigned [the] post on account of ill-health."[123]

This chapter cannot provide a complete picture of Francis Bridgeman's term in office as First Sea Lord, because so many official documents are missing from the Admiralty archives. Nor have his personal papers survived. Further, any assessment of Bridgeman's contribution to Admiralty policy-making is made extremely difficult by the overshadowing personality of Winston S. Churchill. It can be said, however, that probably Bridgeman's greatest strength was his sound critical capability. He had the ability to recognize both a good argument and a bad one. (Under Churchill, perhaps the latter skill was more needed.) Bridgeman, however, was not a gifted administrator, nor an original thinker. He did not leave his mark upon the Admiralty. Although he put forward plenty of good ideas, his proposals were rarely adopted; seldom were they actually rejected. Being perhaps a little politically naive, Bridgeman could normally be persuaded to allow his proposals to be examined "in due course" by a committee of experts.

Undoubtedly, the salient characteristic of Bridgeman's administration was his inability to control either the events or the men around him although not for lack of trying. When Churchill became convinced by another advisor to follow a particular course, Bridgeman simply did not know how to deflect him. His ineffective opposition became more a source of irritation to Churchill than a brake on his interference. After being ousted from the Admiralty, Bridgeman acknowledged that he had found it difficult to keep a tight rein on Churchill but anticipated that his successors would not be able to cope any better. Indeed, he believed they would not even try. "We now have a Board of Admiralty," he wrote to Jack Sanders, "which will be remarkable for its complete submissiveness to the First Lord."[124]

NOTES

Excerpts in this chapter are reproduced with permission of Curtis Brown Group Ltd., London, on behalf of the Estate of Sir Winston S. Churchill. Copyright the Estate of Sir Winston S. Churchill.

1. Churchill to Battenberg, 18 Nov. 1911, Battenberg Mss. T9/46. Bridgeman took office on 9 Dec. 1911.
2. Percy Scott to White, n.d. [November 1911?], White Mss. 172.
3. Diary entry, 4 Oct. 1911, Esher Mss., ESHR 12/1.
4. Percy Scott to White, n.d. [November 1911?], White Mss. 172.
5. *Navy List* [January] *1912.*
6. Sir Winston Churchill, *The World Crisis*, vol. 1, 2nd ed. (Watford: Odhams, 1938), 66.
7. Churchill to Battenberg, 18 Nov. 1911, Battenberg Mss. T9/46. Troubridge to Battenberg, 12 Nov. 1911, Battenberg Mss. T9/47.
8. Notes by Winston Churchill, written in November 1911 after meeting with Fisher, CHART 13/1, f. 70.
9. Churchill to Asquith, 16 Nov. 1911, CHART 13/1, f. 8.
10. Churchill to Asquith, 5 Nov. 1911, Asquith Mss. 13, f. 58.
11. Esher to Fisher, 9 Jan. 1912, in Brett, ed., *Journals and Letters,* 3:78.

12. Fisher to Churchill, 10 Nov. 1911, CHART 13/2, f. 21. Scott to White, 29 Nov. 1911, White Mss. WHI 172. Scott to White, n.d. [? Dec. 1911], WHI 172.
13. Sanders to Balfour, 5 Dec. 1912, Sanders Mss. 765, f. 20. See Sanders to Balfour, 14 Dec. 1911, R. Churchill, Winston S. Churchill, vol. 2, *Young Statesman, 1901-1914* (London: Heinemann, 1967), 541.
14. Churchill to Asquith, 16 Nov. 1911, in Gilbert, (ed.), *Churchill, Companion 2*:1335.
15. Fisher to Churchill, 10 Nov. 1911, CHART 13/2, f. 21.
16. Ibid.
17. Fisher to Jellicoe, 10 Jan. 1911, Add. Mss. 49006, f. 5.
18. Bridgeman to Fisher, 4 Dec. 1911, in Marder, *Fear God*, 2:418.
19. Ibid. Also see Bridgeman to Fisher, 4 Dec. 1911, FISR 1/11.
20. Churchill to Battenberg, 19 Nov. 1911, Battenberg Mss. T9/43.
21. "Naval War Staff", ADM 1/8272.
22. References to Bridgeman in Troubridge diary, Troubridge Mss.
23. Churchill to Battenberg, 19 Nov. 1911, Battenberg Mss. T9/43.
24. Fisher to Churchill, 10 Nov. 1911, CHART 13/2, f. 21.
25. Fisher to McKenna, 8 Nov. 1909, MCKN 3/4, f. 31.
26. Fisher to McKenna, 20 Nov. 1909, in Marder, *Fear God*, 2:280; Fisher to McKenna, 23 Nov. 1909, in Marder, *Fear God*, 2:283.
27. Sanders to Balfour, 12 Feb. 1911, Add. Mss. 49767, f. 99.
28. Bridgeman to Sanders, 7 Dec. 1912, Sanders Mss. 765, f. 27.
29. Jon Sumida "British Naval Administration and Policy in the Age of Fisher", *Journal of Military History*, 54 (Jan. 1990): 1-26.
30. Bridgeman to Hopwood, 8 Dec. 1912, Royal Archive (RA), GV.G414/10.
31. Bridgeman to Churchill, 26 Apr. 1912, CHART 13/9, f. 17. Bridgeman to Battenberg, 23 Apr. 1912, Battenberg Mss. T18/109.
32. Bridgeman to Battenberg, 3 Dec. 1912, Battenberg Mss. T22/169.
33. Churchill to Bridgeman, 14 Dec. 1912, Battenberg Mss. T22/167.
34. "Gunnery in the Royal Navy", Bridgeman to Admiralty, 18 Oct. 1911, ADM 1/8328.
35. Fisher to Churchill, 5 Mar. 1912, in Marder, *Fear God*, 2:439.
36. Bridgeman to Churchill, 2 Sept. 1912, CHART 13/10, f. 45.
37. Churchill to Bridgeman, 27 Sept. 1912, CHART 13/13. See also "Observation force in the North Sea: Remarks on War Orders for, in connection with lessons of 1912 Manoeuvres," 16 Sept. 1912, by Captain G. A. Ballard (DOD), ADM 116/866B, f. 284.
38. Sumida, *In Defence*, 216.
39. Minute by Churchill, dated 27 Oct. 1912, First Lord's Minutes, vol. 1, Naval Historical Branch, (NHB), Ministry of Defence, 117. Churchill to Lloyd-George, 29 Oct. 1912, First Lord's Minutes, 1:119.
40. Sumida, *In Defence*, ch. 2.
41. Draft manuscript of *World Crisis*, CHART 8/59, f. 13.
42. Notes on conversation with F.B. [Francis Bridgeman], 12 May 1909, Sanders Mss. 758, f. 216.
43. Ibid.
44. Churchill to Fisher, 12 Apr. 1912, CHART 8/177, f. 24.
45. Bridgeman to Churchill, 21 May 1912, CHART 13/9, f. 50. See also Fisher to Churchill, 3 Feb. 1912, in Marder, *Fear God*, 2:431.
46. Churchill, *World Crisis*, 1:96.
47. Ibid., 95-96.

48. Fisher to Jellicoe, 12 Dec. 1911, in Marder, *Fear God*, 2:420.
49. Memorandum by Jellicoe, 3 May 1909, Add. Mss. 48990, f. 71.
50. Sumida, *In Defence*, 216.
51. Sir Percy Scott, *Fifty Years in the Navy* (London: John Murray, 1919).
52. "Final report of the Committee on Director Firing", 15 Nov. 1912, Battenberg Mss. T22/161; Bridgeman to Churchill, 26 Nov. 1912, Battenberg Mss. T22/163.
53. "Bridgeman to Churchill, 25 Nov. 1912, Ships Covers No. 294 (Queen Elizabeth class battleships), f. 49.
54. Ibid.
55. "Anti-torpedo Armament of Capital Ships", G01512/12, ADM 1/8367/27. For a review of the arguments, see Jellicoe memorandum, 10 June 1914, G0243/14.
56. Adoption of R'III design at Board meeting, 19 June 1912, Ships Covers No. 294, f. 3.
57. Fisher to Churchill, 14 May 1912, CHART 13/43, f. 14; Fisher to Churchill, 17 May 1912, CHART 13/14, f. 116. Fisher to Esher, 2 Apr. 1912, in Marder, *Fear God*, 2:442.
58. Ottley to Churchill, 12 Dec. 1911, Gilbert, ed., *Churchill, Companion,* 2:1356.
59. Bridgeman to Sanders, 13 Nov. 1914, Sanders Mss. 767.
60. Ibid.
61. "War Plans: pages 1-24. Remarks by C.in.C. H.F.", 9 Jan. 1912, ADM 116/3096.
62. Memorandum sent to 1st Sea Lord, initialed E.T. [Troubridge], May 1912, ADM 116/1169, f. 2.
63. Churchill to Troubridge, 1 Feb. 1912; reply by Troubridge, 7 Feb. 1912; forwarded to Bridgeman, 15 Feb. 1912, ADM 116/3099.
64. Minute by Bridgeman, 8 Mar. 1912, ADM 116/3096.
65. Memorandum sent to 1st Sea Lord, initialled E.T. [Troubridge], May 1912, ADM 116/1169, f. 2.
66. Minute by Bridgeman, 8 Mar. 1912, ADM 116/3096.
67. Churchill to Clementine Churchill, 25 Mar. 1912, Gilbert, ed., *Churchill, Companion* 3:1529.
68. Memorandum sent to 1st Sea Lord, initialled E.T. [Troubridge], May 1912, ADM 116/1169, f. 2.
69. Ibid.
70. Churchill, *World Crisis*, p. 115.
71. "Memorandum Approved for Issue to Flag Officers", 15 Apr. 1912, [not issued], ADM 116/3096.
72. Marder, *From the Dreadnought to Scapa Flow*, 1:370-71.
73. Churchill, *World Crisis*, 1:115.
74. Churchill to Clementine Churchill, 24 Mar. 1912, 25 Mar. 1912, in Gilbert, ed., *Churchill, Companion* 3:1529.
75. Ibid.
76. Churchill, *World Crisis*, 1:115.
77. Bridgeman to Troubridge, 11 May 1912, ADM 116/3096.
78. Admiralty to Callaghan, 9 Apr. 1912, M-001/12, ADM 116/3096.
79. Marginal comment by Bridgeman, 9 Apr. 1912. See resulting "Memorandum approved for issue to Flag Officers", 15 Apr. 1912, (not issued.), M-001/12, ADM 116/3096.
80. "Part 1, General Instructions", M0020, ADM 116/3412.
81. Callaghan to Admiralty, 9 Jan. 1912, ADM 116/3096.

82. Memorandum, 15 Feb. 1912, Churchill, *Young Statesman*, 565. "Naval Situation in the Mediterranean", 5 June 1912, n.b., para. 6, Churchill, *Young Statesman*, 590-92.
83. Paul Halpern, *The Mediterranean Naval Situation 1908-1914* (Cambridge, Mass.: Harvard University Press, 1971), 18.
84. Fisher to Churchill, 16 Jan. 1912, CHART 13/14, f. 18; Fisher to Churchill, 4 Nov. 1911, CHART 13/2, f. 11.
85. Fisher to Churchill, 16 Jan. 1912, CHART 13/14, f. 18.
86. Fisher to Churchill, 5 Mar. 1912, in Marder, *Fear God*, 2:437.
87. Asquith Mss. 107.
88. Hankey to Grey, 30 Apr. 1912, G. P. Gooch and H. V. Temperley, eds., *British Documents on the Origins of the War, 1898-1914, vol. 10, pt. 2*, (London: HMSO, 1926-38), 580.
89. Halpern, *Mediterranean Naval Situation*, 19-30.
90. Kitchener to Grey, 2 June 1912, Gooch and Temperley, eds., *British Documents, 10, pt. 2*:594.
91. "Mediterranean", by Bridgeman, 9 June 1912, ADM 116/3099, ff. 53-57.
92. Ibid.
93. Memorandum for Cabinet, "Naval Situation in the Mediterranean", 18 June 1912, 6, Asquith Mss. 107.
94. "Memorandum to Cabinet", 22 June 1912, Gilbert, ed., *Churchill, Companion* 3:1570.
95. Bridgeman to Sanders, 2 Jan. 1914, Sanders Mss. 766, f. 10.
96. Halpern, *Mediterranean Naval Situation*, 39-40.
97. Asquith to the King, 16 July 1912, Asquith Mss. 6, f. 156. Also note secret enclosure, f. 157.
98. "Memorandum" by Churchill, 6 July 1912, [not issued], in Gilbert, ed., *Churchill, Companion* 3:1588.
99. Fisher memorandum, "Battleships and Trade in the Mediterranean", 24 June 1912, in Marder, *Fear God*, 2:468.
100. Testimony of Lord Fisher given at the 117th CID mtg., 4 July 1912, CAB 2/1.
101. Testimony of Winston Churchill given at 117th CID mtg., 4 July 1912, CAB 2/1.
102. Esher to Balfour, 23 July 1912, in Brett, ed., *Journals & Letters*, 3:103.
103. Sanders to Balfour, 10 Oct. 1912, Add. Mss. 49768.
104. Bridgeman to Churchill, 21 May 1912, CHART 13/9, f. 50.
105. "Mediterranean", 9 June 1912, ADM 116/3099, ff. 53-57.
106. Sanders to Balfour, 16 Oct. 1912, Add. Mss. 49768, f. 27.
107. Troubridge to Churchill, 7 Feb. 1912, ADM 116/3099.
108. Memorandum by Battenberg on "C.I.D. meeting of 4th July 1912," Battenberg Mss. T20/103B.
109. "Considerations as to the best composition of the Mediterranean fleet in 1915," G. A. Ballard, (DOD), 20 Nov. 1912, ADM 116/3099, f. 77.
110. McKenna to Fisher, 20 Nov. 1909, FISR 1/9, FP439.
111. Churchill to Harcourt, 29 Jan. 1912, Gilbert, ed., *Churchill, Companion* 3:1507. See also Asquith to the King, 1 May 1912, Asquith Mss 6, f. 135.
112. Cabinet Memoranda by Winston Churchill, "Naval Expenditure", 18 July 1910; see also "Secret", 6 Feb. 1911, CHART 21/20; Churchill to Crewe, 14 Feb. 1911, Lloyd-George Mss. C/3/15/3.

113. McKenna to Wilson, 6 July 1911, MCKN 3/22, f. 54; Wilson to McKenna, 10 July 1911, MCKN 3/22, f. 54.

114. "Forecast of the reinforcements in the Mediterranean during 1913," Sept. 1912, RA, GV G393/7. See also Winsloe (C-in-C China) to Churchill, 30 Dec. 1912, CHART 13/11, f. 70; Memorandum 22 June 1912, Esher to Spender, 5 June 1912, Esher, *Letters*, 3:93; Gilbert, ed., Churchill, *Companion* 3:1570.

115. "Memorandum to Cabinet," by Churchill, 22 June 1912, in Gilbert, ed., *Churchill, Companion* 3:1570.

116. Australian P.M. to Governor-General, 28 Feb. 1914, ADM 1/8375/108, ff. 154-59. See also N.K. Meaney, *The Search for Security in the Pacific* (Sydney, Australia: Sydney University Press, 1976), ch. 9.

117. Bridgeman to Sanders, 4 Dec. 1912, Sanders Mss. 765, ff. 14-17.

118. Ibid. See also Sanders to Balfour, 10 Oct. 1912, in Gilbert, ed., *Churchill, Companion* 3:1588.

119. Sanders to Balfour, 10 Oct. 1912, in Gilbert, ed., *Churchill, Companion* 3:1653.

120. Battenberg to Churchill, 14 Nov. 1912, CHART 13/11, f. 23.

121. Bridgeman to Hopwood, 8 Dec. 1912, RA, GV.G414/10.

122. Churchill to Bridgeman, 28 Nov. 1912, in Gilbert, ed., *Churchill, Companion* 3:1675.

123. Bridgeman to Sanders, 4 Dec. 1912, Sanders Mss. 765.

124. Bridgeman to Sanders, 7 Dec. 1912, Sanders Mss. 765.

5

Admiral Prince Louis of Battenberg (1912–1914)

John B. Hattendorf

Prince Louis of Battenberg was genuinely popular throughout the Royal Navy and many officers and men had more confidence in his professional abilities than in those of many other senior flag-officers of the time who were holding appointments afloat. In 1911, Captain Charles Ottley, the Secretary of the CID, wrote privately: "There are literally hundreds of naval officers who would be quite ready to believe black was white, if he issued a memo to that effect."[1]

Although his aristocratic connections were important in Prince Louis's private life and in laying the foundations for his early career, they made no obvious difference to his later development as a naval officer. He followed a standard line of training and advancement through the middle ranks of the naval officer corps, proving himself a very effective seaman and leader. Promoted to Commander in 1885, he served in the gunnery and torpedo ships *Excellent* and *Vernon* as well as the ironclad, turret ship *Dreadnought* in the Mediterranean. In 1889, he took up his first independent command, the torpedo cruiser *Scout* in the Red Sea. Promoted to Captain at the end of 1891, he returned to London where, in 1892-94, he served as naval advisor in the War Office. While in that assignment, he became Chief Secretary to a joint Naval and Military Committee of Defence under Lord Sandhurst, the Under Secretary of War. In 1892, he also invented a mechanical course indicator for use in ships. Battenberg returned to sea in 1894 to command the *Cambrian*, one of a new class of light cruisers. Leaving *Cambrian* in 1897, after having won with her a wide range of fleet exercise prizes, he moved on to join *Majestic* as Flag-Captain in the Channel Fleet. Two years later, he returned to the Admiralty as Assistant Director of Naval Intelligence and head of the Mobilization Department. In 1901, he served in the

Mediterranean in commanding a new battleship, *Implacable*. Appointed Director of Naval Intelligence in 1902, he was promoted to Rear Admiral in 1904, then moving on to assume command of the second Cruiser Squadron in 1905 and become second in command of the Mediterranean Station in 1907. Promoted to Vice Admiral, he served as Commander-in-Chief of the Atlantic Fleet from 1907 until 1910, and followed this in the next year by taking command of the 3rd and 4th Divisions of the Home Fleet.

In 1911, as Battenberg took up his new position in the Home Fleet, the German Naval Attaché sent a short estimate of Battenberg's abilities to Berlin: "He is enthusiastic about his career and unites a seaman's judgement, based on long experience in the best commands, with the inborn German thoroughness of a systematic worker."[2] Continuing, the Naval Attaché noted that Prince Louis's greatest organizational talent had been in participating in the development of the Navy's mobilization system, and that he was generally recognized as an outstanding fleet commander. He was an officer who was given the highest respect and was very popular with his subordinates.

Responding to a question in the House of Commons at the end of November 1911, the new First Lord of the Admiralty, Winston Churchill, who had only taken office in the previous month, made the surprising announcement that he was immediately replacing three members of the Admiralty Board.[3] In this change, Admiral Sir Francis Bridgeman replaced Admiral Sir Arthur Wilson as First Sea Lord and Captain William Pakenham replaced Rear Admiral Sir Charles Madden as Fourth Sea Lord. Both Wilson and Madden had entered office in January 1910, and their normal appointment would have lasted just a few months longer, until early 1912. More surprising was Churchill's replacement of the Second Sea Lord, Vice Admiral Sir George Egerton, who had been in office only since February 1911, with Prince Louis of Battenberg. On Churchill's appointment as First Lord in October 1911, Admiral Lord Fisher had unsuccessfully recommended that Battenberg be made First Sea Lord. In Fisher's view, he was "the most capable administrator in the Admiral's List *by a long way*."[4] Politically, Fisher thought that Battenberg would please the Liberal party. "They will say what better proof could we give of our confidence to Germany than selecting a man as First Sea Lord with German proclivities. In reality, he is more English than the English."[5] Acknowledging Fisher's influence in his appointment, Prince Louis wrote him in early November:

I dined with the new First Lord last night and we talked for five hours on end. . . . I am most grateful to you for your warm support with Mr W C & glad to think that he means to avail himself of your advice on many points in the future.[6]

The immediate cause of Wilson's removal had been his strong opposition to establishing a Naval Staff, something that Battenberg had helped to design. Drawing on his own prior experience of the limitations of the existing organization, Battenberg wished to improve the degree of strategic advice and operational planning within the Admiralty.[7]

"It is already rumoured that Lord Fisher had chosen the new Admiralty Board," the German Naval Attaché, Korvettenkapitän Erich von Müller, reported to Berlin. "Bridgeman is always irresolute; Prince Louis of Battenberg has been a convinced follower of Lord Fisher. No wonder, that behind the Board of Admiralty, Fisher's figure emerges again, to begin with only nebulously, but his influence as string-puller will make itself more marked over time."[8] This development, Müller pointed out, was an unfavorable one for Germany. Fisher's anti-German views as First Sea Lord were well remembered in Berlin, and in German eyes, the result of Fisher's influence on a character like Churchill could only be evil for Germany. "The stronger this renewed Fisher influence becomes over time, the less propitious for Germany," Müller commented.[9]

While there was a strong relationship between Battenberg and Fisher, Prince Louis was no blind admirer. In January 1910, for example, just after it was announced Fisher would be succeeded by Wilson, Battenberg had confided to Captain Ernest Troubridge that he felt there was "much danger to be apprehended that Ld F[isher] retains the appointment of Personnel ADC [to the King] & hence always the ear of H.M. & and intends to pull the naval strings in that way."[10]

Battenberg came to the Admiralty Board at the end of 1911 clearly identified as one of Fisher's followers and one of the British officers who saw a serious danger in the growth of the Imperial German Navy. Battenberg's arrival coincided with a distinct change at the Admiralty, not only in terms of its organizational structure, but also in the relationships of the Sea Lords in relation to the First Lord. As von Müller observed: "Only under a weak man, like Mr McKenna, was it possible that the expert, the First Sea Lord, was actually the leader of the Admiralty."[11] Churchill's enthusiasm for his job and his energetic exercise of civilian control over the Navy subtly changed the role of the First Sea Lord while the former was in office. During the latter part of Bridgeman's period as First Sea Lord, observers noted that Bridgeman worked only indirectly with the First Lord through others. At the same time, Churchill seemed to work so easily with

Battenberg that von Müller reported to Berlin: "Admiral Bridgeman was only a 'placeholder' for Prince Louis of Battenberg, whose later promotion to the position of 1st Sea Lord was foreseen for a long time."[12] Battenberg and Churchill found mutual compatibility in their aristocratic family backgrounds. Churchill certainly respected Battenberg's skill and achievements, but more than that, Battenberg's ideas on organization, planning, and personnel were similar to his own. At the same time, Battenberg's continental background and natural ability in languages and diplomacy made him especially attractive at a time when Churchill thought the naval arms race could be avoided by a "holiday" from naval ship construction, followed by direct negotiation on arms control agreements.[13] Thus, it was not surprising that Churchill leaned more toward Battenberg than any other member of the Admiralty Board, a fact Sir Francis Bridgeman increasingly began to resent. In addition, Bridgeman was generally dissatisfied with Churchill's behavior as First Lord, believing that the First Lord was merely *primus inter pares* with the Sea Lords.[14] In trying to mediate these differences in October 1912, Battenberg demonstrated that he was able to accept a strong First Lord and, perhaps, to guide and help him to avoid further disputes with the Sea Lords.

In a private conversation on 14 November, Churchill first intimated to Battenberg that he wanted him to succeed Bridgeman; he informally made this recommendation to the Prime Minister and the King on 29 November.[15] Nevertheless, Bridgeman did not formally agree to resign until 4 December. Immediately following the King's formal approval on 7 December, Battenberg took office.

A week later, the *Morning Post* disclosed that Bridgeman had resigned following an open breach between the First Lord and the Sea Lords.[16] This report was followed by a parliamentary debate in which Churchill was the subject of hostile attack and more details of the change at the Admiralty were disclosed. While this incident was an unpropitious beginning for Prince Louis's term, the public debate focused on the personal dispute between Bridgeman and Churchill and subsided shortly, making little impact on the underlying issue of the institutional relationship between the First Lord and the Sea Lords. Churchill remained successful in maintaining full control at the Admiralty, although not without some continuing resistance.

It is difficult to judge Battenberg's accomplishments as First Sea Lord. The remaining documents leave no clear indications from which to draw a conclusion.[17] His personality, his previous accomplishments, the circumstances of his appointment (with his continuing close, personal, and professional relationship with Churchill), and the annotation on the various official working memoranda that passed between him and the First Lord, all tend to support an argument that he had worked so very closely with Churchill that it is impossible to distinguish an individual role to his conduct in office. There is very little written evidence of any initiative on Prince Louis's part, and he appears to have played the role of judge, mediator, and facilitator behind the First Lord rather than that of an instigator. In contrast to previous First Sea Lords, Prince Louis faced a very unusual situation in regard to the First Lord. Rather than oppose Churchill as Bridgeman had done, Prince Louis clearly chose an alternative path in trying to create a working relationship.

While it appears that Prince Louis was successful in moderating Churchill's behavior in subtle ways without directly standing against the First Lord, and thus avoiding the type of open irreconcilable dispute that had arisen with Bridgeman, there were several occasions when he had to work hard to restrain Churchill from exceeding the bounds of his authority. One of those instances was in the naming of warships. In this case, Churchill found himself in conflict with King George V when Churchill proposed several names for new warships, among them was a suggestion that a new battleship be named *Oliver Cromwell*. Even when King George objected to the name of a republican and regicide, Churchill insisted on it, arguing for Cromwell's contribution in building the fleet in the 1650s. After a series of stiff exchanges between Churchill and the monarch on the subject, Battenberg eventually advised Churchill in writing: [A]ll my experience at the Admiralty & close intercourse with three sovereigns leads me to this; from all times the Sovereign's decisions as to names for H.M. Ships has been accepted as final by all First Lords." He concluded his firm warning by stating unequivocally that "the service as a whole would go against you in this choice."[18]

In another instance, Churchill had embarked on a series of unusual inspections around the coast, during which he took the opportunity to question junior officers about the conduct of their seniors. In one situation, Churchill had told a young lieutenant at HMS *Vernon* to send him a suggestion on torpedoes. When his superior refused to forward it through the chain of command, the lieutenant retorted that he would send it directly to the First Lord. The young officer's commanding officer complained to the Commander-in-Chief (C-in-C), Nore, who in turn passed the complaint to the Second Sea Lord, John Jellicoe. When Jellicoe returned the recommendation, refusing to forward it to the First Lord, Churchill personally intervened in the postal system, obtained it and threatened to dismiss the C-in-C, Nore, and the Captain of *Vernon*, with or without the approval of the

Sea Lords. As a result, the Sea Lords threatened to resign. On 12 November 1913, Prince Louis prepared a letter stating:

According to the very clear terms under which we act, the First Lord has not, in our opinion, the power to issue such an order.

We therefore, cannot share the responsibility for such an act and we have no alternative but to resign our seats on the Board.[19]

Although the Sea Lords had already signed the resignation, Prince Louis was eventually able to restrain them from actually submitting it. In the end, Prince Louis mediated the situation and brought both Churchill and the other Sea Lords around to end the crisis. The Sea Lords privately convinced Admiral Richard Poore, C-in-C, Nore, that Churchill was being irrational and that it would be better to ignore the situation, rather than create a public row. As the Admiralty Additional Civil Lord, Sir Francis Hopwood wrote to the Kings's Secretary, Lord Stamfordham, "*Laus Deo*! it is over for the time, but we shall have it again in some form."[20] Thus, in dealing with Churchill as First Lord, Prince Louis found that he had to try to restrain the First Lord's actions to their proper bounds, not only in terms of the superior authority of the sovereign, but also with internal naval matters and the relationship of civil and professional spheres.

Shortly after instituting the Naval War Staff, Churchill explained its role in a memorandum of 11 March 1912, stressing several new relationships.[21] First among them was the thought that the First Lord was the delegate of the Crown in exercising supreme executive power; under him, the First Sea Lord was, for certain purposes, holding the position of Commander-in-Chief of the Navy, while the Chief of the War Staff, with the Intelligence, Operations, and Mobilisation Divisions, was primarily responsible to the First Sea Lord.

Churchill's actions in relation to the Sea Lords continued to cause comment, and in early 1914, the editor of the *Naval Annual*, Viscount Hythe, felt compelled to stress publicly: "No occupant of this high office of state has made corresponding effort to acquire a practical knowledge of the Navy". But, he stressed:

[A] word of caution is necessary. It is one of the cherished traditions of the Navy that the Board collectively is responsible for all decisions, and it is hoped that his [Churchill's] zeal may not tend to his overstepping the due functions of the First Lord of the Admiralty, and interfering in matters which are the province of his professional advisors.[22]

Within the Admiralty, the role of the Admiralty War Staff, at this stage, was merely advisory in nature, having no executive or administrative authority. As First Sea Lord, Battenberg continued to nurture its development on this basis and saw Vice Admiral Sir Henry Jackson replace Rear Admiral Ernest Troubridge as Chief of the Admiralty War Staff. Prince Louis continued to support the development of the War Staff courses, opening branch War Colleges at Chatham and Devonport, as well as supporting the creation of the *Naval Review* as an organ of informal discussion and initiative.

In 1913, it became increasingly apparent that the Army's General Staff and the Admiralty War Staff needed to cooperate. Lieutenant-Colonel Maurice Hankey, the Secretary of the CID, noted that the General Staff tended to ignore maritime and imperial defense issues and failed thereby to answer the needs of the CID. To develop closer relations in this area, a naval officer was ordered to serve on the General Staff and a military officer was sent to the Admiralty War Staff. Members of the Admiralty War Staff, such as Captain Herbert W. Richmond, remained completely dissatisfied with the situation and urged the development of an offensive naval strategy to complement an offensive military strategy. Both Battenberg and Churchill actively approved and promoted Richmond's initiative to reestablish the CID's 1905 strategic subcommittee for combined operations. Some initial plans for reestablishment were laid, but before they could be put in place or have any effect on contingency planning, war intervened. The Admiralty's decision in 1906 to operate independently of the CID and its committees was not altered in time for the sudden changes of 1914, when the Navy wanted to cooperate in offensive, combined operations.[23]

There were few major, internal organizational changes in the Admiralty under Battenberg. In early 1912, the former Controller's office had been divided in two. To deal with this, an additional Civil Lord was created to conduct the business and commercial transactions of the Admiralty, moving the responsibility for ship design, new inventions, and estimates to the province of the Third Sea Lord. The effects of this change were just coming into place as Battenberg came into office. Additionally, in 1913 the Navigation Department was created, removing this office from the responsibility of the Hydrographer of the Navy. The post of Inspector of Target Practice was abolished, moving some of the responsibilities to the Director of Ordnance.

In terms of fleet organization, Scotland was constituted as a separate command in 1913, under a senior naval officer on the coast of Scotland, with headquarters in Rosyth. Implementing one of the provisions of the 1911 Imperial Conference to establish a new Australian (Commonwealth) Station for the newly established Royal Australian Navy, the limits of the East Indies and China Stations were modified, placing Singapore within the East Indies Command.[24] At the same time, the Admiralty remained concerned that arrangements must be made to ensure that Dominion forces, such as the Royal Australian Navy, as well as the Royal Indian Marine, Royal Canadian Navy, and the even more recently formed New Zealand Naval Forces, be returned to Admiralty control in the event of war.

The subject of Dominion naval force was also enmeshed in the main issues during the twenty peacetime months of Battenberg's tenure as First Sea Lord: the annual naval estimates and, along with them, the political, financial, technical, and international implications they involved. In all this, the tone was set by the plan Churchill had laid before Parliament in March 1912, announcing a "16-10 standard," or a minimum standard of 60 percent British predominance over German dreadnoughts. At the same time, he had made his offer of a naval holiday. In February 1913, some months after Battenberg had taken office, Grand Admiral Tirpitz announced his readiness to accept this standard, proposing a ratio of eight to five battle squadrons. The government's reply to this came in the 1913-14 estimates, which were issued on 13 March and provided for an increase of £1,233,900 over the previous year. In his speech to the Commons, Churchill called the armaments race sheer stupidity and renewed his offer of a naval holiday.

It is significant that Churchill renewed this proposal shortly after Prince Louis became First Sea Lord. In the end, however, the mutual suspicions involved in Germany's repeated rejection of Churchill's proposals for a naval arms limitation agreement, along with Britain's refusal to make a guarantee that would have destroyed the development of the Anglo-French and Anglo-Russian ententes, prevented the renewal of the Anglo-German naval conversations that had taken place in 1910. Thus, Prince Louis did not play the role in an Anglo-German naval arms limitation agreement that he might have performed, had the British government been willing to make a political agreement.

Nevertheless, frequent and substantial naval conversations began to take place with the French in late 1912. Deeply involved with coordinating them, even before becoming First Sea Lord, Prince Louis himself traveled incognito to Paris for detailed discussions with Admiral Le Bris in December 1912 and again in March 1913. Insisting on the need for prudence and caution in the naval plans of the Anglo-French entente, Prince Louis ensured that they remained out of the public view. In the course of these talks, representatives of the two navies made agreements to support their mutual dependence in case of war. Similar arrangements with Russia proceeded more slowly and cautiously. Battenberg did make plans for an incognito visit to St Petersburg in August 1914, but they came to nothing.[25]

The most memorable event of Prince Louis's tenure as First Sea Lord occurred in July 1914. Some nine months earlier Churchill had suggested that to save money, the usual summer naval exercises might be canceled and the normally inactive Third Fleet should instead be mobilized as a test of contingency plans. Battenberg agreed and plans were made for this to take place in mid-July with a fleet review following it. Following the review, the Third Fleet ships were ordered to sail for their various home ports and to demobilize. Before they could carry out their orders, the news arrived in London that Serbia had rejected Austria's ultimatum on the Sarajevo incident. On that day, Prince Louis was at the Admiralty alone, as Churchill, Asquith, Sir Edward Grey, and all the other senior ministers had left town for the weekend. That Sunday, Prince Louis remained in his office, reading all the embassy telegrams as they reported the developing crisis. Knowing that the fleet would disperse and demobilize on Monday morning, Prince Louis took the initiative alone. At 4 o'clock in the afternoon, he countermanded all the previous orders, signaling to "stand fast the fleet." Sending a telegram to the Commander-in-Chief at Portland, Battenberg ordered: "No ships of First Fleet or Flotillas are to leave Portland until further orders."[26] When the ministers hurriedly returned to London late that Sunday night, they congratulated him. Britain's fleet was ready, on a preparatory and precautionary basis. Two days later, within hours after Austria had declared war on Serbia on 28 July 1914, it sailed north to its preliminary war station at Scapa Flow and was soon concentrated, ready to forestall any preemptive attack.[27]

The sudden outbreak of war quickly revealed that the Admiralty was not properly organized to direct a modern war at sea. The Admiralty War Staff was designed for that role, but its members had not been trained in the proper functions of a such a staff in wartime. Probably only the six officers on the war staff who had attended the newly founded War College had ever even considered the broad issues involved in the central direction of a war. In addition, the War Staff was overburdened with detailed information and found it difficult to construct a wide view of the situation with alternative reactions and initiatives. Communications and intelligence support were also poorly organized for this task. Vice Admiral Sir Frederick Doveton Sturdee, who had taken over as Chief of the War Staff in July 1914, made little effective use of his subordinates.

As the senior professional leader, Battenberg, like his immediate predecessors, had failed to prepare the Admiralty for war. He was not alone in this failure; a whole range of naval leaders were collectively responsible for failing to cooperate with the possibilities the CID had offered since 1904, preferring their bureaucratic independence to effective cooperation. Battenberg deserves credit for promoting the Admiralty War Staff and being instrumental in bringing it into existence, however belatedly. Nevertheless, he certainly bears responsibility for its poor organization, ineffective leadership, and incompletely educated staff, as well as for its role as only an advisory body with no authority.

When war broke out, the Admiralty conducted the war through an informally created, ad-hoc committee called the "War Staff Group" or the "Admiralty War Group." It consisted originally of four officials: the First Lord, the First Sea Lord, the Chief of the War Staff, and the Secretary. When the First Sea Lord wished, he added the Second Sea Lord and other advisors, as necessary. Churchill described its workings: "We met every day and sometimes twice a day, read the whole position and arrived at a united decision on every matter of consequence. . . . Besides our regular meetings the First Sea Lord and I consulted together constantly at all hours." More revealingly, however, Churchill continued:

[I]t happened in a large number of cases that seeing what ought to be done and confident of the agreement of the First Sea Lord, I myself drafted the telegrams and decisions in accordance with our policy, and the Chief of Staff took them personally to the First Sea Lord for his concurrence before dispatch.[28]

In fact, there was often no attempt to obtain unanimity, as Churchill admitted:

I accepted full responsibility for bringing about successful results, and in that spirit, I exercised a close general supervision over everything that was done or proposed. Further, I claimed and exercised an unlimited power of suggestion and initiative over the whole field, subject only to the approval and agreement of the First Sea Lord on all operative orders.[29]

Under such circumstances, it is not surprising that Battenberg was rather unfairly dubbed, "I Concur."[30] In fact, Churchill was quite unstoppable and often made no serious attempt to seek the First Sea Lord's approval before making any public announcements on naval policy. Under such circumstances Churchill's egocentric conception of his role and his mercurial temper eliminated the usual methods of staff procedure in presenting alternative views. These circumstances tended to both confuse the situation for subordinates in the Admiralty and overcentralize decision making, while at the same time lessening the authority of the War Staff and the First Sea Lord. Since orders were often issued quickly and tended to be ambiguously written without the advantage of staff analysis, some officers complained that they were unsure of their priorities and often wondered if they were correctly interpreting what was wanted.[31]

Modern electronic communications created two further problems for the Admiralty. On the one hand, it gave the Admiralty the ability to control operations at sea directly in a way that had been unknown in previous European wars. Adding to the personality issues involved, this tended to centralize authority at the Admiralty, allowing more instantaneous action and reaction from the fleet at sea. At the same time, it made the fleet commander more dependant on his orders and instructions, leaving less room for the independent role of commanders at sea. On the other hand, the enemy's use of electronic communications created new opportunities for intelligence and cryptography. The presence of this activity at the Admiralty, in "Room 40," was an additional factor adding to the centralization of command and control within the Admiralty. While Battenberg held tenure during the early months of the war, the Admiralty did poorly in dealing with these new aspects of modern warfare. Delays in communication prevented operational signals from reaching senior commanders at sea in good time, while the Admiralty staff was simultaneously overburdened by deciding issues of unimportant detail better left to subordinate officials.[32] During the same period, the Navy had not yet learned to move beyond cryptography to use their information for the purposes of broader and more effective decision making within the context of intelligence.[33]

The situation within the Admiralty exacerbated the problems that the fleet faced at sea. The first months of the war showed that the Royal Navy was unprepared for modern warfare.[34] A technological revolution had transformed the Navy in the previous decade, and the lack of a well-developed staff system resulted in the influence of individuals rather than integrated and flexible plans based on thoroughly examined analysis. There was little consensus within the Navy on many issues, and few admirals were prepared to compromise. Most seriously, there was no agreement on how the fleet should be employed. This, in turn, led to tactical and material problems, ineffective use of annual exercises to determine capabilities and weaknesses, and the failure to develop tactical doctrine from experience. At the same time, there was a lack of coordination and communication between ship and weapons designers and the operators of this equipment. With the Fleet suddenly engaged in an entirely new type of naval warfare, there was no means to learn effectively from the continual evaluation of recent experience, applying it to ongoing situations. The Navy had failed to obtain in peacetime a sufficient knowledge of the capability and limitations of its technology in order to create an effective strategy, while at the same time it lacked an efficient system to assess its actions and adapt to wartime conditions.[35]

From the point of view of evaluating the First Sea Lord, the most serious deficiency was the ineffective conduct of the War Staff and the War Group in exercising overall, operational control. Much of the reason for this lies in the Admiralty's failure to adopt an appropriate staff system in the years leading up to the war, which was exacerbated by Winston Churchill's concept and conduct of his office as First Lord. Within the first three months of the war, the Admiralty had seen the disastrous escape of the German battlecruiser, *Goeben*, in early August 1914, followed by the problems of conflicting command in the action at Heligoland Bight later in the month. Both revealed the fundamental problems within the Admiralty. The problems created by the appearance of mines and submarines and the subsequent loss of *Pathfinder*, *Aboukir*, *Cressy*, and *Hogue*, followed by *Hawke*, *Hermes*, and *Audacious*, all laid the ground to question the Navy's ability to protect the country from invasion or to safeguard British troops headed for the continent.

It was in the context of these events that public discussion began over Prince Louis and his German family connections, intimating that he was disloyal. The *Daily Mail* noted with restraint: "It is a curious stroke of fortune by which one brother-in-law directs the operations of the British Navy at headquarters and the other in person commands the German Fleets on the sea."[36] Only a few days before, the weekly magazine, *John Bull*, had announced: "Blood is thicker than water; and we doubt whether all the water in the North Sea could obliterate the blood-ties between the Battenbergs and the Hohenzollerens when it comes to a question of a life and death struggle between Germany and ourselves."[37]

Churchill and the Cabinet stood by Prince Louis in this hour of trial, but in the end, Battenberg felt that under the circumstances, it was his patriotic duty to resign. As his naval assistant later wrote, "For years before 1914 he realized that if war came his position would be made hard if not untenable."[38] The Navy's performance in these months, as well as the political liability that Battenberg created at a time when the Conservative party opposition was launching a major attack on the government's management of the war, were reasons enough for a resignation at the Admiralty.[39] For Churchill himself, it offered a chance to let the resignation of his senior professional advisor pay the political price, thus renewing his own lease as First Lord. Apparently, with this in mind, Churchill suggested to Battenberg that he might resign. By this time, however, neither Churchill's opponents nor Battenberg's supporters thought Prince Louis able to restrain Churchill effectively. While no one in a responsible position saw Prince Louis's ancestry as a serious issue, the political outcry it aroused came as an excuse to mask a convenient piece of political expediency.

On 27 October, Churchill saw the King again. Lord Stamfordham recorded the events:

> Ever since the commencement of the War there has been, in certain quarters, an inimical movement against him on account of his name and parentage and this feeling has, to a slight extent, found expression in the Press. Meanwhile, he has been assailed by anonymous letters and these attacks combined with the exacting duties and heavy responsibilities of his office have no doubt affected his general health and nerves so that for the good of the service a change had become necessary.[40]

At the same time, the King initially refused to accept Churchill's recommendation to recall Lord Fisher as First Sea Lord. Prince Louis formally submitted his resignation on 28 October, but Churchill's disagreement with the King caused a delay. Prince Louis, however, could no longer bear the strain. The next day, he wrote to Churchill in anguish: "I beg of you to release me. I am on the verge of breaking down & I cannot use my brain for anything. . . ."[41] That very day, Churchill saw the King, who confided in his private diary his thoughts on Prince Louis: "I feel deeply for him, there is no more loyal man in the country."[42]

Emotionally crushed by the circumstances, Prince Louis left office with the initial understanding that his departure was a temporary one and that he could resume active service after the war with Germany was over, ideally in command of the Mediterranean Fleet.[43] It was a dream that would not be fulfilled, and Prince Louis retired from the service, at his own request, in January 1919.

The public outcry over German names continued to be an issue. It forced Lord Haldane from the War Office in 1915 and culminated in 1917 with King George V deciding to change the name of the royal house. In connection with this, Prince Louis explained to his daughter Louise that King George had told him he could no longer appear to be a German surrounded by German relatives. He asked "us Holsteins, Tecks & Battenbergs to give up using in England our German titles & to assume English surnames. . . . It has been suggested that we shd turn our name into English, viz., Battenhill or Mountbatten. . . . We incline for the latter as having a better sound."[44]

At the same time, the King replaced the German title with an English one, creating him Marquess of Milford Haven. After the war, he was promoted to

Admiral of the Fleet and died, five weeks after his promotion, on 11 September 1921.

At his resignation, the widespread expression of regret from naval officers demonstrated, once again, his great popularity and the respect Prince Louis had earned within the service. As First Sea Lord in the period leading up to the war, Battenberg was prevented by diplomatic and political circumstances from playing a role he was well qualified to undertake in negotiating naval arms control. Later, during the opening months of the war, he faced the dilemma of an Admiralty that was unprepared and poorly organized for fighting a modern war, while at the same time he dealt with a First Lord whose activities, however brilliant and energetic, complicated further the ultimate solution to those problems.

NOTES

1. Quoted in Marder, *From the Dreadnought to Scapa Flow*, 1:407.
2. Bundesarchiv-Militärarchiv, Freiburg im Breisgau, Germany, RM 5/v. 1091, s. 33 [Admiralstab der Marine, A, betreffend England. Personal, Offiziere und Offiziersatz vom Januar 1910 bis April 1919]: "Er ist begeistert von seinem Beruf und vereinigt in sich den durch lange Fahrzeit in besten Kommandos erfahren Seemann mit dem durch angeborene deutsche Gründlichkeit systematischen Arbeiter."
3. The general naval history of this period has been well covered in the following standard works: Winston Churchill, *The World Crisis*, vols. 1, 2; Marder, *From the Dreadnought to Scapa Flow*, vols. 1, 2; Sumida, *In Defence*, ch. 6; Stephen Roskill, *Churchill and the Admirals* (London: Collins, 1977), chs. 1-3.
4. Fisher to J. A. Spender, 25 Oct. 1911, Marder, *Fear God*, 2:398.
5. Ibid.
6. Battenberg to Fisher, 1 Nov. 1911, CHART 13/43.
7. On Battenberg's views on the naval staff, see his letter of 22 November 1911, printed in Kerr, *Prince Louis*, 235-8; on Wilson's removal, see Marder, *From the Dreadnought to Scapa Flow*, 1:257-58.
8. BA-MA. RM 5/v. 1173. s. 69-71. [Admiralstab der Marine. A. Englisch-deutsche Beziehungen vom Dez. 1911 bis Aug. 1914]: Marine Attaché, London, an der Staatssekretär des Reichsmarineamts, 13 January 1912. "Damals munkelte man bereits, dass Lord Fisher das neue Board of the Admiralty ausgewählt habe. Churchill ist sicher nach seiner Wahl, denn nach dem Abgange Lord Tweedmouth's hatte Fisher bereits um ihn an Stelle von McKenna als First Lord gebeten. Bridgeman ist stets ein willenloser, Prinz Louis Battenberg ein überzeugter Anhänger Lord Fisher's gewesen. Kein Wunder, dass hinter dem Board of the Admiralty die Figur Fisher's wieder auftaucht, zunächst zwar nur nebelhaft, aber sein Einfluss als Drahtzieher wird sich mit der Zeit immer fühlbarer machen."
9. Ibid., s. 71: "Je stärker dieser Fischer'sche Einfluss mit der Zeit wieder werden wird, umso ungünstiger für Deutschland."
10. Diary, Tuesday 11 [January 1910], Ernest Troubridge Papers 66/12/1, Imperial War Museum.

11. BA-MA, RM 3/2975, f. 211: Marine-Attaché, London, an den Staatssekretär des Reichmarineamts, 21 December 1912. "Nur unter einem schwachen Mann, wie Mr. McKenna, war es möglich, dass der Fachman, der 1. Sealord, der tatsächliche Leiter der Admiralität war."

12. Ibid., f. 208. "Admiral Bridgeman war zwar nur "Platzhalter" für den Prinzen Ludwig Battenberg, dessen späteres Einrücken in die Stellung des 1. Sealords schon längere Zeit beabsichtigt war."

13. For an analysis of Churchill's naval holiday proposal, see E. L. Woodward, *Great Britain and the German Navy*, 2nd ed. (London: Frank Cass, 1964), 368-72, 408-13; 417-21, 424; Richard Langhorne, "The Naval Question in Anglo-German Relations, 1912-1914," *Historical Journal*, 14, no. 2 (June 1971): 359-70; John H. Maurer, "Churchill's Naval Holiday: Arms Control and the German Naval Race, 1912-1914," *Journal of Strategic Studies*, 15, no. 1 (March 1992): 102-27; John H. Maurer, "The Anglo-German Naval Rivalry and Informal Arms Control, 1912-1914," *Journal of Conflict Resolution*, 36, no. 2 (June 1992): 284-308.

14. Churchill, *Young Statesman*, 610-11, 622-23.

15. Battenberg to Churchill, 14 Nov. 1912, Gilbert, ed., *Churchill, Companion 2, pt.* 3:1663.

16. Ibid., 1684.

17. Papers of Prince Louis of Battenberg, University of Southampton; Chartwell Papers of Winston Churchill, First Lord's Papers, CHART 13/, 1911-1915, Churchill College, Cambridge.

18. Quoted in Churchill, *Young Statesman*, 630.

19. The events are summarized in the documents in Gilbert, ed., *Churchill, Companion* 2:1796-98. The quote from Prince Louis to WSC, 12 Nov. 1913, is to be found on 1797.

20. Hopwood to Stamfordham, 13 Nov. 1913, ibid., 1798.

21. Printed in Lord Brassey et al., *The Naval Annual, 1912* (Portsmouth: Brasseys, 1912), 385-90; Gilbert, ed., *Churchill, Companion* 2:1303-12, 1486-90. The background to Churchill's understanding of his office is outlined in Marder, *From Dreadnought to Scapa Flow*, 2:268-70.

22. Lord Brassey et al., eds., *The Naval Annual, 1914* (Portsmouth: Brasseys, 1914), 2.

23. Nicholas d'Ombrain, *War Machinery and High Policy: Defence Administration in Peacetime Britain, 1902-1914* (London: Oxford University Press, 1973), 111-12.

24. John Bach, *The Australia Station: A History of the Royal Navy in the South West Pacific, 1821-1913* (Kensington: New South Wales University Press, 1986), 193-95.

25. Samuel R. Williamson, *The Politics of Grand Strategy: Britain and France Prepare for War, 1904-1914* (Cambridge, Mass.: Harvard University Press, 1969), 320-27, 334-39; Paul G. Halpern, *The Mediterranean Naval Situation, 1908-1914* (Cambridge, Mass.: Harvard University Press, 1971), 105-6, 108, 112, 124-28, 302-3, 313; E. W. R. Lumby, ed., *Policy and Operations in The Mediterranean, 1912-14* (London: Navy Records Society, vol. 115, 1970), 7, 37, 61, 78, 108-9, 122, 135, 230, 236, 241, 420, 432.

26. Quoted in James Goldrick, *The King's Ships Were at Sea: The War in the North Sea, August 1914-February 1915* (Annapolis, Md.: Naval Institute Press, 1984), 4.

27. Battenberg Papers, File T86: "Stand Fast the Fleet, "University of Southampton; Marder, *From the Dreadnought to Scapa Flow*, 1:432-33; Mark Kerr, *Prince Louis,* 243.

28. Churchill, *World Crisis*, 1:196.

29. Ibid., 194.

30. Patrick Beesly, *Room 40: British Naval Intelligence, 1914-18* (New York: Oxford University Press, 1984), 72.

31. Marder, *From the Dreadnought to Scapa Flow*, 2:39-41.

32. Ibid., 40.

33. Beesly, *Room 40*, 70-72.

34. For an analysis of the problems the Royal Navy faced in the first few months of war, see James Goldrick, *The King's Ships*.

35. Ibid., 311-14, 316.

36. Press cuttings on resignation, *Daily Mail*, 27 October 1914, Battenberg Papers, T44.

37. Quoted in Marder, *From the Dreadnought to Scapa Flow*, 2:86.

38. Quote from a private letter from Rear Admiral Beamish to the Editor, Review of Mark Kerr, *Prince Louis,* in the *Naval Review*, 22 (1934): 814, ftn. 2.

39. Rhodri Williams, *Defending the Empire: The Conservative Party and the British Defence Policy, 1899-1915* (New Haven, Conn.: Yale University Press, 1991), 230-31.

40. George V, Q 711/1, 27 Oct. 1914, RA.

41. Prince Louis to WSC, 29 Oct. 1914, CHART 13/27A.

42. Thursday, 29 Oct. 1914, Buckingham Palace, George V Diary 1914-1917, 97-98, RA.

43. Ibid.

44. Prince Louis to Louise, 6 June 1917, Battenberg Papers, T90.

6
Admiral Sir Henry Bradwardine Jackson (1915–1916)

Malcolm H. Murfett

Once the faltering naval operation at Gallipoli had led to the acrimonious split between Fisher and Churchill in May 1915 and touched off a major political crisis within the Liberal administration into the bargain, even Asquith realized the time had come to make some belated changes to the way that the British were fighting the First World War. Apart from being receptive to the forming of a coalition government, the Prime Minister was made painfully aware that he could no longer ignore the unfortunate situation that had arisen at the Admiralty. He resolved both to ignore Fisher's extraordinary machinations and tactless demands for a return to office and at the same time to dispense with the services of the other protagonist in this affair, Winston Churchill, the First Lord of the Admiralty.

Churchill's post was offered to Arthur James Balfour, the former Conservative Prime Minister, who accepted it with alacrity. An intellectual with a vast fund of ministerial experience, Balfour was a highly respected figure in Whitehall. Nonetheless, even his friends would admit that he was more a philosophical thinker than a man of action. In this and other respects he rather mirrored Prime Minister Asquith. A gifted debater and skilled parliamentarian, Balfour was a cautious individual who was not given to rushing headlong into something or overcommitting himself. A more vivid contrast to his predecessor, Winston Churchill, could hardly be imagined. Instead of the Churchillian drive and energy, Balfour brought a languid disposition to bear on Admiralty business. Unfortunately, there was more than a hint of laziness about the man who was charged with responsibility for picking up the pieces of the Dardanelles campaign and creating a fresh chapter of confidence and stability for the Royal Navy after the disasters of the recent past.

Balfour chose to enter on this new era with a distinguished scientist as his principal colleague on the Board of Admiralty. Sir Henry Jackson, who was appointed to succeed Admiral Fisher as First Sea Lord, had made his name as the copioneer of wireless telegraphy with Guglielmo Marconi—a feat for which he was elected a Fellow of the Royal Society in 1901. Apart from his scientific gifts, Jackson had been a torpedo expert in his early years and had served as a very successful Third Sea Lord and Controller of the Navy (1905-8). Although he had limited command and combat experience at sea, his impressive administrative record within the Admiralty hierarchy and intimate knowledge of the Board's activities (he had been Chief of the War Staff from 1912 to 1914) earmarked him as one of the leading candidates to succeed Fisher as First Sea Lord and Chief of Naval Staff. Even so, it is generally considered that he was only chosen as First Sea Lord because the outstanding candidate—Admiral Sir John Jellicoe—could not be relieved as Commander-in-Chief as there was no ready replacement for him at the head of the Grand Fleet at this time. Although he may have only obtained his post by default, Jackson brought to it the solid reliability of a dour and somewhat pessimistic Yorkshireman. He said little, was rarely expansive on nontechnical items, and preferred caution to flights of fancy. As a result, there was not much dash and verve or reforming zeal about the new First Sea Lord. Jackson was known to be a very private person—someone with a liking for cricket, horse racing, golf, and shooting—and one not given to self-advertisement. On the whole, therefore, he was a somewhat reticent individual who was not a particularly good public speaker or invested with great strategic insight. Moreover, he was liable to be cantankerous on occasion—a fact not unrelated, one suspects, to the relatively poor health from which he suffered in his later years.[1] Despite this list of rather unflattering personal qualities, he was a sound and methodical administrator, who was loyal to his subordinates and especially to Balfour, with whom he developed a close, if occasionally abrasive, working relationship. He listened to advice from all quarters before deciding anything, rarely pontificated about strategic or tactical matters, and did not seek to restrict the freedom of initiative that Jellicoe and the other fleet commanders possessed in fulfilling their operational duties upon the high seas.

When he took up office as First Sea Lord in late May 1915, Jackson was sixty years of age. A veteran with forty-seven years' experience in the Royal Navy, he remained fully committed to the senior service that had offered him so much professional satisfaction. Shrewd, dependable, and conservative, he was not prone to springing major surprises on those with whom he worked. It is little wonder, therefore, that his tenure in office did not herald a radical transformation in the traditional way in which naval business was conducted within the Admiralty. In fact, Jackson jealously guarded his existing administrative privileges, found delegation of authority to subordinates difficult, and took a personal interest in a myriad number of topics, many of which could safely have been left to others. His overzealous working methods were to backfire on him since they often left him little spare time for adequate reflection or much else. He complained bitterly about his work load yet failed to do anything constructive to ease the problem![2]

It is difficult nowadays, blessed as one is with the benefit of hindsight, not to dismiss his appointment as merely a stopgap affair that was not meant to last. Whether Jackson saw it in this way at the outset is difficult to gauge. Even if he did, one suspects that he did not let it inhibit his performance as First Sea Lord. Others were not so charitable. David Beatty was moved to reflect: "God knows what the result will be I fear he is not man enough for the job. What in the world the end will be nobody can tell."[3] Beatty did not speak for the fleet. Jellicoe was not so dismissive about the new First Sea Lord (although he warned Balfour of Jackson's irritability) and Rosslyn Wemyss actually extolled his virtues, seeing him as the best candidate for the job at that time.[4]

Jackson's relations with the other Board members were not especially warm, even if they were officially correct. Sir Frederick Hamilton, Sir Frederick Tudor and Sir Cecil Lambert may have been proficient at their jobs (and there were even some doubts expressed about that), but they could not be described in any sense as outstanding naval officers or administrators. Inheriting them as First Sea Lord, Jackson was curiously loath to dispense with their services in favor of men with far greater ability. Perhaps it suited his purpose to have a string of nonentities working with him. Whatever the reason, they remained at their desks within the Admiralty but enjoyed very little real power. For instance, despite ostensibly supporting them in their drive to increase their executive responsibilities on important matters, such as the conduct of naval war policy, Jackson actually kept them out of the decision-making loop. This aspect of Admiralty policy remained, for all practical purposes, the exclusive province of the First Lord and the First Sea Lord.[5]

Once confirmed in office, Balfour and Jackson were immediately confronted by the need to find an acceptable way through the Dardanelles labyrinth. Jackson, who had never been an enthusiastic advocate of the Gallipoli offensive from the outset (unlike Balfour), remained lukewarm at best to any continuation of the Allied military operation. Once the failure at Suvla Bay (6-29 August 1915) had been recognized for what it was, Jackson's inclination toward evacuation of the peninsula grew apace. He was not wildly sympathtic to the plan for forcing the Straits that had been devised by the tireless Roger Keyes, and he was only prepared to support the scheme if the Army could be relied on to do its fair share of the job by capturing the Narrows forts—a feat that looked well beyond them at this stage. By mid-November, therefore, the odds against any continuation of the Dardanelles operation were lengthening considerably. While Balfour was staunchly against any evacuation of the peninsula, he could not carry the rest of the War Committee with him, and once Field Marshal Lord Kitchener, the Secretary of State for War, had submitted his report to the Cabinet advising evacuation (22 November 1915), the die was finally cast in favor of a military retreat.[6]

After extricating its forces from the Gallipoli adventure as a result of a superbly staged military evacuation (8 December 1915—9 January 1916), the British government was faced by the continuing misfortune in the Balkans, where Bulgaria's entry into the war had helped crush the Serbian Army and tie down an ever-increasing number of Allied troops in Salonika. In addition, enemy submarine activity in the Mediterranean and Adriatic became more disruptive and costly as the weeks proceeded. Although more destroyer patrols were recommended, Jackson did not advocate any convoying procedures. Rather than lament the poor state of antisubmarine detection methods, he preferred instead to pin the blame for the rising U-boat toll on Allied shipping on the inept performance of both the French and the Italian fleets. Accusing them (in private) of being too defensively minded to carry the fight to the underwater aggressor, Jackson wrung his hands in frustration at a situation in which the Royal Navy was forced to take up the slack on behalf of its feeble companions in arms.[7] Although he would have liked to have been able to redeploy a number of his battleships and destroyer strength from Mediterranean to home waters, political considerations always prevailed against such a move. Aggravated beyond measure by this type of situation, Jackson found his patience sorely tested by the necessity for maintaining diplomatic niceties between the Allies. Although he respected and liked Balfour, he had little time for politicians generally—an attitude that was common among all ranks in the services.

This feeling of guarded antipathy was enhanced by the activities of government ministers (who opposed an enforcement of the blockade against Germany which was designed to hit its trading arrangement with neutral countries such as Sweden) and with the industrious amateurs—most notably, Lloyd George—whose increasing control over the distribution of scarce resources as Minister of Munitions wreaked havoc with the Admiralty's new construction plans. Delays over naval building received a bad press within the fleet. Jellicoe was particularly incensed about the shortfall in destroyer strength and Beatty was scarcely less choleric over the slow rate of airship construction, and the tendency was for them and others to accuse the Admiralty of failing to exert sufficient pressure on the relevant authorities to save the production timetable. Jackson felt this criticism keenly (perhaps the product of a guilty conscience) and responded vigorously to it—witness his despatch to the Commander-in-Chief of 2 March 1916.[8] On the whole, however, the criticism that the Admiralty was not punching its requisite weight in government circles was, on balance, justified. Something was undoubtedly missing. Certainly, Balfour was not cast in the Churchillian mold and lacked a good deal of his predecessor's fire. For his part, Jackson could hardly be described as another Fisher. Ironically, the very qualities for which they were now being criticized (their imperturbability and stolidity) had originally been deemed important factors in their appointment to the Admiralty Board in the previous May, when a calming influence was being sought as a antidote to the fevered activity of the Churchill-Fisher era. Now, however, their style was deemed too quiet. Dissatisfaction with the Board's perceived lack of dynamism spilled over into the realms of press and Parliament during the winter of 1915-16. Lord Fisher and his editorial friends in the newspaper world did their best to arouse the country's awareness to what they saw as a Royal Navy ponderously marking time and failing to take the initiative in the war against the enemy. A campaign to restore Fisher as First Sea Lord was whipped up in March 1916, but it failed to make much headway after Balfour finally imposed his scholarly veto on the proposed arrangement in the House of Commons.

Although there was a general feeling that the Admiralty was content to sit back and wait upon events, it would not be true to suggest, as some did, that it preferred inaction to anything more demonstrative. Jackson complained in this sense to Jellicoe in January 1916 when he wrote: "Foreigners can't understand a silent navy and think silence is inaction. Hence the politicians take every chance they have of advertising it."[9] While the Admiralty was aware that the British war effort could be severely compromised if anything went desperately awry with the Grand Fleet, Jackson and Balfour were both anxious to let Jellicoe know that they supported an offensive strategy against the German High Seas Fleet, if one could be successfully orchestrated. Various options for bringing about this desired confrontation were mooted by the Admiralty in the early weeks of 1916, including a suggestion for redeploying the Grand Fleet south from its main base at Scapa Flow in the Orkneys to concentrate it along with Beatty's Battlecruiser Fleet at Rosyth on the Firth of Forth. Despite the fact that Jellicoe was less enamored with this solution than Jackson, Admiral Scheer's "tip and run" raids on Lowestoft and Great Yarmouth (25 April 1916) forced the Commander-in-Chief to discuss the advantages of a more southerly anchorage for his fleet. Despite its attractions, Rosyth did not become the main base for the Grand Fleet until April 1918.[10]

Jackson was to get the battle with the German High Seas Fleet that he wanted, but the action at Jutland (31 May-1 June 1916) was not to be the smashing victory that the Admiralty and the Royal Navy had so eagerly anticipated. Curiously, Jackson seems to have played little part in the actual event—being seemingly content to leave the handling of the Admiralty's part in this battle to Sir Henry Oliver, the Chief of the War Staff, and his less than star-studded team in the Operations Division. For a man who normally found delegation difficult and whose gaze touched most things coming into and going out of the Admiralty, this "hands-off" conduct of the First Sea Lord is almost inexplicable. He may have been too confident about the final outcome and in his subordinates acting on his behalf. If he was, the complacency soon rebounded upon him. Raw intelligence data obtained through the sterling work of the cryptographers and naval analysts in Room 40 failed to be fully appreciated by the staff of the Operations Division, with lamentable results for the seagoing fleets. Although the Battle of Jutland excited heated controversy and much agitation among experts over what were seen as wasted opportunities for worsting an outnumbered and outgunned foe, Jackson did not appear too downcast by the rather tame and inconclusive ending to this important naval encounter in the North Sea. He remarked to Jellicoe that he doubted the Germans would again come out into the North Sea in such strength for some time to come.[11] He also tried to reassure the Commander-in-Chief that the Admiralty Board attached no significance to the criticism that had been expressed in certain quarters over Jellicoe's alleged tactical and strategical shortcomings in the battle. "I hope you are not worrying about the conduct of yourself or anyone else in the action last week. . . . You may rest assured that no criticism has emanated from those qualified to judge."[12] Jackson's note, however, was little compensation for the poor impression given by a tersely worded Admiralty communiqué that had been authorised by Balfour, amended by the First Sea Lord, and issued to the press on 2 June. Far from disputing the German claim that the British had been defeated at Jutland, the communiqué (a public relations disaster) may have unwittingly lent credence to this boast by admitting that the

Royal Navy had indeed lost more ships in the battle than had its European adversary.[13]

Worse was to follow. Instead of grasping the lessons of Jutland and acting on them without delay, the Admiralty seemed reluctant to acknowledge that weaknesses in the matériel resources of the fleet actually existed—it did little, for instance, to test the quality of the armor-piercing shells which had proved so disappointing in the heat of the battle, and it initially resisted the calls that were made for additional armor protection for its ships. A mixture of arrogant complacency and righteous indignation seemed to grip everyone on the Board—Jackson himself was not immune from these feelings and was as guilty as anyone else in ignoring the warning signs that all was not well with the Royal Navy. That was not all. Jellicoe's harsh but justifiable criticism of standard fleet communications and signaling procedures appeared to touch a raw nerve with the First Sea Lord. His correspondence with the Commander-in-Chief, therefore, began to take on a more acrimonious note as the weeks passed.

Matters had scarcely improved between the two men by the time the German High Seas Fleet ventured out into the North Sea again on 19 August and carried out an audacious daylight raid on Sunderland. Jellicoe was unable to meet, much less cripple, Admiral Reinhard Scheer's force before it retreated back to its home base. Once again, another opportunity to defeat the enemy's fleet had been missed. In the frustrating aftermath of this nonevent, relations between the two men cooled even more. Jackson was inclined to agree with those who blamed the Commander-in-Chief for being too defensively minded, while Jellicoe's tactless remarks about the inadequacies and shortcomings of the Admiralty were relayed back to London by Cecil Lambert, to the considerable annoyance of the First Sea Lord. Jackson reacted to this denigration of the institution for which he was personally responsible by telling Jellicoe some home truths in typically trenchant fashion: "Perhaps we have tried to meet your wishes too readily during the past 15 months: that we have done so, as far as the material at our command allows, neither you nor anyone else can deny. Everything else has been starved more or less for the Grand Fleet." He concluded by reminding the Commander-in-Chief that grumbling about authority should be controlled: "Discontent spreads rapidly, especially downwards & may react when least expected. Popularity may sometimes be too dearly bought, plain speaking is sometimes desirable."[14] Given his predilection for plain speaking, Jackson's next missive to Jellicoe was ambiguous to say the least, and ended with what might be construed as a vague warning to the Commander-in-Chief that he should not make the mistake of believing himself indispensable. "If you think, at any time, that you can't stand the strain, you should give us ample warning to prevent a hasty decision being made, and your recommendation would have great influence in the choice of your successor."[15]

Although matters were patched up between them, it would be a mistake to suggest that Jellicoe was alone in finding fault with those running the Admiralty. As the autumn of 1916 wore on, the press and public began to agitate for a change in the administration of the Royal Navy. This latest crisis arose in response to two German "tip and run" raids in the Channel off the Kent and Sussex coasts respectively (26-27 October and 23 November). On neither occasion was the Dover Patrol able to make contact with the German destroyers, let alone deliver them a stinging riposte. Balfour and Jackson were left to pick up the pieces, but they did so inexpertly and the newspaper fraternity turned against what was seen as their ineffectual leadership. A campaign to oust the two men gathered momentum as unseemly political disputes over the control of naval air power and knowledge of an increased U-boat toll on merchant shipping reached the public domain.[16] Balfour and Jackson needed a glittering success to lessen public concern and stave off press criticism of their alleged passivity and inaction. Unfortunately, however, they did not receive such a timely boost to their flagging fortunes, and without a ready answer to the submarine problem, their stock continued to fall in the eyes of friend and foe alike. In the end, Jackson found a partial solution to the problem by offering to resign in favor of Jellicoe. He did so without regret.[17] In his letter to Beatty, Jackson acknowledged truthfully that he was losing touch with naval vessels and command operations:

I think it is quite time I made way for a more energetic & more experienced admiral than I can claim to be, & I offered to go some time ago if it would assist the government to win the war. I have had nearly two years here & it is too long to be away from the sea, if one has to be responsible for naval operations as ships improve to such an extent that it requires personal knowledge of them to properly appreciate their capabilities under all circumstances.[18]

To sum up, therefore, Jackson's tenure as First Sea Lord was a fairly undistinguished one. While it is true that he did not preside over any military disaster during his eighteen month term of office, it must also be admitted that under his stewardship, no notable achievements or major administrative reforms were implemented at the Admiralty. Instead, there is ample evidence of administrative sterility and impotence.

Undoubtedly the most conspicuous failure of Jackson's administration lay in his bewildering inability to spot the potentialities of Room 40's intelligence-gathering facility as a means of providing vital information for operational decision making by both the Admiralty and the fleet. Following from that original mistake, he did nothing to ensure that the valuable material that the staff of Room 40 provided was not wasted by the Admiralty's Operations Division. As if that was not bad enough, he also managed to appear listless and devoid of ideas when it came to coping with the German submarine menace and was strangely reluctant to implement the findings of the post-Jutland committees on improving the readiness of the Royal Navy to meet its German adversary in the future. Although he could be said to have generally worked well with Balfour and been listened to with respect, but without awe, by those in government, his influence on Cabinet ministers should not be exaggerated, for he remained firmly in the shadow of Kitchener until June 1916 and was rarely a match for David Lloyd George from May 1915 onward. Therefore, while his style of doing business may have suited Asquith and Balfour, as a long term desk-bound admiral, remote from the rigors of modern naval command and combat, he was hardly an inspirational figure for the fleet. His retirement to the Presidency of the Royal Naval College at Greenwich (a post that, incidentally, he filled admirably) was greeted with palpable relief in most quarters, and especially at Rosyth and Scapa Flow.

Although Jackson had undoubtedly tried his best as First Sea Lord, it is difficult to rate his performance in office highly. A victim of circumstances largely beyond his control, Jackson in reality paid the price of the Grand Fleet's failure to crush the German High Seas Fleet in the North Sea. Ironically, therefore, it is tempting to see Jackson's ultimate fate as lying almost totally in the hands of the very person who succeeded him as First Sea Lord, namely, Admiral Sir John Jellicoe. If Jellicoe had achieved the stunning Mahanian victory at Jutland that the Grand Fleet was designed to secure, one may speculate that the grave dissatisfaction with the performance at the Admiralty of both Balfour and Jackson may not have arisen, or reached the same fervor, as in late 1916. As it was, however, Jackson was denied this type of smashing victory and soon felt the consequences. While he was not sorry to lay his aside duties as First Sea Lord and Chief of Naval Staff, Jackson passed on to Jellicoe a very daunting challenge and dubious inheritance.

NOTES

1. Poor health seems to have been the main reason why he failed to take up his appointment as Commander-in-Chief of the Mediterranean Fleet in August 1914. He was retained at the Admiralty, where he had been Chief of the War Staff from February 1913. J. R. H. Weaver, ed., *Dictionary of National Biography 1922-1930* (London: Oxford University Press, 1937), 448-50.

2. Letter from Sir Henry B. Jackson to Admiral Sir John Jellicoe, 2 Sept. 1915, f. 5; Jackson to Jellicoe, 3 Oct. 1916, f. 68, Add. Mss. 49009, Jellicoe Papers, British Library, London. See also Marder, *From the Dreadnought to Scapa Flow*, 2:300-1.

3. Sir David Beatty to Lady Beatty, 22 May 1915, BTY/17/33, f. 36, Beatty Papers, National Maritime Museum, Greenwich.

4. Marder, *From the Dreadnought to Scapa Flow*, 2:291. Clear evidence of the friendly relations that existed between Wemyss and Jackson is present in their correspondence. See the batch of letters written from HMS *Euryalus* to the Admiralty, copies of which can be consulted in Rear Admiral H. Miller Papers, 73/11/2, Imperial War Museum, London.

5. Marder, *From the Dreadnought to Scapa Flow*, 2:302-7.

6. Ibid., 308-29.

7. See the Jackson-Jellicoe correspondence of 11 Nov. 1915 and Mar. 1916 cited in Marder, *From the Dreadnought to Scapa Flow*, 2:338-39; see also Jackson to Jellicoe, 2 Oct. 1915, 49009, f. 8, Jellicoe Papers. For an in-depth account of the Royal Navy's problems in the Mediterranean theater, see Paul G. Halpern, *The Naval War in the Mediterranean 1914-1918* (London: Allen and Unwin, 1987), 125-300.

8. Marder, *From the Dreadnought to Scapa Flow*, 2:386-94.

9. Jackson to Jellicoe, 25 Jan. 1916, 49009, f. 20, Jellicoe Papers.

10. Marder, *From the Dreadnought to Scapa Flow*, 2:430-35.

11. Jackson to Jellicoe, 1 June 1916, f. 52, 49009, Jellicoe Papers.

12. Jackson to Jellicoe, 7 June 1916, f. 55; see also his messages of 1 and 3 June 1916, fs. 52, and 54, 49009, Jellicoe Papers.

13. Marder gives the final battle losses as fourteen British ships totaling 111,000 tons as compared to eleven German vessels of 62,000 tons. See Marder, *From the Dreadnought to Scapa Flow*, 3:248-49. On the day after the battle, the Grand Fleet consisted of 31 battleships, 7 battlecruisers, 10 armored cruisers, 35 light cruisers, 135 destroyers and flotilla leaders, and 37 submarines; CAB 37/157.

14. Jackson to Jellicoe, 11 Sept. 1916, Collection 4, Jackson Papers, Ministry of Defence (MOD), Naval Library, London.

15. Jackson to Jellicoe, 14 Sept. 1916, Collection 4, Jackson Papers.

16. Marder, *From the Dreadnought to Scapa Flow*, 3:308-36.

17. Jackson to Jellicoe, 5 Dec. 1916, f. 78, 49009, Jellicoe Papers.

18. Jackson to Beatty, 3 Dec. 1916, BTY/13/20, Beatty Papers.

7
Admiral Sir John Jellicoe (1916–1917)

Donald M. Schurman

Sir Henry Jackson resigned as First Sea Lord on 4 December 1916, and Admiral Sir John Rushworth Jellicoe, who succeeded him, came directly from Scapa Flow, where he had led the Grand Fleet with some distinction for over two exciting, onerous, and stressful years. Born in 1859, Jellicoe could be said to have been an experienced, old Imperial, nineteenth-century naval hand in a Royal Navy entering a new century; he was fifty-five when the war began. His experience of the nineteenth-century Navy had provided Jellicoe with some sense of the proud place it had occupied in Imperial and world affairs; it had also, however, been a time when that Navy moved, not just from sail to steam, but rather, through an immense, fifty-year technological revolution which made the Navy, unlike the Army, thoroughly modern.[1] A gunnery expert, he had served on the senior staff of the Gunnery School in HMS *Excellent* under Admiral (then Captain) J. A. Fisher, whose attention and continuing patronage he enjoyed. His career moved smoothly through sea and battleship appointments, and he held important shore positions, mostly technical, where he developed his interest in the hitting power of the Fleet.[2] He became Second Sea Lord in 1912, and, as Fisher seems to have planned, Commander-in-Chief of the Grand Fleet on 4 August 1914 as the Great War opened.[3]

Under Jellicoe's command, the Royal Navy in the North Sea maintained its supremacy and the blockade on Germany. In this strategic success story, the Battle of Jutland was a significant episode, but it created such an obsession in the minds of professionals that its details have been endlessly reworked. A profound sense of unease with a tactical result of less than Nelsonic proportions has obscured the fact that Jutland provided dividends that stand in comparison with those of

Trafalgar. Notwithstanding, a preoccupation with nautical minutiae appeared almost at once and still continues. Indeed, its bulk makes war gaming respectable.

In the vast global conflict of the war at sea, the Grand Fleet was only a link (although the most important one) in the chain of British naval defense. The responsible British authority was not the Admiralty but the Cabinet and the War Cabinet. Asquith and then Lloyd George were the responsible overall leaders, not Lord Fisher or Jellicoe. Even so, Jellicoe, as the Commander-in-Chief of the Grand Fleet, was an immensely important figure upon whom the government confidently relied to bring the German High Seas Fleet to action and defeat. After moving through nearly two years of war with conspicuous success, the last few months of Jellicoe's command were awkward and controversial ones for the man dubbed the "granite sailor." As a result, therefore, he came to the Admiralty encumbered with a reputation for somehow not annihilating the enemy and for not using the Grand Fleet offensively enough, although both his tactics and his proposals were explicit in the orders he received and carried out.

By late 1916 a second great challenge appeared: German submarines came to constitute a strategic problem of the first magnitude. In the autumn of 1916 the Admiralty, the politicians, and the new First Sea Lord all recognized the serious nature of the submarine threat long before it became a reality. Indeed, Jellicoe literally came to the Admiralty to address this issue.[4] Lord Fisher apart, all held that the translation of Jellicoe from the Grand Fleet to Whitehall was necessary to defend against this expected attack.[5] Even Fisher had no doubt concerning the threat, but he felt, rather, that where Jellicoe was well placed to contribute to the war on board *Iron Duke*, he might not be the man to deal with wily politicians. Nonetheless, Fisher shared Jellicoe's firm view that the greatest menace to all prosecution of the war was the ongoing attempt to substitute for the strategy of weight, or blockade, an aspect of the persistent desire to use the Navy for other, more spectacular, purposes, such as that attempted by Churchill at the Dardanelles.

Jellicoe came to the Admiralty in the same month that Lloyd George became Prime Minister—December 1916. Like Fisher and the outgoing First Lord, Balfour, Jellicoe knew that some constraint on enemy submarines must be devised and operated, but like them, he was not certain of its form.[6] "Convoy" seemed a magic remedy to some planners of the time, as it has to many commentators since, but it was not then so regarded by any consensus of responsible opinion. Certainly, prewar service opinion was that convoying would be unnecessary, and no serious plans were in place for developing it.[7] Moreover, the Navy's fetish for offense, or patrol attack dispositions, lay behind much of the coy attitude to convoys in the service, where it remained through the two world wars.[8] Combinations of these views were used as arguments against convoying, and they waxed and waned according to circumstance as the war unfolded.[9] Jellicoe was not exempt from these views and prejudices. However, he never claimed to have come to London with a detailed program in hand to solve the problem, but rather held the conviction that the submarine war had not been looked at as a whole due to departmentalism and lack of priority planning in London. The idea of convoys certainly did not present itself to his mind as an all-or-nothing choice; rather he saw it as one weapon in the naval armory that might be used against unrestricted submarine warfare.[10]

At the Admiralty he immediately set up what might be called its first wartime reform. The Second, Third, and Fourth Sea Lords were replaced. He established a new office of Fifth Sea Lord, and he created a new Anti-Submarine Division of the Naval Staff with what, he thought, was a wide mandate to coordinate this activity. At the same time a Trade Division was created as part of the Directorate of Naval Intelligence.[11] These changes were significant, since this was the machinery that bridled the submarine menace in 1917-18. Jellicoe could see quite clearly from the beginning that the attack on trade, being such a complex matter, involved the appointment of a strong personality. To head the new Anti-Submarine Division of the Naval Staff, he selected Admiral Alexander Duff, who was also fresh from the Grand Fleet.[12] Duff was to have the task of prescriber, coordinator, and organizer, a huge task that he tackled without much real power. However, it is clear that the First Sea Lord wished to be at the center of these affairs himself so as not to lose contact with, or control of, developing events.[13] Perhaps the most serious flaw in all this was a tendency to seek remedies in the naval system alone when private shipping interests, inland transportation, and wartime goods priorities pointed to wider horizons.

It was, however, quite one thing to predict, in December 1916, that submarines might present an overwhelming challenge in 1917, and quite another to experience it. The committee work necessary for a practical plan to turn back the U-boats was overtaken, two months later, by the high-tonnage losses actually caused by U-boats; these had been anticipated but were still unsettling. Heavy losses in February were followed by worse losses in March and April, which gave rise to projections that were more worrying. Furthermore, a movement that led to friction with the politicians went forward secretly as Commander Reginald Henderson, in the office of the Assistant Chief of Naval Staff (Sir Alexander Duff), fed selected information critical of the new Admiralty to the Secretary of the War Cabinet, through Maurice Hankey, and, so, ultimately to the Prime Minister himself.[14] This movement received support from within the fleet, where Captain Herbert Richmond had strong views on how the war should be prosecuted and who in the Navy should do it. Thus there was built up a set of unsettling cross-purposes, some of them clandestine, that hampered Duff and, ultimately, Jellicoe.

Nevertheless, convoying was not neglected. An experiment, under the practical control of the Grand Fleet, had been conceived in December 1916. It was given a trial in January and February 1917, and then agreed to as a local expedient. This was authorized by Jellicoe's signature on 21 April.[15] Another such experiment, involving the French coal "protected sailings," was also conceived in early December, tried in January-February 1917, and authorized as policy on 17 April.[16] In both cases losses were negligible. During April a convoy route was set up from Gibraltar to the British coastal waters, and again there was negligible loss.

In mid-February, Captain Hankey, Secretary to the War Cabinet, put forward convoy proposals, aided by his relationship with Lloyd George and his information source in Duff's office. This embarrassed Jellicoe, but it got nowhere. No doubt the marine captain was somewhat out of his depth when meeting the admirals face to face. Nonetheless, Hankey's initiative did alert the Prime Minister to the possibilities that convoying seemed to promise. More menacingly for Jellicoe, Beatty, in the Grand Fleet, was of the opinion that, in general, the Admiralty was inefficiently organized, and he informed Lloyd George as such in early April.[17] Jellicoe also held this view when he had commanded the Grand Fleet, and Captain Richmond, who was eager for "reform" and prepared to support Henderson in one way or another, held this view as well. Thus it was that heavy losses, service intrigue, the complicated nature of the submarine problem, and the Prime Minister's suspicions all came together to constitute heavy pressure on Jellicoe to "do something." In fact, the convoy experiments were going forward;[18] the Prime Minister subsequently claimed, however, that it was only his threat to visit the Admiralty, made on 25 April, that caused the Duff report on convoys to be issued on 26 April.[19] Lloyd George's pressure on the Admiralty reflected growing disenchantment. He later wrote that he had galvanized the Admiralty into action.[20] This seems most unlikely, although even Jellicoe's biographer, Temple Patterson, thought it hard to imagine the Prime Minister's provocative moves being ignored.[21] What certainly did happen was that a few days later there was an Admiralty reorganization, directed personally by the Prime Minister, that sent Eric Geddes to the Admiralty as Controller, with responsibility for shipbuilding and procurement. Geddes obviously could have had little *immediate* influence on the antisubmarine operations.

There was another strand in naval affairs that was both significant and very difficult to pinpoint. In 1916, after Jutland, public and service discontent began to emerge concerning the strategic stance of the Navy. This feeling, that timidity and lack of planning lay at the root of the Navy's defensive posture, was widespread and growing. It was this "lack of initiative" that Churchill had deplored before and during the Dardanelles operations and deliberately stirred up in 1916-17.[22] In the service, such views were certainly held by the "Young Turks," and in antisubmarine circles they were held by those who favored a "patrol and attack" approach to the submarine menace. Offensive-minded people may have held very different views on, say, the use of convoys against submarines, but their accusations of timidity and lack of organization at the Admiralty crossed Lloyd George's desk just when he was most suspicious of the Navy's response to the submarine threat. As Lord Fisher had carefully coached them to be, the Admiralty and its service chief were suspicious of any expedients that threatened the blockade of Germany or the power of its main enforcer, the Grand Fleet. Indeed, it was the rigor of the view that the Grand Fleet and the blockade must be kept as priority number one that distressed Fleet Street, some politicians, and the so-called naval reformers. Thus, there were two kinds of attack on the Admiralty, one eclectic and concerned with a supposed specific remedy (convoys) in response to a deadly menace, and the other concerned with general Admiralty organization for war. These two separate attacks, when combined with politics in London and service infighting generally, made Jellicoe's position very difficult and his leadership vulnerable. In an environment where German sinking successes dominated men's minds, when the Admiralty was groping for proper responses, it was easy to mistake short-term cures for overall naval policy. Jellicoe was concerned to maintain the latter against changes of focus in the main strategy. He was pessimistic about the war against the submarines, but he did maintain the central policy.

The charge of pessimism against Jellicoe was undoubtedly true. By April, successes by the German submarines made his projections for the rest of the war bleak. He was right to hold this view, for while German attack successes decreased from May until the end of summer, they continued to be high throughout the autumn. In fact, it has been impossible for anyone writing on this subject since to state clearly when it was that the U-boat was mastered by convoys—or by anything else.[23] This chapter does not challenge the idea that convoys played a central role in the attempt to protect trade against U-boats, but it does suggest that Jellicoe was right to worry about the success or failure of various particular defense mechanisms: he fostered a wide, many-sided approach to the submarine problem. Perhaps he overestimated a fallible foe.[24] Nevertheless, it was Jellicoe, and not his critics, who made the convoy response a reality.

Quite aside from the convoy experiments at Gibraltar and toward Scandinavia, as well as those related to French coal transport, the ship movements that were really crucial to success were focused on the Atlantic oceanic trade. Doubtless, the adoption of protection by the use of convoys was greatly assisted by ships and doctrine from the U.S. Navy.[25] Even so, the Americans did not pioneer nor arrange this expedient. Eventual success grew out of an Admiralty committee that was personally launched by Jellicoe in February 1917. The relatively low-ranking people, comprising the Manisty Committee conducted experiments, measured statistics, and reported to Jellicoe in June.[26] He swiftly approved their plans for convoys on Atlantic routes. These plans involved adherence to iron-clad port-loading and turnaround schedules. The number of merchant ships projected for each convoy was twenty. The success rate was great and probably would have been even more spectacular if habitual convoy numbers had been increased and the prescribed accompanying escort craft reduced.[27] Captain Manisty stated, years after the war, that although Jellicoe was not persuaded of the total potential of convoys, he had nonetheless instituted the program that led to its adoption and then backed what was to him a dark horse through all the subsequent vicissitudes.[28]

The appointment of the shipping expert N. A. Leslie had much to do with the success of the convoy, and there can be no doubt that the contact between Leslie and Commander Reginald Henderson (who worked under Sir Alexander Duff, the ACNS), provided much of the stimulus that launched the Manisty Committee, as Manisty later acknowledged.[29] Henderson's judgment on general Admiralty competence might have been less that omniscient, but his opinions on convoys acting as a bait for submarines, were sound. This quicksilver personality, whatever his ultimate loyalties, was in spite of himself a part of the same Admiralty conglomerate that successfully resisted disaster in the U-boat war. However, any idea that the arrival of newcomers at the Admiralty in May, as a result of Lloyd George's initiative, helped significantly in the antisubmarine war as far as convoys were concerned must be avoided. Admiral Henry Oliver, Chief of the Naval War Staff, contended that the newcomers (among whom he included Duff's helpers in

December) kept him so busy answering obvious questions that he had little time for real work.[30] Oliver was no fool!

Of course, one aspect of Geddes's arrival as Controller—his constant prodding regarding statistics—did become *part* of the general Admiralty response to the submarine war. Jellicoe believed that another insurance against submarine success lay in an increase in shipbuilding. The Admiralty wartime priority for battleship construction was maintained, but Geddes did project a merchant-building program in an attempt to match significant losses due to the U-boat offensive.[31] It may be that his investigations showed Admiralty planning procedures in a bad light, and doubtless this tells us much about the growth of wartime bureaucracy. Nonetheless, the projections and plans finally put forward by Geddes in July 1917 (as Controller and before he was appointed First Lord) were not expected to take serious effect until November 1918.[32] This was an interesting and sound projection. Nevertheless, it is clear that those who wanted instant solutions from Jellicoe were incapable of producing them independently!

Shipbuilding was a supplementary response to the unrestricted U-boat war. Another, to obtain more patrol craft and men to staff them, was to reduce commitments abroad—especially in the Mediterranean.[33] This was a constant in Jellicoe's view of strategic balance. He was a convinced "Westerner" when it came to "sideshows". He wanted his ships at home to help focus support for the army supply line to France, submarine hunting, and of course, the blockade.[34]

At the same time, in the name of the blockade, trade protection, and troop transport, Jellicoe resisted spectacular attempts at diversionary activity nearer home, especially in respect to proposals for raids against Ostende and Zeebrugge,[35] and also respecting proposals for action against Heligoland.[36] The latter proposal Jellicoe was prepared to entertain briefly, not because he believed in its intrinsic value, but because he wished its weaknesses to be laid bare. When it was put to the American Admiral Henry Mayo, he destroyed the whole proposal in a sentence. This was not surprising, and when it did take place, the operation, was a fiasco.[37]

The idea of an attack against the Belgian coast was touted as part of General Sir Douglas Haig's Flanders offensive. Supported by Beatty, Jellicoe firmly agreed to assist the soldiers only if Haig's offensive schedule had reached a certain point by a set date, which it failed to do.[38] The Navy was flat against such an operation by itself, or on resting on naval premises and aims alone. Nothing was able to shift Jellicoe's view.

The real tragedy about Jellicoe was that he seemed to radiate gloom. Many of his views were held by the whole service, yet he was often categorized by opponents of the Navy as "blinkered" or stubborn. He was stubborn, of course; moreover, he required all his powers of control and resistance. The problem of the Admiralty was to maintain its strategic stance in the face of eccentric pressures for change. Fisher never doubted that the naval stance selected was the right one and that the pressures against it should be resisted.[39] He and Jellicoe were at one, except for the fact that Fisher wished to be at the Admiralty in the post to which Jellicoe had been appointed. Fisher's intelligence could not face redundancy. The old genius certainly saw the need for a strong man at the helm in Whitehall, who would keep the game going in the face of shifting pressures and the usual machinations of individuals equipped with no traditional naval judgment.

Personal relationships are not easy to fathom. Nevertheless, Jellicoe treated General Haig, not as the semi-intelligent soldier he was, but rather as a responsible Imperial figure bearing a crushing responsibility. As Jellicoe was a Westerner (although he refused Haig an ultimate strategic blank check), the Admiral gave the General strong personal support. Haig's reaction was to begin a campaign of vilification against Jellicoe that culminated in a whirlwind tour of London in late June. Haig was a friend of the monarch, King George V, who was not keen on Jellicoe, and the General lobbied everyone in power, from the King on down, against his naval opposite.[40] He was so successful that Lloyd George was encouraged to replace Sir Edward Carson as First Lord in July and, so far were all those plotters removed from the world of common sense, that the post was offered, before it went to Geddes, to the CIGS, Sir William Robertson, who had the great good sense to refuse the offer.[41]

Lloyd George was not quite politically strong enough to remove Jellicoe in July 1917 when Geddes became First Lord. Then, as August loomed, another attack was mounted, which proved not strong enough to remove Jellicoe or to sack Oliver.[42] Finally, by September, Geddes was able to advance Admiral Wemyss from the obscurity of the Eastern Mediterranean (no doubt to the delight of Richmond and his king-makers) to the Admiralty.[43] The post dreamed up by Geddes, under a smoke screen of administrative efficiency, was that of Deputy First Sea Lord. The covering document referred to the Admiralty as a kind of deficient General Staff.[44] Jellicoe was not deceived and waited out his time by cementing most of his agenda. Finally, he was casually dismissed at the time of the Christmas festivities in 1917,[45] after fighting a more doubtful, and unsuccessful, rearguard action in support of Admiral Bacon and his Dover

Patrol.⁴⁶ The notion that Admiral Sir Reginald Bacon's replacement, Roger Keyes, was an improvement persists in the service.

Everything seemed to relate to organization. The main point about organization at the Admiralty is that its ultimate test lay in personnel rather than measures: driven concepts rather than mere structures. This is what had happened to the War Staff from the moment of its inception, when it was said of its first head, "all the service is laughing at Troubridge . . . nothing was changed."⁴⁷ Beatty, who somewhat frivolously attacked the Admiralty (a Fleet Commander's hobby), did state clearly that to get things improved in 1917 a wholesale personnel change was required in Whitehall.⁴⁸ That judgment may very well have been true, and if it was, one may well ask, how much good would it have done to sack the First Sea Lord. It would hardly have been helpful to appoint Admiral Wemyss sometime between Easter and Midsummers Day, or before the whole elaborate charade of grooming him began to develop.

It was his relationship to the Prime Minister that ultimately compromised Jellicoe's position at the Admiralty. Information reaching Lloyd George from Beatty, as well as from irresponsible would-be naval reformers of both strategy and organization, was all negative concerning Jellicoe. Hankey, the War Cabinet Secretary, reinforced such views. On the personal level, Jellicoe (perhaps regrettably) was neither unduly affable nor "clubbable." His demeanor among politicians was dull rather than electric, and he was completely without any inclination toward self-advertisement. Notwithstanding these personal impressions, Lloyd George found that when he needed (or wanted) flexibility for political purposes, especially against Haig's larger lunacies, Jellicoe did not (or would not) provide it. In response to his wishes to use the eastern Mediterranean as a counterpoint to Haig's efforts in Europe, or even to flash a short-term diversional success, Lloyd George found Jellicoe stolid, inert, and fixed in his positions. Such a confrontation could have only one ultimate result.⁴⁹

That result did not transpire before Jellicoe had welded the Admiralty organization, through his own dominant position, into a team that allowed the only basically sane strategy, that which the Navy had been trained and equipped to operate: the blockade, the bottling up of the High Seas Fleet, and the control of the German communication and attack systems. While loyally keeping that mandate in place, Jellicoe still found time to facilitate the means of beating the submarine menace. In addition to Jutland, this achievement, which he constructed despite unrelenting pressures against him, was Jellicoe's lasting contribution to the war effort. In many ways he was remarkable and successful, and certainly he has been the most generally undervalued of the entente leaders during World War I.

NOTES

1. The major work is A. J. Marder, *British Naval Policy, 1880-1905: The Anatomy of British Sea-Power* (New York: Alfred Knopf, 1940).
2. For his career, see A. Temple Patterson, *Jellicoe: A Biography* (London: Macmillan, 1969).
3. Marder, *Fear God and Dread Nought*, vol.3 (London: Jonathan Cape, 1959), 33, 35.
4. He was offered the post on 22 November 1916, and he was in place at the Admiralty a week later. See Julian S. Corbett and Henry Newbolt, *History of the Great War: Naval Operations*, vol. 4 (London: Longmans, Green, 1920-31, rev. ed. 1938), 330.
5. Jellicoe to Fisher, 1 Dec. 1916, Marder, *Fear God and Dreadnought*, 3:397.
6. Ibid., 280. Balfour actually set up the first antisubmarine committee at the Admiralty on Jellicoe's suggestion, see Patterson, *Jellicoe*.
7. Marder, *From the Dreadnought to Scapa Flow*, 4:117.
8. See introductory chapter in S. W. Roskill, *The War at Sea, 1939-1945*, vol. 1 (London: HMSO, 1954).
9. Marder, *From the Dreadnought to Scapa Flow*, 4:127-28.
10. A. Temple Patterson, ed., *The Jellicoe Papers, vol. 2, 1916-1935* (London: Navy Records Society, 1968), 90-92.
11. Ibid., 112.
12. The Admiralty changes made on Jellicoe's accession as First Sea Lord are detailed in Marder, *From the Dreadnought to Scapa Flow*, 4:58-62; and Patterson, ed., *Jellicoe Papers*, 2:111.
13. Duff became director of the Anti-Submarine Division, as part of a general shake-up. However, to get things done at the Admiralty it was vital that lines of action passed through the First Sea Lord's office.
14. Barry D. Hunt, *Sailor-Scholar: Admiral Sir Herbert Richmond, 1871-1946* (Waterloo, Ont., Canada: Wilfred Laurier Press, 1982) 56-58.
15. Marder, *From the Dreadnought to Scapa Flow*, 4:140-43.
16. The word *convoy* was deliberately avoided at the Admiralty.
17. Marder, *From the Dreadnought to Scapa Flow*, 4:112.
18. Patterson, ed., *Jellicoe Papers*, 2:114.
19. Ibid., 160.
20. Lloyd George, *War Memoirs, vol. 3* (Boston: Little, Brown and Co., 1934), 70-136.
21. Patterson, ed., *Jellicoe Papers*, 2:114-15.
22. Ibid., 101.
23. The point is that it is impossible to pinpoint a date at which the "turn around" between losses and sinkings occurred. The nearest thing we have is Newbolt's chart of monthly sinkings, which Marder used. See Corbett and Newbolt, *Naval Operations*, 4:403, app. B.
24. Captain H. W. E. Manisty to Jellicoe, 27 Apr. 1928: "It was necessarily feasible, and up to the end of the war it met with many vicissitudes and only escaped others more

serious owing to the lack of enterprise of the German Navy." Manisty Papers, IWM/92/42/1, Imperial War Museum, London.

25. David Trask, *Cabinets and Governments: Anglo-American Naval Relations, 1917-1918* (Columbia, Miss: University of Missouri Press, 1979), 79.

26. Atlantic Trade Convoy, *Report by a Committee*, 6 June, 1917. IWM 92/42/1. The Committee consisted of Captain H. W. E. Manisty, Fleet Paymaster; Captain A. W. Longden; Cdr. J. S. Wilde; Lt. G. E. Burton; N. A. Leslie (Ministry of Shipping); the Secretary to the Admiralty Board.

27. John Terraine, *Business in Great Waters: The U-Boat Wars, 1916-1918.* (London: Leo Cooper, 1989), 63-64.

28. Manisty to Jellicoe 27 Apr. 1928, IWM 92/42/1: "The historian [Newbolt] appears to assume, that it's success was inevitable and ought to have been foreseen; if he is right then, of course, no credit for such success attaches to anyone."

29. Manisty *Report*, acknowledges support from Admiralty Paper M05113, and from Henderson, "who had already given much thought to the subject." Manisty Papers, IWM 92/42/1.

30. Admiral Sir William James, *A Great Seaman: The Life of Admiral of the Fleet, Sir Henry Oliver* (London: Witherby, 1956), 158.

31. There are ongoing and searching investigations into British shipbuilding priorities that open up a whole new field in long-term planning, as opposed to facile expedients. See Jon T. Sumida, "Forging the Trident: British Naval Industrial Statistics, 1914-1918," in John A. Lynn, ed., *Feeding Mars: Essays on Logistics and Resources Mobilization in Western Warfare from the Middle Ages to the Present.* (Boulder: Westview Press, 1993) and Sumida's, "British Naval Operational Logistics, 1914-1918," *Journal of Military History*, 57 (July 1993): 447-80.

32. Marder, *From the Dreadnought to Scapa Flow*, 4:256-7.

33. Corbett and Newbolt, *Naval Operations*, 4:344; Patterson, ed., *Jellicoe Papers*, 2:144; Marder, *From the Dreadnought to Scapa Flow*, 4:69.

34. A whole literature has grown up concerning the value and importance of the blockade, which could not, however, influence men in 1917. The central work is Avner Offer, *The First World War: An Agrarian Interpretation* (Oxford: Clarendon Press, 1989).

35. On the proposed raids against Ostende and Zeebrugge, see Marder, *From the Dreadnought to Scapa Flow*, 4:202-205.

36. David F. Trask, *Captains and Cabinets: Anglo-American Naval Relations 1917-1918* (Columbia, Miss: University of Missouri Press, 1972), 150-51.

37. Marder, *From the Dreadnought to Scapa Flow*, 4:304.

38. Ibid., 203-4.

39. Marder, *Fear God and Dread Nought*, 3:389-90.

40. Among those he lobbied were Sir Max Aitken, King George V, Sir Eric Geddes, Lloyd George, Lord Curzon, Balfour, Asquith and Lord Milner. See Marder, *From the Dreadnought to Scapa Flow*, 4:202-3, 206-7.

41. Ibid., 206-7.

42. Ibid., 216-18.

43. Ibid., 223.

44. Ibid., 218-24.

45. Ibid., 340-41.

46. Ibid., 347.

47. Julian Corbett's comment. See D. M. Schurman, *Julian S. Corbett: 1854-1922: Historian of British Maritime Policy from Drake to Jellicoe* (London: Royal Historical Society, 1981), 142.

48. Marder, *From the Dreadnought to Scapa Flow*, 4:172-73.

49. The position of Sir Eric Geddes in all this seems to have been rather as the Prime Minister's agent at the Admiralty, and not as a powerful First Lord.

8
Admiral Sir Rosslyn Wemyss (1917–1919)
James Goldrick

Rosslyn Erskine Wemyss was fifty-three years of age when he took office, in controversial circumstances, as First Sea Lord on 27 December 1917. His aristocratic connections had been very useful to him in his somewhat unorthodox naval career in the past, and his friendship with King George V was to prove beneficial to him in sustaining his position as First Sea Lord in the 1917-19 period. Wemyss had done well in World War I: first at Mudros and then on the East Indies Station. He had just been appointed C-in-C Mediterranean in the summer of 1917 when Sir Eric Geddes replaced Sir Edward Carson as First Lord. Soon afterwards Geddes, who was unhappy with Jellicoe's direction of the naval war effort, asked Wemyss to become Second Sea Lord. Unfortunately, Jellicoe and Wemyss did not work well together—a fact that confirmed Geddes in his view that Jellicoe must be removed from office. Casting around for an issue to bring about Jellicoe's dismissal, Geddes found one over the performance of Admiral Bacon at the Dover Straits.

Although the rather insensitive and callous way in which Jellicoe was dismissed at Christmas rankled with many senior naval officers, Wemyss rode out the storm and sought to forge a new relationship with the Admiralty Board. Wemyss disliked the manner of Jellicoe's departure as much as the other Sea Lords, but he was aware of Geddes's constitutional rights and did his best to assuage their anger. Duff, the ACNS, commented that the admirals' muddled approach "put us entirely in the wrong and the politicians were quick to seize it."[1] Persuasion by the civil members and by Jellicoe himself that resignation would be both useless and unpatriotic eventually brought the admirals around, although some were to sustain a low opinion of Wemyss for accepting his post in such circumstances.[2]

A visit to Edinburgh placed Wemyss's relationship with Beatty on a secure footing—for the time being—and set at rest fears that the C-in-C had expressed to Jellicoe.[3] Oliver was relieved as Deputy Chief of Naval Staff (DCNS) in January 1918 by Sidney Fremantle. He was due for sea and pleased to go, for he would never have fitted into the new regime. Notably, Wemyss took the newly promoted Rear Admiral George Hope to be Deputy First Sea Lord, believing that seniority was not a factor. The Deputy, the DCNS and ACNS were all assistants to the First Sea Lord. Their capacity to deputize for him derived from their day-to-day involvement in operational matters and from their membership on the Board, through which they could "be charged with that responsibility which it is essential that officers performing those duties should have."[4] Wemyss divided the war into three arenas: Fremantle assumed responsibility for home waters, Duff kept the antisubmarine campaign, and Hope was allocated overseas operations.

Bacon was removed from Dover and Keyes sent in his place by Wemyss with the remark, "You have talked a hell of a lot about what ought to be done in the Dover area, and now you must go and do it."[5] Dudley Pound was sent to Operations, while Sir Cyril Fuller took over Plans. Wemyss thus had his own men in the jobs he saw as key, but he did not change any Board appointments. His policy was to work with the material he had been given. Until the spring of 1919 the only alteration would be the relief of Sir Cyril Halsey by C.M. de Bartoleme in June 1918.

. The organization was only a qualified success. Wemyss's instincts were right, but the lack of staff training among his subordinates meant that the problems of overcentralization had simply been removed one level. The DCNS and ACNS "were inclined to continue in the old way. Several striking examples occurred of important plans being completed without the Plans Division having been counselled or even acquainted with the fact."[6] Wemyss himself was not always innocent,[7] but he realized the need for further reform after the war and adopted wholesale the proposals of Herbert Richmond, which created eight staff divisions under a DCNS and ACNS.[8] Wemyss's last memorandum as First Sea Lord was to a statement of his concept of the Naval Staff.[9]

The Geddes-Wemyss combination proved a good one, despite—or because of—the fact that "probably no two men were ever more unlike each other."[10] Geddes's strengths lay in the matériel side, whereas if this was in good order, it held no interest for Wemyss. The First Lord worked closely with Wemyss in coordinating strategy, and the latter's theme would soon be "Geddes is perfectly straight . . . and will back me up to the last."[11]

The key differences between Wemyss's regime and that of Jellicoe lay in manner, not matter. Wemyss did not pursue any significant innovations in strategy, despite his offensive spirit. The attempts to block the German bases at Zeebrugge and Ostende in April and May 1918 had their origins in 1917, and Jellicoe had approved their preparation. The Admiralty of 1918 was essentially a "continuing on of the same." In an attempt to damn Wemyss (whom he never much liked) with faint praise, Lloyd George later summed up the essential difference: "Wemyss . . . had two special qualities . . . He was not a factionist . . . [T]he second attribute . . . was that he was willing to listen to young officers with ideas. He never stared them out of his room. His eyeglass greeted them with a friendly gleam."[12]

The tone was set early. In January 1918, Wemyss accepted Beatty's proposition that the shortage of destroyers meant that "the correct strategy . . . is no longer to endeavour to bring the enemy to action at any cost, but rather to contain him in his bases until the general situation becomes more favourable."[13] The British programs would not mature until late in 1918,[14] and American commitment to an enlarged escort program had only been secured in July 1917.[15] Limited offensive measures were thus all the more important, and the Admiralty proposed action against the Flanders ports combined with a mining offensive in the Heligoland Bight and renewed emphasis on the antisubmarine barrages in the Channel and the Adriatic.[16] Wemyss' primary contribution was his insistence that the mining campaign be conducted as a coordinated whole through the full integration of forces in home waters.[17]

At heart, Wemyss was not a believer in the efficacy of convoys, though he had been an advocate of convoys in the Mediterranean.[18] He complained: "To counter the submarine menace Defence only had been used. To me it appeared absolutely necessary . . . that we must hunt the enemy submarines instead of their hunting us."[19] Despite his fundamental misunderstanding of the convoy principle, the generally poor results achieved by convoy escorts once contact had been made lent some justification to Wemyss's view.[20] To his credit, however, he did not hinder the continuing development of the convoy system.

Believing that there had been "a loss of touch between the War Office and the Admiralty," Wemyss worked to establish good relations with the Army, relying on private persuasion to overcome what he viewed as the soldiers' "short-sightedness."[21] His strongest stand was to insist upon the holding of the Channel ports in the face of the German offensive of March 1918, a situation in which the French had to be persuaded. With the help of Admiral de Bon, the French Chief of Naval Staff, Wemyss was successful in making his point to Ferdinand Foch and started a friendship that was to last until the Marshal's death.[22]

Much energy was consumed by protracted negotiations with the Allied and Associated powers. To his fluent French and friendship with personalities such as de Bon, Wemyss added the born negotiator's ability to make a point without giving personal offense. Even he was frustrated by the Italians' refusal to play a more active part in the Mediterranean, but he got more cooperation from them than his predecessors. The concern of 1918 was the prospect of a German takeover of the Russian Black Sea Fleet and its use in concert with the *Goeben*. This raised the possibility of defeat in detail in the Mediterranean, and Wemyss and Geddes waged a long campaign to bring the Italians to accept a supreme naval commander. Their proposal to install Jellicoe as a "First Sea Lord in [the] Mediterranean," however, eventually foundered on Italian intransigence.[23]

Wemyss did not maintain the warm relations that Jellicoe had achieved with the Americans, notably Admiral William Benson, the Chief of Naval Operations, but he got on well with Admiral Sims.[24] He had a more realistic view of American sensibilities than Beatty, and he was insistent that support of the American project to create a mine barrage between the Orkneys and Norway was essential to maintain good relations with the United States.

The northern barrage saw the first division between the First Sea Lord and the C-in-C Grand Fleet. Their relationship was not an easy one. Wemyss was Beatty's junior as a flag officer, but he had been placed in the supreme naval appointment to which the C-in-C was formally subordinate. It was a new experience for Beatty to be "passed over," and his reaction, whether conscious or not, was to treat the First Sea Lord as a colleague and not as his senior officer. The problem was complicated by the fact that the Grand Fleet in 1918 had the tendency to constitute an alternative Naval Staff. This had evolved partly in response to obvious inadequacies in the Admiralty Staff capacity earlier in the war.[25] The undemanding operational cycle of the Grand Fleet meant that there were many highly competent senior officers with the time to examine questions of interest to the C-in-C. The committees created in the wake of Jutland confirmed the system. By 1918 it was accepted practice for the Grand Fleet to assemble such bodies to deal with specific problems.

Wemyss initially encouraged this, but it contributed to Beatty's growing inclination to demand the final word. Despite the C-in-C's abilities, his isolation at Rosyth disqualified him from dictating policy at a time when events became ever more complicated. Wemyss was increasingly caught up in complex negotiations which frequently required his presence in Paris and demanded immediate responses to changing situations.

The rapid collapse of the Central Powers in late 1918 brought matters to a head. Beatty did not trust Wemyss's capacity to achieve rigorous naval terms in any armistice. He declared, "Wemyss is none too strong . . . and so might easily be talked around."[26] Wemyss himself was fighting to secure the German Fleet's surrender in the face of opposition from both politicians and the military. Flushed with victory, the latter were inclined to discount the relevance of the Navy's demands. Lloyd George and his colleagues were justifiably eager not to impose terms so harsh that they would cause pride "to overrule reason."[27] At the same time, the First Sea Lord had to moderate the demands of his own Board[28] that the Navy should not be "baulked of her prey."[29] Wemyss maintained the line that the naval terms of the armistice should equate to those of any peace agreement that was to follow.[30]

Lloyd George engineered a compromise by which the German Fleet would be interned rather than surrendered outright, but Wemyss got most of the Admiralty's wants, including maintenance of the blockade and the surrender of the U-boats. This was not enough for Beatty, who claimed—ignoring the fact that the Admiralty carried final authority for operational matters—that he possessed the right "to make the final decision regarding such terms as directly affected him."[31] Beatty was also ignoring the reality that there was simply not enough time to involve him directly.

The C-in-C was enraged by the internment decision and the failure to include the occupation of Heligoland in the armistice, and he communicated his discontent in terms to which any First Sea Lord might have taken exception.[32] Knowing the Grand Fleet's frustration at its inability to force the High Seas Fleet to action, Wemyss soothed Beatty with frequent letters. It was only Beatty's petulant comment on 7 November, "I hope you will find yourself able to take me a little more into your confidence and consultations in the Future than you have in the Past,"[33] that goaded Wemyss to reply: "There can be no naval officer who does not see the end of the war without a feeling of incompleteness . . . [I have had] . . . a hard and difficult time and am quite as irritated as you." He added a postscript: "A smiling face does not always carry a light heart."[34]

Wemyss led the naval team at the signing of the armistice. The German naval representative "made the remark, was it admissable their fleet should be interned seeing that they had not been beaten? . . . [I]t gave me a certain pleasure to observe that they had only to come out!"[35]

The First Sea Lord had also to deal with Anglo-French naval rivalry in the negotiations for an armistice with Turkey. He insisted to Geddes that any Allied force entering the Black Sea be under British command, and he was able to back the local C-in-C, Sir Somerset Gough-Calthorpe, both in the Allied councils and with the dispatch of additional battleships.[36]

Wemyss did his relations with Lloyd George no good when, on Armistice Day, he reported the news to King George V before the Prime Minister had been able to make a triumphant announcement to Parliament. In depriving Lloyd George of his moment in the sun, Wemyss was irrevocably convinced that he had earned the Prime Minister's emnity.[37] More critical, however, was the departure of Geddes in December 1918 to assume the transport portfolio. Wemyss feared the substitution of Churchill, with whom "under no possible circumstances would he serve," but Walter Long was appointed instead.[38] Geddes's drive and experience in management would have proved useful in rebuilding the Royal Navy, for which he already had schemes for "improvements in method and organisation."[39] He could also have dealt with Beatty, to whom Geddes had provisionally offered the post of First Sea Lord, but who was slated to act as chairman of a Post-War Questions Committee until the peace negotiations were concluded.[40] This would have been an ideal solution, since the talks consumed much of Wemyss's energy at a time when the Admiralty required a firm and constant hand. Although a shrewd politician, Long did not possess the energy to give a fundamentally conservative Board the direction it needed.

The months following the armistice were dogged by Beatty's determination to become First Sea Lord on his own terms. Wemyss, who "had no special attraction" to the office, at first intended to leave as soon as the negotiations were complete.[41] He would have been happy enough to admit Beatty to the Admiralty while he worked in Versailles, but he would not accept supercession without a substantial new appointment and would not cater to those who were "trying to push me out."[42] Wemyss rejected any ordinary command and instead devised a scheme by which he could go out to the combined posts of Governor of Malta and C-in-C Mediterranean. This was scotched by Churchill, now at the War Office, who insisted that the governorship of Malta remain with the Army.

Walter Long did his best to achieve a compromise, but the atmosphere was poisoned by Beatty's heated complaints about slights being put on him by the Admiralty and by a vigorous campaign against Wemyss in both the press and society.[43] There was "a very general impression that Her Ladyship [Ethel Beatty] has been extremely active."[44] Wemyss inevitably "stuck his toes in the ground,"

Lady Wemyss mustering her considerable talents in support.[45] The two Admirals' wives had never much liked each other; by spring 1919 they were no longer on speaking terms.[46]

What suffered most was postwar planning. In early 1918, Geddes had created a Reconstruction Committee which, with the aid of its subcommittees, did much useful, if uninspired, work in 1918.[47] What had not been addressed was the central question of the effect of war experience and novel technologies on the future, and Geddes had been eager to undertake an examination. Wemyss was less keen to embark on such a study, since it implied a license to criticize the Admiralty's performance, but he eventually accepted the need.[48]

Wemyss's preoccupation with his future, the peace negotiations, and the Baltic and Balkan crises, combined with the lack of a driving intellect elsewhere on the Board, resulted in the Admiralty pursuing policies that were, albeit sensible, essentially reactive. This was not wholly the Admiralty's fault. It was under pressure to reduce expenditures while it retained considerable operational commitments and the expensive process of demobilization was still in progress. Furthermore, the Admiralty's initial schemes for a peacetime force based on a 20 percent reduction in the 1914 strength soon had to give way to more grandiose ideas in response to the uncertainty created by American plans.[49]

The Board's attitude to personnel was demonstrated by its response to recommendations that promotions from the lower deck be placed on a systematic basis. The Sea Lords shelved the idea, convinced that the first requirement of an officer was that he be a gentleman.[50] Short shift was given to Herbert Richmond's proposal to abolish the thirteen-year-old cadet entry age in favour of an eighteen year old "common" scheme, and Richmond himself was later relieved by Wemyss as Director of the Training and Staff Duties Division. Significantly, one of Wemyss's principal objections to Richmond, whose strong views had made him unpopular within the Admiralty, was that he was too much of a specialist.[51] Even so, there was to be one happy legacy from the Wemyss-Richmond combination. The former was much taken by the suggestion that young officers whose education had been interrupted by the war should enroll in a university to "be put in touch with the world."[52] The Cambridge experiment proved to be a resounding success, which was halted in later years through false economy. It was to be a profound influence on the attitude of the Royal Navy as a whole to tertiary education in later years.

The Board had no desire to make dramatic changes on the lower deck, but Wemyss continued the efforts initiated in January 1918 to improve pay. The First

Sea Lord regarded a just settlement as one of his major goals.[53] Although pay had fallen dangerously behind that of the civilian work force, the Treasury fought a delaying action with claims of unfavorable implications for the other services, but the Admiralty was under no illusion about the state of feeling in the Navy. In April 1919 the First Lord pressed on the Cabinet the findings made for ratings by a committee under Admiral Sir Thomas Jerram, and Wemyss backed this with a stern warning. "Any postponement of an announcement that the Government has accepted the pay and pension recommendations [will mean] serious trouble in the fleet. Under these circumstances I feel it . . . would be my duty to ask the Prime Minister to relieve me of my responsibilities."[54]

The Cabinet's acceptance of the majority of Jerram's recommendations was followed by similar action on officers' pay. Wemyss's shrewd assessment that much apparent interest in "Bolshevism" would dissipate with adequate pay was proved correct, although the limited attempt to provide a channel for the redress of systematic defects through the creation of a Welfare Committee was to founder soon after its inception in 1919.[55] The Admiralty found many of the committee's suggestions too ambitious for its taste, and the Treasury refused to pay for those that did receive Board approval.[56]

In addition to his attempts to find employment for Jellicoe in 1918, Wemyss maintained a careful balance between the veterans of the Grand Fleet and the individuals who were not. Nonetheless, both Beatty and Jellicoe tried Wemyss's patience: Beatty through his public statements and Jellicoe in his book, *The Grand Fleet: Its Creation, Development and Work, 1914-1916*. Both were critical of Admiralty shortcomings in the war, which led, as Wemyss complained, to an impression "that it is the present Board of Admiralty who are the sinners, and that they should immediately be hung, drawn and quartered."[57] Wemyss pleaded with Jellicoe to delay publication[58] and was particularly grieved that his predecessor was propagating the fallacy of a "conservative" Admiralty and a "lively and progressive" fleet.[59]

Wemyss saw the value of objective history, and he gave Julian Corbett Admiralty support in his work, *Naval Operations*.[60] Wemyss also directed Captain J. E. T. Harper to produce a narrative of the Battle of Jutland based on ships' logs and track reconstructions.[61] Harper undertook his work uninterrupted, but he did not complete his record of the battle until a few days before Wemyss's retirement. In the controversy that followed, Wemyss's laudable intention of setting the facts straight was lost.

The Admiralty displayed a less-than-complete understanding of the way in which relations with the Dominions had developed during the war. Wemyss himself had misgivings over the concept of a Whitehall-controlled "Imperial Navy," which he presented to the Imperial Conference in June 1918. It was quickly rejected by the Dominion Prime Ministers.[62] The latter, however, asked for a "highly qualified" Admiralty representative and the armistice was hardly signed before Jellicoe had been invited to tour the Empire. His instructions to advise on "naval organisation and training and types of naval material" seemed explicit enough, but they lacked strategic guidance. Inevitably, Jellicoe developed his own. This focused on the need to defend the Far East against Japan and he proposed the development of powerful British, Australian and New Zealand naval forces in this theater.[63] Wemyss was appalled by Jellicoe's presumption, a reaction suggesting that the latter had been out of mind as well as sight during his tour. Despite the Admiralty's eventual acknowledgment of the Japanese threat, Jellicoe's assessments were effectively disowned.[64]

What Jellicoe had realized was that the Dominions had the potential to take up some of Britain's defense burden and that they required comprehensive and sympathetic education. The Admiralty of 1919 was still in the process of educating itself. Not until October was a memorandum on Far East strategy completed. This largely mirrored Jellicoe's thinking, but he was not made privy to the contents of the paper until late November, nor did the Admiralty accept his detailed proposals.[65]

America concerned the Naval Staff rather more than the Far East. The difficulties of persuading the Americans to defer battleship construction in favor of escort vessels had already given the First Sea Lord food for thought.[66] That the United States might have different postwar aims to those of Britain became uncomfortably clear in the days before the armistice was signed when Admiral Benson, the American Chief of Naval Operations, proved reluctant to agree to the surrender of the High Seas Fleet because of the implications it might have for British naval supremacy. Benson also nursed suspicions that the British wanted to retain German units to increase their own battle line.[67]

What emerged was a total divergence of worldviews, of which Wemyss and Benson were the exemplars. The First Sea Lord recognized Britain's economic weakness, but he was determined that Britain would surrender neither its rights of blockade nor its naval supremacy in favor of an unproven League of Nations. Wemyss, who "conceived a strong dislike [for President Wilson and] instinctively mistrusted his sincerity" had a shrewd idea that the President's advocacy of massive building programs was a club to force the British into the League of Nations.⁶⁸ He could not deny, however, the strength of Benson's absolute conviction that the U.S. Navy should be second to none. The celebrated clash of the admirals before Secretary Daniels, who "feared they would pass the bounds and have an altercation," made it clear that the future health of Anglo-American naval relations required a fundamental revision of British strategy.⁶⁹ This revision would have to come from the politicians; Wemyss was a naval statesman, but he was a naval officer first.

If the Anglo-American naval race remained unsettled, Wemyss still achieved much in the peace negotiations—with the disarmament of Heligoland and the Baltic Coast and the restrictions on the German Fleet—amounting to practically all that the Navy wanted. Despite his antipathy to Lloyd George, the two had worked well together. Even the scuttling of the High Seas Fleet in Scapa Flow did not disturb Wemyss's equilibrium, and his poise may even have contributed to suspicions that the Admiralty had connived at the German action.⁷⁰

With these achievements, Wemyss was embittered by his exclusion from the Victory Honours List. The First Sea Lord's success in arguing for Beatty's Earldom and his own aristocratic background combined to set his sights too high.⁷¹ If a Viscountcy was beyond his desserts, Wemyss was justifiably angered when the other Chiefs of Staff were rewarded with baronetcies and money grants while he was overlooked. He viewed this as "the disavowal of his whole policy"⁷² and immediately resigned.⁷³ Long refused to accept his resignation and Wemyss was persuaded that his departure in such circumstances "would be misconstrued." He agreed to suspend his resignation until "the psychological moment."⁷⁴ He would leave office at the end of October 1919.

Wemyss was unhappy at ending his career at the age of fifty-five and pressed Long for appointment as Ambassador in Rome. He would have filled the post very capably, but all that the First Lord could do was secure him a peerage (which Wemyss accepted reluctantly, with the title of Lord Wester Wemyss) and promotion to Admiral of the Fleet. Without the favor of Lloyd George or Beatty—and Wemyss liked Andrew Bonar Law, the Conservative leader, no better—he was to receive no further official appointments. He retired to Cannes and lived most of the remainder of his life in France, where he died on 24 May 1933. Significantly, the award that gave him most pleasure was that of the French Medaille Militaire, presented at Foch's instigation in 1922.⁷⁵ It was the first and, until Andrew Cunningham, the only such decoration conferred on a British flag officer.

Wemyss's greatest successes as First Sea Lord were personal; his failures were institutional. Despite the reform of the Naval Staff, the Admiralty did not yet understand the concept of delegation, which gravely limited Wemyss's ability to do all that he knew was required. His principal contributions were to restore a sense of confidence within the Admiralty and to steer the peace negotiations successfully in the direction that the Royal Navy wanted. His administrative achievements were limited, but he concentrated on the essentials—such as pay—while under great personal strain, not helped by a poorly timed change of First Lord or by Beatty's tantrums. His balance and his common sense combined with his knowledge of the world to make him a naval statesman of a stature that would have compared well with that of any of the supreme commanders of the Second World War.

NOTES

1. Marder, *From the Dreadnought to Scapa Flow*, 4:345.
2. See Lionel De Chair, *The Sea is Strong* (London: Harrap, 1961), for the part played by Admiral Sir Dudley De Chair. Stephen Roskill's article, "The Dismissal of Admiral Jellicoe", *Journal of Contemporary History* 1, no. 4 (Oct. 1966):69-93 gives a thorough survey of the incident.
3. Letter from Beatty to Jellicoe, 27 Dec. 1917, Patterson, ed., *Jellicoe Papers*, 2:255.
4. Memorandum by First Sea Lord, "Organisation of the Board of Admiralty and Naval Staff," 29 Oct. 1919, WMYS 5/1, Wemyss Papers.
5. Keyes, *Naval Memoirs*, 2:151.
6. Memorandum No. 71, "Co-operation with the British Plans Division," 30 Dec. 1918. Planning Section, U. S. Naval Forces in European Waters, in Michael Simpson, ed., *Anglo-American Naval Relations*, 184. See also Office of Naval Records and Library, *The American Naval Planning Section, London* (Washington, D.C.: Government Printing Office, 1923), 491.
7. Hunt, *Sailor-Scholar*, 96.
8. Ibid., 93-94. See also Marder, *From the Dreadnought to Scapa Flow*, vol. 5 (London: Oxford University Press, 1970), 217-20.
9. Memorandum by First Sea Lord, "Organisation of the Board of Admiralty and Naval Staff," 29 Oct. 1919, WMYS 5/1, Wemyss Papers.
10. Wemyss, *The Life*, 363.
11. Letter from Wemyss to Beatty, 30 Mar. 1918 in B.McL. Ranft, ed., *The Beatty Papers: Selections from the Private and Official Correspondence of Admiral of the Fleet Earl Beatty, vol. 1, 1902-1918* (London: Scolar Press for Navy Records Society, 1989), 524.
12. Lloyd George, *War Memoirs*, 3:1178.
13. Marder, *From the Dreadnought to Scapa Flow*, 5:134.
14. F. J. Dittmar and J. J. Colledge, *British Warships 1914-1919* (London: Ian Allan, 1972), 72-75.

15. David F. Trask, *Captains and Cabinets: Anglo-American Naval Relations 1917-1918* (Columbia, Missouri: University of Missouri Press, 1972), 116.
16. See Marder, *From the Dreadnought to Scapa Flow*, 5:135, and Trask, *Captains and Cabinets*, 190-91.
17. Memoirs. See also Wemyss, *The Life*, 368.
18. Beesly, *Very Special Admiral*, 44.
19. Memoirs. See also Wemyss, *The Life*, 370.
20. See Marder, *From the Dreadnought to Scapa Flow*, 5:77-109.
21. Letter from Wemyss to Beatty, 30 Mar. 1918, Ranft, *Beatty Papers*, 1:524.
22. Marder, *From the Dreadnought to Scapa Flow*, 5:157-58. See also Wemyss, *The Life*, 378-79.
23. Letter from Wemyss to Gough-Calthorpe, 3 Aug. 1918 in the Wemyss Papers. See also letter from Geddes to Jellicoe, 5 June 1918, Patterson, ed., *Jellicoe Papers* 2:279.
24. Letter from Wemyss to Beatty, 23 Aug. 1918, Ranft, *Beatty Papers*, 1:543.
25. See Jon Sumida, "British Naval Administration and Policy in the Age of Fisher," *Journal of Military History*, 54, (Jan. 1990): 1-26.
26. S. W. Roskill, *Naval Policy Between the Wars, vol. 1, The Period of Anglo-American Antagonism* (London: Collins, 1968), 271.
27. Marder, *From the Dreadnought to Scapa Flow*, 5:178.
28. Letter from Wemyss to Beatty, 16 Oct. 1918, Wemyss Papers.
29. Sidney Fremantle, *My Naval Career*, (London: Hutchinson, 1949), 259.
30. Memoirs. See also Wemyss, *The Life*, 356.
31. Letter from Beatty to Wemyss, 19 Oct. 1918, Wemyss Papers.
32. Letter from Beatty to Wemyss, 5 Nov. 1918, Wemyss Papers.
33. Letter from Beatty to Wemyss, 7 Nov. 1918, Wemyss Papers.
34. Letter from Wemyss to Beatty, 14 Nov. 1918, Wemyss Papers.
35. "Armistice Notes," Wemyss Papers. See also Wemyss, *The Life*, 393-94.
36. Letter from Wemyss to Geddes, 30 Oct. 1918, Wemyss Papers.
37. Letter from Dr. the Hon. Alice Cunnack (daughter of Wemyss) to the Author, 20 Mar. 1992.
38. Wemyss, *The Life*, 412.
39. Roskill, *Naval Policy*, 1:113.
40. Ibid.; Marder, *From the Dreadnought to Scapa Flow*, 5:207.
41. Wemyss, *The Life*, 440.
42. Letter from Wemyss to Beatty, 28 Feb. 1919, Beatty Mss. See also Marder *From the Dreadnought to Scapa Flow*, 5:205.
43. Letter from Long to Lord Stamfordham, 9 Mar. 1919, RA, George V 1474/1.
44. Letter from Long to Lloyd George, 15 June 1919, Lloyd George Mss. See Marder, *From the Dreadnought to Scapa Flow*, 5:210.
45. Letter from Long to Stamfordham, 9 Mar. 1919, RA, George V 1474/1. See also Marder, *From the Dreadnought to Scapa Flow*, 5:208. See also letter from Long to Lloyd George, 29 Apr. 1919, in Charles Petrie, *Walter Long and His Times* (London: Hutchinson, 1936), 220-22.
46. The depth of feeling may be indicated by the fact that Lady Wester Wemyss's papers in the Churchill College Archives remain closed, largely due to material relating to the controversy.
47. Roskill, *Naval Policy*, 1:103-104.

48. Memorandum from Geddes to Lloyd George, 18 Nov. 1918, ADM 116/1809. See Roskill, *Naval Policy*, 1:113.
49. Roskill, *Naval Policy*, 1:104-6.
50. Ibid., 121.
51. Arthur J. Marder, *Portrait of an Admiral: The Life and Letters* of Sir Herbert Richmond (Cambridge, Mass.: Harvard University Press, 1952), 329.
52. Schurman, *Julian S. Corbett*, 179. He cites Corbett's diary entry of 15 May 1918 (following a conversation with Wemyss).
53. Wemyss, *The Life*, 440.
54. Ibid., 427.
55. Ibid. See also letter from Wemyss to Gough-Calthorpe, 18 Mar. 1919, Wemyss Papers, for the First Sea Lord's attitude toward communism.
56. Roskill, *Naval Policy*, 1:117-18.
57. Letter from Wemyss to Long, 3 Apr. 1919, Wemyss Papers.
58. Memo from First Sea Lord to First Lord, No. 43, 23 Jan. 1919, Wemyss Papers.
59. Memo from First Sea Lord to First Lord, No. 42, undated, Wemyss Papers.
60. Schurman, *Corbett*, 179.
61. Memorandum from First Sea Lord to First Lord, No. 43, 23 Jan. 1919, Wemyss Papers.
62. Roskill, *Naval Policy*, 1:274-75. See also Patterson, ed., *Jellicoe Papers*, 2:284-87, for a copy of the Admiralty memorandum and the Dominions' reactions to it.
63. Adm 116/1834 contains Jellicoe's report. Patterson, ed., *Jellicoe Papers*, vol. 2, has substantial extracts.
64. Roskill, *Naval Policy*, 1:280.
65. Ibid., 281-82.
66. Letter from Wemyss to Geddes, 3 Oct. 1918, in Simpson, *ed., Anglo-American*, 524.
67. Mary Klachko with David F. Trask, *Admiral William Shepherd Benson: First Chief of Naval Operations* (Annapolis, Md.: U.S. Naval Institute Press, 1987), 130.
68. Wemyss, *The Life*, 410. See also letter from Wemyss to Long, 3 Apr. 1919, Wemyss Papers.
69. Klachko and Trask, *Benson*, 144.
70. Letter from Wemyss to Hope, 22 June 1919, Wemyss Papers.
71. There is an interesting parallel in Mountbatten's indignation at being offered a Barony after the end of the Second World War. After his protest he was given a Viscountcy, see Zeigler, *Mountbatten*, 310.
72. Wemyss, *The Life*, 439.
73. Ibid., 441. See also WMYS 5/3, Wemyss Papers, for his resignation letters and their drafts.
74. Letter from Wemyss to Long, 28 Aug. 1919, in Petrie, *Walter Long*, 223.
75. Letter from Dr. the Hon. Alice Cunnack to the author, 22 July 1992.

9
Admiral David Earl Beatty (1919–1927)

Bryan M. Ranft

Such was Beatty's stature in the Navy and in public esteem that there was no alternative to his appointment as First Sea Lord on 1 November 1919. However, Winston Churchill (the Secretary for War), who had furthered the Admiral's career since 1912, rightly warned the Prime Minister, David Lloyd George, that Beatty would prove a powerful opponent to the heavy cuts in naval strength that the government was determined to impose.[1] Such a struggle was, in fact, to dominate the whole of his term of office. Although he accepted that political and economic factors made such reductions inevitable and that it was the government's responsibility to insist on them, he believed equally strongly that it was his responsibility to confront ministers with the long-term dangers they incurred by reducing the Navy below the strength necessary for it to fulfill its leading role in Imperial defense. From this interpretation of his duty came the protracted and often bitter conflicts with ministers and with the Royal Air Force (RAF), which tested his temperament and health no less severely than had the strains of high command throughout the war. He had to adjust his whole style of work to the world of politics, with all its compromises, conflicts of loyalties, and daily dealings with men whom, he instinctively despised as a class, as did most of his naval contemporaries.

The first essential was to have the sustained support in Cabinet and Parliament of the five First Lords of the Admiralty under whom he served. Obviously his wartime experience and popularity gave him great advantages but surprisingly, considering his initial prejudices, he achieved good personal relations with only one exception. He failed with Lord Lee of Fareham, First Lord during the Washington Naval Conference, a particularly difficult time for Beatty in having to accept the ending of Britain's naval supremacy. He had been helped initially by the ill health of Walter Long, his first political chief, who left even the most important matters at Cabinet level in Beatty's hands. The Admiral also showed considerable political awareness in cultivating other Cabinet members: initially Winston Churchill, before he became Chancellor of the Exchequer; Lord Curzon, Foreign Secretary; and Lord Birkenhead, successively Lord Chancellor and Secretary for India, prominent amongst them. Even with Churchill discharging the Treasury's traditional role as chief critic of the Admiralty, his personal relations remained warm if, on occasion, irritably so. He even found allies in the two Labour administrations of 1924 and 1929: J. H. Thomas, the Colonial Secretary, Stephen Walsh, Secretary for War, and Lord Haldane, the Lord Chancellor. He was agreeably surprised by the strong support of the politically neutral First Lord, Viscount Chelmsford, who had made it a condition of joining the government that he should be allowed to support Beatty's construction program and the development of the Singapore base.[2] Of all his First Lords, Leopold Amery (1922-24) carried most political weight, which enabled him to check one of Beatty's few false political moves when he threatened to lead a mass resignation of Naval Board members over the government's refusal in 1923 to give the Navy control of the Fleet Air Arm.[3]

Convinced that his major role was to be on the political stage, Beatty was determined to be freed of detailed administrative duties by a well-organized Naval Staff. Wemyss had already slimmed down the wartime staff and Beatty rapidly grafted on to it men loyal to himself. Osmond de Brock, his former chief of staff, had already become DCNS in August 1919. Chatfield, his flag-captain throughout the war, became ACNS in 1920 and Controller in 1925. Roger Keyes, a close friend, succeeded de Brock in 1921 and was himself succeeded as DCNS by Frederick Field, whose professionalism Beatty highly respected. All these men eventually commanded the Mediterranean Fleet, and both Chatfield and Field were promoted to become First Sea Lord. Although willing to make small economies, Beatty successfully defended the Naval Staff against major reductions, including those that would have impinged on his own freedom to concentrate on the larger issues. In return, his staff furnished him with the flood of detailed information, draft policy papers, and technical reports without which he could not have achieved the influence he sought in Cabinet, Imperial Conferences, and the CID, or in cultivating popular support for the Navy.[4]

Beatty was at his most traditional in his belief that Britain's security and world influence depended on naval supremacy. Consciously or not, his strategic thought was Mahanian. The ability to use the seas freely depended on fleet supremacy and that, in turn, demanded possession of a battle fleet capable of winning a decisive action against its strongest opponent; not for him the subtlety of Julian Corbett. In this fleet, battleships, suitably modified to meet the threat from submarines and aircraft, would remain the decisive weapon as far into the future as could be predicted. From this creed came his first and continuous campaign to convince governments primarily seeking economies to provide such a fleet, and his ambiguity toward America's naval ambitions. He did not believe in the possibility of war against it and, however reluctantly, accepted its claim to formal naval equality, but he never ceased to argue that Britain's unique sea dependence justified a superiority in cruisers.

Although Beatty, like his American and Japanese counterparts, saw the capital ship as the decisive factor in maritime war, he was fully alert to the potential of airpower. This had already been demonstrated in his final Grand Fleet Battle Instructions giving aircraft offensive and defensive roles in every aspect of fleet operations.[5] It was this realization that led to his second policy objective, to persuade successive governments to give the Navy its own air arm under Admiralty strategic control and manned by aircrew trained as sailors, which could not be achieved under the existing arrangements with the RAF. This was a struggle he lost (as distinct from his American and Japanese counterparts), with disastrous results when war came.

His third objective was to convince governments and influential public opinion that, after the defeat of Germany, the prostration of Bolshevik Russia, and the impossibility of war against America, there remained an increasing threat from Japan, which only a strong Navy could deter or defeat. His political appreciation of the likely development for aggressive Japanese nationalism and the opportunities for expansion offered by the collapse of central government in China, along with the high improbability of American armed intervention, was soundly based. Nevertheless, his deduction that the only remedy for the dangers to Britain's trade and influence in Asia was to develop the capability of operating a fleet superior to that of Japan, resulted in another prolonged struggle. From the first, he insisted that this would demand, not only a superior fleet, but also a fortified base, without which it would be useless. From this began his campaign for Singapore, against inevitable government opposition to the cost, Foreign Office scepticism about Japan's capacity for aggressive war within the ten-year period on which government planning was based, and the claims of the Chief of Air

Staff, Hugh Trenchard, that the RAF should have the predominant role in the defence of the base were it ever constructed.

Beatty's first opportunity to test his powers of political persuasion was to be in the Bonar Law Committee of 1920. As early as August and October 1919, he had concurred in the Admiralty's appeals to the government for a substantial construction response to the expected completion of the U.S. 1916 program. It was a question of quality as well as of numbers. Only *Hood* could match the performance of the new American ships. By 1923 Britain would have become only the second naval power, thus abandoning "the sea supremacy which is vital to us."[6] As the government was demanding a reduction of the Admiralty's 1920/21 estimates from £75 million to £60 million, Lloyd George set up a powerful Cabinet Committee in December 1920. The Committee was mandated "to take evidence on the question of the capital ship in the Royal Navy" and chaired by Bonar Law, who was to succeed him as Prime Minister when the coalition administration broke up in October 1922. Due to Long's illness, Beatty was a full member of the Committee, and not merely "in attendance," and he obviously enjoyed himself in presenting the Admiralty's case, selecting witnesses, and keenly questioning those hostile to the Admiralty's views.[7] Ministerial members saw the cost of the Admiralty's construction proposals as destructive of their basic policy of national economy, as well as having doubts about Beatty's dogmatic assertions that underwater and air weapons did not threaten the future supremacy of the capital ship. This had been suggested by some naval witnesses, including Herbert Richmond and, or course, by Trenchard. In support of his argument that building must begin immediately, Beatty stressed the danger of losing the expertise of the shipbuilding industry which, in fact, was to be a major impediment to naval rearmament in the 1930s.[8]

Although the Committee accepted Beatty's arguments that the case against the capital ship had not been established, it split on his proposals for an immediate replacement program: Law, Geddes, and Sir Robert Horne, President of the Board of Trade, were against; Churchill, Long (in absentia), and Beatty himself were in favor.

In any event these deliberations were superseded by the 1921 Washington Conference, where naval technicalities gave way to international politics, universal demands for lasting peace, and major reductions in armaments. On such a stage Beatty could not hope to play a leading role. His government was now fully convinced that it must avoid naval competition with America, accept its claims to naval parity, and follow its lead to establish this at the lowest possible level.

Beatty accepted the inevitable and concentrated on persuading the leader of Britain's delegation, Arthur J. Balfour, to oppose America's proposal for a five-year holiday from capital ship constructon, arguing that Britain had already had a five-year gap during the war. Instead, he should press for a gradual replacement program, thus preserving industrial capacity and gaining modern ships. Balfour recommended this to the Cabinet but, accepting Lloyd George's lead, it ruled that the advantages, diplomatic and economic, of agreeing with America were overwhelming, despite the admitted soundness of Beatty's reasoning.[9] Thus the treaty was signed, and it was within its limitation of numbers and tonnage of capital ships that the Navy had to develop during the remainder of Beatty's term of office.

The final blow, condemning Beatty to preside over massive naval reductions, was delivered by the Interim Report of the Committee on National Expenditure of 1921.[10] It must be remembered that the Committee also recommended great reductions in civil expenditure in accordance with the accepted doctrine that only by such sacrifices could wider economic disaster and heavier taxation be avoided. The Navy was called on to reduce its 1922-23 estimates from £81 million to £60 million. Beatty left Washington for London to resist this and gained the strong political support of Churchill and Birkenhead, the Lord Chancellor. Churchill, impressed by the economies Beatty had already achieved, suggested a compromise of £62 million while insisting that Geddes's sweeping personnel cuts should be decreased. To Beatty's satisfaction, their joint political skills enabled estimates of just under £65 million to be tabled in Parliament.[11] He had learned the necessity for political compromise and for finding political allies for the struggles that lay ahead.

The year 1921 marked another stage in Beatty's political development: his concern for Imperial defense. Now fully aware of the constraint on Britain's naval strength and, at the same time, increasingly sensitive to the future threat from Japan, he made the first of many appeals for help from the Dominions at the Imperial Conference in July when he took the opportunity to proclaim his strategic doctrine to their leaders. While admitting that Imperial defense was essentially dependent on control of sea communications, he insisted that this "can only be effected by the destruction of the enemy force. . . . The command of the sea is determined by the result of great battles at sea." Such a victory could only be won by concentration of force and unity of effort. "It is therefore necessary to ensure that the various Navies of the Empire be similarly trained and that they adhere to a common doctrine and a common system of command and staff." Aware of

Dominion sensitivity to centralized control from London, he argued that they must be confident that in war the Royal Navy's dispositions would not be designed solely for the defense of the United Kingdom: "It is as much the Navy of Australia, of Canada, of South Africa and of India as it is of the British Isles." Economic weakness had made it necessary for Britain to limit itself to a one-power standard which could not be effective unless the Dominions contributed both ships and shore facilities essential to the mobility of the main fleet.[12]

In the years after Washington and Geddes, Beatty's central concern was to persuade successive administrations to provide the resources needed to maintain a Navy adequate for the global obligations imposed on it. Politicians of all parties continued to be obsessed by the need to reduce national expenditure and hard to convince of the need to modernize the Navy in a world that offered no identifiable maritime threat. Such an attitude throughout his time in office made long-term planning difficult and was largely responsible for the quality of force he handed on to his successors. His task was made more difficult by the advent of the Labour government in January 1924. Ramsay Macdonald and some of his colleagues were pacifists at heart, and the Chancellor, Philip Snowden, with whom Beatty had had long and fierce arguments, was determined to cut defense expenditure to the bone. This administration lasted only until November, but Baldwin's succession brought no relief. The new Chancellor was Winston Churchill, now returning to the Conservatives from the Liberals and determined to excel as an economizer. He reveled in the knowledge of the Admiralty's workings he had gained as First Lord from 1911 to 1915, using it in his sustained efforts to challenge its calls for increased funding, especially for more cruisers and for the payment of a marriage allowance to officers.

The political battle, as always, centered each year on the naval estimates and had been particularly fierce with Baldwin's first administration (1923-24) over the 1924-25 figures because of Beatty's decision to begin a long-term program for cruisers, destroyers, aircraft carriers, and submarines. This had been estimated at £32.5 million over five years. It was badly received by the then Chancellor, Neville Chamberlain, but after heavy pressure from the First Lord, Leo Amery, who strongly backed Beatty, Chamberlain had accepted an overall estimate of £62 million, including enough to begin the construction program.[13] However, the fall of Baldwin's government and the succession of Ramsay Macdonald meant that Beatty had to renew the battle with an ideologically hostile Cabinet.

He began by rapidly building good relations with his new masters, and succeeded not only with the First Lord, Viscount Chelmsford, but also with the two junior ministers. They were both leading trade unionists and well aware of the importance of naval shipbuilding to a wide range of industries. Beatty opened the campaign with an unrealistic bid for a programme costing £260 million over ten years. This, he claimed, would result in a 25 percent superiority in cruisers and destroyers over Japan, as well as providing eighty submarines and four aircraft carriers.[14] Snowden found this totally unacceptable, but a minority government could not turn it down flatly and instead appointed a Cabinet Committee under J. R. Clynes (Lord Privy Seal) to consider both the building program and the future of the Singapore base. Beatty's performance before this body was highly impressive and deserves study that it has not previously received. This is best done in considering the Singapore question, only noting for the present that he had considerable success over the cruiser program, which gained parliamentary approval.

In Baldwin's Conservative government of 1924, the Chancellor was Churchill, who was determined to prove himself a strong defender of the public purse against the spending departments, including the Admiralty. An undated slip of Downing Street paper, probably passed to Beatty early in 1925, indicates the spirit in which the two former allies now clashed over their departmental requirements. "I thought you were masterly. I have never heard such statement by the 1st Sea Lord."[15] In the prolonged discussions over the 1925-26 estimates Churchill shifted away from technical naval questions to an attack on Beatty's political prognostications by casting doubt on Japan's hostility and naval capabilities, especially over the next ten years. However, he did offer a compromise, proposing estimates of £60.5 million. The Admiralty which had asked for £65 million (with no provision for construction), proposing to cover this under a supplementary estimate, rejected the offer. The usual Cabinet Committee, this time under Lord Birkenhead, was appointed to bridge the gulf. Its verbatim minutes show that it was dominated by Beatty and Churchill, with the First Lord, Bridgeman, providing only intermittent support. The result was a deadlock, and after considerable pressure, Baldwin made a binding decision, very much in Beatty's favor, by approving the first five years of the building program at a cost of £58 million but extending the program over seven years.[16]

In 1917 Beatty had welcomed the formation of an independent Air Service embracing the Fleet Air Arm (FAA), as more likely to make better use of air power in furtherance of the war than the then Admiralty. He anticipated that such a service would appreciate the importance of air power in maritime operations and make adequate provision for it.[17] It was perhaps this that led him, in November

1919, to accept Trenchard's proposal that the RAF should be given time to settle down and that the two older services ought to refrain from involving it in any controversial dispute.[18] Beatty's own wide vision of the significant part that aircraft could play in all naval operations was demonstrated in his "Instructions for Aircraft," which were inserted in the Grand Fleet's Battle Instructions in November 1918.[19] This awareness was shared with his predecessor, Wemyss, his successor, Madden, and Chatfield who, as Beatty's ACNS, was responsible for air matters. Geoffrey Till has shown conclusively that the often-made generalization that the weakness of the FAA in 1939 was due mainly to bone-headed admirals is insupportable.

Soon after his arrival at the Admiralty Beatty was made aware of the Naval Staff's strong dissatisfaction with the existing arrangements with the Air Ministry for air work with the fleet. His immediate reaction was that only a radical change, including the abolition of the RAF and its Ministry, would solve the problem and produce effective naval air power at a lower cost.[20] It was only reluctantly that he accepted that such a major political reversal was beyond his power and began to pursue the much more realistic aim of securing the creation of a relatively small force, still organically connected with the Air Ministry but totally dedicated to naval roles. However, his earlier position provided grounds for his opponents to see his more reasonable proposals as the first steps forward toward dismantling the RAF. From this came a long and bitter confrontation with Trenchard over his unshakable commitment to the unity of air power and his long-term hopes for the substitution of air power in operations hitherto discharged by the Army and Navy. Such views gained in political support as time went on, as Beatty was to discover in Cabinet Committees and elsewhere.

Maurice Hankey, as Secretary of the CID, was in the center of this conflict and by 1923 had decided that only a high-level inquiry could resolve it. This resulted in the establishment of the Balfour Committee in 1923, Lords Peel and Weir being its other members. This was where Beatty, as a witness, made his first major effort. As he explained to Brock, now C-in-C Mediterranean, his intention was to avoid the emotional topic of the overall effect of air power on Imperial defense and make only one demand, "that we should have our own Naval Air Arm, without interference from or by the Air Ministry."[21] At the committee's second meeting, he narrowed down the main difficulty of the existing arrangement with the RAF to the shortage of naval officers among aircrew, which was going to intensify as new carriers were built.[22] Three months later in his final statement he encapsulated his whole doctrine on the subject: a fleet commander must in battle be able to rely on air units he has trained and who know his intentions, in other words, "an Air Arm which is just as much a part of the Fleet as the guns that are in the ships, or the Submarines, or the Destroyer or any part of it." Beatty pointed out the advantages of the Admiralty being responsible for the Air Arm:

[T]hey would know how much they could depend upon the Air Arm to do the work of, and possibly replace other units of the Fleet. In doing so it is conceivable that great economies might arise which today are impossible under the existing regime. We are fully awake to the present possibilities that are claimed in the future for the air, and we realise the important part the Air Arm must play in any future Naval operations.

From this it is clear that the Admiralty could not depend on an air arm in the hands of another department when framing its strategic policy. According to Beatty, therefore, the air arm was vital to the Admiralty's future:

Developed for the use of the Navy to meet strategic and tactical requirements, it would be the aim and object of the Admiralty to ensure that a complete understanding of the possibilities of the air and the air sense itself should permeate the Naval Service, and for this reason the Admiralty should endeavour to create a Naval Service, a proportion of the officers of which who should achieve high rank and command should have a complete understanding and knowledge of the requirements of the Navy and its equipment of the Air Arm.[23]

Despite Beatty's repeated claims that such integration of air and sea power could never be achieved by joint control with the Air Ministry, the Committee decided against him. Some progress was made in 1924 to meet the Navy's requirements in negotiations between Trenchard and Keyes under Haldane's guidance.[24] In future, all observers and all ratings on board the new carriers were to be navally entered and trained. It was not until Chatfield's reign that full Admiralty control was achieved.

As for Beatty's "air sense", it is worth recalling that at one of the great social occasions that he skillfully used to educate the public on naval matters, he said: "It may well be that in the future, the Commander-in-Chief of a fleet with his staff will be quartered on board an aircraft carrier during operations, his staff Officers being in the air."[25]

Whatever the mixed record on the question of air power, it was the completion of the fleet base at Singapore that involved all the elements of Beatty's strategic thought. Political and economic restraints made it impossible for Britain to have a two-ocean Navy. Therefore, its fleet had to remain in a central position and only move to the Far East when Japan's attitude demanded it. It could only operate there by possessing a base equipped with every essential supply and facility and capable of self-defense against major attack during the fleet's voyage from the Mediterranean and home waters. The struggle to achieve such a base continued throughout Beatty's term of office against Conservative governments, which were repelled by the cost and skeptical of the Japanese threat, as well as against a Labour government that saw it as a provocative act, threatening their ideals of disarmament and the abolition of war. An additional obstacle was Trenchard's argument that the base could be better defended by aircraft than by the coastal artillery favored by the Army and Navy. This struggle, like his others, was to be fought up to Cabinet level and also in a new forum, the Chiefs of Staff Committee (created in 1923), of which Beatty became Chairman.

By 1921 the CID had accepted the building of the base in principle and Beatty was given the task of explaining the strategic thought behind it to the Imperial Conference of that year.[26] The Admiralty planned to send a force of at least eight capital ships and sixteen cruisers on the six-weeks voyage to Singapore, the base's most vulnerable period. By 1924 he was being more specific. The most likely attack would be by naval gunfire to destroy the base's facilities. The best deterrent or response to this was heavy artillery capable of keeping the Japanese fleet outside bombardment range. After arriving and resupplying the base, the fleet would move out to destroy its enemy counterpart and thus end Japan's threat to British possessions and trade. It was essential, in Beatty's opinion, that the ships be available and the base completed by 1931, when the Washington Treaty limitations on warship building would lapse.

Preliminary construction work had been done by 1925 when the Labour government decided to stop further development. This decision was taken by a Cabinet committee under J. R. Clynes before which Beatty, supported by Dudley Pound as Director of Plans, strongly restated the whole strategic case and dealt effectively with long periods of questioning. The small sum of £150,000 which he requested for continuing the preliminary work in 1924-25 might well have been agreed to over Snowden's objections, as Beatty's arguments had been accepted by some ministers, had it not been for Ramsay Macdonald's objections on wider grounds. He had joined the committee as Foreign Secretary as well as Prime Minister, and, after discussion with Beatty across the table, he accepted that the latter's strategic arguments had been well founded but asserted there were other factors that must be taken into account, particularly the government's determination to resolve international disputes through patience and negotiation. Subsequent private meetings between Beatty and MacDonald failed to overcome this ideological impasse, and Beatty concluded that the only acceptable outcome of such negotiations would be for Japan to give up its whole fleet, a very remote possibility.[27]

An equally deep impasse grew between Beatty and Trenchard over the defense of the base. The main confrontations occurred in the Chiefs of Staff Committee between 1924 and 1926, with Beatty taking advantage of being Chairman and enjoying the support of the successive Chiefs of the Imperial General Staff, Cavan and Milne, who helped shape the discussion. His main contention was that the base must be ready by 1931, with work starting immediately. He accepted Trenchard's claim that torpedo bombers could be effective against the Japanese Fleet, but only in the more distant future. Trenchard's riposte was that they should consider the problem under the Ten Year Rule and not spend money on heavy guns now. Beatty further argued that Trenchard's claim for money saving was based on an underestimate of the number of fighters needed to defend the bombers from the carrier-borne interceptors that Japan was developing. The airman's response was that the bombers' first priority would be to sink the Japanese carriers and thus remove the interceptors' threat. It is noteworthy that in these discussions both Cavan and Milne were skeptical of any major danger from Japanese ground attack.

When Baldwin replaced Macdonald in November 1924, he found his Chiefs of Staff (COS) still unable to agree on how the base should be defended.[28]

By the first half of 1926 the end of Beatty's active service was in sight, and it must be stressed that the dispute with Trenchard was untypical of his general conduct of the business of the COS Committee. His thinking on interservice matters had substantially broadened. In 1925, probably encouraged by Hankey, he had initiated the Chiefs' production of an Annual Review of Defence Policy for the CID. This was supplemented by increased attention to the quality of joint staff work and preparation of war plans. Beatty was even prepared to consider the establishment of a Ministry of Defence provided that the single-service Cabinet ministers disappeared and the COS were made directly responsible to a Secretary of State for Defence. He also took the lead in establishing the syllabus and organization of the Imperial Defence College, which he envisaged as studying problems, supplied by the Chiefs on an interservice basis.[29] This perhaps-surprising encouragement of independent thought on service matters was reinforced in February 1926 by his strong arguments within the Admiralty for the freeing of the *Naval Review* from official censorship.[30]

Beatty's domination of the COS Committee is illustrated by the phraseology and content of the *1926 Review of Defence Policy,* with its stress on "freedom of sea passage throughout the world" as the basis of Imperial strategy. This was reinforced by a memorandum by the CIGS stating that "unless freedom and security of sea passage throughout the Empire was assured, the whole system of Imperial Defence [would break] down." Such an assurance could be provided only by a fleet built up to Washington standards in capital ships and aircraft carriers for, as was included in the *Review*, it was essential that "air developments should be continuously watched with a view to ensuring that full opportunity should be taken of utilising air power towards the maintenance of sea passage."[31]

On 26 October 1926, in what was his last address at an Imperial Conference, Beatty, speaking for all three services, inevitably took the opportunity to repeat his message.[32] After a long detailed elaboration of the problems of all the services he came to a statement of priorities or, as he termed it, an "order of urgency." First, in the absence of any current particular threat, was the maintenance of sea communications to achieve strategic freedom to operate wherever a threat might appear. Second was the acceptance that the Far East was the most vulnerable area for both territory and shipping. This made it essential that the Singapore base, "a cornerstone of Imperial Defence Strategy," should be completed. Next was the necessity to defend the trade routes and ports on the way to the East, including their air and anticraft defences. Behind all these was the security of Great Britain, the essential base for all the resources needed for the defence of the Empire. To this he could see at the time no identifiable danger.[33]

When Beatty died in 1936 the scene had changed for the worse, both in Europe and in the East, which led to great reverses for Britain and for the Navy, particularly at Singapore and in Eastern waters. In a percipient article, Jon Sumida has convincingly argued that these were "attributable less to pre-war technical and tactical conservatism, such as it was, than to inadequate forces stemming from financial restraints and the fortunes of war."[34] Beatty, who had had his share of both as Fleet Commander and as First Sea Lord, would have fully agreed.

There was one distasteful element in Beatty's career as First Sea Lord that cannot be disregarded: his attempts to influence the historical record of the Battle of Jutland to enhance his own reputation and that of the battlecruiser fleet, and to denigrate the contribution of Jellicoe and the battle fleet. The evidence that he did make such attempts is overwhelming. The reasons for his doing so are complex.[35] It was not out of personal vanity, but more the outcome of a pathological anger and sorrow that the Navy, which had given meaning to his whole life, had failed to grasp the one opportunity it was offered to win the decisive victory for which it was designed. There is no evidence that he consciously accepted any personal responsibility for that failure, but there was no doubt about his continuing grief at the heavy losses in ships and men of the battlecruiser fleet or his determination that their reputation and memory should not be tarnished.

As for his overall performance as First Sea Lord, perhaps the best judge was Maurice Hankey, who was closely in sympathy with him during those seven years of political struggle:

You are the only First Sea Lord I have known in my 26 years who could really talk on even terms to the highest cabinet ministers, and stand up to them in argument. Fisher is an exception, but Fisher was a crank. And even he didn't really state a case clearly. . . . You had tremendous achievements to your name, but your successful pilotage of the C.O.S. Committee through its early days, will, I believe, be one of your great contributions to the Empire's welfare.[36]

NOTES

The abbreviation "Doc." refers to documents printed in B. M. Ranft, ed., *The Beatty Papers*, vol. 2 (London: Navy Records Society, 1993). The originals are in the National Maritime Museum, unless otherwise indicated.

1. Ranft, ed., *Beatty Papers*, 2, Doc. 18 (Lloyd George Papers, F/33/2/54).
2. Ranft, ed., *Beatty Papers*, 2, Doc. 135.
3. Ibid., Docs. 127-30.
4. Ibid., Docs. 46, 46A, 103, 115-17.
5. B. M. Ranft, ed., *The Beatty Papers*, vol.1 (London: Navy Records Society, 1989), 481-88.
6. Ranft, ed., *Beatty Papers*, 2, Docs. 25-29.
7. Ibid., Docs. 38, 45, 72, 73.
8. G. Gordon, *British Sea Power and Procurement Between the Wars* (London: Macmillan, 1988).
9. Ranft, ed., *Beatty Papers*, 2, Docs. 93-100.
10. *Cmnd. 1581: Parliamentary Papers 1922.*
11. Ranft, ed., *Beatty Papers*, 2, Docs. 101-9.
12. Address to Imperial Conference, 4 July 1921, CAB 32/3; Doc. 87A.
13. Ranft, ed., *Beatty Papers*, 2, Docs. 120-21.
14. Ibid., Docs. 133-42.
15. Beatty Papers, BTY/14/4/6.
16. Ranft, ed., *Beatty Papers*, 2, Docs. 149-51, 153-66, 168, 172-73.
17. Geoffrey Till, Air Power and the Royal Navy 1914-1945 (London: Jane's, 1979), 115.
18. Ranft, ed., *Beatty Papers*, 2, Doc. 33.
19. Ranft, ed., *Beatty Papers*, 1:481-88.
20. Ranft, ed., *Beatty Papers*, 2, Docs. 85, 91, 101.
21. Ibid., Doc. 121; Beatty to Brock, 13 Mar. 1923, BTY/13/4/3.

22. Ranft, ed., *Beatty Papers*, 2, Doc. 122.
23. Beatty's evidence to the Balfour Committee is in CAB 16/48, 21/226, 32/48; Ranft, ed., *Beatty Papers*, 2, Docs. 123-24, 126.
24. Roskill, *Naval Policy*, 1:390-98.
25. Draft Speech for Lord Mayor's Banquet, 9 Nov. 1923, BTY/11/8/23; Ranft, ed., *Beatty Papers*, 2, Doc. 131.
26. Ranft, ed., *Beatty Papers*, 2, Doc. 87A.
27. Ibid., Docs. 202-12.
28. Ibid., Docs. 213-16.
29. Ibid., Doc. 171.
30. Ibid., Docs. 174, 176.
31. Ibid., Docs. 181-85. The Review is in CAB 4/15 of 22 June 1926 (Doc. 185).
32. Ibid., Doc. 190-91.
33. Ibid., Doc. 192. Beatty's Statement at Imperial Conference, 26 Oct. 1926, CAB 32/46.
34. J. T. Sumida, "'The Best Laid Plans': The Development of British Battle Fleet Tactics, 1919-1942," *International History Review*, 14, (Nov. 1992): 681 ff.
35. Ranft, ed., *Beatty Papers*, 2, pt. 5, covers this in detail.
36. Hankey to Beatty, 30 Apr. 1927, BTY/14/7/5, and Ranft, ed., *Beatty Papers*, 2, Doc. 194.

10

Admiral Sir Charles E. Madden (1927–1930) and Admiral Sir Frederick L. Field (1930–1933)

Nicholas Tracy

Admiral of the Fleet Sir Charles E. Madden, Bart, and Admiral Sir Frederick L. Field successively occupied the office of First Sea Lord from Beatty's retirement on 30 July 1927 until 30 July 1930 and 21 January 1933, respectively. They have been judged failures by their contemporaries and by historians because they were unable to sustain Beatty's valiant defence of the naval estimates* through the Conservative administration of Stanley Baldwin, the Labour administration of Ramsay MacDonald, and the National government headed by MacDonald. At the 1930 London Naval Conference the special needs of the British Empire were given up, and the economies arbitrarily imposed in 1931 on naval rates of pay led to the Atlantic Fleet collectively refusing duty. In the economic and political conditions of the time, however, it may be asked whether any other admirals would have achieved much more. Certainly historians should be careful about accepting the judgment of their contemporaries at face value.

Madden had made a good impression early in his career. Admiral Sir John Fisher believed Madden to be one of the "five best brains in the navy below the rank of Admiral," and when Captain Henry B. Jackson was brought from command of the torpedo school HMS *Vernon* to the Admiralty as Third Sea Lord and Comptroller in February 1905, he asked for Madden, who was a staff officer there, as his naval assistant.[1] Fisher secured Madden's appointment to the "committee on designs" which developed sketch plans for the Dreadnought battleship and the Invincible battlecruiser. There his career became linked with that of Admiral Sir John Jellicoe, who became his brother-in-law when he married Jellicoe's sister-in-law.[2] After a period as Fisher's naval assistant, Madden went to sea in August 1907 as captain of *Dreadnought* and Chief of Staff to Sir Francis

Bridgeman, Commander-in-Chief Home Fleet. In December 1908 he returned to the Admiralty as naval private secretary to the First Lord, Reginald McKenna, and then in December 1910 as Fourth Sea Lord. Four months later he was made a Rear Admiral, and soon after he went to sea in command of the first division of the Home Fleet, and then of the Third and Second Cruiser Squadrons. On the eve of war Jellicoe was appointed Commander-in-Chief Grand Fleet, and he asked for Madden as his Chief of Staff.

Jellicoe found Madden to be a first-rate staff officer. In early 1916 he wrote to Jackson that he would appoint Madden to command the 1st Battle Squadron, if he could spare him "and he would leave me (both of which are doubtful)... But he would be a grievous loss to me."[3] In his Jutland dispatch, little over a month later, Jellicoe wrote:

[T]hroughout a period of 21 months of war his services have been of inestimable value. His good judgment, his long experience in fleets, special gift for organisation, and his capacity for unlimited work, have all been of the greatest assistance to me ... In the stages leading up to the Fleet action and during and after the action he was always at hand to assist, and his judgment never at fault. I owe him more than I can say.[4]

When Jellicoe went to the Admiralty in 1916 he indicated that he thought Madden "was the best fitted" to take command of the Grand Fleet but that Beatty's claim on the basis of seniority would have to be accommodated.[5] Madden was put in command of the 1st Battle Squadron and became second in command of the Grand Fleet with the acting rank of Admiral, which was confirmed in 1919.

In 1916 Fisher had said that he would like to see Madden follow Jellicoe as First Sea Lord, but when Jellicoe was dismissed because of his weak handling of the U-boat crisis, the First Lord, Sir Eric Geddes, appointed Vice Admiral Wemyss for the job, and Beatty succeeded him in 1919. Admiral Sir Reginald Tyrwhitt thought that Madden would be made to suffer by the politicians for the scuttling of the High Seas Fleet at Scapa Flow, but he had taken precautions that could have been adequate had the Admiralty been able to provide some warning.[6] Madden was appointed Commander-in-Chief of the Atlantic Fleet, a command he held until he retired in 1922, when he was appointed first naval aide-de-camp to King George V and promoted Admiral of the Fleet. Between 1923 and 1924 he served as chairman of the committee on functions and training of the Royal Marines, and in 1925 he served on another committee on executive officers of the Navy. He finally retired to private life in 1927, but his retirement was to be short.

Admiral Sir Roger Keyes, hero of Zeebrugge and Commander-in-Chief of the Mediterranean Fleet between 1925 and 1928, claimed that he urged Beatty and

William Bridgeman, who was First Lord, to appoint Madden to succeed Beatty as First Sea Lord "in order to end the Jellicoe vs. Beatty 'talk' which was not in the best interests of the service, Madden having been a loyal subordinate to both."[7] Keyes was Beatty's "service heir," but the appointment of Jellicoe's brother-in-law was an important move in service politics to heal the wounds caused by Jellicoe's dismissal and the Jutland controversy. Moreover, apparently, Keyes also felt it would be a personal convenience that would enable him to remain in command of the Mediterranean Fleet for a third year before he would himself become First Sea Lord. He wrote to Beatty that he had known Madden since their service together in Keyes's first ship and when Keyes had served under him in the Atlantic Fleet, and that he "was absolutely loyal" to Beatty. "I am sure that if he were appointed to relieve you on your recommendation it would be enormously appreciated in the Service who would like to see him get an inning."[8] He also wrote to General Sir Ian Hamilton after Madden's appointment:

[T]he right sort of sailor knows that he was loyalty itself to Beatty when he was 2nd in command to him in the Grand Fleet and has been ever since—and that he was a loyal C.O.S. to his brother-in-law so no one can look upon him—who are in the know—as a partisan or anything but what he is, a good straight loyal fellow.[9]

Considering Beatty's attempts to suppress Rear Admiral J. E. T. Harper's Official Record of the Battle of Jutland, it is clear that he would only have chosen Madden if he thought he could be relied on to back his claims to the starring role at Jutland.[10]

Unfortunately, Keyes is as unreliable as a guide for the historian as he proved to be to Beatty. Years later, after Madden had frustrated his own hopes, he complained to Vice Admiral Dudley Pound that the latter had persuaded him to support Madden "against my better judgment." Beatty, he then claimed, had "grave misgivings, but he acted on the advice you had given and bitterly regretted it for the rest of his life."[11]

It is necessary to discount much of what Keyes wrote but at the same time to learn from it, and Keyes's hyperbole is merely the most extreme instance of an all-too-prevalent bitchiness and vanity among the flag ranks of the interwar era. Too often, the harshest words were written by men who had enjoyed some of the highest postings and exercise of power that Britain had to offer but whose ambition had been thwarted just short of their final triumph. When, in later years, he came to regard Madden and Frederick Field with contempt, Keyes libeled both men's war records, claiming that they had been cowardly and had brought about the disengagement of the fleets at Jutland.[12]

More importance should be given to the opinion of Vice Admiral W. H. Kelly, which he expressed at the time of Madden's appointment. He regarded Madden as "to the service—a *most* unpopular choice" as First Sea Lord. "From every point of view, as I see it, it would be infinitely better for D. B. to stay on here until you have finished your time in the Mediterranean." He continued:

Though I admire Madden in many ways, I cannot think it would be for the good of the Service or of the Country that he should come here. I think he is too re-actionary, too little human, as far as the Service is concerned, and I don't think he would carry any guns at all vis-à-vis with the Politicians.[13]

Although Kelly later came to be unreliable as a source, in this instance there is some corroborative evidence. In 1917 Beatty's wife, Ethel, had responded with a decided negative to Sir Edward Carson's query on whether Madden was the "wonderful man" he had been told he was. "I said he had brain but no [heart? balls?]."[14] There is some reason for thinking that Madden had shown little sensitivity in early 1919, before the signing of the Versailles treaty, towards the hostilities-only ratings who had had enough of service life.[15] As First Sea Lord he was to resist the desire of the Labour government to democratize the officer cadet intake.[16] Kelly was certainly correct about Madden's weakness in dealing with hardened politicians like Winston Churchill who, as Chancellor of the Exchequer in Balfour's administration, pursued with single-minded concentration a policy of economy at the expense of the services. It is worth asking whether Keyes's preference for extending his Mediterranean service was a little influenced by a desire to spare himself the ordeal over procurement that Madden had had to suffer?

Pound, who was Assistant Chief of Naval Staff following a tour as Chief of Staff to Keyes in the Mediterranean, wrote that he did "not feel too happy about the present regime—the combination of C.M. and F.L.F. is *not* a good one." Admiral Frederick L. Field, who had been appointed Deputy Chief of Naval Staff in 1925, had been Britain's naval representative at the Geneva Conference before ill health led Pound to replace him. When Field was made Commander-in-Chief Mediterranean Fleet in June 1928, Madden appointed Vice Admiral William Fisher as DCNS. Pound was delighted because he believed that Vice Admiral Sir Cyril T. W. Fuller wanted the job and that Fuller and Madden would have been at least as bad as Field and Madden had been.[17] Certainly, when Fuller was appointed to the Board as Second Sea Lord on 26 May 1930, he proved to be a major handicap to Admiral Field.

The greatest problem with which Madden was to be faced was the need felt by the government to reach a formal agreement with the U.S. government that extended to smaller ships the limitations on naval armament which had been applied to capital ships at the Washington Conference. The first attempt in 1927 at Geneva, which was still in session when Madden was appointed, was an abject failure and exacerbated the bad feelings existing between the Royal Navy and its U.S. equivalent. If a political confrontation between Britain and the United States was to be avoided, some sort of an accord had to be reached between the two countries. The perceived need for stringent economies to enable the Conservatives to maintain the Gold Standard was an additional incentive to reduce naval armament, with or without a formal American treaty. Beatty wrote to Keyes shortly after Madden's appointment and offered his opinion that "as a result of the Geneva failure Madden will not have an easy time. That was certainly the most gigantic bluff on the part of the Americans to acquire Command of the Sea without having to pay for it or fight for it."[18]

The government was determined to reopen the three-year cruiser-building program to which Beatty had brought his old friend Churchill to agree. Beatty had made it quite clear he would resign if the Cabinet turned down his estimate, and his position was so strong that he could have brought down the administration by so doing.[19] Madden did not have the advantage of Beatty's popularity or his experience of working with Churchill. Pound warned Keyes in November 1927:

For some weeks conversations over the building programme have been taking place as apparently both Winston and First Lord wished to avoid the Cabinet Committee. The First Lord soon dropped out of the negotiations leaving CNS and DCNS to carry them on with W. Winston of course was quite unscrupulous and manoeuvred us into an impossible position with the result that the Cabinet Committee are to sit after all.[20]

He added in a later letter:

The first move was that Winston got the P.M. and First Lord to agree that *he* (Winston) should try and come to an agreement without having to refer the matter to a Cabinet Committee. Personally I think it is bad policy for the Admiralty to agree to treat with anyone except Cabinet or C.I.D.—why should the Chancellor be allowed to dictate or try to dictate Naval policy. . . Winston I gather tried to behave like a bully and interrupted C.M. whenever he spoke, whilst C.M. has not yet learned enough of the game to interrupt Winston and nail his ribs to the [counter?] on the spot with the result that Winston made many statements which he must have known to be inaccurate and talked the meeting out so as to prevent C.M. or Field contraverting it.[21]

Beatty thought the government behaved like "dirty dogs" in turning down the programme "ostensibly to make the 'Beau Geste' to the U.S.A.," but he blamed Madden.

Madden was, poor devil, beat and w[oul]d not go the whole hog and now he is putty in their hands. I am sorry for him but he only had to stick his toes in at the beginning and all w[oul]d have been well, but he lacks guts. This I need hardly say is for your private ear *only* and unfair to him to repeat.[22]

Beatty had learned before the war when he was Naval Secretary to Churchill, as First Lord, that, as he put it to Rear Admiral de Chair, "You have to have a bloody awful row with Winston once a month and then you are all right."[23]

Part of the reason for the Admiralty's inability to stand up to the Chancellor was that it could not agree about what ships it wanted. Field and Admiral Ernle Chatfield, who was the Controller, wanted to build eight-inch gun cruisers, but Madden preferred smaller, six-inch cruisers. Not only did he want to give tangible evidence that the Royal Navy's insistence on a fleet of seventy cruisers for trade defense was genuine, but he, unlike Pound, strongly believed in the value of convoys. Small cruisers were more suitable for the task. The course of the Second World War was to fully vindicate him. However, he did not carry his point. The pressure to reduce the numbers of ships built may have helped to ensure that the few which were authorized in the end were at the top limit of the Washington agreement, namely, 10,000 tons.[24]

It was, of course, absolutely necessary that the animosity between the Royal Navy and the U.S. Navy be addressed by the political leadership. Cruiser programs were merely a manifestation of an underlying distrust. The First World War had reinforced the conviction generated by the American Civil War that naval forces had the capacity to dominate world affairs by controlling maritime trade. The Royal Navy believed that it had perfected the strategy that could protect British interests, if only the Americans did not defend neutral rights from a position of strength, and the American Navy regarded the Royal Navy as a potent threat to American economic growth that only an American Fleet "second to none" could contain. The alternatives to an arms race, which could lead to as deadly an outcome as had the pre-1914 Anglo-German competition, were either to reduce the level of naval armament by treaty so that the Americans felt safe and the British had a free hand in European affairs or to persuade the British government to abandon its claim to belligerent rights to control trade in wartime. Pound summed up the American position at Geneva as:

(a) They want "Freedom of the Seas" by which they mean that when they are neutral no one shall interfere with their ships. (b) To force us to agree to the "F. of the Seas" they want "parity." (c) They want to achieve 'parity' *on the cheap*, i.e. force us by treaty to come back to their level instead of having to build up to our level.[25]

Austin Chamberlain, the Foreign Secretary, was impressed by the danger, and by the emptiness of belligerent rights if they could only be imposed at the expense of good relations with the Americans. "I believe," he recorded in a CID subcommittee report, *Belligerent Rights at Sea and the Relations Between the United States and Great Britain*, that Major General Preston Brown, Commander of the 1st Corps Area in Boston, was right when he said "that any attempt by us to enforce our rights in a future war where the United States were neutral, as we enforced them in the late war, would make war between us 'probable.'"[26] Churchill suggested that it would be well to abandon the right to interdict trade because the ability of the Royal Navy to protect British trade was in such doubt.

Service opinion was clearly against any concession on belligerent rights, however, and with the help and political maneuvering of Maurice Hankey, the Secretary to the Cabinet and to the CID, an international conference on naval strategy was avoided. To avoid packing the CID Sub-Committee on Belligerent Rights with conservatives, Baldwin would only include Madden as an "expert assessor." Pound said of Madden that he was "absolutely sound on the Freedom of the Seas business but I am not too certain of his powers of debate. I knew we should always miss D.B. but never imagined the loss would be so terribly great."[27] Madden, however, did not let him down. When the CID Sub-Committee presented its report in October 1927, Madden refused to agree with either the majority or minority reports. Hankey recorded Madden's objection in any circumstances to submitting belligerent rights to compulsory arbitration.[28] So successful were the stalling tactics that the problem was left for the new Labour administration of Ramsay MacDonald, which was elected and took office in 1929. Madden's term as First Sea Lord had been extended for one year because Bridgeman did not want the confusion of a new appointment at the same time as a general election, and accordingly, it was Madden who had eventually to deal with the two issues of belligerent rights and limitations of cruiser strengths. Ramsay MacDonald was inclined to listen to U.S. President Herbert Hoover's urgent suit to provide food ships with an absolute protection in international law, but he was steered away from making any concession on belligerent rights. Madden dissuaded the Labour First Lord, Albert V. Alexander, from bringing into discussion at the London Naval Conference in 1930 the question of framing new rules of visit and search that could be applied to submarines and aircraft.[29]

The price the Royal Navy had to pay was agreement to the American demand that its cruiser fleet should be cut to fifty ships. Admiral Sir Herbert Richmond later declared that Madden "was nothing short of a calamity and earned the O.M. [Order of Merit] for being subservient to the Labour Government. Madden, whom I had known ever since he was First Liet. of the *Vernon*, never had the glimmerings of anything outside technical matters."[30] In 1916 Jackson had rejected Madden as Grand Fleet Commander because his experience as Chief of Staff had not prepared him for the difficult decision making that "tries and proves the capability of an individual in war."[31] However, it is a little hard on Madden, who had been such a good staff officer, to castigate him for loyally carrying out the clear intentions of the political leadership of the country. He had certainly done his duty in advising and warning the government. In his capacity of Principal Naval Advisor, he had prepared for Alexander a paper in which he made clear the Admiralty's advice on the necessity for eighty cruisers, and a battleship replacement program. The paper was passed to MacDonald, but the Prime Minister preferred to reach an agreement with the Americans to limit the number of light cruisers and to agree to a system of limitations that favored the American naval preference for a smaller number of larger cruisers, rather than to insist on a right to build ships that, in any event, Britain could not afford.[32] After his retirement, Madden claimed that he had not really been forced to reduce the strength of the Navy because Beatty's seventy cruisers were a "myth." The actual number of cruisers was forty-eight and it was only paper growth that he had agreed to axe.[33] Beatty scornfully rejected that argument.

Keyes's expectation of succeeding Madden was dashed, probably as a result of the *Royal Oak* affair in which his incapacity as a personnel manager had been exposed. King George V had expressed his dissatisfaction with Keyes when the latter had hauled down his flag as Commander-in-Chief Mediterranean in 1928.[34] Beatty told Keyes that he had written to the Prime Minister in January 1930 recommending that Keyes should succeed Madden. In February 1929, before his own appointment had been extended, however, Madden had advised Bridgeman that Admiral Sir Frederick Field was "fitted in every respect to deal with this important period" and recommended him in preference to both Sir O. Brock and Keyes.[35] The formation of Ramsay MacDonald's Labour government—which was determined to make a success of the arms limitation discussions—strengthened Madden's preference for Field, because he did not believe Keyes would implement the government's policy but rather thought he would resign and take the board with him.[36] Pound, when he heard of Field's appointment on 30

July 1930, wrote that he could only "suppose that the Gov[ernmen]t want[s] someone who will agree to all their reductions."[37] Madden himself told Field that he had recommended him as a man with "tact, good temper and patience to get a good hearing from a socialist cabinet bent on reducing the Navy." Having commanded the "Dominion Cruise," Field had the additional advantage of knowing the leading Dominion statesmen.[38] Alexander did not ask Beatty for his opinion, and the announcement of Field's appointment was made before Keyes could bring up his own guns in support. Too late, he complained to Ramsay MacDonald that Madden had "sidetracked" and "discredited" him in favor of Field, whom he described as a disruptive influence "on behalf of junior Flag Officers."[39]

Like Madden, Field was a torpedo specialist, having commanded HMS *Vernon* at the beginning of the war. He had joined *Britannia* in 1884 and, like so many naval officers who later rose to high rank, he had distinguished himself during action ashore in the Boxer rebellion. After Field's death in 1945, Keyes wrote to Tomkinson about the former First Sea Lord:

[I have] so many pleasant recollections of Tam Field starting [in] 1885 when he was a third term captain—the most powerfully built and developed boy in the *Britannia*—his basin next to mine, a miserable little specimen 4 ft 10" and a "New." He was awfully good to us and we loved him. Next in China when he did so well—and took it so well my going over his head."[40]

After his period of command at *Vernon*, Field went to sea as flag captain to Sir Martyn Jerram who commanded the 2nd Battle Squadron from HMS *King George V*. He was mentioned in dispatches after the Battle of Jutland for "the great skill" he exercised in handling his ship "under very difficult conditions."

Appointed a Companion, Order of the Bath, (CB), Field served from November 1916 to April 1918 as Madden's Chief of Staff in the 1st Battle Squadron, for which he was appointed a Companion of St. Michael and St. George, (CMG), in 1919. Following the war, Field was first appointed Director of Torpedoes and Mines at the Admiralty and then, in March 1920, he was appointed to the Board of Admiralty as Third Sea Lord and Comptroller. He served as DCNS between May 1925 and May 1928, during which time he stoutly defended at Geneva the British need for seventy cruisers for trade defence. Beatty's view was that Field did a good job of this and was "full of tact and long suffering. Much more so than I should have been."[41] Three months later, when the conference had broken down and "little Bridgeman" had proved to be "putty" in the pacifist hands of "that lunatic Cecil," Beatty was ready to excuse Field. "I don't know now the Inner

History of the whole affair or how Field came to let it get as bad as it was. He poor fellow was very ill or it would never have happened."[42]

In reply to Keyes's letter of congratulations shortly after his appointment, Field wrote in a conciliatory fashion, somewhat unconvincingly asserting that he "didn't ask for the job which I think is going to be very difficult to say the least of it."[43] Keyes, plainly suspicious, wrote to Kelly that he believed Field had "schemed to supplant me as surely as Jacob supplanted Esau."[44] It is hardly safe to judge Field, however, on the basis of what his disappointed fellow admirals said of him. Kelly, for instance, when disappointed in July 1931 about Field's failure to deliver a coveted appointment as Second Sea Lord, wrote to Keyes: "I knew in the Mediterranean, he was weak, and, as his Seniors were concerned, cowardly, but there I thought his defects ended. Now, I feel he is as crooked as a dog's hind leg."[45]

Richmond is on record as having written:

Poor Tam Field, a delightful person and a sick man when he took the job on, had no courage when it came to standing up to Ministers. He allowed the 50 cruiser agreement to go through, and made no protest when Alexander and one or two other Ministers issued a preposterous C[omman]d paper in which it was said that the number of our destroyers was dependent on the number of enemy submarines! I told him it was sheer and disgraceful cowardice on the part of the Board, and of himself in particular, to let that statement go out to the public without protest from the Sea Lords.[46]

In 1942 Richmond blamed Madden, Field, and Chatfield for the loss of Singapore by failing to produce Jellicoe's "Two Ocean Navy."[47] This judgment, however, ignores the fact that shortage of cruisers was perhaps the least significant contributing factor in Britain's defeat in the Pacific. Keyes's 1925 exercise simulating a fleet operation in support of Singapore had made clear the effect torpedo aircraft could have on naval operations in the area.[48] Field, like Madden before him, supplied the Labour government with a clear statement of Britain's need for stronger naval defenses.[49] The importance of reaching an accord with the Americans at the London Conference of 1930 and the financial crisis of 1931 had really put it out of the power of any First Sea Lord to sustain a building program on the scale envisaged by Jellicoe and Beatty.

Criticism of Field is fully deserved, however, over the so-called Invergordon Mutiny. This crisis of a collective refusal of duty in the Atlantic Fleet that occurred in the late summer of 1931, when the government ordered a large reduction in the rates of naval pay, undoubtedly shows the First Sea Lord's handling of personnel problems in a very poor light. His chronic illness was probably the main reason for the failure to anticipate the crisis and devise a more equitable way of securing the ends the government required, but it also appears that the hardship that would be caused to the lower deck, where it was thought the reduction of pay could drive their wives into prostitution, did not interest him as much as did the hardship which would be suffered by the Sea Lords themselves. In a letter written in March 1931 to Sir Warren Fisher, the Permanent Under Secretary of State at the Treasury, he made the following extraordinary suggestion: "When the Order in Council reducing Naval rates of pay on 1st July 1931 is issued, . . . a paragraph should be inserted in it cancelling the Orders in Council now in existence which regulate the reduction of the civil salaries of the Naval Members of the Board." By that means, while the rest of the Navy would suffer cuts in pay, the Sea Lords would have their salaries returned to the 1921 rate.[50] The weakness of the Board of Admiralty, in part because of Field's bad health and in part because of the appointment of Cyril Fuller, as Second Sea Lord with responsibility for personnel, and Admiral F. C. Dreyer as DCNS, was instrumental in bringing about the crisis that was subsequently labeled the "Invergordon Mutiny." Field had promised the post of Second Sea Lord to Admiral Kelly who, it becomes quite clear with hindsight, was the right man for the job, but Alexander had refused to appoint him, no doubt because he could not count on Kelly to carry out Labour's policies.[51] Kelly's resentment was monumental and makes his evocative statements about subsequent events unreliable as evidence. Madden admitted to Field that Fuller had been appointed because he had been Madden's Chief-of-Staff: "This appointment is I think the only one I submitted which could possibly be attributed to favouritism by the Keyes gang." For Dreyer, he wrote, he "certainly held [no?] brief."[52]

In 1924 the Anderson Committee had concluded that lower deck rates of pay had risen too much after the war and ought to be cut by 25 percent, but after several questions in the House of Commons, the pledge was made that there would be no cuts for men already in the service. The Wall Street Crash in 1929, however, and the subsequent financial crisis in Britain in 1931, led the Conservative government, which was committed to the Gold Standard, to change its mind. A committee under Sir George May, which had been struck in March 1931, recommended that armed services pay be cut by eliminating the higher pay of the pre-1924 intake. On 19 August, four days before the financial crisis forced the Labour administration to resign, the Admiralty told the Cabinet that it would agree to the cuts providing they were equivalent to those being borne by other classes of society. At the King's urgent appeal, Ramsay MacDonald agreed to form a National government that could put through a budget tight enough to appease international finance. The new First Lord was Austin Chamberlain. Field was away because of his health, and Dreyer was on leave. Chamberlain took the decision that the May Committee recommendations had to be accepted. The Treasury would not agree to the fleet being told just what loss of pay each rate would suffer before the budget was tabled in the House of Commons, but the Fleet Commanders were sent a warning telegram. Rear Admiral Wilfred Tomkinson, temporary commander of the Atlantic Fleet, did not apparently think any precautions needed to be taken. That he was wrong became abundantly evident when the news of the pay cuts was announced. A shilling was to be cut from every man's pay, reducing a Lieutenant-Commander's pay by 3.7 percent and an Able Seaman's by 25 percent. The cuts made to unemployment insurance and to the salaries of teachers and policemen ranged from 6.5 percent to 15 percent.[53] So shocking was this injustice that the Atlantic Fleet refused to proceed to sea on exercise. Legally, the action, or rather passive inaction, of the men was a mutiny punishable by death under the articles of war, but Chamberlain rightly refused, to label it as such.

The Chilean Navy had also suffered massive pay cuts, which had led to collective refusal of duty, and on 7 September the Chilean government had broken off negotiations with the sailors and launched a massive air and military assault on the ships. A note in Admiral Dreyer's papers indicates that there was discussion among the junior Sea Lords of some sort of military response to the similar troubles in the Atlantic Fleet.[54] There were also those in the Cabinet who felt that no concession could be made to the fleet without the collapse of civil government and that force would have to be used.[55] Field, however, believed that the impasse could be resolved without violence if the men, who refused to go to sea on exercise, were ordered instead to sail to their home ports. Dreyer later insisted that Field's advice was based on a good understanding of lower-deck psychology, especially considering the importance in the whole disgraceful episode of the men's concern for their families.[56] The Cabinet eventually agreed, and a carefully worded order was sent to the fleet in which it was made clear that the Admiralty would review the effect of the pay cuts.[57] There are several reports that King George V asked Admiral Kelly, who was enormously popular with the lower-deck, to come out of retirement and go to Invergordon to talk to the men.[58] On 16 September the fleet sailed, and to stem the run on gold that news of the mutiny had triggered, Chamberlain publicly drew a line under the event and made it clear that there would be no courts martial. When that was insufficient,

Britain had to abandon the Gold Standard. Panicked by new fears of communist plots in the fleet, the Cabinet readily assented to Chamberlain's demand that pay cuts be limited to 10 percent. Apparently at King George V's insistence, Kelly was placed in command of the Atlantic Fleet.[59]

Kelly visited every ship to talk to the men, and afterwards, as he wrote to Keyes and reported to Field:

[I was] astounded, almost appalled, at the *unanimity* of opinion, from the highest to the lowest, that the action of the Board of Admiralty in accepting and publishing the Cuts as originally promulgated was directly responsible for the Mutiny at Invergordon. I told him, further, that the consensus of opinions that I had received was that complete confidence in the Administrative Authority would not be restored as long as the present Board remains in office. And a great deal more, *and* I didn't find it pleasant to do so, for I felt that—having won my fight: when my flag was hoisted—I could sink all bitterness.[60]

Keyes was incensed by the dismissal of Tomkinson before the end of his tour of duty, and also by the inconsiderate way in which he was left to learn of the order on the public news service. "It is an absolute outrage. How Field can have the face to make scapegoats—and in such a cruel way, beats me."[61] Certainly, Field felt himself to be exposed and on the defensive. He believed that Tomkinson should have acted decisively when Atlantic Fleet ratings first met to discuss the pay cuts, but he did not deal with the situation very well.[62] He resented Kelly's criticism very strongly and told him that his offered resignation had been refused by Chamberlain, who had said "it would be quixotic [and] neglecting my duty to do so."[63] The strain seems to have led to Field's suffering a perforated ulcer.

Sir Bolton Eyres Monsell took over as First Lord in November 1931, but Field remained at the Admiralty until January 1933. The Board set up a chain of committees to address the problems thrown into relief by the Invergordon crisis, but Dreyer's continuation as DCNS significantly weakened what appear to have been Field's good intentions.[64] One of the Board's decisions was that people considered to be "troublemakers" should be weeded out despite the promise that there would be no courts-martial. Twenty-four men were dismissed from the service at a time of very high unemployment without much care being taken to discover whether there was any case against them. Field was also thwarted by the junior Sea Lords in his final Review of naval policy, in which he sketched in a building program for the next decade. His successor actually carried out the first five years of his plan, until international events obliged an increase in pace. Field got no credit because his paper was discussed twice by the full Board, heavily amended, and never circulated.[65] As Andrew Gordon wrote, Field's appreciation of the need to be able to keep a "deterrent" fleet in home waters to manage the European situation, should it ever be necessary to confront Japanese aggression in the Pacific, "did at least reflect the strengthening of feeling in the Service whose leadership Sir Ernle Chatfield was about to assume."[66] It was primarily the work of Field in the Committee of Imperial Defence that led to the abandonment of the Ten Year Rule in 1932. He also ensured that Fuller should receive no further employment and that Dreyer should not serve as Commander-in-Chief Atlantic Fleet, which would ensure that he could not rise to First Sea Lord.

Stephen Roskill wrote that "it is difficult not to feel that [Field] was never a big enough man for the job."[67] Clearly he lacked the self-confidence that was needed to cope with the vanities and lust for power that he had to confront, both as naval advisor at the Geneva Conference and as leading naval member of a Board that included a man such as Dreyer, who had been appointed to the Board one month before he was himself. His poor health was, no doubt, both the cause and the effect of his inability to confront such despots and may also have engendered some small-mindedness in his handling of personnel following the Invergordon incident. He, like his predecessor, Madden, however, appears to have had considerable intellectual capacity, which he applied to the problems the Royal Navy faced in the late 1920s and early 1930s. In retrospect, he would have been better suited to a career in a service where more of the officers were gentlemen.

NOTES

1. Fisher to Selborne, 21 Oct. 1904, in P. K. Kemp, ed., *The Papers of Admiral Sir John Fisher*, vol. 1 (London: Navy Records Society, 1960), 5-6.
2. Kemp, *Fisher*, 1, 199-297.
3. Jellicoe to Jackson, 29 Apr. 1916, Temple Patterson, *Jellicoe Papers*, 1, Doc. 221.
4. Jellicoe to Jackson, 25 May 1916, Patterson, *Jellicoe Papers*, 1, Doc. 224.
5. Jellicoe to Jackson, 12 Sept. 1916, *Jellicoe Papers*, 2, Doc. 9b.
6. Tyrwhitt to Keyes, 26 June 1916, in Paul G. Halpern, ed., *The Keyes Papers*, vol. 2 (London: Navy Records Society 1980), Doc. 24; and see Marder, *From Dreadnought to Scapa Flow*, 5:175n.
7. Keyes to First Lord, 3 Mar. 1930, in Halpern, *Keyes Papers*, 2, Doc. 213.
8. Keyes to Beatty, 29 Aug. 1926, in ibid., Doc. 153.
9. Keyes to Hamilton, 4 May 1927, in ibid., Doc. 174; see also Fisher to Jellicoe, 29 Aug. 1914, in Patterson, ed., *Jellicoe Papers*, 1, Doc. 40.
10. *See* Patterson, ed., *Jellicoe Papers*, 2, s.v. part 4, "The Jutland Controversy and the Closing Years," and appendix, "The Harper Papers," 399-490; and Stephen Roskill, *Admiral of the Fleet: Earl Beatty, An Intimate Biography* (New York: Atheneum, 1981), 58.
11. Keyes to Pound, 26 Apr. 1940, in Halpern, *Keyes Papers*, 3, Doc. 18.

12. Beatty to Keyes, 13 Aug. 1926, in Halpern, *Keyes Papers*, 2, Docs. 245-46.
13. Kelly to Keyes, 13 Aug. 1926, in ibid., Doc. 152.
14. Beatty from his wife, 12 May 1917, in Ranft, *Beatty Papers*, vol.1 (London: Navy Records Society, 1989), 376.
15. Madden to Keyes, 23 Apr. 1919, in Halpern, *Keyes Papers*, 2, Doc. 20.
16. Roskill, *Naval Policy*, 2:34.
17. Pound to Keyes, 24 Jan. 1928, in Halpern, *Keyes Papers*, 2, Doc. 193.
18. Beatty to Keyes, 6 Aug. 1927, in ibid., Doc. 182.
19. Roskill, *Beatty,* 351-69; Roskill, *Churchill and the Admirals* (London: Collins, 1977), 78.
20. Pound to Keyes, 9 Nov. 1927, in Halpern, *Keyes Papers*, 2, Doc. 186.
21. Pound to Keyes, 19 Dec. 1927, in ibid., Doc. 185.
22. Beatty to Keyes, 12 Dec. 1927, in ibid., Doc. 185.
23. Roskill, *Beatty*, 58.
24. Stephen Roskill, *Hankey, Man of Secrets,* vol. 2 (London: Collins, 1972), 555-57.
25. Pound to Keyes, 10 Aug. 1927, in Halpern, *Keyes Papers*, 2, Doc. 183.
26. Belligerent Rights at Sea and the Relations Between the United States and Great Britain, 16 and 26 October 1927, CAB 21/307. See Nicholas Tracy, *Attack on Maritime Trade* (London: Macmillan, 1991), 153-73.
27. Pound to Keyes, 19 Dec. 1927, in Halpern, *Keyes Papers*, 2, Doc. 189.
28. Roskill, *Hankey*, 2:549-51.
29. Roskill, *Naval Policy*, 2:49, 60; and Roskill, *Hankey*, 453-59.
30. Richmond to Keyes, 22 Nov. 1940, in Halpern, *Keyes Papers*, 3, Doc. 52.
31. Jackson to Jellicoe, 14 Sept. 1916, in Patterson, ed., *Jellicoe Papers* , 2, Doc. 9c.
32. LNC(29) 4th meeting of 13 Dec. 1929, Cab. 29/117; and see Roskill, *Naval Policy*, 2:52-53, 66; and Roskill, *Hankey*, 2:510.
33. Keyes to Beatty, 1 Dec. 1930, and reply, 6 Dec. 1930, in Halpern, *Keyes Papers*, 2, Docs. 231, 232.
34. Keyes to Monsell, 1 Jan. 1932, and other papers in ADM 230/1 and in Keyes Collection 7/37-42, British Library. See Leslie Gardiner, *The Royal Oak Courts Martial* (Edinburgh, Scotland: William Blackwood and Sons Ltd., 1965), 241-42.
35. Bridgeman Papers, 4629/1/1927/29, 21 Feb. 1929, Shropshire Records.
36. Keyes to Beatty, 1 Dec. 1930, in Halpern, *Keyes Papers*, 2, Doc. 231.
37. Pound to Keyes, 4 Mar. 1930, in ibid., Doc. 214.
38. Madden to Field, 6 June 1932, ADM 230/1.
39. Keyes to Ramsay MacDonald, 28 Feb. 1930, 2 Mar. 1930, and to First Lord, 3 Mar. 1930, 5 Mar. 1930, in Halpern, *Keyes Papers*, 2, Docs. 206, 207, 213. See Madden's defense of his nominations for appointments, Madden to Field, 6 June 1932, ADM 230/1.
40. Keyes to Tomkinson, 3 Nov. 1945, in Halpern, *Keyes Papers*, 3, Doc. 171.
41. Beatty to Keyes, 26 June 1927, in Halpern, *Keyes Papers*, 2, Doc. 180.
42. Beatty to Keyes, 9 Sept. 1927, in ibid., Doc. 184.
43. Field to Keyes, 13 Mar. 1930, in ibid., Doc. 221.
44. Keyes to Kelly, 1 Apr. 1930, in ibid., Doc. 224.
45. Kelly to Keyes, 3 July 1931, in ibid., Doc. 237; and see Keyes to Kelly, 1 Apr. 1930, in ibid., Doc. 224.
46. Richmond to Keyes, 22 Nov. 1940, in Halpern, *Keyes Papers*, 3, Doc. 52; and also 15 Mar. 1941, Doc. 79.
47. Richmond to Keyes, 16 Feb. 1942, in ibid., Doc. 134.

48. Memorandum by Keyes on Exercise "MU," 15 Dec. 1925, in Halpern, *Keyes Papers*, 2, Doc. 136.
49. *See* Roskill, *Naval Policy*, 2:86.
50. Field to Sir Warren Fisher (Treasury), 27 Mar. 1931, ADM 116/3250.
51. *See* Roskill, *Naval Policy*, 2:79.
52. Madden to Field, 6 June 1932, ADM 230/1.
53. Dreyer, "The Board of Admiralty and the Mutiny in the Atlantic Fleet at Invergordon in September 1931," ADM 178/79.
54. DRYR 8/1, Churchill College.
55. Chatfield Papers, CHT/2/2, National Maritime Museum.
56. There is a hint that Field's advice had originated with King George V, who knew the fleet very well, see Alan Ereira, *The Invergordon Mutiny* (London: Routledge and Kegan Paul, 1981), 119.
57. ADM 178/129.
58. Ereira, *Invergordon Mutiny*, 139-45.
59. *See* Roskill, *Naval Policy*, 2:89-124.
60. Kelly to Keyes, 29 Oct. 1931, in Halpern, *Keyes Papers*, 2, Doc. 239. See also "Invergordon Incident 1931, Report by Admiral Sir John Kelly," ADM 178/111.
61. Keyes to Tomkinson, 19 Mar. 1932, in Halpern, *Keyes Papers*, 2, Doc. 244.
62. *See* Sir Oswald Murray to Lord Monsell, "Confidential," 26 Sept. 1934, ADM 230/1.
63. Kelly to Chatfield, 16 May 1932, Chatfield Papers, CHT/2/2; and see Roskill, *Naval Policy*, 2:125. See also remarks by First Sea Lord (Field), 2 June 1932, ADM 230/1.
64. ADM 178/75, 79, 89, 110, 111, 112, 113, 114, 129, 149, 150, see also Roskill, *Naval Policy*, 2:126-32.
65. Memorandum for the Admiralty Board, Field, 14 Nov. 1932, ADM 116/3434, ff.13-21; "A New Standard of Naval Strength," Apr. 1937, ADM 1/9081. See also Roskill, *Naval Policy*, 2:150-51 and Gordon, *British Sea Power* and Procurement, 107-8.
66. Gordon, *British Sea Power and Procurement*,108.
67. Roskill, *Naval Policy*, 2, 154.

11

Admiral Sir (later Baron) Ernle Chatfield (1933–1938)

Eric J. Grove

Alfred Ernle Montacute Chatfield, First Baron Chatfield of Ditchling, was one of the greatest First Sea Lords of all time. Few other British naval officers of the twentieth century made a greater personal impact. From 1900 to 1940 Chatfield played an important role, often disproportionate to his rank. It was, however, his period as First Sea Lord from 1933 to 1938 for which he is most remembered; it was at this time that he ensured the Royal Navy was as prepared as adverse circumstances allowed to face its ultimate test.[1]

A gunnery expert with a wide-range of seagoing experience and several years of important Admiralty staff work behind him, Chatfield came to the post of First Sea Lord after a record of exemplary service in command of the Atlantic and the Mediterranean Fleets. His service in these commands from 1929 to 1932 had been marked by considerable simplification of overcentralized staff work and a tactical revolution in the ability of the Fleets' main units to fight at night. Chatfield had also been able to prevent trouble in the Mediterranean Fleet at the time of the Invergordon Mutiny.[2] Invergordon and its aftermath marked perhaps an all-time low in the morale of the twentieth-century Royal Navy.

It is not an exaggeration to suggest that a senior officer has never had more of a challenge than Chatfield faced when he returned to the Admiralty at the beginning of 1933 to take up his duties as First Sea Lord and Chief of Naval Staff. The Fleet had confidence in him. As Admiral Sir John Kelly, C-in-C Home Fleet, wrote to Chatfield: "[T]he Navy wishes for, and needs strong leadership, and every individual in it, officer or man will know with you at the head of it he will get a square deal."[3]

Chatfield had engaged in correspondence with the First Lord, Sir Bolton Eyres Monsell, after the latter had offered him the post of First Sea Lord in April 1932. Chatfield insisted:

[U]ntil the Sea Lords connected with the events of 1931 have all left it will be impossible to get criticism entirely stopped and to take the strong action that should and must be taken, regardless of persons, to establish the dignity, authority and prestige of the Board without fear or favour.

Chatfield indeed was the last of a group of Sea Lords appointed after the mutiny; Vice Admiral Dudley Pound, Rear Admiral Charles Forbes, and Rear Admiral Geoffrey Blake arrived at the Admiralty before they had become too committed to their own ideas, and Field was forced to depart earlier than he wished.[4]

The new First Sea Lord, a vigorous and tough sixty-year-old, soon exerted his authority. A plan was about to be put into effect to introduce sail training for ratings before promotion to petty officer. Chatfield, who had only narrowly escaped disaster under sail as a Midshipman, had a better conception than most of the dangers of sailing ships. He did not consider that the technically oriented ratings of the 1930s would appreciate or benefit from this enforced obligation. With the support only of his Deputy and Assistant Chiefs of Naval Staff, he blocked the agreed policy of all the Sea Lords and his political chief.[5]

Chatfield was powerful but not overbearing. His ability to delegate enabled the individual Sea Lords to operate without needless interference. The relationship with Reginald Henderson, Forbes's successor as Controller in 1934, was especially important. Chatfield and Henderson were as one on the need to provide ships with the strongest degree of armor protection, as can be seen clearly in the battleship, aircraft carrier, and cruiser designs of the period. Chatfield was determined that his guiding principle of the dominance of the skilled user be asserted, and as soon as he assumed office as Chief of Naval Staff, he reestablished and strengthened the firm rules of a decade before drawing up staff requirements and sketch designs under the close supervision of the First Sea Lord. Chatfield defined his general role thus in a passage worth quoting in full:

The First Sea Lord's office work is largely that of making final decisions, or in certain matters recommendations to the First Lord. In all technical matters he is the final arbiter. Not that it is necessary for the other Sea Lords to refer matters, within their separate administrative tasks, to the First Sea Lord. They are independent, and except perhaps for the Deputy Chief of Naval Staff and Assistant Chief of Naval Staff, they are responsible to the First Lord only. But the First Sea Lord is the experienced leader, who stands behind them and to whom they will come in person, or to whom they will mark the paper under consideration should they be in doubt, or if the problem be of great importance. Such problems may be material ones, affecting the design or production of ships, or their equipment; personal problems affecting the men of the Fleet; problems of pay, fuel or stores; or the constant ones affecting the development of Naval Air Power. When big technical decisions are brought to him, the First Sea Lord must fall back on his wealth of experience to guide him to the right answer—he at any rate has none to whom he can pass them, for as the supreme technical authority he stands so to speak, with his back to the wall.[6]

Restoring morale in the Fleet had to be Chatfield's first priority, and he introduced the custom of the Board appearing in the Fleet in uniform to show the solidarity with the officers and men. This was backed up by dealing with the worst grievances on pay and pensions. Chatfield's own reputation was also a great help. Perhaps uniquely in a backbiting service suffering exceptional stresses, he seems rarely if ever to have been the subject of personal criticism in the Wardroom, or even on the Messdecks.[7]

Having set service morale on the road to recovery, Chatfield could set to work on three policy priorities: building the battlefleet, improving the cruiser fleet in both quality and quantity, and restoring the Fleet Air Arm to complete naval control. Only the cruiser question could be addressed quickly. The Americans and Japanese were exploiting a loophole in the London Treaty of 1930 to build large light cruisers of 10,000 tons that promised to outclass the contemporary British Leander design. Chatfield insisted that the British should build more powerful Southampton class ships.[8]

Chatfield was happy to build smaller cruisers should other powers agree, but he was determined to return cruiser numbers from the London limit of fifty to seventy after 1936. In the Ministerial Committee discussing the forthcoming London Conference, he put it thus to the Prime Minister, MacDonald, who was supporting a Foreign Office compromise figure of sixty vessels: "Supposing we agree, and you build up our cruiser strength too slowly, and in 1939 you say to me 'war is imminent' and I reply 'we are not ready for war, I cannot defend our trade routes.' What would your position be then?"[9] It was duly agreed that British policy should aim at seventy cruisers. Chatfield had both the strength of character to stand up to politicians and the skill to put questions in terms that they found it hard to gainsay.

The same occurred with battleships. Chatfield knew that he had a difficult job given the anti-battleship propaganda of both naval heretics and the air lobby. Both Monsell and the Naval Staff were pessimistic that Chatfield could succeed, but the First Sea Lord was both adamant and confident. As he later put it: "To have a conviction, based on intimate knowledge and the determination to convince others, is bound to bring success in time."[10] Chatfield began a campaign of speeches in which he made the case for higher defence expenditure and a rebuilt battlefleet. This public campaign was perhaps beyond "the customary discretion of the leaders of the Services," but Chatfield regarded it as constitutional and necessary in the serious circumstances. He even took what was for him the extreme measure of writing to the *Times* over the pseudonym "1934" to counter a letter by Admiral Richmond favoring smaller vessels. Against this background, Macdonald, who had been greatly impressed by Richmond's theories, was persuaded that a ship of at least 25,000 tons and armed with twelve-inch guns was necessary for the security of the Empire. In the meantime he obtained authorization to modernise the four existing capital ships that would be required to remain in service the longest.[11]

Before the new conference had opened, Chatfield played a leading role in concluding the Anglo-German Naval Agreement of 1935. He felt that "unless the Governments of this country and France were prepared to use force to stop German rearmament it was wisest to effect this naval agreement for the possibilities it gave of controlling the threat of an armament race both in numbers and sizes of ships throughout Europe."[12] A Navy of 35 percent the size of the Royal Navy might be contained with an affordable British Fleet that could also deal with the threat of Japan. Chatfield was also in favor of qualitative restrictions to diminish the burden of rearmament. Such was the basis of the London Treaty of 1936 whose successful outcome was in large part due to Chatfield's "inexhaustible patience and skill in negotiation."[13] The First Sea Lord worked hand in glove with Robert Craigie, the Foreign Office's naval expert. Chatfield took greater charge of the technical side of the London negotiations than might have been expected because of the necessity to send the able Deputy Director of Plans, Captain V. H. Danckwerts, to sea.[14]

American pressure at London had enlarged the battleship limits to 35,000 tons and fourteen-inch guns. Chatfield was determined that ships to this specification should be started as soon as possible. He had got a commitment to rebuild the battlefleet put into the 1935 Defence White Paper, but he was worried that the continued campaign against battleships in press and parliament might cause a policy reversal. The First Sea Lord prevailed on Sir Bolton Eyres Monsell to persuade Stanley Baldwin to set up the Vulnerability of Capital Ships (VCS) Committee chaired by Sir Thomas Inskip, the Minister for Coordination of Defence, to enquire into the weakness of capital ships if exposed to air attack. Chatfield and Sir Edward Ellington, the Chief of Air Staff, were appointed as "Expert Advisors" and the First Sea Lord took a leading role, relishing the opportunity to cross-examine the various opponents of the capital ship who appeared before the committee.[15]

Chatfield's ability to encapsulate arguments for politicians was also crucial. Returning with a committee member, Lord Halifax, from the Derby in time for an evening meeting of the VCS Committee, Chatfield put it thus:

> If we rebuild the battlefleet and spend many millions in doing so, and then the war comes and the airmen are right, and all our battleships are rapidly destroyed by air attack, our money will have been largely thrown away. But if we do not rebuild it and war comes and the airman is wrong and our airmen cannot destroy the enemy's capital ships, and they are left to range with impunity on the world's oceans and destroy our convoys, then we shall lose the British Empire.[16]

This wording was used in the committee's report. Its findings were a triumph for Chatfield. He had been able to convince the committee that the Admiralty was not ignoring the air menace but had a rational case based on hard evidence to support the construction of a new generation of battleships. He neutralized the Air Ministry by obtaining their agreement that the number of bombers that could be built for the price of a new battleship was only forty-three and by obtaining an admission from the Chief of the Air Staff that although the battleship might eventually become obsolete, that time had not yet arrived. Chatfield overstated his case both as regards the effectiveness of anti-aircraft and anti-submarine measures were concerned, but it was necessary to do so to win the argument. Moreover, this closely reflected the view of the contemporary Fleet Commanders, including those who were actually in danger of air attack.[17] Certainly, without the resulting "King George Vs," the Royal Navy would have been unable to contain the German surface fleet a few years later.

As Chairman of the Chiefs of Staff Sub-Committee and a member of the CID, Chatfield played the key professional role in developing the entire rearmament programme. Lord Hankey, the Cabinet Secretary who had set up the COS system a decade before, wrote to Chatfield in 1938 about the First Sea Lord's importance to the COS Committee:

> [It had not] reached maturity before you took charge of it and I have sat at your feet with growing admiration of that combination of initiative, tact and fearlessness with which you steered it through the conflicting currents service needs and political expediency. It is now much more than the mainspring of the C.I.D. as I conceived it. You have made it an important factor in foreign policy to which it has brought a spirit of realism without a suggestion of aggressive militarism.[18]

Chatfield suggested the strong conclusion to the COS's 1933 Report stating plainly that the armed forces could not, as they stood, accept their current responsibilities and asked for revised instructions. He put it to the CID and this led directly to the first Defence Requirements Committee (DRC), which held its initial meeting in November 1933. It reported four months later on those deficiencies that needed most urgent remedy, and Chatfield could be happy at the emphasis on dealing with naval problems. Unfortunately, however, the Cabinet gave disproportionate attention to the Royal Air Force in its decisions on expenditure. Chatfield and his colleagues maintained pressure for a more comprehensive approach, and the DRC met again in late 1934 to make suggestions without regard to financial constraints. Chatfield insisted that naval rearmament be given due priority and the DRC duly called for a "New Standard of Naval Strength," effectively a new two-power standard. The government would not go as far, but it was willing to sanction building to an expanded one-power "DRC standard."[19] Indeed Chatfield's Board unofficially took as much financial rope as it could in its post-DRC programmes to move towards the "New Standard."[20]

The government's unwillingness to make proper naval provision made it particularly infuriating when, far from diminishing the number of potential enemies, it seemed intent on adding to them, as in the Ethiopian crisis of 1935-36. Chatfield regarded an Italian Ethiopia as a positive strategic advantage that would make the Italian empire more vulnerable to British pressure. He was most reluctant to risk precious ships—even in a victorious war against Italy—given the effects of any losses on Britain's capacity to defend itself and the Empire from the real threats of Japan and Germany. Moreover a friendly, or at least neutral, Italy was a sine qua non for any credible strategy of imperial defense on current, or even projected, resources. Chatfield loyally organized the naval buildup against Britain's former ally, but his worst fears proved justified, and subsequent attempts to rebuild a good relationship with Benito Mussolini, which Chatfield thoroughly supported, proved fruitless.[21]

The same logic drove Chatfield's attitude toward the Spanish Civil War. Like most naval personnel he had no love for the Republicans, who had murdered their officers and driven refugee nuns into British ships in the opening days of the war. He regarded Franco's cause as "noble" and wished to grant the Nationalists belligerent rights. As Temple Patterson put it, Chatfield "deliberately stressed or even exaggerated" the effectiveness of the Nationalist blockade "in order to reduce the risk of our adding to our problems and enemies at a time when he was concerned above anything else that we should remain at peace until our forces were stronger."[22] At Nyon in 1937, however, he and Captain Tom Phillips, his Director of Plans, took the lead in drawing up plans for tough international action to deal with the attacks by Italian submarines on merchant shipping. Foreign Secretary Anthony Eden wrote to Prime Minister Neville Chamberlain about the First Sea Lord: "Chatfield has been of the greatest help possible to us in all this business. . . . All the foreigners have been delighted with him. Indeed he is something of a hero of the ideal British naval type."[23]

Perhaps Chatfield's greatest individual victory during his period as First Sea Lord came in 1937 with the decision to begin a two-year programme to bring the Fleet Air Arm (FAA) under full naval control. This was the only battle which gave him "real anxiety," and it began in 1934 when Chatfield ordered an internal enquiry to look into the workings of dual control.[24] Its critical report formed the basis of a long paper presented by Chatfield to the Board in May 1935. It contained a draft memorandum to the Cabinet that was communicated over Monsell's signature to the Prime Minister, but neither Ramsay Macdonald nor his successor Baldwin would allow Cabinet discussion of its findings. Indeed, Baldwin specifically ruled out reopening the control question and ordered that interdepartmental discussions on manning questions alone be chaired by Hankey. The Air Ministry was predictably obstructive, and it took until early 1936 before it agreed even to consider manning concessions. Then, in March 1936, a neutral arbiter appeared on the scene when Inskip was appointed Minister for the Coordination of Defence.[25]

Inskip showed a willingness to investigate the Admiralty's problems and on 1 May 1936 promised to investigate the manning difficulties without prejudice to the examination of the wider issue of control at a later date. Chatfield's role increased still further when Monsell resigned in June, after writing to Inskip of the "very strong" views of his colleagues on the air issue.[26] Monsell, a former naval officer, had been virtually Chatfield's political agent. Sir Samuel Hoare was a more prominent politician and, to boot, a former Air Minister who was closely associated with the system his department was now trying to destroy. Hoare could not take such a forward position, but he did give Chatfield good political advice on the most telling arguments and was soon fully converted to the naval case, becoming as loyal and well-informed a minister as Chatfield as could have wished for. Chatfield recognised the need to move step by step. He had no intention of accepting the limited conclusions of Inskip's inquiry but hoped that it would convert the Minister for Co-ordination to the Admiralty point of view, as it did.

In his report to Baldwin on 3 November, Inskip wrote: "I cannot say that situation is as yet satisfactory or that my recommendations are likely to make it so."[27]

This was Chatfield's moment to cease maneuvering and open fire. On 16 November he wrote a strongly worded paper to Hoare. Inskip's report, the First Sea Lord insisted, was not "an adequate solution of the problems confronting the Admiralty." The work of the Fleet's aircraft, Chatfield asserted, was second only in importance to the fighting of its guns, and divided responsibility had led to inefficiency and weakness. If the Fleet failed in action because of this, the Admiralty, and not the Air Ministry, would be blamed. Only the transfer of the naval aviation to the Admiralty "at the earliest possible date" would solve the problem. Hoare sent Chatfield's demarche to Baldwin and Inskip three days later and placed his own support behind it, saying it reflected the deeply held views of the Fleet as a whole.[28]

Swinton, the Air Minister, was willing to make only the narrowest of concessions on the manning question and Chatfield therefore saw Hoare again and threatened resignation. The First Lord responded by recommending that Chatfield meet Baldwin and suggest to the Prime Minister that a proper investigation was a political necessity. Baldwin was coming under pressure from the press and backbenches to solve the problem on the Admiralty's terms. Chatfield seems to have had little to do with initiating this directly, as he wanted to avoid the charges of backstairs lobbying that had been held against the Admiralty in its campaigns of the previous decade. The key figure here was Admiral of the Fleet Sir Roger Keyes, a Member of Parliament (MP), who had orchestrated the campaign on his own initiative. He was able to obtain the telling support of Churchill, who normally took a pro-RAF line. Chatfield decided it was important to keep Churchill on board and wrote to him in flattering terms: "To have found a real champion of our cause, which we have been fighting for so many years in the House of Commons and one who . . . carries such weight in the country on such matters, is something for which we have long hoped, but so far only hoped in vain." While Chatfield offered Churchill further contacts, he nonetheless wished to keep his contacts with the backbench critic as secret as possible.[29]

Chatfield spoke plainly to the Prime Minister when he saw him on 11 February 1937. The deep feeling in the Fleet and the seriousness of the situation, the First Sea Lord said, demanded open and straightforward speaking. The present situation of deadlock between the Navy and the RAF was jeopardizing national security. The Navy had tried loyally to make the Balfour system work but had been unable to do so. Chatfield could not do his job of ensuring the efficiency of the Navy, and he was failing in the eyes of the Fleet, where there was a deep sense of injustice. "There is a feeling," Chatfield said, "that everyone has a right to have their grievances investigated and they cannot understand my personal failure in this matter and that I still remain in my post." He claimed always to have acted constitutionally, and despite his secret contacts with Churchill, claimed to have discouraged the campaign in press and parliament. The FAA was dangerously short of personnel and deficient in matériel because of an impossible administrative system. He concluded:

Therefore sir, I feel that my position as First Sea Lord has become intolerable and unless an immediate enquiry is held I shall lose the confidence of the Service, the situation in the Fleet will grow steadily worse and good feeling between the Services—which I have tried for many years to foster—will become impossible. I therefore ask you for an immediate and impartial enquiry.[30]

Chatfield's resignation would have been very damaging and Baldwin had little alternative but to concede a ministerial enquiry. Terms of reference were agreed to, but on 11 March Hoare told Chatfield that Lord Weir was threatening to resign as an advisor to the government if the enquiry was held. A preliminary investigation was, therefore, to be held at the Chiefs of Staff level. Hoare urged Chatfield to accept this, but the First Sea Lord said this was "quite useless" and merely a waste of time.[31] It took a meeting with the Chancellor of the Exchequer Neville Chamberlain, the Chief of the Air Staff and Lord Hankey, who all pleaded with Chatfield to get them off the hook, to do so. Reluctantly, Chatfield conceded, but only as long as Inskip was in the chair; he would be in a position to present his own position to the ministerial inquiry, if and when it met, thus shortening its deliberations.

The COS met three times in April and May, and Chatfield won the argument, but further delay was caused by the resignation of Baldwin and the ensuing government reshuffle. Chatfield was frustrated in the extreme at losing the loyal Hoare and having to brief yet another First Lord, Duff Cooper, on the Admiralty's case. After some Admiralty prodding, Inskip wrote on 23 June that the inquiry would meet on 2 July. Two days later a phone call from Inskip's office abruptly called it off. Clearly, the RAF lobby was once more causing problems. Chatfield was facing perhaps the biggest crisis of his career. On 28 June he presented his ultimatum to Duff Cooper. He had been patient, he wrote, "my critics will no doubt feel . . . unduly so," but if the enquiry were not held before the summer recess, it would "no longer be justifiable for me to continue as First Sea Lord."[32]

Duff Cooper saw Chamberlain, Inskip, and Swinton, and the Minister for Coordination of Defence promised to make an immediate report on his own. It was ready by 20 July when Inskip received a further written prod from the First Sea Lord; Inskip was able to telephone Chatfield that he need not worry. The following day judgment was handed down; the FAA would pass to the Admiralty, but shore-based maritime aircraft would stay with the RAF. Chatfield had for some time been prepared to accept this as the best available deal. If he refused, "the whole matter would have been put back in the melting pot. Time was urgent and the Navy could not wait."[33] Moreover, Chatfield genuinely hoped that the better relations that would ensue with the RAF would help solve the real problems with Coastal Command. Chamberlain did not like having his hand forced by the First Sea Lord, but the Cabinet had little alternative but to give in.[34] It was a remarkable tribute to Chatfield's strength of will, his powers of argument, his political sense, and not least the remarkable moral ascendancy he had achieved over his contemporaries.

This was to continue to be tested. In June 1937 the Cabinet had fixed a "ration" of £1,500 million for defense over five years. Chatfield was against rationing, as regards both the inadequate overall amount and the potential losses to the Navy that direct competition with the RAF for a fixed sum of money implied. Chatfield had always insisted that Britain's diplomatic coat should be cut to the cloth of its military strength. In several appearances in 1937-38, with impeccable strategic reasoning, he urged short-term political settlements, if these were possible, with Germany and Japan, while Britain rearmed to the point where it could deter these members of the Anti-Comintern Pact from embarking upon war.[35] In January 1938 Chatfield obtained an agreement from the COS that Britain would have to reduce its number of enemies or reduce its social services to allow proper servicing of the armament program. This was felt to be too political for the service chiefs formally to minute, but Chatfield sent a private letter on these lines to Inskip with a copy to Duff Cooper.[36]

Chatfield called for the leaders of all the parties to be called together to discuss the situation and take a national decision, above party affiliations.

We are living dangerously and risking everything that our fathers won for us. If we surrender to some extent our idealism we can still use our influence by friendship instead of by criticism. Can it be doubted that leadership to the country on these lines would find a response in our very practical race?

Duff Cooper minuted that he doubted "it would prove possible to persuade the opposition that there are only two alternatives," but Inskip was probably more impressed. Although the meeting of party leaders did not take place, the policy of trying to reduce enemies was more assiduously pursued by the Chamberlain government in 1938.[37]

Chatfield continued his opposition to rationing which came to a head in July. He produced a well argued memorandum for Duff Cooper indicating that as safe *long-term* settlements with Germany or Japan were impossible, the strength of the Navy—a more long term matter than that of the Air Force—had to be safeguarded. If the Foreign Office believed it was safe to do so, reductions in the naval program might be possible, although not as many as required by the Treasury. Rationing as it stood, with money going down the bottomless pit of bomber parity at the Navy's expense, was unacceptable. This was put to the Cabinet by Duff Cooper, and a meeting was arranged for Chatfield, the First Lord, the Chancellor, and Inskip. At the price of sacrificing a destroyer flotilla to obtain fast minelayers, Chatfield obtained an extra £55 million for Admiralty programs. Chatfield has been especially criticized for sacrificing the destroyer flotilla, but it could not have been built for some time and was blatantly surplus to the DRC standard. Moreover, having it in the program would have made no difference to the wartime Fleet.[38]

Chatfield left behind the best possible Navy that any First Sea Lord of the period could have achieved. Existing ships were being modernized, a comprehensive plan of new construction was underway, and the operational Fleet was at a high level of fighting efficiency. Its capabilities against the new threats of submarine and aircraft were undoubtedly overestimated. For example, Chatfield was convinced that existing anti-submarine measures were about eighty percent effective. (He was later big enough to admit that he had, therefore, not put enough stress on the submarine menace and that this had been a factor in his accepting the return of the Irish ports).[39] This reflected a fundamental weakness in Chatfield's philosophy of the dominance of the skilled user; in peacetime, the skilled user's experience was inevitably somewhat artificial. The anti-submarine reports were full of glowing stories of submarines being "pinged" by asdic. Who was the Admiralty to say this was wrong and that the submarine was still a serious problem? The fleets sent back glowing reports of anti-aircraft successes against "Queen Bee" targets. Who was Chatfield to argue that the ships required better high-angle fire control, especially as there were problems in developing the system and it would be even more expensive and hard to produce than the existing equipment? Chatfield's own personal honesty and almost naive belief in the effectiveness of the naval system that had worked so well for him made it unthinkable that these results might have been exaggerated for reasons of branch or fleet self-interest.

Lord Chatfield (he had been ennobled in the previous year) left the Admiralty on 10 August 1938. After being sent out to reorganize Indian defense, he was appointed to replace Inskip as Minister for the Coordination of Defence, in January 1939. Chatfield became a member of Chamberlain's War Cabinet in September until maneuvered out in April 1940 by Churchill. Chatfield, the consummate professional, had always had an uneasy relationship with Churchill, the intuitive amateur. This dated back to before the First World War and an incident on board *Lion*.[40] Although Chatfield had continued to cultivate the government's main backbench critic on rearmament in the late 1930s, giving Churchill special access to anti-submarine trials, engaging in detailed correspondence on Asdic secrets, and even putting his rather strange suggestions through the Naval Staff for comment, the last thing Churchill wanted in office was professional military advice of such political stature.

Chatfield's career demonstrated the power of a straight and upright man with a complete belief in the system of which he was a part. Admiral Sir Thomas Jerram always found him "the soul of probity" and, although he was not entirely humorless, Ernle Chatfield took life very seriously. He had a very "correct" view of how business should be conducted and was intensely loyal both to the service and to his colleagues. Chatfield was always popular and trusted by the service as a whole, and his contemporaries regarded him as "the embodiment of all that was admirable in the naval officer of his day." He firmly believed in the wisdom of authority, both over subordinates and over outside "experts," whom he disliked intensely as being, by definition, ill-informed and irresponsible. Conversely, he got on exceptionally well with permanent heads of government departments, and his correspondence reveals a real friendship with Sir Warren Fisher at the Treasury and Sir Robert Vansittart at the Foreign Office. When he could not put his ideas directly to other ministers in the key departments, he could get their most senior advisors to have a word with them in the Admiralty interest.[41]

Chatfield fitted the Whitehall culture very well. Reserved by nature, he always held himself somewhat aloof, especially when his powers of intense concentration were devoted to the job in hand. Chatfield could weigh both sides of an argument, but he always retained his naval officer's knack for quick decisions and the ability to stick by them. Most important of all, he had a remarkable natural ability to express himself clearly and concisely, both on paper and in speech. In all, Ernle

Chatfield was more than one of the most effective First Sea Lords ever. As Admiral Sir John Kelly wrote to him from retirement in 1936:

[S]uch a Chief as the Navy has not had in my lifetime. I could always feel with confidence that whatever I put up to you would get not only a good but a sympathetic hearing and that if it was refused the refusal would have irrefutable reason behind it. . . . [Y]ou are a great man, how great the modesty innate in your nature will never allow you to recognise.[42]

NOTES

1. Chatfield left a two-volume autobiography, *The Navy and Defence* (London: Heinemann, 1942) and *It Might Happen Again* (London: Heinemann, 1947). Following Chatfield's death, Professor E. Temple Patterson wrote an authorized biography ("Hand on the Torch, The Life of Admiral of the Fleet Lord Chatfield of Ditchling" based on Chatfield's papers before they were deposited in the National Maritime Museum. This was never published, but the late Professor Temple Patterson very kindly passed both the manuscript and his notes to me when I was working on a biography, which is, alas, still incomplete.

2. Chatfield, *The Navy*, 217-52. The evolution in battle instructions can be traced in ADM 186/72 and ADM 186/106. Mediterranean Fleet exercises are covered in ADM 186/148. The Temple Patterson typescript has an interesting section on Invergordon, 185-87.

3. Letter Kelly to Chatfield, 1 Dec. 1932, CHT 4/6.

4. Letter to Monsell, 3 July 1932, CHT 2/1.

5. The Admiralty discussion is in ADM 1/9086. Chatfield's papers connected with the question are in CHT 3/3. See also his correspondence with Sir John Kelly (who supported the scheme) in CHT 4/6.

6. Chatfield, *It Might Happen Again*, 48-49.

7. Letter from Sir John Kelly, 30 July 1936, CHT 4/61; list of improvements in pay and conditions of service, CHT 3/1.

8. They were originally to have been called "Minatours". For their rationale, see contemporary correspondence with the Commanders-in-Chief in CHT 4. See also Chatfield, *It Might Happen Again*, 61-62.

9. *It Might Happen Again*, 65-66.

10. Ibid., 67.

11. Clipping of the letter published on 20 March 1934 is in the Chatfield papers and bears all the hallmarks of the First Sea Lord's normal arguments. See also Chatfield, *It Might Happen Again*, 67-70 and ADM 116/2999.

12. Chatfield, *It Might Happen Again*, 75.

13. Roskill, *Naval Policy*, 2:321.

14. Letter to Backhouse of 27 March 1936, CHT 4/1.

15. Chatfield, *It Might Happen Again*, 95-98. The files of the Vulnerability of Capital Ships (VCS) Committee are to be found in CAB 16/147 and ADM 116/4324.

16. Chatfield, *It Might Happen Again*, 35.

17. See especially Admiral W. W. Fisher's remarkable letter of 6 March 1936, where he refers to the prospect of an attack by a formation of Italian SM-81 bombers as a "pleasant dream"; CHT4/3. Surprisingly, Fisher was actually on Chatfield's list of witnesses.

18. Letter from Hankey to Chatfield, 3 June 1938, CHT 3/1.

19. For COS discussion on the 1933 report, see CAB 53/4. For the first DRC, see CAB 16/109 and ADM 116/3434-6, and for the second, see CAB 16/112. The matter is covered in Roskill, *Naval Policy*, 2:167-72, 216-19. See also the Official History of rearmament, N.H. Gibbs, *Grand Strategy*, vol 1, *Rearmament Policy* (London: HMS0, 1976).

20. The origins of the "DRC standard" in 1934 (not, as is often stated, 1932) are clearly set out in ADM 116/2999. It was drafted by Captain E. L. S. King, Chatfield's Director of Plans at the time. Gordon, *British Sea Power*, shows clearly the extent of Admiralty pressure against the boundaries of Treasury control.

21. For the clearest expression of Chatfield's views on Ethiopia, see his letter to Admiral Dreyer of 16 Sept. 1935, CHT 4/4. Roskill, *Naval Policy*, 2:248-83, has a full account of the Royal Navy's part in the crisis and Chatfield's role.

22. Patterson, "Hand on the Torch", 255. The reference to the "nobler" cause comes from a letter to Backhouse, C-in-C Mediterranean Fleet, 16 Feb. 1937. Chatfield also predicted a Nationalist victory.

23. Lord Avon, *Facing the Dictators* (London: Cassell, 1962), 468-69.

24. Chatfield, *It Might Happen Again*, 102.

25. "Papers relating to the Fleet Air Arm", CHT 3/6, including a most useful chronology which Chatfield used as the basis for his published account. The initial Admiralty papers are in Board Minutes and Memoranda, ADM 167/90.

26. Chronology in CHT 3/6.

27. Ibid.

28. Copy in CHT 3/6.

29. Letter to Churchill of 5 May 1936. Chatfield marked a subsequent letter, "Please keep secret that I have corresponded with him" when he circulated it to the Naval members of the Board.

30. Chatfield took notes and wrote an aide memoire after the interview. These are in CHT 3/6.

31. Chronology in CHT 3/6.

32. Chronology and copy of Memo are in CHT 3/6. The Admiralty and Air Ministry submissions and the COS inquiry are in COS 571 and 572 in CAB 53/31.

33. Chronology in CHT 3/6.

34. Chronology and also correspondence with Duff Cooper on the Cabinet discussion, including Chatfield's pained views of 3 August 1937 on the Prime Minister's adverse comments on the Admiralty's approach to interservice cooperation, are in CHT 3/6.

35. There are three papers on Chatfield's views on the world situation that he sent to the First Lord on 22 July 1937 in CHT 3/1.

36. His views by the beginning of 1938 can be seen in comments forwarding a paper by Phillips, his Director of Plans, in ADM 116/3631 and ADM 205/80.

37. Copy in CHT 3/1.

38. Chatfield, *It Might Happen Again*, 119-20; Roskill, *Naval Policy*, 2:421-26. Gibbs, *Rearmament Policy*, 345-55, contains a full account of the Cabinet discussions.

39. Patterson "Hand on the Torch," 273, quotes Compton MacKenzie on having gained this admission from Lord Chatfield after the war. In his letter to Churchill (see note 29 above) Chatfield claimed 80 percent effectiveness for the Fleet's anti-submarine methods. He later convinced Churchill that this was true following a trip to sea; see letter to Chatfield of 18 June 1938. Correspondence with Backhouse in 1936 (letter of 17 June 1936 in CHT 4/1) reveals equal confidence about the air menace once the fleet was equipped with proper anti-aircraft armament.

40. Correspondence with C. P. Brown, Chatfield's former Flag Lieutenant. See also Chatfield, *The Navy*, 107-8.

41. The correspondence in the Chatfield papers clearly shows this.

42. Letter from Kelly to Chatfield, 30 July 1936, CHT 4/6.

12

Admiral Sir Roger Roland Charles Backhouse (1938–1939)

Malcolm H. Murfett

Chatfield's departure as First Sea Lord was bound to be felt by the Admiralty. His successor, Admiral Sir Roger Backhouse, was nearly sixty years of age, a tireless workaholic who was devoted to the service, which he had joined as a cadet at Dartmouth forty-six years before. On the whole, Backhouse's short tenure at the Admiralty as First Sea Lord usually fails to get much attention or critical acclaim from historians. According to conventional wisdom, Backhouse cut a disappointing figure, both as First Sea Lord and as CNS. He has been described unflatteringly as a weak and indecisive leader who singularly failed to offer his staff any operational guidance. Correlli Barnett dismissed him as the "arch centraliser" and intimated that he was either incapable or unwilling to delegate powers to those in authority around him.[1] This relatively poor assessment of his qualities may be more than a little unfair to the man who was known affectionately throughout the Royal Navy as "RB." Although he may indeed have been dedicated to matériel, he was still a highly intelligent and opinionated First Sea Lord. He was not afraid, for instance, to depart radically from orthodox strategic planning on a number of sensitive issues and was prepared to implement reforms to the administrative structure of the Admiralty.

Apart from being a "five-oner" and a gunnery expert with vast experience of command at sea, RB had also spent over three years on the Admiralty Board as a very successful Third Sea Lord and Controller.[2] At six feet, four inches, in height, fit and lean, he could be said to have had a commanding physical presence. Despite the fact that he had great personal charm, he could also on occasion be extremely withering with those who had made mistakes; he generally had little time for fools and was known to be something of a slave driver.

Nonetheless, because he was not a hypocrite, never spared himself and was a genuinely fair person, RB was well respected throughout the service and was a popular choice to succeed Chatfield, which he did in August 1938.[3]

Within a month he found himself caught up in the traumas of the Munich season as the British government cast around with some desperation for an acceptable answer to the *Sudetendeutsch* problem of September 1938. A war against Germany, which loomed large at this time, was something about which neither the Chiefs of Staff nor the Commonwealth Dominions were enthusiastic. Indeed, severe caution was expressed by them as an initial decision for war by Hitler could end up in pulling in other powers (most notably Italy and possibly Japan) to assist him in forming a fascist axis against the democracies. If this, admittedly worst-case, scenario did take place, the British would be faced by an array of enemy military forces that far exceeded their own. Backhouse realised that the British were in a highly vulnerable position and much preferred to see a political settlement to this crisis, if one could be obtained, rather than resort to war at this time to resolve matters.

His political chief, Alfred Duff Cooper, was well aware of British military weakness but did not agree with Neville Chamberlain's policy of appeasing Germany in order to preserve peace in Europe at any price. Duff Cooper, who had been a surprising success as First Lord of the Admiralty, reacted angrily to the Munich settlement and announced his resignation in early October after the terms of that agreement were made known. Backhouse admired his chief's action in sticking to his principles and regretted his departure since they had formed a useful working relationship in the little time they had had together.[4]

For his part, the Prime Minister was relieved by Duff Cooper's decision. He had proved to be a difficult adversary as First Lord, not least in fighting an enterprising battle with Sir John Simon and Inskip over proposed cuts in the Admiralty estimates.[5] By choosing his friend, the seventh Earl of Stanhope, as First Lord, Chamberlain was hoping he would get a more malleable figure who would accept the need for restraint in the rearmament process and who would share his belief in the wonders of appeasement. Ironically, the fact that Stanhope was largely only a figurehead with little real knowledge of naval matters, ensured that RB took a far more active role as First Sea Lord than he might have had Duff Cooper remained at his post after Munich.

One of Backhouse's first tasks once the Czech crisis had blown over was to establish the Binney Committee (consisting of Vice Admiral T. H. Binney, Rear Admiral L. H. Holland, and Sir Sidney Barnes) to look into the organization of the Naval Staff and make recommendations for a series of reforms to that body. Backhouse felt that the recent crisis had exposed crucial flaws in the administrative structure of the Admiralty, not least in its inflexibility in adapting from a peacetime environment to one of war. Moreover, the First Sea Lord knew from bitter firsthand experience that the existing organizational system was unsound and that work loads among the senior figures on the Naval Staff differed widely and unjustifiably. Both the DCNS and he himself, for instance, had been grossly overstretched throughout the duration of the September crisis and often in urgent need of qualified assistance, while the ACNS (whose duties did not cover either operations or plans) had performed a largely anonymous role throughout that entire episode.[6] RB's criticisms went even further; he was convinced, for example, that the peacetime role of the Naval Staff was basically unsound.

It has led to Plans Division being heavily overburdened and to D.C.N.S. being responsible for every detail connected with War Plans and Operations, not only of the Fleet but of local defence and shipping besides. It is impossible for one man to find time to deal thoroughly with all the great questions involved, in addition to much current work which must be done. . . . No First Sea Lord could get through his work in the Chiefs of Staffs Sub-Committee and the C.I.D. as well as in the Admiralty without properly constituted powers to act for him in addition to the D.C.N.S., who is necessarily fully occupied with current work.[7]

When the Binney Committee issued its authoritative report at the end of October 1938 it made a number of important recommendations that would affect the structure and distribution of Admiralty staff work, including the separation of the Local Defence Section from the Plans Division and its formation into a new division dealing with anti-submarine work, boom defense, minesweeping, and harbor defense among other things. It also put forward a case for merging the existing Training and Staff Duties Division with the Tactical Division and allowed for an increase in both the numbers and status of some Naval Staff appointments. Of all those officials elevated in importance, the ACNS became the most conspicuous beneficiary—a fact recognized in his reassignment to the Admiralty Board in the autumn of 1939. Although these reforms were hardly of a root-and-branch type, they did bring about an improvement in administrative efficiency within the Admiralty. Rather than setting up the Binney Committee to increase his own powers, therefore, Backhouse had used it as a means of delegating and decentralizing policy-making as much as possible.[8]

Contrary to the now-fashionable view that he became enmired in the minutiae of policy implementation and was far more of a tactician than a strategist, Backhouse was prepared to take the long view and sought to refashion the Royal

Navy's war plans as far as Italy and Japan were concerned. It is clear that the state of British military vulnerability, as exposed by the Munich crisis, had deeply impressed him. These weaknesses had to be urgently addressed. To begin with, while recognizing the importance of maintaining British interests in China, he had little trust in the traditional view of the "Singapore Strategy" and thought it a dangerously impractical plan. Sending the bulk of the fleet out to the Far East for an indefinite period of time in the event of an Anglo-Japanese war remained a nightmarish prospect even if that war was contained and involved no other powers than the two former allies. During the Munich crisis, however, Backhouse found himself uncomfortably having to uphold this long-standing strategic doctrine in conversations he was forced to have with Stanley Bruce, the Australian High Commissioner in London. Agitated by the thought that the Japanese military authorities might use the European situation to their own advantage by embarking on a southward advance, Bruce repeatedly pressed the British government for a reaffirmation of its commitment to the Singapore Strategy.

Under these circumstances, with the High Commissioner coming to the Admiralty on virtually a daily basis in the latter stages of the crisis, Backhouse had little room for maneuver. Although admitting the current weakness of the Royal Navy, he could not unilaterally refute the plan on the grounds of its logistic absurdity and was obliged for diplomatic reasons to cover up his own attitude to its implementation. While endeavoring not to spread false hope of an imminent naval reinforcement of Singapore, RB failed to admit that this plan was in the throes of being overhauled. At a celebrated—perhaps even infamous—meeting at the Admiralty on 1 November 1938, Backhouse, in the presence of Stanhope and Bruce, spoke unequivocally of sending seven capital ships (two Nelsons and five Royal Sovereigns) out to Singapore if an Anglo-Japanese war broke out in the future.[9] Such a disingenuous statement did Backhouse no credit at all, even if it satisfied Bruce for the time being. RB appears to have said what Bruce wanted to hear. Whether he was judicious in the choice of the words he used is, alas, impossible to evaluate since Bruce has left the only written record of this meeting, and he can hardly claim to be an objective witness.[10] Whatever way in which this undertaking was presented, however, the charge that the British deliberately deceived the Australians into believing that the Singapore Strategy was inviolable is not difficult to sustain. In fact, owing to the economies that had been inflicted on the Sembawang Naval Base at the outset, even when it was fully operational (which would not be until the summer of 1940 or later), it would not have the facilities available to cope with more than four capital ships at any one time.

Consequently, what Backhouse knew and the Australians should have guessed was that the old concept of sending the bulk of the fleet to the Far East was a total nonsense and that a revision of this plan was long overdue.[11]

Over a fortnight before his meeting with Bruce on All Saints' Day, Backhouse had made the first move in realigning Admiralty war planning toward a set of more realistic strategic objectives. He had decided to bring Admiral Drax, a naval thinker in the Richmond tradition, out of retirement and offer him a temporary and independent appointment within the Admiralty in the expectation that he would be able to develop a series of war plans for the Royal Navy to contemplate in dealing with the menace posed by the German, Italian, and Japanese fleets across the globe.[12] Admiral Drax's unorthodox views on providing an effective naval defense of British overseas interests had already been submitted to the Admiralty in the past. Although these gratuitous submissions had not been enthusiastically received by the Plans Division at the time, they had remained on file and were to appeal to the new First Sea Lord, who was seeking an alternative thesis to that of the traditionalists.

RB supported the Drax line on rethinking the strategic assumptions underlying the Mediterranean and Far Eastern war plans. He believed that the Mediterranean and Middle East region was an area of growing military and economic importance exceeding that of the Far East. Backhouse was supported in this assessment by the Commander-in-Chief, Mediterranean (and his heir apparent), Admiral Sir Dudley Pound, as well as by the Earl of Stanhope. All felt that at the outset of a European or world war, the Mediterranean would have to be cleared of hostile forces, vital stocks of oil reserves in the Middle East defended, and British interests in the region preserved before any Far Eastern expedition could be mounted.

Naturally enough, if this plan was accepted by the government it would mean fundamentally recasting the Singapore Strategy and almost certainly involve lengthening the period before relief at Singapore well beyond seventy days.[13] Such a development would be momentous and disquieting news for both the Australian and New Zealand Dominions as well as for those charged with defending the British colonies and interests throughout the Far East. Backhouse did try to suggest that a revision of the Singapore Strategy was underway in a message he relayed to Vice Admiral Sir Ragnar M. Colvin, the First Naval Member of the Australian Naval Board, on 9 January 1939.

For myself, I regard any large scale expedition against Australia by the Japanese as most improbable so long as we have a fleet at all. It would be a tremendous undertaking on account of the distances and I cannot imagine that the cautious Japanese would ever attempt it. I am sure it is far beyond their resources while they are so occupied in China.... I might mention again the question of our sending capital ships to the East. At the present time we have none to spare, nor shall we have any in 1939. I do not believe there is the least chance of our having a row with Japan unless we first get involved in Europe, when possibly the Japanese might think the opportunity was good. Even so, we should be able to send some heavy ships to the East, not as many as we should like, but some, which should be able to safeguard our communications in the Indian Ocean and their presence would be sure to have an effect on possible operations by the Japanese against Australia or New Zealand.[14]

By beating a tactical retreat in this manner, Backhouse may not have raised the prestige of the British in the eyes of the Australian government, but at least it may be seen as a belated touch of honesty and candor after a long period in which those particular commodities were in short supply. Although he had no authority to inform the Australian government of Robert Menzies that the Singapore Strategy was at an end, he went as far as he could in indicating that the absolute commitment of the past was being revised. Whether the Australians should have heeded this warning and acted accordingly is still a matter of lively debate.[15]

By this time Backhouse actively opposed the oft-repeated phrase that no anxieties or risks associated with British interests in the Mediterranean should be allowed to interfere with the despatch of the Fleet to the Far East. What might be termed the new Drax-Backhouse school of strategy envisaged a concentration of naval and air power in the Mediterranean at the outset of a war on two or three fronts in a concerted effort to defeat the Italians (its weakest enemy) within a few months.[16] Once that military objective had been achieved and the Italian war machine had been broken in North Africa and the Middle East, the Allies would then be able to turn their collective attention to dealing subsequently with either or both the Germans and the Japanese. In the interim period before the Italians had been removed from the war, Admiral Drax favored relying on small, fast mobile forces to deter the Japanese from interfering and overrunning British interests in the Far East. Drax felt that a "flying squadron" of two battleships or battlecruisers, an aircraft carrier, a cruiser squadron, and a destroyer flotilla would be the ideal striking unit for this purpose. This force could be supplemented by an additional fast carrier to extend its coverage westward to the Indian Ocean and southeastward to the Australasian Dominions.[17]

Despite enjoying Backhouse's tacit support, this new, "practical" scheme had a number of serious deficiencies. Although the "flying squadron" was originally designed to be dispatched to Singapore in response to a sudden emergency arising in the region, such as a declaration of war on the British by the Japanese, it was not expected to fulfill anything more than a short-term holding operation in the Far East. For instance, it was never intended to fight the modern Imperial Japanese Navy [IJN] once it had embarked on its long-awaited *Nanshin-ron*, or southward advance. Instead, its very presence in Singapore was supposed to deter the IJN from committing itself to a full-scale invasion of Southeast Asia. Unfortunately, whatever deterrent value it was supposed to have had rested on the (erroneous) presumption that the "flying squadron" could be supplemented by the bulk of the Royal Navy's latest warships if ever a full-scale engagement threatened to take place between the IJN and its own forces in the South China Sea. In reality it was a scheme that could only work if the Japanese were anxious to avoid facing the might of the Royal Navy and if the state of the European war at that time enabled the British to mount such an operation in the Far East. It did not take much imagination to conceive of a scenario in which neither of these theoretical assumptions would actually work in practice. Far from being cowed by the thought of confronting the British, the IJN might actually relish the opportunity of a full-scale encounter in Southeast Asian waters. Moreover, the British might well take more than a few months to subdue the Italians and drive them from the war. If this proved to be the case, a small British task force in Singapore could hardly be reinforced by sufficient vessels from the Mediterranean, Red Sea, or the Atlantic to cope with either the latent or real threat posed by the Japanese in the Far East. As such, it was difficult to see the "flying squadron" serving as an effective short-term, let alone long-term, deterrent to the IJN. Whatever criticism one might level at the wishful thinking that shrouded this concept, the "flying squadron" also had a serious practical shortcoming in that it would be a tempting target for attack and destruction by enemy forces as it steamed east on its long journey toward Singapore. It should not be forgotten that Backhouse was to level exactly the same criticism at the traditional plan of sending the Main Fleet to the Far East.[18]

Clearly, therefore, the new plan was not much of an improvement, if any, on the old Singapore Strategy. One is tempted to state that the British alone were incapable of coping with the Japanese in a two-front, let alone a three-front, war at this time. Although RB was to succumb to his final illness before he had time to prod the Admiralty and government toward a new strategic doctrine for use in a future war in the East, a truncated derivative of the Drax-Backhouse scheme may be seen as the genesis of the ill-fated Churchillian plan for assisting Malaya and Singapore in December 1941 (Force *Z*). It did not work then, and perhaps the only surprise is that so many people thought it would. While the Drax-Backhouse plan for dealing with the IJN is open to severe and justifiable criticism on the grounds of its impracticability, it nonetheless grasped the essential fact that the British government's strategic priorities badly needed to be overhauled in an era when the Royal Navy was desperately weak.[19]

It is evident that at this time Backhouse, like his predecessor, Chatfield, still regarded the capital ship as the ultimate weapon in the fleet's arsenal. His confidence in its ability to accomplish the tasks it had been designed to fulfill never wavered. He did not seem especially worried about its supposed (and demonstrable) vulnerability to air attack on the high seas, pointing to the recent experience of the Spanish Civil War and the poor bombing record of the air crews against moving vessels in that conflict. As far as Backhouse was concerned, therefore, a balanced fleet was one that contained a strong battleship and battlecruiser component as its spearhead. Although somewhat dismissive of aerial bombardment at sea, he was willing to concede the dangers of an aircraft attack on adequately armed naval or merchant vessels caught at anchor in port or in crowded dock areas, such as those in London, where maneuverability was severely restricted.[20]

Inheriting a situation in which four of his fifteen capital ships were laid up for remodernization until the summer of 1939 and with a destroyer force that contained too many obsolete vessels, Backhouse did not need reminding just how weak the Royal Navy was. He was well aware of the fact that the Admiralty could not afford to succumb to any further austerity measures inflicted on it by the Treasury in the post-Munich period. Apart from taking up the struggle against the government's economizing tendencies, which Duff Cooper had laid aside in October 1938, Backhouse also sought to provide value for money in new construction. In a letter to Sir Thomas Inskip, the Minister for Coordination of Defence, RB referred to the horrendous difficulties that would result from a determined submarine campaign waged in war against the British Fleet by any combination of its German, Italian, and Japanese enemies. After giving the matter considerable thought, he had urged his technical staff to design a new type of vessel—smaller than a destroyer and faster than the existing type of escort vessel, but with a strong anti-aircraft armament, which would make it suitable for anti-submarine work, as well as escort and patrol duties. Backhouse suggested that eight of these new ships, which would be described as escort vessels, could be built within sixteen months, and two more could be ready for service a couple of months later.[21] This new vessel would have the singular financial advantage of costing about £390,000 each—almost half as expensive as that of a modern destroyer. Backhouse informed the Board of Admiralty at its meeting on 17 November 1938 that once the original ten vessels had been built, he would like to lay down a further ten. Warming to his theme, RB spoke of the need to both remedy the shortages of minesweepers and overcome a serious deficiency in aircraft within the Fleet Air Arm. He also pointed out the importance of improving port defenses and of protecting stocks of oil fuel, both at home and abroad.[22]

By the time the Admiralty Board met on 15 December, Backhouse had prepared a memo on new construction for 1939 which recommended the building of two new capital ships, a large aircraft carrier, four large cruisers, two flotillas of destroyers, four submarines, twenty fast escort vessels, three escort vessels of the standard type, ten minesweepers, and an assortment of other craft costing a total of £59,936,000. Defending his building program, Backhouse indicated that since the government had not yet set down an authoritative standard of naval strength, the Admiralty ought to seize the initiative and try to offset the Royal Navy's existing inadequacies by approving his plans to provide a better balanced fleet in the future.[23] It did, but RB knew that formal government acceptance of this new construction programme was quite another matter. He was to live to see just what a tenacious hold the Treasury had over the service departments and the defense estimates when the Admiralty was forced to prune £13.2 million from its departmental estimates and accept the loss of both new battleships and two of the four large cruisers from the programme that he had proposed and Stanhope had endorsed for the 1939 financial year.[24]

Although Backhouse dispaired of the parsimonious actions of Sir John Simon and his Treasury mandarins, he had little doubt that the Admiralty's case for an increased level of rearmament had not been pressed with any intensity by Inskip, the Minister for Coordination of Defence. In a letter to Admiral Sir Frederick Dreyer, the First Sea Lord summed up his feelings about the defence debate in no uncertain terms. "Our machine is too slow and ponderous to compete with the instantaneous decisions of the Dictators, who have no regard for people or money and can do anything they like in their own country without a question."[25] When rumors of Inskip's replacement by Lord Chatfield began to surface in late January 1939, RB received the news with pleasure, content in the knowledge that Chatfield, unlike Inskip, at least knew what the services were actually trying to achieve.[26] This did not mean that Chatfield, who was a highly opinionated and respected minister, could be easily manipulated by the Admiralty in the future, however, as Backhouse and Pound were to discover later to their cost. Backhouse neither appreciated Chatfield's intervention in Far Eastern policy formulation in the spring of 1939, nor his establishment of the Strategic Appreciation Committee (SAC) to vet the changes to the Singapore Strategy that RB wished to see implemented.[27]

Once Hitler had broken his promise to Chamberlain and invaded the rump of Czechoslovakia in mid-March 1939, Backhouse became convinced that appeasement could not be resuscitated and that the only way the British were henceforth going to command any sort of respect in the world was if they increased their military preparations for war—a situation that, in his opinion, would entail the introduction of some form of compulsory national service.[28] Hitler's coup against Czechoslovakia occurred at roughly the same time that Backhouse fell sick with what appeared to be influenza. His condition did not improve and he was eventually diagnosed as having a brain tumor, an illness from which, sadly, he never recovered.[29]

During his brief tenure as First Sea Lord, Backhouse held his own on the COS Committee with Air Chief Marshal Sir Cyril Newall (CAS) and Lieutenant-General Viscount Gort (CIGS), dominated the ineffectual Earl Stanhope at the Admiralty, and surrounded himself with men of talent on the Naval Staff, such as Vice Admiral Sir Andrew Cunningham, whom he appointed as DCNS in October 1938. Despite working virtually ceaselessly, RB enjoyed the executive responsibility which he carried as CNS, was alert to the need for change in naval policy both at home and abroad, and may be said to have had a greater impact on the Royal Navy than has been recognized by military historians in the recent past.

NOTES

1 Admiral John H. Godfrey Papers, vol. 5 (II), Churchill College, Cambridge, 300; vol. 8, 32. Correlli Barnett, *Engage the Enemy More Closely* (New York: W. W. Norton, 1991), 50-51, 554. Arthur J. Marder, *Old Friends New Enemies*, vol. 1, *The Royal Navy and the Imperial Japanese Navy, 1936-1941* (Oxford: Clarendon Press, 1981), 31-32.

2 A "five-oner" meant that he had achieved a first class result in each of the five qualifying examinations for promotion to lieutenant. He achieved this distinction in March 1899. His prowess as a gunnery expert soon won him the Egerton Prize in 1902. After his stint at the Admiralty as Third Sea Lord (November 1928-March 1932), RB took command of the First Battle Squadron, became second in command of the Mediterranean Fleet, and in August 1935 was made Commander-in-Chief, Home Fleet. L. G. Wickham Legg, ed., *Dictionary of National Biography 1931-40* (London: Oxford University Press, 1949), 26-27.

3 Backhouse was not an automatic choice as First Sea Lord. Admiral Sir Dudley Pound could easily have been chosen instead. Ultimately, however, Pound was quite pleased to remain as C-in-C, Mediterranean, Marder, *Old Friends*, 31.

4 Letter Backhouse (hereafter, R.B.) to Admiral Sir Charles M. Forbes, 5 Oct. 1938, ADM 205/3.

5 Malcolm H. Murfett, *Fool-proof Relations: The Search for Anglo-American Naval Cooperation During the Chamberlain Years, 1937-40* (Singapore: Singapore University Press, 1984), 168-72.

6 Letter R.B. to Vice Adm. T. H. Binney, 5 Oct. 1938, ADM 205/3.

7 Minute by R.B., 19 Dec. 1938, C.E.3693.1939, ADM 116/4194.

8 Meeting at the Admiralty, 13 Feb. 1939; Minute by R.B., 20 Feb. 1939, M.07778/39, ADM 116/4194. For other material on the Binney Committee, see the Naval Staff Organisation File for 1938/39, ADM 116/4194.

9 Bruce to Joseph A. Lyons, 1 Nov. 1938, No. 315, cited in R. G. Neale, ed., *Documents on Australian Foreign Policy 1937-49*, vol. 1 (Canberra: Australian War Memorial, 1975), 511-12; Murfett, *Fool-proof*, 210.

10 Backhouse's correspondence with Vice Admiral Sir Percy Noble, the Commander-in-Chief on the China Station, is instructive in revealing his apprehensions about the Japanese and the methods needed to deal with them. See his letters to Noble of 11 Oct. 1938 and 14 Nov. 1938, ADM 205/3.

11 Malcolm H. Murfett, "Living in the Past: A Critical Re-examination of the Singapore Naval Strategy, 1918-1941", *War and Society*, 11, no. 1 (May 1993): 73-103.

12 Letter R.B. to Admiral Sir Reginald Aylmer Ranfurly Plunkett-Ernle-Erle-Drax, 15 Oct. 1938, Drax Papers 2/10, Churchill College, Cambridge. See also ADM 205/3.

13 COS 263rd mtg., 23 Nov. 1938; COS 267th mtg., 13 Jan. 1939; COS 276th mtg., 15 Feb. 1939; COS 281st mtg., 15 Mar. 1939, CAB 2/8.

14 Letter R.B. to Colvin, 9 Jan. 1939, ADM 205/3.

15 Murfett, "Living in the Past," 90-97; David Day, *The Great Betrayal: Britain, Australia and the Onset of the Pacific War, 1939-42* (New York: W. W. Norton, 1989).

16 Letter from R.B. to Vice Admiral Sir Percy Noble, 9 Jan. 1939, ADM 205/3.

17 Drax Papers, O.P.C.11, 15 Mar. 1939, 2/9.

18 Backhouse Paper SAC 4, "The Despatch of a Fleet to the Far East", 28 Feb. 1939; see also the minutes of the Strategic Appreciation Committee on 1 March 1939 and 13 March 1939, CAB 16/209.

19 In a letter to Major-General Hastings Ismay on 18 April 1939, Backhouse wrote revealingly: "I have felt for a long time that the Singapore policy has been overstressed by the particular people who have been mixed up in it all along. The Admiralty Plans Division is absolutely soaked in it! Some day, when I get back, I shall hope to have an opportunity to discuss it all freely with you" . . . It was a vain hope. He never returned to work.

20 House of Commons mtg., on "Bombing and Anti-Aircraft Gunfire Experiments," 8 Feb. 1939, ADM 205/1.

21 Letter from R.B. to Inskip, 13 Oct. 1938; see also Letter R.B. to Vice Admiral G. H. D'O Lyon, 21 Nov. 1938, ADM 205/3.

22 Board of Adm. mtg., 17 Nov. 1938, ADM 167/102. Letters R.B. to Admiral the Earl of Cork and Orrery, 12 Dec. 1938; R.B. to Rear Admiral Alfred E. Evans, 23 Jan. 1939, ADM 205/3.

23 Backhouse was in favor of a fleet containing at least nineteen capital ships. This was the figure that the Committee of Imperial Defence accepted at its meeting on 25 October 1938 as being the optimum size for coping with the threat posed by Germany and Japan. See CID 335th mtg., 25 Oct. 1938, CAB 2/8.

24 Board of Adm. mtg, 15 Dec. 1938, ADM 167/102. For the report of the Finance Committee of 2 Feb. 1939, see ADM 167/103. To follow the exchanges between Stanhope and Simon on this issue see ADM 167/104. See also Murfett, *Fool-proof*, 205-6.
25 Letter R.B. to Dreyer, 29 Jan. 1939, ADM 205/3.
26 Letter R.B. to Admiral Sir Cyril T. M. Fuller, 29 Jan. 1939, ADM 205/3.
27 Letter R.B. to Ismay, 18 Apr. 1939, ADM 205/3.
28 Letter R.B. to Earl Stanhope, 27 Mar. 1939, ADM 205/3.
29 Sadly, his successor as First Sea Lord, Admiral Sir Dudley Pound, was also to be stricken with the very same complaint in 1943.

13

Admiral Sir Dudley Pound (1939–1943)

Robin Brodhurst

Admiral of the Fleet Sir Dudley Pound was not an automatic choice for the position of First Sea Lord. He had no real desire for the job originally, and only ended up at the Admiralty because his predecessor died of a brain tumor. Four and a half years later the same disease was to kill him, one of the very few First Sea Lords to have died in office.

Pound had an exemplary career. He was an outstanding young officer, who was promoted Commander in 1909 at the early age of thirty-two. He served his first spell in the Admiralty, in the Ordnance Department, and made his name as Executive Officer on *Superb*. During the First World War he held three crucial appointments: the first of which was as an extra Naval Assistant to the First Sea Lord, the recalled Fisher, from January to July 1915. He was thus at the center of events in Whitehall when the Fisher-Churchill relationship finally blew up. Although his role was only that of a spectator, he would have seen how not to handle a politician. Second, he commanded a battleship, *Colossus*, at Jutland. Like most other British admirals he remained a battleship man. Third, he was the initial head of the Planning Section in the Admiralty, set up in 1917. Originally this was part of the Operations Division, and when a separate Plans Division was established in the autumn of that year, Pound became Assistant Director of Plans to Roger Keyes, under whom he had already served twice. In all three of these appointments, Pound had shown that he was a highly skilled and professional naval officer, who had already been picked out for rapid promotion. His professional judgment and superior intellect were particularly important for keeping Keyes's enthusiasm in bounds at the Admiralty, and also when the latter moved to Dover.

Between the wars Pound served alternately afloat and at the Admiralty, where he held the posts of Director of Plans, ACNS, and Second Sea Lord; all were crucial positions, and in each of them he performed excellently. As Director of Plans he attended both the Lausanne Conference of 1923 and the Geneva Conference of 1924. He was thus involved in the formulation of not just naval policy, but national policy, under both Conservative and Labour politicians. Similarly, as ACNS, Pound had to attend another Geneva Conference in June 1927 when the DCNS, Field, fell ill, and he attended Cabinet meetings while various decisions were taken. In 1932 he spent six months as the British Naval Representative at the Geneva Disarmament Conference, and he then took office as Second Sea Lord in August. His principal role in this job was to assist in the restoration of morale after the Invergordon Mutiny.

Pound took command of the Mediterranean Fleet after the Abyssinian crisis had quietened down in March 1936. He had been originally due to take over in October 1935 for three years, but the Italian invasion had postponed the changeover. In the summer of 1938 he was summoned home and told that he would be extended one year until March 1940, before retirement. He was delighted by this and, in particular, at not being made First Sea Lord. Instead that office was to be filled by the C-in-C Home Fleet, Sir Roger Backhouse. However, early in May 1939 Pound was informed that Backhouse could not carry on and that he was to take over as First Sea Lord as soon as his relief by Cunningham could be arranged.

The choice of Pound as First Sea Lord has not been without criticism. In particular, Stephen Roskill criticized it in his *Naval Policy Between the Wars*.[1] However, his suggested solution of recalling Chatfield was also problematic. Chatfield had not made an impressive Minister for Coordination of Defence, and the comparison with 1914, of "bringing back Jackie," appealed to no one. Forbes had only just taken over the Home Fleet, and Cunningham did not yet have the experience. Roskill cited Pound as being unfit for duty, but for every neurosurgeon called in evidence by him, Professor Marder can supply another to refute him. Many of those who knew Pound best, such as his staff in the Mediterranean (notably Captain John Litchfield and Captain Charles Norris), were happy with his fitness.[2] He was certainly capable of walking long distances when shooting and then working long hours. As one letter to the editor of the Daily Telegraph in 1970 put it: "I wonder what Captain Roskill would have made of a one-eyed, one-armed Admiral of unstable temperament. Unfit for command?"[3] In the circumstances of 1939 there was really no realistic alternative, and Pound arrived at the Admiralty with mixed feelings. He was pleased at his promotion, but worried at what he knew of Britain's world position.

Apart from sitting on the COS Committee as First Sea Lord and contributing to the strategic advice given to the British government, Pound was also head of the Naval Staff. His dual role was different from that of the chiefs of the other two services because the Admiralty, unlike the War Office or the Air Ministry, was an operational center. Since the advent of radio, the Admiralty had had the ability to move ships, squadrons, and fleets, but in World War II it was given a further boost through the extra information it received of enemy planning and operations through Ultra intelligence. Where the War Office and Air Ministry could only give general directions to their C-in-Cs, the Admiralty could, and in certain circumstances did, issue orders to squadrons, convoys, and even individual ships. To give but one example, Ultra intelligence often pinpointed the position of U-boats, allowing convoys to be directed away from them.

There is no doubt that Pound was not always right on the question of Admiralty interference. At the start of the war he had told the Commander-in-Chief Home Fleet that he would "give the c-in-c all the information and leave him to make the necessary dispositions, but that on certain occasions—notably when the fleet was at sea and keeping wireless silence—it might be necessary to alter his dispositions."[4] He did not always carry out this plan, however, the most notable exception being that of Convoy PQ17. The fundamental reason for this lies in the way in which Pound had been brought up. Like the vast majority of naval officers he had been taught that the more gold braid there was on a senior officers' arm the wiser he was. It was thus never done to question a senior officer's decision. The Edwardian Navy had stifled initiative in its officers, as was to be seen in the Grand Fleet Battle Orders, where Jellicoe had laid down what to do in almost every eventuality. As a result, even flag-officers had rarely used their initiative. Pound was simply following a well established tradition. He had done the same in the Mediterranean, as had his predecessors. Things did not change until officers afloat in World War II realized that if they waited for orders, their ships were likely to be sunk under them by aircraft. The tragedy was that Pound never went to sea in his time as First Sea Lord, and he could be said to have, on occasion, rather underestimated the threat to surface craft from modern airpower. That is not to say that Pound did not understand air power. Before the war, while C-in-C Mediterranean, he had given orders for the FAA to look at ways to attack the Italian Fleet, and he always realized the necessity of airpower to help defeat the U-boats.

When Pound arrived at the Admiralty the First Lord was Lord Stanhope, but this soon changed, and the outset of the war saw the return of Churchill. Pound and Churchill had known one another at the Admiralty in 1915. In some ways, therefore, the "Winston is Back" signal sent out by the Admiralty may be seen as just as much a warning as it was a signal of rejoicing. The Churchill that the Royal Navy remembered was not just the energetic First Lord of 1912-14, but also the headstrong, unheeding First Lord of 1914-15 and the Chancellor of the Exchequer from 1924 to 1929. Pound has been heavily criticized for allowing Churchill to interfere in operational matters, not just as First Lord, but also after he became Prime Minister in 1940. The charge was most vigorously made by Captain Roskill in his book, *Churchill and the Admirals*. Pound has been defended by Professor Marder, most notably in his essay, *"Winston Is Back."*[5] Unfortunately, the argument between Roskill and Marder degenerated into little more than a schoolboy quarrel about who could cite the most people to support their own view.

While Pound tried to reaccustom the Royal Navy to war, Churchill began to look for ways of mounting an offensive. His fertile imagination never ceased to conjure up ideas for more effectively carrying the naval war to the enemy. These schemes were excellent for morale but exhausting for the Naval Staff. Pound instilled into the latter the importance of never saying a direct no to Churchill. Instead, a reasoned response was necessary. In the words of Arthur Marder, "Dudley Pound feared neither god, man, nor Winston Churchill" and Churchill was prepared to accept Pound's judgment.[6] He had learned his lesson from 1915 about going against the advice of his naval advisors. Pound saw that Churchill's powers of leadership were such that it was necessary to accept him, warts and all. He wrote to Admiral Forbes: "I have the greatest admiration for W.C., and his good qualities are such and his desire to hit the enemy are so overwhelming, that I feel one must hesitate in turning down any of his proposals."[7] Pound was not prepared to contradict Churchill at a meeting and would only fight him on really vital issues. Thus, when Churchill proposed Operation *Catherine*, the sending of a fleet without air cover into the Baltic in 1939-40, Pound had the operation appreciated by the Naval Staff, the forces necessary assessed, and the full implications laid out. Churchill was eventually brought to the point of saying, "Who thought up this damn fool scheme anyway?" The matter was dropped. Pound summed up the matter in a letter to Cunningham in 1940:

The PM is very difficult these days, not that he has not always been. One has however to take a broad view because one has to deal with a man who is proving to be a magnificent leader, and one just has to put up with his childishness as long as it isn't dangerous. Also with a man like that it is not good policy to present him with a brick wall unless it is about a thing which is really vital.[8]

Many of the schemes that Churchill put forward were purely putative. In the Norwegian campaign, however, we see him actually interfering in operational matters. Here, Roskill is surely correct in saying that Churchill was allowed to intervene too much. A notable case was the appointment of the retired Admiral of the Fleet Lord Cork and Orrery as Flag Officer Narvik. Not only was he senior to the C-in-C Home Fleet, but Churchill had a private line of communication that totally bypassed Pound, the Naval Staff, and the Home Fleet. The language of the signals that were sent directly to Cork and Orrery, over the signature of the Admiralty (i.e. Pound), indicate their origin:

"Pray regard this as my personal opinion"—19 April.
"I shall be glad to share your responsibility"—4 May.

One is entitled to ask why Pound agreed to the appointment of such a senior admiral to this post, and what effect it had on the morale of more junior flag officers who might otherwise have filled it?

Pound also had to cope with the distraction of another retired Admiral of the Fleet, Sir Roger Keyes, who regarded Pound as a protégé and believed that he ought to be First Sea Lord, with Pound operating as his deputy. The correspondence in which Keyes indulged, both to Churchill and to Pound, is bizarre in the extreme. As an example of rampant egomania it is hard to beat, and it shows the sort of problems with which Pound had to deal.

What, however, should Pound have done about Churchill's interference? He certainly made a point of trying to limit it, and one can see that he sometimes succeeded as, for instance, in the Battle of the River Plate, when he refused to allow Churchill's messages to be sent to Harwood. It needs to be pointed out that the Norwegian campaign was a military disaster from the moment when the Germans seized the airfields. There was little the Naval Staff could have done to limit the scale of the disaster, and it is important to remember that the German Navy was severely damaged in the campaign, a fact with important implications for the summer of 1940. The system of running the war was hopelessly incompetent, and the most important result of the military debacle in Norway was the removal of Chamberlain and his replacement by Churchill as Prime Minister and, crucially, also as Minister of Defence. What was dangerous was the precedent it had set. Although by the end of the campaign Churchill was no longer at the Admiralty and a much lesser figure was installed as First Lord, Pound had been seen by the Royal Navy to interfere with the man on the spot. It has been suggested that Pound should have offered his resignation, but that would have solved nothing. There had been few enough choices when he took over in July 1939, and resignation in wartime is not an option.

The same view can be taken of his relationship with Churchill when the latter became Prime Minister. Churchill still expected, as Minister of Defence, to have a hand in naval affairs, particularly in the selection of admirals. There is plenty of evidence that Churchill expected to be consulted over these appointments, but is there evidence of his actual interference in operational matters? The short answer is that he did occasionally interfere. The most poignant was the decision to send the *Prince of Wales* and *Repulse* out to the Far East. This decision was forced on the Naval Staff as a political decision. When, toward the end of 1941, the situation gradually arose in which Britain was faced with war against three major naval powers, the nightmare of all First Sea Lords since the abrogation of the Anglo-Japanese Treaty in 1922 was fulfilled. Something had to be done to try to deter the Japanese from attacking toward the south. The original "Main Fleet to Singapore" strategy simply could not be implemented in 1941 through the necessity to keep capital ships in European waters to contain the threat posed by the German and Italian Fleets. The Royal Navy was in the "position of extraordinary difficulty" envisaged by the then First Lord, Leo Amery, in 1923, of being committed to a war in the Atlantic and Mediterranean and being threatened in the Far East as well. Pound was sensitive to the nature of the problem. In August of 1940 he had written: "There is no object in sending a Fleet to Singapore unless it is strong enough to fight the Japanese Fleet. Singapore is inferior to Trincomalee as a base from which to protect our trade in the Indian Ocean."[9] In August 1941, responding to a call from Churchill as to what he could do, he proposed sending out a fleet of four old slow battleships (those of the Royal Sovereign class—also known as the "Rs") to Trincomalee. In other words there was still little idea of sending out a fleet to act as a firm deterrent since the four Rs could not have engaged the modern Japanese battleships with any prospect of success. Churchill, however, was determined to send out a deterrent force. He wanted to have in the Far East the equivalent of the *Tirpitz*, which he hoped would tie down the Japanese in the same way that the Home Fleet was tied down by the threat of the *Tirpitz*. He wrote in a personal minute to Pound:

Such a force should consist of the smallest number of our best ships. We have only to remember all the preoccupations which are caused to us by the *Tirpitz*—the only capital ship left to the Germans against our 15 or 16 [sic] battleships and battlecruisers—to see what an effect would be produced upon the Japanese Admiralty by the presence of a small but very powerful force in eastern waters.[10]

Pound then engaged in one of his long-drawn-out delaying battles. The matter was brought to a head by the Foreign Secretary, Eden, asking for the matter to be discussed at a Defence Committee meeting on 17 October 1942. Here the Vice Chief of Naval Staff (VCNS), Phillips, represented Pound, who was away visiting the Home Fleet. Phillips reported to Pound:

The First Lord and I defended the position as well as we could, but the PM led other members of the Defence Committee to the conclusion that it was desirable to send the *Prince of Wales* to join the *Repulse* and go to Singapore as soon as possible. The Admiralty expressed its dissent.[11]

A final decision was to be left until after further meetings on 20 October. At the COS meeting Pound fought a lone and unavailing battle against this proposal, but he eventually had to give in. The COS decision was endorsed by the Defence Committee that afternoon, on the grounds that the political need to send the ships to Singapore was so urgent "as to outweigh objections hitherto advanced by the Admiralty on strategical grounds."[12] Here is a classic case of the professional advice being overruled by political necessity. Pound was so disturbed by the decision that he called a meeting of the Sea Lords and other professional members of the Board of Admiralty, who finally wrote a memorandum to the First Lord expressing their unanimous opinion against this strategically unsound disposition. Ultimately decisions in war have to be taken by politicians, and they can sometimes go against professional advice. Churchill and, to a lesser extent, the Admiralty hoped that Force Z would act as a deterrent to the Japanese. As we now know, Japanese decisions had already been taken for war by the time Force Z arrived at Singapore, and nothing would by then have deterred them from action.

Pound's relationship with A. V. Alexander was different to that with Churchill, and not surprisingly. Alexander was a very different character. To put it simply, he did what he was told by Churchill and Pound. He was interested in matters of personnel and the appointment of flag-officers, but in all matters of strategy he took a back seat. Indeed there is some evidence to suggest that many operational matters were not allowed to be shown to him. He carried out a similar role to those politicians who were at the head of the War Ministry and the Air Ministry in time of war and did not interfere in the operational side of things in their ministries.

Pound sat on the Chief of Staff Committee throughout his tenure of office. He was Chairman of the COS from Newall's retirement in October 1940 until he handed over to Brooke on 5 March 1942. It would be fair to say that Pound was not a great committee man. He tended to stay silent unless the COS was discussing naval matters, but when they did, he was definite in his comments. The most common criticism about Pound was that he slept in the COS meetings. We have no way of knowing if that was true, but members of his staff in the Mediterranean were more than used to the way in which he would close his eyes during meetings. Almost without exception they say that he was concentrating and listening. Pound's relationship with the two other members of the COS who served most with him, Brooke and Portal, was excellent. All three were keen fishermen, and when abroad they were happy to go fishing together. They were compatible and enjoyed working with each other. They were to develop a mutual respect that was to become profound, however strong their debates might be. Disagreements there were, but these could not disturb the equilibrium of their working relationship, even when Churchill added a new appointment—the Chief of Combined Operations, the young Mountbatten—to their number. Pound and Portal disagreed on the issue of aircraft for the Battle of the Atlantic, but this never affected their respect for each other, nor for the working of the COS.

From early on in the war both the CIGS and the First Sea Lord felt that they were let down by the air support that they received. To put it simply, the RAF believed that they could defeat Germany by bombing, without the necessity of a land battle. The relationship between the air and the sea became one of the crucial areas of the war. At the level of C-in-C, relations were good. However, among the COS there was less agreement, as there was a fundamental gap between their thinking over the deployment of air power in the Battle of the Atlantic. Pound evidently believed that if the war at sea were lost, the British would lose the entire war. It is often forgotten that by the spring of 1942, the Royal Navy had fought its worst battles, before the Army or the RAF had begun to undertake offensive operations on a major scale. By that time the RAF had still not got the right aircraft or doctrine for effective cooperation with either of the other armed services. Portal was determined that the new aircraft coming into production, the Lancaster in particular, and those coming from the United States were to go to Bomber Command for the offensive against the German cities. Pound was desperate for some to be diverted to Coastal Command so that the air gap could be closed and air cover could be given to the convoys all the way across the Atlantic.

Pound had spent much time in 1941 backing Coastal Command in its requests for more aircraft and also for bombing U-boat bases in France. As to the former request, Coastal Command entered 1941 with only an average of 156 aircraft of all kinds available for service on any day out of a total strength of 505. The Air Staff rejected the need to bomb U-boat bases, and said: "There seemed no justification whatever for a return to this defensive strategy now when conditions at sea had so much improved and we were beginning to develop fully the air offensive to which we must look for winning as opposed to not losing the war."[13] Pound attacked the matter at a meeting of the Defence Committee on 5 March 1942, when he laid down that "we lose the war at sea when we can no longer maintain those communications which are essential to us."[14] He widened the claims of the Admiralty from simply a request for more air power over the oceans to a demand for operational control of all aircraft used on sea operations, similar to that in force with Coastal Command. He finished by demanding a total of 1,940 aircraft, of which 900 were needed in Coastal Command.

The Air Staff retorted with a paper to the Defence Committee on 8 March which restated their belief in the efficacy of bombing German industry rather than the defensive role of supporting the Royal Navy. Matters came to a head in the Defence Committee on 18 March when Portal and Pound clashed on the whole issue of the use of air power. Brooke chimed in with a paper demanding greater support for the Army. This could have effectively led to the complete emasculation of the RAF. This battle continued throughout 1942, and the First Sea Lord's files are full of answers to possible questions put forward by the Air Staff. Pound consulted his Commanders-in-Chief at the Admiralty on 2 June when it was suggested by the C-in-C Home Fleet that the Board of Admiralty should threaten to resign over the issue. Although the Board was not in agreement, it does show the strength of feeling in the Royal Navy. Time and again the decision appeared to go against the Admiralty. For example, in October 1942 Churchill decided in favor of bombing, after Harris had circumvented the chain of command and written a messianic letter direct to the Prime Minister which effectively promised to defeat Germany on his own and called Coastal Command an obstacle to victory.[15]

Pound continued his battle throughout the year. On 18 November 1942, armed with a five page brief, he put the Royal Navy's case yet again to the new Cabinet Anti-U-boat Committee. He asked for just forty Very Long Range (VLR) aircraft. In the previous month, 400,000 tons of shipping had been sunk in the Atlantic, and since the "Battle of the Air" had begun in February, over 4.4 million tons had been sunk in the North Atlantic alone. Portal was prepared to offer only thirty Halifax heavy bombers, and he was not prepared to release any of the new ASV MK III radar for Coastal Command until he was directed by the Cabinet to do so, and then only in very small numbers. Even then, their first operational use was not until March 1943. It was not until January 1943 that Coastal Command received its first VLR Liberators equipped with the American equivalent of the ASV MK III.

By May 1943, the climactic month of the Battle of the Atlantic, Coastal Command had a bare minimum of VLR aircraft to plug the air gap. Although it now had a total of forty-nine VLR aircraft at its disposal, only twelve to fifteen were actually operational at any one time. Dönitz himself recognized the cause of the catastrophic defeat he suffered in May 1943. He wrote: "The enemy Air Force therefore played a decisive part. . . . This can attributed to the increased use of land-based aircraft and aircraft carriers combined with the advantages of radar location."[16] This was a victory won by the sailors and the airmen in the North Atlantic, and won in the teeth of a stubborn refusal by the Air Staff to accept the logical presentation of facts by the Admiralty until it was nearly too late. The bombing offensive was certainly a major factor in the defeat of Germany, but it nearly led to the defeat of Britain. If Dudley Pound had not fought so long and so hard throughout 1942, then the Battle of the Atlantic might easily have gone the other way. To those who are critical of Pound's strategic contribution to the direction of the war, here is refutation indeed. From the very start he saw that the Battle of the Atlantic was not just essential to eventual victory, since no assault against Fortress Europe could be mounted until it was won, but more crucially, Britain would lose the war, as she had nearly lost World War I, if that battle were lost. This guiding belief was probably his most profound contribution to the higher direction of the war, but it was a fact that had to be driven home to both Churchill and Portal, and that they came to accept only very reluctantly.

There were other disagreements among the COS, but this one over air policy was the most profound. It is not surprising that the COS did disagree among themselves, as all three were individuals of forceful views. However, there can be no doubt that they presented a unified force when asked for strategic advice. By March 1942, when Brooke took over as Chairman, the strategic initiative was passing to the Allies and it was appropriate that a soldier should lead their discussions about where Allied manpower should be directed. Pound took part in all the major Allied conferences until his death, and was thus a founder member of the Combined Chiefs of Staff (CCOS). He first encountered his opposite numbers in the American Joint Chiefs of Staff at the Argentia Bay meeting in Newfoundland in August 1941. Here he met Admiral Harold Stark, then CNO, and Admiral Ernest King, who succeeded Stark in March 1942, when the latter became the head of the U.S. Naval Mission in London. On the surface Pound got on well with King, who was the dominant force in U.S. naval thinking, and King says polite things about Pound in his biography. However, King was deeply prejudiced against all things British and was not prepared to listen to advice from the Royal Navy on such basic issues as the introduction of convoys. This resulted in the second "happy time" for the U-boats in early 1942. Pound tried to encourage him to institute convoys, signaling on 19 March 1942 that he regarded "the introduction of convoys as a matter of urgency."[17] King reluctantly accepted this in June, but it was a lesson taught more by Dönitz than by anybody else.

It was at the Washington Conference in December 1941 that Pound really came to grips with his American counterparts, and it was here that the machinery of the CCOS was established. The crucial point about the Washington Conference was that the COS had worked out what they wanted to say while crossing the Atlantic, and could therefore present a united front to the Joint Chiefs of Staff (JCS). In contrast, the Americans were not united. It was Pound who hammered home to the CCOS that the Atlantic was the crucial area. Despite Pound's efforts, Admiral King really had eyes only for the Pacific. Until the end of 1943 the British had the experience and the forces in being to dominate the debates and decisions, but by August 1943 that domination was slipping. According to Correlli Barnett, Pound at Casablanca was "less concerned with the grand strategic issues than with the executive detail of naval operations, and above all the crucial Battle of the Atlantic."[18] This is correct, and he had this confirmed as the Allies' first priority. Pound was happy to let Brooke take the lead in arguing the strategic aim, while agreeing with his basic premise that there was not enough assault shipping or trained manpower in Britain to launch a successful cross-Channel assault in 1943. His actual contribution at Washington and Quebec in 1943 was similarly muted. At the former he was struggling with the Atlantic battle at its height, and during the latter he was dying.

Turning to Pound's relations with his own Navy, we are faced with a strange dichotomy. Those who served on his staff were often devoted to him, but others held equally strong views the other way. S. W. Roskill, who had been Gunnery Officer of Pound's flagship, *Warspite* (1937-39) and a member of the Naval Staff (1939-41), was not an admirer of Pound. His criticisms of Pound in the official history are fairly veiled, but in his book, *Churchill and the Admirals*, he pulled few punches. The tragedy for Pound is that he had no opportunity to set the record straight in the clear light of hindsight, nor did he leave any sort of written record behind.

Pound's relationship with his admirals was mixed. With Cunningham he engaged in a considerable correspondence, and it is instructive to see how much they revealed to each other. Cunningham must have realized that he was likely to succeed Pound, at least after 1942, but he never really wanted the job, preferring to stay in an active command. When Pound asked Cunningham in 1942 whether he should resign, the latter had replied "Glue yourself to your seat."[19] The two men trusted each other, although that is not to say that Cunningham believed Pound got everything right. Pound's relationship with Sir James Somerville was more tricky. For various reasons Churchill believed that Somerville was not sufficiently offensive-minded. This was probably brought about by Somerville expressing his distaste at sinking the French Fleet at Mers-el-Kebir in July 1940. Matters reached a peak when Somerville turned back while chasing an Italian force off Cape Spartivento in November 1940 after realizing he could not catch them. Instead of waiting to receive Somerville's report, the Admiralty precipitately sent out Lord Cork and Orrery to conduct an inquiry. Pound may have acted in this way to stop Churchill from doing anything more outrageous. While a Court of Inquiry was being held, Churchill could be stalled, and once Cork and Orrery had reported it would be clear that Somerville had acted correctly. That was exactly what happened, and thus Churchill could do no damage.

Pound's relationships with the two Commanders-in-Chief Home Fleet were not perfect. Admiral Sir Charles Forbes had been a possible choice as First Sea Lord in 1939, and he might have taken over in 1941 if Pound had retired then. Pound and Forbes had already fallen out over the issue of Admiralty interference with Home Fleet dispositions and operations. Forbes fell foul of Churchill in various matters, notably over the disposition of the Home Fleet to resist possible invasion in 1940, and in Roskill's words, "Pound . . . undoubtedly knew that there was criticism of Forbes in the fleet."[20] Pound told Cunningham in September 1940 that Tovey would be appointed in Forbes's place, and this happened in December 1940. Admiral Sir John Tovey had several areas of disagreement with Pound, although many of them were, in fact, with Churchill. For example, in the chase of the *Bismarck,* Churchill sent Tovey a signal saying "*Bismarck* must be sunk at all costs and if to do this it is necessary for *King George V* [Tovey's flagship] to remain on the scene she must do so even if it subsequently means towing *King George V.*"[21] Although sent by Pound, this extraordinary message originated with

Churchill, as he admitted in his memoirs. Churchill also wanted certain senior officers court-martialed for not reengaging *Bismarck* after *Hood* had been sunk. Tovey's comment that he would haul down his flag and act as prisoner's friend effectively killed that idea, but one must wonder at the state of Pound's relations with Tovey that these sorts of signals could be sent in the first place. Tovey also clashed with Churchill over, among other issues, continuing the Arctic convoys in the summer of 1942 and obtaining more aircraft for Coastal Command. Churchill obviously did not feel confident with Tovey in command and suggested in June 1942 that he be replaced, but Pound told Churchill that such treatment of a man who had proved himself "a capable and successful leader would cause the Navy to lose all confidence in Admiralty administration."[22] This suggestion obviously worked, and Tovey remained in command until he was relieved by Fraser in May 1943.

As C-in-C Home Fleet, Tovey was in command when Convoy PQ17 suffered its disaster in July 1942. The best account of this disaster stresses the fact that in March 1942, Tovey had only been put within striking distance of *Tirpitz* when "the Admiralty . . . intervened to redirect Tovey."[23] This undoubtedly strengthened Pound's belief in Admiralty control. Both Tovey and Pound tried to get the summer convoys abandoned due to the perpetual daylight in the northern latitudes, but they were overruled by Churchill. Pound and Tovey already disagreed on the advisability of scattering a convoy, with Tovey telling Pound that doing so would be "sheer bloody murder."[24] The crux of the matter for Pound was that the Operational Intelligence Centre (OIC) could not specifically tell him whether *Tirpitz* had left Altenfjord. The evidence was not certain about that, and as a result, Pound—who was not prepared to delegate the responsibility for such a crucial decision to anyone else—gave the order to scatter. At the bottom of this must be a very real question about Pound's understanding of how Ultra intelligence worked. Beesly says: "In all intelligence problems there must always be some element of uncertainty, always a last piece of the jigsaw puzzle which can only be filled in with guesswork."[25] Pound ought to have taken the trouble to understand the work of the OIC better, and in particular to get to know such brilliant intelligence officers as Denning and Winn. However, that was not his way, and he took the decision to scatter PQ17. An authority as great as Professor Hinsley feels that Pound had no alternative, but others disagree.[26] Pound was certainly under enormous strain at that time and believed that an immediate decision had to be taken. In hindsight, we can see that this was wrong. Tovey, as well as the escort commander, Jack Broome, always believed so.

Pound could be ruthless in getting rid of admirals who, he believed, were not up to the job. Examples are not difficult to find, and we have already seen that Forbes did not complete his tenure at the Home Fleet. The best known case, however, is the dismissal in 1940 of Admiral Dudley North from his post as Flag-Officer North Atlantic. North could reasonably complain about being told he was derelict in his duty without the issue being investigated at a court-martial. He could not complain about being relieved, however, as the Board of Admiralty had lost confidence in him. Pound made the mistake of attempting to give reasons, and here a stronger Secretary to the Admiralty than Archibald Carter might well have helped matters by making this point more forcibly than he did. In another case, Admiral Harwood was relieved of his post as C-in-C Mediterranean in circumstances that do not cast a particularly good light on Pound. He was sacked principally because General Montgomery did not think him up to the job. There was a similar experience when Pound brought Admiral Sir Frederick Dreyer, an old friend, out of retirement and appointed him Chief of Naval Air Services in July 1942. In the words of Roskill, this was "surely one of Pound's worst misjudgments."[27] Dreyer was fired in April 1943 after failing to make any impression. These instances show the difficulties Pound experienced and that he did not always judge things correctly.

Within the Admiralty, too, not all of his appointments met with universal approval. His appointment of Rear Admiral Tom Phillips as DCNS (later VCNS) was not applauded by all, but he was an energetic and successful deputy to Pound, getting on well with Churchill (both as First Lord and Prime Minister), until they disagreed over the British expedition to Greece in April 1941. Pound and Phillips had first worked together in the Mediterranean in 1925-27, and Pound insisted on Phillips in 1939 even though the job was normally held by a Vice Admiral. The appointment of Harwood as ACNS(F) in December 1940 was probably taken because of Churchill's recommendation of what he considered to be an officer with offensive thoughts. However, there can be little criticism of the appointments of such figures as Admiral Sir Charles Little as Second Sea Lord, Rear Admiral Bruce Fraser as Third Sea Lord, or Captain Arthur J. Power as ACNS(H). It should be noted that Pound refused the appointment of a Deputy First Sea Lord until July 1942, when Admiral Sir Charles Kennedy-Purvis could relieve him of much of the work.

By March 1942, when Brooke took over as Chairman of the COS, and certainly by July 1942, when Kennedy-Purvis became Deputy First Sea Lord, there is a case for saying that Pound was overstretched beyond what was dutiful, and even beyond what was right. In 1942, and later in 1943, however, the question of who was to replace him became a genuine problem. By the end of 1942 his resilience was beginning to flag, and the loss of Lady Pound in the summer of 1943 after a long illness certainly did not help matters. Pound took no leave after giving up the Mediterranean command and was from July 1939 onward tied to a desk and frequent meetings both in and outside the Admiralty. He was at the call of an inconsiderate political chief at any hour of the day or night. There were those around him who were convinced that he was driving himself too hard, for he never took a day off other than to observe his own instructions that all Admiralty officers should absent themselves from duty for one day in seven. One solution to this was provided by an American, Captain Paul Hammond, who rented a hunting lodge in Hertfordshire and invited Pound to shoot there every week starting in the autumn of 1941. Nothing could have been of more benefit to Pound and his work than this chance to get away from his desk. Nonetheless, he believed it was his duty to keep going, and he kept going until the Quebec Conference of August 1943, when he was forced to concede defeat.

What are we to make of him? There is no doubt of his stature as a public servant, his determination to make the best of what he was and what he had. Pound, of all men, was not one to shirk his duty, and to him his duty was plain. Even so, duty sometimes lies in knowing when to quit. Nonetheless, this must be impossibly difficult to gauge when things are going badly. It is only with hindsight that we can see that we were winning. Pound was not bred to the role of First Sea Lord, as Jellicoe had been for the Grand Fleet. Notwithstanding this fact, he was the best that the Royal Navy had to offer in 1939. In the words of Professor Peter Nailor: "He is not a Roosevelt figure, rather a Truman figure; and like Truman he stayed in the kitchen and took the heat."[28]

NOTES

1. Roskill, *Naval Policy*, 2:463-68.
2. Captain John Litchfield has confirmed this fact in conversations with the author.
3. *Daily Telegraph*, 11 March 1970.
4. S. W. Roskill, *The War At Sea*, vol. 1 (London: HMSO, 1954), 27.
5. "Winston Is Back" originally appeared in article form as Supplement No. 5 of the *English Historical Review* in 1972. It was then revised and included in Arthur J. Marder's book, *From the Dardanelles to Oran* (London: Oxford University Press, 1974), 105-78.
6. Marder, *From the Dardanelles to Oran*, 110.
7. Pound to Forbes, 20 Jan. 1940, Cunningham Mss., Add. Mss. 52565, British Museum (BM).
8. Pound to Cunningham, 1 Dec. 1940, Cunningham Mss., Add. Mss. 52560, BM.

9. ADM 205/6.
10. ADM 205/10.
11. Letter of 17 Oct. 1941, photocopy in Roskill Papers, ROSK 4/79, Churchill Archives Centre, Churchill College, Cambridge.
12. DO(41)66, CAB 69/8.
13. Quoted in John Terraine, *The Right of the Line* (London: Hodder and Stoughton, 1985), 413.
14. DO(42)23, CAB 69/4.
15. D. Saward, *Bomber Harris* (London: Buchan and Enright, 1984), 161.
16. ADM 234/578.
17. S. W. Roskill, *The War at Sea*, vol. 2 (London: HMSO, 1956), 97.
18. Correlli Barnett, *Engage the Enemy More Closely*, 615.
19. Ibid., 143.
20. Ibid., 120.
21. Quoted in ibid., 125.
22. Pound to Alexander, 8 June 1942, ADM 205/14.
23. P. Beesly, "Convoy PQ17: A Study of Intelligence and Decision-making," in Michael I. Handel, ed., *Intelligence and Military Operations* (London: Frank Cass, 1990), 301.
24. Ibid., 302.
25. Handel, *Intelligence and Military Operations*, 318.
26. F. H. Hinsley, E. E. Thomas, C. F. G. Ransom, et al., eds., *British Intelligence in the Second World War*, vol. 2 (London: HMSO, 1981), 222.
27. Roskill, *Churchill and the Admirals*, 251.
28. Lecture given by Professor Peter Nailor at the Royal United Services Institute for Defence Studies (RUSI), London, 6 May 1987.

14

Admiral Viscount Cunningham of Hyndhope (1943–1946)

Michael Simpson

A deck sailor rather than a desk sailor, Cunningham's fame rests principally on his command of the Mediterranean Fleet in 1939-42. Indeed, apart from a few months in 1942 as head of the British Admiralty Delegation in Washington, he had spent all the war in the Mediterranean until he was called home in October 1943 to succeed the dying Pound as First Sea Lord. As Pound's protégé, confidant, and chosen heir, he was the generally expected successor.

Cunningham's succession was, however, far from automatic. The First Lord, Albert V. Alexander, was advised that there were three "outstanding" candidates—Cunningham, John Tovey, and Bruce Fraser. Cunningham, it was rightly argued, was "the obvious choice on account of his outstanding pre-eminence in the eyes of the Service and the British public not to mention the Americans."[1] All three interests would be satisfied by his appointment and he would give the Admiralty the firm, steady leadership required to seal victory. However, Churchill defiantly told Alexander, "I have no doubt that we should offer it to Admiral Fraser." Cunningham was still required in the Mediterranean, he was "of the pre-air age" and it was doubtful whether he could cope with the "prolonged ceaseless, detailed work of the Chiefs of Staff Committee." Fraser was younger, more patient, and had technical expertise as well as a year at sea with the Home Fleet.[2] What Churchill really feared was Cunningham's obduracy, which was often revealed in the Mediterranean; the ease and influence he had enjoyed in Pound's time would disappear. Alexander, who was often dismissed as meekly submissive, resisted Churchill determinedly but could not prevent him from offering the post to Fraser, who observed shrewdly: "I believe I have the confidence of my own Fleet. Cunningham has that of the whole Navy."[3]

Churchill conceded to Alexander with a characteristic sting in the tail: "You can have your Cunningham but if the Admiralty don't do as they are told I will bring down the Board in ruins, even if it means my coming down with it."[4]

Cunningham [dubbed "ABC" within the service] was well aware of his limitations. "The office desk was not my strongest suit," he remarked, and he confessed to "an inherent difficulty in expressing myself in verbal discussion." The Admiralty, fortunately, was "running on oiled wheels" and "the foundation of victory had been well and truly laid. . . . [M]y task was to reap where he [Pound] had so ably sown." Furthermore, he was well acquainted with most of the Board, who constituted "a strong team," and he followed his usual policy of letting his subordinates get on with the details while he dealt with external relations and the major strategic and policy issues.[5] The other Chiefs of Staff, Sir Alan Brooke and Sir Charles Portal, proved congenial company and all three resolved their differences among themselves, giving Churchill no opportunity to divide and rule.

Nevertheless, the Prime Minister remained a formidable and persistent antagonist. The approach of victory, the post-Teheran dominance of the superpowers, and the realization that his Victorian world order was crumbling, together with the ravages of age, continuous strain, and intemperance, turned him into the proverbial cannon loose on the gun deck. Dill had warned Cunningham, "You will have great difficulty in controlling your hackles," yet the First Sea Lord kept his temper in the face of Churchill's chicanery, childishness, obstinacy, ignorance, prodding, interference, and selfishness, treating him with a patience and guile unexpected by those subject to ABC's well-known irascibility, bullying, and apparent insensitivity.[6] He appreciated that Churchill "bitterly resent[ed] his choice" and that the Prime Minister believed "I make the other Chiefs of Staff intransigent" (they needed no prompting). Nevertheless, he learned how to manage the sore old lion: "As usual when one gets alongside him on a subject he knows little about I had my way."[7] When Churchill prodded him about operations following D day, asking, "What are the Navy doing on the western flank of the armies? I am convinced that opportunities are passing," Cunningham explained patiently the Navy's support of the post-D day advance.[8] The Prime Minister, who was a fertile source of gadgetal wizardry of schoolboy fiendishness but doubtful utility, suggested lightweight nets to trap U-boats; unsatisfied by Cunningham's reply that they were easily parted and obstructive to British vessels, he concluded, "Well, do not say I did not tell you."[9] If at times ABC humored the Premier, he refused to countenance his interference in the strictly naval sphere, particularly on flag appointments, since he was "such a bad picker." He insisted on the transfer of Admiral Somerville, the C-in-C Eastern Fleet, to Washington despite Churchill's wish to keep the "fighting admiral" in the Indian Ocean. When Fraser succeeded Somerville in the east, Cunningham blocked the Premier's intention of "submitting Fraser to a strategical means test." When Churchill tried to prevent Daniel's appointment as Vice Admiral (Administration) in the British Pacific Fleet, Cunningham announced with finality, "I have no intention of changing him."[10] His rage was confined to his diary. "What a drag on the wheel of war this man is," he exploded in August 1944. "Everything is centralised in him with consequent indecision and waste of time before anything can be done." More seriously, he wrote, "No wonder the US Chiefs of Staff complain of delays in getting things through."[11] Like many of Churchill's associates, ABC was ambivalent about the Prime Minister, acknowledging "with all his faults (and he is the most infuriating man) he has done a great deal for the country," and, the most telling observation, "besides there is no one else."[12]

The major strategic and operational problems faced by Cunningham, involving delicate relationships with civilian and military leaders, both British and Allied, were the shortage of manpower, the final (but unnerving) fling of the U-boats, the elimination of the German surface fleet, the successful conduct of Operation *Neptune/Overlord*, the final destruction of enemy forces in the Mediterranean, and the creation and deployment of a British Pacific Fleet.

The shortage of manpower limited the Navy's expansion and threatened to curtail its operations. The responsibility for naval personnel belonged to the Second Sea Lord, Admiral Whitworth, but Cunningham took an active interest in attempting to solve the Navy's most intractable problem. He had been in office only a week when he was told that "drastic measures are necessary at once."[13] Very few young men would be available in future, yet the Navy had to maintain a powerful surface fleet and large escort forces and also provide for the vast expansion of the Fleet Air Arm and find thousands of crews for the D day landings, while new technology increased ships' companies and enlarged shore establishments were necessary. Skill levels were diluted and much new construction (a large proportion from North America) could not be manned. The prolongation of the European war into 1945 exacerbated the problem, and Cunningham told Fraser: "The Manning Department at present do not see their way to manning more than 60% of the commitments."[14] He ordered old ships to be paid off and exhorted station commanders to comb out surplus personnel, but the conundrum remained unsolved and was made worse by the steady demobilization after VE day.

The most formidable problem, the Battle of the Atlantic, appeared well on the way to solution, but Cunningham was too well aware of the crucial importance of the North Atlantic lifeline and too cautious and experienced to believe that all the pitching and rolling was at last over. Though he was relieved that D day was virtually immune from U-boat attack, he was aware that U-boat production was increasing and that new types with high underwater speeds, great endurance, and advanced torpedoes were about to appear. By January 1945, snorkel-equipped U-boats were sinking merchantmen with familiar regularity and at little cost to themselves. He explained the problem succinctly:

There is no question that we underestimated the immunity which the schnorkel gives to the submarine. He is practically immune from discovery by aircraft as a device on the schnorkel detects the aircraft before the aircraft can detect it. The schnorkel is also very difficult to see. Thus the aircraft are about 90% ineffective. The U-boats have also discovered that, if they come inshore and can operate where there is plenty of land, the tide rips and sea bottom noises will prevent their detection by the asdic.[15]

Churchill, predictably, was "inclined to lash out at all and sundry, rather petulant." The scientists "came in for a bottle for letting the Huns get ahead of them" and Cunningham also chastised them, testimony to the fact that the Battle of the Atlantic had become one of rival technologies as much as of steel and courage.[16] In the absence, for once, of a technical solution, Cunningham responded to Churchill—and Dönitz—with a flurry of desperate measures, acknowledging that "we may be in for a difficult time." Haunted by the likelihood that by the spring of 1945 seventy super-U-boats would be at sea, Cunningham laid down the following guidelines:

[N]o escort vessel that could run however badly was to be paid off and that new ones must be commissioned without paying off corresponding old ones. If necessary commitments to the Far East and East Indies must be deferred. It seems to me a case of putting our greatest effort into holding the U-boats for the next three months and everything must be sacrificed to the object.[17]

He persuaded Churchill to rescind an order releasing trawlers for fishing, recalled destroyers from the Mediterranean, blanketed the narrow seas with mines, and instituted additional coastal convoys on the sound principle of "where the carcase is, there will the eagles be gathered together."[18] This reduced the toll (though few U-boats were sunk). The Admiralty was rescued from a third "happy time" by successful bombing of U-boat shelters and yards and the rapid advance of the Allied armies.

When Cunningham became First Sea Lord, German capital ships based on Norway still threatened the Arctic convoys. The *Scharnhorst* was sunk by Fraser and the Home Fleet on 25 December 1943. Cunningham, after supplying Fraser with all the Admiralty's relevant information, left the conduct of the battle entirely to the C-in-C. The *Tirpitz* was temporarily immobilised by a gallant and skilful FAA attack in April 1944. Cunningham's instinct was to move in for the kill, but Fraser demurred; such favorable circumstances were unlikely to reoccur. Cunningham claimed that Fraser was "in a most truculent and obstinate mood" and that "he would haul his flag down if ordered to repeat TUNGSTEN." Fraser denied having said this but, after tempers on both sides had cooled, he agreed to try again and the FAA made several more strikes. Fraser, ironically, stood up for the autonomy of the local C-in-C, as had Cunningham in the Mediterranean. As CNS, however, Cunningham directed maritime strategy and insisted justifiably that "the Admiralty must be allowed some voice in what operations were to be carried out."[19] The sooner *Tirpitz* was eliminated, the earlier Fraser and the fleet could go to the Pacific. Cunningham and Fraser were not well acquainted and differed in personality and method, factors which may account for their persistently uneasy relationship; if there was any pique over the succession to Pound, it remained unstated.

Detailed planning for D day was in the hands of Admiral Ramsay, in whom Cunningham had total confidence. Given the Navy's global responsibilities, however, he observed with alarm: "The demands for OVERLORD are frightful."[20] As usual, he left the details to Ramsay. As D day drew nearer, however, he remained in constant contact with him, conscious that upon this, the greatest naval operation in history and chiefly a British responsibility, hung the future of the Allied strategy in the West. Like Churchill, he was mightily relieved when it took place with such conspicuous success. He was more publicity-conscious than is generally believed, but on this occasion he remarked that "the greatest compliment paid to the Navy was to take them for granted."[21] He savored a rare tribute from Montgomery: "I have always felt that you personally would see that everything was all right, and this has been so." When Montgomery later reverted to form and complained at the delay in clearing Cherbourg, Cunningham told Brooke firmly: "I wasn't going to have any Tripoli nonsense."[22] He and Ramsay chastised the soldiers for their failure to capitalise on the capture of Antwerp in September 1944, Cunningham himself impressing on the COS that: "Antwerp though completely undamaged was as much good to us as Timbuktu unless the entrance and other forts were silenced and the banks of the Scheldt occupied. I fear this is being overlooked by our generals and the consequence will be the slowing up of our advance."[23] His advice was born of bitter Mediterranean experience and he observed that the soldiers "will and are paying for it by the slowing up or even halting of the advance into Germany."[24] Their failure helped to prolong the European war into 1945. Cunningham, supported by Admiral Ernest J. King, also objected to Eisenhower's swing southward, arguing for the capture of German naval bases and ports close to the front line to maximise logistic efficiency. He was equally critical of the lack of an enterprising coastal strategy: "They should have been into Hamburg and off the Danish coast already."[25]

In the Mediterranean, Cunningham inherited Churchill's disastrous Aegean operation in which the enemy had "practically everything in their favour, distance, adjacent islands, good air reconnaissance and complete air superiority;" the lessons of 1941 had been forgotten and he was relieved when the unequal contest ended.[26] By contrast, the Anzio landings were a model of interservice cooperation, but he was displeased with the soldiers' failure to exploit them, thus imposing on the Navy a further supply burden. Ambivalent about further landings, he bowed to American insistence on operations *Anvil-Dragoon* in southern France but had to fight King to retain sufficient American landing craft. He defended naval interests and autonomy against British commanders, such as Field Marshal Alexander and Sir John Slessor, whose attitudes to the Navy seemed to him cavalier. Britain's Allies caused almost as many problems as the enemy. The civil war in Greece demanded a naval presence, and after the war, Charles de Gaulle attempted to reimpose French authority in the Levant, almost precipitating an Anglo-French naval clash. In these incidents, Cunningham exercised restraint, headed off Prime Ministerial interference, gave his local commanders free rein, and supported their actions.

He regarded the First Lord as "a queer fish, rather a rough diamond," but Alexander gave him few problems.[27] A capable administrator, the First Lord rarely ventured into the professional domain, and he was devoted to the Navy. Cunningham's relations with his principal commanders were generally cordial, and many posts went to longstanding associates: Willis to the Mediterranean, Arthur Power to the East Indies, Rawlings and Vian to the Pacific. It was the Orient that gave him his principal headaches and he had confrontations with Churchill, King, Mountbatten, and Fraser. Perhaps the most serious disagreement of the war was the dispute between the COS and the Prime Minister over British strategy against Japan, which resulted in nine months of "muddle and mismanagement" in 1944. The parties were "at complete loggerheads about the Pacific versus South East Asia Command strategy."[28] The COS, led by Cunningham, held that the principal British contribution should be a powerful fleet cooperating with the U.S. Navy's strike against metropolitan Japan, concentrating strength against the enemy's jugular vein and thus finishing the war quickly, saving many lives. Britain would also exercise an influential voice in the peace settlement and in the future of Asia. Churchill, who was obsessed by the concept of empire, favored an Imperial campaign to recover lost colonies down the eastern flank of the Indian Ocean to Singapore. This would make optimum use of the great base in India, Allied sea and air power, and the drive and imagination of his protégé, Mountbatten. The Americans, whose stated ambition was to decolonize Asia, would not then be able to frustrate the recreation of the British Empire. Cunningham, though not opposed to such operations as Mountbatten could undertake with his modest resources, was determined that they should be secondary to the Pacific thrust. The impasse led the COS to the brink of resignation; they remained "firmly of the opinion. . . that we should put in our major effort in the Pacific on the left of the American forces." Unfortunately, the Prime Minister took diametrically the opposite view. Therefore, as Cunningham indicated in a message to Admiral Sir Percy Noble, a third course was suggested: "[T]he British, using Northern Australia as a base, should fight their way into the China Sea." Since British forces could then move toward South East Asia or Japan, the Prime Minister was "favourably inclined" and ABC found it "quite attractive," as did the Americans.[29] Nevertheless, Churchill soon reverted to his Sumatra-Malaya-Singapore strategy. Cunningham, for his part, was unenthusiastic about the Prime Minister's change of tack and had little difficulty in condemning a policy in which the British appeared to "prefer to hang about outside and recapture [their] own rubber trees."[30] Churchill was finally won over in time for the Quebec Conference (September 1944), at which he "offered the British main fleet for operations in the Central Pacific and it was at once accepted by the President."[31]

Having overcome the Premier, Cunningham had to deal with Admiral Ernest J. King, U.S. Chief of Naval Operations [CNO]. Cunningham's diary records what happened at the subsequent Combined Chiefs of Staff [CCOS] meeting:

All went well till the use of the Navy in the Central Pacific was raised. King flew into a temper. It couldn't be allowed there. He wouldn't have it and so on. I called his attention to the President's acceptance of the Prime Minister's offer. He tried to make out that the acceptance did not mean what it said. . . . In fact King made an ass of himself and having the rest of the US Chiefs of Staff against him had to give way to the fact that the British would operate in the Central Pacific but with such a bad grace.[32]

King continued to throw obstacles in the way of this decision down to the end of the war. He doubted the fleet's ability to maintain itself and refused U.S. assistance. Self-sufficiency was indeed a major headache; British shortages of fast merchantmen, especially tankers, limited severely the size of their force, and Cunningham had a running fight with Lord Leathers, the Minister of War Transport, over the collection of an adequate fleet train. Anticipating King's obstructiveness, Cunningham persuaded his old friend Somerville to go to Washington late in 1944 as head of the British Admiralty Delegation (BAD), a post he had held briefly in 1942, when his prestige and resolution had wrung from King a fragile but effective cooperation. By 1944, Admiral Noble was reporting that King was now feeling the power flowing from the U.S. Navy's Pacific triumphs, was not forthcoming with information and supplies, and seemed reluctant to refit H.M. ships in U.S. yards. "There is no doubt that the Americans have stiffened in their attitude towards us," observed Noble, yet Britain was now even more of a supplicant, being dependent on American largesse. King's antipathy to the Royal Navy derived from 1918, when he had felt the British naval effort lacked energy and ambition; moreover, he had similar grievances in 1944. "The Americans," wrote a liaison officer, "are convinced we are playing a deliberate 'go slow' game in all theatres of the Pacific war." Cunningham pointed out that "for the last year he [Somerville] has had no forces with which to carry out any operations."[33] The Americans were on firmer ground in complaining about the FAA's ineffectiveness, for Cunningham and Churchill were concerned, too, about its appetite for resources, its long working-up periods, and its lack of offensive spirit. Cunningham judged that Somerville had the right personality—a blend of joviality, profanity, charm, forthrightness and firmness—to deal with the CNO. It was an inspired choice. Somerville had "got on with King better than most people" at the *Trident* Conference of 1943, he had over two years' experience in the Eastern War, capped by successful recent air strikes, and he was the Navy's foremost exponent of carrier warfare; with the maritime war now focusing on the Pacific, he had the ideal background. He quickly proved to be the most adept head of BAD, fighting King over Pacific bases, aircraft and other supplies and earning the latter's genuine respect and tangible, if grudging, cooperation. Cunningham still had to confront King at the wartime summits, and he admitted, "I can't bring myself to like that man."[34]

The mutual lack of understanding between ABC and Fraser arose again when the latter became C-in-C British Pacific Fleet. Cunningham found him "rather staff minded" (something of which Cunningham could never be accused), dilatory, impulsive, erratic in judgment, extravagant in his demands, inclined to exceed his brief, and petulant when he failed to get his own way. Thus, in November 1944, when complaining at Admiralty rejection of his plans, he told the First Sea Lord, "I would be very grateful therefore if as soon as possible you would select someone whose judgment you would trust and advice you would follow, to relieve me." Describing it as "an unpleasant letter," Cunningham wondered whether Fraser "is the man for the job the way he has behaved lately."[35] Nevertheless, the fleet performed well, despite immense difficulties, which Cunningham, who never quite grasped the peculiar nature of the war in the Pacific, underestimated. Even after the war, Cunningham continued to complain that Fraser was "a bit troublesome. He will persist that his ideas are better than those of the Admiralty."[36] It was clearly difficult for the two to strike the right balance between Admiralty strategic responsibility and the local knowledge and autonomy of a C-in-C.

Cunningham's difficulties with Mountbatten arose from the latter's appointment in September 1943 as Supreme Allied Commander, South East Asia. A Captain promoted Acting Admiral, Mountbatten, though well known to Cunningham, never enjoyed his approbation, perhaps because of his flamboyant personality and almost certainly because he was Churchill's protégé. The initial problem arose from the clash between Somerville, then C-in-C Eastern Fleet, and Mountbatten over the command of the fleet and operational planning. Cunningham sought to settle their differences without arousing the hostility of either party. He persuaded the Prime Minister to clarify his directive to Mountbatten, reminded Somerville of the Supreme Commander's delicate position vis-à-vis the Americans, and advised both of them that their differences "can only be settled by a considerable amount of give and take."[37] By the time Somerville left the station in August 1944, the essential differences had been removed. However, Mountbatten, commanding the Cinderella theatre, then attempted to keep ships destined for the Pacific, much to Cunningham's annoyance: "I wish that young man would mind his own business."[38]

Like most British leaders, Cunningham grasped only imperfectly that Britain would be a spent force as a global power once the war was over. The empire was beginning to crumble, Germany and Japan had the innate capacity for revival, and the United States was being difficult over many issues, notably bases and air landing rights in the Pacific. It seemed as if a struggle between the old imperialism and the new was now taking place. The U.S. Navy was clearly determined to consolidate its superiority and establish a hegemony over the western Atlantic and the Pacific; the Admiralty placed no reliance on its future assistance and was frankly skeptical about the United Nations. Cunningham's chief worry, however, was the Soviet Union, which Eden discounted as a potential enemy. "Such an ostrich-like attitude," snorted the First Sea Lord. "One cannot close one's eyes."[39] Thus he set about frustrating the Soviet plundering of German naval resources, encouraging the importation of German scientists; "by bringing them over here we prevent the Russians getting at them and also take the advantage of their brains and knowledge."[40] He hustled the Americans into agreeing to a probably illegal seizure of the hundred U-boats in Norway. He had no clear idea of how nuclear weapons would change the art of war. He deplored their use, however, yet warned that we "should enter into every agreement with the utmost suspicion and demand [that] full rights of inspection were accepted."[41]

Though Cunningham considered that Britain's frontier now lay east of Germany, he echoed his Victorian predecessors in emphasising the importance of the Mediterranean in Imperial strategy, condemning Attlee, who "doesn't seem to realise what the Mediterranean means to us."[42] Attlee, quite reasonably, counseled its abandonment as Britain could not keep it open in wartime. Cunningham, however, wished to strengthen the British position there by keeping a base in Egypt and claiming UN Trusteeships over Cyrenaica and Greater Somalia. In terms redolent of the nineteenth century, he stated that "the major military interest was in keeping any powerful potential enemy state away from the shores of the Mediterranean . . . [for] the entry of Russia into the Mediterranean on any terms would be most undesirable."[43] In the Far East, Cunningham felt it was important "to maintain as strong Naval forces as practicable in the Western Pacific and to make an adequate show of force in Japanese and Korean waters . . . to foster our considerable commercial interests in China" and to impress the Chinese, cement the Commonwealth and prevent American hegemony in this region.[44] Though the Admiralty clung to an integrated Imperial defence policy, the Dominions, cutting costs, sought America's protection and were unwilling to accept British naval tutelage. The new Labour Cabinet echoed prewar practice in declaring that there would be no major war for two or three years and no surface fleet threat for even longer; Cunningham reminded it tartly of the submarine threat.

Whatever his grand strategy for the postwar years, Cunningham quickly realized that "there is no question that our financial situation is so bad that it is most urgent that we reduce to essentials only."[45] Initial Board proposals for a fleet of Fisher proportions (12 battleships, 24 carriers, 50 cruisers, 126 destroyers, 190 escort vessels, 86 submarines, and numerous lesser craft) were trimmed substantially. In response to Churchill's doubts (fostered by Cherwell and Sinclair, the Air Minister) "on whether the battleship is not rendered obsolete by new inventions," the Board maintained that it was still "the basis of strength of the Fleet." Cunningham, however, condemned *Vanguard* as "a waste of labour and money."[46]

For all his undoubted conservatism and lack of interest in technology, Cunningham was shrewd enough to see where the future lay. With characteristic peremptoriness, Churchill had told Alexander, "You must realise that after the war the Air will take a very large part of the duties hitherto discharged by the Royal Navy."[47] Though cognizant of the RAF's determination to claim the principal role in both defence and attack, Cunningham took the statesmanlike view that "we do not want eternal friction between the services."[48] Thus he was prepared, subject to guarantees, to permit Air Ministry control of aircraft design and production and made no claim to Coastal Command, believing that naval needs could be satisfied by refining the existing cooperation. Nevertheless, with regard to air power in general, "we looked on it as our principal future weapon and would demand our share of it."[49] He took the lead in shaking up the FAA, whose indifferent performance, despite lavish provision, convinced him that "we must get some acute brains onto the Air side" by strengthening its representation on the Board and setting up flag commands for operations and training.[50] His long Mediterranean exposure to the effects of air power could hardly fail to influence him.

Though he presided over the Navy at a time of rapid technical innovation, he was scornful of much of the new "gadgetry." Of *Solebay*, he observed, "These 'Battles' fulfil my worst expectations. An erection like the Castle Rock Edinburgh on the bridge they call a director and all to control four guns firing a total broadside of about 200lbs. We must get back to a reasonably sized destroyer well gunned." In cruisers, too, he noticed "a grave tendency to sacrifice fighting power for endurance," yet among the war's lessons for the Royal Navy were the lack of endurance of its ships and the inadequacy of their gunnery control.[51] He did share the widespread doubts about the quality of H.M. ships, observing that the design of French and American ships seemed better and he could not help wondering whether British constructors were "skilled enough." Thus he pressed for assurances from the new Ministry of Supply about the future of naval scientific research and was keen to develop missiles and new forms of propulsion. He sought to concentrate the responsibility for combined operations in the Royal Marines, partly to prevent "private navies" and partly to ensure them a distinct and secure future. The Board approved also the liberalisation of officer recruitment and training and agreed, after some deliberation, to retain the Women's Royal Naval Service (WRNS). It was little wonder that Cunningham recorded "there was little or no relaxation in the tempo at the Admiralty" after VE day.[52]

By early 1946, however, the essential transition to peace had been made; the future promised only progressive cuts and unstable world. Cunningham, now sixty-three, and feeling the effects of six years of wartime strain, confessed, "I have to fight against depression all the time," and in the spring of 1946, heart trouble put him in hospital. He had said, "I do not to hang on here keeping other people back so as soon as the fleet gets a bit sorted out I will go." In June 1946 he wrote: "I turned over the Admiralty to John Cunningham the next morning and we came down here [Bishop's Waltham, his home near Winchester]. . . and glad to come."[53] Admiral Sir John Cunningham (no relation) was his own choice as his successor, though only after "many consultations" with Alexander and "many senior officers."[54] Fraser seemed to both Alexander and to Cunningham still to lack the judgment for the post; to one who had been Churchill's first choice in 1943 and had earned high praise in the Pacific, it must have been a grievous disappointment. John Cunningham, who was regarded as more cerebral than the average flag-officer, had not had a spectacular war but he did have two years' seniority over Fraser and was C-in-C Mediterranean, a traditional stepping stone. Andrew Cunningham had a high regard for his abilities and found him congenial, though the Navy must have been surprised at his preferment over Fraser.

Cunningham had been the only possible successor to Pound. Alexander feared that any other choice would have lead to a new "Jellicoe v. Beatty" division in the service and, while King would have been difficult for anyone to deal with, the other American leaders—Roosevelt, Marshall, Arnold, Eisenhower and many flag officers—knew and liked Cunningham and at that stage of the war it was important to take their views into consideration. Cunningham was rightly doubtful of his ability to head the Naval Staff; he had scant interest in staff work and, like many senior officers, little idea of how to handle it properly. Nonetheless, in the previous eighteen months he had made a successful leap from ship to shore, worked harmoniously with the Americans and other British services in the

Mediterranean, and even dealt skilfully and effectively with the French factions in North Africa. This experience was to be invaluable at meetings of the CCOS and in assuring smooth Allied cooperation on D day and in subsequent operations. It was unfortunate that he had to preside over both a decline in the naval share of national resources and a diminishing maritime role in the war. He took over at just about the point at which Neptune's trident passed finally from Britannia to Columbia; for one who was widely regarded as Britain's greatest admiral since Nelson, it was galling to have to play second fiddle to the Americans. It was humiliating to be dependent on American operational assistance, vital supplies, and goodwill, yet every First Sea Lord since Fisher's palmy days had struggled against increasing odds with steadily diminishing resources. Not only were other powers possessed of greater strength, Britain possessed a declining industrial and financial base and a much weaker (and potentially fatal) strategic position, while it also had to meet the demands of a mass army and a huge air force.

As most naval decisions are the collective responsibility of the Board, and as many of the First Sea Lord's papers are drafted for him by subordinates, it is often difficult to determine the Chief of Naval Staff's precise contribution to maritime policy. As he recognized, Cunningham was called on to lead the Navy in the final phase of the war on a course that had already been set. He was a man of limited vision, but that was of little consequence, at least while the war continued. He had the successful executive's capacity for keeping clear of details and keeping to the high ground of first principles. Thus, when the U-boat offensive was renewed, he accorded it at once the highest priority, cognizant of its fundamental strategic significance. When attention began to turn to the Eastern War, he took immediately the firm and sound strategic position that the most rapid and cost-effective way to terminate it was to share in the direct offensive against the Japanese homeland. That the end came before the full British effort could be deployed and that he could not foresee the American determination to exclude all the Allies from any say in the postwar reconstruction of Japan cannot be held against him.

For one with a deserved reputation for abruptness and a severity bordering on the harsh, in the main, he handled awkward personalities and delicate relations with unexpected skill, honing talents that he displayed in Washington and the Mediterranean in 1942-43. He handled Churchill with a discreet blend of tact, patience, and firmness, successfully defending the Royal Navy and his flag-officers from the predatory instincts of the old lion. His relations with the Americans were notably harmonious, and it was a brilliant stroke to put the adroit, experienced, celebrated, and equally tough Somerville in Washington. ABC was diplomatic toward and supportive of, Mountbatten, whom he seems to have both disliked and distrusted. Only with Fraser were his relations less than smooth, a situation attributable probably to differences of temperament and outlook and to lack of a prior acquaintance of any duration or intimacy.

The strength and nature of the postwar Navy was a function of Britain's perceived peacetime role and resources. British politicians of all persuasions were determined that the nation should continue to play a global role and lead an integrated empire. At best, Cunningham, like other leaders, only half appreciated the strategic and economic changes wrought by war. Thus while he was quick to appreciate the potential Soviet threat and to realize the nation's dire economic position, he clung to a positively Victorian perception of the Empire and the significance of the Mediterranean. A continued world role demanded a powerful and balanced surface fleet, a Fleet Air Arm with, not only a major strike capability, but also umbrella provision for the fleet and amphibious operations and a substantial role in antisubmarine warfare. He had digested the war's lessons in air power and recognized also the need to develop the Royal Marines along American lines as the amphibious spearhead, to retain an armada of escorts, landing craft, minesweepers, and fleet auxiliaries, and to reconstruct a chain of fleet bases from Gibraltar to Hong Kong. He supported efforts to bring naval recruitment, training, pay, and conditions more into line with other occupations and postwar society. Though he was defiantly—even aggressively—nontechnical, he was canny enough to grasp the significance of science and technology and pressed for a strong research and development arm, the acquisition of German scientists and their inventions, the provision of a new generation of weapons and propulsion units, and an experimental construction program.

First Sea Lord was not a role for which Cunningham was ideally fitted by background, nature, or temperament, but from the summer of 1942 he had made a remarkable transition from a deck to a desk sailor, albeit much against his will. Duty, diligence, determination, and devotion saw him and the Navy through from war to peace and the reformation of a service capable of profiting from modern technical developments, while carrying out a considerable burden of traditional functions.

NOTES

1. Rear Admiral F.H.G. Dalrymple-Hamilton, the Naval Secretary, to Alexander, 14 Sept. 1943, Alexander Papers, AVAR 5/8/33a, Churchill College Archives Centre, Cambridge.
2. Churchill to Alexander, 25 Sept. 1943, Alexander Papers, AVAR 5/8/36.
3. Fraser, quoted in Richard Humble, *Fraser of North Cape* (London: Routledge, 1983), 177.
4. Cunningham Diary, 19 Feb. 1946, Cunningham Papers, Add. Mss. 52579, British Library.
5. Viscount Cunningham of Hyndhope, *A Sailor's Odyssey* (London: Hutchinson, 1951), 574, 577-8.
6. Field Marshal Sir John Dill, Chairman, British Joint Staff Mission, Washington, to Cunningham, 18 Oct. 1943, *Cunningham Papers*, Add. Mss. 52571.
7. Cunningham to Somerville, 10 Mar. 1944, Somerville Papers, SMVL 8/2, Churchill Archives Centre; Cunningham Diary, 13 Apr. 1945, Add. Mss. 52578.
8. Churchill to Cunningham, 4 Aug. 1944; Cunningham to Churchill, 7 Aug. 1944, ADM 205/36.
9. Churchill to Cunningham, 10 July 1944; Cunningham to Churchill, 11 July 1944; Churchill to Cunningham, 13 July 1944, ADM 205/36.
10. Cunningham Diary, 12 Apr. 1945; 20 Apr. 1944; 19 Apr. 1944, Add. Mss. 52577-78.
11. Cunningham Diary, 8 Aug. 1944; 28 Apr. 1945, Add. Mss. 52577-78.
12. Cunningham Diary, 29 Aug. 1944, Add. Mss. 52577.
13. Rear Admiral E. J. P. Brind, Asst. Chief of Naval Staff (Home), to Cunningham, 24 Oct. 1943, ADM 205/28.
14. Cunningham to Fraser, 19 Jan. 1945, Add. Mss. 52572.
15. Cunningham to Power, 23 Jan. 1945, Add. Mss. 52562.
16. Cunningham Diary, 19 Dec. 1944; 26 Jan. 1945, Add. Mss. 52577-78.
17. Cunningham Diary, 26 Feb. & 1 Mar. 1945, Add. Mss. 52578.
18. Cunningham Diary, 18 Jan. 1945, Add. Mss. 52578.
19. Cunningham Diary, 13 Apr. 1944, Add. Mss. 52577. Humble, *Fraser*, 231-32.
20. Cunningham to Sir John Cunningham, 6 May 1944, Add. Mss. 52562.
21. Cunningham Diary, 13 June 1944, Add. Mss. 52577.
22. Field Marshal Sir Bernard Montgomery to Cunningham, 6 June 1944, Add.Mss.52571; Cunningham Diary, 15 July 1944, Add. Mss. 52577.
23. Cunningham Diary, 7 Sept. 1944, Add. Mss. 52577.
24. Cunningham Diary, 4 Oct. 1944, Add. Mss. 52577.
25. Cunningham Diary, 4 May 1945, Add. Mss. 52578.
26. Vice Admiral A. U. Willis, C-in-C, Levant, to Cunningham, 27 Oct. 1943, Add. Mss. 52571.
27. Cunningham to Aunt Connie May, 15 Mar. 1944, Add. Mss. 52559.
28. Christopher Thorne, *Allies of a Kind: The United States, Britain, and the War Against Japan, 1941-1945* (Oxford: Oxford UP, 1979), 411, 415; Cunningham to Somerville, 10 Mar. 1944, SMVL 8/2.
29. Cunningham to Admiral Sir Percy Noble, BAD, Washington, 8 Apr. 1944, Add. Mss. 52571.
30. Cunningham Diary, 14 July 1944, Add. Mss. 52577.

31. Cunningham Diary, 13 Sept. 1944, Add. Mss. 52577.
32. Cunningham Diary, 14 Sept. 1944, Add. Mss. 52577.
33. Noble to Cunningham, 12 Jan. 1944, and enclosed letter from British N.L.O., U.S. Pacific Fleet, 30 Jan. 1944; Cunningham to Noble, 6 Feb. 1944, Add. Mss. 52571.
34. Noble to Cunningham, 20 Feb. 1944, Add. Mss. 52571. Cunningham Diary, 9 June 1944, Add. Mss. 52577.
35. Cunningham Diary, 30 Oct., 20 and 29 Nov. 1944, Add. Mss. 52577; Fraser to Cunningham, 14 Nov. 1944, Add. Mss. 52571.
36. Cunningham Diary, 28 Sept. 1945, Add. Mss. 52578.
37. Cunningham to Mountbatten, 10 Mar. 1944, Add. Mss. 52571.
38. Cunningham Diary, 31 Aug. 1944, Add. Mss. 52577.
39. Cunningham Diary, 4 Oct. 1944, Add. Mss. 52577.
40. Cunningham Diary, 21 Aug. 1945, Add. Mss. 52578.
41. Cunningham Diary, 8 Oct. 1945, Add. Mss. 52578.
42. Cunningham Diary, 16 Feb. 1946, Add. Mss. 52579.
43. Cunningham Diary, 15 Sept. 1945, Add. Mss. 52578.
44. Cunningham to Fraser, c.7 Mar. 1946, ADM 1/18691.
45. Cunningham to Fraser, 20 Aug. 1945, Add. Mss. 52572.
46. Memorandum by Cunningham on the Empire's Post-War Fleet, ADM 167/120: Churchill to Cunningham, 31 Jan. 1944, ADM 205/36; Board of Admiralty, Memorandum on the Empire's Post War Fleet, 4 May 1944, ADM 167/121; Cunningham, *A Sailor's Odyssey*, 577.
47. Churchill to Alexander, 10 Mar. 1945, ADM 1/19056.
48. Cunningham Diary, 7 Dec. 1944, Add. Mss. 52577.
49. Cunningham Diary, 4 Dec. 1944, Add. Mss. 52577.
50. Cunningham Diary, 17 Apr. 1945, Add. Mss. 52578.
51. Cunningham Diary, 18 Mar. 1946, Add. Mss. 52579; Cunningham, *A Sailor's Odyssey*, 577.
52. Cunningham Diary, 1 June 1945, Add. Mss. 52578; Cunningham, *A Sailor's Odyssey*, 655.
53. Cunningham Diary, 3 Nov. 1945; 10 Aug. 1945, Add. Mss. 52578; Cunningham to Aunt Connie May, 17 June 1946, Add. Mss. 52559.
54. Cunningham, *A Sailor's Odyssey*, 657.

15

Admiral Sir John Henry Dacres Cunningham (1946–1948)

Malcolm H. Murfett

In choosing Sir John Cunningham (aged sixty-one), the Commander-in-Chief of the Mediterranean Fleet, to take over from Admiral Viscount Cunningham of Hyndhope ("ABC") as First Sea Lord in May 1946, Albert Alexander, the First Lord of the Admiralty, brought home arguably the sharpest brain in the service to fight for the Royal Navy at a crucial stage in its history. It was already becoming manifestly obvious that the Labour administration was bent on wholesale disarmament across all three services and that the Royal Navy was going to pay a heavy price so that the Attlee government could afford to implement its plans for the postwar social and economic rehabilitation of the United Kingdom. Another celebrated "five-oner" and the first navigating officer to achieve the distinction of reaching the top of his profession, Cunningham was to be severely tested in his new post. Indeed, it was to take all his skill and tenacity to forestall or delimit the punitive damage that the Cabinet seemed determined to impose upon the military in the aftermath of the Second World War. Although widely respected for his consummate professional abilities, Cunningham was not a very personable character. He was known to be an aloof, disdainful, and sarcastic figure who rarely conveyed emotion and virtually never gave praise to anyone. If personal warmth was not one of his striking qualities, however, he was at least a shrewd and intelligent individual who possessed sound judgment and wide-ranging executive experience, both afloat and ashore.[1] If one had to find a resourceful champion to defend the Royal Navy in a very difficult and fraught era, therefore, Cunningham, for all his personal faults, was probably the man for the job.

He joined A. V. Alexander, a loyal and trusted friend of Clement Attlee, in the struggle to save the Royal Navy from succumbing to a series of drastic cuts in manpower that the Prime Minister had recommended at a meeting of the Defence Committee on 21 January 1946. Working with a brief provided for him by the Treasury which had forecast a financial deficit on the balance of payments of £470 million in 1946, Attlee had stipulated that the United Kingdom could not afford to maintain its armed services at the level recommended by the COS. Without waiting for the COS to revise their target strength downward, the Prime Minister—in his capacity as Minister of Defence—informed the service ministers and their professional advisors that he had decided on a set of new ceilings for the size of each of the armed forces. His figure for the Royal Navy was 330,000 for 30 June 1946 (45,000 fewer than the COS estimate) and 175,000 for the end of the year (50,000 less than the COS target).[2]

It should be noted that Alexander (who was not the lightweight he is often depicted as being) had not been greatly assisted by Cunningham's predecessor in the struggle against the marauding attention of the Treasury mandarins in the early months of 1946. Battling illness and fatigue, ABC had become a spent force as First Sea Lord. His retirement in May 1946 came as a welcome relief for all concerned, since the Admiralty, which he had served so well, now desperately needed someone new on the Board with the energy and resilience to carry on the fight against political encroachment and the initiative and imagination to map out an overall strategy for the Royal Navy to follow in the postwar world.

Sir John Cunningham, who had been chosen as First Sea Lord over the claims of Admiral Lord Fraser of North Cape, felt himself a match for anyone and was in no way intellectually overawed by the prospect of having to defend the Royal Navy against the pro-disarmament lobby in the Cabinet and Defence Committee.[3] He began by seeking to forge a solid partnership with the sixty-one-year-old Alexander—a man whose wily gifts, lengthy ministerial experience at the Admiralty, and long association with Attlee meant that he was listened to with a degree of respect in government circles. Unfortunately, any hopes that Cunningham may have entertained for his working relationship with Alexander were thwarted after only three months when the First Lord was elevated to the post of Minister of Defence.[4] Into Alexander's place at the head of the Admiralty came the ineffectual George Hall, a trade unionist, who had little initiative and even less political weight. If Attlee had wanted deliberately to weaken the Admiralty, he could not have done better than to appoint Viscount Hall to the position of First Lord. Apart from anything else, Hall did not even command a place in the Cabinet—an ominous sign of the times.[5] Despite the fact that the Admiralty had clearly been downgraded in importance as a result of these political changes, Cunningham's own position and influence on the Board had been commensurately strengthened. He was the acknowledged expert and his ideas were always likely to prevail over those of the worthy First Lord, who was largely out of his depth in naval affairs.[6] Moreover, he also possessed, in Sir Rhoderick McGrigor, Vice Chief of Naval Staff, an able and dedicated officer whom he trusted to deputize for him on the COS Committee more often than not.

If Cunningham had hoped to work with, rather than against, the other two Chiefs of Staff in forestalling the government's plans for rapid disarmament, he was destined to be grievously disappointed, for the entry of Field Marshal Viscount Montgomery of Alamein onto the Committee on 1 July 1946 as CIGS did more to sow discord between the three services than anything else. Relations between Montgomery and Lord Tedder, the Chief of Air Staff, were dreadful (each man loathed the other,) and while there was little love lost between Montgomery and Cunningham, these two vain and egotistical men could at least communicate with one another.[7] By contrast, there was an absence of vitriol between Tedder and Cunningham, but it rarely did the latter any good since the demands of each service ensured that each man looked to gain some advantage at the expense of the other. As a result of the savage personal feuding that took place on the COS Committee, the three services were individually, as well as collectively, weakened. Suspicion and envy between them ensured that a broad and cohesive united front against the proposed government cuts could not be constructed.[8] It was a pathetic example of military solidarity.

Frustrated on both the political and COS fronts, Cunningham initially thought it might be possible to appeal for support directly to Alexander in his new capacity as Minister of Defence. He soon found out, however, that such an idea was impractical, and that notwithstanding Alexander's past responsibility for the Royal Navy, expecting him now to favor it over the other two services was totally unrealistic. Sobered by this experience, Cunningham thereafter remained wary of his former chief. By December 1946, therefore, he had come to the conclusion that if the Labour administration's "salami tactics" of slicing the Admiralty estimates bit by bit were to be resisted successfully, the Board would have to look to its own devices to mount a credible defense of the Royal Navy. From this time forward Cunningham became more vocal on a whole range of issues and less willing to seek a compromise on those matters that affected the Admiralty in any way.

Faced by further political demands to reduce manpower in the senior service to a figure of 146,500 by March 1948, Cunningham put forward a vigorously worded paper indicating just what the government would get for these cuts in terms of principal classes of warship. It made depressing reading:

> 2 Battleships
> 2 Fleet Carriers
> 4 Light Fleet Carriers
> 13 Cruisers
> 32 Destroyers
> 23 Escorts
> 17 Submarines

In conclusion, the Admiralty memo pointed out the stark facts of life for the Royal Navy in the modern world:

> It is at once apparent that a Fleet of the size indicated above would not meet our requirements and commitments for training for war; nor for the protection and furtherance of British interests abroad; nor for providing a nucleus for expansion for war. . . . Ships on foreign stations would be so reduced that there would be a continual risk of their being unable to meet all calls for 'police' duties made upon them. . . . It is therefore considered that such a Fleet is inadequate.[9]

Despite its somber tone, Cunningham's dissenting appendix to the COS paper on the future size and strength of the British armed forces did not make the government think again on this issue.

Confronted by a financial calamity that grew worse as the most severe winter weather of the century touched off a major fuel crisis at the start of 1947, Attlee's Cabinet simply could not afford to be sentimental about the Royal Navy. According to the Prime Minister, the existing peacetime fleet was far too large for a naval force that had no obvious rivals and must expect to be streamlined to take account of changes in international relations and economic realities. Alexander vainly tried his best to arrest this development in January 1947. Not surprisingly, he failed to win over a frankly unsympathetic audience in Cabinet, which was demanding a reduction in overseas expenditure and a series of belt-tightening measures at home. Even so, he managed to secure a compromise with Dr. Hugh Dalton, the Chancellor of the Exchequer, the effect of which was to reduce the scale of the cuts that the Treasury had previously demanded in the departmental estimates for all three services and the fledgling Ministry of Supply (the source of the secret funding for the atomic bomb project).

What Alexander and Cunningham sought to avoid was a return to the bad old days of the "Ten Year No War Rule," which had done much to hamstring the British defense effort in the late 1920s and early 1930s. Emanuel Shinwell, the Minister of Power, was known to favor the implementation of this axiom as a guiding principle for the planning of future defense strategy.[10] It had a strong attraction in days of financial restraint since it made disarmament and low departmental estimates a virtual certainty. Neither Alexander nor the First Sea Lord needed reminding that adoption of the "Ten Year Rule" was the thin end of the wedge as far as the armed services were concerned. Consequently, the Minister of Defence set himself the task of derailing this initiative in favor of obtaining political acceptance for a set of security goals that the defense forces were expected to attain in the post-war world. He delineated these objectives as:

i. The ability to defend the resources on which the Commonwealth must draw to prosecute a major war, until with our Allies we can develop an all-out offensive.

ii. The holding of bases, from which this offensive can be launched at the earliest possible moment.[11]

Apart from being able to defend the independence and integrity of the United Kingdom, Alexander pointed out that the British armed forces must be sufficient both to preserve existing sea communications and to maintain a firm hold on the Middle East.[12]

Although the COS were fairly caustic about Alexander's work on their behalf (Montgomery, for instance, thought the Minister of Defence utterly inept), Cunningham was not disposed to attack him since it was difficult to see how anyone else could have achieved more in the face of such ministerial hostility to the military establishment.[13] Even so, he believed that the cuts that had already been agreed to in the departmental estimates were of such an order as to undermine the future viability of the armed services. As far as he was concerned, the latest round of economies had cut everything down to the bone and any further savings could only be made at the expense of taking risks with British security.[14] It was evident to him, therefore, that the future looked extremely bleak for a number of British bases in far-flung corners of the world. Of all of these scattered outposts, the naval bases east of Suez, such as Trincomalee, Singapore, and Hong Kong, seemed especially vulnerable to the wielding of the government's financial axe, as no potential enemy battle fleet existed in the vast areas covered by both the East Indies and the Far East Stations. Nonetheless, as Cunningham lamented, regardless of the capital ship strength of probable enemies in this region, there were still plenty of potentially hostile submarines in this part of the globe, where the British retained many very important assets and investments.[15]

Unfortunately, the sterling crisis of late July and early August 1947 ensured that more stringent demands would be made of the overall military budget in the weeks ahead. Cunningham, Montgomery, and Tedder were equally powerless to prevent these fresh blows from being administered to the armed forces. As expected, foreign stations absorbed most of the punishment. This collective inability on the part of the service ministries to deflect the government from its mission of achieving financial accountability was a matter of grave consternation to the COS. Nagging doubts about the government's likely response to any worsening of the convertibility crisis in the future sparked fears that this might not be the last time the military budget was raided to help pay for the economic dislocation of the country. Cunningham counseled caution and spoke of the risks the Cabinet was running in reducing the combat readiness of the armed forces for any war that might break out suddenly in the future. Speaking of the Admiralty's contribution to future defense policy, Cunningham admitted that since its hands were tied, only minimum forces were available to cope with the tasks of training, the protection of British interests overseas, and the provision of any naval contribution to the UN security forces. He reported that financial constraints had forced it to postpone all hope of creating a balanced war fleet for a period of five years and that it had decided to concentrate its scarce resources in the interim period on the construction of experimental and prototype vessels, the modernization of its aging aircraft carrier fleet, and the maintenance by refitting of its existing forces.[16]

Suspicion that the government would insist on further pruning of the departmental estimates turned to reality when the Minister of Defence instructed the COS to keep the combined defense budget for 1948-49 below £600 million. As mistrust between the three service ministries festered, and broke out into open disagreement between the COS in late August, Alexander reached the conclusion that his original proposal had been too harsh and ought to be revised upward to reach £711 million (£155 million of which was for the Royal Navy). Even so, it was still £114 million below the figure offered by the COS as their revised estimate for the 1948-49 financial year. Disregarding their complaints, Alexander, who was evidently working to the despised "Five Year Rule," sought a further large reduction in the strength of the forces so that a figure of 713,000 could be reached by 31 March 1949 (representing a decline of nearly 300,000 from the approved figure of 1,007,000 for 31 March 1948). In naval terms, these economies would ensure the scrapping of a large number of warships in the Reserve Fleet and significant cuts in the number of vessels on foreign stations, and possibly even in home waters as well. In addition, new construction programs would have to be forfeited, refitting and modernization schemes for older ships postponed, the naval aircraft program would have to be savagely amended, and no new major works projects begun. Alexander was alive to what this meant: "In particular, we shall be virtually abandoning our position in the Pacific, seriously weakening our strength in the Middle East and Germany, and providing no margin to meet unforeseen circumstances."[17] Not surprisingly, Cunningham and the Admiralty Board (with the solitary exception of Viscount Hall) were less than appreciative of Alexander's handiwork when they met on 1 October 1947. Lacking the power to prevent the Minister of Defence from obtaining Cabinet blessing for his plans, however, the Board was advised by Hall to accept the situation for what it was and not to see it as the government attacking the Royal Navy. This was not what the Board wished to hear—even if it made sense—and it did nothing to endear the First Lord to the rest of his senior naval colleagues.[18]

Apart from his participation in the COS's unequal struggle with the government over the departmental estimates during the summer and autumn of 1947, Cunningham's attention had also been increasingly focussed at this time upon another bone of contention—the future system of command in both the Middle East and Far East. This was not so much a fight with the government as an internal dispute between the COS and the services they represented. Cunningham found himself isolated as Montgomery and Tedder for once agreed that the Combined Headquarters for the British forces in the Middle East and Far East should be located at Cyrenaica and Singapore respectively. He was against Montgomery's proposal for a triservice base on practical grounds and felt sympathy with those individuals, such as Sir Denis Boyd, the Commander-in-Chief of the British Pacific Fleet, who regarded Singapore with acute unease as a prospective main base for his fleet.[19] Cunningham's contention that there was no reason to change the existing system of command, while genuine, was never totally convincing. Nonetheless, the First Sea Lord still labored on throughout the winter months in a valiant attempt to thwart Montgomery's plan. He did not succeed, even though his stoical refusal to concede defeat on this issue had the effect of delaying its implementation by several months.[20] Finally, however, Boyd, with much grumbling and foreboding, had to move his headquarters south to the new Far East Station at Singapore. Cunningham's dogged resistance to these arrangements did at least win a concession from Attlee and Alexander to the effect

224 *The First Sea Lords*

that a flag-officer could be retained in Hong Kong as second in command of the Far East Station. It was the Chief of Naval Staff's intention that the flag-officer should remain afloat while the Commander-in-Chief was ashore, and vice versa. It was not a policy that worked very well in practice, however, as the *Amethyst* crisis was to reveal most graphically in 1949.[21]

Much of the first two years of Cunningham's time at the Admiralty had been spent in what may be safely described as damage limitation. While he had been conspicuously unsuccessful in arresting the thrust of the Labour government's plans for the military, it was not through any lack of ability or commitment on his part that the Royal Navy stood in 1948 as a pale imitation of what it had been in the autumn of 1945. One need only look at the following breakdown of warship classes to see the dramatic nature of that somber fact:[22]

<u>Principal Classes of Warship in the Royal Navy (Nov. 1945)</u>
   15 Battleships (5 in Reserve)
   13 Aircraft Carriers (2 in Reserve)
   40 Escort Carriers (2 in Reserve)
   47 Cruisers (2 in Reserve)
   225 Destroyers (18 in Reserve)
   128 Submarines

<u>Disposition of Principal Classes of Warship in the Royal Navy (1 July 1948)</u>

	Home	Med.	Pac.	E.I.	S.At.	A/WI	Train.
Battleships	1	-	-	-	-	-	1
Fleet Carriers	1	-	-	-	-	-	2
Lt.Flt.Carriers	2	2	-	-	-	-	-
Cruisers	4	4	2	2	1	1	2
Destroyers	16	12	5	-	-	-	-
Frigates	18	10	5	5	2	2	21
Submarines	12	8	1	-	-	-	12

Source: DO(48)46, *The Defence Position*, 26 July 1948, 5, CAB 131/6.
Note: Med. = Mediterranean; Pac. = Pacific; E.I. = East Indies; S.At. = South Atlantic; A/WI = America/West Indies; Train. = Training.

In the few remaining months of his tenure as First Sea Lord, however, Cunningham was to witness some easing of the pressure on the senior service as the first of a series of Cold War confrontations began in Europe and Asia simultaneously. Apart from the Berlin Blockade, the communist insurgency problem flared up in Malaya in June 1948. These crises were sufficient in themselves to force the government to think long and hard about its future defense policy. Just months after agreeing to the adoption of the "Five Year Rule" for its defense-planning needs in the medium term, the government found itself under pressure to revise this plan. Up to this point, contingency planning for a future war had envisaged the use of atomic bombs and other methods of mass destruction in any such encounter, but had put the risk of such an unconventional war breaking out before 1957 as relatively small. Cunningham had never really subscribed to this forecast by the Joint Intelligence Committee and was relieved to pronounce the death of the "Five Year Rule" as far as defense preparations were concerned at a COS meeting on 28 July 1948.[23]

While it did not fall to him to devise a new scheme for the defense of British interests around the globe, he remained concerned about the role the Royal Navy would be expected to play in any future conflict. A major area of concern lay in the quality of trained personnel the service would have at its disposal. There was a sad irony in the fact that as the numbers of enlisted personnel in the Royal Navy dropped in response to the government's austerity drive, the level of technical sophistication needed to run the modern fleet increased. This did not augur well for the future. Moreover, he was particularly vexed about the cost in time and money of having to train large numbers of National Service conscripts for a twelve month attachment with the Royal Navy when their long term utility to the fleet was likely to be marginal at best. This was one of the reasons why he argued vigorously for a major reduction in the quota of National Service conscripts entering the service. Once again, however, the government refused to accede to his request and the problem remained unresolved.[24]

Achieving a high standard of training for both officers and crew was but one of the determinants in equipping the Royal Navy for modern warfare. Obviously, keeping pace with advances in weapons technology and radical improvements in military hardware was going to test the viability of all the services in the years to come. In the interim period, however, Cunningham remained faithful to the aircraft carrier—the vessel that, in his opinion, still held the crucial key to future naval operations. Despite not putting any particular emphasis upon the submarine fleet, he did see some value in the continued use of the modern battleship on the grounds that it had shown itself capable in the Second World War of providing the carrier fleet with much-needed protection against surface attack.[25]

It was Cunningham's fate that he should have reached the exalted heights of Chief of Naval Staff at a time when the government, which was beset by a extensive range of economic demands, could least afford an expensive military establishment. He inherited a struggle against enforced disarmament that was to consume vast tracts of his time and make deep inroads into the service he represented. Although he never suffered from low self-esteem, he does not appear to have used his much vaunted intelligence to initiate reforms within either the Admiralty or the peacetime fleet. He was conservative by nature and inclined to pessimism—a trait that shone through in his work. He remained archly suspicious of Germany, and he opposed Mountbatten's plan for a withdrawal from India and Attlee's decision on yielding up the Palestinian mandate.[26] His lack of personal charm and failure to cultivate close political allies counted against him when it came to trying to convince others of the justice of his cause. Honored as a Freeman of the City of London, Cunningham was promoted to the rank of Admiral of the Fleet in January 1948. One senses that by the time he left the Admiralty nine months later to join the Iraq Petroleum Company as Chairman (a post he held for the next ten years), Cunningham was as highly relieved to go as others were content to let him depart.

NOTES

1. E. T. Williams and C. S. Nicholls, eds., *Dictionary of National Biography 1961-1970* (London: OUP, 1981), 257-59.

2. Defence Committee [hereafter DO] (46) 3rd meeting [hereafter mtg.], 21 Jan. 1946, CAB 131/1.

3. It is clear that both ABC and Alexander had made Cunningham their first choice as First Sea Lord. Neither were convinced that Fraser, who had been Churchill's first choice to succeed Pound in 1943, had quite the judgment necessary to be Chief of Naval Staff. Whether the fleet agreed is quite another matter, however.

4. Strictly speaking, Alexander only took up his new post on 19 December 1946 after Parliament had passed the requisite legislation for creating the new Cabinet post of Minister of Defence. From 5 October to 19 December, therefore, Alexander was made Minister without Portfolio.

5. Attlee took the opportunity to replace all three service chiefs in early October 1946. Apart from Alexander, Jack Lawson, the Secretary of State for War, was replaced by Fred Bellenger, and Viscount Stansgate, the Secretary of State for Air, made way for Philip Noel-Baker. Neither Bellenger nor Noel-Baker were given a seat in Cabinet.

6. Hall (aged sixty-four) had been Colonial Secretary in the Attlee government from August 1945 onward. He had been Civil Lord of the Admiralty under Alexander in the 1929-31 MacDonald government.

7. Alun Chalfont, *Montgomery of Alamein* (London: Weidenfeld & Nicolson, 1976), 291.

8. Nigel Hamilton, *Monty: The Field Marshal 1944-1976* (London: Hamish Hamilton, 1986), 641-47.

9. DO(46)135, *Strength of the Armed Forces at 31 December 1946 and 31 March 1948*, 8 Nov. 1946, CAB 131/3.

10. Cabinet Meeting (hereafter C.M.) 13(47), 28 Jan. 1947, CAB 128/9. See also COS(46)307(0), *Service Estimates 1947/48*, 30 Dec. 1946, CAB 80/103; DO(47)4, *Defence Estimates 1947-48*, 7 Jan. 1947, CAB 129/16; DO(47)2snd mtg., 14 Jan. 1947, CAB 131/5; C.P.(47)33, *Defence Estimates 1947/48*, 18 Jan. 1947, CAB 129/16; C.M.10(47), 21 Jan. 1947, CAB 128/9.

11. COS(47)33(0), *Future Defence Policy*, 18 Feb. 1947, 3, DEFE 5/3.

12. These views were echoed by Cunningham himself at the 63rd meeting of the COS held on 10 May 1948, DEFE 4/13.

13. According to Alun Chalfont, Montgomery tried in July 1948 to persuade the other COS to join him in telling Attlee that Alexander ought to be removed as Minister of Defence. After apparently agreeing to complain, both Tedder and Cunningham thought better of it and refused to comply with Montgomery's plan. Alun Chalfont, *Montgomery*, 294-95. Nigel Hamilton confirms this fact in *Monty*, 715.

14. Staff Conference COS(46)176th mtg., 3 Dec. 1946, CAB 79/54.

15. In a Defence Committee meeting of 14 January 1947, Cunningham pointed out that the Royal Navy's superiority in commissioned ships over that of the Russian Navy was small. Apart from its 17 cruisers and 69 destroyers, a large proportion of which were new, the Russian Fleet had a total of 230 submarines. This compared to the German Fleet which had only 65 submarines at the outset of the Second World War. DO(47) 2snd mtg., 14 Jan. 1947, CAB 131/5.

16. COS(47)106th mtg., 20 Aug. 1947, DEFE 4/6.

17. C.P.(47)272, *Defence Requirements*, 30 Sept. 1947, CAB 129/21.

18. Admiralty Board mtg., 1 Oct. 1947, ADM 167/129.

19. Cunningham to Boyd, 31 July 1947, E.47/3, ADM 205/69.

20. Cunningham's opposition to Montgomery's plan may be traced in the papers of the COS Committee, see COS(47)82snd mtg., 2 July 1947, DEFE 4/5; COS(47)103rd mtg., 13 Aug. 1947, DEFE 4/6; COS(47)118th mtg., 10 Sept. 1947; COS(47)123rd mtg., 2 Oct. 1947, DEFE 4/7; COS(47)139th mtg., 12 Nov. 1947, DEFE 4/8; COS(47)150th mtg., 1 Dec. 1947; COS(47)159th mtg., 17 Dec. 1947; COS(47)164th mtg., 31 Dec. 1947, DEFE 4/9; COS(48)7th mtg., 14 Jan. 1948, DEFE 4/10; COS(48)59th mtg., 28 Apr. 1948, DEFE 4/12; COS(48)62snd mtg., 5 May 1948, DEFE 4/13. See also Admiralty Board Minutes for 16 Feb.1948 and 27 May 1948, ADM 167/130; Memo by Cunningham to Viscount Hall, undated (but probably written at the turn of 1947-48), B541; Memo by Cunningham to Hall, 11 May 1948, B553, ADM 167/131.

21. For the background to this Anglo-Chinese dispute and the detailed narrative of the Yangtze incident, see Malcolm H. Murfett, *Hostage on the Yangtze: Britain, China and the Amethyst Crisis of 1949* (Annapolis, Md., Naval Institute Press, 1991).

22. Note should be taken of the fact that of the warships listed in this table, a battleship, three cruisers, twenty-eight destroyers and fifteen submarines were on loan to other navies, *Keesing's Contemporary Archives* (Keynsham), 10-17 Nov. 1945, 7550A.

23. COS(48) 106th mtg., 28 July 1948, DEFE 4/15.

24. COS(47) 148th mtg., 27 Nov. 1947, DEFE 4/9.

25. COS(47) 158th mtg., 16 Dec. 1947, DEFE 4/9. Three days later (19 Dec. 1947) the Defence Committee recommended scrapping five old battleships (*Nelson, Rodney, Queen Elizabeth, Valiant* and *Renown*), showing that there was no room for sentiment in the modern age of financial accountability, DO(47) 27th mtg., 19 Dec. 1947, CAB 131/5.

26. COS(48) 16 th mtg., 2 Feb. 1948, DEFE 4/10; COS(47) 86th mtg., 9 July 1947, DEFE 4/4; COS(47) 97th mtg., 30 July 1947, DEFE 4/6.

16

Admiral Lord Fraser of North Cape (1948–1951)

Tom Frame

Bruce Austin Fraser succeeded Admiral Sir John Cunningham as First Sea Lord on 6 September 1948. He had declined the post when it had first been offered to him by Churchill in 1943 since he thought that it would be more approriate for this accolade to go to Admiral Sir Andrew Cunningham ("ABC"). While five years later he had no further scruples in accepting the post, he may have viewed his appointment as First Sea Lord as something other than the climax of his naval career. He had established his reputation at sea by sinking the German battleship *Scharnhorst*, commanded the massive British Pacific Fleet in wartime, and been accorded the high honors usually associated with the office of First Sea Lord before becoming the professional head of what was a rapidly declining postwar Royal Navy in the late summer of 1948.

A "five-oner" and gunnery officer with a wealth of naval command and administrative experience both afloat and ashore, Fraser was an enigma to many people. He was a very private man who exercised great discipline over his emotions. He was also uncomplicated. At times, he seemed almost too professional and overly devoted to the Navy. This probably explains why he never married. He was a popular flag-officer and enjoyed the goodwill of seagoing officers and sailors, his brother admirals at Whitehall, and politicians on both sides of Parliament.

It was a dispiriting fact that he found the political leadership of the Navy during Fraser's tenure to be comparatively weak. The First Lord of the Admiralty was Viscount Hall. He was ill-suited for the task and described around the Fleet as "the arch aitch-dropper of the Labour Party."[1] Under Hall, the First Lord lost his place in the Cabinet. However, Fraser had an especially close relationship with

Prime Minister Clement Attlee, whom he described as "a very good little man," and with Foreign Secretary Ernest Bevin. Both proved much easier for Fraser to work with than Churchill.

As if to compensate for the ineffectiveness of Viscount Hall, Fraser was fortunately surrounded by a very capable and widely experienced uniformed team at the Admiralty, all of whom had proved themselves in war. The Second Sea Lord was Vice Admiral Cecil Harcourt; the Third Sea Lord was Vice Admiral Sir Charles Daniel (soon to be replaced by Vice Admiral Michael Denny); the Fourth Sea Lord, for most of Fraser's tenure (and by Fraser's personal invitation), was Vice Admiral Earl Mountbatten who replaced Vice Admiral Herbert Packer; and the Fifth Sea Lord was initially Vice Admiral George Creasy, and then Rear Admiral Maurice Mansergh. Vice Admiral Sir John Edelsten, the Vice Chief of Naval Staff, was later replaced by Creasy; Rear Admiral Ralph Edwards was the Assistant Chief of Naval Staff; and Commander Peter Gretton was Fraser's Naval Assistant. Shortly after Fraser took office, the restoration of the Admiralty Board Room, which had been badly damaged in an April 1941 bombing raid, was completed.

For a man of sixty-one years, Fraser was in good health and, given the magnitude of the task before him, he needed to be. Changing the fortunes of a declining organization was to be Fraser's greatest professional challenge. The Navy had not fared well in the three years since the ending of the war. The destruction of two British destroyers by Albania, the deployment of warships by Argentina to challenge British sovereignty over the Falkland Islands, and claims by Guatemala for territory in British Honduras were largely attributed to the Royal Navy's reluctance to demonstrate Britain's naval power and national resolve. As one who had a long experience of naval diplomacy, Churchill lamented the Navy's rapid decline from the Opposition front benches: "Never has the Admiralty given so little fighting value for so much money and so many men, and never has such value as this been so ill-presented to the world."[2]

The major criticism of Sir John Cunningham's tenure was the excessively hasty scrapping and transferring of British ships to other navies rather than their conversion or modernization for postwar use. Cunningham, who admitted to "deliberately accelerating deductions" in the fleet to anticipate future manpower strengths, had failed to devise a persuasive plan for the peacetime Navy and was unsuccessful, as a result, in reviving a large part of the naval construction program that had been halted when the Japanese surrendered. The naval estimates for 1948-49 were reduced by £43.7 million on the previous year to £153 million. Fraser's challenge was to break the spiral of postwar decline and instill the Navy with a new peacetime mind-set which would look toward planning for future peacetime demands rather than preserving what remained of wartime strength for an unspecified future war.

Fraser's time as First Sea Lord was marked by enormous domestic and international transition and change. The Soviet Union had announced its intention to create a blue-water Navy, the North Atlantic Treaty Organisation (NATO) was to be established, the British Empire was being challenged by a host of nationalist movements in the colonies, the Korean War would stretch British resources in the Pacific, defense outlays were being eroded, and naval aviation was under threat. Fraser was confronted by the proliferation of nuclear weapons and the looming specter of defense unification. His task was to provide effective leadership and clear direction to the Navy in the context of rapid strategic, political, and economic change at a time when the future remained uncertain. He would prove equal to the challenge.

When he took over from Cunningham, the key strategic document was "*Future Defence Policy*" which had been endorsed by the Chiefs of Staff in June 1947. The basis of force structure planning was the expectation that Britain would need to be ready for war by 1957.[3] The Admiralty responded with wildly ambitious plans that would see naval construction in the period 1948-57 costing £3.3 billion, with the peak year reaching £465 million.[4] The Minister of Defence, A. V. Alexander, left the COS in no doubt that £600 million each was the most they could expect of total service outlays.

The strategic priorities assigned by Alexander to the services when Fraser took office reflected the uncertainties that affected security planning in the immediate postwar period.

The first priority, which must not be interfered with, is defence research. The second, in the light of the present developing situation, must be to maintain the structure of the Royal Air Force, and its initial striking power. The third priority is for the maintenance of our sea communications, and, therefore, for the most efficient Navy we can get in the circumstances, and then we will do the best we can for the Army.[5]

It was clear to Fraser that the primary task of the Royal Navy was the direct defense of shipping, with the carrier force playing a major role. As he told the Fifth Sea Lord soon after taking office: "Planning can only proceed on something we know we must do, escort safely our convoys."[6]

When he attended his first COS meeting, Fraser found that relations between the three service Chiefs were extremely poor. The Chief of Imperial General Staff

[CIGS], Field Marshal Montgomery, admitted in his *Memoirs* that "there was not harmony and mutual confidence among the Chiefs of Staff themselves," something he ascribed to incompatibility of temperament.[7] Fraser also found that Montgomery and Lord Tedder, Chief of the Air Staff, were locked in a feud with the Minister for Defence, A. V. Alexander. A former First Lord of the Admiralty with a wealth of ministerial experience, Alexander had quickly incurred the wrath of the CIGS to the extent that Montgomery wanted a no-confidence motion in the Minister of Defence brought to Prime Minister Attlee. Montgomery believed that Alexander, whom he continually goaded and deliberately irritated, had "for some reason proved quite incapable of getting a grip on his job as Minister for Defence."[8]

Alexander did not provide the "guiding hand" foreseen by the Ministry of Defence Act.[9] He has also been accused, by one student of this period, of being "unhappy and basically uninterested in his post."[10] He also had to contend with the great personal interest shown in defense matters by Prime Minister Attlee who, more often than not, chaired Defence Committee meetings.[11] Alexander left the post of Minister of Defence for a seat in the House of Lords in 1951, to be replaced by the more vigorous Emanuel Shinwell, former Minister of State for War.

Whereas Cunningham had tended to side with Montgomery and Tedder against Alexander, Fraser tried, in his customary manner, to avoid conflict with his political head. However, the dispute reached crisis point at Fraser's first COS meeting. Montgomery noted that "the First Sea Lord said practically nothing. He had just taken over at the Admiralty. . . . The proceedings seemed to astonish him—as well they might!" Fraser did not get embroiled in this controversy and the crisis passed, helped by Montgomery stepping down as CIGS. He was replaced in this post by General Sir William Slim on 1 November 1948. Fraser also established a good working relationship with Air Chief Marshal Sir John Slessor, who succeeded Tedder on 1 January 1950. Evidence suggests that Fraser was closer to Slim than Slessor, although there is no evidence of great personal tension between any of the Chiefs of Staff during Fraser's tenure. They have even been described as "an unusually compatible group."[12]

Despite his unwillingness to join the campaign against Alexander, Fraser shared the views of Montgomery and Tedder on the state of British defenses and endorsed the staff paper that the three considered on 21 September 1948, which concluded that the state of the armed forces gave cause for the "greatest alarm." Fraser believed that the Royal Navy would soon be unable to meet Britain's global, Commonwealth and home defense needs. At the close of 1948, Fraser stated that if the Naval Estimates for 1949-50 were limited to £177 million, the Home Fleet, the refit programs for the active and Reserve fleets, the recruitment of national servicemen and regular personnel, and the maintenance of adequate naval air power would all be severely affected.

To counter the limit of £700 million that had been offered by the Chancellor, Sir Stafford Cripps, the Chiefs of Staff established a Working Party in November 1948, headed by a civil servant and made up of a senior officer from each of the three services, to show that the services could not fulfill the tasks allotted to them by the government with £700 million.[13] Chaired by Sir Edmund Harwood, the Working Party concluded that in the event of hostilities in the period 1950-53, Britain could only hope to mount operations in the North Sea, the Channel, and the eastern Atlantic. Other than British bases in the Mediterranean and Hong Kong, the remainder of the Commonwealth would be required to make provision for its own defense. Fraser wanted to submit the Harwood Report "to ministers as proof that the present government policy could not be executed" without any comment from the services to shock the Cabinet into action.[14] The other two Chiefs of Staff believed it would be safer for the services to provide a commentary and response with the report given some of the radical recommendations it contained. The majority view prevailed, and the COS tactic was successful.

Defense outlays were increased by £60 million, with the Navy now receiving £189 million.[15] While the existing capital construction program would deliver a number of new units to the Fleet in the ensuing three years, the combined maximum strength of the Royal Navy and Royal Marines was reduced from 167,300 to 153,000. Manning continued to be the most pressing problem. There were shortfalls in recruiting targets, and wastage rates remained high.

Fraser demonstrated that he was prepared to make difficult and painful decisions in reorganising fleet manpower by ordering the paying-off of HMS *Duke of York*, his former flagship in the Home Fleet, in October 1948. Perhaps reflecting his sympathies as a gunnery officer, Fraser decided that the battleships might still play a role in naval warfare and ought to be maintained in reserve.[16] The battleship force was reduced to one operational unit by the end of 1949. The key struggle for Fraser was to protect and enhance the Navy's carrier strength. As for future needs, he told the Defence Committee in June 1949 that the first priority in the naval program was maintaining adequate numbers of destroyers, frigates, and minesweepers, "on which the heaviest immediate fall would be made if an emergency came upon us in the near future."[17]

At the end of May 1949, and after several alterations, the "Revised Restricted Fleet" plan was devised.[18] The Navy would be developed and maintained at a ceiling of £200 million per year in a "normal" year. In other words, Fraser had decided that the decline in estimates had bottomed out. The Navy was to be capable of supporting the government's foreign and diplomatic policies and to be ready by 1957 to act as the expansion base to meet the immediate requirements of war. The peacetime operational fleet would include two fleet carriers, three light carriers, thirteen cruisers, thirty-eight destroyers, thirty-two frigates, and twenty submarines. A further forty large surface vessels and twenty submarines would be dedicated to training. However, a savage rationalization of shore infrastructure became necessary, and a number of H.M. Dockyards and wartime naval establishments were closed at home and abroad.

Fraser considered the plan "very near practical politics."[19] It reflected his realistic and pragmatic approach. This was the upper limit of funding the Royal Navy could expect in the foreseeable future and Fraser instructed the Naval Staff to plan precisely on this figure, rather than on any vague hopes of future increases. The plan also conceded formally that Britain needed to rely substantially on the U.S. Navy in the South Atlantic and the Pacific and on the navies of Australia and New Zealand in the Indian Ocean.

With the naval force structure clearly defined for the first time in several years, Fraser needed to demonstrate that the Royal Navy remained relevant to Britain's defense needs and capable of competently fulfilling its responsibilities. This demonstration came in several unexpected forms.

On 20 April 1949, the frigate HMS *Amethyst* was stranded many miles up the Yangtze River by advancing Chinese Communist troops after providing the British Embassy at Nanking with supplies. In his report to the COS, Fraser stated that further passages up the Yangtze river would be suspended as Britain tried to avoid involvement in the Chinese Civil War. As Malcolm Murfett commented, this must have prompted "memories of the familiar metaphor about shutting the stable door after the horse had bolted!"[20] Fraser faced the problem on several occasions of defending the actions taken by flag officers in response to local crises. At a press conference convened after news of *Amethyst*'s plight was received, Fraser stated: "Our principle is of course the same; leave it to the man on the spot, except where you can give him assistance."[21]

It was soon apparent that the Communists did not plan to allow the ship to sail and would continue to deny her fuel. Fraser was opposed to the abandoning of the ship and the evacuation of her company, but he did not intrude with directions on how the crisis was to be resolved, despite his fears that the Admiralty would be criticized in Parliament for failing to give adequate advice to its officers in China.[22] After protracted diplomacy with the local Communist commander, it was not until 29 July that *Amethyst*'s captain decided to attempt to reach the open sea. At that time, Fraser was not at the Admiralty but rather staying with friends. When told of the plan, he gave instructions to inform the government, while directing the Commander-in-Chief Far East Station (CINCFES), Admiral Sir Patrick Brind, to wait until the Admiralty had authorized *Amethyst*'s planned movements. Fraser's direction was received too late. The daring escape was successful, and *Amethyst* rejoined the Far East Fleet.

After King George VI had approved the immediate award of the Distinguished Service Order (DSO) to Lieutenant Commander John Kerans (who had succeeded in command of the frigate after the death of Lieutenant Commander B. M. Skinner on 20 April), Fraser personally directed CINCFES to make further recommendations for decorations for the men of *Amethyst*. The First Sea Lord met the ship on its return to Plymouth in November 1949. Fraser was delighted with the escape of the *Amethyst* after believing that the ship would be lost. He described it to his biographer, Richard Humble, as one of the "biggest moments" of his later career.

In the months that followed, Fraser opposed giving the Chinese Nationalist (Kuomintang) forces any assistance as they lost their hold over mainland China. Never an avid anti-Communist, Fraser wanted to avoid alienating Britain from the emerging Chinese Communist regime. Nonetheless, Fraser did support naval action against the Nationalists when they refused to allow British ships entry to Shanghai Harbour.

While Fraser was generally a vigorous advocate of deploying warships in support of British foreign policy, he retained the capacity to recognize the limits of naval diplomacy. When the socialist Mossadeq government in Iran repudiated the Anglo-Iranian Oil Concession Treaty in May 1951, some sections of the Cabinet proposed a directly British military response. Fraser did not support the dispatch of a naval task force. Arguing that Britain's force-in-being in the Gulf was insufficient, that ships would need to be withdrawn from other commands to comprise the proposed task force, that Britain had a continuing commitment in Korea, and that supporting a task force in the Gulf would present substantial logistic problems, Fraser advised that Britain's reaction be limited to a naval presence to facilitate the evacuation of British nationals from the by then nationalized oil field at Abadan. The cruiser *Mauritius* was provided for such a role, while the British government would strive to resolve the dispute by legal and economic means. During this incident, Fraser's professional judgment and his close relationship with Attlee were instrumental in determining British policy.

The Cabinet reshuffle, which followed the narrow Labour victory in early 1950, gave ministerial support to a Ministry of Defence attack on the Navy's carrier program.[23] Defence Minister Shinwell also questioned the need for the Navy to engage in its own programme for developing carrier aircraft. It was Fraser's effective use of personal relationships that played a key role. Shinwell found the Royal Navy's administrative style under Fraser irritating.

The trouble with the Navy, the Silent Service, is that it gets away with murder. I remember when I was Minister of Defence and had to preside over the Defence Council the Navy hardly said a word. It always got its own way without saying anything, whereas the Army and the Royal Air Force had to fight for what they wanted. . . . The Navy is like the Russians. It does not have to go to war because it always get what it wants without a struggle.[24]

This appears to be a back-handed compliment to Fraser.

The naval estimates for 1950-51, totaling £203 million, reflected Fraser's emphasis on the need for research. Funds devoted to Production and Research increased from £62,670,000 in 1949-50 to £72,900,000 with an additional £1,750,000 dedicated to scientific research. By this time, all of the battleships except *Vanguard* had been placed in Reserve. However, the new fleet carrier *Ark Royal* would shortly be launched with the carrier *Eagle* to be available in the near future for service. The personnel strength of the Navy had been further reduced by approximately 7,000 to 134,900, of which 6,300 were National Servicemen.

The debate on the naval estimates passed without great controversy, although Churchill made a point of criticizing the adequacy of the Navy's anti-submarine warfare (ASW) capability. The Parliamentary Secretary to the Admiralty, James Callaghan, responded to the Opposition attack and was left by Shinwell to deal with parliamentary questions and answers. Callaghan was a former lieutenant in the Royal Naval Volunteer Reserve (RNVR) and an enthusiastic advocate for the Royal Navy. He would be less admired by the Navy as a later Prime Minister.

Fearing the Navy's intrusion into the air strike role, Slessor wrote to Fraser in April 1950 proposing that the RAF Coastal Command and the Navy's aviation be merged into a Joint Maritime Air Force. Slessor contended that existing plans overstated the performance of ASW aircraft, overemphasised the importance of carrier warfare at the expense of land-based aircraft, and avoided the overconcentration of air assets in a future war at sea.[25] These arguments would be trotted out frequently over the next two decades.

Fraser had no interest in the scheme proposed by Slessor and no intention of compromising over what he believed was the Navy's foremost operational capability. However, the First Sea Lord had earlier shown a reluctance to ascribe a largely offensive role to the carriers. His reaction was interpreted as intransigence by Shinwell, who seemed to believe that the fleet carriers were irrelevant and unaffordable. While the Minister tried to have naval aviation debated at the COS meetings, Slessor continued to appeal to Fraser privately to agree to the establishment of a Joint Maritime Air Force.[26] Slessor argued that the Navy ought to focus on surface fleet and carrier-based ASW, with support from land-based ASW aircraft, and discontinue its efforts to maintain a distinct naval strike and fighter capability. As a veiled threat, Slessor disclosed that if another Harwood Working Party were established, Shinwell might accept a recommendation severely curtailing naval aviation, such as was contained in the Harwood Report.

When the establishment of the Maritime Air Defence Committee was decided in mid-1950, carrier aviation was under serious threat. Fortuitously for the Royal Navy, the Korean War commenced before the committee's first meeting and the Navy was presented with a great opportunity to prove the worth of its carriers. When the committee reported in October 1950, the future of carrier aviation in the ASW and strike role was assured, at least for the time being.

As fears that Britain was becoming marginalized in global security increased, the Korean War served, in Fraser's view, to show that the Royal Navy was neither irrelevant to global collective security nor obsolete for the protection of British interests. In presenting the Chiefs of Staff assessment of Korea to the Cabinet, Fraser recommended that British naval forces be offered to the United Nations and placed under American command.

Fraser did not play a large role in the conduct of the Korean War. He had full confidence in the CINCFES, Admiral Brind, and his second in command, Rear Admiral Andrewes, as both had served under Fraser in the British Pacific Fleet in 1945. Fraser's confidence in his commanders was not misplaced as both they and the Royal Navy performed well in the Korean War. It was reassuring for the First Sea Lord to see that professional standards and operational readiness had not declined in the years since the war. Vice Admiral Sir Peter Gretton, Fraser's

Naval Assistant at the time of the Korean imbroglio, later wrote that the First Sea Lord was most concerned about morale: "He was determined that the men serving in Korea should not think themselves the 'Forgotten Army,' as might easily happen. He maintained morale well by personal messages."[27]

The rapid British response to North Korean aggression also prompted a massive rearmament programme which shifted emphasis away from a "general" war to "limited" warfare. Annual defense spending increased to more than £1 billion over 1951-52. The distribution of outlays was handled arbitrarily and the First Sea Lord had, it seems, limited scope to secure additional funding for his service. Shinwell has provided a rather startling description of the role played by the COS in determining the allocation of defense expenditures in late 1950. "They [The Service Chiefs] produced a programme which involved the expenditure of £6,000 million, and we toned it down to £4,750 million. Who did it? I did it."[28] The Navy quickly directed a percentage of its share of the increase to acquire American carrier aircraft. In October 1950, the "Fraser Plan" for naval expansion was completed.[29] It proposed a "minimum balanced fleet" and concentrated on the construction of destroyers, frigates, and mine-countermeasures vessels. The state of preparedness planned for 1954 would be achieved even earlier. With the threat of war spreading and the Americans seeking a larger British commitment, defense spending was increased again before 1950 was out. An "Accelerated Fraser Plan" was drawn up, although the forces proposed in the plan would not be available until late 1953 and 1954. However, the Admiralty was able to look beyond Korea and anticipate its future requirements.

The Korean War also allowed Fraser to demonstrate his skill in optimizing the contribution that the Dominions could make to Commonwealth defense. This was certainly the case during the Korean War when, in September 1951, the Admiralty was concerned that it could not replace the aircraft carrier HMS *Glory* in Korean waters. Fraser asked the Australian Chief of Naval Staff, Vice Admiral Sir John Collins, whether the Royal Australian Navy (RAN) flagship, the carrier HMAS *Sydney*, might be available to relieve *Glory* for three months while the British carrier was being refitted. The Australian Commonwealth Naval Board adjusted *Sydney*'s program, and Fraser's request was met.

The importance of standardizing doctrine, tactics, and equipment among the navies of Australia, New Zealand, and South Africa was emphasized from the outset. The Royal Canadian Navy would be encompassed by efforts to standardize the Royal Navy and the U.S. Navy. The need to make ships of the Dominion navies interchangeable with British ships was emphasized when Collins advised

Fraser of Australia's inability to provide sufficient escort strength for the planned Australia, New Zealand, and Malaya (ANZAM) Task Group. Collins told Fraser that if the Admiralty could not sell Australia several Daring class destroyers, as local construction of four ships of the class had been delayed, he would consider turning to the U.S. Navy. Fraser's reply was significant.

I have already given much thought to your destroyer problem. We have already made firm plans for the employment of our Darings, and I do not see how we could let any go. Moreover, they have been 'declared' for priority tasks in the NATO plan.

You will understand, I am sure, when I say that we would much prefer that the RAN stuck to British built or British type ships. The reasons are many—standardisation of equipment and subsequent logistic problems, training problems, and last but not least, tradition and sentiment. What is more important is that the US ships are a great deal more expensive than ours. Once a move towards the US has been started I feel it might be difficult to resist further diversions.[30]

Fraser was also no doubt aware that Australia still constituted a valuable market for British shipbuilding firms which would hope to see future orders coming their way.

The Dominion navies also proved to be a valuable source of information on American activities in the Pacific. As early as 1948, Fraser was receiving information on American attitudes to Pacific security from the Australian Chief of Naval Staff (CNS), Vice Admiral John Collins.[31] Fraser was also able to gain an insight into American strategic-level thinking by having Collins provide him with briefs on discussions, which led in February 1951 to the Radford-Collins Agreement, a working-level agreement that divided the Pacific into zones for the naval control of shipping.[32] The agreement also recognized the existence of the Anglo-New Zealand-Australian area of interest in Malaya (ANZAM).

Realizing the decline of British naval power in the East, Fraser tried to moderate American influence over the Dominions. At a meeting between the Australian Prime Minister, Robert Menzies, and the British COS, the minutes record the following statement:

Lord Fraser said that one of the greatest difficulties presented to Australia in deciding on the deployment of forces outside Australia was the lack of information of US plans for the defence of the Pacific. Before sending troops outside their own country Australia would naturally want to know what reliance could be placed on the Americans for defending their coastline.[33]

Fraser's skill in pooling and optimizing available naval strength to support British interests within the Commonwealth reflected his determination to foster cooperation between the British forces and among Britain's European allies. This theme was developed shortly after he took office.

Reflecting Fraser's desire that the Royal Navy should know more about the capabilities and problems faced by the other two services and his enthusiasm for enhanced interservice cooperation, a staff exercise know as "Trident" was held at Greenwich in April 1949. Representatives from the Army and RAF, in addition to American officers, attended the four-day exercise, which sought to use wartime experience in considering future problems. Humble portrayed it as "another masterpiece of delegation by Fraser, whose 'starring' role was to introduce and sum up the proceedings, turning the main burden of the exercise over to the specialists."[34] One of the RAF observers at the exercise concluded: "We should like to think that the Navy will now join with the other two Services in making such an exercise an annual event."[35]

Fraser's timing with "Trident" was perfect. In April 1949, the North Atlantic Treaty was drawn up. From late 1949, NATO became Britain's major defense commitment. Earlier in the year, Fraser had proposed the formation of a committee consisting of naval representatives from Britain, the United States and Canada, to consider the standardization of operations, communications, military equipment, and tactics for the North Atlantic area. Furthermore, in order to foster trust and goodwill, the First Sea Lord took responsibility for establishing close personal ties with his counterparts in NATO. In May 1949, he met with Admiral Lemonnier, the French CNS, and M. Duprez, the Secretary of State for the French Navy. This paved the way in July 1949 for the first combined naval exercises involving the fleets of the Western Union nations—Britain, France, the Netherlands and Belgium—in the Bay of Biscay and the English Channel. In April 1950, Fraser made a five-day visit to the United States, and in the following month toured Scandinavia. This allowed him to visit four other NATO member nations—Norway, Denmark, the Netherlands, and Belgium.

Command of NATO's naval forces was to dominate the latter part of Fraser's term. In October 1950, the U.S. Chief of Naval Operations (CNO), Admiral Forrest Sherman, had persuaded the twelve NATO defence ministers that supreme command of the North Atlantic region (SACLANT) should be given to Admiral William Fechteler, who was also CINC of the U.S. Atlantic Fleet. Sherman also proposed that Admiral Robert Carney be appointed CINC of Allied forces in the Mediterranean. This was the source of personal tension between Fraser and Sherman, who had worked together during the war. Fraser was opposed to the British government agreeing to this arrangement. There was also resentment of

Sherman in Britain when it was felt he had "slandered" the Royal Navy in his comments about Britain's reduced naval strength at the U.S. Congressional hearings into the removal from command in Korea of General Douglas MacArthur. The suggestion that he had hindered trans-Atlantic naval relations was vigorously denied by Sherman in a letter to Carney:

No one has gone to greater lengths than I have for the last ten years fostering Anglo-American friendship and cooperation. If I have been reserved in my recent attitude it has been because of my determination to uphold the dignity of the United States Naval Service and withdraw it as far as possible from a controversy which has an international political basis and which is inevitably damaging to both navies.[36]

Sherman met with General Dwight Eisenhower and Carney on 3 March and proposed a compromise that would involve Carney becoming CINC of a "Southern Region" based in Italy and responsible to Eisenhower, with a British admiral to become Allied CINC Mediterranean under Carney. Eisenhower reluctantly agreed. Two days later, Sherman traveled to Britain for a meeting with the British COS. Unfortunately for the Royal Navy, Fraser was absent, fulfilling a long-standing commitment in Gibraltar. Sherman found that the British were unhappy with both the Atlantic and Mediterranean commands and that little by way of compromise could be achieved.

When the initial round of NATO posts were announced in early April 1951, however, the only Royal Navy officer among them was Admiral Brind, who was appointed CINC, Northern Europe, with responsibility for Italian, French and American air bases in North Africa, and the U.S. Sixth Fleet. Decisions still needed to be made on the North Atlantic, the remainder of the Mediterranean, and the Middle East.

Churchill remained concerned about the proposal that the North Atlantic Command would be given to an American admiral. Churchill believed that, given Britain's standing and influence, its greater success in the war against German U-boats, and its readiness to have General Eisenhower serve as the Supreme Allied Commander, Europe (SACEUR), a British admiral should have been given the naval command. However, the appointment of Montgomery as Deputy SACEUR probably worked against a British officer holding the North Atlantic position. Attlee could only reply that this arrangement was considered by the participating nations to be a fair division of responsibility.

In an attempt to thaw relations with Sherman, Fraser sent what Sherman referred to as "peace feelers" in July 1951. Fraser had previously been told by Carney that Sherman would only return to Britain if he were invited personally by Fraser. Sherman visited in July 1951, and negotiations continued on a cordial basis.

In a subsequent statement to Parliament, Attlee stated that the North Atlantic Naval Command would be divided into an Eastern Command and a Western Command. The Eastern Command would be assumed by CINC Home Fleet. The complex NATO command and control arrangements were the subject of prolonged parliamentary debate in both houses in which fears that Britain had, or would, lose control over her own forces were expressed. Admiral of the Fleet Lord Tovey described the appointment as "entirely unnecessary" and said that it would be considered by British officers and ratings to be a slight against the Royal Navy. There was also criticism that NATO, as well as attempts to standardize equipment and procedures, represented the "Americanization" of the Royal Navy.

In defending the arrangements, the First Lord commented that a number of retired British admirals were in favor of the organization, as were all the COS, "including the Chief of Naval Staff." Fraser had earlier made a rare public statement on the matter. Addressing more than 3,000 officers and ratings of the Home and Mediterranean Fleets at Gibraltar on 5 March 1951, Fraser stated that he was "personally satisfied" with the appointment of an American as Supreme Naval Commander and believed that it was "the best policy for our country." He stressed that the vital area of the Eastern Atlantic would remain under British command, and pointed out that the United States would divert its far larger reserves to assist Britain if the need arose. On his return, Fraser completed his programme of visits to NATO nations with a call on the Spanish Minister of Marine and Chief of Naval Staff.

Sir Peter Gretton explained the details of the speech to Fraser's biographer:

I wrote the first draft of Fraser's speech . . . and he delivered several talks to several assemblies of sailors. He was anxious to reassure the sailors about the future, and said that having an American as SACLANT was all right so long as there was a British officer as commander of the Eastern Atlantic. The Fleet would be in good hands, he said, and he also added that there were some good American admirals.

At one of the speeches, to an assembly of the destroyer command at the seaplane base in Gib., the Rear-Admiral (Destroyers), William-Powlet, had invited the journalist of the local *Gibraltar Chronicle* to attend what was essentially a private talk by the First Sea Lord to his sailors. Fraser had no idea that a journalist was present. A most distorted and offensive despatch was sent to London, which ignored the speech's accent on the end for the British commander in the Eastern Atlantic and stressed Fraser's remarks that American admirals would be all right.[37]

Fraser's remarks landed him in political strife, coming as they did in the midst of a heated party political debate. Brigadier Smyth, a Conservative member of the Commons, asked Shinwell whether Fraser's by now infamous "Gibraltar speech," had been made with the Minister's approval. Shinwell replied that Fraser, who had the support of Attlee, had acted on his own initiative in making the speech and denied that the government had directed it be given "wide and immediate official publicity." Churchill replied by reading a long extract from *King's Regulations* relating to public statements by naval officers and asked Shinwell, "in view of this clear clause," whether Fraser had sought the necessary approval. Shinwell contended that Churchill had not referred to the relevant section in the regulations and stated that there was no need for Fraser to have consulted Shinwell about the speech. The Minister concluded, "So far as I can ascertain, the First Sea Lord did not, in any way, in sense or spirit or in the letter, violate *King's Regulations*."[38]

When it was explained to Churchill that Fraser had not sought any publicity for his views, he wrote privately to the First Sea Lord on 19 March 1951:

I am very glad to have heard from you that you did not intend to make any public pronouncement on the Command arrangements, and to have had your explanation of how the leakage occurred. It is most important that Ministers, who can be criticised, should deal with these controversial matters, and that the Service Chiefs should not be involved.

Despite this rapprochement, Gretton asserted that animosity continued on Churchill's part:

Whatever he may have said in writing, WSC did not forgive Fraser and he never realised how wrong he had been over the whole matter. In the last few weeks of Fraser's period as [First Sea Lord], WSC treated him very off-handedly and failed to consult him on key issues . . . [such as] the command structure in the Mediterranean [that] was discussed at a NATO meeting in Rome which Fraser was not allowed by WSC to attend. As a result of his absence a stupid maritime air command structure was set up, owing to the refusal of Slessor, the Chief of Air Staff, to agree with his 'air' coming under the US Naval Command.[39]

Despite being excluded from the major NATO talks in September 1951, Fraser contributed to other aspects of joint staff planning during his time in Washington and visited Sherman's successor as CNO, Admiral Fechteler. Notwithstanding Churchill's opposition to the arrangements proposed and agreed in principle by Attlee, he and President Harry Truman agreed on the appointment of Admiral Lynde McCormick as SACLANT on 18 January 1952.

As Fraser was drawing to the end of his appointment, the Conservative government returned to power in October 1951. By this time Fraser's successor,

Admiral Sir Rhoderick McGrigor, at that time CINC Plymouth, had been announced, and the Navy enjoyed a much stronger financial position on which to plan for the future. The naval estimates for 1951-52 totaled £278 million, an increase of 40 percent over the 1950 figure.

With the Korean War having reversed the postwar decline of the Navy, Churchill again combined the job of Prime Minister and Minister for Defence. After the short tenure of Lord Pakenham, the future Viscount Cilcennin, James Thomas, was appointed First Lord. His long period of office brought to the Admiralty the benefits of administrative continuity, but he had little chance to make any mark on Fraser's incumbency.

Fraser had learned a great deal from his time as Chief of Staff to Admiral Pound before World War II. Whereas Pound was unable to delegate and accepted more work than he was able to complete, Fraser appears to have had no problem trusting his staff and managing his work load. His service as First Sea Lord had neither exhausted him nor destroyed his enthusiasm for the Navy.

Fraser's preferred successor as First Sea Lord is unknown. However, his invitation to Admiral Earl Mountbatten of Burma to serve as Fourth Sea Lord had created the possibility, if not probability, of Mountbatten later becoming First Sea Lord. Before his departure, Fraser had ensured that Mountbatten's appointment as CINC Mediterranean Fleet was announced. It was, therefore, to be expected that Fraser's farewell dinner in December 1951 was hosted by Mountbatten. The principal guests included the Queen, Princess Elizabeth and the Duke of Edinburgh, Princess Margaret, Lord Porchester, and Noel Coward.

On 2 December 1954, Fraser joined with Admirals Chatfield and Cunningham in criticizing from the House of Lords the omission of any mention in the Queen's Speech at the opening of Parliament of a future construction program for the Royal Navy. Chatfield was critical of the Navy's matériel weakness and the pretext of using the prospects of scientific research to delay new construction. Cunningham contended that the threat of nuclear weapons was a distraction to the naval program in emphasising the continuing place of conventional weapons.[40] Fraser objected to the overreliance on airpower. He pointed out that bad weather precluded the use of airpower in the sinking of *Scharnhorst* in 1943 and alleged: "Even Lord Trenchard will agree that he cannot hope to supply our needs by air within the next twenty five years." In what was an uncharacteristically critical remark, Fraser said that in the period since his retirement, he had noticed "striking evidence of the frustration going through the Royal Naval Service. The reason is lack of sea time, lack of any policy in regard to a replacement programme and lack of encouragement."[41]

Lord Fraser lived a quiet life in Surrey. He did not seek public attention and remained in retirement as self-effacing as he had been in active service. Despite their clash late in his tenure, Fraser retained a great personal affection for Churchill and contributed the chapter on "Churchill and the Navy" for a tribute to the "Former Naval Person" on Churchill's eightieth birthday.[42]

Fraser's tenure as First Sea Lord has been the subject of only passing attention by historians. Much of what he thought and felt was not written down. This very private man kept neither a journal nor a diary. Fraser's authorized biographer, Richard Humble, produced a sympathetic account that concentrated on Fraser's earlier service and tended to gloss over his time as First Sea Lord. Martin Stephen, in *The Fighting Admirals*, described Fraser as "a great man who had great luck, great help and who made on occasion great mistakes. There were other admirals who did more with less."[43] This summation is unfair. Fraser's time as First Sea Lord was not an anticlimax to an already glorious career. Despite the many influences on the Navy and its fortunes that he could not control, Fraser did not recoil from hard decisions and gave the Navy direction. While he could have hastened the Navy's involvement in nuclear weapons and propulsion programs, formulated a more comprehensive role for the carriers and acted to end the battleship era, the Naval force structure was more balanced and forward looking as a result of his stewardship. Fraser had outstanding political acumen. He knew how to achieve compromise, how to have his staff work as a team, and how to anticipate the future. Eric Grove is right when he says that Fraser was "perhaps the greatest of all post-war first sea lords in all-round ability."[44]

At his funeral at Westminster Abbey on 8 April 1981, the then First Sea Lord, Admiral Sir Henry Leach, described Fraser as a man who "made no great mistakes nor great enemies; and was loved and respected by all with whom he came in contact." It was the high personal regard in which Fraser was held that made him an effective First Sea Lord.

NOTES

1. Leslie Gardiner, *The British Admiralty*, 378.
2. Quoted in Richard Humble, *Fraser of North Cape* (London: Routledge and Kegan Paul, 1983), 308.
3. For a detailed assessment of the effects of this approach on postwar planning, see E.J. Grove, "The Post War 'Ten Year Rule'—Myth and Reality," *Journal of the Royal United Services Institute*, (December 1984):48-53.
4. Memo B520, ADM 167/129.

5. ADM 205/69.
6. Ibid.
7. B.L. Montgomery, *The Memoirs of Field Marshal the Viscount Montgomery of Alamein* (London: Collins, 1958), 488.
8. Ibid.
9. The Ministry of Defence Act, legislating Cmd. 6923, was passed by Parliament in October 1946 and took effect on 1 January 1947.
10. Franklyn A. Johnson, *Defence by Ministry: The British Ministry of Defence, 1944-1974* (New York: Holmes and Meier, 1980), 22.
11. In defence of Alexander, it should be remembered that the Ministry of Defence had been established from the Committee of Imperial Defence Secretariat and lacked the necessary administrative authority and staff to discharge its functions. It was not until after the Suez crisis of 1956, when the Minister was delegated definite responsibilities for strategic planning, that he was able to exert greater influence over single-service programs.
12. William Synder, *The Politics of British Defence Policy, 1945-62* (New York: Ernest Benn, 1964), 155. See also Sir John Slessor, *The Central Blue: The Autobiography of Sir John Slessor, Marshal of the RAF* (New York: Praeger, 1957), 450-63.
13. COS (48) 166th and 168th Meetings, DEFE 5/18.
14. Memo B588, ADM 167/133.
15. Harwood had proposed giving the Navy £166 million. See also Memo B577 "Naval Estimates 1949/50," ADM 167/133.
16. ADM 205/72.
17. Eric J. Grove, *Vanguard to Trident: British Naval Policy since World War II* (Annapolis, Md.: Naval Institute Press, 1987), 46.
18. Memo B590, ADM 167/133.
19. Memo for the Board B590, "Revised Restricted Fleet," 23 May 1949, ADM 167/33. See also Board Minute 4285, ADM 167/132.
20. Murfett, *Hostage*, 65.
21. Fraser's press statement, 20 April 1949, ADM 1/21508.
22. Murfett, *Hostage*, 129.
23. Kenneth Harris, *Attlee* (London: Weidenfeld and Nicolson, 1982), 442-47.
24. *Hansard Parliamentary Debates (House of Commons), 5th Series*, [hereafter *Hansard, Commons*], 1959-60, vol. 613, col: 665.
25. ADM 205/74.
26. COS (50) 74th Meeting, DEFE 4/31 and ADM 205/74.
27. Vice Admiral Sir Peter Gretton to Richard Humble, 10 June 1982, in Humble, *Fraser*, 323.
28. *Hansard Commons*, 1957-58, vol. 592, col: 1000. See also Emanuel Shinwell, *Conflict Without Malice* (London: Odhams, 1955).
29. Memo B671, "Shape and Size of the Fleet, Fraser Plan," Board Minute 4407, ADM 167/135.
30. Fraser to Collins, 11 May 1951, ADM 205/76.
31. Collins to Fraser, 20 Dec. 1948, ADM 205/69.
32. Collins to Fraser, 8 Mar. 1951, ADM 205/76.
33. Minutes of meeting between Prime Minister Menzies and the British Chiefs of Staff, 19 July 1950, DEFE 4/33.
34. Humble, *Fraser*, 316.
35. Ibid.

36. Quoted in Robert Love, Jr., ed., *The Chiefs of Naval Operations* (Annapolis, Md.: Naval Institute Press, 1980), 230.
37. Humble, *Fraser*, 326-27.
38. *Hansard Commons*, vol. 485, 1950-51, col: 1539-42.
39. Gretton to Humble, in Humble, *Fraser*, 327.
40. Hansard Parliamentary Debates, House of Lords, 5th Series, vol. 190, 1954-55, cols: 134-46.
41. Ibid., cols: 169-71.
42. Sir James Marchant, *Winston Spencer Churchill: Servant of Crown and Commonwealth* (London: Cassell, 1954).
43. Martin Stephen, The Fighting Admirals, (London: Leo Cooper, 1991), 190.
44. Grove, *Vanguard to Trident*, 417.

17

Admiral Sir Rhoderick McGrigor (1951–1955)

Eric J. Grove

Admiral of the Fleet Sir Rhoderick McGrigor is not one of the better known First Sea Lords, but his tenure of office in the early 1950s laid many of the foundations for the modern Royal Navy, in terms of not only strategy and force posture, but also officer structure and training. That this all took place at a time when the highest secrecy was observed in naval policy-making, and that McGrigor was followed by a successor with a gift for self-publicity has meant that both this service and its significance have never been sufficiently recognized.

By the time McGrigor became First Sea Lord, at the age of fifty-eight in December 1951, he had already achieved much in the service of the Royal Navy. An intelligent officer and torpedo specialist, McGrigor had been successful both afloat and ashore. His experience of Whitehall, where he had been a most effective VCNS to Sir John Cunningham, stood him in good stead now that he had been appointed to succeed Lord Fraser as First Sea Lord.

He reentered Admiralty House with a new Conservative government in office, which was committed in theory to rearmament but in practice to cutting it back to levels that corresponded more closely to economic and strategic realities. At the new First Sea Lord's very first Board meeting on 20 December 1951, the government's proposed cuts in the naval program were discussed.[1] The Admiralty was able to squeeze a little more money out of the Chancellor, R. A. Butler, for the 1952 estimates, but the Treasury kept up the pressure. The main problem was not so much sheer finance as the load the rearmament program was putting on "the metal using industries" and the impact of their exports. Was that load an appropriate one for the nuclear age? When pressed by Churchill, the new Minister of Defence, Lord Alexander of Tunis, asked the COS to produce a fundamental rethinking of policy and strategy. Their Chairman, the Chief of the Air Staff, Sir John Slessor, suggested that the COS leave day-to-day administration to their deputies and lock themselves up in conclave for a week to draw up an agreed document. On 14 April the COS met to discuss a time and a place and McGrigor offered the Royal Naval College Greenwich, a choice that reflected the First Sea Lord's good sense. In these naval surroundings it would be that much harder to write off the Royal Navy.[2]

The service was vulnerable, as the traditional protection of sea communications from the threat of mine, submarine, and aircraft was the main rationale of naval rearmament. McGrigor's predecessor, Fraser, had put convoy escort at the head of all requirements, but there might be little need for convoys to supply a nation devastated by nuclear attack. McGrigor, however, agreed with Fraser that there was still a need for a strong, balanced fleet. He argued in a COS meeting in February 1952 that defending sea communications was still vital and that the rearmament fleet, as designed, was still the best means of doing so. The mine was the chief threat, followed by the submarine. Attack at the source, as touted by the RAF as a role for their new V-bombers, would not be effective against a mining offensive: "[T]he problem of attack at source," McGrigor argued, "was a very complex one" against this particular threat.[3]

McGrigor had the powerful support of a report by Sir Henry Tizard, Chairman of the Defence Research Policy Committee, on the continued importance of sea communications to British security. An attack on these communications, Tizard argued, would be equivalent to a direct attack with nuclear weapons. A subcommittee of the Air Defence Committee reinforced this view by arguing in March that even if the entire Midlands became a radioactive wasteland, "the United Kingdom would not be put out of the war as long as the ports were intact and American industry [continued] sending supplies through them."[4] These reports by independent bodies were great assets to the First Sea Lord at Greenwich. They provided the basis of the case he took with him, that a powerful fleet was vital both at the outset of a war and in its later phases.

McGrigor seemed, at first sight, to be the weakest of the three Chiefs of Staff at Greenwich. Slessor was dominant, articulate, and imbued with the conviction that the next war, if it could not be deterred, would be short and violent. He had been a commandant of the Imperial Defence College, like the CIGS, the distinguished conqueror of Burma, Field Marshal Viscount Slim. McGrigor refused to be intimidated, however, on the important issues. He argued that although the initial phase of the war might indeed be very violent, if a decision were not reached there would follow a "broken-backed" phase "during which both sides would seek to recuperate from the wounds they had sustained and to recover strength for a further intensive effort."[5] Although, as Tizard had argued, the Navy would be crucial in the opening phase, it was in this second "broken-backed" phase that it would really come into its own. The least "broken-backed" theatre would be the maritime one where submarines would continue to be a menace and mines would still have to be swept. McGrigor insisted that all this was written into the Chiefs' "Global Strategy Paper," which also emphasized the peacetime need to protect worldwide interests in the Cold War, another area where the Navy could also make a special contribution.[6]

Slessor's attempt to commit the COS to a short war nuclear deterrent strategy had foundered on the rock of Sir Rhoderick McGrigor who refused to sign a paper that did not reflect his views. As Slessor himself reported in typically patronizing style:

It was essential that we had the Chiefs of Staff behind us and the broken-backed thing I never believed in, and neither did Bill Slim. But we had to put it in for the sake of little Rhoddy McGrigor because otherwise if there was no broken-backed war there was no case for keeping a large Navy.[7]

McGrigor had to accept that provision for "broken-backed" war might not mean much in budgetary terms, but added to the Navy's role in the first intense phase—a point that Slessor seems to have ignored—it would reinforce the case for a powerful fleet equipped with the latest weapons.

For some reason the 1952 Board Minutes and Memoranda remain closed, so it is impossible to obtain a view of detailed Board of Admiralty business for that year. The available files demonstrate, however, that the main problem was the continued pressure on the naval budget from both the Chancellor and the Prime Minister, supported by the Air Ministry. At the end of 1953 the Cabinet, having compromised between the conflicting views of the Treasury and Defence Ministry on the 1953-54 estimates, decided to institute a "Radical Review" of defence policy. McGrigor managed to keep the Navy's role in both the opening phase and "broken-backed" war in the COS recommendations to the Ministerial Committee charged with carrying out the review, but this only led to Churchill, supported by his son-in-law and Minister of Supply, Duncan Sandys, taking matters into his own hands. At a ministerial meeting on 18 June 1953 it was decided that expenditure would be concentrated only on forces that were relevant in peacetime and in the first six weeks of any conflict. This would allow savings of hundreds of millions of pounds.[8]

When Alexander turned this idea into a directive, he argued that Britain's war fighting forces should be those designed to ensure the country"s "survival" while the U.S. Strategic Air Command broke the Soviet "will to fight." McGrigor, who was now an Admiral of the Fleet and had replaced Slessor as Chairman, led the opposition using the form of the June directive to mount a powerful counterattack. In the COS meeting on 22 June, he reasserted the importance of defended sea communications to survival and the assumption of a "broken-backed" phase that "survival" implied. The following month he wrote to his colleagues that although the first six weeks would indeed be "the time when the major atomic attacks on both sides would be delivered," the "survival" forces would, by definition, be those required to ensure the "survival of the United Kingdom during that period in order that she may play her part in the ensuing phase of broken backed war that would lead to victory."[9]

The Admiralty fought a subtle campaign, skillfully manipulating Churchill's reluctance to scrap the King George V class battleships and the older, unmodernized carriers to obtain a Prime Ministerial endorsement of "broken-backed" war in the Defence Committee of the Cabinet in October.[10] McGrigor also got his fellow Chiefs of Staff, Sir William Dickson and Sir John Harding, to assert that their approval had to be obtained for long-term reductions in the defense budget.[11] Against this background, much thought was given within the Admiralty to new ideas on the possibility and desirability of preparing for an extended global war. Rear Admiral Sir Anthony Buzzard, the Director of Naval Intelligence, discounted the possibility of a strategic nuclear campaign achieving its objectives in swiftly knocking out the Soviet Union. Moreover, such a campaign would be suicidal for Britain. Instead, he argued for targets being limited to military objectives. The survival period would, therefore, be at least a year, and the Navy would have to command the sea during this period while accurate limited nuclear attacks were delivered, conventional forces deployed, and a secure reserve force maintained to deter escalation.[12]

Buzzard made these views know to the First Sea Lord in July, but McGrigor was unwilling to espouse such strategic radicalism. At Greenwich he had accepted the premises of relying on the threat of a massive American nuclear attack as the great deterrent to war. Moreover, the main rationale of Britain's V-bomber force was already "counter force," a means of destroying those military targets of special interest to Britain, notably medium-size bomber bases. Buzzard's ideas would make no difference to the British nuclear posture. McGrigor seems to have become increasingly convinced that if the Navy were to develop a stronger case, it needed to argue that it could itself play a vital part in the initial offensive. He was advised as such by his Plans Division which, in October, forwarded a paper on long-term plans for the Navy that emphasized the future potential of a nuclear offensive from carriers and, later, ballistic missiles. This made the Navy's carrier program even more crucial.[13]

McGrigor inherited growing concern about the Navy's carrier strike potential. The advent of the new Sverdlov class cruiser in the Soviet Navy resurrected the concerns about the *Tirpitz* that had dictated much of British naval strategy only a few years before. McGrigor was more concerned than most that the Royal Navy in the future should not suffer from the weaknesses that had vitiated Home Fleet operations in 1944—and that staff studies showed still existed. During 1952, McGrigor's Naval Staff, therefore, reduced still further the proportion of antisubmarine aircraft in Naval Aviation's plans and increased the number of fighters. Even more important, June 1952 saw a requirement issued for a powerful carrier strike aircraft, the NA39. This would be able to attack undetected at low level (no more Mascot fiascos) and kill Sverdlovs with either a projected antiship missile, "Green Cheese," or the "Red Beard," a 2,000 pound nuclear bomb. Simultaneously the Admiralty decided to build a new 50,000 ton fleet carrier. McGrigor was careful not to provoke too much RAF opposition and encouraged further agreement at the vice chief level to work out a division of labor between the services. An agreed document of February 1953 argued for the synergy of both forms of air power, another lesson that was proved off Norway in 1944-45.[14]

The first postwar fleet carrier, HMS *Eagle*, had come into service about the time McGrigor had become First Sea Lord. This left six carriers in the shipyards, five under construction and one being rebuilt. By 1953, *Centaur*, the first of a new class of four larger, Hermes class light fleet carriers laid down during the war, was just approaching completion. To operate first-generation jet aircraft "safely and with a proper degree of efficiency" required fitting the carriers as quickly as possible with an interim version of the newly developed angled deck. To operate the second-generation jets that were planned would require steam catapults and improved arrester gear. These were to be fitted to Eagle's sister HMS *Ark Royal*, due in 1955. Even that vessel, however, would not be fully modernized, that is fitted with a fully angled deck and the new 984 radar, together with the comprehensive display system and digital plot transmission required for the control of the new fighters. That would come, it was hoped, along with a fully angled deck in the rebuilt fleet carrier *Victorious* and the last of the light fleets,

Hermes itself, which was being delayed from completion by more pressing business at the Vickers Yard in Barrow.[15]

On 18 May 1953, at the meeting where it was decided to reintroduce the term "Fleet Air Arm" to improve morale in Naval Aviation (as it had officially been called since 1946), the Board decided to fit an interim angled deck to *Ark Royal* if it could be done without much delay.[16] Over the following months, the Board went ahead as far as it could in the uncertain situation. The *Ark Royal* modification was confirmed, and the interim angling of the two new light fleet carriers, *Albion* and *Bulwark*, was also authorized. It was finally decided to go ahead with *Victorious*—a decision that led to the cancelation of the new fleet carrier and its replacement in the long-term program by a smaller ship. The plan was to have six carriers with interim angled decks by 1956 (*Eagle, Ark Royal, Bulwark, Albion, Centaur*, and the older *Warrior*), the completion of *Victorious* in 1958, and the completion of *Hermes* to the fully modified standard in 1959. The Board, however, still did not feel confident enough to authorize completion of *Hermes* and even considered scrapping the NA39. McGrigor sprang to its defense, however. Only naval strike aircraft, he argued, plus the battleship *Vanguard*, could be expected to deal with powerful enemy ships in any area. Cancelation of the NA39, the First Sea Lord insisted, would entail "the gravest reactions on the Navy's ability to keep the seas clear of enemy heavy ships in war."[17] The Board decided not to cancel the NA39 but to hold further discussion on its future.

By the end of the year the Ministry of Defence had drawn up a compromise. *Ark Royal* would be finished, but it would be forced to operate with a light fleet carrier air group along with the three Hermes class ships. *Eagle* would be relegated to training, the front-line aircraft establishment would be reduced from 250 to 160, and *Victorious* and *Hermes* would be canceled.[18] McGrigor was able to obtain support to attack this idea from an unlikely quarter, the new Chief of the Air Staff, his old friend Sir William Dickson. Dickson agreed that Bomber Command could not substitute for the Striking Fleet. Even if reinforcement allowed attacks on naval facilities, there would not be enough V bombers to take on Northern Fleet air bases as well. Dickson also accepted the crucial point that carrier-based aircraft were more effective than land-based bombers in attacks on northern naval bases and mining in northern waters. He also accepted the argument about the voice that fleet carriers gave Britain in Striking Fleet operations and the wastefulness of completing ships the size of the new *Ark Royal* and then only equipping them for the escort role. Dickson seems to have genuinely agreed with McGrigor on these issues, but he had every interest in getting on well with McGrigor and no reason to like Sandys; the Minister of Supply was pushing an issue as odious to the RAF as his carrier ideas were to the Navy—turning over Coastal Command to the Admiralty. Dickson did not want McGrigor to espouse this idea too enthusiastically.[19]

When illness temporarily removed Duncan Sandys from the scene, therefore, much of the steam went out of the antifleet carrier issue. A sign that things were moving the Admiralty's way came from a ministerial meeting in February 1954 that conceded the Admiralty two full fleet carriers. *Victorious* and the N113 could proceed, but the future of the DH110, the NA39, and *Hermes* was left open. It was also confirmed that Coastal Command should stay with the RAF.[20] Alexander was increasingly impressed by the Admiralty, especially when he asked for a statement of its thinking about the future and McGrigor was able to get the staff rapidly to produce an excellent paper, "The Navy of the Future." This remarkable document looked forward to a nuclear-armed and nuclear-propelled fleet armed with missiles for long-range strike and antiaircraft protection. Long-range submarine detection would revolutionize ASW, and convoys would become less important as effective transit offensives became possible and attacks on bases became more effective and important. Considerable emphasis was placed on the promise of the ballistic missile-firing submarine that would be a "necessary part" of a future strategic air offensive. Helicopters and vertical takeoff fighters would both become key naval assets. It was an assessment that pleased Thomas. He forwarded it to Alexander, who was also duly impressed. At the technical level, it was to prove a remarkably accurate piece of crystal ball-gazing by McGrigor's forward planners.[21]

When this paper was in preparation, McGrigor corresponded with another old colleague, Sir Frederick Brundrett, a former Admiralty scientist who had become Chief Scientific Adviser to the Ministry of Defence. Brundrett helped to persuade the First Sea Lord that the best strategy for the Navy was to accept cuts in the short term and instead to concentrate efforts on restoring as soon as possible its strength to act offensively, with carrier striking forces as an "ancillary deterrent." By the mid-1960s, however, with the advent of the ballistic missile (for which mobile sea-based platforms would have advantages), the Navy might again grow, both in importance and in size. By the 1960s the land-based aircraft had become an ancillary to the ballistic missile submarine.[22]

Brundrett seems to have convinced McGrigor that the strategic tide was running the Navy's way at the very moment a new factor appeared. The shocking power of the American hydrogen bomb test at the beginning of March 1954 caused the COS to begin a new review of defense policy and global strategy. McGrigor, as Chairman, confidently directed this process to produce an agreed paper that included the Navy's new strategic case. The paper, "United Kingdom Defence Policy," put even greater emphasis on deterrence through the threat of massive nuclear and thermonuclear attack than had the 1952 "Global Strategy Paper," but there was an equal emphasis on maritime forces as an "essential complement" to the main deterrent. The Soviet Union had now emerged as "a first class naval power" that would be turned against vital Allied sea communications. Any Soviet attempt to gain command of the sea would be countered by a major offensive against its fleet and bases.[23]

The main task of Britain's defense policy was not, however, "hot war" but rather maintaining its position and influence as a world power and its capacity to discharge its Commonwealth and Colonial responsibilities. The needs of this, plus the requirement to make an effective contribution to prevent "the further encroachments of Communism throughout the world," were to take priority over preparations for a major war that might be averted altogether. The COS concluded that in any case, war was very unlikely for the next four to five years as the USSR would lack the means to retaliate against the U.S. This, however, might make limited war more likely, as the Soviets would see limited advances as their only options and the West would be less deterred from responding militarily. "Cold" and "warm" war duties were thus the "primary task of the Royal Navy in peace," rather than making any preparations for "hot" war. According to the Admiralty, therefore, "preparations for control of sea communications are not only reduced in priority but might well be altered in form."[24] Risks might be taken with the fleet for the rest of the decade, but the need to keep at the technological cutting edge meant that the First Sea Lord was not as keen as the Controller to downgrade too much the technological requirements of the active "Cold War" fleet.[25] Considerable savings, could, however, be made in the Reserve Fleet and the minesweeping programs that had been predicated on the assumption of a global war in the mid-to-late 1950s.

McGrigor ensured that this new directive soon began to shape Admiralty policy. In June 1954 the proposals of Plans Division to abandon completion of both the modernized Tiger class cruisers and the *Hermes* were overruled. McGrigor preferred *Hermes* to *Victorious* because of its longer structural life. It was also decided to try to obtain government approval for the restoration of *Vanguard*—that ultimate naval status symbol—to the active fleet. The First Sea

Lord was also anxious not to sacrifice peacetime deployment to preparation for war.[26]

McGrigor was still not quite out of the wood. In the autumn, Churchill formed a "Defence Review Committee," which was deliberately created to kill the carrier program. It was chaired by Swinton, the former Air Minister, who had opposed the Admiralty's taking over of the Fleet Air Arm in 1939. Its other members were Sandys and Nigel Birch, a former junior Air Minister. While the Committee was still deliberating, McGrigor reported the situation to the Board on 14 October 1954. The Admiralty was willing to offer cuts in its aircraft program, as the angled deck promised less wastage. Equally, it was willing to give up the Seamew aircraft, which had been designed to operate from escort carriers and reflected the old strategic concept. The Volunteer Reserve air squadrons might also be given up to bring Admiralty policy into line with that of the Air Ministry. Nevertheless, these savings would not add up to the maximum that the committee was demanding. McGrigor's friend at court in the Ministry of Defence had, however, ensured Alexander's support for the carrier program. The only disagreement with the Defence Ministry was over the scale of cuts in the minesweeper program.[27]

Only two days later, Churchill, who was approaching his eightieth birthday, reshuffled his Cabinet in an attempt to strengthen his position against those who were seeking his resignation. Alexander, who was now considered insufficiently radical, departed to be replaced by the very different Harold Macmillan. Macmillan was a skilled politician, who was only too aware of the Prime Minister's political weakness and the electoral problems that an open rift with the Admiralty would bring in 1955. Sandys's departure to the Housing portfolio put him into the Cabinet but removed him from a defense-related ministry, whose new chief, Selwyn Lloyd, was soon being briefed by officials (who had disliked Sandys) on the importance of naval war programs, especially the NA39. Churchill himself chaired the final sessions of the committee and was thus closely associated with the final report that was communicated to the Cabinet, with his endorsement, on 2 November 1954. McGrigor's feelings may be imagined when he read the Swinton Committee's assertion that "the relative importance of sea power in our defences is evidently diminishing and there is no sign that this trend will be arrested."[28] The committee called yet again for the abandonment by the Admiralty of the fleet carrier and the reduction of the fleet to an operational force of four ships, all equipped as light fleet carriers for the escort role. Ironically, the committee now used the "broken-backed" war scenario (which appealed to Churchill) against McGrigor as the basis for its rationale for these ships. The proposals were to go to the full Cabinet in a special meeting at the end of the week, Friday, 5 November. At first it was unclear whether the carrier proposals would be discussed or just the minesweeper reductions.[29]

Feelings ran high in the Admiralty and resignation was in the air. Philip Newell, the brilliant Head of "M" Branch of the Secretariat, who had provided well argued drafts and sagacious political advice for McGrigor throughout, minuted to McGrigor on 3 November 1954 his doubts about the Board resigning "more than roughly once in a generation." Even he, however, was not quite sure of the situation. If the carrier question found its way onto the agenda, it was unclear whether Macmillan would defuse the situation by proposing yet more investigations. If he did, then the Admiralty should not object to obtain the Ministry of Defence's support. On the other hand, after two years of radical review, the Admiralty had as good a case as would ever be possible to insist on its carrier program.[30] By 4 November 1954, it was clear that carriers would be discussed, and Newell drafted a powerful paper. He was still hoping for printed support from Macmillan, but when 5 November dawned, none had appeared. It was left to the Admiralty to lead its own defense, although Newell minuted, on 4 November, that he now doubted whether the carriers were under as serious an attack as it had first appeared. Although "fireworks" might be expected from Churchill—a reference to the date of the meeting, Guy Fawkes Night—he now felt, presumably from the Whitehall grapevine, that the Admiralty was being maneuvered only into giving up its minesweepers without too much of a struggle.[31]

Thomas was not able to be present, and it was McGrigor who led for the Admiralty when the Cabinet convened. The absence of the First Lord was a result of the ad hoc nature of the meeting, but it was no bad thing from the Navy's point of view. It would be hard to emasculate the service in the absence of the First Lord, and McGrigor could give the Admiralty case the force of professional advice. It was his finest hour as First Sea Lord. As the Cabinet Minutes drily put it:

The First Sea Lord said that in the war at sea the naval forces which would be deployed on our trade routes and round our coasts would be vulnerable to the powerful surface forces of the Russian Fleet unless they were covered by a strategic force similar to that of the Home Fleet in the last war. The Allied Striking Fleet would provide this covering force and it must contain carriers dealing with Russian cruisers. The United States Government had asked us to contribute three heavy carriers to it, and although we were preparing to contribute only two, it was essential that these should be equipped for this role. We were also relying on these ships to counter the threat of Russian Fleet activities in the early days of war before the United States forces were deployed in the eastern Atlantic. In the course of hostilities it was possible that the Allied Striking Fleet would be employed to counter amphibious operations of the kind the Russians might be expected to launch against Norway but such a task would only be incidental to the primary strategic role which he had outlined.[32]

This was a skilful presentation, as it concentrated on roles that were not competitive with those of Bomber Command. Newell's paper, presented over the First Lord's signature, had made clear that the Board felt "most strongly" on the matter, but envelopes were passed to McGrigor and to Allan Noble, the Parliamentary Secretary, not to say more as things were under control politically.[33] Instead, the new Minister of Supply warned against heavy cuts in the Admiralty's aircraft programs. When Macmillan proposed a further investigation of alternative naval cuts, the Prime Minister's fireworks fizzled out. He made his own views clear, that he regarded the FAA as an expensive luxury, but said he would not press his views if further investigation could produce savings.[34] The Ministry of Defence had played as skillful a game as the Admiralty; its proposals on minesweepers were accepted without a struggle, but after McGrigor's presentation there was no question of Churchill reversing the tide of Cabinet opinion on carriers. For his part, Macmillan preferred to keep his options open on this question.

It was all too typical of the twilight days of Churchill's second ministry that things hung fire for the next few weeks. On 25 November 1954, Thomas and McGrigor informed the Board that there was reason to hope that the attack on the fleet carrier would "die away." At the same meeting, the Board, therefore, approved the ordering of seventy-five DH110s.[35] A few days later, in an interesting comment on interdepartmental communication, Newell minuted McGrigor that the Permanent Secretary had told him that Thomas had received a phone call from Macmillan telling him the position on the carrier was safe.[36] In December the Defence Ministry sent over to the Admiralty for revision a resounding justification of the carrier in the terms that the Admiralty had been articulating for the previous year and more.[37] The Blackburn NA39 design was duly authorized by the Board in January 1955.[38]

Such a complete victory must have been sweet to McGrigor, who was preoccupied now with setting in motion a major review of naval policy in order to reshape the Royal Navy for the thermonuclear era. He reported to the Board on 9 December 1954 that the Naval Staff considered that as time went by, the likelihood of global thermonuclear war would diminish. There was, therefore, a need to balance "ideal" preparations for such a conflict against its declining risk.

The paper presented at this meeting was a remarkable document. It admitted that the unrestricted use of available weapons of mass destruction would be "fatal to mankind." This might not rule out nuclear war in the future, but it made localized conventional war more likely. Indeed, such wars might become more general as nuclear war became more suicidal. The fleet nevertheless still had to prepare for a nuclear war. Improvements in technology meant that navies were better placed than ever before to seek out and destroy the enemy wherever it might be found. If war broke out with the USSR, its naval strength demanded an immediate offensive against the Soviet Union's "maritime forces and facilities." In words that could have come straight out of American strategic pronouncements of the 1980s, great stress was put on "seizing the initiative at the outset" by "offensive action designed to destroy or immobilise the enemy's maritime forces" and in cooperation with shore based bombers, to destroy "his maritime bases and shore facilities which support his ships and aircraft."[39]

The aim, however, was to avoid global war. This meant that the first priority were forces that gave the best chance of preventing and dealing with "local conventional wars [warm wars]," thus preventing them from spreading into global wars (hot wars). This required "in being, a balanced fleet of modern, well found ships capable of dealing with warm wars and major disturbances anywhere in the world." Such ships, the paper went on, "would have an obvious and manifest use in global war." The only fleet that could be relied upon was that available on D day; all the rest would be a useful bonus. The active fleet had to be of high quality and equipped with the best available weapons, including "atomic weapons." In order to minimize the effects of enemy strikes, emphasis would be placed on dispersal as far as practical, "backed by the mobility afforded by afloat support."[40]

Thus was the logic of the Royal Navy of the nuclear age mapped out. The Board thereupon agreed to the setting up of a Steering Group and subordinate committees to look into all aspects of the impact of this assessment on the fleet, its reserve, and its shore infrastructure.[41] Thus was born what would later be christened by Earl Mountbatten the "Way Ahead." This has previously been associated largely with McGrigor's successor, but the belated release of Admiralty documents allows responsibility to be more accurately assigned. Similarly, it was the Thomas-McGrigor Board that was primarily responsible for the reorganization of officer structure that also came to fruition under Mountbatten. This originated in discussions of officer entry and initial training. McGrigor, an early product of the age thirteen entry, would like to have seen it restored, but he clearly recognized the crucial political arguments that led the Board to push for entry at age eighteen; otherwise, the Royal Naval College, Dartmouth would have become a matter of acute controversy. Thomas was most impressed by the way McGrigor loyally presented the agreed Admiralty line to the Cabinet.[42]

This led to the Committee on Officer Structure and Training (COST), which was set up at the Second Sea Lord's suggestion under Admiral Mansergh's chairmanship. Authorized in October 1953, it first of all designed a new scheme for Dartmouth and then went on to propose a more unified list of officers, including engineers and supply officers as well as seamen. Only some officers, however, could be considered for sea command, given the smaller fleet and smaller ships of the future Navy. The committee's proposal was to split the unified list formally into a General List and a Military Command List. McGrigor did not like this. He wanted a completely unified list, with the seagoing officers to continue to have the best prospects of advancement. The whole idea of the COST proposals was, however, to broaden the path to senior shore appointments. McGrigor was again overruled by his colleagues on the Board. His misgivings over the split list were borne out when the General List, which split into "Wet" and "Dry" parts, was eventually introduced by his successor. The split, which caused much ill feeling, eventually had to be abolished.[43]

The First Sea Lord of the 1950s was no dictator but rather part of a well oiled machine that ground out naval policy. He could not even dictate the shape of the Naval Staff. McGrigor was unhappy with the position of Fifth Sea Lord who, although the head of naval aviation, had no formal authority. McGrigor felt that the post should either be abolished or, if it were continued, be given more responsibility, including that for air matériel. This undermined the Controller's traditional responsibilities. Eventually a compromise was reached, with the Fifth Sea Lord becoming additionally DCNS (Air), with increased powers, but still without ultimate responsibility, for air equipment.[44]

McGrigor had, however, achieved an enormous amount when he handed over the reins to Lord Louis Mountbatten in April 1955. Although the exact shape of the building program was not yet finally settled (Mountbatten would have to combine the two guided missile cruisers with the two fleet escorts he inherited in the 1955 program), the frigate force was assuming its early 1960s shape, with fast ASW frigates becoming first-rate general purpose escorts and a second-rate general purpose sloop design (the later Tribal class) having been authorized. Typically, Mountbatten would later claim the credit for much of the McGrigor inheritance. He was the exact opposite of the quiet and modest "Wee Mac," but the latter's dogged and energetic leadership had made a key contribution to the positive and aggressive Admiralty response to the challenge of the Churchill government. McGrigor had not just responded, he had used the opportunity to trace a new path for the Royal Navy in the uncharted waters of the thermonuclear era. This provided the basis, not only for the successful response to Sandys's greatest challenge yet (that came a mere two years later), but for the fleet of the second half of the twentieth century.[45]

McGrigor contributed to smooth departmental performance by an undoubted ability to express himself on paper. He was always able to write powerful documents and, when required, to speak cogently and effectively in committee. It was not McGrigor's nature to exert force of character through special charisma or "style." His ability to work as a team member tended perhaps to cover up his own individual contributions at the time, but the documentary record makes clear that he was more at home in the Admiralty than many thought. He can be criticized for a certain narrowness of view; especially in his prejudice against investment in amphibious capability. He did not support Buzzard in his major critique of the "mass destruction" strategy, but he was strongly opposed to Britain trying to prepare for such a campaign on its own.[46] In this and in much else, McGrigor's Naval Staff provided the basis for the development of the radical thinking of the Mountbatten era.

Most of all, McGrigor's success in maintaining the carriers that would form the foundation of his successor's "East of Suez" policy cannot be underestimated. As he predicted in his last Christmas Message to flag officers, the Cold War would "continue world wide and be very warm in areas such as South East Asia." The Navy would "have a big part to play both in local war at sea and in direct support of the Army ashore in which Naval air power may prove all important in view of the shortage of airfields and the immobility of our Air Force."[47] Only too correctly, McGrigor said that the "final round" in this engagement had not yet been fired, but he had laid the basis for eventual victory in 1957-58. When, on 3 December 1959, McGrigor died (prematurely after surgery in Aberdeen), the NA39 (soon to be christened the Buccaneer) was in the sky and *Hermes* had been in commission for just over a week. He could not have wished for better monuments.

NOTES

1. Board Minute 4526, 20 Dec. 1951, ADM 167/136.
2. Grove, *Vanguard to Trident*, 82-83; Ian Clark and Nick Wheeler, *The British Origins of Nuclear Strategy, 1945-55* (Oxford, U.K.: Clarendon Press, 1989), 160-61.
3. COS (52) 29th Meeting, 19 Feb. 1952, DEFE 4/52.
4. DEFE 8/27 and comments thereon in Clark and Wheeler, *British Origins*, 155-56.
5. Grove, *Vanguard to Trident*, 84.
6. Ibid., 84-85.
7. Quoted in A. Seldon, *Churchill's Indian Summer; The Conservative Government, 1951-55* (London: Hodder and Stoughton, 1981), 335.
8. Grove, *Vanguard to Trident*, 91.
9. Ibid.
10. Ibid., 94-95.
11. Ibid., 96.
12. Ibid., and Clark & Wheeler, *British Origins*, 185-88.
13. PD51/917/1 approved by First Sea Lord, Oct.1953, ADM 205/102.
14. Grove, *Vanguard to Trident*, 29; N. Friedman, *British Carrier Aviation* (London: Conway, 1988), 324, fn. 60.
15. Board Memo B851, 3 Sept. 1953, ADM 167/143. Also see Friedman, *British Carrier*.
16. Board Minutes 4673 and 4669, 18 May 1953, ADM 167/143.
17. Board Minutes 4670 and 4671, 18 May 1953; 4677, 25 June 1953; 4689, 9 July 1953; 4700, 3 Sept. 1953, ADM 167/143. See also memo B851, 3 Sept. 1953, ADM 167/143.
18. Grove, *Vanguard to Trident*, 105-6.
19. Ibid., 107. For the Coastal Command issue, see also Board Minutes 4713 of 29 Oct. 1953, ADM 167/143 and Board Minute 4747, 26 Feb. 1954, ADM 167/144.
20. Board Minute 4747, ADM 167/144.
21. Grove, *Vanguard to Trident*, 107-9.
22. See correspondence of 19 Feb. 1954, 25 Feb. 1954 in ADM 205/102, f. 105. Also McGrigor quoting Brundrett to First Lord, 2 Mar. 1954, ADM 205/102.
23. Grove, *Vanguard to Trident*, 110. Valuable new material on the still closed Chiefs of Staff Review, DP (54) 6 can be obtained from Board Memos, B914 and 915, of 23 June 1954, ADM 167/144.
24. Quotation in paper in ADM 205/182.
25. See correspondence May 1954 in ADM 205/102, f. 91. The Third Sea Lord, the able Ralph Edwards, argued that unsophisticated but impressive vessels would satisfy the peacetime role.
26. Board Minute 4791, Memos B914, B915, 23 June 1954, ADM 167/144.
27. Board Minute 4811, ADM 167/144.
28. Report of the Defence Policy Committee, C (54) 329, CAB 129/171. For the politics of Churchill's second administration see A. Seldon, *Churchill's Indian Summer*.
29. See memorandum in ADM 205/99.
30. Newell to First Sea Lord, 3 Nov. 1954, in ibid.
31. 5 Nov. 1954, f. 56, in ibid.
32. CC 73 (54), CAB 128/27.

33. Newell to First Sea Lord, 29 Nov. 1954, f. 59, ADM 205/99.
34. See note 32 above.
35. Board Minute 4818, 25 Nov. 1954, ADM 167/144.
36. See note 33 above.
37. Grove, *Vanguard to Trident*, 114.
38. Board Minute 4846, 27 Jan. 1955, ADM 167/142.
39. Board Memo, B942 of 3 Dec. 1954 (PD R51/1232/6 of 26 Nov. 1954), ADM 167/144.
40. Ibid.
41. Board Minute 4826, ADM 167/144.
42. Board Minute 4707, 6 Oct. 1953 and holograph note thereon by First Lord, ADM 167/143.
43. Ibid., and Board Minute 4844, ADM 167/142. See Grove, *Vanguard to Trident*, 217.
44. Board Minute 4729, 14 Jan. 1954 and Memo, 23 Dec. 1953, ADM 167/144.
45. Board Minute 4839 of 6 Jan. 1955, ADM 167/142.
46. For McGrigor's doubts on V Bomber numbers, see letter to Lord Cunningham of 15 Mar. 1954, ADM 205/102.
47. Christmas Letter to Flag Officers, 20 Dec. 1954, f. 90, ADM 205/102.

18

Admiral Earl Mountbatten of Burma (1955–1959)

Geoffrey Till

Earl Mountbatten of Burma took over, officially, as First Sea Lord on 18 April 1955, and held that office until 30 April 1959. His was one of the most important periods in the history of the postwar Royal Navy, but it was, nonetheless, no more than a part of a continuing process of adjustment to contemporary conditions that had started long before he assumed office, and arguably, has yet to be complete. In the 1950s, Britain and its Navy were both facing a set of substantial challenges that would end in greatly reducing their power and their role. Mountbatten's function was to be part of this process and to do the best he could to protect the Navy.

The process of naval reduction had, of course, begun well before the end of the Second World War. Mountbatten's predecessors had fought to contain the downward slide, with some success. Indeed, before he took over, Mountbatten was told by his future Vice Chief of the Naval Staff, Admiral Sir William Davis: "[W]e are making progress in getting the Navy's case, i.e. the need for a Navy, across, and I believe the publication of the White Paper will give us a good foundation on which to start a real full scale campaign."[1] The 1955 White Paper certainly gave the impression that all was not yet lost. It vigorously defended the Navy's role and importance in the "Age of Thermonuclear Weapons" and detailed an extensive program of construction which saw four new carriers joining the fleet while twenty-five frigates and over a hundred mine warfare vessels were under construction. New naval aircraft were coming along, and the Navy's dockyards, naval air stations and home ports were all being overhauled and improved.[2]

Nonetheless, there were ominous clouds on the horizon. Starting with the "Long Term Defence Review" of May 1955, the Navy was exposed to very hostile scrutiny for the next several years. There were, essentially, three reasons for this. The first and most obvious was the need for substantial measures of economy. The 1955 study revealed that to keep the Navy at its then level in ships and manpower would require expenditures which, if repeated across all the services, would increase the annual Defence Vote by 25 percent, to £2 billion, by 1960. As Mountbatten later explained to his dismayed Commanders-in-Chief:

We have for years been spending a considerably higher percentage of our national income on defence than any country in the world other than the two giants, the U.S.A. and the U.S.S.R. After two world wars we are not in a position to compete with them and economies were in any case overdue . . .[3]

Excessive levels of defense expenditure were widely held to be a cause of Britain's persistent economic ailments. The need for drastic cuts in defense spending really became crystal clear as a result of the dire effects on the British economy of the run on sterling in the aftermath of the Suez landings of October 1956. This had necessitated desperate measures in the shape of the commitment of British reserves and heavy borrowing from the International Monetary Fund. This made "startling" reductions in defense expenditures absolutely inevitable if national bankruptcy was to be avoided.

In March 1957, Mountbatten announced that the defense estimates were being cut as an immediate step for that year by a draconian 8 percent:

In this reduction, the Navy came down from 349 m[illion] to 316 m[illion], a cut of not less than 33 m[illion] which has been extremely difficult and painful to find so quickly. H.M.G. however require us to prepare a long term plan to run down to an unspecified target figure, but one which I fear will be well below our present one despite rising costs.[4]

Even more worrying was the fact that as a proportion of the total defense budget, the Navy's anticipated share of 22 percent was significantly smaller than those of either of the other two services and was set to fall still further. The Royal Air Force, for example would enjoy 31 percent of the budget in 1958, rising to 33 percent in 1962.

This well illustrated the second major challenge to the Navy, namely the widespread view in the words of Admiral Davis: "that the Air Force is the young, up and coming, and the Navy the old, decrepit and dying." No doubt aided by the fact that "[t]he RAF seem almost to have monopolised Television and much propaganda [sic]," all too many people seemed to think, in a manner eerily reminiscent of the misperceptions of the interwar years, that the RAF could perform virtually all the Navy's tasks, and at a fraction of the cost.[5]

Such thinking produced the startling idea associated with people as diverse as James Callaghan, the Opposition Spokesman on Defense, and Vice Admiral John Hughes Hallett, Conservative MP for Croydon, that the RAF and the Navy should be merged into one service. Mountbatten took this sufficiently seriously to set up a high-level Naval Staff study of the prospect.[6]

The air threat to the Navy was reinforced by the advent of nuclear weapons since this encouraged the "One Big Bang and it is all over" view of future war. In the age of massive retaliation, it was hard to see a place for the sustained conventional operations characteristic of the Navy of prenuclear days. "The Navy, it was widely held, could no longer wield the power modern war demanded; its ships were too vulnerable, its operations too slow."[7]

Clearly, it was necessary for the Navy's professional head to do all he could to argue the Navy's case against such calumnies. Hughes Hallett had himself remarked that skepticism about the Navy's useful future seemed to be based on the assumption that nuclear power was antithetical to naval purposes. Why should this be the case? "Mobile platforms at sea," the invention of guided missiles and ballistic rockets, and the advent of ASW helicopters and small atomic shells might, he thought, change the relative roles of ships and aircraft.[8] There was nothing new about such ideas. They had indeed been forecast in Naval Staff papers written at the very end of the Second World War, which envisaged the arrival both of nuclear propulsion and of submarines capable of firing long-range nuclear missiles.[9]

Mountbatten had no doubts that the acquisition of such technologies would actually help the Navy perform its task more effectively. He was particularly clear about the range and concealment advantage offered by nuclear-propelled submarines, concluding: "If the Royal Navy did not acquire these submarines it would cease to count as a naval force in world affairs."[10]

Mountbatten was also interested in the development of tactical nuclear weapons at sea because in some circumstances they could increase the Navy's offensive and defensive powers. Under Mountbatten, the Navy accordingly explored ideas of producing a nuclear variant of the "Seaslug" surface-to-air missile and developed a naval variant of the "Red Beard" bomb for use against ships, submarines, and bases.[11]

He was, however, much more ambivalent about the prospect of the Navy bidding seriously for a major share in the nuclear deterrence mission by advocating the acquisition of ballistic missile-firing submarines of the Polaris type, which he knew the Americans were developing under the vigorous leadership of

Arleigh Burke and Hyman Rickover. On the one hand, the advantages of putting the deterrent on a mobile, unseen platform at sea were, he thought, obvious. They would be much less vulnerable to attack from the Soviet Union than land-based missiles. This would spare the United Kingdom from preemptive counterforce attack, give British decision makers more time to consider what they should do in ambiguous situations, and make it much more difficult for an enemy to prepare defenses since they "could never be certain from which quarter an attack would come." Less convincingly, the Navy also argued that missile-firing submarines could also have important secondary military tasks.[12]

On the other hand, Mountbatten was consistently skeptical of the need for Britain to have an independent nuclear deterrent in the first place. In his view, such a deterrent was likely to be generally incredible to the Russians, especially in circumstances of nuclear parity and for the benefit of third parties, because the United Kingdom itself was so uniquely vulnerable to nuclear devastation. He could not envisage a situation in which Britain might be singled out for nuclear attack, but if it were, "the United Kingdom must be able to rely on the full weight of the Western deterrent as a whole—if not then the whole fabric of the Western alliance must collapse."[13] He was even more worried about the possible effect that the acquisition of an expensive independent deterrent would have on conventional forces, which were really much more usable and important.

These doubts led Mountbatten to try to orchestrate opposition at the COS level to the government's policy of acquiring any form of nuclear deterrent. However, this was not a successful campaign. Mountbatten was reluctant to challenge government policy directly and was wary about entering into a full scale conflict with the Chief of the Air Staff, Sir Dermot Boyle, who was an enthusiast for a deterrent centered on land-based missiles.[14] Accordingly, the government's deterrent policy survived. Unfortunately, it soon became apparent that with the successive collapses of the Blue Streak and Skybolt programs, the British deterrent was based on false technological premises. In addition, it delayed the acquisition of the much more cost-effective Polaris system by some years. A. J. Pierre's conclusion is that the Royal Navy's failure to make a strong and early case to the government for the acquisition of the Polaris system was "an irresponsible mistake," for which Mountbatten has to share the responsibility.[15] Whether Mountbatten was right to conclude that the United Kingdom did not need an independent deterrent at all is a much more general and important issue, but it is beyond the scope of this chapter.

Mountbatten mounted a much more open and vigorous campaign against the connected notion that conventional forces were less important now than they had been before the advent of nuclear weapons. He kept in close touch with the evolution in strategic thinking in the United States which was to lead to the replacement of the doctrinal concept of "Massive Retaliation" by "Flexible Response" in the early 1960s. This later set of concepts, which were much at variance with Duncan Sandys's Defence White Paper of 1957, allowed for the possibility of more extended conventional operations against the Soviet Union and worked to the strategic benefit of the Navy.

To give but two examples, Mountbatten was very concerned that the fixation on the prospects of strategic nuclear war would blind people to the severe dangers of starvation should shipping to Britain be attacked by a resourceful enemy. He was sympathetic to the argument that a significant submarine threat from the Soviet Navy loomed in the near future. Mountbatten underestimated neither the nature of the threat nor the fact that the lessons of the Second World War would not be lost on those directing the Soviet Navy. Britain was totally dependent on imported food stuffs and had food stocks for no more than three weeks. It was, therefore, acutely vulnerable to an attack on its sea lines of communications. Accordingly, Mountbatten warned: "The main point of this note is to draw attention to the fact that starvation does not appear to have been taken sufficiently into account, and yet this must be the main reason for the Russians keeping up their enormous submarine fleet."[16]

However, it was not only important for the Navy to continue to play its part in the defense of these vital sea lines of communication for the best of operational reasons. The Atlantic bridge was politically crucial, too. The Atlantic connection with the United States was the heart of NATO and of Western defense; accordingly, he thought, the Royal Navy had to be seen to pull its weight in defending it. Mountbatten was supported in this by his admirals. In July 1958, the Commander-in-Chief Home Fleet reminded him, "[T]he fact remains that the maritime side of the NATO alliance might well collapse if we cease to put in the most whole-hearted support into this alliance on the naval side."[17] Nor was it difficult for Mountbatten to secure supportive comments from his U.S. Navy colleagues to the effect that reductions in the British effort in the eastern Atlantic would be a source of serious concern to the United States.

Many of these coalition-building arguments also suggested that the Royal Navy should continue to participate in the offensive operations of the American and NATO Strike Fleets. These operations remained "an integral part of NATO planning and if [Britain] were unilaterally to withdraw from this plan, it would certainly have serious repercussions within the Alliance."[18] Operationally, the Admiralty argued that forward ASW operations might be the best way of defending reinforcement and resupply shipping against Soviet submarine attack. Certainly the Royal Navy could offer the Strike Fleet support against Soviet submarines and might even be able to participate in any attacks it might make on land targets.

In advancing such propositions, however, Mountbatten was challenging the most critical strategic assumptions on which the government based its defense policy, especially when Duncan Sandys was Minister of Defence. Sandys was intent on making deep cuts in defense spending and was sure that in the era of "Massive Retaliation," conventional forces were the obvious target. While there may well have been an element of political calculation in his initial attitudes and negotiating technique, he soon lived up to his fearsome reputation.

Admiral Sir Ralph Edwards, Commander-in-Chief, Mediterranean Fleet, was plainly appalled. He told Mountbatten that Sandys had been "quite the most unpopular visitor Malta has ever had in my time" and thought his naval expertise "infinitesimal. . . . His views on Naval matters shattered me. And I was horribly shocked at his cynical outlook on the S/M [submarine] menace. The idea that the deterrent is the answer to the menace of starvation is crazy."[19]

Mountbatten's most important battle was, therefore, for the mind of his Defence Minister. It fell into two stages. The first was over the concepts and assumptions that were to be built into the government's next Defence White Paper of 1957. This controversial document went through thirteen "final" editions before it eventually emerged. As far as the Admiralty was concerned, the famous phrase in the 1957 Defence White Paper, "The role of the Navy in global war is somewhat uncertain," in fact was considered "quite fair" by the Navy because "global war . . . is uncertain and unpredictable and . . . therefore no firm role for the Navy can be postulated."[20] Nonetheless, the prospect of sustained conventional operations against the Soviet Navy was not an easy case to argue, and Mountbatten continued to need all his diplomatic and presentational skills to wring concessions from his political masters.

The battle was at its most acute in the period immediately after the appearance of the hard fought 1957 Defence White Paper, when the implementation of its general conclusions was at issue. The result was the Defence White Paper of 1958, described by *Time and Tide* as an "astonishing victory" for the Admiralty. The "brilliant and critical" young Lt. Cdr. Mountbatten, who had been told to watch

Sandys's ministerial television broadcast of 7 March 1958, was delighted at how well the Navy had been treated. More practically, the Navy emerged with £24,500,000 more than it had been given in 1957, an effective heavy carrier program, large-strike aircraft, and adequately sized surface flotillas in the Atlantic and East of Suez. Mountbatten's correspondents and much of the press were lavish in their praise for his success in persuading Duncan Sandys into such a volte-face. Thus, a former First Lord, Viscount Cilcennin, was moved to record:

You took on [?over] just when the RN needed you most and when modern warfare history was being written. So you have a far more impressive niche in that history for all the hell you have been through. It is probably very banal and patronising to say that I'm very proud of your performance, but I really am![21]

Mountbatten's campaign for the Navy's surface forces was undoubtedly helped by the much greater acceptability of the Navy's arguments for a continued role East of Suez. In May 1957, Mountbatten passed a draft of a statement on the role of the services onto the First Lord which very nicely summarizes his views on the matter:

Thus to prevent global war, we must do two things—first to present a counter threat to the use of nuclear weapons against this country: second, but just as important, to provide, with our allies, forces which are strong enough and mobile enough to nip any trouble or disturbance in the bud before it has time to spread uncontrollably.

Against this background, then, it is the main role of the Navy to provide flexible, powerful forces which can be deployed at short notice anywhere in the world to ensure stability and tranquillity and to bring under immediate control any disturbance which could threaten the peace of the world. Should a threat to our sea routes develop the Navy would counter it either alone or with our allies according to the circumstances.[22]

Mountbatten organized the Naval Staff to base the case for naval forces on their assessment of the nature of current threats to world stability. In his view, their main characteristic was the absence of reliable warning that impending attacks usually provided: "Limited wars and emergencies nearly always take us by surprise; they boil up suddenly either in unexpected places or at an unexpected time [so] it is essential that the forces we plan to deal with them should be mobile and flexible."[23]

Naval airpower, especially in the form of aircraft carriers, had the mobility and flexibility required and were therefore ideal for the purpose. A speedy response would also be much easier to provide if significant naval forces were deployed permanently into potentially troublesome areas. With his well-organized circle of prestigious contacts in the Commonwealth, it was not difficult for Mountbatten to mobilize influential opinion to argue strenuously for keeping the retention of warships on station all over the world. "We cannot accept less than six ships out here," a correspondent told Mountbatten, "without very grave trouble with Australia and America."[24] The Admiralty argued that at least eighteen frigates were required for such essential purposes.

The government found such arguments for a substantial East-of-Suez role for the Navy generally persuasive, even in the wake of the Suez crisis of 1956, because the process of decolonization produced a level of political turbulence that the Soviet Union under Nikita Khrushchev seemed all too anxious to exploit. On several occasions Mountbatten was able to keep forces by this means that he would probably have lost by deploying more narrowly strategic arguments.

The East-of-Suez role was particularly useful in defending the case for naval airpower. Even before he took over as First Sea Lord, Mountbatten was anxious at every opportunity to stress "the unique value of aircraft carriers, where there are insufficient land-based aircraft, even in narrow waters like the Mediterranean."[25] His assiduous cultivation of the other two services was rewarded in February 1957 by the support of the other two Chiefs of Staff for the Navy's carrier program. In that month, he told Admiral Sir Ralph Edwards that he was having "a real tussle with Duncan Sandys. . . . However, we have already won one major victory over the carriers. The Chiefs put up an excellent paper justifying the need for a Fleet Air Arm which was even *strengthened* by Dickson and Boyle, surely unprecedented—and the Minister had no option but to give in."[26]

The need to prevent the RAF from sinking the Navy's carrier program was an important factor in Mountbatten's reluctance to challenge the Air Ministry over responsibility for the strategic deterrent, even though, he was soon to be convinced that the Polaris system would make better sense should the government decide to proceed after all with the acquisition of an independent deterrent.

In his view, this concession was worth making because "the carrier is the most flexible and valuable unit of the Fleet."[27] The backbone of the future operational fleet of the 1960s was to be its three Carrier Task Groups, each comprising one carrier, one cruiser, four destroyers, and four frigates, and supported by sufficient ships, including one more carrier, at home in refit. Almost any sacrifice was considered worth making to maintain this level of force at sea. The commissioning of the remodeled *Victorious* in 1958 and *Hermes* in 1959 marked the successful culmination of this most important part of Mountbatten's campaign.

He was very nearly as successful in obtaining the aircraft to go into the carriers and to operate from land bases. In 1955, British naval aircraft were thought quite reasonable compared to their RAF equivalents and performed well at Suez.[28] The Scimitar and Sea Vixen fighter-bombers were well under construction; these were effective fighters and could also carry a range of ordnance including "Red Beard" tactical nuclear weapons. These aircraft kept alive the Royal Navy's wish to be able to participate in the offensive land-attack operations of the NATO/U.S. Navy Strike Fleet. Duncan Sandys, however, remained unconvinced that this was a realistic aspiration for the Royal Navy.

The Admiralty lost its campaign for the Saunders Roe P 177 supersonic fighter, however. Mountbatten complained, to no avail, that this "would severely restrict . . . [the Fleet's] . . . ability to carry out its limited war functions," especially as the Soviet Union tended to supply its clients with modern aircraft within two or three years of their first appearance. In Mountbatten's view, this decision increased the Navy's need for air defense missiles.[29]

But the real bone of contention was the Blackburn Buccaneer, the world's first specially designed, low-level high speed strike aircraft. An initial batch of these aircraft was ordered in July 1955, the prototype made its maiden flight in April 1958, and the first deck-landing trials took place on *Victorious* in June 1959. While even the Americans conceded that "you have an aircraft that is at least three years ahead of the United States and more years than that ahead of any other Navy or Air Force in the world," its acquisition had to be defended at every step of the way, especially under Duncan Sandys.[30] The problem was that the RAF wanted the TSR 2 and Sandys did not think (correctly as it turned out) that there was room in the Defense Budget for both. Neither service would compromise on the same plane, but after considerable in-fighting, and much politicking by Mountbatten, both were grudgingly allowed to proceed, at least for the time being.

The rest of the Navy's aircraft program survived reasonably well. Sandys insisted on cuts in the Gannet antisubmarine aircraft, but the Airborne Early Warning version got through. No doubt stimulated by Mountbatten's close and encouraging interest, Westland's ASW helicopter program went from strength to strength.[31]

In one respect of his policy towards naval air power, however, Mountbatten did have to concede defeat. This was in the vexed matter of the control of Coastal Command. It was widely reported in Parliament and the press, when Mountbatten took over as First Sea Lord, that he intended, "getting Coastal Command transferred to the Navy within two months," largely on the basis, it seems, of some discussions he had had with staff and service colleagues in Malta while still C-in-C Mediterranean. Mountbatten was plainly furious, and embarrassed, that this cat had been let out of the bag. There was no doubt that he *did* think the current situation entirely anomalous, and he was scathing about the Air Ministry's arguments in defense of it. In 1956, he agreed with the Chief of the Air Staff, however, that the issue would not be reopened, no doubt because of the need to secure Air Ministry support for the Navy's carrier program.

In his capacity as Minister of Supply, Duncan Sandys *had*, however, written a paper recommending such a transfer and ordering an inquiry into the matter in 1958, whether with or without Mountbatten's tacit encouragement. Dermot Boyle, the Chief of the Air Staff, was furious at what he considered a breach of faith, and Mountbatten, in turn, was angry that Air Marshal Sir William Dickson, the Chief of the Defence Staff, had not been impartial in his conduct of this affair. The matter soon showed signs of getting completely out of hand, with the Air Minister, George Ward, threatening to resign, before the matter was dropped.[32]

The Navy's acquisition of nuclear propulsion for its submarines had, in fact, been started in 1954, while Mountbatten was still in Malta, but progress had been slow until he took as over as First Sea Lord. The Treasury's continued support depended on the project being found neither too uncertain nor too expensive. Getting technical assistance from the Americans would reduce the prospect of both problems, and it was probably in enlisting the support of the U.S. Navy that Mountbatten made his greatest contribution to the Navy's nuclear submarine program.

He made the best possible use he could of his carefully cultivated relationship with the U.S. Chief of Naval Operations, Admiral Arleigh Burke, and did everything he could to win the support of the cantankerous Admiral Hyman Rickover, who ran the U.S. Navy's nuclear program. Rickover stopped Mountbatten from visiting the USS *Nautilus* in October 1955, but after a successful meeting between the two men in London in August 1956, these difficulties melted away and Rickover proved totally cooperative thereafter.

The choice was between the British developing their own reactor, simply acquiring one from the United States, or both. The Prime Minister, Harold Macmillan, and Duncan Sandys both had something of a preference for the British alternative, and Mountbatten himself was initially ambivalent. However, the disappointingly slow progress of the British project and Rickover's openhandedness persuaded Mountbatten to take up the American offer in May 1957. The USS *Nautilus* visited Britain later that year, and Mountbatten arranged for

Sandys to spend five hours on board, a visit which, he later told Burke, "tipped the scale in the minds of our government for the need to press on with the *Dreadnought*."[33]

Mountbatten was playing a complicated game. He wanted the Navy to have nuclear-propelled submarines as quickly and as cheaply as possible and knew that the Treasury was concerned at the high potential costs, especially of the British option. He was anxious to remain on good terms with the Americans and to get as much technical and administrative assistance as he could from them. On the other hand, he did not want the Americans to take the project over, which from time to time seemed more than possible. For this reason he wanted to keep the British project going as well, if at a slower rate. Mountbatten's concern to make the British program as effective as it could be made it possible for a wholly British SSN (nuclear-powered attack submarine) to follow the commissioning of the *Dreadnought*, with its American reactor, in 1963.[34] Mountbatten's keen interest in every aspect of the Navy's nuclear-propelled submarine program was so strong that Rickover was subsequently led to wonder whether the British were really committed to the program after Mountbatten was allowed to leave the Admiralty in 1959, "before the project was properly through."[35]

The biggest apparent loss to the Naval program in Mountbatten's time was probably the 18,000 ton guided missile cruiser that was abandoned in April 1957, but the First Sea Lord had never been enthusiastic about this project, preferring smaller, cheaper guided missile destroyers armed with "Seaslug" missiles, since reliance on these "would be making the best use of the limited resources now available."[36] Ships like these, and the Type 12 frigates, were affordable but capable and could sustain the balanced, flexible fleet that Mountbatten thought Britain needed. Providing a "balanced all purpose naval force" was the rationale behind the so-called "88 Plan" for an enhanced future Navy, which Sandys was eventually persuaded to accept in 1958.

The last constituent of this balanced fleet was Britain's capacity for amphibious warfare. This had been generally neglected since the end of the Second World War and the deficiencies had shown at Suez. The British were very much dependent on the Americans for both the concepts and the "ironmongery" of amphibious operations and there were rumors that the Army might take over the Commando role.[37] Mountbatten had, of course, been Chief of Combined Operations in the war and thought the capacity to project power ashore fundamental to the Navy's capacity to conduct limited war operations.

Whatever his political attitudes towards the Suez operation, he certainly used the opportunities it presented to advance the cause of the Royal Marine Commandos. They had been ready and available from the very beginning and had been able to demonstrate the potentiality of vertical envelopment by means of troop-carrying helicopters. These arguments, both general and specific, fell on fertile soil. Within a year of the operation, plans were being made to convert old carriers to Commando carriers, which led to the commissioning of *Bulwark* in 1960 and *Albion* in 1962. Mountbatten was quite clear on the matter:

Not only is the Commando carrier the most interesting development in Amphibious Warfare since the end of World War II, but the ship will have an important role to play in cold and limited wars. With the ever-increasing uncertainty surrounding our overseas bases it is more than ever necessary that the Navy should be capable of transporting a first-class military force to a potential trouble-spot and landing it there by the quickest possible means.[38]

Mountbatten wanted five Commandos in all, two deployed East of Suez. Once more, it seemed, the Marines were back at the center of the naval case.

While it would be wrong to underestimate the achievements of the Admiralty before Mountbatten in defending the naval case, there could be no doubt that times were difficult in 1955 and that they rapidly worsened in the Duncan Sandys era. This was in many ways, perhaps, the most critical period in the postwar history of the Royal Navy. In the end, however, the Navy went into the 1960s in much better shape than most people would have anticipated. At the time, much of the credit for this was attributed to Mountbatten himself, and this still seems just.

In this most critical campaign, Mountbatten brought a number of qualities and characteristics into play. Perhaps the most important of these was a sense of vision, which he combined with an acute sense of the strategic, political, and economic realities of the time. He knew the Navy was critical to national security, but he was also supremely realistic. He came to his new office knowing very well that the Royal Navy needed drastic surgery if it was to survive the challenges it faced. One of his first steps was to set up the "Way Ahead Committee," which was charged with a radical rationalization of an overlarge, overcomplex, and overexpensive naval shore establishment. The "Way Ahead Committee" and its subcommittees enquired into virtually every aspect of the Navy's infrastructure and felt able to effect large-scale reductions. There were substantial cuts in the logistics tail in shore-training establishments, major economies in the dockyards (though privatization was strenuously resisted), and the closure of bases and subordinate commands. In addition, the Reserve Fleet was effectively cut in half.

The Admiralty machine itself was overhauled with the introduction of everything from "work study methods" to the amalgamation of the empires of the Fifth Sea Lord and the DCNS. Many of these rationalizations involved significant pain and grief, and there was inevitably opposition in some quarters on matters of detail. Generally, though, the reforms were accepted as necessary if the Navy was "to assume its new streamline form for the atomic age."[39]

There needed to be substantial reform, also, in the manpower area. Even before Mountbatten took over, he had privately expressed his concern that the previous Board of Admiralty had overridden some of the recommendations of the Committee on the Officers Structure and Training, which it had set up in 1954. While he did not wish to join the Board "in a spirit of disagreeing," he was alert to the possible need to reverse Board policy in some respects at least. Generally, however, the reforming recommendations of the COST Committee were carried through, which did much to reverse morale problems in the fleet.[40] These reforms set the manpower agenda for the next generation.

Mountbatten's other major advantage in the forthcoming battle was his superlative skill as a "Whitehall warrior." This was a unique blend of a whole set of characteristics. One of his predecessors had remarked on the Navy's need for leadership by "a colourful personality well in the Public eye," and that is exactly what it got. Socially, Mountbatten moved in the most exalted of circles and was apt to pepper his personal correspondence with references to such as "My younger sister—the Queen of Sweden," and casually to mention to a correspondent in AFNORTH (Allied Forces Northern Europe) that on a forthcoming visit to Oslo, "I may stay with the Crown Prince or the King who are relations of mine." When in May 1958, General Lauris Norstad and his wife visited London, Mountbatten got them splendid theatre seats to see "My Fair Lady" and told Norstad that there would only be two others in the party, his first cousins, Prince and Princess Louis of Hesse and the Rhine. He provided the Norstads with a concise account of their genealogy and their principal seat. No doubt this appealed to Norstad a Lutheran minister's son from Red Wing, Minnesota. Vain himself, Mountbatten knew very well how to appeal to the vanity of others, and he made the most of his royal and aristocratic connections, and the lure of his country seat at Broadlands in Hampshire.[41]

Personally and naturally charming, Mountbatten was assiduous in his cultivation of good relations with anyone he came across, but especially with people who might later be useful. With individuals as personable as the American CNO, Arleigh Burke, this was easy enough, but with more difficult people or those whose views needed to be changed, Mountbatten was at his very best. The conversion of Duncan Sandys and Hyman Rickover must be counted as among his most impressive achievements. Montgomery was another example. Shortly after Mountbatten took over as First Sea Lord, Montgomery gave a talk at the Royal United Services Institute which the Navy thought disparaging of its future role. Mountbatten "had a very good go at him," and he kept the pressure on; in consequence, when Mountbatten departed the Admiralty, Montgomery wrote, in very different terms, that he hoped he had "been able to play some small part in ensuring that the mighty weapon of sea power is given its rightful place in the planning of military operations today and in the future."[42]

Mountbatten was also very assured politically. This quality had been demonstrated and developed while he was Supreme Commander at South-East Asia Command (SEAC) in 1945-46 and later when he supervised the independence process of India and Pakistan. He understood the political realities better than some politicians, as his considerable reservations about the wisdom of the Suez operation may suggest, and he was always confident in their company. Not for him the self-doubting despair of his successor in the Mediterranean, and indeed the Admiralty, the otherwise impressive Admiral Sir Charles Lambe, who wrote of his need "for a Foreign Office chap alongside me. . . . [T]his whole area is getting so damned political that I simply can't keep track."[43]

However, this was not Mountbatten's effort alone. He assembled a trusted, first class team around him, and he went out of his way to develop good working and social relations with his political and civil service colleagues. He got the best out of people and inspired them into constructive team effort. This is not to say, though, that all was harmony and light. John Lang, Secretary to the Admiralty, was not easy to get along with and was alert to the possibility that the civilian/political side of the Admiralty could be marginalized by their new confident and charismatic First Sea Lord. There were disputes and disagreements, but Mountbatten's voluminous personal correspondence shows that they rarely resulted in long-lasting antipathies. His relations with his VCNS, Admiral Sir William Davis, were, perhaps, typical. On Davis's departure, Mountbatten wrote:

You will remember that I told you the first day that I wanted to decentralise the whole of the routine control of the navy to you: you took it over and so far as I was concerned, it took a very large load off my shoulders. . . . During the two years we were together, I cannot remember any major disagreement and that says a good deal for you because I realise I am not a particularly easy person to serve.[44]

The result of this was a very impressive level of Naval Staff work. At the grand strategic level, this meant that the Admiralty was able to produce first-class papers on the role of the Navy in the atomic age, its policy towards the acquisition of Polaris and so on, while at the tactical level, it meant that when Mountbatten went to an American football game, it turned out that he knew more about the rules than did Arleigh Burke.[45]

This quality of professional preparation and careful consideration was at its most noticeable when Mountbatten was dealing with the masters of other important empires. Mountbatten's professional specialization was as a communicator, and this showed. He knew the power of the press and went out of his way to cultivate good relations by constantly writing to editors and, in particular, making the best use of retired naval officers to say what he felt he himself could not say. This was not always successful. Mountbatten had his enemies, especially in the Beaverbrook press, who were only to ready to fall on any indiscretion or contentious judgment. "Operation Fairlead," held at the Royal Naval College Greenwich in 1957, was yet another discreet and effective bid to put the naval case to British and Commonwealth politicians, industrialists, and to the Navy itself.[46]

Foreign and Commonwealth opinion was sometimes mobilized in a bid to influence, or even wholly to change, the trend in government policy. The American connection was especially important for making it possible, cheaper, or quicker for the Navy to get equipment it wanted (such as nuclear reactors and, eventually, the Polaris missile). Consequently, whenever the result of government policy would have been unpopular with the United States, Commonwealth leaders, or NATO, Mountbatten did his best to make sure that foreigners told the government so.

However, it was probably in his dealings with the other services that the task confronting Mountbatten was at its most complex. There was, first of all, a strong need for them to stand together against the likes of Duncan Sandys. On the other hand, however, their interests were far from identical. Mountbatten had no particular problems with the Army, but the Royal Air Force was a different matter, for the potential rivalries were acute, and indeed always had been. In such crucial matters as the carrier program, he got what he wanted. Over Polaris and the Buccaneer, he won partial victories that kept alive projects that would eventually prevail over their RAF competitors, but only after great costs in time, money, and political rancor. In the matter of Coastal Command he was defeated, permanently as it turned out. It has been argued that he should have pushed the Air Force further on these and other matters, but he was aware of the need for mutual support against the Treasury.

He also believed that the logic of Britain's strategic circumstances required the increasing integration of the services, a policy he pursued strongly in his next appointment, as Chief of the Defence Staff. Integration, he thought, would work, resulting in long-term benefits to the Navy. When considering the whole idea of merging the Navy and the RAF in 1957, Mountbatten concluded:

[W]e ought to be in no hurry to raise this question of integration, as the longer the discussion of the subject is delayed the weaker the position of the Royal Air Force will become and any form of integration is more likely to be on our terms rather than theirs in the future.[47]

In his prediction that there would, and should, be more integration between the services, Mountbatten was certainly right. In regard to the assumption that this would work to the relative benefit of the Navy, however, the 1960s and the collapse of the Navy's carrier program were to render this a far more debatable conclusion.

Whatever the future held, there can be few doubts about Mountbatten's level of achievement as First Sea Lord. Chief M(E) R. Tupper, the President of the Chief's Mess at the Royal Navy Barracks, Portsmouth, summed it all up as well as anyone: "You have during the past difficult years been our defence against a general apathy and even almost a deliberate campaign by some sections of the press to decry our service to the nation, but because of you, we have preserved our pride and regained our status."[48] Few would dispute the validity of this general verdict.

NOTES

The opinions expressed in this paper are the author's own and should not be thought necessarily to represent official opinion in any way. The author is indebted to Eric Grove for these and other references.

1. Vice Adm. Sir William Davis to Mountbatten [hereafter M], 12 Feb. 1955, MB1 I/270, Mountbatten Mss. [hereafter M/Mss.], Southampton University.
2. David Brown, "Mountbatten as First Sea Lord," in *Journal of the Royal United Services Institute*, (June 1986): 63-68.
3. To Commanders-in-Chief and others, *The Ides of March 1957*, MBI I/106, M/Mss.
4. Ibid.

5. Davis letter, 12 Feb. 1955, MB1 I/270, M/Mss. For the interwar period antecedents of this, see Geoffrey Till, *Air Power and the Royal Navy* (London: Jane's, 1979), 192-94.

6. For this see, Philip Ziegler, *Mountbatten (New York: Alfred A. Knopf, 1985)*, 526 and Mountbatten's correspondence with Hughes Hallett in MB1 I/217, M/Mss.

7. Vice Adm. John Hughes Hallett to M, 31 Mar. 1955, MB1 I/217, M/Mss.

8. Ibid.

9. For example, "*The Influence of the Atomic Bomb on Naval War*," Admiralty Paper of 15 Aug. 1945, ADM 1/17259.

10. Board Minute 5161, 15 Oct. 1957, ADM 167/149.

11. See Eric Grove, *Vanguard to Trident*, 212.

12. See Ziegler, *Mountbatten*, 560-61 and *The Polaris Project*, Draft Paper for Chiefs of Staff by VCNS, Vice Admiral Sir Caspar John, Mar. 1958, ADM 205/179.

13. Ibid.

14. For Mountbatten's effort to agree a policy with the then Chief of the General Staff, Field Marshal Sir Gerald Templar of June 1958, see MB1 I/106, M/Mss.

15. A. J. Pierre, *Nuclear Politics* (Oxford, U.K.: Oxford University Press, 1972), 220-21.

16. Rear Adm. C. D. Howard Johnstone, Allied Naval Forces Central Europe to M, 17 Jan. 1955, MB1 I/106 and M to VCNS, 31 Mar. 1959, MB1 I/106, M/Mss.

17. C-in-C, Home Fleet, Admiral Sir William Davis, to M, 3 July 1958, MB1 I/106, M/Mss.

18. See memorandum by First Lord of the Admiralty, *Role of the Navy*, D(57) 29, 15 Nov. 1957, CAB 131/18.

19. Vice Adm. Davis to M, 28 Aug. 1957, MB1 I/277, M/Mss.

20. See comments by Director of Plans and M Branch, 14 Mar. 1957, ADM 205/114.

21. *Time and Tide*, 1 Mar. 1958, *The Battle of Storey's Gate*; report on Sandys broadcast and Cilcennin to M, 17 Feb. 1958, MB1 I/326, M/Mss.

22. Draft memo to First Lord, Earl of Selkirk, 28 May 1957, MB1 I/228, M/Mss.

23. To Vice Adm. G. Barnard, Adm. President Royal Naval College, Greenwich, 1 July 1957, MB1 I/106, M/Mss.

24. Adm. Sir Alan Scott-Moncrief to M, 20 May 1957, MB1 I/143 (ii), M/Mss.; For M's use of the Commonwealth connection, see D(57)29, CAB 131/18; also Ziegler, *Mountbatten*, 532-33, 552.

25. M to Vice Adm. P. G. K. Cazalet, Chief of Allied Staff Med, 18 Mar. 1955, MB1 I/59, M/Mss.

26. To Vice Adm. Sir Ralph Edwards, C-in-C Med, 25 Feb. 1957, MB1 I/276, M/Mss.

27. 14th Meeting of COS Committee, 19 Feb. 1957, DEFE 4/95.

28. Vice Adm. Sir Ralph Edwards, 5th Sea Lord, memo for Vice Adm. Grantham, 14 Dec 55, MB1 I/276 (i), M/Mss.

29. To Sir Frederick Brundrett, Chief Scientific Advisor to Admiralty, 24 Sept. 1956, MB1 I/106(ii), M/Mss.

30. To First Lord, Earl of Selkirk, 10 Oct. 1958, MB1 I/106 (i), M/Mss.

31. See correspondence with Westland's personnel in MB1 I/106 (i), M/Mss.

32. Ziegler, *Mountbatten*, 589; see correspondence with Air Marshal B. V. Reynolds, 3 Mar. 1955, in MB1 I/325; Marshal Sir Dermot Boyle, Chief of the Air Staff, 20 Nov. 1958, and Air Marshal Sir William Dickson, Chief of the Defence Staff, 14 Jan. 1959 in MB1 I/326, M/Mss.

33. To Adm. Arleigh Burke, 14 Nov. 1957, ADM 205/178.

34. See Grove, *Vanguard to Trident*, 229-33.

35. To Vice Adm. Sir Charles Lambe, C-in-C Med, 29 Jan. 1959, in MB1 I/63, M/Mss.
36. Board Minute 5111, 11 Apr. 1957, ADM 167/149.
37. Major-General C. F. Phillips, RM, to M, 29 Apr. 1955, MB1 I/63 and Vice Adm. Sir Ralph Edwards, 23 Nov. 1953, MB1 I/87, M/Mss.
38. Quoted in Ziegler, *Mountbatten*, 549.
39. To First Lord, Lord Cilcennin, 3 Sept. 1956, MB1 I/149, M/Mss.
40. To Vice Adm. John Hughes-Hallett, in MB1 I/217, M/Mss.; also Grove, *Vanguard to Trident*, 217.
41. Admiral of the Fleet Sir Andrew Cunningham, quoted in Ziegler, *Mountbatten*, 522; to Vice Adm. Grantham, C-in-C Med, 2 Sept. 1956, MB1 I/276 (i); to Vice Adm. G. V. Gladstone, Cdr. Allied Naval Forces, Northern Europe, 15 June 1956, MB1 I/180; to General Lauris Norstad, SACEUR, 7 May 1958, MB1 I/307, M/Mss.
42. To Vice Adm. James Fife, U.S.N., 8 Feb. 1955, MB1 I/147 and from Lord Montgomery to M, 19 Sept. 1958, MB1 I/326, M/Mss.
43. See Peter Dennis, *Troubled Days of Peace: Mountbatten and South East Asia Command, 1945-46* (Manchester, U.K.: Manchester University Press, 1987); see also Ziegler, *Mountbatten*, 537-47. Vice Adm. Sir Charles Lambe, C-in-C Med, 3 June 1958, MB1 I/276 (ii), M/Mss.
44. To Vice Adm. Sir William Davis, VCNS, 11 June 1957, MB1 I/33, M/Mss.
45. Ziegler, *Mountbatten*, 557-58.
46. For Operation "Fairlead," see MB1 I/143, M/Mss.
47. Memo of 26 Feb. 1957, MB1 I/228, M/Mss.
48. Chief M(E) R. Tupper to M, 16 Apr. 1959, MB1 I/106 (i), M/Mss.

Select Bibliography

MANUSCRIPT SOURCES

United Kingdom: Official Records (Public Record Office, Kew Gardens, London).

Admiralty

ADM. 1.	Papers of the Admiralty and Secretariat
ADM. 116.	Cases of the Admiralty and Secretariat
ADM. 137.	Operational Records
ADM. 167.	Board of the Admiralty: Minutes and Memoranda
ADM. 178.	Station Records
ADM. 181.	Navy Estimates
ADM. 182.	Confidential Admiralty Fleet Orders
ADM. 199.	War History: Cases and Papers
ADM. 205.	First Sea Lord: Papers

Air Ministry

AIR. 8.	Chief of the Air Staff: Records
AIR. 9.	Director of Plans: Records
AIR. 19.	Correspondence

Cabinet Office

CAB. 2-5.	C.I.D.: Minutes and Memoranda
CAB. 16.	*Ad-hoc* Sub-Committees of Enquiry: Proceedings and Memoranda
CAB. 21.	Cabinet Registered Files

CAB. 23.	Cabinet Minutes	
CAB. 24.	Cabinet Memoranda	
CAB. 27.	Committees: General Series	
CAB. 29.	Anglo-French Staff Conversations	
CAB. 32.	Imperial Conferences: Minutes and Memoranda	
CAB. 53.	C.O.S. Committee: Minutes and Memoranda	
CAB. 54.	Deputy C.O.S. Committee: Minutes and Memoranda	
CAB. 55.	C.I.D. Joint Planning Committee: Minutes and Memoranda	
CAB. 57.	Sub-Committees	
CAB. 64.	Minister for Coordination of Defence: Registered Files	
CAB. 65.	War Cabinet: Minutes	
CAB. 66-8.	War Cabinet: Memoranda	
CAB. 69.	Cabinet Defence Committee (Operations)	
CAB. 79	C.O.S. Committee: Minutes	
CAB. 80.	C.O.S. Committee: Memoranda	
CAB. 82.	Deputy C.O.S. Committee: Minutes and Memoranda	
CAB. 83.	Ministerial Committee on Military Coordination: Minutes and Papers	
CAB. 84.	Joint Planning Committees: Minutes and Memoranda	
CAB. 94.	Oversea Defence Committee: Minutes and Papers	
CAB. 99.	Supreme War Council 1939-1940: Minutes and Memoranda	
CAB. 100.	Summaries of Information: Central War Room	
CAB. 103.	Cabinet Office Historical Section: Periodical Progress Reports	
CAB. 115.	Central Office for North American Studies	
CAB. 118.	Various Ministers: Files	
CAB. 128.	Cabinet Minutes	
CAB. 129.	Cabinet Memoranda	
CAB. 130.	Cabinet Committees	
CAB. 131.	Defence Committee Papers	

Ministry of Defence

DEFE. 4.	C.O.S. Committee Minutes (from Jan. 1947)
DEFE. 5.	C.O.S. Committee Memoranda (from Jan. 1947)

DEFE. 6.	Joint Planning Committee
DEFE. 7.	Register Files: General Series
DEFE. 8.	C.O.S. Committees and Sub-Committees
DEFE. 10.	Major Committees: Minutes and Papers

Dominions Office

DO. 3.	Registers of Correspondence
DO. 35.	Original Correspondence
DO. 114.	Confidential Print—Dominions
DO. 121.	Private Office Papers

Foreign Office

FO. 371.	General Correspondence Files
FO. 436.	Far Eastern Affairs: Further Correspondence
FO. 800.	Foreign Office Personnel

Prime Minister's Office

PREM. 1-8.	Correspondence and Papers

Treasury

T. 160.	Treasury Correspondence and Finance
T. 172.	Chancellor of the Exchequer Office: Miscellaneous Papers

War Office

WO. 32.	War Office: Registered Papers, General Series
WO. 33.	Committees: Reports and Papers
WO. 190.	Appreciation Files

United Kingdom: Private Papers

Bodleian Library, Oxford

Earl of Oxford and Asquith Papers
Earl Attlee Papers
Jack Sanders Papers
Earl of Selbourne Papers

286 *Select Bibliography*

Cambridge University Library
    Earl Baldwin Papers
    Viscount Templewood Papers

Churchill College Archive Centre, Cambridge
    Earl Alexander of Hillsborough Papers
    William Bridgeman Papers
    The Chartwell Papers (Winston S. Churchill)
    Admiral Sir R. A. R. Plunkett-Ernle-Erle-Drax Papers
    Admiral Sir Frederick Dreyer Papers
    Viscount Esher Papers
    Baron Fisher of Kilverstone Papers
    Admiral J. H. Godfrey Papers
    Reginald McKenna Papers
    S. W. Roskill Papers
    Admiral Sir James Somerville Papers
    Lord Wester Wemyss Papers

British Library, London
    Admiral Viscount Cunningham of Hyndhope Papers
    Admiral Viscount Jellicoe Papers
    Admiral Sir Roger Keyes Papers
    Additional Manuscripts

Imperial War Museum, London
    Admiral Sir Dudley de Chair Papers
    Rear-Admiral Sir H. W. E. Manisty Papers
    Rear-Admiral H. Miller Papers
    Admiral Sir Ernest Troubridge Papers
    Admiral Sir William Whitworth Papers

House of Lords Records Office
    Andrew Bonar Law Papers
    Earl Lloyd-George Papers

National Maritime Museum, Greenwich
    Earl Beatty Papers
    Baron Chatfield Papers
    Lord Fraser of North Cape Papers

Vice Admiral Sir Frederick Hamilton Papers
Admiral Sir William May Papers
Admiral Sir Herbert Richmond Papers
Admiral Sir Edmond Slade Mss.
Arnold White Papers

Naval Library M3, Ministry of Defence Whitehall Library, London

Captain Thomas Crease Papers
Admiral Sir Henry Bradwardine Jackson Papers

University of Southampton Library

Prince Louis of Battenberg Papers
Earl Mountbatten of Burma Papers

Royal Archives, Windsor Castle

Papers relating to the reigns of King Edward VII and King George V.

Privately Held Papers

L. S. Amery Papers

Germany: Official Records

Bundesarchiv-militärarchiv, Freiburg im Breisgau

Admiralstab der Marine. A. betreffend England. Personal, Offiziere und Offiziersatz vom Jan. 1910 bis Apr. 1919.
Admiralstab der Marine. A. Englisch-deutsche Beziehungen vom Dez. 1911 bis Aug. 1914.

PRINTED SOURCES

Primary Sources

Official Command Papers

Cmnd. 2335.	*Parliamentary Papers*, 1905, vol. 68.
Cmnd. 256.	*Parliamentary Papers*, 1909.
Cmnd. 1581.	*Parliamentary Papers*, 1922.
Cmnd. 6743.	*Statement Relating to Defence*: 1946.
Cmnd. 6923.	*The Central Organisation for Defence*: 1946.
Cmnd. 7042.	*Statement Relating to Defence*: 1947.
Cmnd. 7327.	*Statement Relating to Defence*: 1948.

288 Select Bibliography

    Cmnd. 7631.   *Statement on Defence*: 1949
    Cmnd. 7895.   *Statement on Defence*: 1950.
    Cmnd. 8146.   *Defence Programme*: 1951.

Official Histories

Bullen, Roger, and Pelly, Margaret, eds., *Documents on British Policy Overseas*, ser. 1, vols. 3-4. London: HMSO, 1986-87.

Gooch, G. P., and Temperley, H., eds., *British Documents on the Origins of the War*. London: HMSO, 1926-38.

Hinsley, F. H., Thomas, E. E., Ransom, C. F. G., et al., eds., *British Intelligence in the Second World War*. vol. 2. London: HMSO, 1981.

Medlicott, W. N. and Dakin, D., eds., *Documents on British Foreign Policy 1919-1939*. 2nd ser., vols. 13, 18, 19. London: HMSO, 1973-82.

Neale, R. G., ed., *Documents on Australian Foreign Policy 1937-49*. vol. 1. Canberra: Australian War Memorial, 1975.

Woodward, E. L., and Butler, R., eds., *Documents on British Foreign Policy 1919-1939*, 3rd ser., vols. 2-9. London: HMSO, 1949-55.

Yasamee, Heather, and Hamilton, Keith, eds., *Documents on British Policy Overseas*, ser. 2, vol. 4. London: HMSO, 1991.

Parliamentary Debates

Hansard Official Report, Commons. 4th and 5th Series. 1904-59.
Hansard Official Report, Lords. 4th and 5th Series. 1904-59.

The Royal Navy List

The Royal Naval List. London: Witherby. 1902-04.
The Royal Navy List and Naval Recorder. London: Witherby, 1905-14.
The Royal Navy List. London: Witherby, 1915-.

Autobiographies, Biographies, Diaries, and Memoirs

Avon, Lord. *Facing the Dictators*. London: Cassell, 1962.

Bacon, Sir R. H. *Life of Admiral of the Fleet Lord Fisher of Kilverstone*. 2 vols. London: Hodder and Stoughton, 1929.

Beesly, Patrick. *Very Special Admiral: The Life of Admiral J. H. Godfrey, CB*. London: Hamish Hamilton, 1980.

Bradford, Sir Edward. *Admiral of the Fleet Sir Arthur Knyvett-Wilson*. London: John Murray, 1923.

Brett, M. V., ed. *The Journals and Letters of Reginald Viscount Esher.* London: Nicholson & Watson, 1934.

Burridge, Trevor. *Clement Attlee.* London: Jonathan Cape, 1985.

Chalfont, Alun. *Montgomery of Alamein.* London: Weidenfeld & Nicolson, 1976.

Chatfield, Lord. *The Navy and Defence.* London: Heinemann, 1942.

———. *It Might Happen Again.* London: Heinemann, 1947.

Churchill, R. *Winston S. Churchill.* vol. 2, *Young Statesman, 1901-1914.* London: Heinemann, 1967.

Connell, Brian. *Manifest Destiny: A Study in Five Profiles of the Rise and Influence of the Mountbatten Family.* London: Cassell, 1953.

Cunningham of Hyndhope, Viscount. *A Sailor's Odyssey.* London: Hutchinson, 1951.

Dewar, K. G. B. *The Navy From Within.* London: Gollancz, 1939.

Fremantle, Sidney. *My Naval Career.* London: Hutchinson, 1949.

Fyfe, Hamilton. *Northcliffe: An Intimate Biography.* London: George Allen and Unwin, 1930.

Halpern, Paul G., ed. *Selection from the Private and Official Correspondence of Admiral of the Fleet Baron Keyes of Zeebrugge.* 2 vols. London: Navy Records Society, 1972-80.

Hamilton, Nigel. *Monty: The Field Marshal, 1944-1976.* London: Hamish Hamilton, 1986.

Harris, Kenneth. *Attlee.* London: Weidenfeld and Nicolson, 1982.

Hough, Richard. *First Sea Lord.* London: George Allen and Unwin, 1969.

Humble, Richard. *Fraser of North Cape.* London: Routledge and Kegan Paul, 1983.

Hunt, Barry D. *Sailor-Scholar: Admiral Sir Herbert Richmond, 1871-1946.* Waterloo, Ontario, Canada: Wilfrid Laurier Press, 1982.

James, Sir William. *The Eyes of the Navy: A Biographical Study of Admiral Sir Reginald Hall.* London: Methuen, 1955.

———. *A Great Seaman: The Life of Admiral of the Fleet, Sir Henry Oliver.* London: Witherby, 1956.

Jellicoe, Sir John. *The Grand Fleet.* London: Cassell, 1919.

Kemp, P. K., ed. *The Papers of Admiral Sir John Fisher.* vol. 1. London: Navy Records Society, 1960.

Kerr, Mark. *Prince Louis of Battenberg.* London: Longmans Green, 1934.

Keyes, Sir Roger. *The Naval Memoirs of Admiral of the Fleet Sir Roger Keyes.* vol. 2, *Scapa Flow to the Dover Strait, 1916-1918.* New York: Dutton, 1935.

Klachko, Mary, with Trask, David F. *Admiral William Shepherd Benson: First Chief of Naval Operations.* Annapolis, Md., U.S.: Naval Institute Press, 1987.

Mackay, Ruddock. *Fisher of Kilverstone.* Oxford, U.K.: Clarendon Press, 1973.

Marchant, Sir James. *Winston Spencer Churchill: Servant of Crown and Commonwealth.* London: Cassell, 1954.

Marder, Arthur J. *Portrait of an Admiral: The Life and Letters of Sir Herbert Richmond.* Cambridge, Mass.: Harvard University Press, 1952.

Montgomery, B. L. *The Memoirs of Field Marshal the Viscount Montgomery of Alamein.* London: Collins, 1958.

Ollard, Richard. *Fisher and Cunningham: A Study in the Personalities of the Churchill Era.* London: Constable, 1991.

Patterson, A. Temple. *Jellicoe: A Biography.* London: Macmillan, 1969.

Patterson, A. Temple, ed. *The Jellicoe Papers, 2 vols.* London: Navy Records Society, 1966-68.

Petrie, Charles. *Walter Long and His Times.* London: Hutchinson, 1936.

Ranft, B. McL., ed. *The Beatty Papers: Selections from the Private and Official Correspondence of Admiral of the Fleet Earl Beatty.* 2 vols. London: Scolar Press for Navy Records Society, 1989-93.

Roskill, S. W. *Hankey: Man of Secrets, 3 vols.* London: Collins, 1970-74.

———. *Admiral of the Fleet, Earl Beatty, An Intimate Biography.* New York: Atheneum, 1981.

Saward, D. *Bomber Harris.* London: Buchan and Enright, 1984.

Schurman, D. M. *Julian S. Corbett, 1854-1922: Historian of British Maritime Policy from Drake to Jellicoe.* London: Royal Historical Society, 1981.

Scott, Sir Percy. Fifty Years in the Navy. London: John Murray, 1919.

Shinwell, E. *Conflict Without Malice.* London: Odhams, 1955.

Slessor, Sir John. *The Central Blue: The Autobiography of Sir John Slessor, Marshal of the RAF.* New York: Praeger, 1957.

Warner, Oliver. *Cunningham of Hyndhope: Admiral of the Fleet.* London: John Murray, 1967.

Wemyss, Lady W. *The Life and Letters of Lord Wester Wemyss.* London: Eyre and Spottiswoode, 1935.

Wemyss, Lord W. *The Navy in the Dardanelles Campaign.* London: Hodder and Stoughton, 1934.

Zeigler, Philip. *Mountbatten.* New York: Alfred Knopf, 1985.

Biographical Dictionaries

Smith, George, ed. *Dictionary of National Biography 1912-1921.* London: Oxford University Press, 1927.

Weaver, J. R. H., ed. *Dictionary of National Biography 1922-1930.* London: Oxford University Press, 1937.

Wickham Legg, L. G., ed. *Dictionary of National Biography 1931-1940.* London: Oxford University Press, 1949.

Wickham Legg, L. G., and Williams, E. T., eds. *Dictionary of National Biography 1941-1950.* London: Oxford University Press, 1959.

Williams, E. T. and Palmer, Helen M., eds. *Dictionary of National Biography 1951-1960*. London: Oxford University Press, 1971.
Williams, E. T. and Nicholls, C. S., eds. *Dictionary of National Biography 1961-1970*. London: Oxford University Press, 1981.

The Naval Annual

Brassey, Lord, et al. *The Naval Annual, 1912*. Portsmouth and London: Brassey's, 1912.
———. *The Naval Annual, 1914*. Portsmouth and London: Brassey's, 1914.

Newspapers, Periodicals and Scholarly Journals

Blackwood's Magazine
Canadian Hostorical Review
The Cornhill Magazine
The Daily Telegraph
The Economist
Historical Journal
International History Review
Journal of Conflict Resolution
Journal of Contemporary History
The Journal of Military History
Journal of Modern History
The Journal of the Royal United Services Institute
The Journal of Strategic Studies
Keesing's Contemporary Archives
Manchester Guardian
The Mariner's Mirror
The Naval Review
Pointer
South China Morning Post
The Spectator
The Straits Times
Time and Tide
The Times
War and Society

Secondary Sources

Books, Articles and Dissertations

Bach, John. *The Australia Station: A History of the Royal Navy in the South West Pacific, 1821-1913*. Kensington: New South Wales University Press, 1986.
Barker, Dudley. *Prominent Edwardians*. London: George Allen and Unwin, 1969.

Barnett, Correlli. *Engage the Enemy More Closely*. New York: W. W. Norton, 1991.
Beesly, Patrick. *Room 40: British Naval Intelligence, 1914-18*. New York: Oxford University Press, 1984.
Blake, Robert and Louis, William R., eds. *Churchill: A Major New Assessment of His Life in Peace and War*. New York: W. W. Norton, 1993.
Briggs, Sir John H. *Naval Administrations 1827 to 1892: The Experience of 65 Years*. London: Sampson, Low, Marston, 1897.
Brown, David. "Mountbatten as First Sea Lord," *Journal of the Royal United Services Institute*, (June 1986): 63-68.
Busch, Briton C. *Britain, India, and the Arabs, 1914-1921*. Berkeley: University of California Press, 1971.
Campbell, John. *The Fighting at Jutland*. London: Conway, 1983.
Churchill, W.L.S. *The World Crisis*, 3 vols. London: Thornton Butterworth, 1923.
Clark, Ian and Wheeler, Nick. *The British Origins of Nuclear Strategy 1945-55*. Oxford, U.K.: Clarendon Press, 1989.
Clowes, W. Laird. *The Royal Navy*. London: Sampson, Low and Co., 1897-1913.
Corbett, Julian S. and Newbolt, Henry. *History of the Great War: Naval Operations*, 5 vols. London: Longmans, Green, 1920-31. Rev. ed. 1938.
Day, David. *The Great Betrayal: Britain, Australia and the Onset of the Pacific War 1939-42*. New York: W. W. Norton, 1989.
De Chair, Lionel. *The Sea is Strong*. London: Harrap, 1961.
Dennis, Peter J. *Troubled Days of Peace: Mountbatten and South East Asia Command, 1945-46*. Manchester, U.K.: Manchester University Press, 1987.
D'Ombrain, Nicholas. *War Machinery and High Policy: Defence Administration in Peacetime Britain, 1902-1914*. London: Oxford University Press, 1973.
Dorling, Taprell. *Men o' War*. London: Phillip Allan, 1929.
Douglas, W. A. B., ed. *The RCN in Transition, 1910-1985*. Vancouver, B.C., Canada: University of British Columbia Press, 1988.
Ereira, Alan. *The Invergordon Mutiny*. London: Routledge and Kegan Paul, 1981.
Frere Cook, G. *The Attacks on the Tirpitz*. London: Ian Allan, 1974.
Gardiner, Leslie. *The Royal Oak Courts Martial*. Edinburgh, Scotland: William Blackwood and Sons, 1965.
———. *The British Admiralty*. Edinburgh, Scotland: William Blackwood and Sons, 1968.
Gibbs, Norman H. *Grand Strategy*. vol.1, *Rearmament Policy*. London: HMSO, 1976.
Goldrick, James. *The King's Ships Were at Sea: The War in the North Sea August 1914-February 1915*. Annapolis, Md.: Naval Institute Press, 1984.
Gordon, D. C. "The Admiralty and Dominion Navies, 1902-1914," *Journal of Modern History*, 33 (1961): 407-22.
Gordon, G. A. H. *British Sea Power and Procurement Between the Wars*. London: Macmillan, 1988.

Grove, Eric J. "The Post War 'Ten Year Rule'—Myth and Reality." *Journal of the Royal United Services Institute*, Dec. 1984: 48-53.

———. *Vanguard to Trident: British Naval Policy since World War II*. Annapolis, Md: Naval Institute Press, 1987.

———. *Fleet to Fleet Encounters*. London: Arms and Armour Press, 1991.

Halpern, Paul G. *The Mediterranean Naval Situation, 1908-1914*. Cambridge, Mass.: Harvard University Press, 1971.

———. *The Naval War in the Mediterranean 1914-1918*. London: Allen and Unwin, 1987.

Hampshire, A. C. *The Royal Navy since 1945*. London: Kimber, 1975.

Handel, M. I., ed. *Intelligence and Military Operations*. London: Frank Cass, 1990.

Hankey, Lord. *The Supreme Command 1914-1918*. vol.1. London: George Allen and Unwin, 1961.

Hattendorf, John B., and Jordan, Robert S., eds. *Maritime Strategy and the Balance of Power; Britain and America in the Twentieth Century*. New York: St. Martin's Press, 1989.

Jackson, Sir William, and Bramall, Field Marshal Lord. *The Chiefs*. London: Brassey's, 1992.

Johnson, F. A. *Defence by Committee*. London: Oxford University Press, 1960.

———. *Defence by Ministry: The British Ministry of Defence, 1944-1974*. New York: Holmes and Meier, 1980.

Kemp, P. K., ed. *The Oxford Companion to Ships and the Sea*. Oxford: Oxford University Press, 1976.

Lambert, Nicholas A. "The Influence of the Submarine upon Naval Strategy: 1898-1914." Unpublished D.Phil. dissertation, Oxford University, 1992.

Langhorne, R. "The Naval Question in Anglo-German Relations, 1912-1914." *Historical Journal*, 14, no.2 (June 1971): 359-70.

Lewis, Julian. *Changing Direction: British Military Planning for Post-War Strategic Defence, 1942-1947*. London: Sherwood Press, 1988.

Lloyd George, D. *War Memoirs*. vol. 3. Boston: Little, Brown and Co., 1938.

Love, Jr., Robert, ed. *The Chiefs of Naval Operations*. Annapolis, Md.: Naval Institute Press, 1980.

Lumby, E. W. R., ed. *Policy and Operations in the Mediterranean, 1912-14*. London: Navy Records Society, 1970.

Lynn, John A., ed. *Feeding Mars: Essays on Logistics and Resources Mobilization in Western Warfare from the Middle Ages to the Present*. Boulder, Col.: Westview Press, 1993.

Marder, Arthur J. *British Naval Policy 1880-1905: The Anatomy of British Sea Power*. New York: Alfred Knopf, 1940.

———. *Fear God and Dread Nought*. 3 vols. London: Jonathan Cape, 1952-59.

Marder, Arthur J. *From the Dreadnought to Scapa Flow: The Royal Navy in the Fisher*

Era, 1904-1919. 5 vols. London: Oxford University Press, 1961-70.

———. *From the Dardanelles to Oran.* London: Oxford University Press, 1974.

———. *Old Friends, New Enemies.* vol. 1, *The Royal Navy and the Imperial Japanese Navy, 1936-1941.* Oxford: Clarendon Press, 1981.

Marder, Arthur J., Jacobsen, Mark, and Horsfield, John. *Old Friends, New Enemies: The Royal Navy and the Imperial Japanese Navy.* vol. 2, *The Pacific War, 1942-1945.* Oxford: Clarendon Press, 1990.

Maurer, John H. "Churchill's Naval Holiday: Arms Control and the German Naval Race, 1912-1914." *Journal of Strategic Studies,* 15, no. 1 (March 1992): 102-27.

———. "The Anglo-German Naval Rivalry and Informal Arms Control, 1912-1914." *Journal of Conflict Resolution,* 36, no. 2 (June 1992): 284-308.

McIntyre, W. D. *The Rise and Fall of the Singapore Naval Base.* London: Macmillan, 1979.

Meaney, N. K. *The Search for Security in the Pacific.* Sydney, Australia: Sydney University Press, 1976.

Miller, Francis H. *The Origin and Constitution of the Admiralty and Navy Boards.* London: HMSO, 1884.

Murfett, Malcolm. "Strategic Necessity or Naval Extravagance? The Role of Hong Kong and Singapore in British Naval Defence Policy in the Far East, 1945-49," *Pointer,* 14, no.4. (July-Sept. 1988): 48-69.

———. *Fool-proof Relations: The Search for Anglo-American Naval Cooperation During the Chamberlain Years, 1937-40.* Singapore: Singapore University Press, 1984.

———. *Hostage on the Yangtze: Britain, China and the Amethyst Crisis of 1949.* Annapolis, Md.: Naval Institute Press, 1991.

———. "Living in the Past: A Critical Re-examination of the Singapore Naval Strategy, 1918-1941," *War and Society,* vol.11, no.1 [May 1993]: 73-103.

———. *In Jeopardy: The Royal Navy and British Far Eastern Defence Policy, 1945-51.* Kuala Lumpur: Oxford University Press, 1994.

Murray, Sir O. "The Admiralty," *The Mariner's Mirror,* 23-25 (1937-39).

Offer, Avner. *The First World War: An Agrarian Interpretation.* Oxford: Clarendon Press, 1989.

Pierre, A. J. *Nuclear Politics.* London: Oxford University Press, 1972.

Rodger, N. A. M. *The Admiralty.* Lavenham: Terence Dalton, 1979.

Roskill, Stephen. *The War at Sea 1939-1945.* 3 vols. London: HMSO, 1954-61.

———. "The Dismissal of Admiral Jellicoe," *Journal of Contemporary History,* 1, no. 4. (Oct. 1966): 69-93.

———. *Naval Policy Between the Wars.* 2 vols. London: Collins, 1968-76.

———. *Churchill and the Admirals.* London: Collins, 1977.

Sarty, Roger. "Canadian Maritime Defence, 1892-1914." *Canadian Historical Review,* 71, 4 (1990):462-90.

Seldon, A. *Churchill's Indian Summer: The Conservative Government 1951-55.* London: Hodder and Stoughton, 1981.
Simpson, M., ed. *Anglo-American Naval Relations, 1917-1919.* Aldershot: Scolar Press for the Navy Records Society, 1991.
Smith, P. *Hit First, Hit Hard.* London: Kimber, 1976.
Snyder, William. *The Politics of British Defence Policy, 1945-62.* New York: Ernest Benn, 1964.
Stephen, Martin. *The Fighting Admirals.* London: Leo Cooper, 1991.
Sumida, Jon. *In Defence of Naval Supremacy.* London: Unwin Hyman, 1989.
———. "British Naval Administration and Policy in the Age of Fisher." *Journal of Military History*, 54 (January 1990): 1-26.
———. "British Naval Operational Logistics, 1914-1918." *Journal of Military History*, 57 (July 1993): 447-80.
———. "'The Best Laid Plans': The Development of British Battle Fleet Tactics, 1919-1942." *International History Review*, 14 (November 1992): 681-700.
Sydenham, Lord, et al. *The World Crisis by Winston Churchill: A Criticism.* 2nd ed. London: Hutchinson, 1927.
Taylor, A. J. P. *English History 1914-1945.* Oxford: Clarendon Press, 1965.
Terraine, John. *The Right of the Line.* London: Hodder and Stoughton, 1985.
———. *Business in Great Waters: The U-Boat Wars, 1916-1918.* London: Leo Cooper, 1989.
Thorne, Christopher. *Allies of a Kind: The United States, Britain, and the War Against Japan, 1941-1945.* London: Oxford University Press, 1979.
Till, Geoffrey. *Air Power and the Royal Navy.* London: Jane's, 1979.
Tracy, Nicholas. *Attack on Maritime Trade.* London: Macmillan, 1991.
Trask, David. *Captains and Cabinets: Anglo-American Naval Relations 1917-1918.* Columbia: University of Missouri Press, 1972.
———. *Cabinets and Governments: Anglo-American Naval Relations, 1917-1918.* Columbia: University of Missouri Press, 1979.
Warner, Sir G., ed. *The Libelle of Englyshe Polycye.* Oxford, U.K.: Clarendon Press, 1926.
Warner, Oliver. *Admiral of the Fleet.* London: Sidgwick and Jackson, 1969.
Williams, Rhodri. *Defending the Empire.* New Haven, Conn.: Yale University Press, 1991.
Williamson, Samuel R. *The Politics of Grand Strategy: Britain and France Prepare for War, 1904-1914.* Cambridge, Mass.: Harvard University Press, 1969.
Woodward, E. L. *Great Britain and the German Navy.* 2nd ed. London: Frank Cass, 1964.

Index

Abadan, 236
Abyssinian Crisis 186
Admiralty: Anti-Submarine Division of, 103; Board of, 2, 4, 6-7, 12, 14, 20, 22, 25, 27-29, 38, 40, 49, 55-56, 58, 62, 69, 76, 95-97, 113-14, 117-20, 128, 150-51, 153-54, 157, 162-63, 175, 180-81, 191, 193, 198, 202, 211-13, 218-19, 223, 249, 251, 254, 257-61, 277; Directorate of Naval Intelligence, 103; Local Defence Section, 175; "M" Branch, 258; Mobilization Department, 75; Naval Intelligence Division, 1, 48, 57; Naval Staff, 15, 48, 57, 77, 116, 121, 123, 128, 134, 175, 182, 187-90, 195, 253, 259, 261-62, 267, 271; Naval War Staff, 1, 4-5, 48, 57, 59, 62-64, 67, 80-81, 83-84, 86; Navigation Department, 81; Operations Division, 96, 99, 114, 185; Ordnance Department, 185; Planning Section, 185; Plans Division, 114, 175, 177, 183 n.19, 185, 253, 256; Room 40, 85, 96, 99; Staff, 116; Steering Group, 260; Tactical Division, 175; Trade Division 103; Training and Staff Duties Division, 175; Transport Department, 48; War Staff Group, 84, 86

Adriatic, 94, 115
Aegean Sea, 206
Agadir Crisis (1911), 47
Air Defence Committee, 250
Air Ministry, 15, 161, 187, 191, 211, 251, 257, 272; and Fleet Air Arm, 134-35, 163-64, 170 n.32; control of Coastal Command, 274
Air Staff, 193-94
Aitken, Sir Max (Lord Beaverbrook), 111 n.40
Albania, 230
Alexander, Albert Victor (Earl), 11; as First Lord (1929-31), 147-51; (1940-45), 191, 201, 206, 211-12; (1945-46), 217-18, 226 n.3; as Minister of Defence (1946-50), 219-23, 226 n.4, 227 n.13, 231-32, 246 n.11
Alexander Forts, 21
Alexander of Tunis, Lord, 206, 249, 252, 255, 257
Alexandretta, 27
Alexandria, 66-67
Allied Forces Northern Europe (AFNORTH), 277
Allied Striking Fleet, 258-59
Altenfjord, 197
Amery, Leopold, 128, 132, 190
Amethyst Crisis (1949), 224
Anderson Committee, 151

Andrewes, Sir William, 237
Anglo-American Naval Relations, 8-9, 15, 115-16, 121-22, 129, 241, 274-75. *See also* U.S. Navy
Anglo-French Entente (1904), 82
Anglo-German Naval Agreement (1935), 160
Anglo-Iranian Oil Concession Treaty (1951), 235
Anglo-Russian Agreement (1907), 82
Anti-Comintern Pact, 166
Antwerp, 205-6
Anzam (Australia, New Zealand and Malaya), 239
Anzio, 206
Appeasement, 10, 181
Arabian Gulf, 27, 235
Arctic Convoys, 197, 205
Argentina, 230
Argentia Bay Meeting (1941), 195
Argo Company, 61
Armistice, 18
Armstrong-Whitworth & Co. Ltd., 60
Army, 26, 48, 192-93, 231, 236, 240, 262, 275, 279; Council, 22; General Staff, 81
Arnold, Henry H. (Hap), 212
Arnold-Forster, Hugh O., 22
Asdic, 167-68, 204
Asia, 13
Asquith, Herbert Henry (Earl of Oxford and Asquith), 37, 48, 83, 99, 102, 111 n.40; his relations with Battenberg, 4, 55; his relations with Fisher, 17, 28-30, 65, 91
ASV MK III Radar, 194
Atlantic Command, 23
Atlantic Fleet, 76, 141-43, 150, 152-54, 157
Atlantic Ocean, 23, 106, 179, 190, 194-95, 204, 271; Battle of, 11, 192-95, 204; Eastern Atlantic 233, 242, 259; North Atlantic, 204, 240-41; South Atlantic, 224, 234; Western Atlantic, 23, 210
Attlee, Clement (Earl), 210, 226, 226 n.6; and Defence Policy 217-18, 220, 223, 226 n.5, 227 n.13, 232; his

relations with Fraser; 230, 236; and the North Atlantic Command Controversy, 241-43
Australia, 24, 68-69, 132, 176-78, 207, 234, 238-39, 272
Australian Commonwealth Naval Board, 177, 238
Austria-Hungary, 83

Backhouse, Sir Roger, 170 n.22; as First Sea Lord, 10, 173-83, 186
Bacon, Sir Reginald, 41, 43, 108-9, 113
Baldwin, Stanley (Earl), 132-33, 137, 141, 147, 160, 163-65
Balfour, Arthur James (Earl), 28, 67, 102, 111 n.40, 131; as First Lord, 6, 91-96, 98-99, 110 n.6
Balfour Committee (1923), 134
Baltic Scheme, 26-27
Baltic Sea, 26, 28, 122, 188
Barham, Lord (Charles Middleton), 19
Barnes, Sir Sidney, 174
Barnett, Correlli, 30 n.4, 173, 195
Barrow-in-Furness, 254
Bartoleme, C. M. de, 114
Battenberg, Prince Louis of, 4, 22, 61, 69; as First Sea Lord, 5, 25, 78-88; his early career, 75-77; his relations with Churchill, 55-57, 62; his views on a Mediterranean Strategy, 65, 67
Battle of the Air, 193
Battle of the Atlantic, 192-95, 204
Battle of the River Plate (1939), 189
Bayly, Sir Lewis, 46
Bay of Biscay, 240
Beatty, Earl David, 65, 69, 104, 142, 148-49; as First Sea Lord, 3, 8-9, 127-39; his relations with Jellicoe, 107, 109, 143, 212; his relations with Wemyss, 114-18, 120, 122-23; his support for naval construction, 141, 145-46, 150; his views on Jackson, 93, 95, 98
Beatty, Ethel, 118, 144
Beaumont, Sir Lewis, 35
Beesly, Patrick, 197
Belgium, 240

Bellenger, Fred, 226 n.5
Benson, William, 8, 116, 121-22
Beresford, Sir Charles, 3, 24, 35-36, 44, 49
Berlin Blockade (1948-49), 224
Bethell, Sir Alexander, 47
Bevin, Ernest, 230
Binney, Sir T.H., 174
Binney Committee, 10, 174-75
Birch, Nigel, 257
Birkenhead, Lord, 128, 131, 133
Bismarck, 196-97
Blackburn Buccaneer, 273, 279
Black Sea, 118
Blake, Sir Geoffrey, 158
Blue Streak, 268
Board of Invention and Research, 30
Bomber Command, 192, 254, 259
Bon, Admiral de, 115
Bonar Law Committee, 130
Bosphorus, Straits of, 94
Boxer Rebellion (1900), 149
Boyd, Sir Denis, 223
Boyle, Sir Dermot, 268, 272, 274
Bridge, Sir Cyprian, 24
Bridgeman, Sir Francis Bridgeman-, 36, 38-39, 45-47, 76-79, 88 n.8, 89 n.12, 142; as First Sea Lord, 4-5, 55-70
Bridgeman, William, 133, 143, 147-49
Briggs, Sir Charles, 60
Brind, Sir Patrick, 235, 237, 241
Britain, 17-18, 23, 26, 47, 82
British Admiralty Delegation (BAD), 201, 208
British Empire, 17, 68, 141, 161-62, 207, 209, 214, 231
British Expeditionary Force, 28
British Honduras, 230
British Pacific Fleet (BPF), 68-69, 203, 209, 229, 223, 237
Broadlands, 277
Brock, Sir Osmond de, 128, 134, 148
"Broken-backed war," 251-52, 257
Brooke, Sir Alan (later Viscount Alanbrooke), 192-95, 198, 202, 205
Broome, Jack, 197
Brown, Preston, 147
Bruce, Stanley, 176-77

Brundrett, Sir Frederick, 255
Bulgaria, 94
Burke, Arleigh, 15, 268, 274-75, 278-79
Butler, Richard Austen (Baron Butler of Saffron Walden), 249
Buzzard, Sir Anthony, 252, 262

Cabinet Anti-U-Boat Committee, 193
Callaghan, Sir George, 39, 45-47, 63-64
Callaghan, James, 236, 267
Callwell, Charles, 27
Canada, 23-24, 68-69, 132, 240
Cape Spartivento, 196
Caribbean, 23
Carney, Robert, 240-41
Carrier Task Groups, 272
Carson, Sir Edward, 113, 108, 144
Carter, Archibald, 198
Casablanca, 195
Cavan, Earl of, 137
Cawdor, Earl, 23
Cawdor Memorandum (1905), 23-24
Cecil, Viscount David, 149
Central Powers, 25, 117
Chalfont, Lord Alun, 227 n.13
Chamberlain, Austen, 147, 152-53
Chamberlain, Neville, 10, 132, 163, 165-68, 174, 181, 189
Channel Command, 23
Channel Fleet, 36, 38-40, 42, 44, 75
Chatfield, Sir Ernle (Baron), 128, 134-35, 146, 150, 154, 173-74, 180, 244; as First Sea Lord 2, 9, 157-71; as Minister for Coordination of Defence, 181, 186
Chatham, 81
Chelmsford, Viscount, 128, 132
Cherbourg, 205
Cherwell, Lord, 211
Chiefs of Staff (COS), 2, 201; with Backhouse as First Sea Lord, 175, 182; with Beatty as First Sea Lord, 136-37, 139; with Chatfield as First Sea Lord, 9, 161-62, 165-66; with Pound as First Sea Lord, 187, 191-92, 194-95; with ABC as First Sea Lord, 206-7; with J.D.H. Cunningham as First Sea Lord, 218-23, 225, 227 ns.12-13; with Fraser

as First Sea Lord, 231-32, 237-39, 241-42; with McGrigor as First Sea Lord, 249-52, 256; with Mountbatten as First Sea Lord, 268, 272
Chile, 152
China, 21, 129, 176-77, 207, 210, 235
China Station, 68, 81, 183 n.10
Chinese Civil War, 234
Churchill, Sir Winston, 1, 17, 95, 105, 128, 146, 168, 185, 211-12, 226 n.3, 229-30, 245; as First Lord (1911-15), 4-6, 10-11, 21, 25-29, 48-49, 55-60, 62-70, 76-84, 86-87, 88 n.8, 91, 102; as First Lord (1939-40), 188-89; as a Backbencher, 164-65; as Leader of the Opposition (1945-51), 236, 241, 243; as Secretary of State for War, 118, 127, 130-31; as Chancellor of the Exchequer, 132-33, 144-45, 147; as Prime Minister (1940-45), 11, 190-94, 196-97, 201-9, 213; as Prime Minister (1951-55), 14, 244, 249, 251-52, 257-59, 262
Cilcennin, Viscount (formerly James Thomas), 244, 271
Clarke, Sir George, 26
Clynes, J. R., 133, 136
Coastal Command, 166, 192-94, 197, 211, 236, 255, 273, 280
Cold War, 224, 256, 262
Collins, Sir John, 238-39
Colonial Conference (1909), 68
Colville, Sir Stanley, 49
Colvin, Sir Ragnar M., 177
Combined Chiefs of Staff (CCOS), 11, 194-95, 207, 213
Committee of Imperial Defence (CID), 2, 22, 58, 62, 137, 161, 175; and the Admiralty, 81, 84, 145; and Anglo-American Relations, 147; and Naval Rearmament, 154, 162, 183 n.23; and the Mediterranean, 65-67; and the Singapore Naval Base, 136; with Wilson as First Sea Lord, 36, 38, 44, 47
Committee on National Expenditure, 131
Committee on Officer Structure and Training (COST), 261, 277

Commonwealth, 238-39, 271, 279
Conservative and Unionist Party, 86, 145, 267
Convoy, 7, 94, 102-3, 105-6, 187, 197, 231
Cooper, Alfred Duff (Viscount Norwich), 165-67, 170 n.34, 174, 180
Corbett, Sir Julian, 120, 129
Cork and Orrery, Lord, 189, 196
Craigie, Sir Robert, 160
Creasy, Sir George, 230
Cripps, Sir Stafford, 233
Cunningham, Sir John H. D., 212, 229-30, 232, 249; as First Sea Lord, 12-13, 217-27
Cunningham of Hyndhope, Viscount, (ABC), 122, 182, 186, 217, 244; as First Sea Lord, 11-12, 201-14, 218; his relations with Fraser, 229; his relations with Pound, 188, 196; his views on his successor, 226 n.3
Curzon, Lord, 111 n.40, 128
Curzon-Howe, Sir Ashton, 35
Custance, Sir Reginald, 35
Cyrenaica, 210, 223
Czechoslovakia, 174, 181-82

Daily Mail, 86
Daily Telegraph, 186
Dalton, Hugh (Baron), 220
Danckwerts, Victor H., 160
Daniel, Sir Charles, 203, 230
Daniels, Josephus, 122
Dardanelles, 1, 6, 10, 18, 25, 27-28, 91, 93-94, 102, 105
Dardanelles Inquiry, 27, 30
Dartmouth, 173
Davis, Sir William, 265-66, 278
De Chair, Sir Dudley, 146
Declaration of London, 45
D Day, 202-5, 213
Defence Committee, 191-93, 218, 227 nn.15, 25, 232-33, 252
Defence Council, 236
Defence Requirements Committee (DRC), 162; DRC Standard, 167, 170 n.20

Defence Research Policy Committee, 250
Defence Review Committee, 257
Defence White Paper: (1935), 160; (1955), 265-66; (1957), 269-70; (1958), 270
De Gaulle, Charles, 206
Denmark, 206, 240
Denning, Sir Norman E., 197
Denny, Sir Michael, 230
Devonport, 81
DH 110, 255, 259
Dickson, Sir William, 252, 254-55, 272, 274
Dill, Sir John, 202
Dogger Bank, 27
Dominions, 23-24, 68-69, 121, 131-32, 174, 177-78, 210, 238-39
Dönitz, Admiral Karl, 194-95, 204
Dover Patrol, 98, 109, 185
Dover Straits, 113-14
Drax, Sir Reginald, 10, 177-79
Dreyer, Sir Frederick, 40-42, 151-54, 181, 198
Drury, Sir Charles, 36
Duff, Sir Alexander, 103-4, 106, 110, 113
Dunston, Sir John, 39
Duprez, M., 240
Durnford, Sir John, 56

Eastern Command, 23, 242
Eastern Fleet, 203, 209
Eastern Front, 27
East Indies Station, 81, 113, 204, 206, 221, 224
Edelsten, Sir John, 230
Eden, Anthony (Earl of Avon), 163, 191, 210
Edinburgh, 40-41
Edward VII, 17
Edwards, Sir Ralph, 230, 263 n.25, 270, 272
Egerton, Sir George, 32, 76
Egypt, 210
Eisenhower, Dwight D., 206, 212, 241
Ellington, Sir Edward, 160

Elswick Ordnance Company, 60
England, 18, 63
English Channel, 98, 115, 233, 240
Esher, Lord, 19, 22, 29-30,
Esquimalt Dockyard, 23
Ethiopia, 162, 170 n.21
Europe, 10, 13, 18, 26, 68, 178, 224

Falkland Islands, 5, 25, 230
Far East, 10, 121, 135, 138, 176-79, 181, 190, 204, 210, 221, 223-24
Far East Fleet, 235
Farquhar, Sir Arthur Murray, 69
Fawkes, Sir Wilmot, 36
Fechteler, William, 240, 243
Field, Sir Frederick, 3, 128, 141, 143-46, 148, 158, 186; as First Sea Lord, 9, 149-54, 156 n.56
First Cruiser Squadron, 69
Fisher of Kilverstone, Lord John Arbuthnot (Jackie), 1, 39, 88 n.8, 92, 95, 101-2, 108, 139, 141, 185-86, 213; as First Sea Lord, 3, 5-6, 15 n.1, 17-30, 68; his relations with Battenberg, 76-77; his relations with Bridgeman, 56, 60, 62, 65-66, 68; his relations with Churchill, 5-6, 25-29, 87, 91; his relations with the Syndicate of Discontent, 3, 35-37, 44; his relations with Wilson, 35, 38, 43, 45, 49
Fisher, Sir Warren, 151, 168
Fisher, Sir William, 144, 170 n.17
Five Year Rule, 222, 225
Flanders, 107, 115
Fleet Air Arm, 180, 187, 205, 254, 257, 259, 272; American complaints about, 208; and the attack on the *Tirpitz* (April 1944), 205; Beatty's influence on, 8, 128, 133-35; Chatfield and, 159, 163, 165-66; Cunningham's involvement with, 203, 211, 214
Flexible Response, Doctrine of, 269
Flotilla Defense, 67
Foch, Marshal Ferdinand, 116, 122
Forbes, Sir Charles, 158, 188, 196, 198
Force Z, 179, 191

Foreign Office, 65, 129, 159, 167-68, 278
Forgotten Army, 238
Fortress Europe, 194
France, 23, 47, 65-66, 82, 107, 115, 160, 206, 213, 240-41
Franco, Francisco, 162
Fraser of North Cape, Lord, 197-98, 201, 249; as First Sea Lord, 13, 229-45; his relations with ABC, 203, 205-6, 209, 214; and the succession to ABC, 212, 218, 226 n.3; his views shared by McGrigor, 250
Fraser Plan, 238
Fremantle, Sir Sidney, 114
French Coal Protected Sailings, 104, 106
French Navy, 59, 94, 196, 211, 240
Fuller, Sir Cyril T. W., 114, 144, 151, 154

Gallipoli Peninsula, 27, 91, 93-94
Gannet (Anti-Submarine Aircraft), 273
Geddes, Eric, 111 n.40, 130, 142; and the Committee on National Expenditure, 131; as Controller, 104-5, 107; as First Lord, 7-8, 108, 112 n.49, 113-14, 116, 118-19
Geddes Axe (1921), 8
General List, 261
Geneva Conference (1927), 145-46, 149, 154, 186
Geneva Disarmament Conference (1932-34), 186
George V, 17, 78-79, 87, 108, 111 n.40, 113, 118, 142, 148, 151-53, 156 n.56
George VI, 235
German Coast, Blockade of, 44-48, 64, 94, 101, 105, 107
German High Seas Fleet, 26, 45, 64, 77; its future after the armistice, 117, 121; its scuttling, 122, 142; post-Jutland effects of, 99, 102; the Royal Navy's blockade of, 109; the Royal Navy's confrontations with, 5-6, 95-97; the Royal Navy's preparations for war with, 42, 44-48, 59, 63, 67-68. *See also* Imperial German Navy

German Naval Law (*Novelle*), 64-65
German Navy (post-1935), 177, 189-90, 227 n.15
Germany, 23, 76-77, 82, 115, 160, 174; and the Agadir Crisis (1911), 47; and the Axis (post-1936), 10, 162, 166-67, 178, 180, 183 n.23; and World War I, 25-27, 30, 95-97, 115; and World War II, 189-90, 192-94, 203, 206; Post-1945, 209-10, 223, 226
Gibraltar, 23, 64-66, 104, 106, 214, 241-42
Gibraltar Chronicle, 242
Global Strategy Paper (1952), 251
Goeben, 86, 116
Gold Standard, 145, 151, 153
Gordon, Andrew, 153
Gort, Viscount, 182
Gough-Calthorpe, Sir Somerset, 118
Goschen, George (Viscount), 20
Graham, Sir James, 20
Grand Fleet, 25, 27, 99, 100 n.13, 101-5, 116-17, 120, 142-43, 199
Grand Fleet Battle Instructions, 129, 134, 187
Greece, 198, 206
Green Cheese, 253
Gretton, Sir Peter, 230, 237, 242-43
Grey, Sir Edward, 83
Groome, Robert L., 48
Grove, Eric, 245
Guatemala, 230

Hague Conference on Disarmament (1899), 22
Haig, Earl, 7, 107-9
Haldane, Lord, 87, 128, 135
Halifax, Lord, 161
Halifax Aircraft, 194
Halifax Dockyard, 23
Hall, Sydney S., 44
Hall, Viscount George, 12, 218, 223, 226 n.6, 229-30
Hallett, Sir John Hughes, 267
Halsey, Sir Cyril, 114
Hamburg, 206
Hamilton, Sir Frederick, 93

Hamilton, Sir Ian, 143
Hammond, Paul, 199
Hankey, Lord, 27, 57, 81, 104, 109, 147; his relations with Beatty, 134, 137, 139; his relations with Chatfield, 161, 163, 165
Harcourt, Sir Cecil, 230
Harcourt, Viscount (Lewis), 68
Harding, Sir John, 252
Harper, J. E. T., 120, 143
Harris, Sir Arthur, 193
Harwood, Sir Edmund, 233
Harwood, Sir Henry, 189, 198
Harwood Working Party, 233, 237
Heligoland, 46, 48-49, 107, 117, 122
Heligoland Bight, 46-47, 86, 115
Henderson, Sir Reginald, 103-4, 106, 158
Hermes Class (Light Fleet Carriers), 253-54
Hinsley, Sir Harry, 197
Hitler, Adolf, 174, 181-82
HMAS *Sydney*, 238
HMS *Aboukir*, 86
HMS *Albion*, 254, 276
HMS *Amethyst*, 13, 234-35
HMS *Ariadne*, 42
HMS *Ark Royal*, 236, 253-54
HMS *Audacious*, 86
HMS *Britannia*, 149
HMS *Bulwark*, 254, 276
HMS *Cambrian*, 75, 81
HMS *Centaur*, 253-54
HMS *Colossus*, 185
HMS *Cressy*, 86
HMS *Dreadnought* (1906), 23, 41-42, 59, 75, 141; (1963), 275
HMS *Duke of York*, 233
HMS *Eagle*, 236, 253-54
HMS *Euryalus*, 100 n.4
HMS *Excellent*, 21, 75, 101
HMS *Glory*, 238
HMS *Hawke*, 86
HMS *Hermes*, 86, 254-56, 262, 272
HMS *Hogue*, 86
HMS *Hood*, 130, 197
HMS *Implacable*, 76
HMS *Indomitable*, 69

HMS *Inflexible*, 21
HMS *Invincible*, 21, 59, 141
HMS *Iron Duke*, 102
HMS *King George V*, 149, 196
HMS *Lion*, 168
HMS *Majestic*, 75
HMS *Mauritius*, 236
HMS *Nelson*, 227 n.25
HMS *New Zealand*, 69
HMS *Pathfinder*, 86
HMS *Prince of Wales*, 190-91
HMS *Queen Elizabeth*, 227 n.25
HMS *Renown*, 227 n.25
HMS *Repulse*, 190-91
HMS *Rodney*, 227 n.25
HMS *Royal Oak*, 148
HMS *Scout*, 75
HMS *Solebay*, 211
HMS *Superb*, 185
HMS *Thunderer*, 61
HMS *Valiant*, 227 n.25
HMS *Vanguard*, 211, 236, 254, 256
HMS *Vernon*, 75, 79, 141, 148-49
HMS *Victorious*, 253-56, 272-73
HMS *Victory*, 30 n.2
HMS *Warrior*, 254
HMS *Warspite*, 195
Hoare, Sir Samuel (Viscount Templewood), 163-65
Hohenzollerns, 86
Holland, L. H., 174
Home Fleet, 36, 76; under Wilson as First Sea Lord, 43, 46; with Bridgeman as First Sea Lord, 55, 63, 65; in World War II, 186, 189-91, 196-98, 205; post-1945, 233, 242, 253, 258, 269
Hong Kong, 68, 214, 221, 224, 233
Hoover, Herbert, 147
Hope, Sir George, 114
Hopwood, Sir Francis, 80
Horne, Sir Robert, 130
House of Commons, 20, 76, 82, 95, 151-52, 164, 243
House of Lords, 232, 244
Humble, Richard, 235, 240, 245
Hythe, Viscount, 80

Imperial Conference: (1911), 81; (1918), 121; (1921), 131, 136; (1926), 138
Imperial Defence College, 137, 250
Imperial German Navy, 5-6, 30
India, 68, 132, 207, 226, 278
Indian Ocean, 178, 190, 203, 207, 234
Inskip, Sir Thomas, 160, 163-68, 174, 180-81
International Monetary Fund (IMF), 266
Invergordon Mutiny, 9, 150-54, 157, 169 n.2, 186
Iran, 235
Ismay, Lord Hastings, 183 n.19
Italian Navy, 10, 94, 177, 187, 190, 196
Italy, 65, 116, 162-63, 175, 178-80, 186, 241

Jackson, Sir Henry, 1, 57, 81, 101; as First Sea Lord, 6-7, 91-99, 100 n.4; on Madden, 141, 148
Japan, 23, 60, 166-67; and World War II, 190-91, 207, 213; post-1945, 209-10; threat posed by, 10, 121, 129, 131, 135-36, 160, 162, 174-80, 183 nn.10, 23; Anglo-Japanese Alliance, 68
Japanese Fleet, 133, 137, 159, 177-79, 190
Jellicoe, Sir John (Earl), 26, 113, 138, 150, 187, 199, 212; and Bridgeman, 56, 64; and Churchill, 79; and the Grand Fleet, 27, 92, 96-97; and Jackson, 93, 95, 97-99; and Madden, 141-43; and Wemyss, 115-16, 120-21; and Wilson, 39, 41-43, 47, 49; as First Sea Lord, 7-8, 101-10
Jerram, Sir Martin, 149
Jerram, Sir Thomas, 120, 168
John Bull, 86
Joint Intelligence Committee, 225
Joint Maritime Air Force, 236-37
Jutland, Battle of, 6-7, 18, 30 n.3, 96-97, 99, 101, 109, 116, 120, 138, 143, 149, 185

Kelly, Sir John, 150-53, 157, 169
Kelly, Sir W. H., 144
Kennedy-Purvis, Sir Charles, 198
Kerans, John, 235
Kerr, Lord Walter, 39
Keyes, Sir Roger (Baron), 29-30, 41, 44, 94, 109, 114, 128; and Field, 149-50, 153; and Naval Aviation, 135, 164; and Pound, 145, 185, 189; and the succession to Beatty, 142-44, 148
Khrushchev, Nikita, 272
King, E. L. S., 170 n.20
King, Ernest J., 11, 195, 206-8, 212
King George V Class Battleships, 252
King's Regulations, 243
Kitchener, Lord, 27, 65, 94, 99
Korea, 13, 210, 231, 235, 237-38, 241, 244
Kuomintang, 235

Lambe, Sir Charles, 278
Lambert, Sir Cecil, 93, 97
Lambton, Sir Hedworth, 56
Lancaster Aircraft, 192
Lang, John, 278
Lausanne Conference (1923), 186
Law, Andrew Bonar, 122, 130
Lawson, Jack, 226 n.5
Leach, Sir Henry, 245
League of Nations, 121-22
Leathers, Lord Edward, 208
Le Bris, Admiral, 82
Lee of Fareham, Lord, 127
Lemonnier, André Georges, 240
Leslie, Sir Norman A., 106
Levant, 206
Liberal Party, 76
Lion Class Battlecruisers, 60
Litchfield, John, 186
Little, Sir Charles, 198
Lloyd, Selwyn (Baron), 257
Lloyd George, David (Earl), 99, 102, 111 n.40; and Jellicoe, 7, 104-5, 108-9; and Wemyss, 8, 115, 117-18, 122; as Minister for Munitions (1915-16), 94-95; as Prime Minister, 18, 27, 127, 130-31

London Docks, 180
London Naval Conference: (1930), 9, 141, 147, 150, 159; (1935-36), 159
London Naval Treaty (1936), 160
Long, Walter, 118, 122, 128, 130
Long Term Defence Review, 265
Lowestoft, 96

MacArthur, Douglas, 241
MacDonald, J. Ramsay, 132, 136-37, 141, 147-49, 151, 159-60, 163, 226 n.6
Macmillan, Harold (Earl of Stockton), 257-59, 274
MacKenzie, Sir Compton, 171 n.39
Madden, Sir Charles, 3, 47, 76, 134, 150-51, 154; as First Sea Lord, 8-9, 141-49
Main Fleet to Singapore, 10, 179, 190
Malaya, 179, 207, 225
Malta, 64-67, 270, 274
Manisty, H. W. E., 106
Manisty Committee, 106, 111 n.26
Mansergh, Sir Maurice, 230, 261
Marconi, Guglielmo, 92

Marder, Arthur J., 30 n.3, 110 n.23, 186, 188, 199 n.5
Maritime Air Defence Committee, 237
Marshall, George Cattrell, 212
Mascot Fiasco, 253
Massive Retaliation, Doctrine of, 269-70
May, Sir William, 36, 43, 45-46, 56
May Committee, 9, 151-52
Mayo, Sir Henry, 107
McCormick, Lynde, 243
McGrigor, Sir Rhoderick, 219, 244; as First Sea Lord, 13-14, 249-63
McKenna, Reginald, 4, 47-48, 56, 58, 68, 142; how he was viewed by von Müller, 77, 88 n.8, 89 n.11; as First Lord of the Admiralty, 24, 35-39
Mediterranean, 10, 64, 94, 100 n.7, 107, 115-16, 144, 150, 177, 187; and Far Eastern Strategy, 178-79, 190; and World War II, 203-6, 213; Bridgeman's views on, 66-67;
Churchill's policy towards, 65, 69; post-1945 British policy towards, 210-11, 214, 224, 233, 240-41, 243, 272
Mediterranean Command, 23, 199
Mediterranean Fleet, 27, 157, 169 n.2, 201
Mediterranean Station, 21, 76
Menzies, Robert, 178, 239
Mers-el-Kebir, 196
Middle East, 177-78, 221, 223, 241
Middleton, Charles (Lord Barham), 19
Military Command List, 261
Milne, George (Baron), 137
Milne, Sir Berkeley, 46,
Milner, Lord Alfred, 111 n.40
Minatours, 169 n.8
Ministry of Defence, 20, 22, 137, 236, 246 n.11, 251, 254, 257-58
Ministry of Supply, 212, 220
Monsell, Sir Bolton Eyres (Viscount), 153, 157, 159-60, 163
Montgomery of Alamein, Viscount, 198, 205, 241, 278; as CIGS, 12, 219, 221-23, 227 n.13, 232; appointed Deputy SACEUR, 241
Moore, Sir Arthur, 35, 37
Morning Post, 78
Mossadeq, Dr. Muhammad, 235
Mountbatten of Burma, Earl, 3, 125 n.71, 192, 206-7, 209, 214, 230, 244, 260-62; as First Sea Lord, 14-15, 265-80
Mudros, 113
Müller, Erich von, 76-78, 88 n.8, 89 n.11
Munich Crisis (1938), 176
Munich Settlement, 174
Murfett, Malcolm, 234
Mussolini, Benito, 162

N113 (Naval Aircraft), 255
NA39 (the future Buccaneer), 14, 254-55, 257, 259, 262
Nailor, Peter, 199
Nanking, 234
Nanshin-Ron, 178

Narrows Forts, 94
Narvik, 189
National Service, 225
Naval Annual, 80
Naval Aviation, 254
Naval Defence Act (1889), 22
Naval Review, 81, 137
Naval War College, 35, 38
Naval War Council, 47
Nelson, Lord Horatio, 18-19, 30 n.2
Netherlands, 240
Neville, Sir George, 41
Newall, Sir Cyril, 182, 192
Newbolt, Henry, 110 n.23, 111 n.28
Newell, Philip, 258-59
Newfoundland, 195
New Standard of Naval Strength, 162
New Zealand, 68, 178, 234, 238
New Zealand Naval Forces, 82
Nicholas II (Czar of Russia), 27
Noble, Alan, 259
Noble, Sir Percy, 183 n.10, 207-8
Noel-Baker, Philip John (Baron), 226 n.5
Norris, Charles, 186
Norstad, Lauris, 277
North, Sir Dudley, 198
North Africa, 178, 213, 241
North America Station, 21, 23
North Atlantic Naval Command, 242

North Atlantic Treaty Organization (NATO), 13, 231, 240-43, 269, 273, 279
Northern Fleet, 254
North Sea, 26, 28, 43, 45, 64-65, 67-68, 96-97, 99, 101, 233
Norway, 63, 116, 189, 205, 210, 240, 253, 259
Nyon Conference, 163

Oliver, Sir Henry, 96, 106-7, 114
Oliver Cromwell, 79
Operational Intelligence Centre (OIC), 197
Operation *Anvil*, 206
Operation *Catherine*, 188

Operation *Dragoon*, 206
Operation *Fairlead*, 279
Operation *Neptune*, 203
Operation *Overlord*, 203, 205
Operation *Tungsten*, 205
Orkneys, 116
Ostende, 107, 115
Ottley, Sir Charles, 47, 57, 75

Pacific Ocean, 23, 68, 154, 207-10, 223-24, 231, 234, 239
Packer, Sir Herbert, 230
Pakenham, Baron (Earl of Longford), 244
Pakenham, Sir William, 76
Pakistan, 278
Palestinian Mandate, 226
Patterson, A. Temple, 104, 162, 169 nn.1, 2
Pax Britannica, 18
Peel, Lord, 134
People's Liberation Army (PLA), 234
Persian Gulf, 27
Phillips, Sir Tom Spencer V., 163, 170 n.36, 191, 198
Pierre, A. J., 268
Plymouth, 235, 244
Poe, Sir Edmond, 56
Polaris, 267-68, 272, 279
Pollen, Arthur, 40, 61
Pollen Fire Control System, 41-42
Pomeranian Coast, 26
Poore, Sir Richard, 79-80
Porchester, Lord, 244
Portal, Lord Charles, 11, 192-94, 202
Portland, 64, 83
Port Royal Dockyard, 23
Portsmouth, 22, 42
Post-War Questions Committee, 118
Pound, Lady, 199
Pound, Sir Dudley, 114, 136, 146-48, 158, 182 n.3, 183 n.29, 201-2, 244; as First Sea Lord, 10-11, 185-99; his relations with Keyes, 143-45
Power, Arthur, 198, 206
PQ 17 (Convoy), 187, 197

Quebec Conference: (1943), 195, 199; (1944): 207
Queen Bee, 167
Queen Elizabeth Class Battleships, 62
Queen's Speech (1954), 244

Radar (984), 253
Radford-Collins Agreement (1951), 239
Ramsay, Sir Bertram, 205
Rawlings, Sir Bernard, 206
Reconstruction Committee (1918), 119
Red Beard, 253, 267, 273
Red Sea, 75, 179
Reserve Fleet, 223, 233, 256, 277
Review of Defence Policy (1926), 137-38
Richmond, Sir Herbert W., 81, 104, 108, 114, 119, 130, 148, 150, 160
Rickover, Hyman, 15, 268, 274-75, 278
Robertson, Sir William, 108
Room 40 (Admiralty), 85, 96, 99
Roosevelt, Franklin Delano, 207, 212
Roskill, Stephen, 154, 186, 188-89, 195-96, 198
Rosyth Dockyard, 24, 81, 96, 99, 116
Royal Air Force (RAF), 127, 130, and Naval Aviation, 129, 134, 164-66; and rearmament, 162, 167; role in defence policy 192-93, 211; post-1945 policy on, 231, 236, 240, 250, 253, 255, 262, 266-67, 272-73, 279-80
Royal Australian Navy (RAN), 81-82, 239
Royal Canadian Navy (RCN), 82, 238
Royal Indian Marine, 82
Royal Marines, 212, 214, 233, 276
Royal Naval Barracks (Portsmouth), 280
Royal Naval College (Dartmouth), 261
Royal Naval College (Greenwich), 99, 250, 252, 279
Royal Naval College (Osborne), 22
Royal Naval Volunteer Reserve (RNVR), 236
Royal United Services Institute (RUSI), 278
Russia, 23, 26-27, 129, 210, 259
Russian Black Sea Fleet, 116
Russian Fleet, 227 n.15, 258

Salami Tactics, 219
Salonika, 94
Sanders, Jack, 67
Sandhurst, Lord, 75
Sandys, Duncan, 14, 251, 255, 257, 270-76, 278-79
Sarajevo, 83
Saunders Roe P177, 273
Scandinavia, 106, 240
Scapa Flow (Orkney Islands), 27, 83, 96, 99, 101, 122, 142
Scharnhorst, 205, 229, 244
Scheer, Reinhard, 96-97
Scheldt, River, 206
Scimitar Fighter Bombers, 273
Scotland, 81
Scott, Sir Percy, 61
Scott Director, 41, 61
Seamew Aircraft, 257
Seaslug Missile, 267, 275
Sea Vixen Fighter Bombers, 273
Selborne, Earl of, 19-20, 23, 32 n.14, 38-39
Sembawang Naval Base (Singapore), 8, 128, 133, 135, 138, 176
Serbia, 83
Serbian Army, 94
Shanghai, 235
Sherman, Forrest, 240-42
Shinwell, Emanuel (Baron), 221, 232, 236-38, 243
Simon, Sir John, 167, 174, 180
Sims, William, 8, 116
Sinclair, Sir Archibald (Viscount Thurso), 211
Singapore, 81, 129, 136, 150, 177-79, 190-91, 207, 221, 223; Naval Base (Sembawang), 8, 128, 133, 135, 138, 176
Singapore Strategy, 176-79, 181, 183 n.19
Skinner, Bernard Morland, 235
Skybolt Missile, 268
Slessor, Sir John, 206, 232, 236-37, 243, 250-52
Slim of Burma, Viscount, 232, 250-51
Smyth, Brigadier, 243
Snowden, Philip (Viscount), 132-33, 136

Somalia, 210
Somerville, Sir James, 196, 203, 208-9, 214
South Africa, 23, 68, 132, 238
South China Sea, 179
South East Asia, 179, 207, 262
South East Asia Command (SEAC), 207, 209, 278
Soviet Navy, 253, 269-70
Soviet Union (USSR), 210, 214, 231, 252, 256, 260, 266, 268-70, 272-73
Spain, 65
Spanish Civil War, 162, 180
Spee, Graf Maximilian von, 5, 25
Splendid Isolation, 23
St. Petersburg, 83
Stamfordham, Lord, 80, 87
Stanhope, Earl of, 174, 176-77, 181-82, 188
Stansgate, Viscount, 226 n.5
Stark, Harold, 195
Stephen, Martin, 245
Sterling Crisis (1947), 222
Strategic Appreciation Committee (SAC), 181
Sriking Fleet, 254
Sturdee, Sir Doveton, 43, 46, 83
Sudetendeutsch, 174
Sudetenland, 10
Suez, 221, 246 n.11; and the 1956 crisis, 15, 266, 273, 275-76, 278; East of Suez policy, 271-72
Sumatra, 207
Sumida, Jon Tetsuro, 138
Sunderland, 97
Suvla Bay, 93
Sverdlov Class Cruisers, 253
Sweden, 94
Swinton, Earl of, 164-65, 257
Syndicate of Discontent, 35, 37, 49

Tedder, Lord, 219, 222-23, 227 n.13, 232
Ten Year Rule, 137, 154, 220
The Times, 160
Third Fleet, 83
Thomas, J.H., 128

Thomas, James, (Viscount Cilcennin), 244, 255, 258-61, 271
Tiger Class Cruisers, 256
Till, Geoffrey, 134
Time and Tide, 270
Tirpitz, 190, 197, 205, 253
Tirpitz, Admiral Alfred von, 82
Tizard, Sir Henry, 250-51
Tomkinson, Wilfred, 149, 152-53
Tovey, Lord John, 196-97, 201, 242
Trafalgar, Battle of, 19, 21, 30 n.2, 102
Treasury, 13, 120, 152; and Backhouse, 180-81; and Chatfield, 9-10, 167-68, 170 n.20; and J.D.H. Cunningham, 12, 218, 220; and McGrigor, 249, 251; and Mountbatten, 15, 274-75, 280
Trenchard, Lord, 130, 134-37, 244
Trident Conference (1943), 208
Trident Staff Exercise (1949), 240
Trincomalee, 190, 221
Triple Alliance, 65
Tripoli, 205
Troubridge, Sir Ernest, 1, 4, 39, 57, 62-64, 67, 69, 77, 81, 109
Truman, Harry S., 243
TSR 2 (Vertical Take-off Fighter), 273
Tudor, Sir Frederick, 93
Tupper, R., 280
Turkey, 27-28, 118
Two-Ocean Navy, 150
Tyrwhitt, Sir Reginald, 142
Tweedmouth, Lord, 24, 88

U-boats, 117, 241; in World War I, 7, 94, 98, 102-3, 105-7; in World War II, 187, 193, 195, 202-5, 210, 213
Ultra Intelligence, 187, 197
United Kingdom, 9, 13, 132, 217-18, 221, 250, 252, 268
United Nations Organization (UNO), 210, 222, 237
United States, 23, 206-10, 213, 237-42, 250, 252, 256, 258-60, 266-67, 269, 272-75, 279
U.S. Atlantic Fleet, 240
U.S. Joint Chiefs of Staff, 195, 203, 208

U.S. Navy, 8-9, 15, 106, 119, 122, 145-46, 207-8, 210-11, 234, 238-41, 243, 269, 273-74. *See also* Anglo-American Naval Relations, and United States
U.S. Strategic Command, 252
USS *Nautilus*, 274

V Bombers, 250, 252, 254
Vansittart, Sir Robert (Baron), 168
Versailles Peace Conference, 8, 118, 144
Very Long Range (VLR) Aircraft, 193-94
Vian, Sir Philip, 206
Vickers Yard, 254
Victoria, Queen, 17
Victory Honours List, 122
Volunteer Reserve Air Squadrons, 257
Vulnerability of Capital Ships (VCS) Committee, 160-61, 169 n.15

Wall Street Crash (1929), 151
Walsh, Stephen, 128
War Cabinet, 22
War College, 57, 81, 83
War Council, 27-28
War Ministry, 191
War Office, 22, 27, 48, 75, 87, 115, 118, 187
War Orders, 44, 47, 63
Ward, George, 274
Washington, 195, 208
Washington Conference: (1921-22), 8, 127, 130, 136, 145; (1941), 195

Way Ahead Committee, 260, 276
Weir, Lord, 134, 165
Welfare Committee, 120
Wemyss, Lady, 119, 124 n.46
Wemyss, Lord Wester (Sir Rosslyn), 69, 100 n.4, 108-9, 128, 134, 142; as First Sea Lord, 7-8, 113-23; on Jackson as First Sea Lord, 93
Western Command, 242
Western Front, 26
Western Squadron, 19
West Indies, 224
West Indies Station, 21
Westland Helicopter Company, 273
White, Sir William H., 39
Whitehall, 12, 20, 22, 38-39, 57, 64, 249, 258
Whitehead Torpedo, 36
Whitworth, Sir William Jock, 203
William-Powlett, Sir Peveril, 242
Willis, Sir Algernon U., 206
Wilson, Sir Arthur Knyvett-, 25, 35-38, 55-56, 63-64, 68, 76-77; as First Sea Lord, 3-4, 39-49
Wilson, Woodrow, 121
Winn, Sir Rodger, 197
Women's Royal Naval Service (WRNS), 212
World War I, 21, 25-29, 83-86, 93-99, 101-10, 115-17, 120, 194
World War II, 13, 187-97, 202-9, 225

Yangtze River, 13, 234

Zeebrugge, 28, 107, 115, 142

Contributors

ROBIN BRODHURST, B.A., is the Head of History at Pangbourne College near Reading, Berkshire. He is currently working on a full length biography of Admiral Sir Dudley Pound which he expects to publish in 1996.

TOM FRAME, Ph.D., recently retired from the Royal Australian Navy (RAN) in order to become ordained as a parish priest in New South Wales. He has written several books in addition to his best-selling *Where Fate Calls: The HMAS Voyager Tragedy* (1992). His latest piece of published work is *Pacific Partners: A History of American-Australian Naval Relations* (1993). He is currently working on a book dealing with the controversy surrounding the cruiser HMAS *Sydney*.

Commander JAMES GOLDRICK, Ph.D., RAN, is currently attached to the RAN Surface Warfare School, HMAS *Watson*, Watson's Bay, New South Wales, Australia. Despite his full-time naval career, Commander Goldrick also wrote the excellent book *The King's Ships Were at Sea: The War in the North Sea, August 1914-February 1915* (1984). He and Professor John B. Hattendorf recently coedited a volume entitled *Mahan is not Enough* (1993).

BARRY M. GOUGH, Ph.D., F.R.Hist.S., is Professor of History at Wilfrid Laurier University in Waterloo, Ontario, Canada. Among his numerous published works on maritime and naval subjects, Professor Gough wrote the critically acclaimed *The Royal Navy and the Northwest Coast of North America, 1810-1914* (1971) and *The Falkland Islands/Malvinas: The Conquest for Empire in the South Atlantic* (1992). He is currently working on a biographical study of Lord Fisher of Kilverstone.

312   Contributors

ERIC J. GROVE, M.A., is a Lecturer in International Relations in the Department of Politics, University of Hull, United Kingdom. Among his prodigious output of books and articles, *Vanguard to Trident* (1987) is an outstanding work on British naval policy since the Second World War, and his *Fleet to Fleet Encounters* (1991) has added to his already considerable reputation in the field. He is currently engaged in writing a life of Lord Chatfield.

JOHN B. HATTENDORF, D.Phil., F.R.Hist.S., is Ernest J. King Professor of Maritime History at the U.S. Naval War College, Newport, Rhode Island. A prolific author on many naval subjects, Professor Hattendorf is well known for his work *England in the War of the Spanish Succession: A Study in the English View and Conduct of Grand Strategy, 1702-1713* (1988) and for coediting, with Robert S. Jordan, *Maritime Strategy and the Balance of Power in the Twentieth Century* (1989). He is currently completing a research project on the state of naval and maritime history around the world.

NICHOLAS A. LAMBERT, D.Phil., is currently a Visiting Fellow at Wolfson College, Oxford. His doctoral thesis at Oxford University, "The Influence of the Submarine upon Naval Strategy: 1898-1914," will soon appear in print.

MALCOLM H. MURFETT, D.Phil., F.R.Hist.S., is an Associate Professor in the Department of History at the National University of Singapore. Apart from his edited works, he is the author of *Fool-proof Relations: The Search for Anglo-American Naval Cooperation During the Chamberlain Years, 1937-1940* (1984), *Hostage on the Yangtze: Britain, China and the Amethyst Crisis of 1949* (1991), and *In Jeopardy: The Royal Navy and British Far Eastern Defence Policy, 1945-1951* (1995).

BRYAN M. RANFT, D.Phil., F.R.Hist.S., is Professor Emeritus at the Royal Naval College, Greenwich, London. Apart from his other major works, Professor Ranft edited both volumes of *The Beatty Papers* (1989-1993) as well as *Ironclad to Trident: 100 Years of Defence Commentary* (1986).

DONALD M. SCHURMAN, Ph.D., F.R.Hist.S., is Professor Emeritus at the Royal Military College, Kingston, Ontario, Canada. He is the author of two well-known works, *Julian S. Corbett: 1854-1922: Historian of British Maritime Policy from Drake to Jellicoe* (1981) and *The Education of a Navy* (1965).

MICHAEL SIMPSON, M.Litt., F.R.Hist.S., is a Senior Lecturer in United States History in the Department of History, University of Wales-Swansea. He is the editor of *Anglo-American Naval Relations, 1917-1919* (1991) and the author of *Franklin D. Roosevelt* (1989). He is currently working on an edition of Viscount Cunningham of Hyndhope's papers for the Navy Records Society in London.

Contributors 313

GEOFFREY TILL, Ph.D., F.R.Hist.S., is Professor of History at the Royal Naval College, Greenwich, London. He has written extensively on naval topics in the modern era, and his work on the Fleet Air Arm, entitled *Air Power and the Royal Navy* (1979), is regarded as the standard work in its field. He is also the author of *The Future of British Sea Power* (1984) and the editor of *Britain and Nato's Northern Flank* (1988).

NICHOLAS TRACY, Ph.D., is a freelance author and was formerly Associate Professor of History at the National University of Singapore. He is the author of *Navies, Deterrence and American Independence: Britain and Seapower in the 1760s and 1770s* (1988) and a number of thought-provoking articles. His latest book, *Attack on Maritime Trade* (1991), has attracted wide critical acclaim.

ND | Springer Series in **Nonlinear Dynamics**

Springer Series in **Nonlinear Dynamics**

Series Editors: F. Calogero, B. Fuchssteiner, G. Rowlands, H. Segur, M. Wadati and V. E. Zakharov

Solitons – Introduction and Applications
Editor: M. Lakshmanan

What Is Integrability?
Editor: V. E. Zakharov

Rossby Vortices and Spiral Structures
By M. V. Nezlin and E. N. Snezhkin

Algebraic-Geometrical Approach to Nonlinear Evolution Equations
By E. D. Belokolos, A. I. Bobenko, V. Z. Enolsky, A. R. Its and V. B. Matveev

Darboux Transformations and Solitons
By V. B. Matveev and M. A. Salle

Optical Solitons
By F. Abdullaev, S. Darmanyan and P. Khabibullaev

V. B. Matveev   M. A. Salle

Darboux Transformations and Solitons

With 12 Figures

Springer-Verlag
Berlin Heidelberg New York
London Paris Tokyo
Hong Kong Barcelona
Budapest

Professor Dr. Vladimir B. Matveev
Department of Physics, Leningrad State University,
Ulyanovskaya 1, 198904 Leningrad, USSR

Dr. Mikhail A. Salle
Leningrad Institute of Aviation Instrumentation,
Gertsena 67, 190000 Leningrad, USSR

Series Editor:
Professor Dr. Miki Wadati
Institute of Physics
College of General Education
University of Tokyo
Komaba 3-8-1, Meguro-ku
Tokyo 153, Japan

ISBN 3-540-50660-8 Springer-Verlag Berlin Heidelberg New York
ISBN 0-387-50660-8 Springer-Verlag New York Berlin Heidelberg

Library of Congress Cataloging-in-Publication Data. Matveev, V. B. (Vladimir B.), 1944– Darboux transformations and solitons / V. B. Matveev, M. A. Salle. p. cm.– (Springer series in nonlinear dynamics) Includes bibliographical references (p.) and index. ISBN 3-540-50660-8 (Springer-Verlag Berlin, Heidelberg, New York).– ISBN 0-387-50660-8 (Springer-Verlag New York, Berlin, Heidelberg) 1. Solitons. 2. Darboux transformations. 3. Differential equations, Partial–Numerical solutions. I. Salle, M. A. (Mikhail A.), 1953– . II. Title. III. Series. QC174.26.W28M37 1991   530.1'4–dc20   90-22644

This work is subject to copyright. All rights are reserved, whether the whole or part of the material is concerned, specifically the rights of translation, reprinting, reuse of illustrations, recitation, broadcasting, reproduction on microfilms or in other ways, and storage in data banks. Duplication of this publication or parts thereof is only permitted under the provisions of the German Copyright Law of September 9, 1965, in its current version, and a copyright fee must always be paid. Violations fall under the prosecution act of the German Copyright Law.

© Springer-Verlag Berlin Heidelberg 1991
Printed in Germany

The use of registered names, trademarks etc. in this publication does not imply, even in the absence of a specific statement, that such names are exempt from the relevant protective laws and regulations and therefore free for general use.

Typesetting: Springer T$_E$X inhouse system

57/3140-543210 – Printed on acid-free paper

Preface

The modern theory of solitons was born in 1967 when Gardner, Greene, Kruskal and Miura related the solution of the Cauchy initial value problem for the Korteweg-de Vries equation to the inverse scattering problem for a one-dimensional linear Schrödinger equation. Soliton theory is now a large part of theoretical and mathematical physics. An important method used to solve related equations is based on the Inverse Scattering Transform (IST). This IST method has been extended and applied to a large variety of (analytically) solvable nonlinear evolution equations, including many important examples describing phenomena in nonlinear optics, solid state physics, hydrodynamics, theory of general relativity, plasma physics, etc.

In the about twenty years of development the necessary mathematical tools have become rather sophisticated. They include the methods of algebraic geometry, the machinery of group representations, the theory of the local and nonlocal Riemann-Hilbert problem and many other "higher" levels of contemporary mathematics.

Almost from the beginning, it was realized that one of the most important results of soliton theory – the construction of multisoliton solutions – may be obtained by using rather elementary tools applying the so-called Bäcklund transformations. These transformations were first discovered for the famous sine-Gordon equation at the end of the 19th century. Usually they are treated as nonlinear superpositions which allow one to create new solutions of a nonlinear evolution equation from a finite number of known solutions. In practice, however, Bäcklund transformations are not very straightforward to apply in the construction of multisoliton solutions, despite the numerous statements of various authors.

Our aim is to propose and to systematically generalize another, but closely related, elementary approach which also dates back to the 19th century. The idea of this approach was originated by Darboux (1882) in his study of the linear Sturm-Liouville problem. In this volume it is shown that Darboux's idea may be applied to construct the solutions of linear and nonlinear partial differential equations including the nonstationary Schrödinger equation, Korteweg-de Vries and Kadomtsev-Petviashivili equations, $1 + 1$ and $2 + 1$ Toda lattice equations, sine-Gordon and nonlinear Schrödinger equations, and many others.

This approach should provide an advanced student or experimental physicist with a very convenient way of studying solitons and their interactions in various systems where a complete analysis based on the IST is more difficult. Our teaching experience shows that this way is quite appropriate for beginners who are familiar with some topics of linear algebra and the Fourier integral. The new results presented herein will also be of interest to specialists in soliton theory. To draw attention to important related developments and results we are not directly concerned with a short section with comments on the literature is added.

Leningrad, *V. B. Matveev*
August 1990 *M. A. Salle*

Contents

1. **Introduction** 1

2. **Darboux Transformations and Linear Equations** 7
   2.1 Darboux and Crum Theorems 7
   2.2 Reflectionless Potentials and Their Properties 10
   2.3 Darboux Transformations
       for the Linear Nonstationary Schrödinger Equation
       and Higher Order Linear Evolution Equations 16
   2.4 Binary Darboux Transformations 19
   2.5 Darboux Transformations for a Lattice Evolution Equation .. 23
   2.6 Darboux Transformations
       and Supersymmetric Quantum Mechanics 24
   2.7 Factorization Method for Multidimensional Hamiltonians ... 26
   2.8 Binary Darboux Transformation
       and the $\partial_p \partial_q \psi + u\psi = 0$ Equation 27

3. **Exact Solutions of the KdV and KP Equations** 29
   3.1 The KdV and KP Equations in Physics 29
   3.2 The KdV Equation and the Associated Linear System 31
   3.3 Some Exact Solutions of the KP Equation 33
   3.4 Elastic and Inelastic Collisions of KP Solitons.
       Instability of Lumps 38
   3.5 Soliton Propagation on an Arbitrary Background 41
   3.6 The Boussinesq Equation 43
   3.7 The Johnson Equation and its Equivalence to the KP Equation 45
   3.8 The Cylindrical KdV Equation and its Exact Solutions 47

4. **Darboux Transformations for the Zero Curvature Equations
   and Nonlocal Nonlinear Evolution Equations** 49
   4.1 Darboux Transformations for Nonlinear Evolution Equations
       and the Generalized Zakharov-Shabat Linear Problem 49
   4.2 Multisoliton and Periodic Solutions
       of the Nonlinear Schrödinger Equation 51
   4.3 Interactions of the NS Solitons with an Arbitrary Background 55
   4.4 Bloch Equations, the Reduced Maxwell-Bloch System
       and SIT Equations 59

4.5	Generation of the Second Harmonic	67
4.6	The Nonlocal KdV Equation	68
4.7	The Kaup Equation	75

5. Nonlinear Lattice Equations and Related Systems ... 77
5.1 Darboux Transformations and the Two-Dimensional Toda Lattice ... 77
5.2 The Lattice Burgers Equation ... 85
5.3 Nonabelian Toda Lattice ... 86
5.4 Multisoliton Solutions of the Sine-Gordon Equation ... 88
5.5 The Nonlinear Network Equations and Related Systems ... 92
5.6 The Lattice Silin-Tikhonchuk Equation ... 94

6. Darboux Transformation for 2+1 Nonlinear Evolution Equations and Localized Soliton Solutions ... 97
6.1 The Davey-Stewartson Equation ... 97
6.2 The Veselov-Novikov Equation ... 102

7. Hamiltonian Interpretation of the Darboux Transformations and Other Problems ... 104
7.1 Darboux Transformation as a Canonical Transformation ... 104
7.2 The Relationship Between the Zakharov-Shabat Dressing Method and Darboux Transformations ... 105
7.3 Phase Shifts in Soliton Interaction ... 106

Comments on the Literature ... 108

Summary and Outlook ... 112

References ... 113

Subject Index ... 119

List of Abbreviations

DS   Davey-Stewartson equation
DT   Darboux transformation
EDS   Extended Davey-Stewartson equation
ISM   Inverse scattering method
KdV   Korteweg–de Vries equation
KP   Kadomtsev–Petviashvili equation
NEE   Nonlinear evolution equations
NS   Nonlinear Schrödinger equation
RMB   Reduced Maxwell–Bloch system
SIT   Self-induced transparency
SG   Sine–Gordon equation
2D   Two-dimensional

1. Introduction

A fascinating development in our knowledge of the behaviour of solutions of nonlinear partial differential equations has taken place in the past two decades. The crucial point was the understanding of the nature of a special type of elementary solutions now called solitons. Remarkably, these solutions satisfy some simple superposition rules which can be considered as being "asymptotically linear". The nature of these superposition rules may be explained very simply, using only elementary algebraic tools. A related idea, which was proposed more than a century ago by the French mathematician Gaston Darboux, was recently rediscovered and applied to a broad class of nonlinear evolution equations of considerable physical interest and importance. His idea seems to be the most transparent in applications to linear differential equations. Darboux's original result was related to the theory of the Sturm-Liouville equation

$$y'' + [\lambda - u(x)]y = 0 \tag{1.1.1}$$

Equation (1.1.1) is also well known in quantum mechanics where it is usually referred as the one-dimensional Schrödinger equation. Let φ be some fixed solution of (1.1.1) with $\lambda = \lambda_1$, and $\sigma = \varphi_x \varphi^{-1}$. *Darboux* [1.1] proved that (1.1.1) is covariant with respect to the following tranformation:

$$y \to \tilde{y} = y_x - \sigma y, \quad u \to \tilde{u} = u - 2\sigma_x \tag{1.1.2}$$

In other words $\tilde{y}$ satisfies the Schrödinger equation with the potential $\tilde{u}$. Varying y in (1.1.2) we recover all the solutions of this new differential eqation. This provides the possibility to construct from one solvable Schrödinger equation another solvable equation of the same type. In 1979, *Matveev* realized [1.21] that the same covariance property also holds for all evolution equations of the form

$$\frac{\partial f}{\partial t} = \sum_{m=0}^{n} u_m(x,t) \frac{\partial^m f}{\partial x^m} \tag{1.1.3}$$

with scalar or matrix valued coefficients. It was shown that there exists a reasonable lattice generalization of the Darboux theorem [1.3] valid for differential difference equations of the form:

$$\frac{\partial f_n}{\partial t} = \sum_{m=k_1}^{k_2} b_m(n,t) f_{n+m}, \quad n = 0, \pm 1, \pm 2, \ldots . \tag{1.1.4}$$

Thus, it should be possible to construct an infinite series of explicitly solvable partial differential or differential-difference linear evolution equations by applying the Darboux transformation to an initial solvable equation an infinite number of times.

An example of the applications of this method to nonlinear systems is provided by the famous Kadomtsev-Petviashvili equation derived in 1971 [1.4] for the description of propagation of two-dimensional dispersive waves on shallow water:

$$3\alpha^2 u_{yy} + (u_t - 6uu_x - u_{xxx})_x = 0 \,. \tag{1.1.5}$$

Zakharov and *Shabat* [1.5] and independently *Druma* [1.6] have shown that (1.1.5) may be represented as the condition for compatibility of the following system of linear partial differential equations:

$$\alpha \psi_y + \psi_{xx} + u(x,y,t)\psi = 0 \,, \tag{1.1.6}$$

$$\psi_t + 4\psi_{xxx} + 6u(x,y,t)\psi_x + v(x,y,t)\psi = 0 \,. \tag{1.1.7}$$

Both (1.1.6, 7) are of the same type as (1.1.3) and hence are Darboux covariant. Now let $u(x,y,t)$ be some known solution of (1.1.5), for instance $u = 0$, and the associated system (1.1.6, 7) may be solved explicitly. Let us fix an arbitrary solution φ of this system. Now from the Darboux covariance of the system it turns out that:

1) the potential $\tilde{u} = u(x,y,t) + 2\partial_x^2 \ln \varphi$ is a new solution of the Kadomtsev-Petviashvili equation;

2) the linear system obtained from (1.1.6, 7) by the change $u \to \tilde{u}$, $v \to \tilde{v}$ is also explicitly solvable. Its solutions $\tilde{\psi}$ are defined by

$$\tilde{\psi} = \psi_x - \sigma \psi \,, \quad \sigma = \varphi_x \varphi^{-1} \,.$$

Taking $u = 0$, and choosing φ to be

$$\varphi = \int_\Omega \varrho(k) \exp(kx - \alpha^{-1}k^2 y - 4k^3 t) dk$$

we already get a family of solutions of the KP equation depending on the functional parameter $\varrho(k)$ given by $\tilde{u} = 2\partial_x^2 \ln \varphi$. The described construction may be easily generalized by iterating the Darboux transformation. The required formulas (Chap. 3) may be converted into compact form involving a Wronskian determinant [1.2]. For the case of the Sturm-Liouville equation this type of formula was first obtained by *Crum* (1955) [1.7]. For the Korteweg-de Vries equation, the formula for a multi-soliton solution involving Wronskians was found by *Wahlquist* [1.8] in 1976. Below it is shown that the results of Crum and Wahlquist follow very easily from the general approach developed in [1.2].

Different extensions and generalizations of the described approach for solving linear and nonlinear problems are thoroughly discussed in subsequent chapters of this volume. It is necessary to mention that the presented technique is not able to recover all the solutions or to give a solution of the Cauchy problem with arbitrary initial data. But, at the same time, it allows one to obtain rather nontrivial classes of solutions and to study their properties in many cases where the complete analysis based on the local or nonlocal Riemann-Hilbert problem approach is many times more complicated.

The book is organized as follows. In Chap. 2 we describe various versions of the Darboux transformations for linear stationary and evolution equations. The theory of the reflectionless potentials is treated independently from the general spectral theory of the Schrödinger operator, starting from explicit formulas for the Jost solutions. In the same chapter we obtain a natural generalization of the Liouville formula for the nonstationary Schrödinger equation. This generalization allows one to combine the Darboux transformations for an initial linear system and its conjugated version in a rather useful formula called the "binary Darboux transformation", first introduced in [1.9].

Chapter 3 contains applications of the Darboux transformation and its binary version to the Kadomtsev-Petviashvili equation and its stationary reductions – the Korteveg-de Vries and Boussinesque equations. Localized solutions of the KP equation called lumps and their instability are discussed. We have shown also how easy the rational solutions of the KP equation may be constructed in our approach. The cylindrical version of the KP equation usually referred to as the Johnson equation is shown to be equivalent to the KP equation for initial data decreasing at infinity. This equivalence discovered in 1986 [1.10] is described by a three-dimensional change of variables which makes it possible to solve the Cauchy initial problem for the Johnson equation by using the solution of the same problem well known for the KP case [1.11–12]. The discussion of the cylindrical KdV equation

$$u_t + (2t)^{-1}u + 6uu_x + u_{xxx} = 0 , \qquad (1.1.8)$$

completes this chapter. Chapter 4 discusses nonlinear evolution equations obtained as the conditions for compatibility of the system

$$\Psi_t = U(\lambda, x, t)\Psi , \quad \Psi_x(\lambda, x, t) = V(\lambda, x, t)\Psi , \qquad (1.1.9)$$

where U and V are the matrix valued functions with rational or polynomial dependence on the spectral parameter λ. They have to also satisfy some complementary requirements (reductions) to produce "physically interesting" nonlinear evolution equations. Study of the covariance properties of (1.1.9) with respect to gauge transformations preserving reduction constraints leads to a natural extension of the Darboux dressing method [1.13]. This extension provides a construction of the multisoliton solutions on the arbitrary background for a Nonlinear Schrödinger (NS) equation

$$i\psi_t + \psi_{xx} + \kappa|\psi|^2\psi = 0 \qquad (1.1.10)$$

arising in various problems of nonlinear optics, hydrodynamics and quantum statistical physics. In the same chapter we construct the solutions of the reduced Maxwell-Bloch (RMB) system and the self induced transparency (SIT) equations also describing some important phenomena in nonlinear optics. We also discuss nonlocal generalizations of the KdV equation describing the propagation of internal waves in a stratified fluid of finite depth:

$$u_t = -\varepsilon H u_{xx} + 2\varepsilon \delta^{-1} u_x + 2u u_x, \quad H = (T+1)(T-1)^{-1},$$
$$(Tf)(x) = f(x+i\delta).$$
(1.1.11)

In the limit $\delta \to 0$ (1.1.11) reduces to the KdV equation. The solutions of the Benjamin-Ono equation describing the propagation of long internal waves in the fluid of infinite depth are also discussed in Chap. 4.

Chapter 5 is devoted to the theory of the nonlinear one-dimensional and two-dimensional Toda-lattice equations generated by the consistency conditions for the systems of differential-difference or difference linear equations. The one-dimensional Toda-lattice equation reads

$$\ddot{x}_n = \exp(x_{n+1} - x_n) - \exp(x_n - x_{n-1}), \quad n = 0, \pm 1, \pm 2, \ldots.$$
(1.1.12)

Its integrability was discovered in 1974 independently by Manakov and Flaschka. The two-dimensional Toda-lattice equation

$$x_{n\xi\eta} = \exp(x_{n+1} - x_n) - \exp(x_n - x_{n-1}), \quad n = 0, \pm 1, \pm 2, \ldots,$$
(1.1.13)

was first considered by *Darboux* [1.14] but its integrability by the method of the inverse scattering transform was established only in 1979 by *Mikhailov* [1.15].

In the same chapter following the work [1.16, 17] we consider the nonabelian Toda lattice introduced by Polyakov (1979) and the sine-Gordon equation which can be treated as the minimal n-periodic reduction of the two-dimensional Toda lattice.

Chapter 6 involves some multidimensional problems intensively studied last ten years: the so-called Davey-Stewartson equation arising in hydrodynamics and plasma physics and describing the propagation of surface wave packets in deep water. In recent years it has been extensively studied as a two-dimensional integrable generalization of the nonlinear Schrödinger equation. The technique developed in Chap. 2 enables one to construct a large family of explicit solutions containing, in particular, recently discovered dromion and multidromion solutions [1.18–20]. Some of these solutions are briefly discussed here. A discussion of the so-called Novikov-Veselov equation [1.21] completes this chapter.

Chapter 7 deals with different aspects of the Darboux transformation involving its Hamiltonian interpretation, and its relation to the Zakharov-Shabat dressing method. The last section of this chapter discusses the long-time asymptotic behavior of multisoliton solutions.

The diagrams presented below help to simplify the reading of this book. The user of this volume may choose the optimum path among the numbered sections according to his personal interests by moving from the tops to the bottoms of the figures.

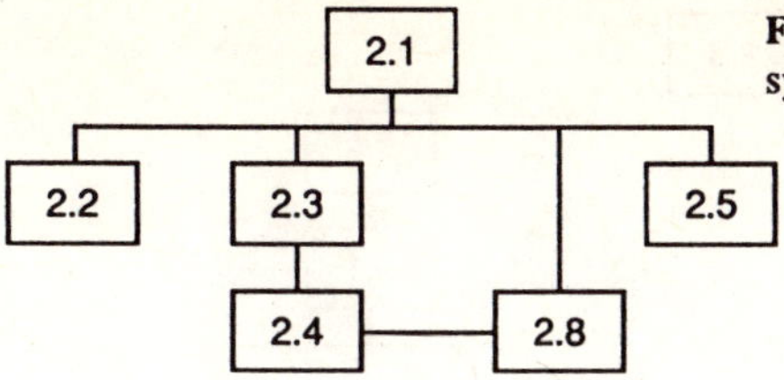

Fig. 1.1. Darboux transformations for linear systems

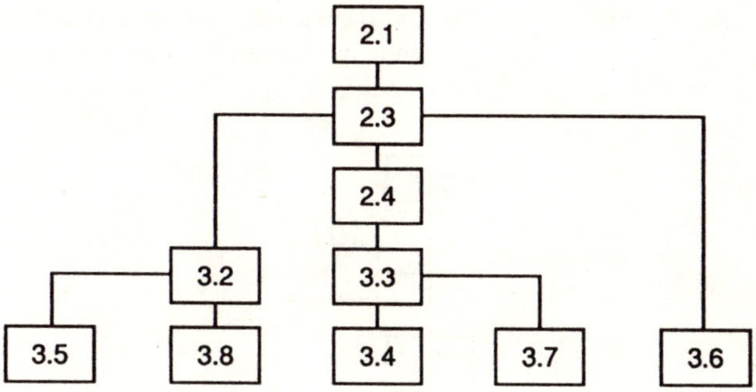

Fig. 1.2. KdV, KP, Boussinesque equations, cylindrical KdV and Johnson equations

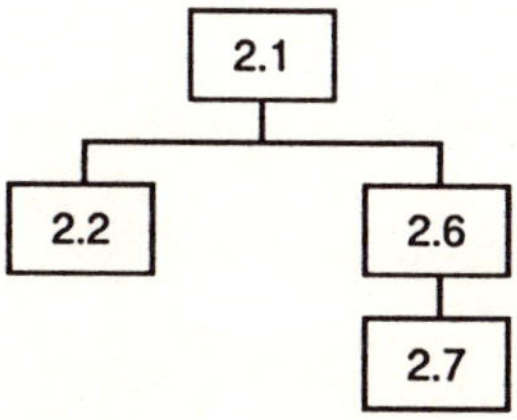

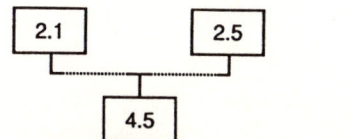

Fig. 1.3. Quantum mechanics and supersymmetry

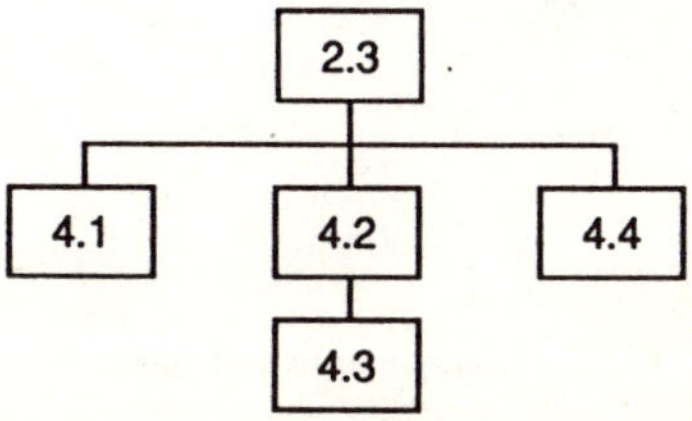

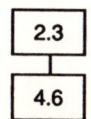

Fig. 1.4. Nonlinear Schrödinger equation, SIT, RMB, N-wave equations, principal chiral field equation

Fig. 1.5. Nonlocal KdV, Burgers equation, Benjamin-Ono equations

Fig. 1.6. Kaup equation

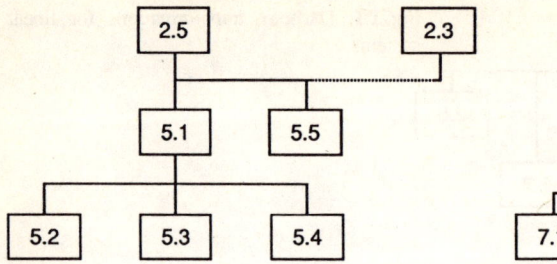

Fig. 1.7. Discrete systems and the sine-Gordon equation

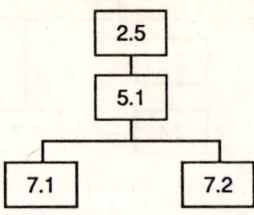

Fig. 1.8. Hamiltonian interpretation and its relation to the Zakharov-Shabat method

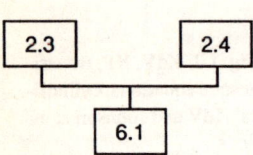

Fig. 1.9. Darboux transformation for the Davey-Stewartson equation

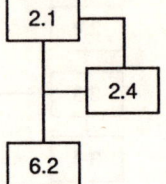

Fig. 1.10. Darboux transformation for the Veselov-Novikov equation

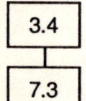

Fig. 1.11. Asymptotics of multisoliton solutions

2. Darboux Transformations and Linear Equations

Here we consider some covariance properties of the ordinary and partial differential equations with respect to the gauge transformation first studied in 1882 by *Darboux* [2.1] in the special case of the Sturm-Liouville equation. The results of this chapter provide a key to the construction of multisoliton solutions and their generalizations for various nonlinear equations discussed in the following chapters. But the results obtained in this chapter are in themselves of some interest, since they describe an infinite series of the exactly integrable linear differential or differential-difference equations with variable coefficients. In particular, the results of these sections give us the simplest possible way to construct the so-called reflectionless potentials. This chapter also includes some remarks on the relation between the Darboux transformation and supersymmetric quantum mechanics.

2.1 Darboux and Crum Theorems

Consider the Sturm-Liouville equation

$$-\Psi_{xx} + u\Psi = \lambda\Psi . \tag{2.1.1}$$

We denote the fixed solution of (2.1.1) taken at the point $\lambda = \lambda_1$ by Ψ_1, $\Psi_1 = \Psi_1(x, \lambda_1)$ and define σ_1 to be the logarithmic derivative of Ψ_1: $\sigma_1 = \Psi_{1x}\Psi_1^{-1}$. Now the Darboux transformation (DT) $\Psi \to \Psi[1]$ of the arbitrary solution of (2.1.1) is defined by

$$\Psi[1] = \left(\frac{d}{dx} - \sigma_1\right)\Psi = \Psi_x - \frac{\Psi_{1x}}{\Psi_1}\Psi = \frac{W(\Psi_1, \Psi)}{\Psi_1} , \tag{2.1.2}$$

where $W(\Psi_1, \Psi) = \Psi_1\Psi_x - \Psi_{1x}\Psi$ is the ususal Wronskian determinant.

Theorem. [2.1] The function $\Psi[1]$ satisfies the differential equation

$$-\Psi_{xx}[1] + u[1]\Psi[1] = \lambda\Psi[1] , \tag{2.1.3}$$

$$u[1] = u - 2\sigma_{1x} = u - 2\frac{d^2}{dx^2}\ln\Psi_1 . \tag{2.1.4}$$

In other words Darboux's theorem declares the Sturm-Liouville equation (2.1.1) is covariant with respect to the action of the Darboux transformation $\Psi \to \Psi[1]$, $u \to u[1]$.

Proof. The proof of the Darboux theorem is trivial. Substituting $\Psi[1]$ into (2.1.3) we get

$$-\Psi_{xxx} + \sigma_{1xx}\Psi + 2\sigma_{1x}\Psi_x + \sigma_1\Psi_{xx} + u[1](\Psi_x - \sigma_1\Psi) = \lambda\Psi_x - \lambda\sigma_1\Psi.$$

Taking into account that $\Psi_{xx} = (u - \lambda)\Psi$ we can rewrite the last equation in the form

$$-u_x\Psi - (u - \lambda)\Psi_x + \sigma_{1xx}\Psi + 2\sigma_{1x}\Psi_x + \sigma_1(u - \lambda)\Psi + u[1](\Psi_x - \sigma_1\Psi)$$
$$= \lambda\Psi_x - \lambda\sigma_1\Psi.$$

After obvious simplifications we may represent the last equation in the form

$$(u[1] - u + 2\sigma_{1x})\Psi_x + (-u_x + \sigma_{1xx} + \sigma_1 u - \sigma_1 u[1])\Psi = 0$$

Setting the coefficients of Ψ and Ψ_x equal to zero we obtain the relations:

$$u[1] = u - 2\sigma_{1x}, \tag{2.1.5}$$

$$\sigma_{1xx} - u_x + \sigma_1 u - \sigma_1 u[1] = 0. \tag{2.1.6}$$

Substitution of (2.1.5) into (2.1.6) produces the relation

$$\sigma_{1xx} + 2\sigma_1\sigma_{1x} - u_x = 0,$$

which is evidently satisfied by virtue of the definition of σ_1. □

The importance of the Darboux theorem lies in the possibility of obtaining another solvable equation (2.1.3) starting from the solvable equation (2.1.1). This will be illustrated by several examples. In fact, by varying Ψ in (2.1.2) we recover all the solutions of (2.1.3). In Sect. 2.2 we shall see that this possibility leads to nontrivial results even in the simplest case of $u = 0$.

It is evident that the Darboux transformation may be applied to (2.1.3) once more producing some new solvable Sturm-Liouville equation and that this operation may be repeated an arbitrary number of times. For the second step of this procedure we have

$$\Psi[2] = \left(\frac{d}{dx} - \frac{\Psi_2'[1]}{\Psi_2[1]}\right)\left(\frac{d}{dx} - \frac{\Psi_1'}{\Psi_1}\right)\Psi,$$

where $\Psi_2[1]$ is the fixed solution of (2.1.3) with $\lambda = \lambda_2$, generated by some fixed solution $\Psi_2(x, \lambda_2)$ of (2.1.1)

$$\Psi_2[1] = \Psi_{2x} - \frac{\Psi_{1x}}{\Psi_1}\Psi_2.$$

The potential of the linear Sturm-Liouville equation corresponding to $\Psi[2]$ is given by

$$u[2] = u[1] - 2\frac{d^2}{dx^2} \ln \Psi_2[1] = u - 2\frac{d^2}{dx^2} \ln W(\Psi_1, \Psi_2) \,. \qquad (2.1.7)$$

Formula (2.1.7) may be generalized to include the case of N-times repeated Darboux transformation, expressed completely in terms of the solutions of the initial equation (2.1.1) without any use of the solutions related to the intermediate iterations of the process.

Let $\Psi_1, \ldots, \Psi_N$ be solutions of (2.1.1) fixed arbitraryly at $\lambda = \lambda_1, \ldots \lambda_N$, respectively. We define the Wronskian determinant W of k functions $f_1, f_2, \ldots, f_k$ by

$$W(f_1, \ldots, f_k) = \det A \,, \qquad A_{ij} = \frac{d^{i-1} f_j}{dx^{i-1}} \,, \qquad i, j = 1, 2, \ldots, k \,.$$

The following generalization of the Darboux theorem was discovered by *Crum* [2.2]:

Theorem. The function

$$\Psi[N] = W(\Psi_1, \ldots, \Psi_N, \Psi)/W(\Psi_1, \ldots, \Psi_N) \,, \qquad (2.1.8)$$

satisfies the differential equation

$$-\Psi_{xx}[N] + u[N]\Psi[N] = \lambda \Psi[N] \,, \qquad (2.1.9)$$

with the potential

$$u[N] = u - 2\frac{d^2}{dx^2} \ln W(\Psi_1, \ldots, \Psi_N) \,. \qquad (2.1.10)$$

The Darboux theorem follows from the result of the Crum theorem in the case of $N = 1$.

Proof. The proof of the Crum theorem is based on the premise that the action of the N-times repeated Darboux transformation on the initial solution Ψ may be represented in the form

$$\Psi[N] = D[N]\Psi = \Psi^{(N)} + s_1 \Psi^{(N-1)} + \ldots + s_N \Psi \,. \qquad (2.1.11)$$

The coefficient of the N-th order differential operator $D[N]$ may be determined from the condition $D[N]\Psi|_{\Psi=\Psi_k} = 0$. This idea becomes clear from the definition of $\Psi[1]$ and $\Psi[2]$. In other words, for the coefficients of s_k we have the system of linear algebraic equations

$$\sum_{k=1}^{N} s_k \Psi_j^{(N-k)} = -\Psi_j^{(N)} \,, \qquad j = 1, 2, \ldots, N \,, \qquad (2.1.12)$$

which can be solved by the Kramer rule.

The explicit representations of s_k are

$$s_k = -W_k/W(\Psi_1, \ldots, \Psi_N), \quad k = 1, 2, \ldots, N, \qquad (2.1.13)$$

where W_k is obtained by replacing the k-th column of W by the column of N-th derivatives of the same functions $\Psi_1, \ldots, \Psi_N$. In particular, s_1 is given by the following expression:

$$s_1 = -\frac{\begin{vmatrix} \Psi_1 \Psi_1' & \cdots & \Psi_1^{(N-2)} \Psi_1^{(N)} \\ \vdots & \vdots & \vdots \\ \Psi_N \Psi_N' & \cdots & \Psi_N^{(N-2)} \psi_N^{(N)} \end{vmatrix}}{W(\Psi_1, \ldots, \Psi_N)} = -\frac{\partial}{\partial x} \ln W(\Psi_1, \ldots, \Psi_N); \qquad (2.1.14)$$

the last equality follows from the well known rule for the differentiation of determinants.

Substitution of the ansatz (2.1.11) into (2.1.9) by using (2.1.14) leads to the following formula for $u[N]$:

$$u[N] = u + 2s_{1x} = u - 2\frac{\partial^2}{\partial x^2} \ln W(\Psi_1, \ldots, \Psi_N) .$$

Now to complete the proof of Crum's theorem we have to verify that the obtained function Ψ satisfies the equation (2.1.9).

2.2 Reflectionless Potentials and Their Properties

Other Quantum Mechanical Applications

The simplest implementation of the Darboux theorem is to choose $u = 0$ as the starting potential. Let $\lambda_1 = -\kappa_1^2$, $\kappa_1 > 0$. Now we can take Ψ_1 in one of the forms $\exp(\pm\kappa_1 x)$, $\cosh \kappa_1(x - x_1)$, or $\sinh \kappa_1(x - x_1)$. The first choice is not interesting because it does not generate any new potentials. Taking

$$\Psi_1 = \cosh \kappa_1 x \qquad (2.2.1)$$

we find

$$\sigma = \kappa_1 \tanh \kappa_1 x, \quad u[1] = -2\sigma_1' = -\frac{2\kappa_1^2}{\cosh^2 \kappa_1 x}. \qquad (2.2.2)$$

Now we put in (2.1.2) $\Psi = e^{ikx}$, $\lambda = k^2$. So far we obtain for (2.1.3) the following particular solution

$$\Psi[1] = (ik - \kappa_1 \tanh \kappa_1 x)e^{ikx} . \qquad (2.2.3)$$

It can be shown for smooth potentials $u(x)$ decreasing faster than $|x|^{-1-\varepsilon}$, $\varepsilon > 0$, when $x \to \pm\infty$ that there exists a so-called Jost solution $f(x, k)$ fixed uniquely by its asymptotic behavior at infinity:

$$f(x,k) = e^{ikx} + o(1), \quad x \to +\infty.$$

For $x \to -\infty$ this solution behaves like

$$f(x,k) \sim a(k)e^{ikx} - \overline{b(k)}e^{-ikx}. \tag{2.2.4}$$

The coefficients $a(k)$ and $b(k)$ are usually called the reflection and transmission coefficients. Equation (2.2.3) shows that the potential (2.2.2) is remarkable in many senses. First of all, from (2.2.3) after simple renormalization we obtain the explicit form of the Jost solution. In fact,

$$\Psi[1] \sim (ik - \kappa_1)e^{ikx}, \quad x \to +\infty$$

and hence

$$f(x,k) = \frac{ik - \kappa_1 \tanh \kappa_1 x}{ik - \kappa_1} e^{ikx}. \tag{2.2.5}$$

The second even more remarkable fact follows from the consideration of the behavior of (2.2.5) at negative infinity:

$$f(x,k) \sim \frac{ik + \kappa_1}{ik - \kappa_1} e^{ikx}. \tag{2.2.6}$$

Comparing (2.2.6) with (2.2.4) we conclude that in our case $b(k) = 0$, and the coefficient $a(k)$ is given by the formula

$$a(k) = \frac{ik + \kappa_1}{ik - \kappa_1}, \tag{2.2.7}$$

and for the real values of k we have $|a(k)| = 1$. The potentials $u(x)$ with the property $b(k) = 0$ are called reflectionless. Thus (2.2.2) represents the simplest example of the nonsingular, real reflectionless potentials.

Taking $\Psi_1 = \sinh \kappa_1 x$ we also obtain a reflectionless real potential with a singularity at the point $x = 0$.

Taking $k = i\kappa$, $\kappa > 0$ it is easy to verify that for $\lambda = \lambda_1 = -\kappa_1^2$ the solution (2.2.5) decreases exponentially when $x \to \pm\infty$ and that this is a unique value of λ with such a property. Really the function $f(x,k)$ for $\text{Im}\{k\} > 0$, $k \neq i\kappa_1$ behaves as (2.2.6) when $x \to +\infty$, in other words, it is increasing at $+\infty$.

When $k = i\kappa_1$, we have

$$f(x,k) = \frac{-\kappa_1(1 + \tanh \kappa_1 x)e^{-\kappa_1 x}}{-2\kappa_1}.$$

The last factor in the numerator grows exponentially at $-\infty$. But the first factor $(1+\tanh \kappa_1 x)$ decreases even faster than $\exp(\kappa_1 x)$ by virtue of the following asymptotic approximation

$$\tanh \kappa_1 x = -[1 - \exp(2\kappa_1 x)][1 + \exp(2\kappa_1 x)]^{-1} = -1 + O(e^{2\kappa_1 x})$$

$$f(x,k) \sim e^{\kappa_1 x}, \quad x \to -\infty.$$

Thus the analytic continuation of the Jost solution into the upper half-plane produces at $k = i\kappa_1$ the bound-state eigenfunction exponentially decreasing at $\pm\infty$. The corresponding value of $k = i\kappa_1$ is the zero of the function $a(k)$ lying on the imaginary axis in the upper half-plane. Thus $\lambda = -\kappa_1^2$ is the unique bound-state eigenvalue of the Schrödinger operator

$$H = -\frac{d^2}{dx^2} + u(x)$$

with the potential (2.2.2).

The Crum theorem gives the construction for all reflectionless smooth and real potentials. In order to describe them, we put $u = 0$, $\kappa_1 < \kappa_2 < \ldots < \kappa_N$, and define the functions Ψ_j by the formulas

$$\Psi_1 = \cosh \kappa_1(x - x_1), \quad \Psi_2 = \sinh \kappa_2(x - x_2), \quad \Psi_3 = \cosh \kappa_3(x - x_3), \ldots$$

$$\Psi_N = \begin{cases} \cosh \kappa_N(x - x_N), & N = 2j - 1, \\ \sinh \kappa_N(x - x_N), & N = 2j. \end{cases} \tag{2.2.8}$$

In (2.2.8) x_j are real numbers chosen arbitraryly. The fact that the potentials $u[N]$ given by (2.1.10), (2.2.8) are nonsingular will be proved later (Chap. 3). The fact that all smooth and real reflectionless potentials are included in our construction may be established, for example, by calculating the associated transmision coefficients and referring to the general results obtained in the solution of the inverse scattering problem for the Schrödinger operator. One more interesting way is to study the analytic properties of the Jost functions of the arbitrary reflectionless potentials. It is not difficult to prove that these analytic properties enable one to reconstruct the Jost functions explicitly from some $2N$ real parameters. Performing this reconstruction we see that for the obtained structure of the Jost solution corresponding to the general reflectionless potentials is just the same as (2.1.10) with $u = 0$, and $\Psi_1, \ldots, \Psi_N$ chosen as in (2.2.8). In this section we restrict ourselves to the contruction of the Jost solutions of these potentials and to the calculation of the coefficients $a(k)$, $b(k)$.

As in the case $N = 1$ it is easy to verify that the solution of (2.1.9) with $u = 0$, and $\Psi_1, \ldots, \Psi_N$ chosen as in (2.2.8)

$$\Psi[N] = \frac{W(\Psi_1, \Psi_2, \ldots, \Psi_N, e^{ikx})}{W(\Psi_1, \ldots, \Psi_N)}, \tag{2.2.9}$$

differs by an x-independent factor from the Jost solution. Replacing the Ψ_j in (2.2.9) by their asymptotics and taking into account that these asymptotics are differentiable we get

$$\Psi[N] \sim \frac{\begin{vmatrix} 1 & 1 & \cdots & 1 \\ \kappa_1 & \kappa_2 & \cdots & ik \\ \vdots & & & \vdots \\ \kappa_1^N & \kappa_2^N & \cdots & (ik)^N \end{vmatrix}}{\begin{vmatrix} 1 & \cdots & 1 \\ \kappa_1 & \cdots & \kappa_{N-1} \\ \vdots & & \vdots \\ \kappa_1^{N-1} & \cdots & \kappa_{N-1}^{N-1} \end{vmatrix}} e^{ikx} = \prod_{j=1}^{N}(ik - \kappa_j)e^{ikx}, \qquad (2.2.10)$$

by virtue of the well known formulas for the Van-der-Mond determinant. Hence Jost solutions for the potentials considered here are determined by

$$f(x,k) = \frac{W(\Psi_1, \Psi_2, \ldots, \Psi_N, e^{ikx})}{W(\Psi_1, \ldots, \Psi_N) \prod_{j=1}^{N}(ik - \kappa_j)}. \qquad (2.2.11)$$

Looking at the asymptotic when $x \to -\infty$ we find that $u[N]$ with $u = 0$ is really reflectionless and the transmission coefficient $a(k)$ is

$$a(k) = \prod_{j=1}^{N} \frac{k - i\kappa_j}{k + i\kappa_j}. \qquad (2.2.12)$$

It is easy to verify that by replacing Ψ in (2.2.9) by $\exp(-ikx)$ we get the solution which is linearly independent with $f(x,k)$ for $k \neq 0$. For $k = 0$ we get the fundamental system of solutions simply by replacing the plane wave by 1 and x.

As in the case $N = 1$ it is easy to verify that for $\text{Im}\{k\} > 0$ the solutions (2.2.11) decrease exponentially when $x \to \pm\infty$ if $k = i\kappa_j$, $\lambda = -\kappa_j^2$. Thus these values of λ give the spectrum of discrete eigenvalues of the associated Schrödinger operator

$$H = -\frac{d^2}{dx^2} + u(x)$$

The solutions (2.2.9) at the points $k = i\kappa_j$ represent the corresponding bound-state eigenfunctions.

A singular periodic potential can also be obtained from our construction. Taking $u = 0$, $\Psi_j = \sin \kappa_j x$, or $\cos \kappa_j x$, $\kappa_j > 0$ we get

$$\sigma_1 = \kappa_1 \cot \kappa_1 x, \quad u[1] = -2\sigma_{1x} = \frac{2\kappa_1^2}{\sin^2 \kappa_1 x}.$$

Taking now $\Psi = e^{ikx}$ we have for its Darboux transformation

$$\Psi[1] = \left(\frac{d}{dx} - \sigma_1\right)e^{ikx} = (ik - \kappa_1 \cot \kappa_1 x)e^{ikx}, \quad k^2 = \lambda,$$

and the linearly independent solution is given by replacing e^{ikx} by e^{-ikx}, or by $\overline{\Psi[1]}$. Note that the functions $\Psi[1]$, $\overline{\Psi[1]}$ are the so-called Bloch solutions for this case. They are multiplied by the x-independent factor upon the translation of the argument by the period of the potential

$$\Psi[1]\left(x + \frac{2\pi}{\kappa_1}\right) = \exp\left(ik\frac{2\pi}{\kappa_1}\right) \Psi[1](x) .$$

It is interesting to compare this result with the general structure of the Bloch solutions of the Schrödinger equation with a periodic potential

$$-y'' + p(x)y = \lambda y , \quad p(x + T) = p(T) . \tag{2.2.13}$$

It is well known [2.3] that in general there exist two linearly independent solutions $\Psi_{1,2}$ of (2.2.13)

$$\Psi_{1,2} = \chi_{1,2}(x) \exp(\pm \mu(\lambda)x) , \quad \chi_{1,2}(x + T) = \chi_{1,2}(x) ,$$

called Bloch solutions. In our case the functions $\pm \mu(\lambda)$ describing the dependence of the quasimomentum on the energy variable becomes trivial: $\mu(\lambda) = \sqrt{\lambda}$, i.e., just as for the potential $u = 0$.

The construction described above may be trivially generalized following the reasoning of the Crum formula to produce a large family of "integrable" Schrödinger equations with singular periodic potentials. All these potentials obtained from a zero background $u = 0$ have the same property: trivial dependence of quasimomentum on the energy variable.

Special Sturm-Liouville Problem with Dirichlet Boundary Conditions

Consider the same formulas for singular periodic potentials, taking for simplicity $\kappa_1 = 1$, $\Psi_1 = \sin x$, $u[1] = 2/\sin^2 x$, looking for the Dirichlet boundary conditions:

$$-y'' + u[1]y = \lambda y , \quad y(0) = y(\pi) = 0 . \tag{2.2.14}$$

Construct the eigenfunctions of this problem starting from the appropriate linear combination of $\Psi[1]$ and $\overline{\Psi[1]}$:

$$\varphi(x, k) = (\Psi[1] - \overline{\Psi[1]})/2i = k \cos(kx) - \cot(x) \sin(kx) .$$

For $k = 1$ this solution become trivial. It is evident that the RHS of the obtained solution is nonsingular and $\varphi(0, k) = 0$. Now let $x = \pi$. The eigenvalues of the problem coincide with $\lambda = k^2$ for k satisfying the condition $\lim_{x \to \pi} \varphi(x, k) = 0$. This will be satified for $k = 2, 3, \ldots$. In fact, $n \cos(n\pi) = n(-1)^n$ and

$$\lim_{x \to \pi} (\sin(nx)/\sin x) = (-1)^{n+1} ,$$

which proves the result.

So the spectrum of the Dirichlet problem (2.2.14) with zero boundary conditions is just the same as for $u = 0$, only the eigenvalue $\lambda = 1$ is absent. Continuing the iterations of Darboux transformations leads to a family of singular potentials with a Dirichlet spectrum which differs from the case of the zero potential by the absence of some of the first eigenvalues.

Now turn to the case of a harmonic starting potential, i.e., put $u = x^2$ in the Crum formula. The Schrödinger equation is then

$$-\Psi'' + x^2\Psi = \lambda\Psi \,, \tag{2.2.15}$$

one of the most important and most famous exactly solvable models in quantum mechanics.

Taking $\lambda_1 = -1$, $\Psi_1 = \exp(x^2/2)$ we get

$$\Psi[1] = \left(\frac{d}{dx} - x\right)\Psi \,, \quad u[1] = x^2 - 2 \,, \tag{2.2.16}$$

i.e., $\Psi[1]$ satisfies the equation

$$-\Psi''[1] + x^2\Psi[1] = (\lambda + 2)\Psi[1] \,, \tag{2.2.17}$$

or $\Psi[1](x, \lambda) = \Psi(x, \lambda + 2)$.

In this case the Darboux transformation acts as a Dirac creation operator [2.4].

Equations (2.2.16, 17) enable one to obtain the exact representation for the Hermite polynomials [2.5]. Taking

$$\Psi(x, 1) = \exp(-x^2/2)$$

from (2.2.16, 17) we obtain

$$\Psi(x, 3) = -2x \exp(-x^2/2) = -H_1 \exp(-x^2/2) \,,$$
$$\Psi(x, 5) = (4x^2 - 1) \exp(-x^2/2) = -H_2 \exp(-x^2/2) \,, \ldots$$

etc.

In general,

$$H_n = (-1)^n \exp(x^2/2) \left(\frac{d}{dx} - x\right)^n \exp(-x^2/2) \,.$$

The Darboux transformation with the starting function $\Psi_1 = \exp(-x^2/2)$ acts as the annihilation operator [2.4]. Taking $\Psi_1 = x \exp(-x^2/2)$ we get

$$u[1] = x^2 + 2/x^2 + 2 \,.$$

In the last case we obtain the eigenfunctions of the Schrödinger operator corresponding to a spherically symmetric potential wall of a harmonic oscillator with angular momentum $l = 1$. In the case $u = 0$, $\lambda_1 = 0$, $\Psi_1 = x$,

$$\Psi[1] = \left(\frac{d}{dx} - \frac{1}{x}\right)\Psi \,, \quad u[1] = \frac{2}{x^2} \,,$$

and we have the radial Schrödinger equation for free motion with angular momentum $l = 1$:

$$-\Psi''[1] + \frac{2}{x^2}\Psi[1] = \lambda\Psi[1] .$$

For the zero energy $\lambda = 0$ this equation is satisfied by the function $\Psi_2[1] = x^2$. Performing the Darboux transformation once more we get $u[2] = 6/x^2$, i.e. $l = 2$, etc. In general, the formula for the transformed eigenfunctions corresponds to the well known recurrence relation for the Bessel functions.

In concluding this section we remark that almost all exactly solvable stationary problems of one-dimensional quantum mechanics may be treated with the Darboux transformations. The related formulas are well known and far from the main focus of this volume. Therefore we will stop this discussion at this level and turn to the consideration of nonstationary linear problems.

2.3 Darboux Transformations for the Linear Nonstationary Schrödinger Equation and Higher Order Linear Evolution Equations

The original result of Darboux [2.1] discussed in the previous section may be easily generalized to include linear partial differential equations even with matrix-valued coefficients [2.6]. The simplest but also the most interesting case is the evolution equation

$$\alpha\Psi_t = -\Psi_{xx} + u(x,t)\Psi , \tag{2.3.1}$$

which we shall call the nonstationary Schrödinger equation even in the case $\alpha \neq i$.

We fix a solution $\Psi_1(x,t)$ of (2.3.1) and denote as σ its logarithmic derivative, i.e., we put $\sigma = \Psi_{1x}\Psi_1^{-1}$. Then, exactly as in the case of the stationary Schrödinger equation, one can check that the Darboux-transformed function

$$\Psi[1] = \Psi_x - \sigma\Psi$$

satisfies the linear equation

$$-\alpha\Psi[1]_t = -\Psi[1]_{xx} + u[1]\Psi[1] ,$$
$$u[1] = u - 2\sigma' = u - 2\sigma_x^2 \ln\Psi_1 .$$

The "nonstationary" generalization of the Crum theorem is also straightforward: We take in $\Psi_1, \ldots, \Psi_n$ to be various linearly independent fixed solutions of (2.3.1) different from Ψ; then (2.1.8) defines the solution of the nonstationary Schrödinger equation with the potential $u[1]$ given by (2.1.10). In other words, (2.3.1) is covariant with respect to the Darboux transformation when $u, \Psi_1, \ldots, \Psi_N$ are correctly defined. Due to the fact that the space of the solutions of (2.3.1) is infinite-dimensional, in contrast to the situation in the stationary case, there is a much greater possibility to create new solvable equations by use of the Darboux transformations technique.

The covariance of (2.3.1) will be used in the further study of the two-dimensional analogy of the KdV equation – the Kadomtsev-Petviashvili equation. But the possibility of creating in a simple way an infinite family of exactly solvable nonstationary Schrödinger equations ($\alpha = i$) or the heat equation ($\alpha = -1$) is of independent interest.

Thus, starting from $u(x,t) = 0$ we obtain a large variety of exactly solvable equations of the form (2.3.1) with the potential depending on an arbitrary number of functional parameters.

The property of Darboux covariance is even more general, it is not restricted by the second order scalar differential equations. The remarkable fact, first established in [2.6], is that Darboux covariance holds also for the case of an *arbitrary* linear partial differential equation of the form

$$\frac{\partial \Psi}{\partial t} = \sum_{k=0}^{N} u_k(x,t) \frac{\partial^k \Psi}{\partial x^k} \tag{2.3.2}$$

even if the coefficients are matrix-valued or operator-valued functions of x and t. In the case of $N \times N$ matrix coefficients $u_k(x,t)$ we can define the Darboux transformation by the same formula, taking for Ψ and $N \times N$ matrix solution of (2.3.2) and defining φ to be a fixed invertible matrix solution of (2.3.2), i.e.,

$$\Psi[1] = \Psi_x - \sigma \Psi, \quad \sigma = \varphi_x \varphi^{-1}.$$

It can be proved that $\Psi[1]$ satisfies the equation

$$\Psi_t[1] = \sum_{k=0}^{n} \tilde{u}_k(x,t) \Psi[1]^{(k)}, \quad \Psi[1]^{(k)} = \frac{\partial^k \Psi[1]}{\partial x^k}.$$

The functions $\tilde{u}_k(x,t)$ are defined by some simple recurrence relations [2.6] and for the first coefficients we get[1]

$$\tilde{u}_n = u_n, \quad \tilde{u}_{n-1} = u_{n-1} + u_{n-1}^{(1)} + [u_n, \sigma],$$
$$\tilde{u}_{n-2} = u_{n-2} + u_{n-1}^{(1)} + u_n^{(1)} \sigma + n u_n \sigma^{(1)} + [u_{n-1}, \sigma] + [u_n, \sigma]\sigma.$$

Taking $n = 2$, $u_2 = 1$, $u_1 = 0$, $u_0 = u(x)$, $\Psi = \exp(\lambda x)\Psi_0(x,t)$, $\varphi = \exp(\lambda_1 x)\varphi_0(x, \lambda_1)$ we recover once more the original results of Darboux cited above.

In the scalar case the formulas for the coefficients $\tilde{u}_k$ become more simple, particularly for the scalar differential equation of the form (2.3.2) with $u_n = 1$, $u_{n-1} = 0$, we have the following formulas for the coefficients $\tilde{u}_k$:

---

[1] Here and below $[A, B]$ denotes the commutator of the matrices A and B, i.e. $[A, B] = AB - BA$.

$$u_{n-2} = -n\sigma' + \tilde{u}_{n-2},$$
$$u_{n-3} + u'_{n-2} - \sigma u_{n-2} = -C_n^2 \sigma'' + \tilde{u}_{n-3} - \tilde{u}_{n-2}\sigma,$$
$$u_0 + u'_1 - \sigma u_1 = -C_n^1 \sigma^{(n-1)} + \tilde{u}_0 - \sum_{m=1}^{n-2} \tilde{u}_m C_m^1 \sigma^{(m-1)}.$$

The explicit expression of u_{n-3} is

$$\tilde{u}_{n-3} = u_{n-3} + u'_{n-2} - 2\sigma u_{n-2} + C_n^2 \sigma'' - 4\sigma\sigma'.$$

For further applications we need to have some generalization of the Darboux theorem involving a rational dependence on the spectral parameter [2.7]. Let Ψ be a vector solution of the following spectral problem

$$\Psi_x = \sum_n \sum_{k=1}^{N(n)} U_{kn}\Psi \frac{1}{(\lambda - a_n)^k} + \sum_{j=0}^N V_j \Psi \lambda^j, \qquad (2.3.3)$$

with $m \times m$ matrix coefficients, $\Psi = (\varphi_1, \ldots, \varphi_m)^{\mathrm{T}}$. It is clear that the analysis of (2.3.3) may be regarded as a particular case of the following equations for an $m \times m$ matrix-valued function Ψ:

$$\Psi_x = \sum_n \sum_{k=1}^{N(n)} U_{kn}\Psi M_n^k + \sum_{j=0}^N V_j \Psi \Lambda^j, \qquad (2.3.4)$$

where M_n and Λ are diagonal matrices:

$$\Lambda = \mathrm{diag}(\lambda_1, \ldots, \lambda_m),$$
$$M_n = \mathrm{diag}\left((\lambda_1 - a_n)^{-1}, \ldots, (\lambda_m - a_n)^{-1}\right).$$

Consider the following version of the Darboux transformation $\Psi \to \Psi[1]$:

$$\Psi[1] = \Psi\Lambda - \sigma\Psi, \quad \sigma = \Psi_1 \Lambda_1 \Psi_1^{-1}, \qquad (2.3.6)$$

where Ψ_1 is a fixed solution of the system (2.3.4) with fixed λ_j specified by the second index i.e., $\lambda_1 = \lambda_{11}$, $\lambda_2 = \lambda_{21}$, etc. Then the following holds:

Theorem. Equation (2.3.4) is covariant with respect to the Darboux transformation (2.3.6). The transformed coefficients $U_{kn}[1]$, $V_j[1]$ are defined by

$$V_N[1] = V_N,$$
$$V_{N-k}[1] = V_{N-k} + \sum_{j=1}^k [V_{N-k+j}, \sigma]\sigma^{j-1}, \quad k = 1, \ldots, N$$
$$U_{N(n),n}[1] = \sigma_n U_{N(n),n} \sigma_n^{-1},$$
$$U_{N(n)-k,n}[1] = \sigma_n (U_{N(n)-k,n} + \sum_{j=1}^k [U_{N(n)-k+j,n}, \sigma_n^{-1}]\sigma_n^{1-j})\sigma_n^{-1},$$
$$k = 1, 2, \ldots, N(n) - 1, \quad \sigma_n = \sigma - a_n. \qquad (2.3.7)$$

The proof of this theorem is given by straightforward but tedious calculation. We therefore leave it as an exercise for the reader.

Note that (2.3.6,7) remain valid also in another case when

$$M_n^k \Lambda = \Lambda M_n^k = M_n^{k-1} + a_n M_n^k, \quad M_n^{-1} = \Lambda - a_n E, \tag{2.3.8}$$

where E is the unit matrix. Note also that we can choose Λ in a more general form than given in (2.3.5). If we can modify (2.3.8) appropriately we can generate a modified version of (2.3.7) which, however, we omit here.

2.4 Binary Darboux Transformations

In this section we expand the set of applications of the Darboux transformation and look at conjugated linear systems. Namely together with the equation

$$\alpha \psi_y^+ + \psi_{xx}^+ + u\psi^+ = 0, \tag{2.4.1}$$

we consider the conjugate relation

$$-\alpha \psi_y^- + \psi_{xx}^- + u\psi^- = 0. \tag{2.4.2}$$

Each of the equations (2.4.1,2) is covariant with respect to the Darboux transformation introduced in Sect. 2.1. For (2.4.1) this transformation is given by

$$\begin{aligned}\psi^+ \to \psi^+[+1] &= \psi_x^+ - \frac{\psi_{1x}^+}{\psi_1^+} \psi^+, \\ u \to u[+1] &= u + 2\frac{\partial^2}{\partial x^2} \ln \psi_1^+.\end{aligned} \tag{2.4.3}$$

The Darboux transformation for (2.4.2) is defined by

$$\begin{aligned}\psi^- \to \psi^-[-1] &= \psi_x^- - \frac{\psi_{1x}^-}{\psi_1^-} \psi^-, \\ u \to u[-1] &= u + 2\frac{\partial^2}{\partial x^2} \ln \psi_1^-.\end{aligned} \tag{2.4.4}$$

Now the following natural question arises. How should one construct the solutions of the conjugate equation (2.4.2) with the potential u replaced by $u[+1]$?

We define the differential form $\Omega(f, g)$ and the function $\psi^-[+1]$ by

$$\Omega(f, g) = fg\, dx + \alpha^{-1}(fg_x - f_x g) dy \tag{2.4.5}$$

$$\psi^-[+1] = \left(A_1 + B_1 \int_{(x_0, y_0)}^{(x,y)} \Omega(\psi_1^+, \psi^-) \right) \bigg/ \psi_1^+. \tag{2.4.6}$$

The answer to this question is given by the following theorem.

Theorem. Equations (2.4.1, 2) are covariant with respect to the transformation

$$\psi^+ \to \psi^+[+1], \quad \psi^- \to \psi^-[+1], \quad u \to u[+1]$$

and $\psi^-[+1]$ is defined by (2.4.5) in which A_1, B_1 are arbitrary constants, and the integral is taken over an arbitrary path joining the points (x_0, y_0) and (x, y) in the (x, y) plane.

The proof of this theorem is given by direct calculation and we leave it to the reader. Note that the differential form $\Omega(f, g)$ is closed for the solutions of the corresponding linear system.

The theorem demonstrates the possibility of creating new integrable evolution equations combining Darboux transformations applied to the "+" (2.4.1) or to the "−" (2.4.2) equations. This is done by setting in (2.4.6) the function ψ^- to be equal to ψ_2^- of the "−" equation with the potential $u[+1]$ and performing the Darboux transformation

$$\psi^-[+1] \to \psi^-[+1, -1] = \psi^-[+1]_x - \frac{\psi_2^-[+1]_x}{\psi_2^-[+1]}\psi^-[+1],$$

$$u[+1, -1] = u + 2\frac{\partial^2}{\partial x^2}\ln\psi_1^+ + 2\frac{\partial^2}{\partial x^2}\ln\psi_2^-[+1]$$

$$= u + 2\frac{\partial^2}{\partial x^2}\ln\left(A_1 + B_1\int_{(x_0, y_0)}^{(x, y)}\Omega(\psi_1^+, \psi_1^-)\right). \tag{2.4.7}$$

We can easily solve both equations (2.4.1, 2) with u replaced by $u[+1, -1]$. At this point we are able to create a new integrable potential by applying the Darboux transformation to (2.4.1) or to its conjugate version. The "tree" of the obtainable integrable potentials is represented by Fig. 2.1. The commutativity of this diagram may be easily proved.

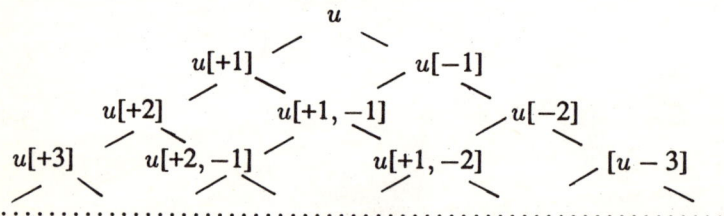

Fig. 2.1. "Tree" of all obtainable potentials produced by Darboux transformation of (2.4.1, 2)

Below we will need an exact formula for the potential $u[+N, -M]$. Without loss of generality we assume that $N \geq M$. Then we get

$$u[+N, -M] = u + 2\frac{\partial^2}{\partial x^2}\ln\Delta, \tag{2.4.8}$$

2.4 Binary Darboux Transformations

$$\Delta = \begin{vmatrix} J_{1,N+1} & J_{2,N+1} & \cdots & J_{N,N+1} \\ J_{1,N+2} & J_{2,N+2} & \cdots & J_{N,N+2} \\ \cdots & \cdots & \cdots & \cdots \\ J_{1,N+M} & \cdots & \cdots & J_{N,N+M} \\ \psi_1^+ & \psi_2^+ & \cdots & \psi_N^+ \\ \psi_{1x}^+ & \psi_{2x}^+ & \cdots & \psi_{Nx}^+ \\ \cdots & \cdots & \cdots & \cdots \\ \partial_x^{N-M-1}\psi_1^+ & \partial_x^{N-M-1}\psi_2^+ & \cdots & \partial_x^{N-M-1}\psi_N^+ \end{vmatrix},$$

$$J_{jk} = A_{jk} + B_{jk} \int_{(x_0,y_0)}^{(x,y)} \Omega(\psi_j^+, \psi_k^-). \qquad (2.4.9)$$

When $M = 0$ we recover (2.1.10). When $N = M$ we get

$$u[+N, -N] = u + 2\frac{\partial^2}{\partial x^2} \ln \det(J_{j,N+k}), \quad 1 \leq j, k \leq N. \qquad (2.4.10)$$

The appearance of (2.4.6) may be understood by turning back to the stationary Schrödinger equation with the real-valued potential $u(x)$

$$-\psi_{xx} + u\psi = \lambda\psi. \qquad (2.4.11)$$

Let ψ_1 be a solution of (2.4.11) with $\lambda = \lambda_1$. Then the linearly independent solution is given by the Liouville fomula

$$\psi_2 = \psi_1 \int \frac{dx}{\psi_1^2}. \qquad (2.4.12)$$

The Darboux transformation of (2.4.12) is

$$\left(\psi_1 \int \frac{dx}{\psi_1^2}\right)_x - \frac{\psi_{1x}}{\psi_1} \psi_1 \int \frac{dx}{\psi_1^2} = \frac{1}{\psi_1},$$

i.e., one of solutions of the Schrödinger equation with $\lambda = \lambda_1$ and the potential $u[+1]$ is ψ_1^{-1}. The linearly independent solution $\psi_2[+1]$ is once more given by the Liouville Formula

$$\psi_2[+1] = \frac{1}{\psi_1} \int \psi_1^2 \, dx. \qquad (2.4.13)$$

Hence, performing the Darboux transformation with generating solution ψ_1^{-1} we return back from the potential u. Taking (2.4.13) for the generating solution we get

$$u[2] = u[1] - 2\frac{\partial^2}{\partial x^2} \ln \left(\frac{1}{\psi_1} \int \psi_1^2 \, dx\right)$$

$$= u - 2\frac{\partial^2}{\partial x^2} \ln \left(\int \psi_1^2 \, dx\right). \qquad (2.4.14)$$

Comparing (2.4.7, 14) it is easy to realize that (2.4.7) is a nonstationary generalization of (2.4.14) and that (2.4.6) is a natural extension of the Liouville formula in the case of a linear partial differential evolution equation of the second order.

Note in addition that when applied to the stationary situation in the self-adjoint case, the binary Darboux transformation may be obtained by the simple degeneration of (2.1.10). In particular, looking for $u[2]$,

$$u[2] = u - 2\frac{\partial^2}{\partial x^2} \ln \begin{vmatrix} \psi_1 & \psi_2 \\ \psi_{1x} & \psi_{2x} \end{vmatrix} \qquad (2.4.15)$$

with $\psi_1 = \psi_1(x, \lambda_1)$, $\psi_2 = \psi_1(x, \lambda_1 + \delta)$, $\delta \ll \lambda_1$, and expanding ψ_2 in a series in δ we get

$$u[2] = u - 2\frac{\partial^2}{\partial x^2} \ln \begin{vmatrix} \psi_1 & \psi_1 + \psi_{1\lambda}\delta + \psi_{1\lambda\lambda}\delta^2/2! + \cdots \\ \psi_{1x} & \psi_{1x} + \psi_{1\lambda x}\delta + \psi_{1\lambda\lambda x}\delta^2/2! + \cdots \end{vmatrix}$$

$$= u - 2\frac{\partial^2}{\partial x^2} \ln \begin{vmatrix} \psi_1 & \psi_{1\lambda}\delta + \psi_{1\lambda\lambda}\delta^2/2! + \cdots \\ \psi_{1x} & \psi_{1\lambda x}\delta + \psi_{1\lambda\lambda x}\delta^2/2! + \cdots \end{vmatrix}.$$

When $\delta \to 0$

$$u[2] \to u - 2\frac{\partial^2}{\partial x^2} \ln(\psi_1 \psi_{1\lambda x} - \psi_{1\lambda}\psi_{1x}) . \qquad (2.4.16)$$

It is clear that

$$(\psi_1\psi_{1\lambda x} - \psi_{1\lambda}\psi_{1x})_x = \psi_1\psi_{1\lambda xx} - \psi_{1\lambda}\psi_{1xx} . \qquad (2.4.17)$$

Taking into account that

$$-\psi_{1xx\lambda} + u\psi_{1\lambda} = \lambda_1 \psi_{1\lambda} + \psi_1 ,$$

from (2.4.17) we get

$$(\psi_1\psi_{1\lambda x} - \psi_{1\lambda}\psi_{1x})_x = -\psi_1^2 .$$

From this and (2.4.16) we conclude that (2.4.14) may be regarded as a degenerate case of (2.4.15). Nevertheless, we shall see below that a formula similar to (2.4.14) may be useful for the construction of some classes of solutions of nonlinear integrable equations particularly for the KdV equation or its cylindrical version.

The described procedure may be easily extended to include N-times iterated Darboux transformations. We let $\lambda_k \to \lambda_1$, $k = 2, \ldots, N$. Then the formula for the N-times iterated Darboux transformation of the potential may be reduced to the form

$$u[N] = u - 2\frac{\partial^2}{\partial x^2} \ln \begin{vmatrix} \psi_1, & \psi_{1\lambda}, & \psi_{1\lambda\lambda}, & \cdots & \partial_\lambda^{N-1}\psi_1 \\ \psi_{1x}, & \psi_{1\lambda x}, & \psi_{1\lambda\lambda x}, & \cdots & \partial_\lambda^{N-1}\partial_x\psi_1 \\ \partial_x^{N-1}\psi_1 & \cdots & \cdots & \cdots & \cdots \\ \partial_x^{N-1}\psi_1 & \cdots & \cdots & \cdots & \partial_\lambda^{N-1}\partial_x^{N-1}\psi_1 \end{vmatrix}.$$

(2.4.18)

It is also not difficult to describe the intermediate degenerations of $u[N]$, corresponding to the case when some part of $\{\lambda_i\}$ tends to the same value, but here we omit this discussion.

2.5 Darboux Transformations for a Lattice Evolution Equation

It is worth noting that it is possible to define a reasonable lattice version of the Darboux transformation [2.8] for solving a linear differential-difference equation of the form

$$\dot{\psi}_n = \sum_{m=0}^{N} u_{nm}(t)\psi_{m+n}, \quad \dot{\psi}_n = \partial\psi_n/\partial t. \qquad (2.5.1)$$

The lattice Darboux transformation $\psi_n \to \psi_n[1]$ is defined by the formula

$$\psi_n[1] = \psi_n - \sigma_n\psi_{n-1}, \quad \sigma_n = \psi_{n,1}\psi_{n-1,1}^{-1}, \qquad (2.5.2)$$

where $\psi_{n,1}$ is a fixed solution of the system (2.5.1).

Theorem. Function $\psi_n[1]$ satisfies the equation

$$\dot{\psi}_n[1] = \sum_{n=0}^{N} u_{nm}[1]\psi_{n+m}[1], \quad u_{nN}[1] = u_{nN},$$

$$u_{nk}[1] = \frac{1}{\psi_{n+k,1}}\left\{\sum_{j=k}^{N-1}(u_{nj} - \sigma_n u_{n-1,j+1})\psi_{n+j,1} + u_{nN}\psi_{n+N,1}\right\}. \qquad (2.5.3)$$

In other words, (2.5.1) is covariant with respect to the action of the Darboux transformation (2.5.2). The proof of this theorem is given by straightforward calculation [2.8].

As in the continuous case, the Darboux transformation may be repeated an arbitrary number of times. The solution of the associated linear equation $\psi_n[N]$, where N is the number of iterations, is defined by the formula first obtained in [2.8]:

$$\psi_n[N] = \frac{W_n(\psi_1, \psi_2, \ldots, \psi_N, \psi)}{W_{n-1}(\psi_1, \psi_2, \ldots, \psi_N)},$$

$$W_n(f_1, f_2, \ldots, f_l) = \det(f_{n+1-k, l+1-j}), \quad 1 \leq k, j \leq 1. \qquad (2.5.4)$$

The unique difference between this and the continuous case is that now the Wronskian determinant is replaced by its difference analog, the Cazorati determinant. We omit the general expression for the coefficients $u_{nm}[N]$ of the linear equation for $\psi_n[N]$. In real applications, in particular, for the famous Toda lattice equations, these formulas may be substantially simpler than the general case. Related results will be presented in Chap. 5.

In complete analogy with the results of Sect. 2.4, we can define the binary Darboux transformation [2.9] for (2.5.1) and its conjugate. We shall discuss a particular case of the binary lattice Darboux transformation, looking for the solution of the two-dimensional Toda equation, first introduced by Darboux [2.10]. We would like to mention that [2.8] also contains nonabelian and difference-difference generalizations of the results of this section, which are omitted here.

2.6 Darboux Transformations and Supersymmetric Quantum Mechanics

Consider two Schrödinger equations

$$-\psi_{xx} + u\psi = \lambda\psi ,\qquad(2.6.1)$$

$$-\varphi_{xx} + v\varphi = \lambda\varphi \qquad(2.6.2)$$

related by the Darboux transformation

$$v = u - 2\frac{\partial^2}{\partial x^2}\ln\psi_1 ,\qquad(2.6.3)$$

$$\varphi = \psi_x - \frac{\psi_{1x}}{\psi_1}\psi .\qquad(2.6.4)$$

The function $\varphi_1 = 1/\psi_1$ satisfies (2.6.2) for $\lambda = \lambda_1$. Performing a Darboux transformation with the generating function φ_1 we transform (2.6.2) into (2.6.1). In fact, we then have

$$v - 2\frac{\partial^2}{\partial x^2}\ln\varphi_1 = u - 2\frac{\partial^2}{\partial x^2}\ln\psi_1 - 2\frac{\partial^2}{\partial x^2}\ln(1/\psi_1) = u .$$

In other words, we have

$$u = v - 2\frac{\partial^2}{\partial x^2}\ln\varphi_1 \qquad(2.6.5)$$

$$\psi = \left(\varphi_x - \frac{\varphi_{1x}}{\varphi_1}\varphi\right)(\lambda_1 - \lambda) , \quad \varphi_1\psi_1 = 1 .\qquad(2.6.6)$$

Formulas (2.6.3–6) define the direct and inverse Darboux transformations.

Introducing

$$\sigma = \psi_1'\psi_1^{-1} = -\varphi_1'\varphi_1^{-1} ,\qquad(2.6.7)$$

we can represent the potentials u and v in the form

$$u = \sigma' + \sigma^2 + \lambda_1 , \quad v = \sigma^2 - \sigma' + \lambda_1 .\qquad(2.6.8)$$

We define operators of supercharge

$$B^+ = -\partial + \sigma, \quad B^- = \partial + \sigma, \qquad (2.6.9)$$

which effect the direct and inverse Darboux transformations. Then we have the relations

$$B^+B^- = -\partial^2 + \sigma^2 - \sigma' = -\partial^2 + v - \lambda_1,$$
$$B^-B^+ = -\partial^2 + \sigma^2 + \sigma' = -\partial^2 + u - \lambda_1.$$

We introduce the operators

$$H^+ = -\partial^2 + u \quad H^- = -\partial^2 + v,$$
$$H = \begin{pmatrix} H^+ & 0 \\ 0 & H^- \end{pmatrix}, \quad Q_+ = \begin{pmatrix} 0 & 0 \\ B^+ & 0 \end{pmatrix}, \quad Q_- = \begin{pmatrix} 0 & B^- \\ 0 & 0 \end{pmatrix}. \qquad (2.6.10)$$

It is easy to check that the matrix Hamiltonian H and the operators $Q_\pm$ satisfy the relations

$$\{Q_+, Q_-\} \equiv Q_+Q_- + Q_-Q_+ = H - \lambda_1, \quad [H, Q_\pm] = 0. \qquad (2.6.11)$$

In other words they form the simplest superalgebra with "even" elements $Q_\pm$ and an "odd" element $H - \lambda_1$, and the superpotential σ. The Schrödinger matrix equation ($H\Psi = \lambda\Psi$) may be rewritten in the form

$$(-\partial^2 + U)\Psi = \lambda\Psi, \qquad (2.6.12)$$

where $\Psi = (\psi, \varphi)^T$,

$$U = W^2 + W', \quad W = \begin{pmatrix} \sigma & 0 \\ 0 & -\sigma \end{pmatrix}. \qquad (2.6.13)$$

The relation between (2.6.12) and the Darboux transformation was noted by *Borisov, Andrianov* and *Ioffe* in their study of multidimensional matrix Hamiltonians [2.11–13].

This section makes it evident that the fact of the Darboux covariance opens the possibility of constructing a series of exactly solvable equations of supersymmetric quantum mechanics, having interesting physical interpretations.

2.7 Factorization Method for Multidimensional Hamiltonians

In this section we restrict ourselves to the contruction of two-dimensional supersymmetric Hamiltonians. We introduce the operators

$$B_1^\pm = \pm\partial_x + \sigma_1 \quad B_2^\pm = \pm\partial_y + \sigma_2,$$
$$\sigma_1 = \psi_{1x}\psi_1^{-1}, \sigma_2 = \psi_{1y}\psi_1^{-1}, \quad (2.7.1)$$

and the matrix Hamiltonian

$$H = \begin{pmatrix} H_{11} & 0 \\ 0 & H_{22} \end{pmatrix},$$
$$H_{11} = B_1^+ B_1^- + B_2^+ B_2^-, \quad H_{22} = B_1^- B_1^+ + B_2^- B_2^+,$$
$$H_{11} = -\Delta - \sigma_{1x} - \sigma_{2y} + \sigma_1^2 + \sigma_2^2, \quad (2.7.2)$$
$$H_{22} = -\Delta + \sigma_{1x} + \sigma_{2y} + \sigma_1^2 + \sigma_2^2,$$
$$\Delta = \partial_x^2 + \partial_y^2.$$

The Schrödinger equation may be written in the form

$$H\begin{pmatrix} \psi \\ \varphi \end{pmatrix} = \lambda \begin{pmatrix} \psi \\ \varphi \end{pmatrix}. \quad (2.7.3)$$

We define the Darboux transformation of the two-component wave function $(\psi, \varphi)^T$ by the formula

$$\begin{pmatrix} \tilde{\psi} \\ \tilde{\varphi} \end{pmatrix} = \begin{pmatrix} B_1^- & B_2^+ \\ B_2^- & -B_1^+ \end{pmatrix} \begin{pmatrix} \psi \\ \varphi \end{pmatrix}. \quad (2.7.4)$$

Then it is easy to show that

$$\tilde{H}\begin{pmatrix} \tilde{\psi} \\ \tilde{\varphi} \end{pmatrix} = \lambda \begin{pmatrix} \tilde{\psi} \\ \tilde{\varphi} \end{pmatrix}, \quad \tilde{H} = \begin{pmatrix} \tilde{H}_{11} & \tilde{H}_{12} \\ \tilde{H}_{21} & \tilde{H}_{22} \end{pmatrix}, \quad (2.7.5)$$

$$\tilde{H}_{11} = B_1^- B_1^+ + B_2^+ B_2^-, \quad \tilde{H}_{12} = B_1^- B_2^+ - B_2^+ B_1^-,$$
$$\tilde{H}_{21} = B_2^- B_1^+ - B_1^+ B_2^-, \quad \tilde{H}_{22} = B_2^- B_2^+ + B_1^+ B_1^-. \quad (2.7.6)$$

or

$$\tilde{H} = \begin{pmatrix} -\Delta + \sigma_{1x} - \sigma_{2y} + \sigma_1^2 + \sigma_2^2, & \sigma_{1x} + \sigma_{2y} \\ \sigma_{1y} + \sigma_{2x}, & -\Delta + \sigma_{2y} - \sigma_{1x} + \sigma_1^2 + \sigma_2^2 \end{pmatrix}.$$

The related algebra of supersymmetry is generated by the Hamiltonian $\hat{H}$ and the supercharge operators $Q^\pm$:

$$\hat{H} = \begin{pmatrix} H_{11} & 0 & 0 & 0 \\ 0 & H_{11} & H_{12} & 0 \\ 0 & H_{21} & H_{22} & 0 \\ 0 & 0 & 0 & H_{22} \end{pmatrix},$$

$$Q^+ = \begin{pmatrix} 0 & 0 & 0 & 0 \\ B_1^- & 0 & 0 & 0 \\ B_2^- & 0 & 0 & 0 \\ 0 & B_2^- & -B_1^- & 0 \end{pmatrix}, \quad Q^- = \begin{pmatrix} 0 & B_1^+ & B_2^+ & 0 \\ 0 & 0 & 0 & B_2^+ \\ 0 & 0 & 0 & -B_1^+ \\ 0 & 0 & 0 & 0 \end{pmatrix},$$

$$[\hat{H}, Q^\pm] = 0, \quad \{Q^+, Q^-\} = \hat{H}.$$

The basic point of the previous formula was to use an expression of the potential in terms of the fixed ψ-function allowing us to factorize the corresponding Hamiltonian. The close relation between Darboux transformations and factorization methods may be studied in arbitrary space dimensions [2.11–13].

2.8 Binary Darboux Transformation and the $\partial_p \partial_q \psi + u\psi = 0$ Equation

Here we discuss the potentials u for which the equation

$$\partial_p \partial_q \psi + u\psi = 0 \tag{2.8.1}$$

may be solved explicitly. We do not specify variables p and q but wish to recover simultaneously the hyperbolic case $p = x - y$, $q = x + y$, and the elliptic case $p = x + iy$, $q = x - iy$. We introduce the differential form

$$\Omega = (f\partial_p g - g\partial_p f)dp - (f\partial_q g - g\partial_q f)dq. \tag{2.8.2}$$

Then the following proposition holds:

Theorem. Equation (2.8.1) is covariant with respect to the Darboux transformation $\psi \to \psi[1]$, $u \to u[1]$,

$$\psi[1] = \theta(\psi, \psi_1)\psi_1^{-1}, \quad \theta(f, g) = \int_{(p_0, q_0)}^{(p,q)} \Omega. \tag{2.8.3}$$

$$u[1] = u + 2\partial_p \partial_q \ln \psi_1 \tag{2.8.4}$$

where ψ_1 is a fixed solution of (2.8.1), and the integral in (2.8.3) is path independent because on the solution of (2.8.1) $d\Omega = 0$.

The proof of this theorem is given by a straightforward calculation. It is easy to verify that

$$\psi_1[1] = \psi_1^{-1}.$$

The result of the action of N-times repeated Darboux transformation may be expressed, as in the one-dimensional case, in terms of the solutions of the starting equation (2.8.1):

$$\psi[2N] = \frac{\sum_{\langle 0,1,\ldots,2N+1\rangle}(-1)^{[i_1,\ldots,i_{2N+1}]}\psi_{i_1}\theta_{i_2 i_3}\theta_{i_4 i_5}\ldots\theta_{i_{2N} i_{2N+1}}}{\sum_{\langle 0,1,\ldots,2N\rangle}(-1)^{[i_1,\ldots,i_{2N}]}\theta_{i_1 i_2}\theta_{i_3 i_4}\ldots\theta_{i_{2N-1} i_{2N}}}, \tag{2.8.5}$$

$$u[2\hat{N}] = u + 2\partial_p \partial_q \ln \sum_{\langle 1,\ldots,2N\rangle} (-1)^{[i_1,\ldots,i_{2N}]} \theta_{i_1 i_2} \ldots \theta_{i_{2N-1} i_{2N}}, \qquad (2.8.6)$$

$$\psi[2N-1] = \frac{\sum_{\langle 1,\ldots,2N\rangle}(-1)^{[i_1,\ldots,i_{2N}]}\theta_{i_1 i_2}\theta_{i_3 i_4}\ldots\theta_{i_{2N-1}i_{2N}}}{\sum_{\langle 1,\ldots,2N-1\rangle}(-1)^{[i_1,\ldots,i_{2N-1}]}\psi_{i_1}\theta_{i_2 i_3}\ldots\theta_{i_{2N-2}i_{2N-1}}}, \qquad (2.8.7)$$

$$u[2N-1]$$
$$= u + 2\partial_p \partial_q \ln \sum_{\langle 0,\ldots,2N-1\rangle} (-1)^{[i_1,\ldots,i_{2N-1}]} \psi_{i_1}\theta_{i_2 i_3}\ldots\theta_{i_{2N-2}i_{2N-1}}. \qquad (2.8.8)$$

In (2.8.5–8) ψ is a transformed function. The sum taken over all permutations of the indices specified by the condition $i_k < i_{k+1}$. $[i_1,\ldots,i_m]$ is the signature of the permutation. The pfaffians entering into (2.8.5–8) can be written also in the form of the determinants.

Note that all out transformations are invertible, and the inverse of the Darboux transformation generated by the function ψ_1 is given by the Darboux transformation with the generating function $\psi_1[1] = \psi_1^{-1}$.

Taking $u = 0$ for the starting potential we have

$$\psi_k = a_k(p) + b_k(q), \qquad (2.8.9)$$

where a_k and b_k are arbitrary functions. The simplest integrable potentials have the following form

$$u[1] = 2\partial_p \partial_q \ln[a_1(p) + b_1(q)].$$

$$u[2] = 2\partial_p \partial_q \ln[c + b_1 a_2 - b_2 a_1 + \int_{M_0}^{M}(a_1 a_2' - a_2 a_1')dp + (b_1 b_2' - b_2 b_1')dq],$$

$c = \text{const}$.

The important special case $b_2 = a_1 = 0$ leads to the formula

$$u[2] = 2\partial_p \partial_q \ln[c + b_1(q)a_2(p)]$$

The restrictions $q = \bar{p}$, $b_1 = \bar{a}_1$ isolate the real potentials $u[1]$. The complementary requirement $\psi_2 = \bar{\psi}_1$ includes the reality of the potential $u[2]$ etc.

Equations (2.8.2, 3) may be considered as a natural generalization of the one-dimensional Darboux transformation (2.1.1) and the binary transformation (2.4.14). If we let $p = (x+y)/2$, $q = (y-x)/2$, then we have

$$-\psi_{xx} + u\psi = -\psi_{yy},$$
$$\psi_1[1] = \theta(\psi,\psi_1)/\psi_1, \quad u[1] = u + 2(-\partial_x^2 + \partial_y^2)\ln\psi_1.$$

$$\theta(f,g) = \int_{(x_0,y_0)}^{(x,y)} (fg_y - f_y g)dx - (fg_x - f_x g)dy.$$

Assuming that $u = u(x)$, $\psi = \varphi(x)\exp(\lambda x)$, $\psi_1 = \varphi_1(x)\exp(\lambda_1 x)$, we get

$$-\varphi_{xx} + u\varphi = -\lambda^2 \varphi, \quad u[1] = u - 2\partial_x^2 \ln\varphi_1.$$

3. Exact Solutions of the KdV and KP Equations

3.1 The KdV and KP Equations in Physics

Korteweg and de Vries originally derived their equation

$$u_t = 6uu_x - u_{xxx} \tag{3.1.1}$$

in 1885 in the course of their studies of long wave propagation in shallow water. Later, in the 1950s, it was realized that the KdV equation is valid in a very large variety of physical situations when a few general assumptions about the structure of nonlinearity and dispersion are made. In particular, the KdV equation arises quite naturally in plasma physics, solid state physics, biology and many other areas. The reader may consult the textbooks [3.1–3] for numerous references to applications of the KdV equation. Here we present a brief summary of the origin of the KdV equation.

Consider a plane wave given by the exponential

$$u = \exp(ikx - i\omega t) \,.$$

Assume that the dispersion law is of the form

$$\omega = \alpha k + \beta k^3 \,.$$

Under such an assumption u satisfies the linearized version of the KdV equation

$$u_t + \alpha u_x + \beta u_{xxx} = 0 \,.$$

Now consider a medium where the following conservation law holds:

$$\partial_t u + \partial_x j = 0 \,.$$

For the linearized version of the KdV equation the related current j is given by the formula

$$j = \alpha u + \beta u_{xx} + 2^{-1}\gamma u^2 \,.$$

The requirement that the same conservation law still holds leads immediately to the KdV-like equation

$$u_t + \alpha u_x + \beta u_{xxx} + \gamma u u_x = 0 \,.$$

This last equation may be reduced to the form of (3.1.1) by a simple scale transformation.

The fundamental importance of the KdV equation, in the contemporary view, is defined by the remarkable discovery of *Gardner*, *Green*, *Kruskal* and *Miura* [3.4]. In their work the ingenious idea to relate the solution $u(x,t)$ of the KdV equation to the evolution of the spectral data of the linear Schrödinger operator

$$-\partial_x^2 + u(x,t)$$

was first introduced. Further development of this idea undertaken by different workers became a new branch of modern theoretical and mathematical physics, the theory of solitons.

In 1970, while studying the stability of the KdV soliton-like solutions with small transverse perturbations, *Kadomtsev* and *Petviashvili* [3.5] arrived at the following two-dimensional version of the KdV equation:

$$(u_t - 6uu_x - u_{xxx})_x = -3\alpha^2 u_{yy}, \tag{3.1.2}$$

which is now known as the *Kadomtsev-Petviashvili* (KP) equation. Historically (3.1.2) was the first integrable nonlinear evolution equation with two space and one time variables which was solved by the inverse scattering transform method. A large class of solutions of the KP equation was found by *Zakharov* and *Shabat* (1974), by starting from the Marchenko-like integral equation [3.6]. In 1976 *Krichever* [3.7] constructed a large family of explicit solutions generated by a compact, arbitrary fixed, Riemann surface which generalizes the *Its-Matveev* formula [3.8] obtained in 1974 to describe periodic finite gap solutions of the KdV equation. For detailed information about the solutions of the KP and KdV equations generated by compact Riemann surfaces the interested reader may consult the forthcoming monograph [3.9].

In 1977, localized rational solutions, called lumps, were isolated by *Bordag et al.* [3.10] for the KP equation with $\alpha = i$. Finally in 1981–1983, using the technique of the nonlocal Riemann problem, or $\bar{\partial}$-problem, the Cauchy problem for rapidly decreasing initial data was solved by *Manakov*, *Ablowitz* and *Fokas* [3.11–13].

The number of physical applications of the KP equation is even larger than for the KdV case. In this chapter we restrict ourselves to results which can be obtained by the method of Darboux transformations, using a straightforward approach to the study of the solutions with rather interesting and complicated behavior [3.14–17].

3.2 The KdV Equation and the Associated Linear System

In 1968 Lax [3.18] explained in a very transparent way the greater part of the results of [3.4] by introducing the following operators:

$$L = -\partial_x^2 + u(x,t), \quad A = -4\partial_x^3 + 6u\partial_x + 3u_x . \tag{3.2.1}$$

He noted that the commutator of L and A gives exactly the RHS of (3.1.1), i.e.,

$$[L, A] = 6uu_x - u_{xxx}.$$

Hence, the KdV equation may be represented in the following form:

$$\partial_t L = [L, A], \tag{3.2.2}$$

usually called the Lax representation. Equation (3.2.2) is equivalent to the consistency condition for the following system of partial differential equations:

$$\begin{cases} L\Psi = \lambda\Psi \\ \Psi_t = A\Psi \end{cases} \leftrightarrow \begin{cases} -\Psi_{xx} + u\Psi = \lambda\Psi & (3.2.3) \\ \Psi_t = -4\Psi_{xxx} + 6u\Psi_x + 3u_x\Psi & (3.2.4) \end{cases}$$

The equivalence follows from the fact the system (3.2.3, 4) means that

$$(\partial_t L - [L, A])\Psi = 0 .$$

For fixed t, $\partial_t - [L, A]$ is an operator of multiplication on the λ-independent function $(u_t - 6uu_x + u_{xxx})$. Thus it is evident that if the system (3.2.3, 4) admits a family of solutions depending on λ, (3.2.2) must also be satisfied.

Equation (3.2.3) is covariant with respect to the action of Darboux transformation (2.1.2, 4) and it is easy to verify that the same is true for (3.2.4). The covariance of the system (3.2.3, 4) allows one to create new solutions of the KdV equation, starting from some known solution $u(x, t)$ for which we are able to solve (3.2.3, 4) explicitly. In fact, from the Darboux covariance it follows that the function $\Psi[1]$ defined by (2.1.2), where Ψ_1 and Ψ are some pair of solutions of (3.2.3, 4), satisfies the system of differential equations of the same structure with the potential u replaced by $u[1]$. The consistency of the system satisfied by $\Psi[1]$ shows that $u[1]$ is a new solution of the KdV equation. Looking for the N-times repeated Darboux transformation we shall obtain an infinite family of the solutions of the KdV equation. For a given N these solutions are of the form first discovered by *Wahlquist* [3.19],

$$u[N] = u - 2\partial_x^2 \ln W(\Psi_1, \Psi_2, \Psi_3, \ldots, \Psi_N) , \tag{3.2.5}$$

where $\Psi_1, \ldots, \Psi_N$, are fixed linearly independent solutions of (3.2.3, 4). In particular, taking $u = 0$ for the simplest starting solution of the KdV equation and choosing Ψ_1 in the form

$$\Psi_1 = \cosh[\kappa_1(x - x_1) - 4\kappa_1^3 t], \quad \lambda_1 = -\kappa_1^2 , \tag{3.2.6}$$

we get
$$u[1] = -2\partial_x^2 \ln \Psi_1 = -2\kappa_1^2 \cosh^{-2}[\kappa_1(x - x_1) - 4\kappa_1^3 t] . \tag{3.2.7}$$

The obtained solution of the KdV equation describes the propagation of a solitary wave moving with constant velocity $4\kappa_1^2$, its amplitude and velocity are proportional to each other. Following the proposal of N. Zabussky, (3.2.7) is referred to as a soliton solution, or simply soliton. A smooth multisoliton solution (i.e., the solution describing nonlinear interaction between N solitons) is obtained from (3.2.5) after choosing the functions Ψ_i to be

$$\begin{aligned}\Psi_{2k-1} &= \cosh\left(\kappa_{2k-1}(x - x_{2k-1}) - 4\kappa_{2k-1}^3 t\right) , \\ \Psi_{2k} &= \sinh\left(\kappa_{2k}(x - x_{2k}) - 4\kappa_{2k}^3 t\right) , \quad \kappa_1 \leq \kappa_2 \leq \ldots \leq \kappa_N . \end{aligned} \tag{3.2.8}$$

There are many ways to check that a solution constructed in this way is nonsingular. We prefer the method presented in Sect. 3.3 based on the derivation from the solution of the KP equation.

It is also possible to take for Ψ_1 the following function

$$\Psi_1 = \cos[k_1(x - x_1 + 4k_1^2 t)] , \quad \lambda_1 = k_1^2 , \tag{3.2.9}$$

$$\Psi_1 = x - x_1 , \quad \lambda_1 = 0 . \tag{3.2.10}$$

Equations (3.2.9) and (2.1.4) produce a singular periodic solution. The choice of (3.2.10) leads to the stationary rational solution

$$u[1] = 2/(x - x_1)^2 . \tag{3.2.11}$$

Iteration of the Darboux transformation with a mixed choice of the functions $\Psi_1, \ldots, \Psi_N$ corresponding to the possible forms (3.2.6, 7, 9) describes the nonlinear superpositions of the simplest solutions considered above.

To conclude this section we focus on the rational solutions of the KdV equation. We shall start from the degenerate N-times iterated solution (2.4.18) in which we put $u = 0$. For $u[N]$ we get

$$u[N] = -2\partial_x^2 \ln \begin{vmatrix} \Psi_1 & \Psi_{1\lambda} & \cdots & \partial_\lambda^{N-1}\Psi_1 \\ \Psi_{1x} & \Psi_{1x\lambda} & \cdots & \partial_\lambda^{N-1}\Psi_{1x} \\ \cdots & & & \\ \partial_x^{N-1}\Psi_1 & \cdots & \cdots & \partial_x^{N-1}\partial_\lambda^{N-1}\Psi \end{vmatrix} . \tag{3.2.12}$$

Now in the limit $\lambda \to 0$ we obtain from (3.2.12) the rational solutions of the KdV equation. The simplest of these solutions, corresponding to the $N = 2$ case, is of the form

$$u[2] = -2\partial_x^2 \ln(x^3/3 + t + C) , \tag{3.2.13}$$

where C is an arbitrary constant.

A somewhat different approach for the construction of rational solutions was proposed by *Moser* and *Adler* [3.20], *Krichever* [3.21], *Nimmo* and *Freeman* [3.22] and *Hirota* [3.23]. More interesting, however, are the rational solutions of the KP equation discussed in the next section.

3.3 Some Exact Solutions of the KP Equation

The KP equation

$$(u_t - 6uu_x - u_{xxx})_x = -3\alpha^2 u_{yy} \tag{3.3.1}$$

appears in physical applications in two different forms with $\alpha = 1$ and $\alpha = i$, usually referred to as the KP-I and the KP-II equations. Most of the information about their solutions may be extracted from the Zakharov-Shabat representation of (3.3.1):

$$\begin{aligned} & L_t - A_y = [A, L], \\ & A = -4\partial_x^3 - 6u\partial_x - 3(u_x - \alpha w), \quad L = -(\partial_x^2 + u)/\alpha. \end{aligned} \tag{3.3.2}$$

It is more convenient to consider (3.3.1) as the compatibility condition of the following linear system of partial differential equations:

$$\alpha \psi_y^+ = -\psi_{xx}^+ - u\psi^+, \tag{3.3.3}$$

$$\psi_t^+ = -4\psi_{xxx}^+ - 6u\psi_x^+ - 3(u_x - \alpha w)\psi^+. \tag{3.3.4}$$

The compatibility of this system, which we shall also call the (+)-system, means that $(\psi_y^+)_t = (\psi_t^+)_y$. This condition may be transformed into

$$\begin{aligned} & w_x = u_y, \\ & u_t - 6uu_x - u_{xxx} = -3\alpha^2 w_y. \end{aligned} \tag{3.3.5}$$

Eliminating w we obtain the KP equation (3.3.1). The KP equation may also be represented as a condition of compatibility of the system

$$-\alpha \psi_y^- = -\psi_{xx}^- - u\psi^- \tag{3.3.6}$$

$$\psi_t^- = -4\psi_{xxx}^- - 6u\psi_x^- - 3(u_x + \alpha w)\psi^-, \tag{3.3.7}$$

which is conjugated with respect to (3.3.3,4). We shall call (3.3.6,7) the (−)-system.

The first equations of the (±)-systems are covariant with the Darboux transformation and the same is true for the second equations. Hence it is possible to apply all the formulas for Darboux dressing given in Sect. 2.4. In particular, (2.8.4) is valid up to a modification in the differential form Ω, and the integrals J_{ik}:

$$\begin{aligned} \Omega(f, g) = & fg\, dx + \alpha^{-1}(fg_x - f_x g) dy \\ & - (4fg_{xx} - 4f_x g_x + 4f_{xx} g + 6ufg) dt, \end{aligned} \tag{3.3.8}$$

$$J_{ik} = A_{ik} + B_{ik} \int_{(x_0, y_0, t_0)}^{(x, y, t)} \Omega(\psi_i^+, \psi_k^-). \tag{3.3.9}$$

In contrast to the KdV case, the binary Darboux transformation, when applied to the KP-I and KP-II equations produces classes of solutions that are extremely important in physical applications.

We now consider some exact solutions of the KP equation. We set $u = 0$. The auxiliary linear system takes the form

$$\pm\alpha\psi_y^\pm = -\psi_{xx}^\pm, \quad \psi_t^\pm = -4\psi_{xxx}^\pm. \tag{3.3.10}$$

A rather general solution of the system (3.3.10) may be constructed in the form

$$\psi_1^+ = \int_{s_1} f_1(\omega) \exp(\omega_1 x - \alpha^{-1}\omega_1^2 y - 4\omega_1^3 t) d\sigma_1, \tag{3.3.11}$$

where f_1 is an arbitrary function of the complex variable ω_1, and σ_1 is some measure. The integration is taken over a domain s_1 on the complex plane. A one-step Darboux transformation generated by this function already produces the solution of the KP equation depending on the functional parameter $f_1(\omega_1)$:

$$u[+1] = 2\partial_x^2 \ln \int_{s_1} f_1(\omega_1) \exp(\omega_1 x - \alpha^{-1}\omega_1^2 y - 4\omega_1^3 t) d\sigma_1. \tag{3.3.12}$$

The simplest solution (soliton wall) of the KP equation may be obtained by taking f_1 to be a linear combination of two δ-functions. In other words, we define ψ_1^+ by the formula

$$\psi_1^+ = \exp(\theta_1) + \exp(\theta_2), \quad \theta_k = \kappa_k(x - x_k) - \kappa_k^2 \alpha^{-1} y - 4\kappa_k^3 t. \tag{3.3.13}$$

From this we get

$$\psi_1^+ = \exp[(\theta_1 + \theta_2)/2] \cosh[(\theta_1 - \theta_2)/2],$$
$$u[+1] = 2\partial_x^2 \ln \cosh[(\theta_1 - \theta_2)/2], \tag{3.3.14}$$

When $\kappa_2 = -\kappa_1$, the solution (3.3.14) is y-independent and satisfies the KdV equation. Looking at the solution obtained by use of the N-times repeated Darboux transformations, let us first consider $u[+N]$, produced by the choice of $\psi_1^+, \ldots, \psi_N^+$ in the form of (3.3.11) with f_1, σ_1, ω_1 replaced by f_i, σ_i, ω_i, respectively:

$$u[+N] = 2\partial_x^2 \ln \Delta_N,$$
$$\Delta_N = \int_{s_1} \ldots \int_{s_N} F_N(\vec{\omega}) \exp(\theta) \det(\omega_k^{j-1}) d\sigma_1 \ldots d\sigma_N,$$
$$j \leq k, \; j \leq N, \tag{3.3.15}$$
$$F_N = \prod_1^N f_l(\omega_l), \quad \theta = \sum_1^N (x\omega_l - \alpha^{-1} y \omega_l^2 - 4t\omega_l^3).$$

We can reduce this solution to a more elegant form by assuming that

3.3 Some Exact Solutions of the KP Equation

$\alpha = 1, \quad d\sigma_k = d\omega_k, \quad \omega_k \in \mathbf{R}:$

$$u[+N] = 2\partial_x^2 \ln \iint_\Omega \int G(\xi_1, \xi_2, \xi_3) \exp(\xi_1 x - 2\xi_2 y - 12\xi_3 t) d\xi_1 d\xi_2 d\xi_3,$$

$$\xi_k = k^{-1} \sum_{j=1}^{N} \omega_j^k, \quad k = 1, 2, 3, \ldots, N;$$

$$G = \iint \ldots \int F_N(\vec{\omega}(\xi)) d\xi_4 d\xi_5 \ldots d\xi_N.$$

The obtained solutions should be nonsingular under the assumption that the functions f_k are different from zero only on the sets $[A_k, B_k] \cup [C_k, D_k]$ and their signs are chosen by the rule

$f_k(\omega_k) > 0$ if $\omega_k \in [C_k, D_k]$,

$f_k(\omega_k) > 0$ if $\omega_k \in [A_k, B_k]$, $k = 2n - 1$, $n = 1, 2, \ldots$,

$f_k(\omega_k) < 0$ if $\omega_k \in [A_k, B_k]$, $k = 2n$, $n = 1, 2, \ldots$,

$\ldots < A_2 < B_2 < A_1 < B_1 < C_1 < D_1 < C_2 < D_2 \ldots$.

In such a case the factor

$$\prod_{l=1}^{N} f_l(\omega_l) \det(\omega_k^{j-1})$$

entering into the integral in (3.3.15) will be nonnegative. In particular, a multi-soliton solution of the KdV equation corresponds to the choice

$$f_k(\omega_k) = A_{k1} \delta(\omega_k - \kappa_k) + A_{k2} \delta(\omega_k + \kappa_k), \quad 0 < \kappa_1 < \kappa_2 < \ldots < \kappa_N.$$

The choice of the signs of f_k described above means that

$A_{ki} > 0$, $k = 1, 2, \ldots, N$,

$A_{2N-1,2} > 0$, $A_{2N,2} < 0$.

After simple transformations we get (3.2.8) for smooth real multisoliton solutions.

Consider one class of solutions containing a number of simplest soliton walls joined together. Let

$$\psi_k = \sum_{j=1}^{L_k} A_{kj} \exp \theta_{kj},$$

where $\theta_{kj} = \omega_{kj} x - \alpha^{-1} \omega_{kj}^2 y - 4\omega_{kj}^3 t$, and assume that $u[+N]$ depends only on the $x - v_1 t$ and $y - v_2 t$. In other words, we set a restriction such that $u[+N]$ evolves without changing its profile. After tedious calculations it is possible to show that with this assumption $L_k \leq 3$ and

$$\omega_{kj} = -\frac{v_2}{12\alpha} + \sqrt{\frac{v_2^2}{36\alpha^2} + \frac{v_1}{3}} \sin\left(\theta_k - \frac{2\pi j}{3}\right),$$

θ_k are arbitrary constants.

The advantage of the use of the binary Darboux transformation is best seen for the KP-II equation, i.e., for $\alpha = i$. First of all it allows one to isolate real-valued solutions of the form $u[+N, -N]$ by putting $\psi_{k+N}^- = \overline{\psi_k^+}$, $B_{kj} = \overline{B_{jk}}$. The corresponding formulas for $\alpha = i$, $u = 0$ coincide with those obtained by the Zakharov-Shabat dressing method [3.6].

The advantage of our approach is that we can also study the case $\alpha = 1$, $u \neq 0$ without any additional difficulties. Note that systematic use of the (+) and (−) systems with the Zahkharov-Shabat method should allow generalization of their results, which has not yet been relized.

In the case of $\alpha = i$, together with the solutions exponentially decreasing in some directions and nondecreasing in other directions, there exists a class of solutions decaying as $(x^2 + y^2)^{-1}$ in all directions. These solutions, discovered in 1977 [3.10], are the rational functions of x, y and t. Usually these solutions are referred to as lumps. One soliton (lump) solution of this kind is obtained when

$$\psi_1^+ = \exp(\kappa x + i\kappa^2 y - 4\kappa^3 t)(x + 2i\kappa y - 12\kappa^2 t), \quad \psi_2^- = \overline{\psi_1^+}. \tag{3.3.16}$$

Such a choice for ψ^+ corresponds to f being a derivative of a δ-function. The associated solution $u[+1, -1]$ of the KP-II equation is

$$u[+1, -1] = 2\frac{\partial^2}{\partial x^2} \ln \left\{ \left[x - \frac{1}{2\beta} - 2\gamma y - 12(\beta^2 - \gamma^2)t \right]^2 \right.$$
$$\left. + (2\beta y - 24\gamma\beta t)^2 + \frac{1}{4\beta^2} \right\} \tag{3.3.17}$$

$\beta = \text{Re}\{\kappa\}, \quad \gamma = \text{Im}\{\kappa\}$.

It is also possible to let f_k be linear combinations of derivatives of δ-functions. The corresponding form of ψ_k is then given by

$$\psi_k = \sum_{m=0}^{N_k} A_{km} \frac{\partial^m}{\partial \omega_k^m} \exp(\omega_k x - \alpha^{-1}\omega_k^2 y - 4\omega_k^3 t)$$
$$= \mathbf{P}_k \exp(\omega_k x - \alpha^{-1}\omega_k^2 y - 4\omega_k^3 t). \tag{3.3.18}$$

It is evident that $\mathbf{P}_k$ in (3.3.18) is a polynomial depending on x, y and t. It is clear that the exponentials in each column of the Wronskian determinant may be omitted and the related solution $u[+N]$ is a rational function of x, y and t. It is possible to construct rational solutions of the KP equation such that they decay at long times. Below we shall see that solutions with such properties exist for many other nonlinear integrable equations, and are called then exultons. The construction of the KP exulton solution is given by

$$u = 2\frac{\partial^2}{\partial x^2} \ln \frac{\partial^4}{\partial \omega^2 \partial \bar{\omega}^2} \exp(\theta + \bar{\theta}), \quad \theta = \omega x + i\omega^2 y - 4\omega^3 t, \quad (3.3.19)$$

which can be also rewritten as

$$u = 2\partial_x^2 \ln(|\vartheta + \theta^2|^2 + 4\kappa^2 |\theta - \kappa|^2 + 4\kappa^4),$$
$$\vartheta = 2iy - 24\omega t + \kappa^2, \kappa = (\omega + \bar{\omega})^{-1}.$$

To conclude this section we describe a few specific solutions representing a mixture of the exponential and rational solutions. The simplest form of such a solution is described by $u[3]$ with

$$\psi_{1,2}^+ = \theta_{1,2} \exp \theta_{1,2}, \quad \theta_{1,2} = x + 2i\omega_{1,2} y - 12\omega_{1,2}^2 t \pm \kappa^2 \beta / 4,$$
$$\omega_1 = -\bar{\omega}_2 = \gamma/\sqrt{3} + i\kappa,$$
$$\psi_3^+ = \exp(\theta_{3,1} + \theta_0) + \exp(\theta_{3,2} + \theta_0).$$
$$\theta_{3,j} = \omega_{3j} x + i\omega_{3j}^2 y - 4\omega_{3j}^3 t, \quad \omega_{31} = -\bar{\omega}_{32} = \gamma + i\kappa,$$
$$\theta_0 = \text{const}.$$

Introducing new variables ξ and η we get

$$\xi = x - 12(\kappa^2 + \gamma^2/3)t - 2\kappa(y - 12\kappa t), \quad \eta = y - 12\kappa t$$
$$u[+3] = 2\partial_x^2 \ln \left\{ \left[(\xi - 3/2\gamma)^2 + 4\gamma^2 \eta^2/3 + m^2 \right] \exp(\gamma \xi + \theta_0) \right.$$
$$\left. + \left[(\xi + 3/2\gamma)^2 + 4\gamma^2 \eta^2/3 + m^2 \right] \exp(-\gamma \xi - \theta_0) \right\},$$
$$m^2 = 3/4\gamma^2 + 27\kappa^4/(2\gamma)^4.$$

The set of exact solutions of the KP equation is extremely rich and far from complete. The solutions described above represent the simplest classes of exact solutions of the KP equation. Other possibilities related to the construction of rational solutions are discussed in (3.24, 25). The variety of exact solutions of the KP equation may be significantly enlarged by the use of the methods of algebraic curves which generate the large families of solutions of the KdV and KP equations together with the exact solutions of associated linear systems, usually called Baker-Akhiezer functions [3.26, 27]. Evidently such solutions allow application of the Darboux transformation method. This is not very interesting for the KdV case where the discussed solutions may be obtained by simple degeneration of the finite gap solutions. But for the KP case the class of solutions obtained by Darboux dressing of finite-gap solutions is considerably more rich. The relations of this class to the so-called higher range solutions introduced by *Novikov* and *Krichever* [3.15] are not yet well understood. See, however, the work of *Bobenko* [3.16].

3.4 Elastic and Inelastic Collisions of KP Solitons. Instability of Lumps

In this section we consider the interactions of solitons. It is well known that in the KdV case a multisoliton solution at large times asymptotically splits into a sum of simple solitons. The difference between asymptotic behavior in "past infinity" and "future infinity" is the order of the solitons. Their amplitudes and velocities are the same at both infinities and the result of an interaction is analytically described by phase shifts defined by the discrete spectrum of the associated Schrödinger operator and by the rearrangement of the ordering of the solitons. At past infinity more rapid solitons are situated to the left of slower solitons, moving from left to right. At future infinity the slower solitons are situated to the left of more rapid solitons.

The results obtained in this section are more or less universal. The reason is that multisoliton solutions of the numerous integrable nonlinear equations have similar structure. Note that the method of calculations of the phase shifts produced by the interactions of solitons presented here [3.17] is considerably simpler than other approaches reported in the literature.

Consider the expression

$$u = 2\partial_x^2 \ln \det[b_{1k}^{j-1} \exp(\theta_{1k}) + b_{2k}^{j-1} \exp(\theta_{2k})] . \tag{3.4.1}$$

In the case

$$b_{lk} = \kappa_{lk} , \quad \theta_{lk} = \kappa_{lk}(x - x_k) - \kappa_{lk}^2 \alpha^{-1} y - 4\kappa_{lk}^3 t + \theta_{lk0} ,$$

(3.4.1) describes a multisoliton solution of the KP equation. We shall consider the more general situation

$$\theta_{lk} = a_{lk}x + c_{lk}t + g_{lk}(y) , \quad l = 1,2 ; \quad k = 1, 2, \ldots, N ,$$

taking into account future applications to some other nonlinear equations. Equation (3.4.1) may be rewritten as

$$u = 2\partial_x^2 \ln \det A , \quad A_{jk} = b_{1k}^{j-1} \exp(\varphi_k) + b_{2k}^{j-1} \exp(-\varphi_k) ,$$
$$\varphi_k = (\theta_{1k} - \theta_{2k})/2 . \tag{3.4.2}$$

We shall call φ_k the phase of the k-th soliton. Now we fix the phase of the p-th soliton, i.e., $\varphi_p = $ const, when $t \to \pm\infty$. In other words, we choose a reference frame related to the p-th soliton. We get

$$x = [2\varphi_p - (c_{1p} - c_{2p})t - (g_{1p} - g_{2p})](a_{1p} - a_{2p})^{-1} ,$$

$$\varphi_k = (a_{1k} - a_{2k})(a_{1p} - a_{2p})^{-1}\varphi_p$$
$$+ 2^{-1}[c_{1k} - c_{2k} - (a_{1k} - a_{2k})(c_{1p} - c_{2p})/(a_{1p} - a_{2p})]t$$
$$+ 2^{-1}[g_{1k} - g_{2k} - (g_{1p} - g_{2p})/(a_{1p} - a_{2p})] .$$

3.4 Elastic and Inelastic Collisions of KP Solitons. Instability of Lumps

Hence the function r_{kp} defined by the formula

$$r_{kp} = \text{Re}[c_{1k} - c_{2k} - (a_{1k} - a_{2k})(c_{1p} - c_{2p})/(a_{1p} - a_{2p})],$$

determines the behavior of the k-th solution when $t \to \pm\infty$. Assume for a moment that $r_{kp} < 0$ when $k < p$ and $r_{kp} > 0$ when $k > p$. Then the function u behaves like

$$u \sim 2\partial_x^2 \ln \Delta^{\pm} \tag{3.4.3}$$

when $t \to \pm\infty$, where Δ^+ and Δ^- are defined by:

$$\Delta^+ = \begin{vmatrix} 1, \ldots, 1, & e^{\varphi_p} + e^{-\varphi_p}, & 1, \ldots, 1 \\ b_{21}, \ldots, b_{2,p-1}, & b_{1p}e^{\varphi_p} + b_{2p}e^{-\varphi_p}, & b_{1,p+1}, \ldots, b_{1N} \\ b_{21}^2, \ldots, b_{2,p-1}^2, & b_{1p}^2 e^{\varphi_p} + b_{2p}^2 e^{-\varphi_p}, & b_{1,p+1}^2, \ldots, b_{1N}^2 \\ b_{21}^{N-1}, \ldots, b_{2,p-1}^{N-1}, & b_{1p}^{N-1} e^{\varphi_p} + b_{2p}^{N-1} e^{-\varphi_p}, & b_{1,p+1}^{N-1}, \ldots, b_{1N}^{N-1} \end{vmatrix}$$

$$\Delta^- = \begin{vmatrix} 1, \ldots, 1, & e^{\varphi_p} + e^{-\varphi_p}, & 1, \ldots, 1 \\ b_{11}, \ldots, b_{1,p-1}, & b_{1p}e^{\varphi_p} + b_{2p}e^{-\varphi_p}, & b_{2,p+1}, \ldots, b_{2N} \\ b_{11}^2, \ldots, b_{1,p-1}^2, & b_{1p}^2 e^{\varphi_p} + b_{2p}^2 e^{-\varphi_p}, & b_{2,p+1}^2, \ldots, b_{2N}^2 \\ b_{11}^{N-1}, \ldots, b_{1,p-1}^{N-1}, & b_{1p}^{N-1} e^{\varphi_p} + b_{2p}^{N-1} e^{-\varphi_p}, & b_{2,p-1}^{N-1}, \ldots, b_{2N}^{N-1} \end{vmatrix} \tag{3.4.4}$$

From (3.4.3) it is clear that for $t \to -\infty$

$$u \sim 2\partial_x^2 \ln[W_1 \exp(\varphi_p) + W_2 \exp(-\varphi_p)],$$

in other words,

$$u \sim 2\partial_x^2 \ln \cosh(\varphi_p + 2^{-1} \ln(W_1/W_2)), \tag{3.4.5}$$

$$W_1 = W(b_{11}, b_{12}, \ldots, b_{1,p-1}, b_{1p}, b_{2,p+1}, \ldots, b_{2N}),$$

$$W_2 = W(b_{11}, \ldots, b_{1,p-1}, b_{2p}, b_{2,p+1}, \ldots, b_{2N}),$$

and W denotes the Van-der-Mond determinant:

$$W(z_1, \ldots, z_N) = \det A, \quad A_{jk} = z_k^{j-1}, \quad 1 \le j, \quad k \le N.$$

From (3.4.3 – 5) we conclude that the p-th soliton phase shift reduced to the x-variable is given by

$$\delta_p = (a_{2p} - a_{1p})^{-1} \ln(W_1 W_3 / W_2 W_4). \tag{3.4.6}$$

In the KP case b_{lm} must be replaced by κ_{lm} and $a_{lm} = \kappa_{lm}$. In the KdV case, in addition we have to put $a_{2k} = -a_{1k}$. Under these assumptions we get

$$W_1 = W(a_{11}, \ldots, a_{1,p-1}, a_{1p}, -a_{1,p+1}, \ldots, -a_{1N}),$$

$$W_2 = W(a_{11}, \ldots, a_{1,p-1}, -a_{1p}, -a_{1,p+1}, \ldots, -a_{1N}),$$

$$W_3 = (-1)^N W_2, \quad W_4 = (-1)^N W_1,$$

and hence

$$\delta_p = -(2a_p)^{-1} \ln(W_2^2/W_1^2) \, . \tag{3.4.7}$$

This last formula, after substitution of the well known product representation for W

$$W(z_1,\ldots,z_N) = \prod_{\substack{i,j \\ i<j}} (z_i - z_j) \, ,$$

gives the answer usually discussed in textbooks containing the calculation of the KdV soliton phase shifts.

Note that we never imposed the nonsingularity conditions on the discussed solutions of the KP equation nor of the KdV equation. Our formulas describe not only the collisions of nonsingular solitons but also the collisions of "singular solitons". We can also apply these formulas to the analysis of the long time behavior of some "mixed" solutions containing, asymptotically, a number of singular and nonsingular solitons.

The analysis performed above was based on the assumption that one of the exponentials $\exp(\varphi_p)$ or $\exp(-\varphi_p)$ vanishes when $t \to \pm\infty$. In particular, it is clear that the rational solitons of the KP equation generated by the solutions $\psi = P(x,y,t) \exp\vartheta$, where P is some polynomial, of the auxiliary linear system are unshifted by the collision process.

We have discussed above the situation with $r_{kp} \neq 0$. The case $r_{kp} = 0$ corresponds to bound states of the solitons.

To conclude this section we present the solution describing the instability of the rational soliton of the KP equation:

$$\begin{aligned}u[+1,-1] = 2\partial_x^2 \ln\{ & [x - (2\beta)^{-1} - 2\gamma y - 12(\beta^2 - \gamma^2)t]^2 \\ & + [2\beta y - 24\gamma\beta t]^2 + (2\beta)^{-2} + A \exp[-2\beta(x - 2\gamma y) \\ & - 4(\beta^2 - 3\gamma^2)t]\} \, , \quad A \neq 0 \, .\end{aligned}$$

This solution corresponds to the following choice of ψ_1^+, ψ_2^+:
$\psi_1^+ = \psi_2^- = (x + 2i\kappa y - 12\kappa^2 t) \exp(\kappa x + i\kappa^2 y - 4\kappa^3 t) \, , \quad \kappa = \beta + i\gamma$. It is clear that when $t \to -\infty$, this solution represents a mixture of the exponential soliton and of the rational soliton. When $t \to +\infty$, the rational part disappears, and only the exponential soliton determines the leading term of the asymptotics of the solution. $A = 0$ corresponds to the lump rational solution localized in the x-y plane.

3.5 Soliton Propagation on an Arbitrary Background

In this section, following from [3.26], we consider the Darboux-dressing of an arbitrary small amplitude solution of the KdV equation. The associated formulas describing the interaction between one soliton solution or multisoliton solution and the background are asymptotic.

We rewrite the linear system associated with the KdV equation in the form

$$-\psi_{xx} + u\psi = \lambda\psi, \tag{3.5.1}$$

$$\psi_t = 2u\psi_x + 4\lambda\psi_x - u_x\psi. \tag{3.5.2}$$

We represent the asymptotic solution of (3.1.5) in the form

$$\psi_1 = \exp\left[\kappa \int_s^x v(z,t)\,dz + p(t)\right]$$
$$+ \exp\left[-\kappa \int_s^x w(z,t)\,dz + q(t)\right], \tag{3.5.3}$$

$$s = x_0 + 4\kappa^2 t, \quad \lambda_1 = -\kappa^2,$$

$$v = \sum_{n=0}^{\infty} \kappa^{-n} v_n(x,t), \quad w = \sum_{n=0}^{\infty} \kappa^{-n} w_n(x,t), \tag{3.5.4}$$

$$p(t) = \sum_{n=-\infty}^{\infty} \kappa^{-n} p_n(t), \quad q(t) = \sum_{n=-\infty}^{\infty} \kappa^{-n} q_n(t). \tag{3.5.5}$$

Substituting anzatz (3.5.3) into (3.5.1) and equating the coefficients of the same powers of κ, we get the following recurrence relations for v_n and w_n:

$$(v_n)_x = u\delta_n^1 - \sum_{k=0}^{n+1} v_k v_{n+1-k}, \quad n \geq 0,$$

$$-(w_n)_x = u\delta_n^1 - \sum_{k=0}^{n+1} w_k w_{n+1-k}, \tag{3.5.6}$$

The temporal dynamics of (3.5.3) determined by (3.5.2) lead to the relation

$$\int_s^x (v_n(z,t))_t\,dz - 4\hat{v}_{n+2} + (p_{n-1})_t = 2uv_n - 4v_{n+2} - u_x\delta_n^1,$$

$$-\int_s^x (w_n(z,t))_t\,dz + 4\hat{w}_{n+2} + (q_{n-1})_t = -2uw_n + 4w_{n+2} - u_x\delta_n^1,$$

$$\hat{v}_n = v_n(s(t),t), \quad \hat{w}_n = w_n(s(t),t). \tag{3.5.7}$$

Differentiating (3.5.7) by x we get

$$(v_n(z,t))_t = 2(uv_n)_x + 4(v_{n+2})_x - u_{xx}\delta_n^1,$$

$$-(w_n(z,t))_t = -2(uw_n)_x + 4(w_{n+2})_x - u_{xx}\delta_n^1. \tag{3.5.8}$$

The consistency of (3.5.6, 8) may be established easily by the method of mathematical induction.

In [3.26] it was proved that the following relation holds

$$(v_n)_t = \partial_x F_n, \quad (w_n)_t = \partial_x G_n. \tag{3.5.9}$$

The function F_n and G_n are given in [3.27].

Using (3.5.7, 9) we get a recipe for calculating the quantities

$$a_n = (p_n)_t, \quad b_n = (q_n)_t,$$
$$a_{n-1} = F_n + 4\hat{v}_{n+2}, \quad b_{n-1} = -G_n - 4\hat{w}_{n+2}.$$

From (3.5.6, 8, 9) we deduce that

$$F_n = (-1)^n G_n, \quad a_{n-1} = (-1)^{n-1} b_{n-1}, \quad n \geq 0.$$

The expression for the first a_n in terms of the potential u looks like

$$a_{-1} = 2u|_{x=s(t)}, \quad a_0 = -u_x|_{x=s(t)}, \quad a_1 = u^2|_{x=s(t)},$$
$$a_2 = -uu_x/2|_{x=s(t)}, \quad a_3 = (uu_{xx} - u^3)/4|_{x=s(t)}, \quad \ldots.$$

Taking this into account we can represent formal solution (3.5.6) in the form

$$\psi_1 = \exp(\theta_1 + \theta_2 + r_1 + r_2) + \exp(-\theta_1 + \theta_2 - r_1 + r_2)$$
$$= 2\exp(\theta_2 + r_2)\cosh(\theta_1 + r_1), \tag{3.5.10}$$

$$\theta_1 = \int_s^x (\kappa + v_2/\kappa + v_4/\kappa^3 + \ldots)dz,$$
$$\theta_2 = \int_s^x (v_3/\kappa^2 + v_5/\kappa^4 + \ldots)dz, \tag{3.5.11}$$

$$r_1 = \int_0^t (\kappa a_{-1} + a_1/\kappa + a_3/\kappa^3 + \ldots)d\tau,$$
$$r_2 = \int_0^t (a_0 + a_2/\kappa^2 + a_4/\kappa^4 + \ldots)d\tau. \tag{3.5.12}$$

Now performing a Darboux transformation we obtain the following solution of the KdV equation

$$u[1] = u - 2\partial_x^2 \ln \psi_1 = u - 2(\theta_2 + r_2)_{xx} - 2\partial_x^2 \ln \cosh(\theta_1 + r_1). \tag{3.5.13}$$

Substituting (3.5.11, 12) into (3.5.13) we obtain the asymptotic expansion

$$u[1] = u + 2\kappa^{-2}u_{xx} - 8\kappa^{-4}(4u_x^2 + 4uu_{xx} - u_{xxxx}) + \ldots - \kappa^{-1}u_x \tanh f$$
$$- 2(\kappa + (2\kappa)^{-1}u + \ldots)^2/\cosh^2 f,$$

$$f = \kappa(x - x_0) - 4\kappa^3 t + \int_0^t (2\kappa\hat{u} + \kappa^{-1}\hat{u}^2 + \ldots)d\tau$$
$$+ \int_{x_0+4\kappa^2 t}^x [(2\kappa)^{-1}u + \ldots]dz. \tag{3.5.14}$$

When $u = 0$, $u[1]$ given by (3.5.14) reduces to the soliton solution of the KdV equation. Hence it is reasonable to treat the term proportional to $\cosh^{-2}$ as a deformend soliton. The term containing tanh may be interpreted as describing the interaction between the soliton and the background $u(x,t)$. Other terms may be interpreted as describing the deformation of the background in the presence of the soliton.

The leading term in the asymptotics of $u[1]$ when $\kappa \to \infty$ (large amplitude soliton) is given by the formula

$$u[1] = u - 2\kappa^2 \cosh[\kappa(x - x_0) - 4\kappa^3 t + 2\kappa \int_0^t u(s(\tau), \tau) d\tau] \, .$$

Multisoliton solutions on an arbitrary but small background may be studied in the same manner, taking the functions Ψ_k in the form (3.5.3) and defining $u[N]$ by (3.2.5).

It is interesting to study the phase shift of the soliton produced by the interaction with an arbitrary background. We fix the phase of an unperturbed soliton $\xi = \kappa(x - x_0) - 4\kappa^3 t$. Let $u(x,t)$ and all its derivatives tend to zero when x tends to infinity and let $\xi = $ const. Then we have

$$u \sim -2\kappa^2 / \cosh^2 \sigma^{\pm}, \quad x \to \pm \infty \, ,$$

$$\sigma = \xi + \int_0^{\pm \infty} h(x_0, t) dt \, ,$$

$$h(x_0, t) = [2\kappa u + u^2/\kappa + (uu_{xx} - u^2)/(4\kappa^2) + \ldots]|_{x=x_0+4\kappa^2 t} \, ,$$

hence, the phase shift Δ_x is given by

$$\Delta_x = \kappa^{-1}(\sigma^+ - \sigma^-) = \kappa^{-1} \int_{-\infty}^{\infty} h(x_0, t) dt \, . \tag{3.5.15}$$

In the case when $u(x,t)$ represents a one soliton solution, (3.5.15) reduces to the well known formula for the asymptotic behavior of a two soliton solution.

3.6 The Boussinesq Equation

In this section we consider the so-called Boussinesq nonlinear equation

$$w_{tt} - w_{xx} + (w^2)_{xx} + w_{xxxx}/3 = 0 \, , \tag{3.6.1}$$

describing t-independent solutions of the KP equation. The corresponding linear system is

$$\psi_{xxx} + (3w/2 - 3/4)\psi_x + u\psi = \lambda\psi \, , \quad \psi_t = -\psi_{xx} - w\psi \, . \tag{3.6.2}$$

The conditions of compatibility of the system (3.6.2) are

3. Exact Solutions of the KdV and KP Equations

$$u_{\tilde{x}} = 3w_{xx}/4 - 3w_t/4 \,,$$

$$u_t = w_{xxx}/4 + 3(w^2)_x/4 - 3w_x/4 + 3w_{xt}/4 \,.$$

Excluding u from the last system we obtain (3.6.1).

The system (3.6.2) is Darboux-covariant, i.e., covariant with respect to the transformation

$$\psi \to \psi[1] = \psi_x - \frac{\psi_{1x}}{\psi_1}\psi \,, \quad w \to w[1] = w + 2\partial_x^2 \ln \psi_1 \,.$$

Solitons of the Boussinesq equation are obtained by taking $w = 0$

$$\psi_{xxx} - 3\psi_x/4 = \lambda\psi \,, \quad \psi_t = -\psi_{xx} \,. \tag{3.6.3}$$

The position of λ is responsible for different types of solitons. Consider the following cases

1. $|\lambda| < 1/4$, then we have

$$w[1] = 2\partial_x^2 \ln[A_1 \exp\theta_1 + A_2 \exp\theta_2 + A_3 \exp\theta_3] \,, \tag{3.6.4}$$

where $\theta_k = \kappa_k x - \kappa_k^2 t$, A_k is an arbitrary constant, κ_k are the roots of the algebraic equation

$$\kappa^3 - 3\kappa/4 = \lambda \,.$$

2. $\lambda = 1/4$. Then

$$\begin{aligned}w[1] &= 2\partial_x^2 \ln[C \exp(3x/2 - 3t/4) - x - t] \\ &= 2\frac{[3 - 9(x+t)/4]C \exp(3x/2 - 3t/4) - 1}{[C \exp(3x/2 - 3t/4) - (x+t)]^2} \,.\end{aligned} \tag{3.6.5}$$

The solution (3.6.5) is rather amazing because it describes the collapse arising from a smooth initial condition at the moment

$$t = 4[\ln(3C/2) + 1]/9 \,.$$

Obviously we can construct more complicated multicollapse solutions by examining the repeated Darboux transformation.

3.7 The Johnson Equation and its Equivalence to the KP Equation

In this section we consider the axially symmetric version of the KP equation usually called the Johnson equation:

$$(u_t + 6uu_x + u_{xxx} + u/(2t))_x = -3\alpha^2 u_{yy}/t^2 \ . \tag{3.7.1}$$

The reader may consult the original work of *Johnson* [3.27] for a discussion of its physical derivation. For a long time the Johnson equation was thought to be essentially different from the KP case [3.28, 29] and in some aspects this opinion is justified. But this is not the case in the most important situation of rapidly decreasing initial conditions.

Let $v(x, y, t)$ be an arbitrary solution of the KP equation

$$(v_t + 6vv_x + v_{xxx})_x = -3\alpha^2 v_{yy} \ . \tag{3.7.2}$$

In recent work [3.30, 31] it was discovered that under this assumption the function

$$v(x - y^2 t/12\alpha^2, yt, t) \tag{3.7.3}$$

satisfies the Johnson equation.

The corresponding change of variables is invertible. Each solution $u(x, y, t)$ of the Johnson equation generates the solution of the KP equation defined by the formula

$$v = u(x + y^2/12\alpha^2 t, y/t, t) \ . \tag{3.7.4}$$

It is easy to see that the mappings $u \to v$, $v \to u$, defined by (3.7.3, 4) preserve the class of functions rapidly decreasing at infinity [i.e., when $(x^2 + y^2)^{-1} \to 0$]. Consequently all the results obtained in the theory of the KP-I or KP-II equations with rapidly decreasing initial data can be simply and directly applied to solve the Johnson equation. However, this is not the case for periodic initial data: it is evident that the class of periodic solutions is not invariant with respect to the action of the described transformation. Instead of the wall-soliton localized near some moving straight lines in the xy plane, in the Johnson case we get a solution with a parabolic profile.

Nevertheless, independent analysis of the solutions of the Johnson equation is of some interest, taking into account that the solutions different from those rapidly decreasing at infinity may be applied in some realistic situations. In particular, the solutions periodic in y may be useful.

The ($\pm$) system associated with the Johnson equation is of the form

$$\begin{aligned}\pm \alpha \psi_y^\pm &= t\psi_{xx}^\pm + (tu - x/12)\psi^\pm \ , \\ \psi_t^\pm &= -4\psi_{xxx}^\pm - 6u\psi_x^\pm - (3u_x \pm 3\alpha v/t)\psi^\pm \ .\end{aligned} \tag{3.7.5}$$

The compatibility condition of (3.7.5) is equivalent to the following relations:

$$v_x = u_y ,$$
$$u_t + u/2t + 6uu_x + u_{xxx} = -3\alpha^2 v_y/t^2 . \qquad (3.7.6)$$

This leads to the Johnson equation after substitution of the first formula of (3.7.6) into the second. The Darboux transformations are

$$\psi^+[+1] = \psi_x^+ - \frac{\psi_{1x}^+}{\psi_1^+}\psi^+ , \quad \psi^-[-1] = \psi_x^- - \frac{\psi_{1x}^-}{\psi_1^-}\Psi^- ,$$

$$u[\pm 1] = u + 2\partial_x^2 \ln \psi_1^\pm ,$$

$$\psi[+1] = (\psi_1^+)\left[B_1 + \int_{(x_0,y_0,t_0)}^{(x,y,t)} \Omega(\psi_1^\pm, \psi) \right] , \qquad (3.7.7)$$

$$\Omega(f,g) = fg\, dx - \alpha^{-1} t(fg_x - f_x g) dy$$
$$+ (-4f_{xx}g + 4f_x g_x - 4fg_{xx} - 6ufg) dt .$$

The formula for $u[+M,-N]$ coincides with similar representations for the solutions $u[+M,-N]$ for the KP up to a redefinition of the differential form Ω. We fix $\alpha = 1/12$, $u = 0$, and choose ψ_1^+, ψ_2^- as follows:

$$\psi_1^+ = \int_s A_1(\omega) \exp(-x(y-\omega) + 4t(y-\omega)^2) d\sigma ,$$
$$\psi_2^- = \int_s A_2(\omega) \exp(x(y+\omega) - 4t(y+\omega)^3) d\sigma . \qquad (3.7.8)$$

Construction of the soliton and multisoliton solutions in such a case may be performed in a manner completely analogous to the KP case. A particular soliton of the Johnson equation with $\alpha = 1/12$ is

$$u = 2\partial_x^2 \ln[(12t)^2 |x/12t + y^2 - \gamma^2 - 2i\gamma y|^2 + 1/4\gamma^2] .$$

Obviously in this formula x and y (but not t) may be replaced by $x - x_0$, $y - y_0$.

The periodic solution in y may be obtained in the same case $\alpha = i/12$ under the following choice of ψ_1^+:

$$\psi_1^+ = t^{-1/3} \sum_{-\infty}^\infty \left[A_k \operatorname{Ai}\left(\frac{x-k}{\sqrt[3]{12t}}\right) + B_k \operatorname{Bi}\left(\frac{x-k}{\sqrt[3]{12t}}\right) \right] \exp(iky) ,$$

where $\operatorname{Ai}(z)$ and $\operatorname{Bi}(z)$ are the solutions of the Airy equation

$$w'' - zw = 0 \qquad (3.7.9)$$

defined by the integral representations

$$\operatorname{Ai}(z) = \pi^{-1} \int_0^\infty \cos(t^3/3 + tz) dt , \qquad (3.7.10)$$

$$\operatorname{Bi}(z) = \pi^{-1} \int_0^\infty [\exp(-t^3/3 - zt) + \sin(t^3/3 + zt)]\, dt . \qquad (3.7.11)$$

Using the change of variables (3.7.4) we can also obtain a large family of solutions of the KP equation involving the Airy functions. Solutions of this type were first obtained by *Nakamura* [3.32].

3.8 The Cylindrical KdV Equation and its Exact Solutions

The cylindrical KdV equation

$$u_t + u/2t + 6uu_x + u_{xxx} = 0 \tag{3.8.1}$$

describes y-independent solutions of the Johnson equation. The corresponding linear system first found by *Druma* [3.33] is

$$\begin{aligned} t\psi_{xx} + (tu - x/12) &= \lambda\psi \,, \\ \psi_t &= -4\psi_{xxx} - 6u\psi_x - 3u_x\psi \,. \end{aligned} \tag{3.8.2}$$

A direct transformation discovered by *Lugovtsov* and *Lugovtsov* [3.34] allows one to obtain the solutions of the cylindrical KdV equation from the known solutions of the usual KdV equation and vice versa. In contrast to (3.7.3, 4) the Lugovtsov transformation does not preserve the class of rapidly decreasing initial data. That is, in order to obtain the decreasing solutions of (3.8.1) from their transformation, we need to take the growing solutions of the KdV equation of the form $x/2t$ plus terms added by Darboux dressing [3.35].

We can generate the solutions of (3.8.1) from the solution of the Johnson equation by taking into account that the system (3.7.5) reduces to (3.8.2) under the assumption

$$\psi^+(x,y,t) = \exp(\pm\lambda y)\varphi(x,t) \,,$$

corresponding to the case of y-independent solutions of the Johnson equation. All the formulas of the DT machinery applied to the Johnson equation remain valid up to the replacement of the expression (3.7.7) for Ω by

$$\Omega(f,g) = fg\,dx + (-4fg_{xx} + 4f_x g_x - 4f_{xx}g - ufg)dt \,.$$

In contrast to the KdV case, where the solutions interesting for physical applications were given by $u[+N]$ for the cylindrical KdV case, we need to apply a binary DT to get nonsingular solutions.

In particular, looking for $u[+1]$ we get

$$u[+1] = 2\partial_x^2 \ln \operatorname{Ai}\left(\frac{x-\lambda_1}{\sqrt[3]{12t}}\right) \,, \tag{3.8.3}$$

i.e., the singular solution with an infinite number of poles. At the same time the formula

$$u[+1,-1] = 2\partial_x^2 \ln\left\{ Bt^{1/3} + [\text{Ai}'(0)]^2 - \int_0^\xi \text{Ai}^2(\eta)d\eta \right\},$$

$$\xi = (x - \lambda_1)/\sqrt[3]{12t}$$

defines a nonsingular real solution of the cylindrical KdV equation.

The general formula for $u[+N, -N]$ with the solutions ψ_i defined by (3.8.2) with different λ_i defines multisoliton nonsingular solutions first obtained by a different method in [3.36].

It is also easy to construct the solutions corresponding to Darboux-dressing of a nonzero background solution. For example, the starting solution $u = x/12t$ generates the nonsingular growing solution

$$u(x,t) = \frac{x}{12t} + \frac{2\lambda_1^2}{t \cosh^2[\lambda_1(x + 8\lambda_1^2)/\sqrt{t}]}.$$

Starting from the slowly decaying $u = at^{-1/2}$ we get from a one-time applied Darboux transformation

$$u = at^{-1/2} + 2\partial_x^2 \ln\left\{ Bt^{1/3} + [\text{Ai}'(0)]^2 - \int_0^\xi \text{Ai}^2(\eta)d\eta \right\},$$

$$\xi = (x - 12at^{1/2})(12t)^{-1/3}.$$

It is clear that in both these cases the system (3.8.2) is explicitly solvable and we can construct solutions $u[+N, -N]$ in the same manner.

4. Darboux Transformations for the Zero Curvature Equations and Nonlocal Nonlinear Evolution Equations

In this chapter we consider the applications of the DT method to various nonlinear evolution equations (NEE) related to auxiliary linear problems with the matrix coefficients involving the nonlinear Schrödinger equation, self-induced transparency equations, the reduced Maxwell-Bloch system, and the sine-Gordon equation. We discuss also some nonlocal generalizations of the KdV equation describing the propagation of internal waves in deep water or in water of a finite depth. The associated linear problem involves a shift operator and may be considered as infinite-dimensional.

4.1 Darboux Transformations for Nonlinear Evolution Equations and the Generalized Zakharov-Shabat Linear Problem

Consider the linear system

$$\Psi_t = I\Psi\Lambda + V\Psi, \quad \Psi_x = J\Psi\Lambda + U\Psi, \qquad (4.1.1)$$

where I and J are constant matrices satisfying the condition

$$[I, J] = 0 .$$

The consistency condition of the system (4.1.1) reads

$$[I, U] = [J, V], \quad U_t - V_x = [V, U] . \qquad (4.1.2)$$

Taking U and V in the form $U = [J, Q]$, $V = [I, Q]$, we get

$$[J, Q_t] - [I, V_x] = [[I, Q], [J, Q]] . \qquad (4.1.3)$$

For the moment we are not interested in further reductions of the system (4.1.2) since (as was shown in [4.1]), already general systems such as (4.1.2) are widely applied and well known in physics.

Equations (4.1.1) are included in the family of linear systems considered in the Sect. 2.3. In the particular case considered here, the general formulas of the

Sect. 2.3 are substantially simplified. In terms of Q we get the following formulas for the Darboux-transformed coefficients of the system (4.1.1):

$$Q[1] = Q + \sigma, \quad Q[N] = Q - s_1, \quad \sigma = \Psi_1 \Lambda_1 \Psi_1^{-1}, \tag{4.1.4}$$

where s_1 is defined from the following system of the linear matrix equations:

$$s_1 \Psi_1 \Lambda_k^{N-k} + \ldots s_N \Psi_k = -\Psi_k \Lambda_k^N, \quad k = 1, 2, \ldots, N \tag{4.1.5}$$

fixed by the choice of $\Psi_1, \ldots, \Psi_N$, $-N$ fixed invertible matrix solutions of the system (4.1.1).

The N-soliton solution corresponds to the choice $Q = 0$, and Ψ_k satisfies the system

$$\Psi_t = I\Psi\Lambda, \quad \Psi_x = J\Psi\Lambda.$$

The interesting evolution equation

$$V_\zeta = U_\eta = [V, U]/2 \tag{4.1.6}$$

arises as a consistency condition of the linear system

$$\Psi_\zeta = U\Psi M_1, \quad \Psi_\eta = V\Psi M_2,$$
$$M_1 = \mathrm{diag}\,[(\lambda_1 - 1)^{-1}, \ldots, (\lambda_m - 1)^{-1}], \tag{4.1.7}$$
$$M_2 = \mathrm{diag}\,[(\lambda_1 + 1)^{-1}, \ldots, (\lambda_m + 1)^{-1}].$$

Assuming that $U = \mathrm{i}\Phi_\zeta$, $V = \mathrm{i}\Phi_\eta$ we get for Φ the nonlinear equation

$$\Phi_{\zeta\eta} = \mathrm{i}[\Phi_\eta, \Phi_\zeta]. \tag{4.1.8}$$

The same machinery described in Sect. 2.3 is applicable also to the systems (4.1.6–8). For the Darboux-transformed coefficients we have

$$U[1] = U - \sigma_x, \quad V[1] = V - \sigma_t, \quad \Phi[1] = \Phi + \mathrm{i}\sigma,$$
$$U[N] = U + s_{1x}, \quad V[N] = V + s_{1t}, \quad \Phi[N] = \Phi - \mathrm{i}s_1, \tag{4.1.9}$$

where σ and s_1 are defined as in (4.1.4, 5).

Note that the problem of satisfying the complementary reduction constraints may be solved by appropriate choice of $\lambda_1, \ldots, \lambda_N$ in Λ and by appropriate choice of the matrix solutions Ψ of the starting linear system.

4.2 Multisoliton and Periodic Solutions of the Nonlinear Schrödinger Equation

The nonlinear Schrödinger (NS) equation

$$ir_t + r_{xx} + 2\alpha|r|^2 r = 0 \tag{4.2.1}$$

arises in various physical contexts. For example, it describes the effects of self-focusing of the envelope of a monochromatic plane wave propagating in nonlinear media [4.2]. The NS equation also appears in the theory of surface waves on shallow water [4.3]. Just recently it was recognized that the NS equation also appears in quantum correlation functions in some solvable models of statistical mechanics [4.4]. Equation (4.2.1) may also be considered as the Hartree-Fock equation for a one-dimensional quantum Boson gas with δ-point interaction. Then α plays the role of a coupling constant: the case $\alpha > 0$ corresponds to attractive interaction between the particles, and $\alpha < 0$ is the repulsive case. The two cases are essentially different in optical applications, describing selffocusing or defocusing of the light rays in nonlinear wave guides [4.2]. Mathematically these two cases are also very different because the first one corresponds to a selfadjoint linear problem while the second one is generated by a nonselfadjoint linear problem. The nonlinear Schrödinger equation was first solved by the inverse scattering method by *Zakharov* and *Shabat* [4.5] in 1971. In our treatment we shall follow [4.6, 7] with slight modifications. After the publication of [4.6], part of the results of this section were rediscovered by the several other authors [4.8, 9]. It is necessary to mention the work of *Wadati* [4.10] who first treated a Bäcklund transformation for the NS equation in the framework of the inverse scattering method.

Consider the following linear system for a 2×2 matrix function Ψ:

$$\Psi_x = J\Psi\Lambda + U\Psi,$$
$$\Psi_t = 2J\Psi\Lambda^2 + 2U\Psi\Lambda + (JU^2 - JU_x)\Psi,$$
$$U = \begin{pmatrix} 0 & iq \\ ir & 0 \end{pmatrix}, \quad J = \begin{pmatrix} i & 0 \\ 0 & -i \end{pmatrix}, \quad \Lambda = \begin{pmatrix} \lambda_1 & 0 \\ o & \lambda_2 \end{pmatrix}. \tag{4.2.2}$$

The consistency condition $\Psi_{xt} = \Psi_{tx}$ of the system (4.2.2) is equivalent to the so-called nonlinear Schrödinger system

$$iq = q_{xx} + 2q^2 r, \quad ir_t = -r_{xx} - 2qr^2. \tag{4.2.3}$$

Equation (4.2.3) reduces to the original NS equation with $\alpha = 1$ under the condition

$$q = r^*. \tag{4.2.4}$$

It is clear that the Zakharov-Shabat system (4.2.2) is included into the general scheme of the DT method described in Sect. 2.3. For example, for $U[1]$ we get

$$U[1] = U + [J, \Psi_1 \Lambda_1 \Psi_1^{-1}], \quad U[N] = U - [J, s_1]. \tag{4.2.5}$$

In terms of the dressed solutions $r[1]$, $q[1]$ the last formula takes the form

$$q[1] = q - 2(\lambda_{11} - \lambda_{21})\psi_1\psi_2(\psi_1\varphi_2 - \varphi_1\psi_2)^{-1},$$

$$r[1] = r - 2(\lambda_{21} - \lambda_{11})\varphi_1\varphi_2(\psi_1\varphi_2 - \varphi_1\psi_2)^{-1},$$

$$\Lambda_1 = \text{diag}[\lambda_{11}, \lambda_{21}], \quad \Psi_1 = \begin{pmatrix} \psi_1 & \psi_2 \\ \varphi_1 & \varphi_2 \end{pmatrix}.$$

The result of the action of the N-times repeated Darboux transformation is described by

$$U[N] = U - [J, s_1], \tag{4.2.6}$$

and the matrix s_1 is determined by the system (2.3.9). Equation (2.3.9) may be easily solved and we get the following result written in terms of the dressed solutions $r[N]$, $q[N]$ of the NS system:

$$r[N] = r - 2\Delta_1/\Delta_2,$$

$$\Delta_1 = \begin{vmatrix} \lambda_1^N \varphi_1, & \lambda_2^N \varphi_2, & \cdots, & \lambda_{2N}^N \varphi_{2N} \\ \lambda_1^{N-1} \varphi_1, & \lambda_2^{N-1} \varphi_2, & \cdots, & \lambda_{2N}^{N-1} \varphi_{2N} \\ \cdots & \cdots & \cdots & \cdots \\ \varphi_1, & \varphi_2, & \cdots, & \varphi_{2N} \\ \lambda_1^{N-1} \psi_1, & \lambda_2^{N-1} \psi_2, & \cdots, & \lambda_{2N}^{N-1} \psi_{2N} \\ \cdots & \cdots & \cdots & \cdots \\ \psi_1, & \psi_2, & \cdots, & \psi_{2N} \end{vmatrix}$$

$$\Delta_2 = \begin{vmatrix} \lambda_1^{N-1} \psi_1, & \lambda_2^{N-1} \psi_2, & \cdots, & \lambda_{2N}^{N-1} \psi_{2N} \\ \cdots & \cdots & \cdots & \cdots \\ \psi_1, & \psi_2, & \cdots, & \psi_{2N} \\ \lambda_1^{N-1} \varphi_1, & \lambda_2^{N-1} \varphi_2, & \cdots, & \lambda_{2N}^{N-1} \varphi_{2N} \\ \cdots & \cdots & \cdots & \cdots \\ \varphi_1, & \varphi_2, & \cdots, & \varphi_{2N} \end{vmatrix}$$

$$\tag{4.2.7}$$

Interchanging φ_k and ψ_k, $k = 1, 2, \ldots, 2N$ in Δ_1 we obtain the formula for $q[N]$.

We assume that in (4.2.7) Ψ_k, Λ_k, ψ_i, φ_j, λ_j are related by the formula

$$\Lambda_k = \begin{pmatrix} \lambda_{2k-1} & 0 \\ 0 & \lambda_{2k} \end{pmatrix}, \quad \Psi_k = \begin{pmatrix} \psi_{2k-1} & \psi_{2k} \\ \varphi_{2k-1} & \varphi_{2k} \end{pmatrix}.$$

The reduction requirement $q = r^*$ will be realized when

$$\lambda_{2k} = \lambda_{2k-1}^*, \quad \varphi_{2k} = \pm \psi_{2k-1}^*, \quad \psi_{2k} = \pm \varphi_{2k-1}^*. \tag{4.2.8}$$

Multisoliton solutions are obtained when $r = 0$,

$$\psi_{2k-1} = A_{2k-1} \exp(i\lambda_{2k-1}x + 2i\lambda_{2k-1}^2 t) ,$$
$$\varphi_{2k-1} = B_{2k-1} \exp(-\lambda_{2k-1}x - 2i\lambda_{2k-1}^2 t) , \qquad (4.2.9)$$

Formula (4.2.7) under the condition (4.2.8) defines the multisoliton solution of the nonlinear Schrödinger equation.

The single soliton solution is described by the formula

$$r[1] = -2(\lambda_1 - \lambda_1^*)\varphi_1\psi_1^*/(|\psi|^2 + |\varphi|^2)$$
$$= -2i \operatorname{Im}\{\lambda\} \exp(-2i \operatorname{Im}\{\theta\} + i\Phi_1)/\cosh(2\operatorname{Re}\{\theta\} + \Phi_2) , \qquad (4.2.10)$$

where Φ_1, Φ_2 are arbitrary real constants defined by A and B, and

$$\theta = i\lambda_1 x + 2i\lambda_1^2 t .$$

A very interesting solution is obtained by applying the Darboux transformation to the simplest periodic solution r,

$$r = A \exp(iS) , \quad S = ax + (2A^2 - a^2)t , \qquad (4.2.11)$$

where, without loss of generality, we can take A to be real valued. The solution of the system (4.2.2) corresponding to this choice of r with $q = r^*$ is given by the formula

$$\psi = u \exp(-iS/2) , \quad \varphi = v \exp(iS/2) , \quad \psi_2 = -\varphi_1^* , \quad \varphi_2 = \psi_1^* .$$

Here u and v are determined from the solution of the system of linear equations with constant coefficients.

Consider the following possibilities.

A. The eigenvalues $\mu_1 = \mu_2 = 0$. The characteristic equation is

$$(\lambda + a/2)^2 = -A^2 .$$

We find

$$u = x - x_0 - 2at \pm 1/2A \pm 2iAt ,$$
$$v = \pm i(x - x_0 - 2at \pm 1/2A \pm 2iAt) ,$$
$$r[1] = A[4A^2/3 - 4A^2 t^2 - \zeta^2 + 4it][\zeta^2 + 1/4A^2 + 4A^2 t^2]^{-1} ,$$
$$\zeta = x - x_0 - 2at , \qquad (4.2.12)$$
$$|r[1]|^2 = A^2 + 2(p(t) - \zeta^2)/(p(t) + \zeta^2)^2 ,$$
$$p(t) = 4A^2 t^2 + 1/4A^2 .$$

When $t \to \pm\infty$ the rational solution (4.2.12) loses the sharpness of its profile and $r[1] \to r$. Below we shall call such a solution the exulton solution.

B. The general case. The characteristic equation takes the form

$$\mu^2 + (\lambda + a/2)^2 + A^2 = 0 ;$$

$$u = c_1 \exp(\theta) + c_2 \exp(-\theta) , \quad \theta = \mu[x + (2\lambda - a)t] ,$$
$$v = (c_1/iA)[\mu - i(\lambda + a/2)] \exp(\theta)$$
$$\quad - /c_2/iA)[\mu + i(\lambda + a/2)] \exp(-\theta) . \quad (4.2.13)$$

For brevity we write down only a formula for $|r[1]|^2$ of the obtained solution,

$$|r[1]|^2 = A^2 + \partial_x^2 \ln[\cosh(2\mu_R(x - ct) + 4(\lambda_R\mu_R - \lambda_I\mu_I)t)$$

$$+ \sqrt{\frac{A^2 + |\lambda + a/2|^2 - |\mu|^2}{A^2 + |\lambda + a/2|^2 + |\mu|^2}}$$

$$\times \cos(2\mu_I(x - at) + 4(\lambda_I\mu_R + \lambda_R\mu_I)t + \varphi_0)] ,$$

$$\mu = \mu_R + i\mu_I , \quad \lambda = \lambda_R + i\lambda_I . \quad (4.2.14)$$

The special case

$$\lambda_R = -a/2 , \quad \mu_R = 0 , \quad \mu_I = \sqrt{A^2 - \lambda_I^2} , \quad |A| > |\lambda_R| ,$$

of the formula (4.2.13) is of particular interest:

$$|r[1]|^2 = A^2 - \frac{4|\lambda_I/A|^2(A^2 - \lambda_I)^2 + 4|\lambda_I/A|^2(A^2 - \lambda_R)^2 \cosh p \cos q}{(\cosh p + |\lambda_R/A| \cos q)^2} ,$$

$$p = 4\lambda_I t\sqrt{A^2 - \lambda_I^2} , \quad q = \sqrt{A^2 - \lambda_R^2}\,(x - 2at) .$$

For fixed values of t this solution is periodic in x. It tends to A^2 when $t \to \pm\infty$. Thus this solution describes selfgeneration and decaying of an x-periodic solution of the NS equation.

Multisoliton solutions on the periodic background describing periodic modulations of multiexultons and their interactions are given by (4.2.7) with ψ_{2k-1}, φ_{2k-1} given by

$$\psi_{2k-1} = u_{2k-1} \exp(-iS/2) , \quad \varphi_{2k-1} = v_{2k-1} \exp(iS/2) ,$$

with u_{2k-1}, v_{2k-1} chosen as the points A and B.

4.3 Interactions of the NS Solitons with an Arbitrary Background

In this section we describe the technique of analysis of solitons on an arbitrary background adopted to the nonlinear Schrödinger case, following [4.7]. Our approach here is slightly different from that used in the Sect. 3.6 for the KdV case.

The study of solutions of this kind is of special importance. The reason is that one possible physical interpretation of the solutions of the NS equation is that they represent the propagation of the envelope of a monochromatic plane wave in an optical fiber in the presence of noise. The noise leads to the deformation of solitons and forces them to move slower than when they propagate freely. This effect can be described analytically.

Let us represent the solutions of the system (4.2.2) with $q = r^*$ in the form:

$$\psi = C_1 \exp(\kappa x/2 - i\kappa^2 t/2 + n_1) + C_2 h_2 \exp(-\kappa x/2 + i\kappa^2 t/2) ,$$
$$\varphi = C_1 h_1 \exp(\kappa x/2 - i\kappa^2 t/2) + C_2 \exp(-\kappa x/2 + i\kappa^2 t/2 + n_2) . \quad (4.3.1)$$

We try to construct n_1, n_2, h_1, h_2 in the form of the asymptotic series

$$h_1 = \sum_{n=1}^{\infty} \kappa^{-n} \int_x^{\infty} f_n(x',t) dx' ,$$

$$n_2 = \sum_{n=1}^{\infty} \kappa^{-n} \int_{-\infty}^{x} g_n(x',t) dx' , \quad (4.3.2)$$

$$n = \sum_{n=1}^{\infty} \kappa^{-n} b_n , \quad h = \sum_{n=1}^{\infty} \kappa^{-n} c_n , \quad \kappa = 2i\lambda . \quad (4.3.3)$$

Substitution of (4.3.1–3) into the linear system leads to the recursion relations

$$f_1 = -|r|^2 , \quad f_2 = r^* r_x ,$$

$$f_{k+1} = r^* \frac{\partial}{\partial x} \left(\frac{f_k}{r^*} \right) - \sum_{j=1}^{k-1} f_j f_{k-j} , \quad k \geq 2 , \quad (4.3.4)$$

$$g_k = (-1)^k f_k^* , \quad k \geq 1 ,$$

$$(b_{k+1})_x f_1 + b_{k+1} f_2 = - \sum_{j=1}^{k} (b_j f_{k-j+3} + b_j f_{k-j+2}) , \quad c_k = (-1)^k b_k^* . \quad (4.3.5)$$

At the same time

$$b_1 = ir , \quad b_2 = -ir_x + ir \int_x^{\infty} |r|^2 dx' - \frac{ir}{2} \int_{-\infty}^{\infty} |r|^2 dx' .$$

The recursion relation (4.3.5) arose for the first time in the pioneering paper [4.11]. g_n and f_n are polynomial densities of the integrals of motion.

Now, when ψ and φ corresponding to the arbitrary background $r(x,t)$ have been constructed, we dress this background in accordance with (4.2.5). For this we substitute (4.3.1) and (4.3.2–5) into (4.2.5), and we obtain

$$r[1] = r - 4\mathrm{i}\beta \frac{A_1 \exp(\mathrm{i}\chi) + B_1 \exp(-\mathrm{i}\chi) + A_2 \exp\theta + B_2 \exp(-\theta)}{A_3 \exp(\mathrm{i}\chi) + B_3 \exp(-\mathrm{i}\chi) + A_4 \exp\theta + B_4 \exp(-\theta)}$$

where

$$\chi = 2\alpha(x - x_0) + 4(\alpha^2 - \beta^2)t, \quad \theta = 2\beta(x - x_0) + 8\alpha\beta t,$$
$$\kappa = 2\mathrm{i}\lambda = -2\beta + 2\mathrm{i}\alpha,$$

$$A_1 = h_1 h_2^*$$
$$= \left[\mathrm{i}r\kappa^{-1} + \kappa^{-2}\left(-\mathrm{i}r_x + \mathrm{i}r\int_x^\infty |r|^2 d\xi - \mathrm{i}r\int_{-\infty}^\infty |r|^2 d\xi/2\right) + \ldots\right]$$
$$\times \left[-\mathrm{i}r\kappa^{-1} + \kappa^{-2}\left(-\mathrm{i}r_x - \mathrm{i}r\int_{-\infty}^x |r|^2 d\xi + \mathrm{i}r\int_{-\infty}^\infty |r|^2 d\xi/2\right) + \ldots\right]$$

$$B_1 = \exp(n_1^* + n_2) = \exp\left\{\int_x^\infty \left(\frac{|r|^2}{\kappa} - \frac{rr_x^*}{\kappa^2} + \ldots\right) dx \right.$$
$$\left. + \int_{-\infty}^x \left(\frac{|r|^2}{\kappa} + \frac{rr_x^*}{\kappa^2} + \ldots\right) dx\right\},$$

$$A_2 = h_2^* \exp n_2$$
$$= \left[-\mathrm{i}r\kappa^{-1} + \kappa^{-2}\left(-\mathrm{i}r_x - \mathrm{i}r\int_{-\infty}^x |r|^2 d\xi + \mathrm{i}r\int_{-\infty}^\infty |r|^2 d\xi/2\right) + \ldots\right]$$
$$\times \exp\left\{\int_{-\infty}^x \left(\frac{|r|^2}{\kappa} + \frac{rr_x^*}{\kappa^2} + \ldots\right) dx\right\},$$

$$B_2 = h_1 \exp n_1^*$$
$$= \left[\mathrm{i}r\kappa^{-1} + \kappa^{-2}\left(-\mathrm{i}r_x + \mathrm{i}r\int_x^\infty |r|^2 d\xi - \mathrm{i}r\int_{-\infty}^\infty |r|^2 d\xi/2\right) + \ldots\right]$$
$$\exp\left\{\int_x^\infty \left(\frac{|r|^2}{\kappa} - \frac{rr_x^*}{\kappa^2} + \ldots\right) dx\right\},$$

$$B_3 = A_3^*, \quad A_3 = h_2^* \exp n_1 + h_1 \exp n_2^*$$
$$= \left[-\mathrm{i}r\kappa^{-1} + \kappa^{-2}\left(-\mathrm{i}r_x - \mathrm{i}r\int_{-\infty}^x |r|^2 d\xi + \mathrm{i}r\int_{-\infty}^\infty |r|^2 d\xi/2\right) + \ldots\right]$$
$$\times \exp\left\{\int_x^\infty \left(\frac{|r|^2}{\kappa} - \frac{rr_x^*}{\kappa^2} + \ldots\right) dx\right\} + \ldots,$$

$$A_4 = |h_2|^2 + \exp(n_2 + n_2^*), \quad B_4 = |h_1|^2 + \exp(n_1 + n_1^*).$$

If we set $r(x,t) = 0$, then (4.3.6) goes over into the simplest single-soliton solution of the NS$_+$ equation:

$$r[1] = -2i\beta \frac{\exp(-2i(\alpha(x-x_0)+2(\alpha^2-\beta^2)t)}{\cosh[2\beta(x-x_o)+8\alpha\beta t]}. \tag{4.3.6}$$

If we put in (4.3.1) $c_1 = 0$, we get

$$r[1] = r - 4i\beta \frac{\bar{h}_2 \exp n_2}{h_2 \bar{h}_1 + \exp(n_2 + \bar{n}_2)}.$$

For $c_2 = 0$ we have

$$r[1] = r - 4i\beta \frac{h_1 \exp \bar{n}_1}{h_1 \bar{h}_1 + \exp(n_1 + \bar{n}_1)}.$$

Now we consider the solution phase shift following scattering by an arbitrary decreasing background.

Theorem. The phase shift of a soliton passing through a rapidly decreasing background is determined by the expression

$$\begin{aligned}\Delta\Phi &= \frac{\Phi_+ + \Phi_-}{\beta} = \frac{1}{2\beta} \sum_{n=1}^{\infty} \frac{\bar{\kappa}^n - \kappa^n}{|\kappa|^{2n}} \int_{-\infty}^{\infty} (g_n - (-1)^n \bar{g}_n) dx \\ &= -\frac{1}{\alpha^2+\beta^2} \int_{-\infty}^{\infty} |r|^2 dx + \frac{i\alpha}{2(\alpha^2+\beta^2)^2} \int_{-\infty}^{\infty} (r\bar{r}_x - r_x \bar{r}) dx \\ &+ \frac{2\alpha^2-\beta^2}{4(\alpha^2+\beta^2)^3} \int_{-\infty}^{\infty} (|r|^2 - |r_x|^2) dx + \ldots, \end{aligned} \tag{4.3.7}$$

i.e., it is an asymptotic series whose coefficients are integrals of the motion of the background — the particle number, momentum, energy etc.

Suppose $r(x,t) \to 0$ as $x \to \infty$; to be specific, we take $\alpha < 0$ and $\beta < 0$. We see that

$$\chi = \frac{\alpha^2+\beta^2}{\alpha} x + \frac{\alpha^2+\beta^2}{2\alpha\beta}\theta. \tag{4.3.8}$$

Let's let x tend to $+\infty$ in such a way that θ remains constant. Then

$$n_1, h_1, h_2 \to 0, \quad n_2 \to n_2^{\infty} = \sum_{n=1}^{\infty} \int_{-\infty}^{\infty} \frac{g_n(x,t)}{\kappa^n} dx. \tag{4.3.9}$$

Comparing (4.3.9) and (4.3.8) it is easy to deduce (4.3.7) for the phase shift.

One more interesting property of the NS solitons propagating on an arbitrary background is that for polynomial densities of the first three integrals of the NS equation, corresponding to a Darboux-dressed background, the following formulas hold:

$$|r[1]|^2 = |r|^2 + \frac{\partial^2}{\partial x^2} \ln \Delta, \tag{4.3.10}$$

4. Darboux Transformations for the Zero Curvature Equations

for the momentum density

$$\frac{1}{2}(r[1]\overline{r[1]}_x - r[1]_x\overline{r[1]})$$

$$= \frac{1}{2}(r\bar{r}_x - r_x\bar{r}) + \frac{\kappa - \bar{\kappa}}{2}\frac{\partial^2}{\partial x^2}\ln\Delta + \frac{\partial}{\partial x}\frac{\bar{r}a - r\bar{a}}{2}, \qquad (4.3.11)$$

for the energy density

$$|r[1]|^4 - |r[1]_x|^2 = |r|^4 - |r_x|^2 + \frac{(\kappa-\bar{\kappa})^2}{4}\frac{\partial^2}{\partial x^2}\ln\Delta$$

$$+ \frac{\partial}{\partial x}\left(\frac{\Delta_x\Delta_{xx}}{\Delta^2} - \frac{2}{3}\left(\frac{\Delta_x}{\Delta}\right)^3 + 2|r|^2\frac{\Delta_x}{\Delta} + \frac{\kappa-\bar{\kappa}}{2}\frac{\bar{r}a-r\bar{a}}{\Delta}\right), \qquad (4.3.12)$$

where $\Delta = |\theta|^2 + |\varphi|^2$, $a = i(\kappa + \bar{\kappa})\varphi\bar{\theta}$.

Because the higher integrals do not have a physical meaning, we shall not give the analogical expressions for their densities. Formulas (4.3.10–12) may be proved by direct calculations. We did not use any assumptions about the asymptotic behavior of $\vartheta(x,t)$, $\varphi(x,t)$ or $r(x,t)$. Thus, the terms additional to background densities can be interpreted as the particle number density, momentum, energy, etc., which correspond to the solution in the background–soliton interaction situation when the background behaves arbitraryly at $\pm\infty$. Thus, we obtain the possibility of describing the soliton behavior also in the situation when the energy of the background is infinite, for example, for a periodic or random background. In the case of a decreasing background, we can show for the solution $r[1]$ that

$$\int_{-\infty}^{\infty}|r[1]|^2 dx = \int_{-\infty}^{\infty}|r|^2 dx + 4\beta, \qquad (4.3.13)$$

$$\frac{1}{2}\int_{-\infty}^{\infty}(r[1]\overline{r[1]}_x - r[1]_x\overline{r[1]})^2 dx$$

$$= \frac{1}{2}\int_{-\infty}^{\infty}(r\bar{r}_x - r_x\bar{r})^2 dx + 8i\alpha\beta, \qquad (4.3.14)$$

$$\int_{-\infty}^{\infty}(|r[1]|^4 - |r[1]_x|^2)dx$$

$$= \int_{-\infty}^{\infty}(|r|^4 - |r_x|^2)dx + 16\beta\left(\frac{\beta^3}{3} - \alpha^2\right). \qquad (4.3.15)$$

Thus, each integral of motion of the solution $r[1](x,t)$ can be represented as a sum of the corresponding integrals of motion in terms of the scattering data. Additivity can also be proved for higher integrals.

4.4 Bloch Equations, the Reduced Maxwell-Bloch System and SIT Equations

In this section we discuss the so-called Bloch equations, reduced Maxwell-Bloch equations (RMB-equations) and the self-induced transparency equations (SIT-equations) within the theory of the Darboux transformations.

Consider the system:

$$\psi_t = i\lambda\psi + iE\varphi$$
$$\varphi_t = iE\psi - i\lambda\varphi ,\qquad(4.4.1)$$

where $E(t)$ is some real valued function. We introduce the following variables:

$$M_1 = \psi\varphi^* + \varphi\psi^*, \quad M_2 = i(\varphi\psi^* - \psi\varphi^*),$$
$$M_3 = |\psi|^2 - |\varphi|^2, \quad \Delta\omega = \lambda/2, \quad \omega(t) = -2E,\qquad(4.4.2)$$

and impose the condition

$$|\psi|^2 + |\varphi|^2 = 1 .\qquad(4.4.3)$$

Then (4.4.1) may be rewritten

$$M_{1t} = \Delta\omega M_2$$
$$M_{2t} = -\Delta\omega M_1 + \omega(t)M_2 \qquad(4.4.4)$$
$$M_{3t} = -\omega(t)M_2$$

The system (4.4.2) is important, for example, in the theory of nuclear magnetic resonance (NMR) phenomena where the vector

$$B = (\omega(t), 0, \Delta\omega)$$

describes an external magnetic field [4.12].

Equation (4.4.1) may also be represented in matrix form

$$\Psi_t = J\Psi\Lambda + U\Psi ,$$
$$J = \begin{pmatrix} i & 0 \\ 0 & -i \end{pmatrix}, \quad \Lambda = \begin{pmatrix} \lambda_1 & 0 \\ 0 & \lambda_2 \end{pmatrix}, \quad U = i\begin{pmatrix} 0 & E \\ E & 0 \end{pmatrix},$$
$$\Psi = \begin{pmatrix} \psi_1 & \psi_2 \\ \varphi_1 & \varphi_2 \end{pmatrix} .\qquad(4.4.5)$$

The columns of the matrix Ψ satisfy (4.4.1) with $\lambda = \lambda_1$ and $\lambda = \lambda_2$, respectively. Obviously (4.4.5) is Darboux covariant and it is necessary to satify the reduction requirement. Further analysis leads to the following algorithm of solution of the system (4.4.2):

1) Take the known starting solution E.
2) Find ψ_1, φ_1 solving (4.4.1) for $\lambda = \lambda_1$ – the fixed pure imaginary value of λ – under the complementary condition

4. Darboux Transformations for the Zero Curvature Equations

$$\psi_1 \varphi_1^* + \varphi_1 \psi_1^* = 0 \,. \tag{4.4.6}$$

3) Find Ψ_1,

$$\Psi_1 = \begin{pmatrix} \psi_1 & \varphi_1 \\ \varphi_1 & \psi_1 \end{pmatrix}, \quad \text{corresponding to} \quad \Lambda = \Lambda_1 = \begin{pmatrix} \lambda_1 & 0 \\ 0 & -\lambda_1 \end{pmatrix}.$$

4) Define single Darboux dressing by the formula

$$\Psi[1] = (\Psi\Lambda - \Psi_1 \Lambda_1 \Psi_1^{-1} \Psi)/\sqrt{\lambda^2 - \lambda_1^2} \,, \tag{4.4.7}$$

$$U[1] = U + [J, \sigma] \,, \quad \sigma = \Psi_1 \Lambda_1 \Psi_1^{-1} \,. \tag{4.4.8}$$

The normalization factor $(\lambda^2 - \lambda_1^2)^{-1}$ in (4.4.7) is introduced in order to preserve the constraint (4.4.3). From (4.4.8) we get

$$E[1] = E - 4\lambda_1 \varphi_1 \psi_1^* (|\psi_1|^2 + |\varphi_1|^2)^{-1} \,.$$

Equation (4.4.7) defines the associated solutions $\psi[1], \varphi[1]$ corresponding to real values of λ:

$$\begin{pmatrix} \psi[1] \\ \varphi[1] \end{pmatrix} = \lambda \begin{pmatrix} \psi \\ \varphi \end{pmatrix} + \sigma \begin{pmatrix} \psi \\ \varphi \end{pmatrix} \,.$$

5) Construct the vector $M[1]$ from $\varphi[1], \psi[1]$ with help of (4.4.2). N-times repeated Darboux transformation may be obtained in complete analogy with (4.2.3). The associated generating functions $\Psi_1, \Psi_2, \ldots, \Psi_N$ may be constructed from pure imaginary values of λ: $\lambda_1, \lambda_2, \ldots, \lambda_N$, as described in Sect. 2.3. $M[N]$ is constructed from $\Psi[N], \varphi[N]$, corresponding to the real values of λ.

An interesting result is the possibility to parameterize the solutions of (4.4.1,2) in terms of an arbitrary function $M_1(t)$. We have

$$M_2(t) = -M_{1t}/2\lambda_0 \,, \quad M_3(t) = \pm\sqrt{1 - M_1^2 - M_{1t}^2/4\lambda_0^2} \,,$$

$$E = \pm\lambda_0 (M_1 + M_{1tt}/4\lambda_0^2)(1 - M_1^2 - M_{1t}^2/4\lambda_0^2)^{-1/2} \,,$$

where λ_0 represents some fixed value of λ. The corresponding expression for ψ and φ are

$$\varphi = \sqrt{(1 - M_3)/2} \, \exp(i\theta) \,,$$

$$\psi = (M_1 + iM_2)(2(1 - M_3))^{-1/2} \exp(i\theta) \,,$$

$$\theta = EM_1(1 - M_3)^{-1} - \lambda_0 \,.$$

The next nonlinear problem discussed in this section is the so-called self-induced transparency or SIT system

4.4 Bloch Equations, the Reduced Maxwell-Bloch System and SIT Equations

$$E_x = \langle \varrho \rangle ,$$
$$\varrho_t + 2\mathrm{i}\varrho = NE ,$$
$$N_t = -(E^*\varrho + E\varrho^*)/2 .$$
(4.4.9)

This system describes various effects arising in the interaction of dielectric media with an external magnetic field near the resonance frequency. In (4.4.9) $\langle \varrho \rangle$ denotes the average

$$\langle \varrho \rangle = \int_{-\infty}^{\infty} \varrho(x,t,\eta) g(\eta) d\eta , \quad \int_{-\infty}^{\infty} g(\eta) d\eta = 1 , \qquad (4.4.10)$$

where $g(\eta)$ is some normalized probability density. E is the complex envelope of the electric field, N and ϱ depend on η. In the case of an infinitely narrow line $g(\eta) = \delta(\eta)$, E is real valued, $N = \cos\varphi$, $\varrho = \sin\varphi$, and the SIT system reduces to the sine-Gordon equation

$$\varphi_{tt} - \varphi_{xx} = \sin\varphi .$$

A detailed discussion of the physical origin of the SIT equations and a list of known exact solutions, not covering all the solutions presented below, however, may be found in *Dodd* et al. [4.13].

The linear system associated with SIT equations reads

$$\Psi_t = J\Psi\Lambda + U\Psi , \quad \Psi_x = \langle M\Psi P \rangle ,$$
$$\Lambda = \begin{pmatrix} \lambda_1 & 0 \\ 0 & \lambda_2 \end{pmatrix}, \quad U = \begin{pmatrix} 0 & -E \\ E^* & 0 \end{pmatrix}/2 , \quad M = -\mathrm{i}\begin{pmatrix} N & \varrho \\ \varrho^* & -N \end{pmatrix}/4 ,$$
$$P = \begin{pmatrix} (\eta - \lambda_1)^{-1} & 0 \\ 0 & (\eta - \lambda_2)^{-1} \end{pmatrix} . \qquad (4.4.11)$$

Equations (4.4.11) are of the type already discussed in Sect. 2.3. These equations are Darboux covariant and for Darboux transformed coefficients we get

$$U[1] = U + [J, \sigma_1] , \quad \sigma_1 = \Psi_1 \Lambda_1 \Psi_1^{-1} , \qquad (4.4.12)$$
$$M[1] = M + \sigma_{1x} = (\eta - \sigma_1) M (\eta - \sigma_1)^{-1} . \qquad (4.4.13)$$

The physical derivation of the SIT equation is based on the assumption of the absence of impure states. This fact is taken into account by the condition

$$N^2 + |\varrho|^2 = 1 .$$

In terms of M this condition reads

$$M^2 = -1/16 .$$

These restrictions are preserved by the action of the Darboux transformation,

$$M^2 = -(N^2 + |\varrho|^2)E/16 ,$$
$$M[1]^2 = ((\eta - \sigma_1) M (\eta - \sigma_1)^{-1})^2 = -(N^2 + |\varrho|^2)E/16 ,$$

4. Darboux Transformations for the Zero Curvature Equations

where E is the unit matrix. The reduction restrictions would be satisfied under the following choice of Ψ_1 and Λ_1:

$$\Psi_1 = \begin{pmatrix} \psi_1 & -\varphi_1^* \\ \varphi_1 & \psi_1^* \end{pmatrix}, \quad \Lambda_1 = \begin{pmatrix} \lambda_1 & 0 \\ 0 & \lambda_1^* \end{pmatrix}. \tag{4.4.14}$$

For N-times repeated Darboux transformation we have to take

$$\lambda_{2k} = \lambda_{2k-1}^*, \quad \varphi_{2k} = \psi_{2k-1}^*, \quad \psi_{2k} = -\varphi_{2k-1}^*, \quad k = 1, \ldots, N.$$

The simplest dressing formulas for the solutions of the SIT equations corresponding to a single Darboux transformation are of the form

$$E[1] = E + 4i(\lambda_1 - \lambda_1^*)\psi_1\varphi_1^*(|\psi_1|^2 + |\varphi|^2)^{-1}, \tag{4.4.15}$$

$$N[1] = N + 4i \left(\frac{\lambda_1|\psi_1|^2 + \lambda_1^*|\varphi_1|^2}{|\psi_1|^2 + |\varphi_1|^2} \right)_x$$

$$= N - 4\mathrm{Im}\{\lambda_1\} \left(\frac{|\psi_1|^2 - |\varphi_1|^2}{|\psi_1|^2 + |\varphi_1|^2} \right)_x, \tag{4.4.16}$$

$$\varrho[1] = \varrho + 4i \left(\frac{(\lambda_1 - \lambda_1^*)\psi_1\varphi_1^*}{|\psi_1|^2 + |\varphi_1|^2} \right)_x. \tag{4.4.17}$$

N-times repeated Darboux transformation leads to the formulas strongly resembling the NS case. For brevity we include here only the formula for $E[N]$:

$$E[N] = E - 4i\Delta_1/\Delta,$$

$$\Delta = \begin{vmatrix} \lambda_1^{N-1}\psi_1 & \lambda_1^{N-1}\varphi_1 & \lambda_1^{N-2}\psi_1 & \lambda_1^{N-2}\varphi_1 & \cdots & \psi_1\varphi_1 \\ \lambda_2^{N-1}\psi_2 & \lambda_2^{N-1}\varphi_2 & \lambda_2^{N-2}\psi_2 & \lambda_2^{N-2}\varphi_2 & \cdots & \psi_2\varphi_2 \\ \cdots & \cdots & \cdots & \cdots & \cdots & \cdots \\ \lambda_{2N}^{N-1}\psi_{2N} & \lambda_{2N}^{N-1}\varphi_{2N} & \lambda_{2N}^{N-2}\psi_{2N} & \lambda_{2N}^{N-2}\varphi_{2N} & \cdots & \psi_{2N}\varphi_{2N} \end{vmatrix}$$

$$\varphi_{2k} = \psi_{2k-1}^*, \quad \psi_{2k} = -\varphi_{2k-1}^*, \quad \lambda_{2k} = \lambda_{2k-1}^*.$$

Δ_1 is obtained from Δ by replacing the second column of Δ by

$$(\lambda_1^N\psi_1, \lambda_2^N\psi_2, \lambda_1^{N-1}\psi_1, \lambda_2^{N-1}\psi_2, \ldots,)^T.$$

Let us consider a few exact solutions of (4.4.9).

A. Choose the starting solution to be

$$E = 0, \quad \varrho = 0, \quad N = N(x).$$

The case $N = \pm 1$ corresponds to the pure states. We can, however, forget the origin of the SIT equations and consider them as describing the density matrix omitting the condition $N^2 + |\varrho|^2 = 1$, i.e., allowing the existence of nonpure states.

At the first step we obtain the soliton-like solution

$$E[1] = -8\lambda_I \left(\frac{\exp\{-2i\lambda_R t - 2i \int \kappa_R dx\}}{\cosh\{2\lambda_I t + 2 \int \kappa_I dx\}} \right),$$

$$N[1] = N - 8\lambda_I \kappa_I / \cosh^2(2\lambda_I t + 2 \int \kappa_I dx),$$
(4.4.18)

$$\lambda_1 = \lambda_R + i\lambda_I, \quad \kappa = \kappa_R + i\kappa_I, \quad \kappa = \langle N(x)/(\eta - \lambda_1) \rangle / 4.$$

B.

$$E = A \exp(ikx + i\omega t),$$

$$\varrho = \frac{iA^2 H(\eta)}{(\omega + 2\eta)^2 + A^2} \exp(ikx + i\omega t),$$
(4.4.19)

$$N = -\frac{(\omega + 2\eta)AH(\eta)}{(\omega + 2\eta)^2 + A^2},$$

where the function H may be chosen arbitraryly as long as it satisfies the normalization condition

$$\langle \frac{AH(\eta)}{(\omega + 2\eta)^2 + A^2} \rangle = k.$$

To exclude nonpure states we have to impose the complementary restriction on H

$$\langle 1/AH \rangle = k.$$

Under these assumptions the system (4.4.11) may be solved explicitly. Introducing the new variables

$$\psi = u \exp\theta, \quad \varphi = v \exp(-\theta), \quad \theta = i(kx + \omega t)/2,$$

we get a linear system for u and v. Now

$$E[1] = E - \frac{8\lambda_I u v^*}{|u|^2 + |v|^2} \exp\theta, \quad \lambda_I = \text{Im}\{\lambda_1\}.$$

The obtained solution describes the propagation of a soliton on a periodic background. The same formula contains a exulton-like solution

$$|E[1]| = |A| \, |1 + 4(ip_I x - 1)(4z^2 + 1)^{-1}|,$$

$$z = |t - 2A^{-1}px|, \quad p_I = \text{Im}\{p\},$$
(4.4.20)

$$p = A^2 \langle H/[(\omega + 2\eta)^2 + A^2](\eta - \lambda_1) \rangle.$$

C. The system (4.4.10) may be easily solved also for background solution

$$\varrho = EN/2i\eta, \quad \langle N/\eta \rangle = 0, \quad E = \text{const}, \quad N = \text{const}.$$

This case includes usual soliton-like solutions containing cosh-terms as well as rational solutions of the form

$$E[1] = E\frac{2|E|^{-2} - 2(\theta^* - \theta)|E|^{-1} - |\theta|^2}{|\theta|^2 + |E|^{-2}},$$

$$\theta = t - ipx|E|^{-1} + c, \quad c = \text{const},$$

$$p = \langle N/(\eta - i|E|2^{-1})\rangle = p_R + ip_I.$$

(4.4.21)

In the case $p_R = 0$, (4.4.21) reduces to the rational soliton

$$E[1] = -E(1 - 3/(|E|^2(t + p_I x|E|^{-1}) + 1)).$$

In the case $p_I = 0$, we get from (4.4.21) the exulton-like solution

$$E[1] = -E\left\{1 - \frac{3 - 4ip_R x}{p_R^2 x^2 + |E|^2 t^2 + 1}\right\}.$$

In general (4.4.21) describes a soliton-exulton mixed solution.

D. Of considerable interest is the Darboux dressing of the starting solution

$$E = E_0 \exp\left\{i\omega t - i\int_{x_0}^{x} \langle N/(\omega + 2\eta)\rangle dx\right\},$$

$$\varrho = -\frac{iNE_0}{\omega + 2\eta} \exp\left\{i\omega t - i\int_{x_0}^{x} \langle N/(\omega + 2\eta)\rangle dx\right\},$$

$$N = N(x, \eta).$$

By introducing the notation

$$\theta = i\omega t - i\int_{x_0}^{x} \langle N/(\omega + 2\eta)\rangle dx,$$

we find φ_1 and ψ_1 in the form

$$\psi_1 = u(z)\exp(\theta/2), \quad \varphi_1 = v(z)\exp(-\theta/2),$$

$$z = t + \frac{1}{4}\int_{x_0}^{x} \langle N/(\omega/2 + \eta)(\eta - \lambda)\rangle dx,$$

(4.4.22)

with u and v satisfying the system

$$u_z = -i(\lambda_2 + \omega/2)u - 2^{-1}E_0 v$$

$$v_z = 2^{-1}E_0^* u + i(\lambda_1 + \omega/2)u.$$

(4.4.23)

System (4.4.23) is straightforward to solve. As a result of applying the Darboux dressing we get interesting solutions which are easiest to study for the case of an infinitely narrow line. Actually we do allow the presence of nonpure states, so there are no solutions with similar behavior in the sine-Gordon case.

4.4 Bloch Equations, the Reduced Maxwell-Bloch System and SIT Equations

Let $g(\eta) = \delta(\eta)$. Then for the dressed solution $N[1]$ we get

$$N[1] = N\left\{1 - \frac{2\lambda_I}{|\lambda|\cosh(2\lambda_I t + 2^{-1}|\lambda|^{-2}\lambda_I \int_{x_0}^{x} N(x)dx + \beta)}\right\}.$$

Taking in the last expression

$$x_0 = \beta_0 = 0, \quad N(x) = \begin{cases} c_1, & x > 0 \\ c_2, & x < 0 \end{cases}, \qquad (4.4.24)$$

we find

$$N[1] = c_1\left(1 - \frac{2\lambda_I}{|\lambda|^2\cosh^2(2\lambda_I t + 2^{-1}|\lambda|^{-2}\lambda_I c_1 x)}\right), \quad x > 0,$$

$$N[1] = c_2\left(1 - \frac{2\lambda_I}{|\lambda|^2\cosh^2(2\lambda_I t + 2^{-1}|\lambda|^{-2}\lambda_I c_2 x)}\right), \quad x < 0.$$

Now let $c_1 = -1$, $c_2 = 1$, $t \to +\infty$. Then we get

$$N[1] \sim \begin{cases} -1, & x > 0 \\ 1, & x < 0 \end{cases}.$$

When $t \to -\infty$, $N[1]$ represents two solitons propagating in opposite directions. Hence in the case $c_1 = 1$, $c_2 = -1$ our solution describes the annihilation of solitons. An exact step structure for the starting solution N is chosen above only to simplify the analysis. The same qualitative behavior remains valid in the case when N represents a step function only asymptotically. It is not difficult to treat the case $g \neq \delta(\eta)$ in the same manner. We can also consider, quite similarly, the case $c_1 = 1$, $c_2 = -1$ in which the opposite effect will be observed.

The next nonlinear system discussed below is that of the Maxwell-Bloch equations:

$$r_{1\zeta} = -\omega r_2, \quad r_{2\zeta} = \omega r_1 + E r_2, \quad r_{3\zeta} = -E r_2,$$
$$E_\tau = -\langle r_{1\zeta}\rangle, \quad \langle f \rangle = \int_0^\infty f(\omega)g(\omega)d\omega. \qquad (4.4.25)$$

In (4.4.25) the r_i are linear combinations of the matrix elements of the density matrix

$$r_1 = \varrho_{21} + \varrho_{12}, \quad r_2 = i(\varrho_{21} - \varrho_{12}), \quad r_3 = \varrho_{22} - \varrho_{11}.$$

The system (4.4.25) was first introduced by *Eilbeck* [4.14] and studied in [4.13–15]. In these works multisoliton solutions and breather-like solutions were explicitly constructed. The corresponding linear system is of the form

$$\Psi_\zeta = J\Psi\Lambda + U\Psi, \quad \Psi_\tau = \langle M_1\Psi P_1 + M_2\Psi P_2\rangle,$$

$$J = \begin{pmatrix} -i & 0 \\ 0 & i \end{pmatrix}, \quad U = \frac{i}{2}\begin{pmatrix} 0 & E \\ E & 0 \end{pmatrix},$$

$$M_1 = \frac{\omega}{8}\begin{pmatrix} ir_3 & r_2+ir_1 \\ -r_2+ir_1 & -ir_3 \end{pmatrix},$$

$$M_2 = \frac{\omega}{8}\begin{pmatrix} ir_3 & r_2-ir_1 \\ -r_2-ir_1 & -ir_3 \end{pmatrix}, \quad (4.4.26)$$

$$P_1 = \begin{pmatrix} (\lambda_1-\omega/2)^{-1} & 0 \\ 0 & (\lambda_2-\omega/2)^{-1} \end{pmatrix},$$

$$P_2 = \begin{pmatrix} (\lambda_1+\omega/2)^{-1} & 0 \\ 0 & (\lambda_2+\omega/2)^{-1} \end{pmatrix}.$$

All the results of the Sect. 2.3 are surely applicable to the system (4.4.26). The structure of (4.4.26) is conserved under the action of Darboux transformation for the following choice of Λ_1, Ψ_1:

$$\Lambda_1 = \begin{pmatrix} \lambda_1 & 0 \\ 0 & -\lambda_1 \end{pmatrix}, \quad \Psi_1 = \begin{pmatrix} \psi_1 & \varphi_1 \\ \varphi_1 & \psi_1 \end{pmatrix},$$

for one step Darboux transformation an

$$\Lambda_k = \begin{pmatrix} \lambda_{2k-1} & 0 \\ 0 & \lambda_{2k} \end{pmatrix}, \quad \lambda_{2k} = -\lambda_{2k-1}, \quad \Psi_k = \begin{pmatrix} \psi_{2k-1} & \psi_{2k} \\ \varphi_{2k-1} & \varphi_{2k} \end{pmatrix}, \quad (4.4.27)$$

$$\varphi_{2k} = \psi_{2k-1}, \quad \psi_{2k} = \varphi_{2k-1}, \quad k = 1,\ldots,N.$$

for the N-step Darboux transformation.

Darboux dressing formulas for U are of the same form as above; for M_1 and M_2 we have:

$$M_1[1] = (\omega/2 - \sigma_1)M_1(\omega/2 - \sigma_1)^{-1},$$

$$M_2[1] = (\omega/2 + \sigma_1)M_2(\omega/2 + \sigma_1)^{-1},$$

$$\sigma_1 = \Psi_1\Lambda_1\Psi_1^{-1},$$

$$M_1[N] = \tilde{s}_1 M_1 \tilde{s}_1^{-1}, \quad M_2[N] = \tilde{s}_2 M_2 \tilde{s}_2^{-1},$$

$$\tilde{s}_{1,2} = \sum_{j=0}^{N}(\pm\omega/2)^{N-j} s_j, \quad (4.4.28)$$

where s_j are defined by (2.3.9), $s_0 = E$. The sums representing $\tilde{s}_{1,2}$ may be easily converted to more compact expressions [4.12]. Turning back to the inital variables $E, r_{1,2,3}$ in the first step of Darboux dressing we obtain

$$E[1] = E - 8\frac{\lambda_1\psi_1\varphi_1}{\psi_1^2 - \varphi_1^2}, \quad r_1[1] = \omega^{-1}(r_{2\zeta}[1] - E[1]r_3[1]),$$

$$r_2[1] = r_2 - \frac{8\lambda_1}{\omega}\left(\frac{\varphi_1\psi_1}{\psi_1^2-\varphi_1^2}\right)_\tau, \quad (4.4.29)$$

$$r_3[1] = r_3 + \frac{4i\lambda_1}{\omega}\left(\frac{\psi_1^2+\varphi_1^2}{\psi_1^2-\varphi_1^2}\right)_\tau.$$

The simplest solutions should be obtained if we let $r_2 = 0, r_1, r_3, E$, be some constants defined by the relation

$$\omega_1 r_1 + E r_3 = 0.$$

Then, when $\lambda_1 = iE/2$, we get

$$\psi_1 = \eta + E^{-1} \quad \varphi_1 = i(\eta - E^{-1})$$

$$\eta = \zeta - \zeta_0 + \langle \frac{\omega r_3}{E^2 + \omega^2}\rangle t,$$

and (4.4.27) should describe a rational soliton.

In the case $\lambda_1 \neq iE/2$ we get a solution depending on η

$$\eta = \zeta - \zeta_0 - \langle \frac{\omega r_3}{E^2 + \omega^2}\rangle t,$$

$$\begin{pmatrix}\psi_1 \\ \varphi_1\end{pmatrix} = C_1 \begin{pmatrix} 1 \\ 2(\nu + \lambda_1)E^{-1}\end{pmatrix} \exp(i\nu\eta)$$

$$+ C_2 \begin{pmatrix} 1 \\ 2(\lambda_1 - \nu)E^{-1}\end{pmatrix} \exp(-i\nu\eta),$$

$$\nu = \sqrt{\lambda_1^2 + E^2/4},$$

the branch of the square root may be chose arbitrarily.

In the case $\mathrm{Re}\{\nu\} = 0$ (4.4.27) produces the usual cosh-like soliton. In the case $\mathrm{Im}\{\nu\} = 0$, we obtain the simplest periodic solution

$$r_1 = f(\omega) \cos k\zeta, \quad \langle f(\omega) \rangle = 0,$$

$$r_2 = k\omega^{-1} f(\omega) \sin k\zeta, \quad r_3 = [c - f^2(1 - k^2/\omega^2) \cos(2k\zeta)/2]^{1/2}$$

$$E = -\omega f(\omega)(1 - k^2/\omega^2) \cos(k\zeta) \{c - f^2(\omega)[1 - k^2 \cos(2k\zeta)/\omega^2]/2\}^{-1/2}.$$

4.5 Generation of the Second Harmonic

An interesting example of the application of a technique quite similar to that applied above involves the nonlinear equation describing second harmonic generation [4.16]:

$$q_{1\xi} = q_2 q_1^*, \quad q_{2\eta} = -2q_1^2. \tag{4.5.1}$$

The associated linear system is of the form

$$\Psi_\xi = J\Psi\Lambda + U\Psi, \quad \Psi_\eta = V\Psi\Lambda^{-1},$$

$$U = \begin{pmatrix} 0 & q_2 \\ q_1^* & 0 \end{pmatrix}, \quad J = \begin{pmatrix} 1 & 0 \\ 0 & -1 \end{pmatrix}, \quad V = \begin{pmatrix} -|q_1|^2 & q_1^2 \\ -q_1^{*2} & |q_1|^2 \end{pmatrix}. \tag{4.5.2}$$

The method of the DT is formulated quite similarly to the previous section except for the structure of Λ_1, Ψ_1 which have to be taken in the form

$$\Lambda = \begin{pmatrix} \lambda_1 & 0 \\ 0 & -\lambda_1^* \end{pmatrix}, \quad \Psi_1 = \begin{pmatrix} \psi_1 & \varphi_1^* \\ \varphi_1 & \psi_1^* \end{pmatrix},$$

and we have

$$q_2[1] = q_2 - \frac{2i\lambda_1 \psi_1 \varphi_2^*}{|\psi_1|^2 - |\varphi_1|^2}.$$

Let us consider the application of the DT-method to the description of the solution of the system (4.5.1) which involves two functional parameters. Let

$$q_1 = \exp s, \quad q_2 = s_\xi, \quad s \in \mathbf{R}.$$

Then it turns out that s must be a solution of the Liouville equation:

$$s_{\xi\eta} = -2\exp(2s).$$

Taking the well known solution of the last equation involving two arbitrary functions $u(\xi)$, $v(\eta)$,

$$s = \frac{1}{2}\ln\frac{u'(\xi)v'(\eta)}{2(u(\xi)-v(\eta))^2}$$

we can reconstruct q_1 and q_2 by the formulas

$$q_1 = \frac{\sqrt{u'(\xi)v'(\eta)}}{\sqrt{2}(u(\xi)-v(\eta))}, \quad q_2 = \frac{u''(\xi)}{2u'(\xi)} - \frac{u'(\xi)}{u(\xi)-v(\eta)}.$$

4.6 The Nonlocal KdV Equation

The nonlocal KdV equation reads

$$u_t = -i\varepsilon H u_{xx} + 2\varepsilon \delta^{-1} u_x + 2uu_x,$$
$$H = (T+1)(T-1)^{-1}, \quad (Tf)(x) = f(x+i\delta). \tag{4.6.1}$$

It can be rewritten in the form

$$u = -\frac{\varepsilon}{\delta}\int_{-\infty}^{\infty}\left[\coth(\pi\delta^{-1}(x-\xi)) - \text{sign}(x-\xi)\right]u_{\xi\xi}d\xi + 2uu_x.$$

The nonlocal KdV equation describes internal waves in a stratified fluid of finite depth and reduces to the KdV equation in the limit $\delta \to 0$, $\varepsilon \sim 2\delta^{-1}$. When $\delta \to \infty$, $\varepsilon = 1$ (4.6.1) reduces to the Benjamin-Ono equation

$$u_t = \frac{1}{\pi} \int_{-\infty}^{\infty} \frac{u_{\xi\xi}}{x - \xi} d\xi + 2uu_x \ . \tag{4.6.2}$$

In this section we derive a broad class of solutions of (4.6.1). This class includes, in particular, multisoliton solutions similar to those constructed in [4.17–19]. These solitons are constructed by using of the appropriate version of the Darboux transformation introduced in [4.20, 21]. These works also contain a discussion on the two-dimensional version of the nonlocal KdV (NKdV) equation.

The starting point for the investigation of the NKdV equation is its representation as a consistency condition for the following system of linear equations:

$$\psi_x = i\alpha T\psi + i\varepsilon^{-1}u\psi + i\mu\psi \ , \tag{4.6.3}$$

$$\psi_t = i\varepsilon\alpha^2 T^2\psi + iv\alpha T\psi + w\psi \ , \tag{4.6.4}$$

$$v = Tu + u + 2\varepsilon\delta^{-1} \ , \quad w = Hu_x + 2i\delta^{-1}u + i\varepsilon^{-1}u^2 \ .$$

where α and μ play the role of spectral parameters. The system (4.6.3–4) is a slightly modified, by introduction of the second spectral parameter α, and corrected version of the Lax representation for (4.6.1) proposed by *Kupershmidt* [4.22].

Following [4.21], we introduce the Darboux transformation for the system [4.6.3–4] by the formulas

$$\psi[1] = \alpha T\psi - \sigma\psi \ , \quad \sigma = \alpha_1(T\psi_1)/\psi_1 \ , \tag{4.6.5}$$

$$u[1] = u - i\varepsilon(T - 1)\partial_x \ln \psi_1 = Tu + \varepsilon(T - 1)\sigma \ . \tag{4.6.6}$$

Then the following proposition holds:

Theorem. The system (4.6.3–4) is covariant with respect to the Darboux transformation (4.6.5–6).

The proof includes the following steps. First replace ψ by $\psi[1]$ and u by $u[1]$ in (4.6.3). Equating the coefficients of ψ and $T\psi$ on both sides of the resulting equation we get

$$i\alpha\varepsilon^{-1}T - i\alpha\sigma = -i\alpha T\sigma + i\varepsilon^{-1}\alpha u[1] \ ,$$

$$-\sigma_x - i\varepsilon^{-1}\sigma = -i\varepsilon^{-1}\sigma u[1] \ .$$

From this we find (4.6.6) for $u[1]$. The proof of covariance of (4.6.4) is also straightforward and we leave it to the reader.

Note that the Darboux transformation (4.6.5) may be rewritten as

$$\psi[1] = (\partial_x - i\mu)\psi - \psi_1^{-1}(\partial_x - \mu_1)\psi_1\psi \ . \tag{4.6.7}$$

In this form it looks quite similar to the classical Darboux transformation for the Sturm-Liouville equation.

In complete analogy with the considerations of Chap. 2 we can derive the formulas describing the action of the N-times repeated DT (4.6.5–6):

$$\psi[N] = W(\psi_1, \psi_2, \ldots, \psi_N, \psi)/(W(\psi_1, \ldots, \psi_N),$$
$$u[N] = u - i\varepsilon(\mathbf{T} - 1)\partial_x \ln W(\psi_1, \ldots, \psi_N), \qquad (4.6.8)$$
$$W(f_1, \ldots, f_M) = \det(\alpha_k^{j-1} \mathbf{T}^{j-1} f_k), \quad 1 \le j, k \le M.$$

In (4.6.8) $\psi_1, \ldots, \psi_N$ are the fixed solutions of the system (4.6.3–4), corresponding to the fixed values of the two-dimensional spectral parameter (μ, α): $\psi_k = \psi_k(x, t, \mu_k, \alpha_k)$. The simplest solutions are obtained when we choose starting solution $u = 0$. Substitution of the exponential

$$\psi_1 = \exp(ax + bt)$$

into (4.6.3, 4) leads to the following equations for a and b:

$$a = i\alpha \exp(i\delta a) + i\mu, \qquad (4.6.9)$$

$$b = i\varepsilon\alpha^2 \exp(2i\delta a) + 2i\alpha\varepsilon\delta^{-1} \exp(i\delta a). \qquad (4.6.10)$$

A large class of complex valued solutions may be obtained by taking for ψ_1

$$\psi_1 = \sum_k A_k \exp(a_k x + b_k t),$$

where a_k are different solutions of (4.6.9) and b_k are determined from a_k by using (4.6.10). But it is more convenient to take a_1, a_2 as fixed parameters determining the corresponding values of the spectral data α and μ

$$\alpha = \frac{i(a_1 - a_2)}{\exp(i\delta a_1) - \exp(i\delta a_2)}, \quad \mu = \frac{ia_2 \exp(i\delta a_1) - ia_1 \exp(i\delta a_2)}{\exp(i\delta a_2) - \exp(i\delta a_1)}.$$

Taking ψ_1 in the form

$$\psi_1 = \exp(a_1 x + b_1 t) + A \exp(a_2 x + b_2 t)$$

and imposing the reality condition $u[1] = u^*[1]$ we get the following solutions:

1. $a_2 - a_1 = 2p, \quad p \in \mathbf{R},$

$$u[1] = \frac{\varepsilon\delta \sin(\delta p)}{\cosh^2(p\xi) \cos^2(\delta p/2) + \sinh^2(p\xi) \sin^2(\delta p/2)}, \qquad (4.6.11)$$

$$u[1] = \frac{-\varepsilon\delta \sin(\delta p)}{\sinh^2(p\xi) \cos^2(\delta p/2) + \cosh^2(p\xi) \sin^2(\delta p/2)}, \qquad (4.6.12)$$

$$\xi = x - x_0 + Vt, \quad V = 2\varepsilon\delta^{-1} - 2\varepsilon p \cot \delta p.$$

In the limit $\delta \to 0$, $\varepsilon \sim 2\delta^{-1}$ the soliton (4.6.11) becomes the soliton solution of the KdV equation

$$u[1] \to 2p^2 \cosh^{-2}(p(x - x_0) + 4p^3 t/3).$$

The soliton (4.6.12) becomes in the same limit, a singular KdV soliton

$$u[1] \to -2p^2 \sinh^{-2}(p(x - x_0) + 4p^3 t/3) .$$

Solitons of the Benjamin-Ono equation are obtained from (4.6.12) in the limit $\delta \to \infty$, $\varepsilon = 1$ under the complementary conditions

$$\delta p = 2\pi k \left(1 + r\delta^{-1} + o(\delta^{-1})\right) \quad r = \text{const}, \quad k \in \mathbb{N}, \quad \alpha = -\mu .$$

At this limit we have

$$u[1] \to -r(\xi^2 + r^2/4)^{-1} , \quad \xi = x - x_0 - 2t/r .$$

2. $a_2 - a_1 = 2iq$, $q \in \mathbb{R}$,

$$u[1] = -\frac{2\varepsilon q \sinh(\delta q)}{\cos(2q\xi) + \cosh(\delta q)} .$$

In the KdV limit this solution goes to a singular periodic solution. In the infinite depth (Benjamin-Ono) limit this solution reduces to a constant.

It is not difficult to compute the solutions generated by the following choice of the starting solution:

$$u = -x/2t - \varepsilon/\delta .$$

The associated system (4.6.3, 4) may be easily solved by using Fourier integral. For $u[1]$ we get

$$u[1] = -x/2t - i\varepsilon(T - 1)\partial_x \ln \left(\int_{-\infty}^{\infty} \exp(i\theta) d\omega\right) ,$$

$$\theta = \omega x + \varepsilon \omega^2 t + 2\alpha \varepsilon \delta^{-1} t \exp(-\omega \delta) - 2\mu \varepsilon \omega t .$$

It is interesting to see what happens in the two limiting cases considered above in Lax representation. It is clear that the L, A-pair for (4.6.1) goes to the KdV Lax representation when $\delta \to 0$. Let us show that in the limit $\delta \to \infty$ we get the Lax representation [4.23] for the Benjamin-Ono equation. The limiting transition may be found by performing the following steps

a) put $\alpha = -\mu$, $\varepsilon = 1$;
b) using (4.6.3), replace the shift operator by differentiation by x;
c) multiply (4.6.3) by the Hilbert operator $\mathcal{H}$:

$$\mathcal{H}\psi = \frac{1}{\pi} \int_{-\infty}^{\infty} \frac{\psi(\xi)}{x - \xi} d\xi .$$

As a result we get

$$(\mathcal{H} + i)\psi_x - i(\mathcal{H} + i)u\psi = \lambda \psi , \quad \lambda = -2\mu , \tag{4.6.13}$$

$$\psi_t = -\psi_{xx} + \lambda \psi + (i\mathcal{H}u_x - u_x + i\mu^2)\psi . \tag{4.6.14}$$

From (4.6.13) it is easy to see that $\mathcal{H}\psi = i\psi$. Multiplying (4.6.13) by $(\mathcal{H}+i)$ we get

$$2i\psi_x - u\psi - \lambda\psi = \varphi, \quad \mathcal{H}\varphi = -i\varphi.$$

By virtue of (4.6.14) the time evolution of φ is given by

$$\varphi_t = -i\varphi_{xx} + \lambda\varphi_x - i[(\mathcal{H}+i)u_x]\varphi.$$

Consider now the general nonlinear equation of KdV type

$$u_t = Su_{xx} - uu_x, \qquad (4.6.15)$$

where S is some linear transformation. Equation (4.6.15) may be represented as a consistency condition of the linear system

$$\psi_t = A\psi = \left(\mu\partial_x^2 + \lambda\partial_x - (2\mu)^{-1}(Su_x) + u_x/2\right)\psi,$$
$$\varphi_t = B\varphi = \left(\mu\partial_x^2 + \lambda\partial_x - (2\mu)^{-1}(Su_x) - u_x/2\right)\varphi, \qquad (4.6.16)$$
$$\varphi = L\psi = (2\mu\partial_x + u + \lambda)\psi.$$

The operator form of (4.6.15) is

$$L_t = BL - LA, \quad [\partial_x, S] = 0. \qquad (4.6.17)$$

The representation (4.6.17) is often called the *Manakov triad*.

Theorem. The equation

$$\psi_t = \mu\psi_{xx} + \lambda\psi_x + w\psi$$

is covariant with respect to the transformation

$$\psi \to \psi[1] = D\psi - (D_1\psi_1)\psi\psi_1^{-1},$$
$$D = \partial_x + \lambda/2\mu, \quad D_1 = \partial_1 + \lambda_1/2\mu, \qquad (4.6.18)$$

$$w \to w[1] = w + 2\mu\partial_x^2 \ln\psi_1. \qquad (4.6.19)$$

Using this theorem it is easy to show that the system (4.6.16) is also covariant with respect to the Darboux transformation (4.6.18) and for the transformed coefficients we get

$$u[1] = u + 2\mu\partial_x \ln(\psi_1\varphi_1^{-1}), \qquad (4.6.20)$$

$$Su[1] = Su - 2\mu^2\partial_x \ln(\psi_1\varphi_1). \qquad (4.6.21)$$

From this we conclude that the generating functions ψ_1, φ_1 of the DT (4.6.20, 21) have to satisfy the consistency equation

$$S\left(\psi_{1x}\psi_1^{-1} - \varphi_{1x}\varphi_1^{-1}\right) = -\mu\left(\psi_{1x}\psi_1^{-1} + \varphi_{1x}\varphi_1^{-1}\right). \qquad (4.6.22)$$

For N-times repeated DT we get

$$\psi[N] = W(\psi_1, \ldots, \psi_N, \psi)/W(\psi_1, \ldots, \psi_N),$$
$$W(f_1, \ldots, f_M) = \det(D_k^{j-1} f_k), \qquad (4.6.23)$$
$$1 \leq j, \ k \leq M, \ D_k = \partial_x + \lambda_k/(2\mu),$$
$$u[N] = u + 2\mu \partial_x \ln \frac{W(\psi_1, \ldots, \psi_N)}{W(\varphi_1, \ldots, \varphi_N)},$$
$$Su[N] = Su - 2\mu \partial_x \ln\bigl(W(\psi_1, \ldots, \psi_N) W(\varphi_1, \ldots, \varphi_N)\bigr)$$

and the generating functions ψ_i, φ_i have to satisfy the relation

$$\begin{aligned}
&S\left(\frac{W_x(\psi_1, \ldots, \psi_N)}{W(\psi_1, \ldots, \psi_N)} - \frac{W_x(\varphi_1, \ldots, \varphi_N)}{W(\varphi_1, \ldots, \varphi_N)}\right) \\
&= -\mu\left(\frac{W_x(\psi_1, \ldots, \psi_N)}{W(\psi_1, \ldots, \psi_N)} + \frac{W_x(\varphi_1, \ldots, \varphi_N)}{W(\varphi_1, \ldots, \varphi_N)}\right)
\end{aligned} \qquad (4.6.24)$$

or

$$\begin{aligned}
&S\{\partial_x \ln[W(\psi_1, \ldots, \psi_N)/W(\varphi_1, \ldots, \varphi_N)]\} \\
&= -\mu \partial_x \ln[W(\psi_1, \ldots, \psi_N) W(\varphi_1, \ldots, \varphi_N)].
\end{aligned} \qquad (4.6.25)$$

Note that the consistency conditions (4.6.25) have to be satisfied only in the last step of the repeated application of the DT and it is not necessary to impose the condition (4.6.22) on each of the functions ψ_i, φ_i.

Let us consider the particular cases related to the Burgers equation and the Benjamin-Ono equation as an application of the general approach of the integration of the KdV-like equations. In the case of the Burgers equation

$$u_t = u_{xx} - u u_x, \quad Su = u. \qquad (4.6.26)$$

The consistency condition (4.6.22) takes the form

$$(1 + \mu)\frac{\psi_{1x}}{\psi_1} = (1 - \mu)\frac{\varphi_{1x}}{\varphi_1}. \qquad (4.6.27)$$

Consider the following possibilities:

A. $\mu = 1$. Then from (4.6.16, 27) it is easy to conclude that $\psi_1 = $ const and

$$\varphi_{1t} = \varphi_{1xx} + \lambda_1 \varphi_{1x} - u_x \varphi_1, \quad \varphi_1 = (u + \lambda_1)\psi_1.$$

From these expressions and from (4.6.20) we deduce that the Burgers equation is covariant with respect to the transformation

$$u \to u[1] = u - \frac{2u_x}{u + \lambda_1}.$$

B. Now let $\mu = -1$. Then $\varphi = $ const. Without loss of generality we can take $\varphi = 2$. Then we get

$$\psi_t = -\psi_{xx} + \lambda \psi_x + u_x \psi, \quad 2 = -2\psi_x + (u + \lambda)\psi.$$

When $u = 0$ we have $\psi_1 = -\kappa_1^{-1} - c_1 \exp(-\kappa_1 x + \kappa_1^2 t)$, where $\kappa = -\lambda_2/2$, $D = \partial_x - \lambda/2 = \partial_x + \kappa$. Hence

$$u[1] = -2\partial_x \ln[\kappa_1^{-1} + C_1 \exp(\theta_1)], \quad \theta_1 = -\kappa_1 x + \kappa_1^2 t. \tag{4.6.28}$$

Equation (4.6.28) represents the simplest travelling-wave solution of the Burgers equation. N-times repeated DT produces the formula

$$u[N] = -2\partial_x \ln \begin{vmatrix} \psi_1 & D_1\psi_1 & \ldots & D_1^{N-1}\psi_1 \\ \psi_2 & D_2\psi_2 & \ldots & D_2^{N-1}\psi_2 \\ \vdots & & & \\ \psi_N & D_N\psi_N & \ldots & D_N^{N-1}\psi_N \end{vmatrix},$$

$$\psi_k = -\kappa_k^{-1} - c_k \exp\theta_k, \quad \theta_k = -\kappa_k x + \kappa_k^2 t.$$

Hence

$$u[N] = -2\partial_x \ln \begin{vmatrix} \kappa_1^{-1} + c_1 \exp\theta_1, & 1, & \kappa_1, & \ldots, & \kappa_1^{N-2} \\ \kappa_2^{-1} + c_2 \exp\theta_2, & 1, & \kappa_2, & \ldots, & \kappa_2^{N-2} \\ \kappa_N^{-1} + c_N \exp\theta_N, & 1, & \kappa_N, & \ldots, & \kappa_N^{N-2} \end{vmatrix}. \tag{4.6.29}$$

Formula (4.6.29) represents the "multisoliton" solution of the Burgers equation. In the limit $N \to \infty$ (4.6.28) reduces to

$$u[\infty] = -2\partial_x \ln \int_{-\infty}^{\infty} g(\omega) \exp(-\omega^2 t - i\omega x) d\omega. \tag{4.6.30}$$

Of course (4.6.30) may be derived in a more simple manner by searching for a solution in the form

$$u = -2\partial_x \ln h$$

known as the *Hopf-Kowl* anzatz. Then the direct substitution into the Burgers equation shows that it is sufficient to take for h some solution of the heat equation

$$h_t = h_{xx}$$

in order to obtain the solution of (4.6.26) from the Hopf-Kowl anzatz.

In the case of the Benjamin-Ono equation

$$\mathbf{S}f = \mathcal{H}f = \frac{1}{\pi} \int_{-\infty}^{\infty} \frac{f(\xi)}{x - \xi} d\xi, \tag{4.6.31}$$

i.e., the $\mathbf{S}$ operator corresponds to a Hilbert transformation.

Here we restrict ourselves to the construction of the multisoliton solutions. Let $\mu = -i$, $u = 0$. Then

$$\psi_t = -i\psi_{xx} + \lambda\psi_x, \quad \varphi_t = -i\varphi_{xx} + \lambda\varphi_x, \quad \varphi = -2i\psi_x + \lambda\psi.$$

The consistency conditions for φ_1, ψ_1 are satisfied for $\lambda > 0$ because

$$\mathcal{H}\frac{1}{x-x_0+\lambda t\pm i/\lambda}=\pm\frac{i}{x-x_0+\lambda t\pm i/\lambda}=\mp\mu\frac{1}{x-x_0+\lambda t\pm i/\lambda},$$

i.e., $\mathcal{H}(\psi_{1x}/\psi_1)=-\mu\psi_{1x}/\psi_1$, $\mathcal{H}(\varphi_{1x}(\varphi_1)=\mu\varphi_{1x}/\varphi_1$. The general formula for $u[1]$ produces immediately a one-soliton solution

$$u[1]=\pm 2i\partial_x\ln\frac{x-x_0+\lambda t\mp i/\lambda}{x-x_0+\lambda t\pm i/\lambda},\quad(\lambda>0)$$

or

$$u[1]=-4\left(\lambda(x-x_0+\lambda t)^2+\lambda^{-1}\right)^{-1}.$$

Multisoliton solutions follow directly from (4.6.24) under the choice $\mu=-i$.

$$\psi_k=x-x_0+\lambda_k t+i/\lambda_k+\beta_k,$$
$$\varphi_k=\lambda_k(x-x_0+\lambda_k t-i/\lambda_k+\beta_k).$$

The consistency conditions (4.6.25) lead to the restrictions

$$\beta_k=-\Delta'_k/\Delta,\quad\Delta=\det A,\quad A_{kj}=(i\lambda_k/2)^{j-1},\quad\Delta'_k=\frac{\partial}{\partial(i\lambda_k/2)}\Delta.$$

This may be checked by direct calculation.

Note that in the case of the Benjamin-Ono equation the main problem – how to satisfy the condition (4.6.22) – is solved in a rather elementary way: we have to find ψ_1 and φ_1 with the property that their logarithmic derivatives are analytic in the corresponding half-planes.

In the case of a general equation of the form (4.6.15) the problem of finding the Darboux-dressing may be reduced to finding the solutions ψ_1,φ_1 of (4.6.16) having the property that their logarithmic derivatives are the eigenfunctions of the operator S. The general solution of this problem is still unknown.

4.7 The Kaup Equation

Kaup [4.24] was the first to consider the following equation

$$\partial_{x_j}p_j=p_i^*p_k^*,\quad(4.7.1)$$

where i,j,k run over all cyclic permutations of the numbers $1,2,3$. Actually (4.7.1) represents the unique known example of the solvable three-dimensional system in which all independent variables enter in the same way. In this section we show how to construct the multisoliton solutions of (4.7.1) by the method of Darboux transformations. Here from the beginning, we need to use a binary DT.

Consider two linear systems:

$$\partial_i\psi_k=p_j\psi_i,$$
$$\partial_i\psi_j=q_k\psi_i,\quad(4.7.2)$$

$$\partial_i \varphi_k = q_j \varphi_i ,$$
$$\partial_i \varphi_j = p_k \varphi_i , \qquad (4.7.3)$$
$$\partial_i = \partial_{x_i} .$$

The consistency conditions of the system (4.6.2–3) are the nonlinear equations

$$\partial_j p_j = q_i q_k , \quad \partial_i q_i = p_k p_j . \qquad (4.7.4)$$

Equations (4.7.4) reduce to (4.7.1) under the complementary restriction $q_k = p_k^*$.
Darboux transformations for the system (4.7.2) are defined as

$$\psi_k[1] = \psi_k - \psi_k^{(1)} \Omega(\psi, \varphi^{(1)}) / \Omega(\psi^{(1)}, \varphi^{(1)}) ,$$
$$\Omega(f,g) = \int_{M_0}^{M} \sum_{n=1}^{3} f_n g_n dx_n , \qquad (4.7.5)$$

$$p_j[1] = p_j - \psi_k^{(1)} \varphi_i^{(1)} / \Omega(\psi^{(1)}, \varphi^{(1)}) , \qquad (4.7.6)$$

where $\psi^{(1)}, \varphi^{(1)}$ are the fixed families of the solutions of (4.7.2, 3). The reduction to (4.7.1) may be obtained by the choice $\varphi = \psi^*$.

Note that (4.7.6) may be rewritten in the form

$$p_j[1] = p_j - D_j \Omega(\psi^{(1)}, \varphi^{(1)}) , \qquad (4.7.7)$$

where D_j is determined by the formula

$$D_j \int_{M_0}^{M} \sum_{n=1}^{3} \psi_n^{(1)} \varphi_n^{(1)} dx_n = \psi_k^{(1)} \varphi_i^{(1)} . \qquad (4.7.8)$$

where j, k, i is a cyclic permutation of $1, 2, 3$.

The iterations of Darboux transformation may be easily expressed in terms of the starting solutions

$$p_j[N] = p_j - D_j \ln \det \left(\Omega(\psi^{(l)}, \varphi^{(m)}) \right) , \quad 1 \leq l, m \leq N ,$$
$$D_j \ln f = f^{-1} D_j f .$$

In the case of $\varphi_k^{(m)} = (\psi_k^{(m)})^*$ we obtain the solutions of the reduced equation. The simplest solutions are obtained under the choice $p = 0$, $q = 0$. Then

$$\partial_i \psi_k = 0 , \quad \partial_i \psi_j = 0 ,$$

and hence $\psi_i = \psi_i(x_i)$ are arbitrary functions depending on one variable. For $p_j[1]$ we get

$$p_j[1] = \frac{\psi_k(x_k)\psi_i^*(x_i)}{\sum_{n=1}^{3} \int_{x_{n_0}}^{x_n} |\psi_n|^2 dx_n} .$$

Further study of the obtained solutions is left to the reader.

5. Nonlinear Lattice Equations and Related Systems

5.1 Darboux Transformations and the Two-Dimensional Toda Lattice

In 1915 Darboux [5.1] introduced the nonlinear differential-difference equation

$$h_{n+1} + h_{n-1} = 2h_n - \partial_\zeta \partial_t \ln h_n, \quad n = 0, \pm 1, \ldots \qquad (5.1.1)$$

By introducing a new variable x_n related to h_n by

$$h_n = \exp(x_{n-1} - x_n),$$

we can represent (5.1.1) in the form

$$x_{n\zeta t} = \exp(x_n - x_{n+1}) - \exp(x_{n-1} - x_n). \qquad (5.1.2)$$

When we additionally assume $x_n = x_n(\pm\zeta + t)$, (5.1.2) reduces to a system of coupled ordinary differential equations

$$\pm x_{ntt} = \exp(x_n - x_{n+1}) - \exp(x_{n-1} - x_n). \qquad (5.1.3)$$

Equation (5.1.3) is usually referred to as the Toda lattice equation. Its soliton-like solutions were first found by *Toda* [5.2]. The integrability of (5.1.3) by the IST method was discovered independently by *Manakov* [5.3] and *Flaschka* [5.4] in 1974. The integrability of (5.1.2) was established by *Mikhailov* [5.5] only as late as 1979. The Darboux transformation which is valid for both equations (5.1.2,3) and their higher versions, as well as for some nonabelian generalizations, were proposed in [5.6] and applied to several examples in [5.7–12]. A binary version of the lattice Darboux transformation dealing with the associated linear system and its conjugate version was simultaneously introduced in [5.12].

Note that (5.1.2) is closely related to the sine-Gordon and the sinh-Gordon equations. This fact was mentioned already by *Darboux* [5.1] who stated the problem of solving (5.1.1) under the condition

$$h_{n+2} = h_n$$

i.e., for the case when (5.1.1) reduces to the *sinh*-Gordon equation

$$s_{\zeta t} = 4 \sinh s, \quad h_n = \exp s, \quad h_{n+1} = \exp(-s). \qquad (5.1.4)$$

Pure imaginary solutions of $s = iu$ of (5.1.4) generate real solutions of the sine-Gordon equation

$$u_{\zeta t} = 4\sin u .\qquad(5.1.5)$$

Equation (5.1.5) is one of the most famous and most important completely integrable nonlinear evolution equations (NEE) of mathematical physics. Its applications in nonlinear optics [5.13, 14], theory of Josephson junctions [5.15], various models of statistical mechanics on lattices [5.16], and differential geometry [5.17, 18] are being actively pursued by numerous researchers. The sine-Gordon equation will be discussed more thouroughly below in Sect. 5.3.

To solve (5.1.2) we introduce new dependent variables

$$v_n = x_{nt} , \quad u_n = \exp(x_n - x_{n+1}) .$$

Now the system (5.1.2) may be rewritten as

$$\begin{aligned} v_{n\zeta} &= u_n - u_{n-1} , \\ u_{nt} &= u_n(v_n - v_{n+1}) . \end{aligned}\qquad(5.1.6)$$

The possibility to apply the DT method to (5.1.6) requires representation in a form of the consistency condition

$$\psi^+_{nt\zeta} = \psi^+_{n\zeta t} ,$$

of the linear system

$$\begin{aligned} \psi^+_{nt} &= v_n \psi^+_n + \psi^+_{n-1} , \\ \psi^+_{n\zeta} &= u_n \psi^+_{n+1} . \end{aligned}\qquad(5.1.7)$$

In complete analogy to the KP case it is reasonable to explore together with (5.1.7) the conjugate system

$$\begin{aligned} -\psi^-_{nt} &= v_n \psi^-_n + \psi^-_{n+1} , \\ -\psi^-_{n\zeta} &= u_{n-1} \psi^-_{n-1} . \end{aligned}\qquad(5.1.8)$$

The consistency condition of (5.1.8)

$$\psi^-_{n\zeta t} = \psi^-_{nt\zeta}$$

is also equivalent to (5.1.6). Both systems (5.1.7, 8) are covariant with respect to the following Darboux transformation already discussed in Sect. 2.6 :

$$\begin{aligned} \psi^+_n &\to \psi^+_n[+1] = \psi^+_n - \frac{\psi^+_{n,1}}{\psi^+_{n+1,1}} \psi_{n+1} , \\ u_n &\to u_n[+1] = u_{n+1} \psi^+_{n,1} \psi^+_{n+2,1} (\psi^+_{n+1,1})^{-2} , \\ v_n &\to v_n[+1] = v_{n+1} + \partial_t \ln(\psi^+_{n,1}/\psi^+_{n+1,1}) , \\ x_n &\to x_n[+1] = x_{n+1} + \ln(\psi^+_{n,1}/\psi^+_{n+1,1}) . \end{aligned}\qquad(5.1.9)$$

$$\psi_n^- \to \psi_n^-[-1] = \psi_n^- - \frac{\psi_{n,1}^-}{\psi_{n-1,1}^-}\psi_{n-1}^-,$$

$$u_n \to u_n[-1] = u_{n-1}\psi_{n+1,1}^-\psi_{n-1,1}^-(\psi_{n,1}^-)^{-2}, \quad (5.1.10)$$

$$v_n \to v_n[-1] = v_{n-1} + \partial_t \ln(\psi_{n-1,1}^-/\psi_{n,1}^-),$$

$$x_n \to x_n[-1] = x_{n-1} + \ln(\psi_{n-1,1}^-/\psi_{n,1}^-).$$

Here $\psi_{n,1}^+$ and $\psi_{n,1}^-$ denote some fixed solutions for the starting systems (5.1.7,8) respectively.

In complete analogy with the continuous case we can apply the Darboux transformation many times. The result of the action of N-times repeated application of the lattice DT is given by

$$u_n[+N] = u_{n+N}\frac{W_n^+(N)W_{n+2}^+(N)}{(W_{n+1}^+(N))^2},$$

$$v_n[+N] = v_{n+N} + \partial_t \ln[W_n^+(N)/W_{n+1}^+(N)], \quad (5.1.11)$$

$$x_n[N] = x_{n+N} + \ln[W_n(N)/W_{n+1}(N)],$$

$$W_n^+(N) = \det(\psi_{n+j-1,k}^+), \quad 1 \le j, \quad k \le N.$$

Similar expressions may also be obtained for the system (5.1.8). In particular,

$$x_n[-N] = x_{n-N} + \ln[W_{n-1}^-(N)/W_n^-(N)], \quad (5.1.12)$$

$$W_n^- = \det(\psi_{n-j+1,k}^-), \quad 1 \le j, \quad k \le N.$$

As in the KP case, we can introduce the binary version of the lattice Darboux transformation. In particular, the formulas

$$\psi_n^-[+1] = (\psi_{n,1}^+)^{-1}\{c_1 + b_2\Omega_n(\psi_{k,1}^+, \psi_k^-)\},$$

$$\Omega_n(f_k^+, g_k^-) = \int_{(\zeta_0,t_0)}^{(\zeta,t)} \omega_n + \sum_{k=m}^n f_k^+(\zeta_0, t_0)g_k^-(\zeta_0, t_0),$$

$$\omega_n = u_n f_{n+1}^+ g_n^- d\zeta - f_n^+ g_{n+1}^- dt, \quad (5.1.13)$$

$$\sum_{k=m}^n b_k = \begin{cases} b_m + b_{m+1} + \ldots + b_n, & n > m \\ -(b_n + b_{n+1} + \ldots + b_m), & n < m, \end{cases}$$

describe the solutions of the system

$$-\psi_{nt} = v_n[+1]\psi_n + \psi_{n+1}, \quad (5.1.14)$$

$$-\psi_{n\zeta} = u_{n-1}[+1]\psi_{n-1}$$

i.e., the solutions of (−) system with the coefficients obtained by the one-step Darboux dressing of the (+) system (5.1.7).

Note that the 1-form ω_n is closed for the solutions f_n^+, g_n^- of the systems (5.1.7,8) and hence the integral in (5.1.13) is path independent.

The bilinear expression Ω_n may also be represented in the form

$$\Omega_n = \int_{(\zeta_0,t_0)}^{(\zeta,t)} \omega_m + \sum_{k=m}^{n} f_k^+(\zeta,t) g_k^-(\zeta,t) . \tag{5.1.15}$$

When the solutions f_m^+, g_m^- are rapidly decreasing when $t \to -\infty$, Ω_n may also be represented as a convergent series,

$$\Omega_n = \sum_{k=-\infty}^{n} f_k^+ g_k^- - \sum_{k=-\infty}^{m-1} f_k^+(\zeta_0,t_0) g^-(\zeta_0,t_0) . \tag{5.1.16}$$

Performing the Darboux transformation (5.1.11) with the generating function $\psi_{n,1}^+$ we can also proceed differently. One way is to perform the next Darboux transformation of the obtained (+) system with the generating function $\psi_{n,2}^+[+1]$. This leads to a new solution $x_n[+2]$ of [5.1.2]. Another way is to take $\psi_{n,2}^-[+1]$ as a generating function for the Darboux transformation applied to a conjugate system. This leads to the following solution $x_n[+1,-1]$ of (5.1.2):

$$x_n[+1,-1] = x_n + \ln \frac{c_1 + b_1 \Omega_{n-1}(\psi_{k,1}^+ \psi_{k,2}^-)}{c_1 + b_1 \Omega_n(\psi_{k,1}^+ \psi_{k,2}^-)} .$$

Here, $u_n[+1,-1]$ and $v_n[+1,-1]$ are constructed quite similarly. All the possibilities of the multiple application of the Darboux transformation to the (+) system or the (−) system are represented by the diagram

$$x_n$$

$$x_n[+1] \qquad x_n[-1]$$

$$x_n[+2] \qquad x_n[+1,-1] \qquad x_n[-2]$$

$$x_n[+3] \qquad x_n[+2,-1] \qquad x_n[+1,-2] \qquad x_n[-3]$$

For $N \geq M$ we have

$$x_n[+N, -M] = x_{N+n-M} + \ln(\Delta_{n-1}/\Delta_n) , \tag{5.1.17}$$

$$\Delta = \begin{vmatrix} P_n(1, N+1) & P_n(2, N+1) & \dots & P_n(N, N+1) \\ P_n(1, N+2) & P_n(2, N+2) & \dots & P_n(N, N+2) \\ \vdots & & & \vdots \\ P_n(1, N+M) & P_n(2, N+M) & \dots & P_n(N, N+M) \\ \psi_{n,M+1}^+ & \dots\dots & & \psi_{n+N-1,M+1}^+ \\ \vdots & & & \vdots \\ \psi_{n,N-1}^+ & \dots\dots & & \psi_{n+N-1,M+1}^+ \end{vmatrix} ,$$

$$P_n(j,s) = c_{js} + b_{js} \Omega_n(\psi_{k,j}^+, \psi_{k,s}^-) .$$

Let us consider some particular solutions of (5.1.2, 6). Let

$$x_n = 0, \quad v_n = 0, \quad u_n = 1.$$

Then the solutions $\psi_n^{\pm}$ of (5.1.7, 8) may be constructed explicitly:

$$\psi_n^{\pm} = \int_{\Omega} A^{\pm}(\omega_R, \omega_I) \exp\{n \ln \omega \pm \omega \zeta \pm \omega^{-1} t\} d\sigma(\omega_R, \omega_I), \quad (5.1.18)$$

$$\omega = \omega_R + i\omega_I, \quad \text{Im}\{\omega_{R,I}\} = 0,$$

and σ is some measure on the Ω-plane. Substituting solutions (5.1.18) with different densities $A_j^{\pm}(\omega_1, \omega_2)$ into (5.1.11, 12, 17), we obtain a large class of solutions of the two-dimensional Toda-Darboux lattice equation depending on the functional parameters.

As in the KP case, [compare with (3.3.11)], the simplest soliton-wall solution is obtained when A is a linear combination of two δ-functions in (5.1.18). From this we get

$$\psi_n^{+} = b_1 \omega_1^n \exp(\omega_1 \zeta + \omega_1 t) + b_2 \omega_2^n \exp(\omega_2 \zeta + \omega_1 t).$$

Now, from (5.1.9) we obtain

$$x_n[+1] = \ln \frac{b_1 \omega_1^n \exp \theta_1 + b_2 \omega_2^n \exp \theta_2}{b_1 \omega_1^{n+1} \exp \theta_1 + b_2 \omega_2^{n+1} \exp \theta_2}, \quad (5.1.19)$$

$$\theta_{1,2} = \omega_{1,2} \zeta + \omega_{1,2}^{-1} t,$$

The solution describing a bound state of a finite number of solitons is produced by the following choice of ψ_n^{+}:

$$\psi_n^{+} = \sum_k A_k \exp \theta_k, \quad \theta_k = n \ln \omega_k + \omega_k \zeta + \omega_k^{-1} t. \quad (5.1.20)$$

It is easy to show that $x_n[+1]$, generated by (5.1.20), depends only on $n - v_1 t$, $\zeta - v_2 t$, *under the condition that* ω_k *satisfy the functional equation*

$$v_1 \ln \omega_k + v_2 \omega_k + \omega_k^{-1} = C, \quad (5.1.21)$$

where C is an arbitrary constant.

The solution similar to (3.3.15) for a 2D Toda lattice is given by the formula

$$x_n[+N] = \ln(W_n/W_{n+1}),$$

$$W_n = \int_{\Omega_1} \int_{\Omega_2} \cdots \int_{\Omega_N} \prod_{k=1}^N A_k(\omega_k) \omega_k^n \prod_{k<j} (\omega_k - \omega_j) \exp \theta \, d\sigma_1 \ldots d\sigma_N, \quad (5.1.22)$$

$$\theta = \zeta \sum_{k=1}^N \omega_k + t \sum_{k=1}^N \omega_k^{-1}.$$

A subset of nonsingular real solutions may be isolated from (5.1.22) in complete analogy with the KP-case. The special case of the solution $x_n[+N]$ in which it depends only on $n - v_1 t$, $\zeta - v_2 t$ may be extracted from (5.1.22) under the choice

$$\psi_{n,j} = \sum_k A_{k,j} \exp \theta_{k,j}, \quad \theta_{k,j} = n \ln \omega_{k,j} + \zeta \omega_{k,j} + \omega_{k,j}^{-1} t.$$

Then W_n becomes

$$W_n = \sum_{k_1,\ldots,k_N} c_{k_1 k_2 \ldots k_N} \exp(\theta_{k_1,1} + \ldots + \theta_{k_1,N}),$$

where $c_{k_1 k_2 \ldots k_N}$ are some constant coefficients. It is clear that under the condition

$$v_1 \sum_{j=1}^N \ln \omega_{k,j} + v_2 \sum_{j=1}^N \omega_{k,j} + \sum_{j=1}^N \omega_{k,j} = C,$$

the solution $x_n[+N]$ described above generalizes (5.1.20, 21) and also represents some bounded cluster involving a finite number of the simplest solitons.

Under the condition

$$\psi_{n+m} = \lambda \psi_n,$$

imposed on the solutions of the auxiliary linear systems, m-periodic solutions should be obtained. These conditions surely would be satisfied if we put in (5.1.18)

$$A_k(\omega_k) = \sum_{j=1}^m A_{kj} \delta(\omega_k - \varepsilon_j \exp[2\pi i j/m]), \quad \varepsilon_j^m = \lambda.$$

Rational solutions of (5.1.2) are generated by the choice of a zero background solution taking for ψ_n^+

$$\psi_n^+ = \sum_k b_k \partial_\omega^k [\omega^n \exp(\omega \zeta + \omega^{-1} t)],$$

which is equivalent to taking in (5.1.18) some linear combination of the δ-functions and their derivatives for $A(\omega_1, \omega_2)$.

Reduction of the previous results to a one-dimensional Toda lattice equation may be obtained by imposing on the obtained solutions the complementary restriction: $x_n(\zeta, t) = x_n(t \pm \zeta)$. The 1D Toda equation may also be treated independently. In particular, the system

$$x_{ntt} = \exp(x_{n-1} - x_n) - \exp(x_n - x_{n+1}) \tag{5.1.23}$$

after the change of variables

$$v_n = x_{nt}, \quad u_n = \exp(x_n - x_{n+1}),$$

(5.1.23) goes to a system

$$v_{nt} = u_{n-1} - u_n, \quad u_{nt} = u_n(v_n - v_{n+1}), \tag{5.1.24}$$

which is equivalent to the consistency condition of the linear system

$$\psi_{nt} = v_n \psi_n + \psi_{n-1} , \tag{5.1.25}$$
$$v_n \psi_n + u_n \psi_{n+1} + \psi_{n-1} = \lambda \psi_n .$$

The multiple Darboux transformation of this system is described by

$$\psi_n[N] = W_n(\psi_{k,1}, \ldots, \psi_{k,N}, \psi_k)/W_{n-1}(\psi_{k,1}, \ldots, \psi_{k,N}) ,$$
$$v_n[N] = v_{n-N} + \partial_t \ln \frac{W_n(\psi_{k,1}, \ldots, \psi_{k,N})}{W_{n-1}(\psi_{k1}, \ldots, \psi_{kN})} , \quad \psi_{k,j} \equiv \psi_{kj} , \tag{5.1.26}$$
$$u_n[N] = u_{n+N} - \frac{W_n(\psi_{k1}, \ldots, \psi_{kN})W_{n+2}(\psi_{k1}, \ldots, \psi_{kN})}{W_{n+1}^2(\psi_{k1}, \ldots, \psi_{kN})} ,$$
$$W_n(\psi_1, \ldots \psi_N) = \det(\psi_{n+1-j, N+1-k}) , \quad 1 \le j , k \le N .$$

We omit here the formulas for the binary Darboux transformation for the reason that they may be obtained by a simple reduction of the corresponding expression for the 2D Toda lattice.

Soliton solutions for a one-dimensional Toda lattice are obtained with the trivial starting solution $x_n = 0$ in (5.1.26) as well as multisoliton solutions. Another interesting family of solutions would be obtained if we put $x_n = cnt$ for the starting solution. The corresponding solutions of the linear problem may be expressed in terms of the Bessel functions. In particular, in the case $c = 2$, we find

$$\psi_n = \{a(-1)^n J_{n-\lambda/2}[\exp(-t)] + b J_{\lambda/2-n}[\exp(-t)]\}$$
$$\times \exp[(n + \lambda/2)t] ,$$

where J_ν is the Bessel function, $\lambda \ne 2k$, $k \in \mathbb{N}$. In the case $\lambda = 2k$,

$$\psi_n = (a J_{n-k}(\exp(-t)) + b Y_{n-k}(\exp(-t))(-1)^n) \exp[(n + k)t] ,$$

where Y_ν is the Neumann function [5.19]. The associated solution is a smooth function for sufficiently large and positive values of t. For $t \to -\infty$ it behaves like $\ln|\tan \exp|t||$, i.e., for large negative t singularities occur. The solution itself may be expressed in terms of the elementary functions

$$x_n = 2(n+1)t + \ln(B_n/B_{n+1}) ,$$

$$B_n = \sum_{m=0}^{n} \frac{(n+m)! \exp(mt)}{m!(n-m)! 2^m} \cos(e^t + \beta + 2^{-1}\pi(n+m)) ,$$

$$\beta = \text{const} .$$

A discussion of the spectral interpretation of the resulting class of the solutions $x_n[N]$ may be found in [5.11].

Of course we can also construct a class of growing solutions of the 2D Toda lattice equation [5.8] by taking

$$u_n = f(t) , \quad v_n = -n f_t(t)/f(t)$$

as initial solutions of the system (5.1.6). Then for the solutions of the associated linear system (5.1.7) we get

$$\psi_n^+ = \int_\Omega A(\omega)\omega^n f^{-n} \exp(\omega^{-1} \int f(t)dt + \zeta\omega)d\omega .$$

The following system of ordinary differential equations arising quite naturally in plasma physics [5.3], and ecology [5.20] is closely related to the Toda lattice equation:

$$a_{nt} = a_n(a_{n-1} - a_{n+1}) . \tag{5.1.27}$$

This is often referred to as the discrete KdV equation or Volterra system [5.20]. Equation (5.1.27) may be considerd as a consistency condition of the linear system

$$a_n\psi_{n+1} + \psi_{n-1} = \lambda\psi_n , \quad -a_n a_{n+1}\psi_{n+2} = \psi_{nt} . \tag{5.1.28}$$

System (5.1.28) is covariant with respect to the Darboux transformation:

$$\psi_n \to \psi_n[1] = \lambda_1 \frac{\psi_{n-1,1}}{\psi_{n,1}}\psi_n - \lambda\psi_{n-1} ,$$
$$a_n \to a_n[1] = \frac{\psi_{n-2,1}\psi_{n+1,1}}{\psi_{n-1,1}\psi_{n,1}} a_n . \tag{5.1.29}$$

For an N-times repeated Darboux transformation we get

$$\psi_n[N] = W_n(\psi_1,\ldots,\psi_N,\psi)/W_n(\psi_1,\ldots,\psi_N) ,$$
$$a_n[N] = a_n \frac{W_{n-2}(\psi_1,\ldots,\psi_N)W_{n+1}(\psi_1,\ldots,\psi_N)}{W_{n-1}(\psi_1,\ldots,\psi_N)W_n(\psi_1,\ldots,\psi_N)} , \tag{5.1.30}$$
$$W_n(\psi_1,\ldots,\psi_N) = \det(\psi_{n-2j+2,k}) , \quad 1 \leq j,k \leq N .$$

Taking $a_n = a = $ const for the starting solution of (5.1.27) we get

$$\psi_n = Az_1^n \exp(-a^2 z_1^2 t) + Bz_2^n \exp(-a^2 z_2^2 t) ,$$
$$az_{1,2} + (z_{1,2})^{-1} = \lambda , \tag{5.1.31}$$

for the solutions of (5.1.28). The initial solution

$$a_n = n/2t$$

also allows one to solve (5.1.28) explicitly:

$$\psi_n = \frac{\sqrt{t}}{2\pi i} \oint_{|z|=1} z^{-n} \exp(-(z-\lambda)^n) dz . \tag{5.1.32}$$

Substituting these solutions into (5.1.30) we obtain multisoliton solutions of (5.1.27) and multisoliton solutions on the increasing background.

Additional applications of the technique described above arise in the theory of periodic (with respect to a discrete variable n), or almost periodic solutions, expressed in terms of multidimensional theta functions of compact Riemann surfaces, of the 1D and 2D Toda lattice equations [5.21–23]. For these solutions the associated linear systems also may be solved explicitly in terms of multidimensional theta functions. However, we will not discuss these possibilities here.

5.2 The Lattice Burgers Equation

Here we consider a nonlinear system which represents a lattice version of the Burgers equation discussed in Sect. 4.5

$$r_{nt} = r_n(r_{n+1} - r_n), \quad n = 0, \pm 1, \ldots . \tag{5.2.1}$$

This equation also arises in some ecological problems describing the evolution of an infinite number of competing species [5.20]. It should be noted that as in the continuous case, the Cauchy problem for (5.2.1) may be solved explicitly [5.8]. The structure of this solution relates the rapidly decreasing, when $n \to \pm\infty$, initial data to the solutions meromorphic in time. The finite in n initial data generate the solutions which are rational functions of t. From the general formulas it is easy to also isolate the periodic solutions and the solutions corresponding to increasing initial data: $r_n(0) = n/a$.

Let

$$\varphi_n = \frac{1}{2\pi i} \oint_{|\omega|=1} A(\omega) \omega^{-n-1} \exp(-t/\omega) d\omega, \tag{5.2.2}$$

then we have

$$A(\omega) \exp(-t/\omega) = \sum_{n=-\infty}^{\infty} \omega^n \varphi_n(t),$$

$$\varphi_n(0) = \frac{1}{2\pi i} \oint_{|\omega|=1} A(\omega) \omega^{-n-1} d\omega, \tag{5.2.3}$$

$$\varphi_n(t) = \sum_{k=0}^{\infty} \varphi_{n+k}(0) \frac{(-t)^k}{k!} .$$

Now it is easy to check that the formula

$$r_n = -\varphi_n \varphi_{n-1}^{-1}, \tag{5.2.4}$$

defines the solution of (5.2.1). From (5.2.4) we find

$$r_n(t) = \frac{\sum_{k=1}^{\infty} \frac{t^{k-1}}{(k-1)!} \prod_{j=0}^{k-1} r_{n+j}(0)}{1 + \sum_{k=1}^{\infty} \frac{t^k}{k!} \prod_{j=0}^{k-1} r_{n+j}(0)}. \qquad (5.2.5)$$

From (5.2.5) it is easy to see that if $r_n(0) = 0$ for some value of n, then the series in (5.2.5) transforms to a finite sum and $r_n(t) \to 0$ when $t \to \infty$.

It is not difficult to isolate the periodic solutions of (5.2.1) from (5.2.5) which satisfy the condition $r_n(t) = r_{n+N}(t)$. Let

$$z = \prod_{j=1}^{n} r_j(0), \quad r_{n+N}(0) = r_n(0), \quad n = 1, 2, \ldots, N,$$

$$S_m(t, z, N) = N^{-1} z^{(1-m)/N} \sum_{k=0}^{N-1} \exp\left[tz^{1/N} \exp(2\pi i k/N) - \frac{2\pi i k(m-1)}{N}\right].$$

Then the periodic solution $r_n(t)$ is given by the formula

$$r_n(t) = \frac{zS_N + \sum_{m=2}^{N} S_{m-1} \prod_{j=0}^{m-2} r_{n+j}(0)}{S_1 + \sum_{m=2}^{N} S_m \prod_{j=0}^{m-2} r_{n+j}(0)}. \qquad (5.2.6)$$

Note that when $t \to \infty$,

$$r_n(t) \to \left(\prod_{j=1}^{N} r_j(0)\right)^{1/2}.$$

One more interesting solution of (5.2.1) having the form of a simple wave is

$$r_n(t) = \kappa v (\sinh \kappa)^{-1} \cosh \kappa(n - vt - \beta) / \cosh \kappa(n - 1 - vt - \beta).$$

Taking, in the last formula, κ to be pure imaginary we obtain a singular solution which depends periodically on n and t.

5.3 Nonabelian Toda Lattice

The nonabelian Toda chain was introduced by *Polyakov* [5.24]. Later it was studied by *Mikhailov* [5.5] and in a periodic case by *Krichever* [5.23]. Our exposition follows [5.9]. The nonabelian generalization of the Toda lattice equation reads

$$(g_{nt} g_n^{-1})_\zeta + g_{n+1} g_n^{-1} - g_n g_{n-1}^{-1} = 0. \qquad (5.3.1)$$

Here g is an $M \times M$ invertible matrix function. We introduce new matrices

$$v_n = g_{nt} g_n^{-1}, \quad u_n = -g_n g_{n-1}^{-1}.$$

In this notation (5.3.1) may be rewritten in the form

$$v_{n\zeta} = u_{n+1} - u_n,$$
$$u_{nt} = v_n u_n - u_n v_{n-1}. \tag{5.3.2}$$

Equations (5.3.2) may be represented as the consistency condition for the linear system

$$\psi_{n\zeta} = u_n \psi_{n-1},$$
$$\psi_{nt} = v_n \psi_n - \psi_{n+1}. \tag{5.3.3}$$

The Darboux transformation for (5.3.3) is a combined version of the lattice DT and of the DT for the *Zakharov-Shabat* system used in Chap. 4:

$$\psi_n[1] = \psi_n - \psi_{n,1}\psi_{n-1,1}^{-1}\psi_{n-1},$$
$$u_n[1] = \psi_{n,1}\psi_{n-1,1}^{-1}u_{n-1}\psi_{n-2,1}\psi_{n-1,1}^{-1} = u_n - (\psi_{n,1}\psi_{n-1,1}^{-1})_\zeta,$$
$$v_n[1] = v_n + \psi_{n,1}\psi_{n-1,1}^{-1} - \psi_{n+1,1}\psi_{n,1}^{-1},$$
$$g_n[1] = \psi_{n,1}\psi_{n-1,1}g_{n-1}. \tag{5.3.4}$$

The expressions for the N-times repeated Darboux transformation take the form

$$\psi_n[N] = \psi_n - \sigma_{n1}\psi - \ldots - \sigma_{nN}\psi_{n-N}, \tag{5.3.5}$$

where σ_{nk} are defined by the system of linear algebraic equations

$$\sigma_{n1}\psi_{n-1,j} + \ldots + \sigma_{nN}\psi_{n-N,j} = \psi_{nj}, \quad j = 1, 2, \ldots, N, \tag{5.3.6}$$

where $\psi_{k,j}$ are the fixed $M \times M$ matrix solutions of (5.2.3),

$$u_n[N] = u_n - (\sigma_{n1})_\zeta,$$
$$v_n[N] = v_n + \sigma_{n1} - \sigma_{n+1,1}, \tag{5.3.7}$$
$$g_n]N] = \sigma_{n1}g_{n-1}.$$

For the simplest starting solutions $g_n = I$, $v_n = 0$, $u_n = -I$, (5.3.3) reduces to the system

$$\psi_{n\zeta} = -\psi_{n-1}, \quad \psi_{nt} = -\psi_{n+1},$$

which may be easily solved:

$$\psi_n = \int_\Omega \{A_n(M)\exp(\theta) + \exp(\theta)B_n(M)\}d\sigma(\omega),$$

where $A_n(M)$ and $B_n(M)$ are the matrix valued functions and

$$A_n = (-1)^n A\omega^n, \quad B_n = (-1)^n \omega^n B.$$

From this we can obtain soliton and multisoliton solutions of the nonabelian Toda lattice equation in the usual way. The natural nonabelian version of the lattice KdV equation

$$a_{nt} = a_{n-1}a_n - a_n a_{n+1}, \tag{5.3.8}$$

for $m \times m$ matrix functions a_n is also generated by the consistency condition of the linear system

$$a_n \psi_{n+1} + \psi_{n-1} = \psi_n \Lambda,$$
$$\psi_{nt} = -a_n a_{n+1} \psi_{n+2},$$

where ψ is an $m \times m$ matrix solution of (5.3.9) and Λ is a matrix spectral parameter. The related Darboux transformation is given by

$$\psi_n[1] = \psi_{n-2} - \sigma_n \psi_n, \quad \sigma_n = \psi_{n-2,1} \psi_{n,1}^{-1}, \quad a_n[1] = \sigma_n a_n \sigma_{n-1}^{-1}.$$

The expressions describing the result of the action of N-times repeated DT are quite similar to the Toda lattice case and will not be discussed. Taking $a_n = a$ as the starting solution of (5.3.8), where a is a constant matrix, we find

$$\psi_n = \sum_k \exp(-a^2 \omega_k^2 t) \omega_k^n A_k,$$

and ω_k are the matrix roots of the equation

$$\omega^2 a - \omega \Lambda + I = 0,$$

which commutes with a, i.e.,

$$[\omega_k, a] = 0.$$

5.4 Multisoliton Solutions of the Sine-Gordon Equation

The sine-Gordon equation

$$s_{xt} = 4 \sin s \tag{5.4.1}$$

first appeared in 19th century in the study of surfaces of constant mean curvature [5.17]. Its multisoliton solutions were constructed in 1953 by *Seeger* et al. [5.25]. In this century it was realized that the same equation describes various interesting phenomena in nonlinear optics, in the theory of dislocations, and in the description of Josephson junctions. Equation (5.4.1) also arises in the scaling limit of the Ising model in statistical physics of lattices. At first, construction of the multisoliton solutions of (5.4.1) was based on the use of the Bäcklund transformations [5.25]. The inverse scattering transform method for (5.4.1) was developed in 1973–1974 by *Ablowitz* [5.14], and by *Tahtadjian* [5.13]. Here, following [5.9], we obtain multisoliton solutions on an arbitrary background. The obtained results may be applied to the case of periodic or multiperiodic backgrounds which have been treated thoroughly in [5.26].

We introduce the notations

$$v = is_x/2, \quad w = \exp(is).$$

In this notation (5.4.1) may be rewritten in the form

$$v_t = w - w^{-1}, \quad w_x = 2vw. \tag{5.4.2}$$

The corresponding linear system reads

$$\psi_x = v\psi + \lambda\varphi, \quad \varphi_x = \lambda\psi - v\varphi,$$
$$\psi_t = \lambda^{-1}w\varphi, \quad \varphi_t = (\lambda w)^{-1}\psi. \tag{5.4.3}$$

The Darboux transformation for this system may be introduced in many ways, for example, by starting as in the Zakharov-Shabat system studied in Chap. 4, and applying the general theorems of Chap. 2 on the covariance properties of matrix systems with rational dependence on the spectral parameter. Here, however, we prefer to start by noting that the sine-Gordon equation may be considered as a periodic reduction of the 2D Toda lattice. This leads directly to the following definition of the Darboux transformation for (5.4.1):

$$\psi \to \psi[1] = \lambda\varphi - \lambda_1\varphi_1\psi_1^{-1}\psi,$$
$$\varphi \to \varphi[1] = \lambda\psi - \lambda_1\psi_1\varphi_1^{-1}\varphi,$$
$$v \to v[1] = v + \partial_x \ln(\varphi_1/\psi_1), \tag{5.4.4}$$
$$w \to w[1] = w(\varphi_1/\psi_1)^2,$$
$$s \to s[1] = s - 2i \ln(\varphi_1/\psi_1).$$

N-times iterated Darboux transformations are described by the formulas

$$\psi[N] = \Delta_1(N+1)/\Delta_1(N), \quad \varphi[N] = \Delta_2(N+1)/\Delta_2(N),$$
$$v[N] = v + \partial_x \ln\left(\Delta_2(N)/\Delta_1(N)\right),$$
$$w[N] = w\left(\Delta_2(N)/\Delta_1(N)\right)^2,$$
$$s[N] = s - 2i \ln\left(\Delta_2(N)/\Delta_1(N)\right),$$
$$\Delta_1(N) = \det(\lambda_k^{j-1}\chi_{kj}), \quad 1 \le j, k \le N, \tag{5.4.5}$$
$$\chi_{k,2p-1} = \psi_k, \quad \chi_{k,2p} = \varphi_k,$$
$$\Delta_2(N) = \det(\lambda_k^{j-1}\zeta_{kj}), \quad 1 \le j, k \le N,$$
$$\zeta_{k,2p-1} = \psi_k \quad \zeta_{k,2p} = \varphi_k,$$

The soliton solution will be obtained by choosing $s = 0$:

$$\psi = A \exp\theta + B \exp(-\theta),$$
$$\varphi = A \exp\theta - B \exp(-\theta), \qquad (5.4.6)$$
$$\theta = \lambda x + \lambda^{-1} t,$$

and

$$s[1] = -4 \operatorname{arccot} \exp 2[\lambda(x - x_0) + \lambda^{-1} t].$$

Two soliton solutions are obtained from (5.4.5) when we choose ψ_i, φ_i in the form of (5.4.6):

$$s[2] = -2i \ln \frac{\lambda_1 \psi_1 \varphi_2 - \lambda_2 \psi_2 \varphi_1}{\lambda_1 \varphi_1 \psi_2 - \lambda_2 \varphi_2 \psi_1}.$$

The reality of the solutions should be guaranteed by the choice $\lambda_1, \lambda_2 \in \mathbb{R}$, $\varphi_1 = \psi_1^*$, $\varphi_2 = \psi_2^*$. Taking $\lambda_1 = \lambda_2^*$ we get the so-called breather solution

$$s = 4 \operatorname{arccot} \left(\frac{\operatorname{Im}\{\lambda_1\}}{\operatorname{Re}\{\lambda_1\}} \frac{\cosh\theta}{\cos\varrho} \right),$$

$$\theta = \frac{\operatorname{Re}\{\lambda_1\}}{2} \left[(1 + |\lambda_1|^{-2})t + (1 - |\lambda_1|^{-2})(x - x_0) \right],$$

$$\varrho = \frac{\operatorname{Im}\{\lambda_1\}}{2} \left[(1 - |\lambda_1|^{-2})t + (1 + |\lambda_1|^{-2})(x - x_0) \right],$$

$$s[2] = \pm 2i \ln \frac{\begin{vmatrix} \lambda_1 \psi_1 & \lambda_2 \psi_2 \\ \varphi_1 & \varphi_2 \end{vmatrix}}{\begin{vmatrix} \lambda_1 \varphi_1 & \lambda_2 \varphi_2 \\ \psi_1 & \psi_2 \end{vmatrix}}, \qquad (5.4.7)$$

An interesting solution arises in the limit $\lambda_2 \to \lambda_1$ and when ψ_i, φ_i in $s[2]$ are chosen as in (5.4.6). Then for $\lambda_1 \in \mathbb{R}$ we get

$$s = 4 \operatorname{arccot} \frac{8\lambda(x - \lambda^{-2} t)}{\cosh 2(\lambda x + \lambda^{-1} t)}. \qquad (5.4.8)$$

In a similar manner we can consider the degeneracies of higher orders. For instance, the degenerate breather solution is described by the formula

$$s = 4 \operatorname{arccot} \frac{2\lambda_I \lambda_R \left\{ \begin{array}{l} \lambda_R^2 (\cos\theta_I + \theta_I \sin\theta_I) \cos\theta_R + \\ + \lambda_I^2 (\cosh\theta_R + \theta_R \sinh\theta_R) \cos\theta_I \end{array} \right\}}{\lambda_R^4 (\theta_I^2 - \cos^2\theta_I) + \lambda^4 (\theta_R^2 + \cosh\theta_R^2)},$$

$$\lambda_1 = \lambda_R + i\lambda_I,$$

$$\theta_R = \frac{\lambda_R}{2} \left[(1 + |\lambda_1|^{-2})t + (1 - |\lambda_1|^{-2})x \right],$$

$$\theta_I = \frac{\lambda_I}{2} \left[(1 - |\lambda_1|^{-2})t + (1 + |\lambda_1|^{-2})x \right].$$

Now let us discuss the connection between the so-called Bäcklund transformation and the DT for the sine-Gordon equation. We denote the ratio ψ_1/φ_1 by h. It is clear that

$$w[1] = h^{-2}w, \quad v[1] + v = \lambda_1(h - h^{-1}).$$

Hence

$$i(s[1] + s)_x = 2\lambda_1(h - h^{-1}),$$
$$h = \exp[-i(s[1] - s)/2].$$

Eliminating h from this equation we get

$$(s[1] + s)_x = 4\lambda_1 \sin[(s - s[1])/2]. \tag{5.4.9}$$

In the same manner we can derive the relation

$$(s - s[1])_t = 4\lambda_1^{-1} \sin[(s + s[1])/2]. \tag{5.4.10}$$

Equations (5.4.9,10) are exactly what is called the Bäcklund transformation for the sine-Gordon equation. Its direct application to the construction of the exact solutions of (5.4.1) seems to be rather inconvenient in comparison with our approach. The same remark may be made about many other situations where nonlinear superposition principles similar to (5.4.5,6) have been treated directly, without the use of the solutions of the auxiliary linear problem. Our approach is also more convenient for different degeneracies, interactions of solitons with a small background and also for the calculation of phase shifts describing the long-time asymptotic behavior of multisolitons.

We now turn to a brief discussion of the nonabelian version of the sine-Gordon equation. We consider (5.2.1) and impose the requirement that the solutions be periodic. Then (5.2.1) reduces to

$$(g_{1t}g_1^{-1})_\xi + g_2 g_1^{-1} - g_1 g_2^{-1} = 0,$$
$$(g_{2\xi}g_2^{-1})_t + g_1 g_2^{-1} - g_2 g_1^{-1} = 0,$$

Introducing new variables $v = g_{1t}g_1^{-1}$, $w = g_{2\xi}g_2^{-1}$, it is easy to check that

$$v_\xi = w - w^{-1}, \quad w_t = vw + wv. \tag{5.4.11}$$

Below, following [5.27, 28] we shall call (5.4.11) the *nonabelian sine-Gordon equation*. The associated linear system follows easily from the Lax representation of a 2D nonabelian Toda lattice

$$\Psi_\xi = v\Psi + \Phi\Lambda, \quad \Phi_\xi = \Psi\Lambda - v\Phi,$$
$$\Psi_t = w\Phi\Lambda^{-1}, \quad \Phi_t = w^{-1}\Phi\Lambda^{-1}. \tag{5.4.12}$$

The corresponding Darboux transformation is

$$\Psi \to \Psi[1] = \Phi\Lambda - \Phi_1\Lambda_1\Psi_1^{-1}\Psi,$$

$$\Phi \to \Phi[1] = \Psi \Lambda - \Psi_1 \Lambda_1 \Phi_1^{-1} \Phi ,$$
$$v \to v[1] = -v + \Psi_1 \Lambda_1 \Phi_1^{-1} - \Phi_1 \Lambda_1 \Psi_1^{-1} ,$$
$$w \to w[1] = \Phi_1 \Lambda_1 \Psi_1^{-1} w \Phi_1 \Lambda_1^{-1} \Psi_1^{-1} .$$

Matrix solitons correspond to the case $v = 0$, $w = E$

$$\Psi = \sum_k A_k \exp(p_k \xi + p_k^{-1} t) ,$$

$$\Phi = \sum_k A_k \exp(p_k \xi + p_k^{-1} t) p_k \Lambda^{-1} ,$$

where p_k are the matrix solutions of the equation $p^2 = \Lambda^2$.

5.5 The Nonlinear Network Equations and Related Systems

Let a_n in (5.2.8) be represented in the following form:

$$a_n = (E + B_n B_{n+1}) \otimes E + (B_n - B_{n+1}) \otimes \sigma ,$$

where $\sigma = \begin{pmatrix} 0 & -1 \\ 1 & 0 \end{pmatrix}$, B_n are 2×2 matrices. The B_n satisfy the nonlinear equation [5.9]:

$$B_{n_t} = B_{n-1} - B_{n+1} + B_{n-1} B_n^2 - B_n^2 B_{n+1} .$$

When $B_n = b_n$, $b_n \in \mathbf{R}$ (5.4.1) reduces to nonlinear filter equations

$$\begin{aligned} V_{n_t} &= (1 + V_n^2)(J_n - J_{n+1}) , \\ J_{n_t} &= (1 + J_n^2)(V_{n-1} - V_n) . \end{aligned} \tag{5.5.1}$$

In fact, when taking $v_n = b_{2n}$, $J_n = b_{2n-1}$ we get (5.5.2). Now let $B_n = \kappa^n U_n$.

$$\kappa = \begin{pmatrix} -i & 0 \\ 0 & -i \end{pmatrix} , \quad U_n = \begin{pmatrix} 0 & u_n^* \\ u_n & 0 \end{pmatrix} .$$

Then (5.4.1) may be reduced to the discrete version of the nonlinear Schrödinger equation

$$i u_{n_t} = u_{n+1} + u_{n-1} + |u|^2 (u_{n+1} + u_{n-1}) . \tag{5.5.2}$$

Note that in the abelian case there exists a change of variables [5.9] which transforms the discrete NS equation into the 1D Toda lattice equation

$$v_n = a_{2n} + a_{2n+1} , \quad u_n = a_{2n} a_{2n-1} . \tag{5.5.3}$$

5.5 The Nonlinear Network Equations and Related Systems

It is necessary to also mention the formulas transforming the solutions of (5.5.2) into the solutions of the Toda lattice equation found by *Wadati* [5.30]

$$v_n = J_n(V_n + V_{n-1}) + i(V_{n-1} - V_n) ,$$

$$u_n = (1 + V_{n-1}^2)(1 + J_{n-1}J_n) + i(1 + V_{n-1}^2)(J_{n-1} - J_n) .$$

The existence of these mappings demonstrates the close relation between the two systems.

We now turn to the discrete version of the Miura transformation [5.9] which maps the solutions of the KdV equation to the modified KdV equation. Consider

$$s_n = \psi_n \psi_{n+1}^{-1} , \qquad (5.5.4)$$

where ψ_n satisfy (5.1.8). Using (5.1.8) it is easy to see that s_n satisfy the nonlinear equation

$$s_{n_t} = (s_n^2 - \lambda s_n)(s_{n+1} - s_{n-1}) . \qquad (5.5.5)$$

Comparing (5.4.4, 5) we find that

$$b_n = \varphi_n \varphi_{n-1} - i , \qquad (5.5.6)$$

where φ_n are the solitons of (5.1.8) corresponding to the choice $\lambda = 2i$, satisfy the nonlinear equation

$$b_{n_t} = (1 + b_n^2)(b_{n+1} - b_{n-1}) , \qquad (5.5.7)$$

which is equivalent to (5.5.2). Taking

$$p_n = i\varphi_{n-1}(\varphi_n^*)^{-1} ,$$

where φ_n satisfy (5.1.8) with $\lambda = 0$, we find that p_n satisfy

$$p_{n_t} = |p_n|^2(p_{n-1} - p_{n+1}) \qquad (5.5.8)$$

which seems to be of some interest to potential applications.

The Darboux transformation may be combined with the Miura transformation. We demonstrate this by examining the system (5.5.7). Our way to construct the solitons of this system involves the following steps:

1. Take the a priori known starting solution of (5.1.8).
2. Construct associated solutions $\psi_{n,1}, \ldots \psi_{n,N}$ corresponding to $\lambda = \lambda_1, \ldots, \lambda_N$ and the solution ψ_n, corresponding to $\lambda = 2i$.
3. Using (5.1.10) for the repeated DT, construct $\psi_n[1]$ corresponding to the choice $\lambda = 2i$.
4. Using (5.5.6), and taking $\varphi_n = \psi_n[N]$, construct the solution $b_n[N]$ of (5.5.7).

5.6 The Lattice Silin-Tikhonchuk Equation

Here, following [5.29] we consider the system

$$\omega \partial_\Omega p(\omega, \Omega) = p(\omega, \Omega)[q(\omega + \Omega, \Omega) - q(\omega - \Omega, \Omega)] ,$$
$$- \omega \partial_\Omega q(\omega, \Omega) = q(\omega, \Omega)[p(\omega + \Omega, \Omega) - p(\omega - \Omega, \Omega)] . \quad (5.6.1)$$

These equations were first derived by *Silin* and *Tikhonchuk* [5.31]. Equation (5.6.1) describes the distribution of the number of Langmuir waves in a spatially inhomogeneous plasma. The interference of waves is due to the induced scattering off of sound oscillations.

Assuming a weak dependence of $p(\omega, \Omega)$ and $q(\omega, \Omega)$ on ω we can write the discrete version of (5.6.1)

$$p_{n_t} = p_n(s_{n+1} - s_{n-1}) ,$$
$$- s_{n_t} = s_n(p_{n+1} - p_{n-1}) , \quad (5.6.2)$$

called below the *lattice Silin-Tikhonchuk* (LST) equation.

We introduce the matrices

$$K_n = \begin{pmatrix} -p_n & 0 \\ 0 & s_n \end{pmatrix} , \quad \sigma = \begin{pmatrix} 0 & 1 \\ 1 & 0 \end{pmatrix} , \quad R_n = \sigma K_n \sigma K_{n+1} ,$$

and rewrite (5.5.2) in the form

$$K_{n_t} = K_n \sigma K_{n+1} \sigma - \sigma K_{n-1} \sigma K_n . \quad (5.6.3)$$

Equation (5.6.3) may be represented as a consistency condition of the linear system

$$K_n \Psi_{n+1} + \Psi_{n-1} = \sigma \Psi_n \Lambda , \quad \Psi_{n_t} = R_n \Psi_{n+2} , \quad (5.6.4)$$

where $\Psi_n = \text{diag}(\psi_n, \varphi_n)$, $\Lambda = \begin{pmatrix} 0 & \lambda \\ \mu & 0 \end{pmatrix}$ is a matrix spectral parameter.

The Darboux transformation for (5.6.3,4) is defined by

$$\Psi_n[1] = \Psi_{n-2,1} \Psi_{n,1}^{-1} \Psi_n - \Psi_{n-2} ,$$
$$K_n[1] = \sigma \Psi_{n-2,1} \Psi_{n,1}^{-1} \sigma K_n \Psi_{n+1,1} \Psi_{n-1,1}^{-1} , \quad (5.6.5)$$

where $\Psi_{n,1}$ is the solution corresponding to the fixed value of the matrix spectral parameter $\Lambda = \Lambda_1$.

The N-times iterated DT is given by

$$K_n[N] = \sigma \Delta_{n-2} \Delta_n^{-1} \sigma K_n \Delta_{n+1} \Delta_{n-1} , \quad (5.6.6)$$

$$\Delta_n = \begin{vmatrix} \Psi_{n,1} & \Psi_{n,2} & \cdots & \Psi_{n,N} \\ \Psi_{n-2,1} & \Psi_{n-2,2} & \cdots & \Psi_{n-2,2} \\ \cdots \\ \Psi_{n-2N+2,1} & \Psi_{n-2N+2,2} & \cdots & \Psi_{n-2N+2,N} \end{vmatrix} .$$

In (5.6.6) $\Psi_{n,k}$ denote the diagonal matrices satisfying (5.6.4) and the matrix-valued determinant is defined by

$$\Delta_n = \sum_{j_1,\ldots,j_N} (-1)^{[j_1,\ldots,j_N]} \prod_{k=1}^{N} \Psi_{n+2-2j_k,k} ,$$

where the summation is taken over all permutations of $j_1,\ldots,j_N$ and $[j_1,\ldots,j_N]$ is the signature of the permutation.

Note that the same statement (i.e., the formula for DT) remains valid also for the general case of nondiagonal matrices Ψ_n and K_n.

Several interesting solutions of (5.6.2) may now be obtained by taking $p_n = p = $ const, $s_n = s = $ const as the initial solution. In this case the linear system (5.6.4) takes the form

$$\psi_{n_t} = -ps\psi_{n+2} , \quad \varphi_{n_t} = -ps\varphi_{n+2} ,$$
$$-p\psi_{n+1} + \psi_{n-1} = \mu\varphi_n , \quad s\psi_{n+1} + \varphi_{n-1} = \lambda\psi_n . \quad (5.6.7)$$

Searching for the solution of (5.5.7) in the form of "Fourier" integrals we find

$$\psi_n = \int f(\omega)\omega^n \exp(-ps\omega^2 t) d\omega ,$$
$$\varphi_n = \int g(\omega)\omega^n \exp(-ps\omega^2 t) d\omega , \quad (5.6.8)$$

$$f(\omega) = C_1^+ \delta(\omega - \omega_1) + C_1^- \delta(\omega + \omega_1) + C_2^+ \delta(\omega - \omega_2) + C_2^- \delta(\omega - \omega_2) ,$$
$$g(\omega) = \frac{-p\omega_1^2 + 1}{\omega_1 \mu} \left[C_1^+ \delta(\omega - \omega_1) + C_1^- \delta(\omega + \omega_1) \right]$$
$$+ \frac{-p\omega_2^2 + 1}{\omega_2 \mu} \left[C_2^+ \delta(\omega - \omega_2) + C_2^- \delta(\omega - \omega_2) \right] , \quad (5.6.9)$$

where $\pm\omega_{1,2}$ are the roots of the fourth order algebraic equation

$$-ps\omega^4 + (-p + s - \lambda\mu)\omega^2 + 1 = 0 . \quad (5.6.10)$$

In the case of multiple roots of (5.6.10) we get

$$f(\omega) = A^+ \delta(\omega - \omega_1) + B^+ \delta'(\omega - \omega_1) + A^- \delta(\omega + \omega_1) + B^- \delta'(\omega + \omega_1) ,$$
$$g(\omega) = \frac{-p\omega_1^2 + 1}{\omega_1 \mu}$$
$$\times \left[A^+ \delta(\omega - \omega_1) + B^+ \delta'(\omega - \omega_1) - A^- \delta(\omega + \omega_1) + B^- \delta'(\omega + \omega_1) \right] . \quad (5.6.11)$$

The simplest solitons are given by the formulas

$$p_n[1] = p \frac{\psi_{n+1,1}}{\psi_{n-1,1}} \frac{\varphi_{n-2,1}}{\varphi_{n,1}} ,$$
$$s_n[1] = s \frac{\psi_{n-2,1}}{\psi_{n,1}} \frac{\varphi_{n+1,1}}{\varphi_{n-1,1}} .$$

For (5.6.8, 10) we get

$$p_n[1] = p \frac{\cosh(\theta_n^- + \beta)\cosh(\theta_{n-1}^+ + \theta - \beta)}{\cosh(\theta_n^- - \beta)\cosh(\theta_{n-1}^+ + \theta + \beta)},$$

$$s_n[1] = s \frac{\cosh(\theta_{n-1}^- - \beta)\cosh(\theta_n^+ + \theta + \beta)}{\cosh(\theta_{n-1}^- + \beta)\cosh(\theta_n^+ + \theta - \beta)},$$

$$\beta = \frac{1}{2}\ln(\omega_1 \omega_2^{-1}), \quad \theta = \frac{1}{4}\ln\frac{-p\omega_1^2 + s\omega_2^2 + ps + 1}{-p\omega_2^2 + s\omega_1^2 + ps + 1},$$

$$\theta_n^\pm = -\frac{ps(\omega_1^2 - \omega_2^2)}{2}t + \frac{n}{2}\ln\frac{\omega_1}{\omega_2} + \frac{1}{2}\ln\frac{C_1^+ \pm (-1)^n C_1^-}{C_2^+ \pm (-1)^n C_2^-}.$$

(5.6.12)

Darboux dressing of the starting solution in the case of mltiple roots leads to a rational solution which may be obtained by degeneration of (5.6.11)

$$p_n = p\frac{(\zeta_n - \kappa_n^+ + \omega_1^{-1})(\zeta_{n-1} - \kappa_{n-1}^- - \omega_1^{-1})}{(\zeta_n - \kappa_n^+ - \omega_1^{-1})(\zeta_{n-1} - \kappa_{n-1}^- + \omega_1^{-1})},$$

$$s_n = s\frac{(\zeta_n - \kappa_n^- + \omega_1^{-1})(\zeta_{n-1} - \kappa_{n-1}^+ - \omega_1^{-1})}{(\zeta_n - \kappa_n^- - \omega_1^{-1})(\zeta_{n-1} - \kappa_{n-1}^+ + \omega_1^{-1})},$$

(5.6.13)

where $\zeta_n = n\omega^{-1} - 2ps\omega_1 t$,

$$\kappa_n^\pm = (A^+ \pm (-1)^n A^-)/(B^+ \pm (-1)^n B^-).$$

Equation (5.5.12) may be rewritten also in the form

$$p_n = p\frac{z_n^2 - 9\omega_1^2/4}{z_n^2 - \omega_1^2/4}, \quad z_n = \frac{2n-1}{\omega_1} - 2ps\omega_1 t - \frac{A^+ - (-1)^n A^-}{B^+ + (-1)^n B^-}.$$

All these formulas are invariant with respect to time-shifts. In other words, we can replace t by $t - t_0$, $t_0 = $ const in all our constructions. As usual, an N-times repeated Darboux transformation leads to a multisoliton solution. The asymptotic behavior of the multisoliton solutions will be studied in Sect. 7.3.

6. Darboux Transformation for 2 + 1 Nonlinear Evolution Equations and Localized Soliton Solutions

The general results obtained in Chap. 2 for linear partial differential equations with matrix valued coefficients together with the concept of the binary Darboux transformation enable one to construct a large family of exact solutions of the so called Davey-Stewartson system. The DS system is a natural 2+1 generalization of the nonlinear Schrödinger (NS) equation. In this chapter we also discuss another very interesting 2+1 evolution equation often referred to as the Novikov-Veselov equation for which we construct some new solutions.

6.1 The Davey-Stewartson Equation

Here we consider the Davey-Stewartson system

$$iu_t - u_{xx} - \alpha^{-2}u_{yy} + 2\kappa\alpha^{-2}|u|^2 u - Su = 0,$$
$$\alpha^2 S_{xx} - S_{yy} = 4\kappa(|u|^2)_{xx}.$$
(6.1.1)

The case $\kappa = \pm 1$, $\alpha = 1$ is usually referred to as the DS-I system, $\alpha = i$ corresponds to the DS-II system. The DS equations were derived in [6.1] and were studied in a considerable number of works especially in the last three years [6.2–12]. In particular in [6.4, 5] solitons and multisoliton solutions exponentially decaying in all spatial directions in the xy plane were first constructed. A Hamiltonian interpretation of the DS-I system was given in [6.10]. In [6.7–9] different versions of the spectral transform method were worked out which led to many new features in the behavior of related localized coherent structures. Below we present a simple algebraic construction [6.12, 13], based on the results of [6.14] producing a large family of exact solutions with very interesting properties.

Consider an auxiliary linear system for a 2×2 matrix valued Ψ-function:

$$\Psi_y = J\Psi_x + U\Psi,$$
(6.1.2)

$$\Psi_t = 2i\alpha^{-1}J\Psi_{xx} + 2i\alpha^{-1}U\Psi_x + V\Psi,$$
(6.1.3)

$$J = \begin{pmatrix} \alpha & 0 \\ 0 & -\alpha \end{pmatrix}, \quad U = \begin{pmatrix} 0 & u \\ v & 0 \end{pmatrix},$$

$$V = \begin{pmatrix} (w+iQ)/2 & i\alpha^{-2}(\alpha u_x + u_y) \\ i\alpha^{-2}(\alpha v_x - v_y) & (w-iQ)/2 \end{pmatrix}.$$

The consistency condition of the system (6.1.2, 3) is equivalent to the following nonlinear equations:

$$iu_t = -\left(u_{xx} + \alpha^{-2} u_{yy}\right) - uQ, \tag{6.1.4}$$

$$iv_t = v_{xx} + \alpha^{-2} v_{yy} + vQ, \tag{6.1.5}$$

$$w_y = i\alpha Q_x - 2i\alpha^{-1}(uv)_x, \tag{6.1.6}$$

$$w_x = i\alpha^{-1} Q_y + 2i\alpha^{-3}(uv)_y. \tag{6.1.7}$$

Equations (6.1.4, 5) may be reduced to

$$\alpha^2 Q_{xx} - Q_{yy} = 2\left[(uv)_{xx} + \alpha^{-2}(uv)_{yy}\right].$$

We shall call (6.1.4, 7) the extended DS system or EDS system. Under the complementary constraint

$$v = \alpha u^*, \quad \mathrm{Im}\{Q\} = 0, \tag{6.1.8}$$

and the change of variables

$$Q = -2\kappa\alpha^{-2}|u|^2 + S,$$

the EDS system reduces to (6.1.1). Now we can use the results of Chap. 2 [6.14], showing that the system (6.1.2, 3) is covariant with respect to the action of the Darboux transformation:

$$\Psi \to \Psi[1] = \Psi_x - \sigma\Psi, \quad \sigma = \Psi_{1x}\Psi_1^{-1},$$

$$U \to U[1] = U + [J, \sigma], \quad V \to V[1] = V + 2i\alpha^{-1}(\sigma_y + J\sigma_x).$$

As usual, Ψ_1 is a fixed invertible matrix solution of (6.1.2, 3) corresponding to the starting matrix potentials U and V. $U[1]$, $V[1]$ determine some new solution of the EDS system given by

$$\begin{aligned}
u[1] &= u + 2\alpha\sigma_{12} = u + 2\alpha\frac{-\psi_{1x}\psi_2 + \psi_{2x}\psi_1}{\Delta}, \\
v[1] &= v - 2\alpha\sigma_{21} = v - 2\alpha\frac{\varphi_{1x}\varphi_2 - \varphi_{2x}\varphi_1}{\Delta}, \\
w[1] &= w + 2i\alpha^{-1}\left(\sigma_{11_y} + \sigma_{22_y} + \alpha\sigma_{11_x} - \alpha\sigma_{22_x}\right), \\
Q[1] &= Q + 2\alpha^{-1}\left(\sigma_{11_y} - \sigma_{22_y} + \alpha\sigma_{11_x} + \alpha\sigma_{22_x}\right), \\
\Psi_1 &= \begin{pmatrix} \psi_1 & \psi_2 \\ \varphi_1 & \varphi_2 \end{pmatrix}, \quad \Delta = \psi_1\varphi_2 - \varphi_1\psi_2, \quad \sigma = \begin{pmatrix} \sigma_{11} & \sigma_{12} \\ \sigma_{21} & \sigma_{22} \end{pmatrix}.
\end{aligned} \tag{6.1.9}$$

As in Chap. 2, N-times repeated Darboux transformation of Ψ may be represented by

$$\Psi[N] = \partial_x^N \Psi - \left(s_1 \partial_x^{N-1} \Psi + \ldots + s_N \Psi\right),$$
$$U[N] = U + [J, s_1]. \tag{6.1.10}$$

The coefficients $s_1, \ldots, s_N$ are determined by the system of linear algebraic equations

$$s_1 \partial_x^{N-1} \Psi_k + s_2 \partial_x^{N-2} \Psi_k + \ldots + s_N \Psi_k = \partial_x^N \Psi_k, \quad k = 1, 2, \ldots, N. \tag{6.1.11}$$

where Ψ_k are some fixed solutions of the system (6.1.2, 3).

Now let us show how to apply the described construction to find the solutions exponentially decaying in all spatial dimensions, first discovered by *Boity* et al. [6.4]. Let $\alpha = 1$, $u = v = Q = 0$. In this case (6.1.2, 3) reduces to the system

$$\begin{aligned} \psi_y &= \psi_x, & \psi_t &= 2i\psi_{xx}, \\ \varphi_y &= -\varphi_x, & \varphi_t &= -2i\varphi_{xx}. \end{aligned} \tag{6.1.12}$$

Now taking in (6.1.10) ψ_k and φ_k satisfying (6.1.12) we get new solutions $u[N]$, $v[N]$, $Q[N]$ from (6.6.10). For a one step Darboux transformation these solutions depend on four functional parameters. We restrict ourselves to the following choice of ψ_k and φ_k:

$$\psi_k = \left[A_k \exp\left(\mu(x + y - 4at)\right) + B_k \exp\left(-\mu(x + y - 4at)\right)\right] \exp(i\theta),$$

$$\varphi_k = \left[C_k \exp\left(\lambda(x - y + 4pt)\right) + D_k \exp\left(-\lambda(x - y + 4pt)\right)\right] \exp(i\vartheta),$$

$$\theta = a(x + y) + 2(\mu^2 - a^2)t,$$

$$\vartheta = p(x - y) + 2(p^2 - \lambda^2)t. \tag{6.1.13}$$

The complementary restrictions $\mu, \lambda, A_k, B_k, C_k, D_k \in \mathbf{R}$

$$\lambda(m^2 - n^2) = \kappa\mu, \tag{6.1.14}$$

ensure that the constraint (6.1.7) is satisfied. The obtained solution of the DS-I system is

$$u[1] = \frac{2\mu}{m \cosh f_1 + n \cosh f_2} \exp(ih), \tag{6.1.15}$$

$$f_1 = (\mu + \lambda)x + (\mu - \lambda)y - 4(\mu a - \lambda p)t + f_{10},$$
$$f_2 = (\mu - \lambda)x + (\mu + \lambda)y - 4(\mu a + \lambda p)t + f_{20},$$
$$h = \theta - \vartheta + h_0,$$

$f_{10}, f_{20}, h_0, m, n$, are arbitrary constants, which may be expressed in terms of A_k, B_k, C_k and D_k.

Formula (6.1.15) describes the spatially localized soliton propagating in the xy plane with the velocity $v = 2(a - p, a + p)$. The corresponding $Q[1]$ is given by

$$Q[1] = 4\frac{C + 2mn\left[(\mu^2 + \lambda^2)\cosh f_1 \cosh f_2 - (\mu^2 - \lambda^2)\sinh f_1 \sinh f_2\right]}{(m\cosh f_1 + n\cosh f_2)^2},$$
$$C = (m^2 + n^2)(\mu^2 + \lambda^2). \tag{6.1.16}$$

In contrast with $u[1]$, $Q[1]$ is nondecreasing in the directions $f_2 = \pm f_1 + \text{const}$.

In the considered example the restrictions (6.1.7) are satisfied by virtue of the choice of φ_k and ψ_k. Using the technique of the binary Darboux transformation we can satisfy the constraint (6.1.7) also for N-times repeated DT. To do this we introduce the linear system formally conjugated to (6.1.2, 3):

$$\Phi_y = \Phi_x J - \Phi U,$$
$$\Phi_t = -2i\Phi_{xx}J + 2i\Phi_x U + \Phi W, \tag{6.1.17}$$

$$J = \begin{pmatrix} 1 & 0 \\ 0 & -1 \end{pmatrix}, \quad W = \begin{pmatrix} -(w + iQ)/2 & i(u_x - u_y) \\ i\kappa(u_x^* + u_y^*) & -(w - iQ)/2 \end{pmatrix}.$$

Now the DS-I system may be represented also as the condition of compatibility of the linear system (6.1.17). We introduce the matrix function $\Phi[-1]$ by the formula

$$\Phi[-1] = \Omega(\Phi, \Psi_1) \cdot \Psi_1^{-1},$$
$$\Omega(\Phi, \Psi) = \int_{M_0}^{M} \omega, \quad d\omega = 0, \tag{6.1.18}$$
$$\omega = \Phi\Psi dx + \Phi J\Psi dy + 2i(\Phi U\Psi + \Phi J\Psi_x - \Phi_x J\Psi)dt.$$

It is easy to check that $\Phi[-1]$ is the solution of the system obtained from (6.1.17) by the change of the potential $U \to U[+1]$,

$$U[+1] = U + [J, \sigma_1]. \tag{6.1.19}$$

The system (6.1.17) is covariant with respect to DT:

$$\Phi \to \Phi[-1] = \Phi_x - \Phi\Phi_1^{-1}\Phi_{1x}, \quad U \to U[-1] = U + [J, \Phi_1^{-1}\Phi_{1x}]. \tag{6.1.20}$$

The function $\Psi[-1]$ solving the system (6.1.2, 3) with the potential U replaced by $U[-1]$ may be defined by

$$\Psi[-1] = \Phi_1 \Omega(\Phi_1, \Psi). \tag{6.1.21}$$

From this it turns out that we can "dress" the potential U in two ways: by using (6.1.19) or (6.1.20). Each of the next iterations of the DT may be done by applying (6.1.19, 20) in an arbitrary order. So far we get an infinite series of solutions $U[+N, -M]$ corresponding to N-times iterated DT (6.1.19) and consequent M-times repeated DT (6.1.20). Most interesting for us are the solutions $U[+N, -N]$. The simplest of them is $U[+1, -1]$

$$U[+1, -1] = U + [J, \Psi_1 \Omega^{-1}(\Phi_1, \Psi_1)\Phi_1], \tag{6.1.22}$$

where Ψ_1 and Φ_1 are the fixed solutions of the associated linear systems. By direct calculation it is possible to check that the solutions of the linear systems corresponding to $U[+N,-N]$ are

$$\Psi[+N,-N] = \Psi - \sum_{k=1}^{N} \sigma_k \Omega(\Phi_k, \Psi),$$

$$\Phi[+N,-N] = \Phi - \sum_{k=1}^{N} \Omega(\Phi, \Psi_k) s_k,$$

where the coefficients σ_k, s_k, are determined from the system of the linear algebraic equations

$$\sum_{k=1}^{N} \sigma_k \Omega(\Phi_k \Psi_j) = \Psi_j, \quad \sum_{k=1}^{N} \Omega(\Phi_j, \Psi_k) s_k = \Phi_j, \quad (6.1.23)$$

$$j = 1, 2, \ldots, N.$$

The solution $U[+N,-N]$ itself is given by

$$U[+N,-N] = U + \left[J, \sum_{k,j=1}^{N} \sigma_j \Omega(\Phi_k, \Psi_j) s_k \right]. \quad (6.1.24)$$

Now assume that U satisfies the constraint $v = \kappa u^*$. The same would be true for $U[-1]$ if we put

$$\Phi_k = \Psi_k^* T, \quad T = \begin{pmatrix} 1 & 0 \\ 0 & -\kappa \end{pmatrix}.$$

The simplest solution obtained by this way from (6.1.22) is

$$u[+N,-N] = u + 2\kappa \Delta^{-1}$$
$$\times \left(-\psi_1 \varphi_1^* \theta_{22} - \psi_2 \varphi_2 \theta_{11} + \psi_2 \varphi_1^* \theta_{12}^* + \psi_1 \varphi_2^* \theta_{12} \right), \quad (6.1.25)$$
$$\Delta = \theta_{11} \theta_{22} - |\theta_{12}|^2,$$

where θ_{ik} is defined by

$$\theta_{ik} = \int_{M_0}^{M} (\psi_i^* \psi_k - \kappa \varphi_i^* \varphi_k) \, dx + (\psi_i^* \psi_k + \kappa \varphi_i^* \varphi_k) \, dy$$
$$+ 2i \left(u \psi_i^* \varphi_k - u^* \varphi_i^* \psi_k + \psi_i^* \psi_{k_x} + \kappa \varphi_i^* \varphi_{k_x} - \psi_{i_x}^* \psi_k - \kappa \varphi_{i_x}^* \varphi_k \right) dt.$$

For $|u[+1,-1]|^2$ the following more simple representation holds:

$$|u[+1,-1]|^2 = |u|^2 + \kappa^{-1}(\partial_x^2 - \partial_y^2) \ln \Delta. \quad (6.1.26)$$

The important particular case of $u = 0$ already produces a large variety of explicit solutions defined by (6.1.26) because in this case the solution of (6.1.2,3) and (6.1.17) is trivial.

In the case of the DS-II system where $\alpha = i$, a possible choice of the starting solution of the auxiliary linear problem providing that $U[+N]$ satisfies the conditions $v = \alpha u^*$, $\text{Im}\{Q\} = 0$ is

$$\Psi_k = \begin{pmatrix} \psi_k & \varphi_k^* \\ \varphi_k & \kappa\psi_k^* \end{pmatrix}.$$

In particular, for $u[+1]$ we get

$$u[+1] = u + 2i\frac{-\psi_{1x}\varphi_1^* + \varphi_{1x}^*\psi_1}{\kappa|\psi_1|^2 - |\varphi_1|^2}. \tag{6.1.27}$$

In the case $u = 0$, ψ_1 and φ_1 satisfy the system

$$\psi_y = i\psi_x, \quad \psi_t = 2i\psi_{xx},$$
$$\varphi_y = -i\varphi_x, \quad \varphi_t = -2i\varphi_{xx}.$$

The choice of ψ and φ in the form

$$\psi = \int f(\omega) \exp\left[\omega(x+iy) + 2i\omega^2 t\right] dm(\omega),$$
$$\varphi = \int g(\omega) \exp\left[\omega(x-iy) - 2i\omega^2 t\right] dm(\omega), \tag{6.1.28}$$

where the integration is performed over some domain in the complex m-plane, produces a class of solutions having very different types of behavior. In particular in the case $\kappa = -1$, the obtained solutions are nonsingular.

Another possibility is to take as the starting solutions of the DS-system some solutions of the nonlinear Schrödinger equation with the known solutions of the auxiliary linear problem. A large variety of this type of solution expressed in terms fo multidimensional theta functions is obtained by the so-called method of finite gap integration [6.15]. We omit the discussion of these solutions here in order to preserve the elementary character of this volume.

More details about the behavior of the solutions of the DS-system obtained by the use of the IST method may be found in the references cited above.

6.2 The Veselov-Novikov Equation

In this section, starting from the results of Sect. 2.8, we consider the following system:

$$u_t = \left(\partial^3 + \bar{\partial}^3\right)u + 3\partial(uv) + 3\bar{\partial}(v^*u),$$
$$\partial v^* = \bar{\partial}u, \quad \bar{\partial}v = \partial u, \quad \partial = \frac{\partial}{\partial z}, \quad \bar{\partial} = \frac{\partial}{\partial z^*}, \tag{6.2.1}$$

usually called the Novikov-Veselov equation. Equation (6.2.1) may be represented as a compatibility condition of the linear system

$$\partial \bar{\partial} \psi + u\psi = 0 , \qquad (6.2.2)$$

$$\psi_t = \left(\partial^3 + \bar{\partial}^3 + 3v\partial + 3v^*\bar{\partial}\right)\psi . \qquad (6.2.3)$$

The system (6.2.2, 3), as follows from the results of Sect. 2.8, is covariant with respect to the action of the Darboux transformation (2.8.3, 4) up to the redefinition of the functions θ:

$$\begin{aligned}
\theta(\psi, \psi_1) &= \psi_1^{-1} \int_{M_0}^{M} \gamma , \\
\gamma &= (\psi \partial \psi_1 - \psi_1 \partial \psi) dz - (\psi \bar{\partial} \psi_1 - \psi_1 \bar{\partial} \psi) dz^* \\
&\quad + \left[\psi \partial^3 \psi_1 - \psi_1 \partial^3 \psi + \psi_1 \bar{\partial}^3 \psi - \psi \bar{\partial}^3 \psi_1 + 2(\partial^2 \psi \partial \psi_1 - \partial \psi \partial^2 \psi)\right] dt .
\end{aligned} \qquad (6.2.4)$$

In particular (6.2.3) is covariant with respect to these transformations and the transformed coefficient $v[1]$ is

$$v[1] = v + 2\partial^2 \ln \psi_1 .$$

Hence (2.8.6–8) determine a sequence of solutions of the Novikov-Veselov equation up to the redefinition of θ_{ij} mentioned above. In particular, by starting from $u = 0$ we get a family of solutions of (6.2.1). The simplest of the solutions $u[1]$ should be singular. Nonsingular solutions correspond to higher iterations of the Darboux transformation. The simplest nonsingular solution is $u[2]$:

$$\begin{aligned}
u[2] &= 2\partial \bar{\partial} \ln(C + |f|^2) , \\
\partial \bar{\partial} f &= 0 , \quad f_t = \partial^3 f .
\end{aligned} \qquad (6.2.5)$$

Taking f in the form

$$f = \sum_L C_L \sum_{l=0}^{(L/3)} \frac{z^{L-2l} t^l}{(L - 3l)! l!} , \qquad (6.2.6)$$

where C_L are the constants chosen in arbitrary way and $[m]$ denotes the entire part of m, we get from (6.2.4) the simplest family of nonsingular rational solutions. A "soliton" solution is obtained under the following choice of f:

$$f = \exp(ikx) g(z - ct) , \quad g''' + cg' - ikg = 0 .$$

The list of exact solutions may be easily continued by the reader.

7. Hamiltonian Interpretation of the Darboux Transformations and Other Problems

7.1 Darboux Transformation as a Canonical Transformation

Flaschka and *McLaughlin* [7.1] were the first to establish that the classical Darboux transformation is canonical with respect to the symplectic structure related to the KdV equation. Their result was generalized by *Bobenko* [7.2] for the Toda lattice equation, NS equation, and SG equation. In this section we restrict ourselves to reproducing his result for the Toda lattice case with some slight modifications.

Let us rewrite (5.1.13) in the form

$$\dot{q}_n = p_n ,$$
$$\dot{p}_n = \exp(q_{n-1} - q_n) - \exp(q_n - q_{n+1}) . \tag{7.1.1}$$

We introduce the Hamiltonian function H by

$$H = \sum_n p_n^2/2 + \exp(q_{n-1} - q_n) .$$

It is easy to check that (7.1.1) may be rewritten as

$$\dot{q}_n = \frac{\partial H}{\partial p_n} , \quad \dot{p}_n = -\frac{\partial H}{\partial q_n} . \tag{7.1.2}$$

The Darboux transformation (5.1.6) may be represented in the form

$$P_n = p_n - \sigma_n + \sigma_{n-1} ,$$
$$Q_n = q_{n+1} + \ln \sigma_n ,$$

where $P_n = p_n[1]$, $Q_n = q_n[1]$, $\sigma_n = \psi_{n,1}/\psi_{n+1,1}$, and, as before, ψ_n is a fixed solution of (5.1.5). This Darboux transformation is canonical with respect to the Poisson bracket

$$\{F, G\} = \sum_n \left(\frac{\partial F}{\partial q_n} \frac{\partial G}{\partial p_n} - \frac{\partial F}{\partial p_n} \frac{\partial G}{\partial q_n} \right) .$$

The generating function of this canonical transformation is given by

$$F = \sum_n [\exp(Q_n - q_{n+1}) - \exp(q_n - Q_n) + \lambda_1 q_n - \lambda_1 Q_n] ,$$

and we have
$$P_n = -\frac{\partial F}{\partial Q_n}, \quad p_n = \frac{\partial F}{\partial q_n}.$$

The proof of this statement is based on the identity
$$\exp(q_n - q_{n+1}) = (\lambda_1 - \sigma_{n-1} - p_n)\sigma_n,$$
following from (5.1.15).

7.2 The Relationship Between the Zakharov-Shabat Dressing Method and Darboux Transformations

We shall illustrate the connection between the Zakharov-Shabat dressing method and the method of Darboux transformations on the example of a 2D Toda lattice. We recall the main idea of the Zakharov-Shabat method following [7.3].

Let us introduce the operator F satisfying the conditions
$$(F\psi)_n = \sum_{k=-\infty}^{\infty} F_{nk}\psi_k,$$
$$[\partial_t - A^+, F] = 0, \quad [\partial_\xi - L^+, F] = 0,$$
(7.2.1)

where A^+ and L^+ are defined by
$$A^+_{nm} = u_n\delta_{nm} + \delta_{n+1,m}, \quad L^+_{nm} = u_n\delta_{n-1,m}.$$

We assume that F admits the triangular (Volterra) factorization
$$F = (1 + K^+)^{-1}(1 + K^-),$$
$$(K^+\psi)_n = \sum_{j=n}^{\infty} K^+_{nj}\psi_j, \quad (K^-\psi)_n = \sum_{j=-\infty}^{n-1} K^-_{nj}\psi_j.$$
(7.2.2)

We shall define the operators $\tilde{A}$ and $\tilde{L}$ by the equations
$$(\partial_t - \tilde{A})(1 + K^+) - (1 + K^+)(\partial_t - A) = 0,$$
$$(\partial_t - \tilde{L})(1 + K^+) - (1 + K^+)(\partial_t - L) = 0.$$
(7.2.3)

The $\tilde{A}$ and $\tilde{L}$ are commuting and have the same matrix structure as A^+ and L^+. The associated coefficients may be found from (7.2.3) and determine a new solution of the 2D Toda lattice equation.

To find K^+ it is necessary to solve the Gelfand-Levitan-Marchenko equation
$$K^+_{nm} + F_{nm} + \sum_{k=n}^{\infty} K^+_{nk}F_{km} = 0, \, m \geq n.$$
(7.2.4)

One of the possible realizations of this approach is to take the "kernel" F_{nm} in the form (degenerate kernel)

$$F_{nm} = \psi_n^+ \psi_m^- ,$$

where $\psi_n^\pm$ are determined by (5.1.7–8). In this case the system (7.2.4) may be easily solved and we get

$$K_{nm}^+ = -\frac{\psi_j^+ \psi_j^-}{1 + \sum_{j=n}^\infty \psi_j^+ \psi_j^-}, \quad n \geq m . \tag{7.2.5}$$

It is easy to obtain from (7.2.3) the dressing formulas

$$\begin{aligned}\tilde{v}_n &= v_{n-1} + \partial_t \ln(1 + K_{n-1,n-1}^+) , \\ \tilde{u}_n &= u_{n-1} \frac{1 + K_{nn}^+}{1 + K_{n-1,n-1}^+} , \\ \tilde{x}_n &= x_{n-1} - \ln(1 + K_{n-1,n-1}^+) .\end{aligned} \tag{7.2.6}$$

Substituting (7.2.5) into (7.2.6) we get the formula (5.1.17) for $x_n[+1,-1]$.

The obvious generalization is obtained under the choice of F_{nm}

$$F_{nm} = \sum_{j=1}^N \psi_{n,j}^+ \psi_{m,j}^- .$$

In this case we have

$$\begin{aligned}K_{nm}^+ &= -(\psi_{m,1}^-, \ldots, \psi_{m,N}^-) M^{-1} (\psi_{n,1}^+, \ldots, \psi_{n,N}^+)^T , \\ M_{ik} &= \delta_{ik} + \sum_{j=1}^\infty \psi_{jk}^+ \psi_{ji}^- , \quad 1 \leq j, k \leq N .\end{aligned} \tag{7.2.7}$$

The associated solution coincides with the previously obtained solution $x_n[+N, -N]$ written in a slightly modified form. This coincidence between $x_n[+N, -N]$ and the formula obtained by the Zakharov-Shabat dressing method illustrates the relationship between these approaches.

7.3 Phase Shifts in Soliton Interaction

Let us consider a multisoliton solution $u(x,t)$ of any nonlinear equation. In many cases characterized by the absence of bounded soliton clusters the asymptotic behavior of $u(x,t)$ may be described by the formula

$$u(x,t) \sim \sum_{k=1}^N u_k(x - v_k t + \varphi_k^\pm) \quad \text{for} \quad t \to \pm\infty . \tag{7.3.1}$$

Thus the result of the interaction is described by the spectrum of total phase shifts $\delta_k^\pm = \varphi_k^+ - \varphi_k^-$.

This behavior was already demonstrated when we considered the asymptotic behavior of the solitons of KP and KdV equations in Sect. 3.4. As was mentioned there, the major part of the calculations is more or less universal and may be also used in certain other situations.

In the case of the nonlocal KdV equation considered in Sect. 4.5 the multi-soliton solution is given by the formula

$$u = -i\varepsilon(T-1)\partial_x \ln[b_{1k}^{j-1}\exp\varphi_k + b_{2k}^{j-1}\exp(-\varphi_k)] ,$$
$$b_{mk} = \alpha_k \exp(i\delta a_{mk}) , \quad \varphi_k = (\theta_{1k} - \theta_{2k})/2 , \qquad (7.3.2)$$
$$\theta_{mk} = a_{mk}x + c_{mk}t + g_{mk} , \quad g_{mk} = \text{const} ,$$

where a_{mk}, c_{mk} are defined by (4.5.9–10):

$$a = i\alpha \exp(i\delta\alpha) + i\mu ,$$
$$c = i\varepsilon\alpha^2 \exp(2i\delta\alpha) + 2i\alpha\varepsilon\delta^{-1}\exp(i\delta\alpha) .$$

Thus (3.4.3) is true for the nonlocal KdV equation.

In the case of a 2D Toda lattice we can rewrite the multisoliton solution in the form

$$x_n = \ln \frac{\Delta_n}{\Delta_{n-1}} .$$

where

$$\Delta_n = \det[a_{1k}^{j-1}\exp\varphi_k + a_{2k}^{j-1}\exp(-\varphi_k)] ,$$
$$\varphi_k = (a_{1k} - a_{2k})\xi/2 - (a_{1k}^{-1} - a_{2k}^{-1})t/2 - [n \ln(a_{1k}/a_{2k})]/2 + g_k ,$$
$$g_k = \text{const} .$$

It can be shown that (3.4.3) is appropriate for this case if we put $b_{mk} = a_{mk}$.

These results are also valid for q-periodic reduction if

$$a_{mk}^q = \lambda_k , \qquad (7.3.3)$$

where λ_k are arbitrary complex constants. In the case of the *sine-Gordon* equation ($q=2$) we have

$$a_{2k} = -a_{1k} .$$

In the case $r_{kn} = 0$ (Sect. 3.4) our equation has bounded cluster solutions. This occurs, for example, for the KP equation and the *2D Toda lattice*. Multisoliton solutions of other equations can be involved in this scheme without any difficulties.

We should mention that the absence of the phase shift of lump solutions of the KP equation is due to trivial fact that ψ- functions of such solutions have only one exponential and the $W_k^\pm$ are equal.

Comments on the Literature

Chapter 1

In addition to [1.8] which contains many references to works on Bäcklund transformations, we should mention three books [1.22–24] also devoted to the algebraic aspects of the theory of solitons. However, these books have only very limited overlap with the approach used in this volume. In particular, it should be remarked that the so-called "generalized Bargmann potentials" considered in [1.24] represent a very particular case of the general construction proposed in [1.2].

For a systematic approach to the theory of solitons involving the solution of the Cauchy initial problem based on the inverse scattering method the reader may consult the excellent books [1.25–28], also containing many interesting historical materials.

A modern exposition of the hamiltonian approach to the theory of solitons, based on the notion of the classical R-matrix may be found in *Faddeev* and *Tahtajian* [1.29].

The periodic version of the IST method is closely related to the theory of algebraic curves (compact Riemann surfaces). The reader can find several expositions of the related theory, for example, in [1.28–1.29]. It should be mentioned that the approach of this volume gives an alternative description of the degeneration of the so-called finite gap solutions. One of the crucial properties of these solutions is that associated linear problems may be solved explicitly in terms of multidimensional Riemann theta-functions [1.30].

A diffent approach to construct explicit solutions of the KdV equation, which is based on the projection technique, was recently proposed by *Marchenko* [1.31]. This approach provides, in particular, a new way to obtain Wronskian representations for the multisoliton solutions of the nonlinear KdV-like equations.

The solutions of the Cauchy initial problem for the KdV-like equations are rather complicated. Remarkably, it is possible to derive the exact asymptotic formulae describing their long-time behavior in terms of special functions [1.25, 28].

It is necessary to mention that Crum transformations, within the framework of soliton theory, were first used by *Wadati*, *Sanuki* and *Konno* [1.32] in 1975 to explain why the Bäcklund transformation can add a soliton to the given background solution. In their work it was also shown how to derive the Bäcklund transformations from the inverse scattering formulation and also how to obtain the conservation laws from the Bäcklund transformations.

Chapter 2

The fundamental results of Darboux were not used for a long time, although they were included in a textbook by *Ince* [2.14] on ordinary differential equations. Even in the work of Crum there is no exact reference to Darboux's original work [2.1]. Often his result, referred to as the Crum transformation, was used in the solution of the inverse scattering problem to exclude the angular momentum term in the radial Schrödinger equation [2.15]. For some other important applications the reader may consult *Sabatier* [2.16] and *Chadan, Sabatier* [2.15].

The expression "Darboux transformation" was first proposed by *Matveev* in [2.6, 8] where the original approach of Darboux was generalized to include the partial differential linear and nonlinear integrable equations as well as their lattice and some matrix generalizations.

The results of Sects. 2.3–5 were obtained by the present authors. The relation between supersymmetric quantum mechanics and the Darboux transformation was discovered by *Borisov, Andrianov, Ioffe* [2.11–13]. In their works the reader may also find applications to the real problems of nuclear physics.

More general theorems on the Darboux covariance of linear problems with matrix valued or operator valued coefficients, including the case of discrete time difference difference equations may be found in [2.8, 18].

Very recently *Bleuler* and *Stahlhofen* [2.19–20] proposed an extension of the Infeld factorization method based on a natural generalization of the oscillator algebra. Their work is also closely connected with the content of this chapter.

Chapter 3

The study of the KdV equation from the inverse problem viewpoint which was started in the famous work in [3.4] later followed different directions. It is necessary to mention the fundamental contribution of *Lax* [3.18], and the hamiltonian treatment of the KdV dynamics given by *Zakharov* and *Faddeev* [3.36]. An algebrogeometrical approach to construct periodic and almost periodic solutions was developed in 1974–1976 by Novikov, Dubrovin, Matveev, Its, Krichever, Lax, Van Moerbeke, McKean, Marchenko, Kac, Tanaka, Date and others. For detailed exposition see [3.9, 38, 40].

Formulas similar to that denoted by $u[N]$ in this volume were first obtained by *Wahlquist* [3.19], but the original derivation was rather complicated. The generalizations, including the KP case, and the general theorems on Darboux covariance of linear partial differential equations and also the differential-difference and difference-difference equations were established in [3.25]. The particular case corresponding to the trivial background solution and scalar coefficients in the associated linear problem was treated by *Chudnovsky* and *Chudnovsky* [3.41].

Binary Darboux transformations were introduced in [3.14, 42]. The Johnson equation has been studied by several authors. We should mention in particular [3.27–29]. The cylindrical KdV equation in the framework of the Darboux transformation approach was first studied in [3.35].

In recent years there has been a surge in efforts to obtain Wronskian representations for the solutions of KP- or KdV-like equations, including representations for their discrete versions. In particular we wish to mention the works of *Nakamura* [3.43, 44], *Miyaka, Ohta* and *Satsuma* [3.45] which originate, in a sense, from the work of *Nimmo* and *Freeman* [3.22]. A significant part of the results of these works follows directly, and easily, from our general approach proposed in 1979–1981 and presented here.

Chapter 4

Bäcklund transformation involving the KdV equation solutions of associated linear systems for the AKNS system and, particularly for the NS case, were first studied by *Wadati* et al. [4.10], *Konno* and *Wadati* [4.11]. However, in their approach, starting from the IST method, the multisoliton solutions on an arbitrary background were not obtained.

Results similar to those in [4.6] were later rediscovered in [4.8]. The reader is also referred to [4.9].

Chapter 5

The inverse scattering method for the differential-difference and difference-difference versions of the AKNS NEE was developed by *Ablowitz* and *Ladik* [5.32].

The relationship between nonlinear network equations and the Toda lattice equation was first noted by *Wadati* [5.30]. Casorati determinant representations for 1D and 2D Toda lattice equations were first introduced in [5.6–9] and later were rediscovered through different approaches by several authors. The interested reader may find additional references in J. Phys. Soc. Jpn. between 1986 and 1989, in particular [5.33–35, 37] and also in [5.36]. For the study of master symmetries and recursion operators for various new discrete systems see *Fuchssteiner* [5.38]. The τ-functional approach to the integrable lattice equations was recently developed by *Nijhoff* [5.39]. Closely related with the τ-functional approach is the projection method of *Marchenko* [5.40] also leading to Casorati determinant representations for the discrete Toda-like systems. It is important to note that in this chapter we have mostly restricted ourselves to considering the simplest well known examples of integrable discrete systems, and numerous other known integrable systems of this kind were not mentioned to limit the scope of this book to a reasonable breadth. Discrete time nonlinear difference systems may also be considered following the reasoning of this chapter by applying associated version of the Darboux transformation proposed in [5.6].

Chapter 6

The Davey-Stewartson system is closely related to the two-dimensional version of the Heisenberg ferromagnetic isotropic equation usually referred to as the Ishimori equation. As was shown by *Lipovsky* and *Shirokov* [6.11] there exists an exact gauge equivalence between these two systems. Thus all results obtained here are also applicable to the Ishimori equation.

Chapter 7

For other approaches to studying the asymptotic behavior of multisoliton solutions see *Zakharov* et al. [7.4] and *Fuchssteiner* [7.5] where hamiltonian interpretation of the multisoliton solutions is also discussed. For the R-matrix treatment of the hamiltonian structure of nonlinear integrable systems the reader may consult *Faddeev* and *Tahtajian* [7.6].

The long-time behavior of solutions in the presence of nontrivial solitons and with reflection coefficients different from zero has been studied by *Schuur* [7.7].

Summary and Outlook

We have presented in this volume the most illustrative examples of applications of the Darboux transformation method. However, several closely related topics have been omitted for several reasons. First, in following a purely algebraic treatment we have not explained how to derive the Darboux or Bäcklund transformations within a general formulation of inverse scattering. This subject has been thoroughly discussed by *Calogero* and *Degasperis* [1.27] and in the recent book by *Konopelchenko* [1.33]. The last book also contains a number of additional references on the Bäcklund transformations relevant to this volume.

We have also not discussed in detail the important class of finite-gap solutions of nonlinear integrable equations, which is very important in applications of the Darboux transformation. The interested reader may consult, for example, the forthcoming book by *Belokolos et al.* [3.9] for a detailed discussion of the finite-gap solutions and their properties. Most interesting, and not yet completely studied, is the class of solutions obtained by application of Darboux dressing to the finite-gap solutions of 2+1 integrable NEE similar to the KP equation or the 2D Toda lattice equation. For 1+1 systems this is less interesting; the same results can be obtained by different methods, for example, by degenerating the associated compact Riemann surface (the related effects are described for the nonlinear Schrödinger equation by *Bobenko* et al.).

Another class of systems for which the Darboux transformation approach can be generally applied is in the so-called deformed zero curvature equations recently introduced by *Burtzev et al.* [7.8]. One member of this family is the linear system introduced by *Maison* [7.9] and independently, in another form, by *Zakharov* and *Belinski* [7.10] to show integrability of the vacuum axially symmetric stationary Einstein equations. For this example the Darboux transformation approach was developed by *Neugebauer* [7.11] and later generalized by *Neugebauer* and *Kramer* [7.12] to the case of an electromagnetic field interacting with the field of gravity. General Darboux dressing formulas for the class of equations of *Burtzev*, *Zakharov* and *Mikhailov* were reported in the Ph.D thesis of *A. Rybin* [7.13].

We do believe, however, that the reader already somewhat familiar with the background material can easily fill in the omitted parts of the theory and successfully apply the DT method.

References

Chapter 1

1.1 G. Darboux: Compt. Rend. **94**, 1456–1459 (1882)
1.2 V.B. Matveev: Lett. Math. Phys. **3**, 213–216 (1979)
1.3 V.B. Matveev: Lett. Math. Phys. **3**, 217–222 (1979)
1.4 B.B. Kadomtsev, V.I. Petviashvili: Dokl. Akad. Nauk SSSR **192**, 753–756 (1970)
1.5 V.E. Zakharov, A.B. Shabat: Funkt. Anal. Pril. **8**(3), 43–53 (1974)
1.6 V.S. Druma: Pisma Zh. Eksp. Teor. Fiz. **19**(12), 219–220 (1973)
1.7 M. Crum: Quat. J. Math. **6**, 121–128 (1955)
1.8 H. Wahlquist: in *Bäcklund Transformations*, ed. by R. Miura, Lect. Notes Math. Vol. **515** (Springer, Berlin Heidelberg 1976) pp. 162–175
1.9 M.V. Babich, V.B. Matveev, M.A. Salle: Zap. Semin. LOMI **145**, 34–45 (1985)
1.10 V.B. Matveev, M.A. Salle: "On some new class of the solutions of the KP equation and Johnson equation" in *Some Topics on Inverse Problems*, ed. by P. Sabatier (World-Scientific, Singapore 1988) pp. 182–212
1.11 V.D. Lipovsky, V.B. Matveev, A.O. Smirnov: Zap. Semin. LOMI **150**, 70–75 (1986)
1.12 S.V. Nanakov: Physica D **3**(1), 420–427 (1981)
1.13 A.S. Fokas, M.J. Ablowitz: Phys. Lett. A. **94**(2), 67–70 (1983)
1.14 G. Darboux: *Leçons sur la Theorie des Surfaces* Vol.2 (Gauthier-Villars, Paris, 2nd ed. 1915) pp. 214–215
1.15 A.V. Mikhailov: Pisma Zh. Eksp. Teor. Fiz. **30**(7), 443–448 (1979)
1.16 M.A. Salle: Teor. Mat. Fiz. **53**(2), 227–237 (1982)
1.17 M.A. Salle: Zap. Semin. LOMI **161**, 72–76 (1987)
1.18 M. Boity, J. Leon, M. Martina, F. Pempinelli: "A New Spectral transform for the Davey-Stewardson Equation", PM/ 89-10 Montpellier (1989)
1.19 A.S. Fokas, P.M. Santini: "Coherent Structures and a boundary value problem for the DS-I equation", Preprint INS # 121, Clarkson University, 1989
1.20 P.M. Santini, A.S. Fokas: How to Generate and Drive Coherent Structures in Multidimensions, Preprint No.684 Universita di Roma "La Sapienza"
1.21 S.P. Novikov, A.P. Veselov: Dokl. Akad. Nauk SSSR **279**(1), 20–24 (1984)
1.22 C. Rodgers, W. Shadwick: "Bäcklund Transformations and their Applications" in *Mathematics in Science and Engineering* Vol. 161 (Academic, New York 1982)
1.23 R. Hermann: *Toda Lattices, Cosymplectic Manifolds, Bäcklund Transformations and Kinks* Vol.**I–II**, Interdisciplinary Mathematics (Brooklyn 1977)
1.24 A.N. Leznov, M.V. Saveliev: *Group Approach to Integration of Nonlinear Dynamical Systems* (Nauka, Moscow 1985) [in Russian]
1.25 M.J. Ablowitz, H. Segur: *Solitons and the Inverse Scattering Transform* (SIAM, Philadelphia 1981)
1.26 G.L. Lamb: *Elements of Soliton Theory*, (Wiley-Interscience, New York 1980)
1.27 F. Calogero, A. Degasperis: *Spectral Transform and Solitons* Vol. **I** , (North Holland, Dordrecht 1982)
1.28 S.V. Manakov, S.P. Novikov, L.P. Pitaevsky, V.E. Zakharov: *Theory of Solitons* (Nauka, Moscow 1980) [in Russian]

1.29 L.D. Faddeev, L.A. Tahtajian: *Hamiltonian Approach in the Theory of Solitons* (Nauka, Moscow 1986) [in Russian]
1.30 E.D. Belokolos, A.I. Bobenko, V.Z. Enolsky, A.R. Its, V.B. Matveev: *Algebraic-Geometrical Approach to Nonlinear Evolution Equations*, Springer Series in Nonlinear Dynamics (Springer, Berlin Heidelberg 1992) (in preparation)
1.31 V.A. Marchenko: *Nonlinear Equations and Operator Algebras* (Naukova Dumka, Kiev 1986)
1.32 M. Wadati, H. Sanuki, K. Konno: Progr. Theor. Phys. **53**(2), 419–436 (1975)
1.33 B.G. Konopelchenko: *Nonlinear Integrable Equations* Lect. Notes Phys. Vol. 270 (Springer, Berlin Heidelberg 1987)

Chapter 2

2.1 G. Darboux: Compt. Rend. **94**, 1456–1459 (1882)
2.2 M. Crum: Quat. J. Math. **6**, 121–128 (1955)
2.3 E.T. Whittakker, G.N. Watson: *Course of Modern Analysis* (Cambridge University Press, London 1915)
2.4 P.A.M. Dirac: *Quantum Mechanics* (Oxford 1928)
2.5 H. Wahlquist: in *Bäcklund Transformations*, ed. by R. Miura, Lect. Notes Math. Vol. **515** (Springer, Berlin Heidelberg 1976) pp. 162–175
2.6 V.B. Matveev: Lett. Math. Phys. **3**, 213–216 (1979)
2.7 M.A. Salle: Zap. Semin. LOMI **161**, 72–76 (1987)
2.8 V.B. Matveev: Lett. Math. Phys. **3**, 217–222 (1979)
2.9 M.V. Babich, V.B. Matveev, M.A. Salle: Zap. Semin. LOMI **145**, 34–45 (1985)
2.10 G. Darboux: *Leçons sur la Theorie des Surfaces* Vol. 2 (Gauthier-Villars, Paris, 2nd ed. 1915) pp. 214–215
2.11 A.A. Andrianov, N.V. Borisov, M.J. Ioffe: Theor. Math. Fiz. **61**(2), 183–198 (1984)
2.12 A.A. Andrianov, N.V. Borisov, M.J. Ioffe: Phys. Lett. B **181**(1,2), 141–144 (1986)
2.13 A.A. Andrianov, N.V. Borisov, M.J. Ioffe: Teor. Mat. Fiz. **61**(1), 17–28 (1984)
2.14 E.L. Ince: *Ordinary Differential Equations*, (Dover 1956)
2.15 K. Chadan, P.C. Sabatier: *Inverse Problems in Quantum Scattering Theory*, Second ed. (Springer, Berlin Heidelberg 1989)
2.16 P.C. Sabatier: Nuovo Cimento **78B**, 235–245 (1983)
2.17 V.B. Matveev, M.A. Salle: "On some new class of the solutions of the KP equation and Johnson equation" in *Some Topics on Inverse Problems*, ed. by P. Sabatier, (World-Scientific, Singapore 1988) pp. 182–212
2.18 V.B. Matveev: "Darboux Transformations and Nonlinear Equations" in *Problemes Inverses, Evolution Non-Lineaire*, Proc. of the Workshop R.C.P. 264, ed. by P.C. Sabatier, (CNRS 1980) pp. 247–264
2.19 K. Bleuler: "The Infeld Factorization in Relation to Various Problems in Mathematical Physics", Preprint Theor. Nucl. Phys. Inst., Univ. of Bonn (1990)
2.20 A. Stahlhofen, K. Bleuler: Nuovo Cimento **104B**(4), 447–465 (1989)

Chapter 3

3.1 M.J. Ablowitz, H. Segur: *Solitons and the Inverse Scattering Transform* (SIAM, Philadelphia 1981)
3.2 G.L. Lamb: *Elements of Soliton Theory* (Wiley-Interscience, New York 1980)
3.3 F. Calogero, A. Degasperis: *Spectral Transform and Solitons* Vol. I (North-Holland, Dordrecht 1982)
3.4 C.S. Gardner, J.M. Green, M.D. Kruskal, R.M. Miura: Phys. Rev. Lett. **19**, 1095–1097 (1967)
3.5 B.B. Kadomtsev, V.I. Petviashvili: Dokl. Akad. Nauk SSSR **192**, 753–756 (1970)
3.6 V.E. Zakharov, A.B. Shabat: Funkt. Anal. Pril. **8**(3), 43–53, (1974)

3.7 I.M. Krichever: Dokl. Akad. Nauk SSSR **227**(2), 291–294 (1976)
3.8 A.R. Its, V.B. Matveev: Teor. Mat. Fiz. **23**(1), 51–67 (1975)
3.9 E.D. Belokolos, A.I. Bobenko, V.Z. Enolsky, A.R. Its, V.B. Matveev: *Algebraic-Geometrical Approach to Nonlinear Evolution Equations*, Springer Series Nonlinear Dynamics (Springer, Berlin Heidelberg 1992) (in preparation)
3.10 L.A. Bordag, A.R. Its, S.V. Manakov, V.B. Matveev, V.E. Zakharov: Phys. Rev. Lett. A **63**(3), 205–208 (1977)
3.11 S.V. Manakov: Physica D **3**(1), 420–427 (1981)
3.12 A.S. Fokas, M.J. Ablowitz: Phys. Lett. A **94**(2), 67–70 (1983)
3.13 A.S. Fokas, M.J. Ablowitz: J. Math. Phys. **25**, 2505–2521 (1984)
3.14 R.A. Sharipov: Dokl. Akad. Nauk SSSR **292**(6), 1356–1359 (1987)
3.15 I.M. Krichever, S.P. Novikov: Funkt. Anal. Pril. **12**(4), 41–52 (1978)
3.16 A.I. Bobenko: Vestn. Leningrad. Univ. **22**, 74–77 (1984) [in Russian]
3.17 V.B. Matveev, M.A. Salle: Zap. Semin. LOMI **120**, 136–141 (1981)
3.18 P.D. Lax: Comm. Pure and Appl. Math. **21**, 467–490 (1968)
3.19 H. Wahlquist: in *Bäcklund Transformations*, ed. by R. Miura, Lect. Notes Math. Vol. **515** (Springer, Berlin Heidelberg 1976) pp. 162–175
3.20 J. Moser, M. Adler: Comm. Math. Phys. **61**, 1–30 (1978)
3.21 I.M. Krichever: Funkt. Anal. Appl. **12**(1), 76–78 (1978)
3.22 N.C. Freeman, J.J.C. Nimmo: Phys. Lett. A **95**(1), 1–6 (1983)
3.23 R. Hirota: in *Solitons*, ed. by R.K. Bullough, P.J. Caudry (Springer, Berlin Heidelberg 1980)
3.24 V.B. Matveev: "Darboux Transformations and Nonlinear Equations" in *Problemes Inverses, Evolution Non-Lineaire*, Proc. of the workshop R.C.P. 264, ed. by P.C. Sabatier, (CNRS 1980) pp. 247–264
3.25 V.B. Matveev: Lett. Math. Phys. **3**, 503–512 (1979)
3.26 A.V. Rybin, M.A. Salle: Teor. Mat. Fiz. **63** (3), 333–339 (1985)
3.27 R.S. Johnson: J. Fluid Mech. **97**(4), 701–719 (1980)
3.28 Yu. Stepanyanz: in *Proc. of the Kiev Workshop on Nonlinear Phenomena* Vol.2 (Naukova Dumka, Kiev 1985) pp. 150–154
3.29 V.S. Druma: Dokl. Akad. Nauk SSSR **268**(1), 15–17 (1983)
3.30 V.D. Lipovsky, V.B. Matveev, A.O. Smirnov: Zap. Semin. LOMI **150**, 70–75 (1986)
3.31 V.B. Matveev, M.A. Salle: "On some new class of the solutions of the KP equation and Johnson equation" in *Some Topics on Inverse Problems*, ed. by P. Sabatier (World-Scientific, Singapore 1988) pp. 182-212
3.32 A. Nakamura: J. Math. Phys. **23**(8), 1422–1426 (1982)
3.33 V.S. Druma: Izv. Mold. Akad. Nauk **21**, 120–123 (1977) [in Russian]
3.34 A. Lugovtsov, B. Lugovtsov: in *Dynamics of Continuous Media* I (Nauka, Novosibirsk 1969) pp. 195–200 [in Russian]
3.35 L.A. Bordag, V.B. Matveev: "Explicit Increasing Solutions of the KdV Equation and their Applications to the Cylindrical KdV Equation" Preprint Lab. Phys. Teor. Hautes Energies, Orsay, 79/6 (1979)
3.36 F. Calogero, A. Degasperis: Preprint No.93 Inst.G.Marconi, 1978
3.37 V.E. Zakharov, L.D. Faddeev: Funkt. Anal. Appl. **5**(4), 18–28 (1971)
3.38 S.V. Manakov, S.P. Novikov, L.P. Pitaevsky, V.E. Zakharov: *Theory of Solitons* (Nauka, Moscow 1980) [in Russian]
3.39 V.A. Marchenko: *Nonlinear Equation and Operator Algebras* (Naukova Dumka, Kiev 1986) [in Russian]
3.40 D. Mumford: *Tata Lectures on Theta* Vol.1,2 (Birkhauser, Boston 1983, 1984)
3.41 D.V. Chudnovsky, G.V. Chudnovsky: Lett. Nuovo Cimento **25**(9), 263–265 (1979)
3.42 M.V. Babich, V.B. Matveev, M.A. Salle: Zap. Semin. LOMI **145**, 35–45 (1985)

3.43 A. Nakamura: J. Phys. Soc. Jpn. **58**, 412 (1989)
3.44 A. Nakamura: J. Phys. Soc. Jpn. **57**, 3309 (1988)
3.45 Sh. Miyaka, Y. Ohta, J. Satsuma: J. Phys. Soc. Jpn. **59**(1), 48–55 (1990)

Chapter 4

4.1 A.A. Ignatov: Zh. Eksp. Teor. Fiz **87**(5), 1652–1659 (1984)
4.2 S.A. Akhmanov, R.V. Khokhlov, A.P. Sukhorukov: in *Laser Handbook*, ed. by F.T. Arecchi, E.O. Schulz-Dubois (North Holland, Amsterdam 1982)
4.3 T.B. Benjamin, J.E. Feir: J. Fluid Mech. **27**, 417–427 (1966)
4.4 A.R. Its, A. Izergin, V.E. Korepin, A. Slavnov: Preprint University of Canberra, FMA-R-26-89 (1989)
4.5 V.E. Zakharov, A.B. Shabat: Zh. Eksp. Teor. Fiz. **61**(1), 118–134 (1971)
4.6 M.A. Salle: Teor. Mat. Fiz. **53**(2), 227–237 (1982)
4.7 A.R. Its, M.A. Salle, A.V. Rybin: Teor. Mat. Fiz. **74**(1), 29–45 (1988)
4.8 G. Neugebauer, R. Meinel: Phys. Lett. A **100**(9), 467–470 (1984)
4.9 D. Levi, O. Ragnisco, A. Sym, Preprint No.369 Universita di Roma "La Sapienza" (1983)
4.10 M. Wadati, H. Sanuki, K. Konno: Progr. Theor. Phys. **53**(2), 419–436 (1975)
4.11 K. Konno, M. Wadati: Progr. Theor. Phys. **52**(6), 1652–1656 (1975)
4.12 V.B. Matveev, M.A. Salle, A.V. Rybin: Inverse Problems **4**, 173–183 (1988)
4.13 R. Dodd: *Solitons and Nonlinear Wave Equations* (Academic, New York 1984)
4.14 J.C. Eilbeck: J. Phys. A **5**, 1355–1363 (1972)
4.15 J.C. Eilbeck, J.D. Gibbon, P.J. Caudrey, R.K. Bullough: J. Phys. A **6**, 1337–1347 (1973)
4.16 D.J. Kaup: Stud. Appl. Math. **59**, 25–35 (1978)
4.17 M.J.Ablowitz, H. Segur: Stud. Appl. Math. **62**, 249–262 (1980)
4.18 H.H. Chen, Y.C. Lee: Phys. Rev. Lett. **43**, 264–266 (1979)
4.19 T. Kubota, D. Ko, L. Dobbs: AIAA J. Hydronautics **12**, 157–165, (1978)
4.20 V.B. Matveev, M.A. Salle: Dokl. Akad. Nauk SSSR **261**(3), 533-537 (1981)
4.21 A.I. Bobenko, V.B. Matveev, M.A. Salle: Dokl. Akad. Nauk SSSR **265**(6), 1537–1560 (1982)
4.22 J. Gibbons, B. Kupershmidt: Phys. Lett. A **79**, 31–32 (1980)
4.23 J. Satsuma, M. Ablowitz, Y. Kodama: Phys. Lett. A **73**, 283–286 (1979)
4.24 D.J. Kaup: J. Math. Phys. **22**(6), 1176–1181 (1981)
4.25 M.A. Salle: Zap. Semin. LOMI **161**, 72–76, (1987)

Chapter 5

5.1 G. Darboux: *Leçons sur la Theorie des Surfaces* Vol.2, 2nd ed. (Gauthier-Villars, Paris 1915) pp. 214–234
5.2 M. Toda: J. Phys. Soc. Jpn. **34**, 18 (1977)
5.3 S.V. Manakov: Zh. Eksp. Teor. Fiz. **67**(2), 543–552 (1974)
5.4 H. Flaschka: Progr. Theor. Phys. **51**, 703–718 (1974)
5.5 A.V. Mikhailov: JETP Lett. **30**(7), 443–448 (1979)
5.6 V.B. Matveev: Lett. Math. Phys. **3**, 217–222 (1979)
5.7 V.B. Matveev, M.A. Salle: Lett. Math. Phys. **3**, 425–429 (1979)
5.8 V.B. Matveev, M.A. Salle: Zap. Semin. LOMI **101**, 111–117 (1981)
5.9 M.A. Salle: Teor. Mat. Fiz. **53**(2), 227–237 (1982)
5.10 V.B. Matveev, M.A. Salle: Zap. Semin. LOMI **120**, 136–141 (1981)
5.11 M.V. Babich: Vestn. Leningrad. Univ. **22**, 70–73 (1984) [in Russian]
5.12 M.V. Babich;, V.B. Matveev, M.A. Salle,: Zap. Semin. LOMI **145**, 34–45 (1985)
5.13 L.A. Tahtajian: Zh. Eksp. Teor. Fiz. **66**(2), 476–482 (1974)
5.14 M. Ablowitz: Phys. Rev. Lett. **30**, 1262–1264 (1973)
5.15 S.M. Tinkham: *Introduction to Superconductivity* (McGraw Hill, New York 1975)

5.16   M. Sato, T. Miwa, M. Jimbo: Publ. RIMS Kyoto Univ. **16**, 531–584 (1980)
5.17   L. Bianchi : *Lezioni di Geometria Diferenzial* (Spoerri, Pisa 1896)
5.18   R. Sasaki: Nucl. Phys. B **154**, 343 (1979)
5.19   E.T. Whittakker, G.N. Watson: *Course of Modern Analysis* (Cambridge University Press, London 1915)
5.20   V. Volterra: *Leçons sur la Théorie Mathématique de la Lutte sur la Vie* (Gautier-Villars, Paris 1931)
5.21   I.M. Krichever: Usp. Mat. Nauk **33**(4), 215–216 (1978)
5.22   I.M. Krichever: Dokl. Akad. Nauk SSSR **265**(5), 1054–1058 (1982)
5.23   I.M. Krichever: Usp. Mat. Nauk **36**(2), 79–80 (1981)
5.24   A.M. Polyakov: Phys. Lett. B **103**, 207–212 (1981)
5.25   A. Seeger, H. Donth, A. Kochenforfer: Z. Phys. **134**, 173–193 (1953)
5.26   E.D. Belokolos, A.I. Bobenko, V.Z. Enolsky, A.R. Its, V.B. Matveev: *Algebraic-Geometrical Approach to Nonlinear Evolution Equations*, Springer Series Nonlinear Dynamics (Springer, Berlin Heidelber 1990) (in preparation)
5.27   A.S. Budagov, L.A. Tahtajian: Dokl. Akad. Nauk SSSR **235**, 805–812 (1977)
5.28   A.V. Mikhailov, V.E. Zakharov: Zh. Eksp. Teor. Fiz. **74**(6), 1953–1973 (1978)
5.29   S.B. Leble, M.A. Salle: Dokl. Akad. Nauk SSSR **284**(1), 1311–1313 (1985)
5.30   M. Wadati: J. Phys. Soc. Jpn. **40**, 1517–1520 (1976)
5.31   A. Silin, V.Tikhonchuk: Zh. Eksp. Teor. Fiz **81**(6), (1981)
5.32   M. Ablowitz, J. Ladik: J. Math. Phys. **16**, 598–603 (1975)
5.33   F. Yuase: J. Phys. Soc. Jpn. **56**(2), 423–424 (1987)
5.34   N. Saitoh: J. Phys. Soc. Jpn. **55**, 1827 (1986)
5.35   A. Nakamura: J. Phys. Soc. Jpn. **52**, 380 (1983)
5.36   Z. Popowicz, O. Raignisco: Phys. Lett. A **125**(5), 247–249 (1987)
5.37   K. Narita: J. Phys. Soc. Jpn. **56**(1), 1212–1215 (1987)
5.38   B. Fuchssteiner: Progr. Theor. Phys. **81**(2), 294–308 (1989)
5.39   F.W. Nijhoff: Phys. Lett. A **110**(1), 10–14 (1985)
5.40   V.A. Marchenko: *Nonlinear Equations and Operator Algebras* (Naukova Dumka, Kiev 1986)

Chapter 6

6.1   A. Davey, K. Stewartson: Proc. Roy. Soc. London A **338**, 101–110 (1974)
6.2   A. Nakamura: J. Math. Phys. **23**(8), 517–523 (1982)
6.3   V.E. Zakharov, A.B. Shabat: Funkt. Anal. Pril. **8**(3), 43–53 (1974)
6.4   M. Boity, J. Leon, L. Martina, F. Pempinelli: "Solitons in Two Dimensions", Preprint PM/88–59 Montpellier (1988)
6.5   M. Boity, J. Leon, M. Martina, F. Pempinelli: "A new Spectral Transform for the Davey-Stewartson Equation", PM/89-10 Montpellier (1989)
6.6   A.S. Fokas, P.M. Santini: "Coherent Structures and a Boundary Value Problem for the DS-I Equation". Preprint INS # 121, Clarkson University (1989)
6.7   P.M. Santini, A.S. Fokas: "How to Generate and Drive Coherent Structures in Multidimesions", Preprint No. 684 Universita di Roma "La Sapienza", 1–36 (1989)
6.8   M. Boity, J. Leon, L. Martina, F. Pempinelli: Phys. Lett. A **132**, 432 (1988)
6.9   A.S. Fokas, M.J. Ablowitz: J. Math. Phys. **25**, 2494 (1984)
6.10   P.P. Kulish, V.D. Lipovsky: Zap. Semin. LOMI **161**, 54–71 (1987)
6.11   V.D. Lipovsky, A.V. Shirokov: Funkt. Anal. Pril. **23**(3), 65–66 (1989)
6.12   M.A. Salle: Zap. Semin. LOMI **180**, 161–169 (1990)
6.13   M.A. Salle, S.B. Leble, A.V. Yurov: In *Nonlinear World, Proc. of the IV Int. Workshop on Nonlinear and Turbulent Processes in Physics*, ed. by A.G. Sitenko, V.E. Zakharov, Vol. 2 (Naukova Dumka, Kiev 1989) pp. 287–291
6.14   V.B. Matveev: Lett. Math. Phys. **3**, 213–216 (1979)

6.15 E.D. Belokolos, A.I. Bobenko, V.Z. Enolsky, A.R. Its, V.B. Matveev: *Algebraic-Geometrical Approach to Nonlinear Evolution Equations*, Springer Ser. Nonlinear Dynamics (Springer, Berlin Heidelberg 1992) (in preparation)

References 6.16–21 are suggested as general background reading

6.16 V.D. Lipowsky: Vestn. Leningrad. Univ. Ser. Phys. Chem. **4**, 67–70 (1987) [in Russian]
6.17 S.P. Novikov, A.P. Veselov: Dokl. Akad. Nauk SSSR **279**(1) (1984)
6.18 P.G. Grinevich, R.G. Novikov: Funkt. Anal. Pril. **19**(4), 32–42 (1985)
6.19 P.G. Grinevich, S.V. Manakov: Funkt. Anal. Pril. **20**(2), 14–24 (1985)
6.20 L.V. Bogdanov, S.V. Manakov: J. Phys. A **21**, L537–538 (1988)
6.21 V.D. Lipovsky, A.V. Shirokov: J. Funkt. Anal. Appl. **23**(3), 65–66 (1989)

Chapter 7

7.1 H. Flaschka, D.Mc. Laughlin: in *Bäcklund Transformations*, ed. by R. Miura, Lect. Notes Math. Vol. **515** (Springer, Berlin Heidelberg 1976) pp. 225–230
7.2 A.I. Bobenko: Vestn. Leningrad. Univ. Ser. Phys. Chem. **22**(4), 14–21 (1982) [in Russian]
7.3 M.V. Babich, V.B. Matveev, M.A. Salle: Zap. Semin. LOMI **145**, 34–45 (1985)
7.4 S.V. Manakov, S.P. Novikov, L.P. Pitaevsky, V.E. Zakharov: *Theory of Solitons* (Nauka, Moscow 1980) [in Russian]
7.5 B. Fuchssteiner: Progr. Theor. Phys. **78**, 1022–1050 (1987)
7.6 L.D. Faddeev, L.A. Tahtajian: *Hamiltonian Approach in the Theory of Solitons* (Nauka, Moscow 1986) [in Russian]
7.7 P.C. Schuur: *Asymptotic Analysis of Soliton Problems*, Lect. Math. Vol. 1232 (Springer, Berlin Heidelberg 1986)
7.8 V.A. Burtzev, V.E. Zakharov, S.M. Mikhailov: Teor. Mat. Fiz. **70**(3), 323–341 (1987)
7.9 G. Maison: Phys. Rev. Lett. **41**, 521 (1987)
7.10 V.E. Zakharov, A.I. Belinski: Zh. Eksp. Teor. Phys. **75**, 1953 (1978)
7.11 G. Neugebauer: J. Phys. A **12**, L67 (1979)
7.12 G. Neugebauer, A. Kramer: J. Phys. A **16**, 1927-1936 (1983)
7.13 A. Rybin: Ph.D. Thesis (Leningrad State University, 1987)

Subject Index

$\bar{\partial}$-problem 30

Airy
- equations 46
- functions 46, 47

background solution 41, 55
Bäcklund transformation 51, 88, 91
Baker–Akhiezer functions 37
Benjamin–Ono equation 4, 68, 71, 73, 75
Bessel functions 16, 83
binary Darboux transformation 3, 19, 27, 35, 47, 100
Bloch
- equation 59
- solution 14
Bose gas 51
Boussinesq equation 3, 43
breather 65, 90
Burgers equation (BE) 73, 74
  lattice version of BE 85

Cauchy problem 3
Crum
- formula 14, 15
- theorem 9, 10, 12, 16
cylindrical KdV equation 22, 47

Darboux
- dressing 33, 37, 41, 47, 57, 59, 64, 65, 77, 79
- transformation, inverse 24, 25
- theorem 1, 7
Darboux transformation for
- $-\partial_p \partial_q \psi + u\psi = 0$ 27
- $V_\xi = U_\eta = [V, U]/2$ 49
- $\Phi_{\xi\eta} = i[\Phi_\eta, \Phi_\xi]$ 49
- Benjamin–Ono equation 4, 75
- Bloch equations 55
- Boussinesque equation 3, 44
- cylindrical KdV equation 3, 47, 48
- Davey–Stuartson equation 98
- Johnson equation 3, 46

- Kadomtsev–Petviashvili equation 2, 3, 33, 37
- KdV type equation 72
- KdV equation 1, 3, 31, 37
- discrete version of KdV 84
- discrete nonabelian version of KdV 88
- nonlocal KdV 69
- lattice equations 23
- lattice Silin-Tikhonchuk equation 94
- linear matrix equations 18
- linear systems 3, 5, 17
- nonlinear filter equations 18
- nonlinear Schrödinger equation 3, 52
- nonstationary Schrödinger equation 16
- reduced Maxwell-Bloch equations 4, 65
- second harmonic generation equation 67
- self-induced transparency equation 4, 61
- sine-Gordon equation (SG) 89
  nonabelian SG 91
- Sturm-Liouville equation 78
- Toda lattice (TL) 4, 78, 79, 82, 84
  - nonabelian TL 87
two dimensional (2D) TL 4, 78–81, 83, 89
- Veselov-Novikov equation 103
Davey-Stewartson equation (DS) 4, 97, 102
  extended DS 98
differential–difference equations 7
Dirac operators 15
discrete KdV equation 84
nonabelian version of KdV 88
Exulton 53, 63

factorization method 26

Gelfand-Levitan-Marchenko equation 105

Hamiltonian 25, 26
- interpretation 4, 97
- function 104
  multidimensional Hamiltonian 25, 26
harmonic oscillator 15
Hartree-Fock equation 51
Hermite polynomials 15

Hopf-Kowl ansatz 74
inverse scattering
– method 51
– transformation 4, 77, 102

Johnson equation 45, 47
Josephson junction 78, 88
Jost solution 10-13

Kadomtsev-Petviashvili equation 2, 17, 30-36, 39, 40, 43, 45-47, 78, 79, 81, 107
Kaup equation 75
KdV type equation 72
KdV equation 3, 4, 17, 29-36, 40-43, 47 49, 50, 70, 104, 107

Lax representation 31
Liouville
– equation 68
– formula 3, 21
lump 3, 30, 35, 37

Manakov triad 72

Neumann function 83
nonlinear filter equation 92
nonlocal KdV equation 68, 69
Novikov-Veselov equation 97, 102

phase shift 39, 43, 57, 106, 107

reduced Maxwell-Bloch equation 4, 49, 59, 65
reflection coefficients 11
reflectionless potential 3, 11
Riemann problem 30

second harmonic equation 67
self-induced transparency, see SIT

sine-Gordon equation (SG) 4, 49, 61, 64, 77, 78, 89, 91, 104, 107
nonabelian SG 91
sinh-Gordon equation 77
SIT, see self-induced transparency
SIT equation 4, 49, 59-62
Sturm-Liouville
– equation 1, 2, 7-9, 69
– problem with Dirichlet boundary conditions 14
Schrödinger equation (SE) 1, 14-16, 21, 24, 97, 104
matrix SE 25, 26
nonstationary SE 3, 16
radial SE 16
nonlinear SE 4, 49, 51, 53-57, 97, 102
discrete nonlinear SE 92
– system, discrete nonlinear 51
– operator 12-15, 38
Silin-Tikhonchuk equation 94
–, discrete version 94
superalgebra 25
supercharge 25, 26
supersymmetry 24, 26

Toda lattice equation (TDL) 4, 24, 77, 104
–, two dimensional (2D) 4, 24, 77, 91, 105, 107
–, nonabelian 77, 86
transmission coefficients 11, 12

Veselov-Novikov equation 4
Volterra system 84

Zakharov-Shabat
– method 4, 35, 105, 106
– representation 33, 51

D. Park, Williams College, Williamstown, MA

Classical Dynamics and Its Quantum Analogues

2nd enl. and updated ed. 1990. IX, 333 pp. 101 figs. Hardcover DM 78,–
ISBN 3-540-51398-1

The primary purpose of this textbook is to introduce students to the principles of classical dynamics of particles, rigid bodies, and continuous systems while showing their relevance to subjects of contemporary interest. Two of these subjects are quantum mechanics and general relativity. The book shows in many examples the relations between quantum and classical mechanics and uses classical methods to derive most of the observational tests of general relativity. A third area of current interest is in nonlinear systems, and there are discussions of instability and of the geometrical methods used to study chaotic behaviour. In the belief that it is most important at this stage of a student's education to develop clear conceptual understanding, the mathematics is for the most part kept rather simple and traditional.

This book devotes some space to important transitions in dynamics: the development of analytical methods in the 18th century and the invention of quantum mechanics.

A. Hasegawa, AT & T Bell Laboratories, Murray Hill, NJ

Optical Solitons in Fibers

2nd enl. ed. 1990. XII, 79 pp. 25 figs. Softcover DM 48,– ISBN 3-540-51747-2

Already after six months high demand made a new edition of this textbook necessary. The most recent developments associated with two topical and very important theoretical and practical subjects are combined: **Solitons** as analytical solutions of nonlinear partial differential equations and as lossless signals in dielectric **fibers.** The practical implications point towards technological advances allowing for an economic and undistorted propagation of signals revolutionizing telecommunications. Starting from an elementary level readily accessible to undergraduates, this pioneer in the field provides a clear and up-to-date exposition of the prominent aspects of the theoretical background and most recent experimental results in this new and rapidly evolving branch of science. This well-written book makes not just easy reading for the researcher but also for the interested physicist, mathematician, and engineer. It is well suited for undergraduate or graduate lecture courses.

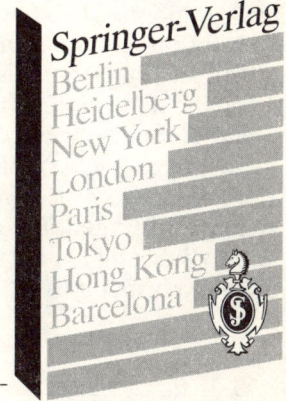

B.N. Zakhariev, Moscow; **A.A. Suzko**, Minsk

Direct and Inverse Problems
Potentials in Quantum Scattering

1990. XIV, 223 pp. 42 figs. Softcover DM 48,– ISBN 3-540-52484-3

This textbook can almost be viewed as a "how-to" manual for solving quantum inverse problems, that is, for deriving the potential from spectra and/or scattering data. The formal exposition of inverse methods is paralleled by a discussion of the direct problem.
In part differential and finite-difference equations are presented side by side. A variety of solution methods is presented. Their common features and (dis)advantages are analyzed. To foster a better understanding, the physical meaning of the mathematical quantities are discussed in detail. Wave confinement in continuum bound states, resonance and collective tunneling, and the spectral and phase equivalence of various interactions are some of the physical problems covered.

R.M. Dreizler, University of Frankfurt; **E.K.U. Gross**, University of Würzburg

Density Functional Theory
An Approach to the Quantum Many-Body Problem

1990. XI, 302 pp. 18 figs. Hardcover DM 148,– ISBN 3-540-51993-9

Density Functional Theory is a rapidly developing branch of many-particle physics that has found applications in atomic, molecular, solid state and nuclear physics. This book describes the conceptual framework of density functional theory and discusses in detail the derivation of explicit functionals from first principles as well as their application to Coulomb systems. Both non-relativistic and relativistic systems are treated. The connection of density functional theory with other many-body methods is highlighted. The presentation is self-contained; the book is thus well suited for a graduate course on density functional theory.

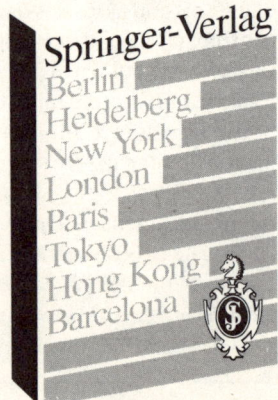